CW00495682

SCHIRMER'S
COMPLETE
RHYMING
DICTIONARY
FOR SONGWRITERS

PAUL ZOLLO

SCHIRMER
TRADE
BOOKS

A Part of **The Music Sales Group**
New York/London/Paris/Sydney/Copenhagen/Berlin/Tokyo/Madrid

Omnibus Press
A Division of Music Sales Corporation, New York

Exclusive Distributors:
Music Sales Corporation
257 Park Avenue South, New York, NY 10010 USA

Music Sales Limited
14-15 Berners Street, London W1T 3LJ England

Music Sales Pty. Limited
120 Rothschild Street, Rosebery, Sydney, NSW 2018, Australia

Order No. OP52250
International Standard Book Number: 978-0-8256-7349-8

Printed in the United States of America

Copyright © 2007 Paul Zollo

All rights reserved. No part of this book may be reproduced or transmitted in any form or by any means, electronic or mechanical, including photocopying, recording, or by any information storage and retrieval system, without permission in writing from the Publisher.

Visit Omnibus Press on the web at www.omnibuspress.com

Library of Congress Cataloging-in-Publication Data

Zollo, Paul, 1958-
Schirmer's complete rhyming dictionary : for songwriters / Paul Zollo.
   p. cm.
ISBN-13: 978-0-8256-7332-0 (pbk.)
1. Lyric writing (Popular music) 2. English language--Rhyme--Dictionaries. I. Title.
 MT67.Z58 2007
423'.1--dc22

2006030507

TABLE OF CONTENTS

Part One:
Introduction

INTRODUCTION

> "Rhymes…are like servants. If the master is fair enough to win their affection and firm enough to command their respect, the result is an orderly happy household. If he is too tyrannical, they give notice; if he lacks authority, they become slovenly, impertinent, drunk, and dishonest."
>
> —W.H. Auden

> "History doesn't repeat itself. At best it sometimes rhymes."
>
> —Mark Twain

Rhymes. For songwriters, they are like the intricate machinery inside of a clock—you don't see them work, or know how they got in there. They are sometimes mysterious, sometimes magical, occasionally pedestrian, sometimes smooth, shiny, or rough. But without them, the clock wouldn't run and it would be tough to tell time. Rhymes are among the most potent and fundamental ingredients in the construction of a good song.

In a song, be it rock 'n' roll, rap, folk, blues, funk, or hip-hop, rhymes are integral to the solidity of the lyric; a great rhyme adds a beautiful completion to a line that nothing else can replace. Rhymes not only complete a line sonically by matching sounds, they also link words in terms of associative meaning. "All there is to thought is feats of association," wrote the poet Robert Frost, who proposed that the act of rhyming was emblematic of the associative nature of verbal thought. "Now," he wrote, "wouldn't it be a pretty idea to look at that as the under part of every poem: a feat of association, putting two things together and making a metaphor... Carry that idea a little further, to think that perhaps the rhyming, the coupling of lines is an outward symbol of this thing that I call feats of association." The 19th century British poet Gerald Manley Hopkins pointed to the dual virtues of rhyming, connecting two words in terms of sound that are not connected in terms of connotation. "…there are two elements that the beauty of rhyme has to the mind," he wrote, "the likeness or sameness of sound and the unlikeness or difference of meaning." The usage of inner rhymes (discussed later) and intricate, interlocking rhyme schemes (also discussed later) adds an unassailable richness to lyrics by adding more sonic and associative links.

I recently interviewed Aimee Mann in Aspen. The interview was part of the Aspen Writer's Foundation's *Lyrically Speaking* series, in which many of the world's great songwriters are invited to this glorious mountain city to discuss their writing and to consider if popular lyrics are on par with literature. Mann was an ideal choice for the program, as she's one of the most gifted songwriters around. Rarely does she ever settle for a false rhyme (false vs. true rhymes are discussed later) in her songs, and like Dylan and some of the great poets of the past, she often employs intricate rhyme schemes such as the interlocking Byronic and Dylanesque *abab* rhyme scheme (in which every line rhymes). I asked her about this, and she said, "Yeah, I do that because real rhymes add a resonance to a song. But I don't think Bob Dylan ever uses a rhyming dictionary." So I asked her if she used one and she answered in the affirmative, explaining that which every savvy songwriter knows—that a rhyming dictionary is a useful tool, but it doesn't do all the work for you. It doesn't write the song. It simply provides you with all the options for rhymes at hand—the elements—and how you use those elements has to do with your talent and mastery of the craft.

This is a compendium of those elements.

This book might be useful for poets as well as for songwriters, though I tend to believe more songwriters than poets will use it. Rhymes are of diminished importance in the poetry of modern times, as most poems these days are written now in free verse, which does not rely on rhymes. And which, of course, makes it a wholly different artform from what it was when rhymes were an integral part of the whole. As the poet Robert Frost said, "Writing free verse is like playing tennis with the net down." Indeed, it is a different game. Which doesn't mean the stakes are any lower—the aim of a poet working in free verse, or "blank verse" as it's sometimes unfortunately termed, is different than a poet using rhymes, but does not imply a diminishment of the power or passion of the poem itself. The actor John Barrymore once said, "I've read some of your modern free verse and wonder who set it free." This comment, though funny, betrays a clinging to the past. The evolution of the poem from rhymed verse into free verse is not unlike the evolution of the symphony from tonality to atonality. All expressions in every artform must be explored. And just as tonality has not been completely replaced by atonal explorations, rhymed verse has not been totally replaced, either. "Rhyme has fallen out of fashion in most contemporary poetry," said Mark Salerno, author of *Hate, Method* and other compilations of his poetry. "It seems that, in our age of irony and satire, we have become impatient with rhyme's candor and directness. But we welcome rhyme in popular song, where it continues to feel appropriate and unselfconscious."

Salerno is quite right. When it comes to songs, rhymes are still of fundamental importance for many reasons, all of which I will explore in the following pages.

What you hold in your hands is a rhyming dictionary, the purpose of which is to make your job as a rhyming songwriter or rhyming poet easier.

This brings up many issues. What is a rhyme? Why rhyme? Is rhyming necessary? What is a perfect rhyme and what is a false rhyme? Should rhymes always be perfect rhymes? And is it ethical to use a rhyming dictionary? Shouldn't a savvy songwriter or poet have all the rhymes in the universe at his fingertips without having to resort to a reference book such as this one?

I'll answer the last question first. A rhyming dictionary is a tool. Despite what some songwriters have expressed, I don't feel there's anything at all wrong with using every tool one has. Songwriting is both an art and a craft. It's the fusion of inspiration with knowledge and confidence. A rhyming dictionary is an important tool in enabling the craftsman in the service of his craft. There are purists who quarrel with the fact that Vladimir Horowitz had his piano manipulated in such a way that the action was extra-light, thus making it possible to achieve some of his digital gymnastics. Some have suggested that this was cheating, somehow, not unlike using a corked bat in baseball. I disagree. An artist should use any tool that exists to enable him to realize that vision which remains unrealized. No other musicians could create the kind of magic on Horowitz's piano that he did. Similarly, the way any songwriter or poet uses a rhyming dictionary is individual and unique. There is no context given in this or any rhyming dictionary; there is no key to unlock the mystery of a great rhymed couplet, or directions to follow to discover an ideal intertwined *abab* rhyme scheme. All I am offering here are the essential elements—the list of rhymes—but as to how to use these rhymes in a song or poem, that's up to you.

And it's important to recognize that this is a book of rhymes in the English language, and English is actually one of the most difficult languages in which to rhyme words. Whereas the word "love" in French—"amour"—offers many rhymes, in English there are only a handful of good rhymes for the word "love"—"above," "dove," "glove," "of," and 'shove.' In English, as opposed to many other languages, most words end with consonants rather than vowels. And there are fewer rhymes for words ending in consonants. English is simply a difficult language to use in a poetic way, as the words do not dance and sing with the same kind of lyricism inherent in romance languages, such as French, Italian, and Spanish. Vladimir Nabokov, the legendary author of *Lolita* and many other books, and who was fluent in Russian, French, and other languages, once commented about the difficulty of making English sing; he said English, compared to other languages, was not unlike a blank canvas. It takes a lot of paint—in the right places—to make it beautiful.

The use of rhyme is not only effective in linking the sound of words and lending a lyrical grace to a line, it's also valuable in linking the significance of words. "Rhyme is powerful in the way it can associate the meanings of words," said Mark Salerno. "For example, in the famous cliché of 'love' rhymed with 'dove,' we are happy to associate the emotion of love with that most spiritual and peaceful of birds. By the same token, we wince when the poetaster fumbles a rhyme and inadvertently creates inappropriate associations, as when 'love' is rhymed with 'shove.' Who's doing the shoving? Why is love being shoved?"

The artistry involved in songwriting does not have to do with the remembrance of all great rhymes past (though, of course, any purveyor of rhymed words does in time build up an internal lexicon of remembered rhymes); it has to do with how one uses those rhymes. Dylan, for example (and he is one of my favorite examples, as he is a masterful songwriter and rhymer), has used countless rhymes that thousands, if not millions, of songwriters, have used. But his brilliance and amazing artistry lies not simply in the choice of rhymes—the rhymes offered here in this book— but in the *usage* of those rhymes.

For example, in Dylan's astoundingly cinematic song "Joey," which employs an *aabb* rhyme scheme (much more on various rhyme schemes to follow), he rhymes "fork" and "New York" in the final verse of this epic narrative song. He then introduces a couplet founded on two simple long "e" rhymes—"Italy" and "family." But he uses them in such a beautiful and effortless way that one can easily understand that it's the artist's inspired imagination and ability to combine images, description, and action all in beautifully metered rhythm, more than simply knowing simple rhymes, that creates this powerfully visual effect:

One day they shot him down in a clam-bar in New York
He could see it coming through the door as he lifted up his fork
He pushed the table over to protect his family
And staggered out into the streets of Little Italy.

—"Joey" by Bob Dylan

It's clear that the use of a rhyming dictionary to assist in the process of writing songs is not a form of cheating. The only real form of cheating in songwriting is plagiarism—using somebody else's melody or lyrics. Many songs, of course, do share the same title, as a title cannot be secured by copyright. (Though Sammy Cahn told me he went out of his way not to use a title that had been previously used, because he was worried ASCAP—the organization that collects performance royalties on songs for songwriters—might get confused.) But using a book such as this to give you a list of rhymes is certainly not cheating and many of our greatest songwriters, including the brilliant Stephen Sondheim, regularly use rhyming dictionaries. When asked about this, Sondheim reasoned that no songwriter should be expected to have at his fingertips every rhyme for the word "askew," for example, when a book can provide those for you.

What Is a Rhyme?

"Rhyme" is both a verb and a noun. The verb "rhyme" refers to the linking of two or more words in terms of sound. Each linking word is a "rhyme." The definition of the noun "rhyme," according to Webster, is "a correspondence in terminal sounds of two or more words, lines of verse, or other units of composition."

In simpler terms, a rhyme is when two words match in every way except for the letter (or letters) with which they begin. The ending of the word must match perfectly for it to be considered a true rhyme, or a perfect rhyme. For example, a rhyme for the word "sky" is "die." Other rhymes for it include "eye," "my," "fly," and "try." A rhyme for "corn" that is "storm" is a false rhyme, or assonant rhyme, in that the vowel sound does rhyme, but the final consonant does not. False rhymes are extremely common and used with great frequency in popular songs.

In the following example, those words in bold are rhymes:

*Woody walks in sorrow all along the lonely **climes***
*Thinking of tomorrow and of other happy **times***
*Wondering what happened to the cat who played the **blues***
*On a pawnshop Stratocaster in his Jackson Pollack **shoes***
—"Unfinished Blues" by Henry Crinkle

The beauty of a rhyme lies in its ability to connect lines, phrases, and ideas in terms of sound and meaning. Rhymes can structure words in a pleasing and memorable order, such that throughout history—even prior to the advent of the printing press—rhymes have been used as mnemonic devices to enable people to remember key facts. For example, the calendar:

"Thirty days has September
April, June, and November…"

Or wisdom about the weather:

"Red sky at night
Shepherd's delight
Red sky at morning
Shepherds take warning."

Or this axiom about house and home:

"A house is made of bricks and beams,
A home is made of love and dreams."

And this:

"Never judge someone by their looks or a book by the way it is covered
Because within those tattered pages, there is a lot to be discovered."

In this way, songwriters, and, to a lesser extent these days, poets, can use rhymes to beautifully connect and combine lines of our language, so that, rather than tell us about the calendar or weather, Ira Gershwin can tell us about the timelessness of love in a song he wrote with his brother George, "Our Love Is Here To Stay." In this song, the famous title line is rhymed perfectly with a rhyme that emphasizes the eternal quality of love:

It's very clear our love is here to stay
Not for a year, but ever and a day...
> —"Our Love Is Here To Stay" by George and Ira Gershwin

Must a Song Rhyme?

The use of rhymes in a song is certainly not mandatory. Time was when there were more accepted rules for songwriting that professional songwriters obeyed. For example, songs had to be a specific number of matching measures—32 bars was the accepted length for a song. But as with all rules applying to songs, this limitation was transcended. Two legendary songwriters—the composer Harold Arlen and the lyricist Johnny Mercer—collaborated to write "That Old Black Magic." Their publishers at Paramount told them it was unacceptable, because it was too long; it had a 64-bar melody, twice as long as the norm. But Arlen and Mercer were established and seasoned professionals at this point and were wise and brave enough to insist that their form was perfect for this song and that no changes were necessary. Paramount grudgingly gave in and "That Old Black Magic" became a classic standard and has since been recorded by a veritable universe of singers, actors, and musicians, including Frank Sinatra, Billie Holiday, Judy Garland, Kevin Spacey, Glenn Miller, Sammy Davis, Jr., Tommy Dorsey, Ella Fitzgerald, Miles Davis, Johnny Mathis, Tony Bennett, Mel Torme, Oscar Peterson, and even Marilyn Monroe (who performed a sultry rendition of it in the movie *Bus Stop*). It's evidence that no predetermined restrictions of songwriting—be it length, use of rhyme, or structure—ever matter, if the song works. That's what it comes down to. Is it a good song? None of the craft elements of songwriting, including rhyme, matter as much as the overall effect. As the late great Laura Nyro (writer of "And When I Die" and countless classics) told me, "... I'm from the school that there are no limitations with a song. That's the beauty of it. To me a song is a little piece of art. It can be whatever you like it to be."

It was Ray Evans (the great lyricist of such standards as "Silver Bells," "Que Sera," and "Mona Lisa," all created with the composer Jay Livingston) who told me this story about "That Old Black Magic," and went on to say, "You see, there shouldn't be rules at all in songwriting. Nobody can predict a hit. Every hit we had got turned down all over the place." (This, incidentally, is an important lesson for songwriters to learn: no one opinion of a song is the ultimate opinion; any response to a song is always a subjective response.)

So one certainly can write a song with no rhymes. But it isn't that easy to do and still create an effective song. Rhymes, as previously stated, are a fundamental ingredient in the creation of a sturdy song, just as a traditional song structure, such as the common but effective verse-chorus-verse-chorus-bridge-chorus structure, is an effective tool to use in the design of a durable song. One might think of rhyme or song structure as a limitation—and it's part of the artistic sensibility to rebel against any limitations to be free. But as Krishnamurti once said, "Limitations create possibilities." And this is so true when it comes to the art and craft of songwriting. By working within the limitations, a songwriter can be freer to express ideas that have previously been unexpressed, but do so in a form where they will be effective. "I like the structure of pop songs," Aimee Mann told me. "When you have a strong structure like that, you can be much freer with the other aspects of the song, the words, and the tune." And as Mark Salerno said (and we will discuss later), "the form generates the poem."

So a songwriter is wise to use all the elements and tools at hand, and rhymes—and a rhyming dictionary—are both effective means to achieving a powerful result. There are some examples, though not many, of great songs that have no rhymes at all. The one that astounds me most of all is the beautiful and epic "America," by Paul Simon, first recorded by Simon and Garfunkel on the album *Bookends,* and often performed by them in concerts and on subsequent live albums. That Simon managed to create such a beautiful song—with both an astounding lyric and beautiful melody—without any rhymes is something of a miracle. It's the only one of his songs I know of that exists without any rhymes. Yet it's a beautifully detailed lyric, and much of that beauty has to do with his masterful use of concrete detail and a lilting meter that goes a long way in making up for the lack of rhyme:

> *Let us be lovers, we'll marry our fortunes together*
> *I've got some real estate here in my bag*
> *So we bought a pack of cigarettes, and Mrs. Wagner's pies*
> *And walked off to look for America...*
>
> —"America" by Paul Simon

Note that Simon is a brilliant rhymer, and has used rhymes to great effect for decades. In his song "Thelma," which he wrote and recorded for his *Rhythm of the Saints* album, but ultimately discarded, including it on his boxed set *Paul Simon 1964-1993,* he links lines with rhymes, but in the chorus actually strings together four rhymes in one line, unprecedented in his work: *"I will need you, feed you, seed you, plead with you..."*

The standard "Moonlight In Vermont," written by John Blackburn and Karl Suessdorf, also succeeds beautifully even with no rhymes. A vast swath of artists have recorded it, namely Sinatra, Sam Cooke, Rosemary Clooney, Tommy Dorsey, Nat King Cole, and even Captain Beefheart. Much of its ability to transcend the lack of rhymes has to do, like Simon's "America," with its beautiful melody—which holds the structure together—as well as a masterful use of concrete imagery, and a savvy use of meter. Some students of songwriting have suggested that the short three-line verses in the song are like haikus—lovely succinct little packages of imagery. This is quite accurate:

> *Pennies in a stream*
> *Falling leaves, a sycamore*
> *Moonlight in Vermont*
> *Icy finger-waves*
> *Ski trails on a mountainside*
> *Snowlight in Vermont*
> —"Moonlight In Vermont" by John Blackburn and Karl Suessdorf

But the example of great songs that succeed without any rhymes are extremely rare. It's much more common for a songwriter to employ rhymes, and with good reason, as the songwriter Steve Forbert explained to me. "I think the order of it gives a person a feeling of security which is pleasant," he said. "Because you set it up: 'I'm going away, baby, and I won't be back till fall.' It sets up anticipation, right? 'And if I find me a good loving woman, child, I do believe I won't be back at all.' In your mind you feel a sense of release and order there because you were anticipating and then were rewarded with the rhyme. And that's why rhymes have stood the test of time and remain essential."

One of the primary and essential techniques for making a song sturdy and effective is by using a compelling title, and setting up that title in every way: musically (so that the melody culminates at the title line), rhythmically, and lyrically. And to set up a title lyrically, there's no better method than the use of a rhyme. Dylan has done this masterfully so many times, emphasizing the title by using a rhyme—but not an overt, obvious rhyme—not a rhyme that is put into place only to set up the title, but a rhyme that flows naturally and contributes to the meaning and content of the song as well as setting up the title. That is the fusion, again, of art and craft. Doing both. Using the craft in a way that is seamless and appears inevitable.

For example, look at Dylan's classic song, "I Shall Be Released." The title line is set-up by a preceding rhyme that is perfectly crafted, as it's a real rhyme, but also adds to the poetry and content of the lyric:

> *I see my light come shining*
> *From the west unto the east*
> *Any day now, any day now*
> *I shall be released.*
>
> —"I Shall Be Released" by Bob Dylan

Or from his song "Tangled Up In Blue," from the classic album *Blood On The Tracks:*

> *And when finally the bottom fell out*
> *I became withdrawn,*
> *The only thing I knew how to do*
> *Was to keep on keepin' on like a bird that flew,*
> *Tangled up in blue.*
>
> —"Tangled Up In Blue" by Bob Dylan

In the preceding song, rather than have a single repeating chorus in which the title is anchored, Dylan has expansive verses that end with the title, using different words to set up the title each time. It's a form often used by Leonard Cohen, and always to great effect. In his astonishing song, "Democracy," his central line is "Democracy is coming to the U.S.A.," and in each verse he explores the odd and unexpected ways in which an idea of historic democracy and theoretical democracy is discovered in America. And in each verse, he sets up the central line with a long 'a' sound to rhyme with U.S.A. It's a great example of the use of rhyme in songs, as it never gets conventional or banal, but retains the dynamism of great poetry. From one of the first verses:

> *"It's coming from the silence on the dock of the bay,*
> *from the brave, the bold, the battered heart of Chevrolet:*
> *Democracy is coming to the U.S.A."*

And later in the song:

But I'm stubborn as those garbage bags
that Time cannot decay,
I'm junk but I'm still holding up this little wild bouquet:
Democracy is coming to the U.S.A.

—"Democracy" by Leonard Cohen

And Paul Simon has shown us countless times in his songs an artful approach to setting up a title with a rhyme. There are many famous examples in his body of work, but I'll choose "Still Crazy After All These Years," as this is a song—like "Tangled Up In Blue" and "Democracy" which doesn't have a chorus. It sets up the title that ends with the word "years"—in its verses by using a different rhyme each time. The first verse uses the word "beers" as the set-up rhyme: "*And we talked about some old times, and drank ourselves some beers / still crazy after all these years.*" The second verse uses the word "ears" as the set-up: "*And I ain't no fool for love songs that whisper in my ears / still crazy after all these years.*" Now "beers" and "ears" are both somewhat common rhymes for "years." But his third and final set-up rhyme is less conventional, and reflects Simon's ingenuity. It's the word "peers," but he makes it work seamlessly by setting it up in the context of the verse, using the phrase "jury of my peers." Without that phrase, the line would stick out like the proverbial sore thumb. With that phrase and its surrounding phrase, it works beautifully. It's inventive, intriguing, modern, American, and uniquely Simon:

"Now I sit by my window and watch the cars
I fear I'll do some damage one fine day
But I would not be convicted by a jury of my peers
Still crazy after all these years..."

—"Still Crazy After All These Years" by Paul Simon

Influenced and informed by Dylan, Cohen, Simon, and all the other great songwriters who have come before me, I have learned a lot about the art of setting up a title. If you use a set-up rhyme that precedes the title, then the title will fall in such a way that it seems inevitable and gives the listener a feeling of completion and order. It's a feeling that is so rare to come by in the real world, which is always full of disorder and incompletion. An example is my song, "What Jesus Meant," which is an extended song with many verses that reflect on the meaning of Jesus in the modern-world. I'll admit one of the reasons I was drawn to the title is that I knew that "meant" is any easy word to rhyme. There are a profusion of excellent rhymes for it, and so rather than write only one chorus of lyrics that repeats many times throughout the song, I changed the words in the chorus every time, setting up the title differently in each instance. For example, my first chorus uses the word 'bent' to set up the title:

> *And we persist in going straight*
> *Although our backs are bent*
> *Will we be left at heaven's gate*
> *Wondering what Jesus meant?*
>
> —"What Jesus Meant" by Paul Zollo

(Notice, too, in that chorus I linked all the lines together by the use of the *abab* rhyme scheme, in which the first and third lines rhyme, as well as the second and fourth lines. Much more on this rhyme scheme and others to follow.)

In a later chorus, I set up the same title with a different rhyme, "continent":

> *Still we walk through burning sands*
> *And we cross the continent*
> *We see the work of unseen hands*
> *Wondering what Jesus meant*
>
> —"What Jesus Meant" by Paul Zollo

Again, as with all ingredients that combine to create a song, there is both art and craft involved. The craft involves knowing where to place the rhyme and how to use a real rhyme. The art has to do with doing it in a seamless, non-obvious fashion. You never want the set-up rhyme to call attention to itself. It must fall in the line with a natural and graceful simplicity, so that when the title emerges, it does so in a way that seems organic. There are thousands of examples of a poor set-up—even Dylan is guilty of this, using set-ups that obviously exist more to set up the title than because they are essential to the lyric. In his song "When I Paint My Masterpiece," for example, he sets up the title by mentioning a date he has with "Botticelli's niece." It's certainly an interesting line, and characteristic of the inventive and colorful nature of Dylan's work. And as Sondheim has explained, a song is such a short form that the slightest flaw seems enormous. And so every song needs what Sondheim calls "polish." It needs to be revised until it's close to perfection.

Of course, all of these statements can be qualified. No song is ever perfect. But unlike a sprawling novel, or a movie, or an epic poem, or any art of a longer form, it's easier to approach perfection in a song than in other artforms. But as the legendary dancer and choreographer Martha Graham explained, no art is ever perfect, yet there is a certain "divine dissatisfaction" that all artists know, that is born in the yearning to achieve perfection, but which allows that any such attempt is doomed to failure. It's this very knowledge that perpetuates the artist's desire to continue in the pursuit of artistic perfection.

Differences Between Writing Lyrics and Writing Poetry

What is the difference between a song and a poem? The answer is complex. Some have suggested that songs are spiritual and poems are intellectual. I don't agree—there are intellectual songs and spiritual poems.

Song lyrics, though they have been printed on albums and CDs since the advent of The Beatles, are not meant to be read—as is a poem—but are meant to be heard. And they do not stand on their own. They are delivered wrapped in melody, harmony, rhythm, and a rainbow of instrumental colors. Poetry exists on the page and though poems are often spoken, they are meant primarily to be read and must stand up to repeated readings. "Poetry exists in its conciseness," said Stephen Sondheim in a 1971 interview with *Time* magazine, "how much is packed into it; it's important to be able to read and reread it at your own speed. Lyrics exist in time, second to second to second. Therefore lyrics always have to be underwritten. You cannot expect an audience to catch more than the ear is able to catch at the tempo and richness of the music. The perfect example of this is 'Oh, What a Beautiful Morning,' the first part of which I'd be embarrassed to put down on paper. I mean, you just don't put down: *'Oh, what a beautiful mornin', Oh, what a beautiful day . . .'* It's just ridiculous. What Oscar knew was that there was music to go with it. The minute that Dick Rodgers' music is added, the whole song has an emotional weight. I really think that *Oklahoma!* ran seven years on that lyric."

The legendary songwriter Van Morrison, who has written a profusion of magical, soulful, and classic songs, said that Bob Dylan is the world's greatest poet. He didn't say Dylan was the world's greatest *songwriter*— but called him a poet. But is Dylan a poet? When I interviewed Bob Dylan, some two decades after Sondheim related his story to *Time*, I asked him what he felt about Van Morrison's declaration. Dylan responded with an inspirational, contemplative, and wondrously Whitmanesque inventory of veracities about the poet in modern times, the kind of answer that only a man with a genuinely poetic perspective could conceive:

Author: *Van Morrison said that you are our greatest living poet. Do you think of yourself in those terms?*

Dylan: [*Pause*] Sometimes. It's within me. It's within me to put myself up and be a poet. But it's a dedication. [*Softly*] It's a big dedication.

[*Pause*] Poets don't drive cars. [*Laughs*] Poets don't go to the supermarket. Poets don't empty the garbage. Poets aren't on the PTA. Poets, you know, they don't go to picket the Better Housing Bureau, or whatever. Poets don't… they don't even speak on the telephone. Poets don't ever *talk* to anybody. Poets do a lot of listening… and *usually they know why they're poets*!

… Poets live on the land. They behave in a gentlemanly way. And live by their own gentlemanly code.

[*Pause*] And die broke. Or drown in lakes. Poets usually have very unhappy endings. Look at *Keats'* life.

From *Songwriters On Songwriting,* Expanded Edition by Paul Zollo

Usages of Rhyme

As Dylan and other great songwriters have shown us countless times in their work, there is a fusion of craft and art in songwriting. One of the chief craft elements is the use of rhyme. But the artistry comes with knowing how to use a rhyme, to rhyme lines but do so in a way that they flow in a colloquial and conversational way, and to link those associative thoughts that Frost discussed in a coherent and cohesive way. As one Dylan scholar wrote when asked to provide what he felt were Dylan's greatest rhymes, "If I am conscious of Dylan's rhymes, then he has not done a good job." This is an important point to consider. A songwriter does not rhyme to point attention to the *rhyme.* A songwriter rhymes to hold a line together. Rhymes are often like glue that holds together a collection of thoughts. A songwriter rhymes to accent a certain word or thought: in a song, a rhyme doesn't only link two lines because of the sonic syllabic concord of the rhyming words. A rhyme highlights a line, or a specific word. It draws attention to it. It crystallizes a thought. And it helps direct a specific thought to a listener, even if the listener is not conscious of the rhyme.

"I work on [rhymes] as much as anything," Aimee Mann told me. "I also try to get the best rhyme scheme I can… I do spend a *lot* of time trying to get a perfect rhyme. That is important to me because I think that helps a lot in communicating certain ideas to a listener. I think it makes a nice little surprise that helps you connect with a song. Even if the listener doesn't realize it, subconsciously they feel it. I don't always have perfect rhymes, but I work hard to get them." She went on to explain that it's the business of the songwriter to utilize rhymes and other craft elements of songwriting to give solidity to a song. "I feel as a songwriter that's your job [to find good rhymes.] There's not only the *thing* that you are saying, but there's the best way to say it. It's your job to find out the best way to say it; to make sure the meter is good, the rhyme is good, and that it sounds very conversational."

The songs of Aimee Mann, like those by Dylan, are excellent examples of our purpose here, which is to explore the use of rhymes in popular songs. Like Dylan, and like the songwriters of previous generations who went to great pains to avoid the use of a false rhyme, Mann will often use great rhymed couplets and quatrains that are ideal examples of the synthesis of craft and art. The opening to her famous song "Save Me" (used to great effect in the film *Magnolia*) is a couplet that could have come from Cole Porter or one of his peers, as it contains an engaging mix of cleverness, conversation, content, and rhyme:

> *You look like a perfect fit*
> *for a girl in need of a tourniquet*
>
> —"Save Me" by Aimee Mann

This is a good example because, although it's a clever rhyme and use of words, it's the content of the couplet more than the perfect rhyme that matters. Using a perfect rhyme is not successful in a song if the content is not clearly and conversationally conveyed. It's the same as with any of the other poetic craft elements that go into songwriting, such as the use of alliteration. Alliteration is effective in a lyric, as it adds a percussive element to a succession of words and also accents those words in a way that's similar to the use of rhymes. But alliteration just for the sake of alliteration is useless in a song. The same thing holds true with a rhyme. The aim of a songwriter must always be to merge craft with artistry, to achieve a rhyme in a way that doesn't draw attention to the rhyme itself, but to the intended meaning of the line.

That line—which rhymes "tourniquet" with "fit"—links a polysyllabic word with a monosyllabic word. It's a technique that Mark Salerno referred to when discussing the use of rhymes in popular songs. "There are countless ways for a writer to achieve different effects with rhyme," he said. "For example, I am always delighted by Smokey Robinson's rhyming of a monosyllable with a polysyllable in 'The Tracks of My Tears': '*Although she may be cute / She's just a substitute…*' The relatively big word 'substitute' delays the '-ute' sound and in doing so creates a little anticipation, as does the leap from the one-syllable 'cute' to the more complicated three-syllable 'substitute.' That complicating word 'substitute'—which normally receives its strongest accent on the first syllable, but here, due to the rhyme, gets an extra push on the third syllable as well—seems fitting, since the song is about the complicated and ambivalent emotions of being with one woman while desiring another."

When I interviewed Dylan in 1991 (an interview he did precisely because my aim was to focus strictly on songs and songwriting), I took the opportunity to ask him about rhyming. As mentioned, Dylan's certainly famous for the free-flowing, expansive, poetic, and often abstract nature of his lyrics. But he's also a meticulous craftsman, who will work and rework his songs, even after some of them have been recorded. So I was especially interested to discover what he thought about this process of combining the craft of rhyming with the art of songwriting. Since his rhymes are so spacious and inspired, I started by asking him if rhyming was fun for him.

"Well, it can be," he said, "but you know, it's a game. You know, you sit around… it gives you a thrill. It gives you a thrill to rhyme something you might think, well, that's never been rhymed before."

He then expounded on his method of combining the dictates of the craft with the spontaneity of this art. "My sense of rhyme used to be more involved in my songwriting than it is," he said. "Still staying in the unconscious frame of mind, you can pull yourself out and throw up two rhymes first and work it back. You get the rhymes first and work it back and then see if you can make it make sense in another kind of way. You can still stay in the unconscious frame of mind to pull it off, which is the state of mind you have to be in anyway."

I followed up on that, asking him if working backwards like that, in essence, was something he often did. "Oh, yeah," he answered. "Yeah, a lot of times. That's the only way you're gonna finish something. That's not uncommon, though." This understanding is key to the conception and completion of a good song—one works backwards and forwards at the same time, much as a rhyme simultaneously propels the listener of a song backwards and forwards. To work forward towards the linear conclusion of a song constructed with rhymes, the only sensible way of doing it is to put rhymes in place first, and work backwards from there. A song is a puzzle of sorts, and creating one is not unlike constructing a crossword puzzle. As any cruciverbalist worth his weight in words will tell you, nobody creates a crossword puzzle by writing the questions first, and then assembling the answers together into an order. One must assemble the answers first, and work backwards and forwards simultaneously, and the same is true with the creation of a sturdy song.

When I spoke to Mark Salerno about the use of rhymes in poetry and songs, he spoke about this dynamic, and about the inherent power in the recurring sound of a rhyme—in the almost magical way rhymes connect lines. "The repeat is one of the oldest tricks in any artist's magic bag," he said. "Whenever something is repeated—whether it is a word or phrase in a written text, or a line or color in a visual text—the process of shaping begins. Rhyme is a repeated sound with variation. Once it is put into play, it establishes a pattern that gives form to a piece of writing. It also sets up a current of energy: We anticipate the coming rhyme and, when we hear it, we are reminded of, and sent back to, the preceding rhyme. Thus, the rhyme sound sends us forward and backward at the same time, effectively binding the text together. Rhyme lends a shape to writing through the use of sound effects and making sounds with words is what distinguishes poetry from prose."

Stephen Sondheim, an avid user of rhyming dictionaries who brilliantly employs real rhymes to propel a narrative and to flesh out characters, wrote this in an e-mail to an author: "I use a rhyming dictionary, you know. It's craft, nothing personal..." A careful scrutiny of his lyrics is beneficial for any student of songwriting. Though he's now well established as both a legendary lyricist and composer of songs, his professional career started when he wrote only lyrics. Though he always yearned to do both, opportunities arose first for him to write the lyrics for the songs for *West Side Story,* for which Leonard Bernstein wrote the music, and then for *Gypsy,* with music by Jule Styne.

As early as *West Side Story*, his mastery of rhymes is evident. Keep in mind, however, that Sondheim is not attempting to write popular songs (though some of his songs, such as "Send In The Clowns," from *A Little Night Music,* have become popular songs), he is writing songs for musicals, in which they are sung by characters and are intended to shed light into the characters of those who are singing. It's one of Sondheim's steadfast beliefs that the use of rhymes in his character songs speaks volumes about the character. In Sondheim's creative universe, only an intelligent, erudite person would sing in rhyme. Of course, nobody sings his thoughts in real life—unless they're crazy—so that any song in a musical necessarily relies on a suspension of disbelief, and an acceptance of this conceit that actual communication can occur in a song. Yet within this framework of the musical in which Sondheim works, this conceit is ever-present:

> "You…have to know when and where to use rhyme," Sondheim said in a 1972 interview with the *Washington Post*. "One function of rhyme is that it implies education. And one of the most embarrassing moments of my life was after a run-through of *West Side*, when some of my friends were out front. I asked Sheldon Harnick after the show what he thought, knowing full well that he was going to fall to his knees and lick the sidewalk. Instead he said, 'There's that lyric, 'I Feel Pretty.' I thought the lyric was terrific. I had spent the previous two years of my life rhyming 'day' and 'way' and 'me' and 'be' and with 'I Feel Pretty' I wanted to show that I could do inner rhymes, too. That's why I had this uneducated Puerto Rican girl singing, 'It's alarming how charming I feel.' You must know she would not be unwelcome in Noel Coward's living room.' …So there it is to this day embarrassing me every time it's sung, because it's full of mistakes like that…"

It's always striking to me that Sondheim considers that a mistake, as it's a fine song, and does everything a song should do: It propels the narrative, it encompasses the character of the singer, and it has an effective marriage of lyric with melody. Yet he subscribes to this notion of a rhyme implying education, and he's not alone in this perspective. But it does point to one of the many functions of rhymes in a song. And it points to the fact that Sondheim is one of the few songwriters carrying on the great tradition of the serious song craftsmen of the Broadway theater. Though Sondheim never got to meet Gershwin, he did get to meet another classic songwriter of that era, Cole Porter—and even had the opportunity to play him a song. Porter had been in a terrible horse-riding accident, and by this time both of his legs had been amputated; his butler would literally carry him from room to room. This was the year when Sondheim was writing lyrics for *Gypsy,* with music by Jule Styne. Notably, it was Sondheim's ingenious use of rhyme that most impressed the elder songwriter, as Sondheim recalled in Meryle Secrest's excellent biography of him:

> "Cole was very depressed," Sondheim says. "He was carried in like a sack of potatoes by a burly manservant. But he couldn't have been more charming. On that line in 'Together'—*No fits, no fights, no feuds and no egos, amigos'*—he chortled, and I knew I got him. He didn't see the last rhyme coming. It was a real Cole Porter rhyme — he inserts foreign words into lyrics — an homage to Cole Porter without meaning to be. He got such a moan of pleasure, it was absolutely sexual. *It was a great moment!"*

Spontaneous Creation

While this dictionary concerns itself primarily with the use of rhymes, by no means do I suggest to any songwriter or poet that the use of rhymes—an element of craft—is meant to take precedence over spontaneous, inspired writing—embracing inspiration. Songwriting, as I've written, is both an art and a craft—music, at its best, is inspirational. Good music can often inspire a lyric, as a good lyric can inspire a melody. It's that fusion of art and craft again—of using the craft to shape the art, while allowing for an artistic usage of craft.

Almost all the songwriters I've interviewed, who belong to many generations and write songs in many genres, have said that songwriting is more an act of *following* than it is *leading.* The creator is moving in two directions at once, forward and backwards simultaneously. And the form itself, as Mark Salerno explained, will often lead one both forward to a new rhyme and backwards to link to the preceding one. It's a process of following inspiration—of discovering where the song wants to go—as well as leading it. It's not a new concept. Even the ancient philosopher Plato wrote that the truest poetry cannot be predetermined, but must follow inspiration. He contended that poetry came not from knowledge or reason but from inspiration—the muses that sing through us. Similarly, the English romantic poet William Wordsworth felt that the best poetry was inspired, not invented. "All good poetry is the spontaneous overflow of powerful feelings," he wrote. Interesting that he qualified this to 'good' poetry. Indeed, bad poetry can certainly be planned. Similarly, any experienced songwriter knows that it's easy to sit down and write a song. But to write a great song—a song that will resound for years to come— a song that is inspirational and timeless—that is another matter altogether. It has to do with plugging into that electric current of creative inspiration. John Lennon said that he could easily craft a song any day of the week, but that writing a truly great song—and he wrote so many in his short lifetime—required a transcendent process, a process of bypassing concrete reality and connecting with the force of inspiration. Much of the greatness inherent in songs is outside of the songwriter's hands in a sense—some of it comes from chance, perhaps, or from luck, or from a more spiritual source, maybe—a concept many songwriters have suggested. In an 1892 letter to Wilkie Collins, Charles Dickens put it this way: "These are the ways of Providence, of which ways all art is but a little imitation." Indeed there is a sense when writing songs often that you are not inventing something new, but finding something which already exists—imitating Providence, if you will. You are going backwards and forwards simultaneously. Backwards to find that essential truth of the form which already exists in time, and forward in time to set it down, to preserve it.

There are countless examples in songs that make it clear the songwriter is participating in a process in which he's not altogether in charge. Look at The Beatles' famous song "The Word." The key line of the song contains a perfect inner rhyme: "Have you heard the word is love?" Certainly when Lennon and McCartney wrote "The Word" (and they did write it together, according to John, though, he said in 1980, "It's mainly mine."), they did not plan in advance that they could rhyme 'heard' and 'word.' It's a happy circumstance that came from moving forward in the heady creation of a new song, inspired by music, collaboration, and the positive message of love itself, as well as moving backwards—from the sound of the word 'word' to the quick realization of linking it with 'heard' to create a musical question and its answer all in one simple rhymed line: "Have you heard the word is love?" Because not only does it contain that perfect inner rhyme, it also links up in a perfect couplet with the preceding line, using one of the very few rhymes for 'love' in English, the word 'of': "Say the word I'm thinking of/Have you heard the word is love." In this couplet, the word 'word' in the first line comes at the exact same spot—the third syllable of the line—as the word 'heard' in the next line, setting up yet another rhyming link. So in this one couplet Paul and John created not one but three perfect rhymes. And it's fairly evident that the creation of those three rhymes came about not from a predetermined plan, but from being open to the artistic rush of inspiration fused with craft.

Paul Simon amplified this understanding of consciously embracing the unconscious when I interviewed him the first time. Like many songwriters, he has found ways of diverting the conscious mind, so that you can delve underneath the surface, underneath the pool of conscious, predetermined thoughts to discover something deeper, something richer, and, according to Simon, something that is more true. "As soon as your mind knows that it's on," he explained, "and it's supposed to produce some lines, either it *doesn't* or it produces things that are very predictable. And that's why I say I'm not interested in writing something that I thought about. I'm interested in *discovering* where my mind wants to go, or what object it wants to pick up. It *always* picks up on something true. You'll find out much more about what you're thinking that way than you will if you're determined to say something. What you're determined to say is filled with all your rationalizations and your defenses and all of that. And as a *lyricist,* my job is to find out what it is that I'm thinking. Even if it's something that I don't want to be thinking."

I've learned in writing lyrics for my own music, and in writing lyrics to fit a collaborator's melody, the job of a good lyricist is not to *impose* lyrics onto a song, but to listen carefully to a melody and determine what lyrics are meant to be there. It brings up the old example of Michelangelo stating that a sculpture was inside a block of marble; his job was merely to cut away all the excess material. In the same way, a songwriter must discover the essential song that already exists in one sense—to hear the true song, and capture it—rather than to invent it. As Paul Simon told me that he is much more interested in lyrics that he *discovers* than lyrics that he *invents*. In a way, he said, he considers himself more of an editor of his songs than a writer.

"I don't consciously think about what a song should say," he said. "In fact, I consciously try *not* to think about what a song should say... Because I'm interested in what... I *find,* as opposed to... what I'm planting. I like to be the audience, too. I like to *discover* it rather than plot it out. So I let the songs go this way and that way and whatever way it is and basically what I do is be the *editor:* 'Oh, that's interesting. Never mind *that,* that's not so interesting. That's good, *that's a good line.'* And the *most* I can do is say, 'There's a good line, and the rhyming pattern, I don't know, let me see how I will set up that line.'"

What Simon is describing, with an insight and eloquence that is manifest in all of his lyrics, is that aforementioned need for a songwriter to be conscious while writing, while simultaneously reaching into the subconscious; to be a craftsman and an artist at the same time. To combine what my former teacher Jack Segal (lyricist of "When Sunny Gets Blue," "Scarlet Ribbons," and many other songs) used to describe as the intersection of "inspiration and perspiration." And that's an accurate way of describing it, as it is a fusion of work and play—one does not *work* music, after all—one *plays* music. Inherent in the act of making music is the sense of *play,* of joy, of creating pleasure. It's serious play, as Laura Nyro explained to me, "… it's like a playground," she said. "I find it to be like that, that all these other responsibilities kind of drift away and you are really there with your essence. And you are really with delight. There can be delight there. There can be self-discovery. You can dance there. And there are swings, there are monkey bars, you can play. I think of it as a serious playground."

But as with any playground, a structure is necessary. Just as an architect can be creative in the creation of a building, he still must rely on the basic principles of structure—of building a firm foundation, etc.—so that the creation does not collapse. The use of rhyme is a foundational form in the structure of a song.

I asked Simon—half-expecting him not to be able to answer—how one can distinguish between discovery and invention. Don't they overlap, I asked? But Simon did have an answer, and a good one. "Yes, they do [overlap]," he said. "You just have no idea that that's a thought that you had. It surprises you. It can make me laugh, or make me emotional. When it happens and I'm the audience and I react, I have faith in that because I'm already reacting. I don't have to question it. I've already been the audience. But if I make it up, knowing where it's going, it's not as much fun. It *may* be just as good, but it's more *fun* to discover it."

Many songwriters have told me they feel more like receivers of songs than creators. Felix Cavaliere, who wrote "Groovin'" and "It's A Beautiful Morning" said, "I really believe that we are all sort of like beacons from another source. It's the same thing as the radio stations that are going through this room at this point. Yet until we turn on a tuner, we're not aware that KXJ or whatever station is going through. I feel some of us as human beings are tuners to this vibration that comes through us. What we have to do is train the basic fundamentals of music so that it has a way to come out and speak."

And Paul Simon put it this way: "You don't really possess it. That's the feeling that it comes through, that you're a transmitter. It comes through you. But you don't possess it. You can't control it or dictate to it. You're just waiting… You're just waiting… Waiting for the show to begin."

True Rhymes vs. False Rhymes

This book contains only true, or perfect, rhymes, and not false, or imperfect rhymes. A true rhyme is one in which both the vowel sound of a word and the ending consonants match. For example, "corn" and "born" are perfect, true rhymes. "Corn" and "storm" are false, or imperfect, rhymes because the ending consonants do not match.

Rhymes can be multisyllabic; this book contains one-, two-, and three-syllable rhymes. A two-syllable example of a true rhyme would be "after" and "laughter." A false rhyme with two syllables would be "after" with "factor." Close, but not quite. As the famous and funny line from the movie *The Sunshine Boys* goes, "'Lady' he rhymes with 'baby'! No wonder he's dead!"

Carolyn Leigh, who wrote all the lyrics for *Peter Pan* and many famous songs such as "Witchcraft" and "Young At Heart," used to lecture on writing lyrics and was well-known for her distress over false rhymes. "…'home' and 'alone' don't rhyme," she said, "'time' and 'mine' don't rhyme, and 'friend' and 'again' rhyme only in the area bounded by Nashville and God knows what."

And George Gershwin's brother Ira, who wrote most of the great lyrics to George's melodies, once commented on a record of one of their songs that he felt was rather offensive, as the singer had changed some of the words to the extent that Ira's perfect rhymes became imperfect. "It changes tense and sense," he said, "and suddenly rhyme doesn't chime."

As mentioned, previous generations of songwriters cared much more about perfect rhymes—and the use of rhymes in general—than do the generations of songwriters since the era of rock 'n' roll. Irving Gordon, who wrote the words and music of the classic song "Unforgettable," told me that he was always ashamed of one of his rhymes in this song which is his most famous, and which was made popular by Nat King Cole's rendition:

> *"That's why, darling, it's incredible*
> *That someone so unforgettable*
> *Thinks that I am unforgettable, too…"*
>
> —"Unforgettable" by Irving Gordon

Gordon, who spoke to me over a lunch of apple sauce (I don't think he was feeling too great that day), said that rhyming 'unforgettable' with 'incredible' was bad writing—that one has a 't' sound, while one has a 'd' rhyme. Truth is, as I told him, rhyming 'incredible' and 'unforgettable' would be a good rhyme for most songwriters today. Many subscribe to the attitude that Jackson Browne expressed to me. Jackson, who is a great songwriter and a gifted purveyor of rhymes, said that he now feels the direct expression of content should take priority over the use of perfect rhymes. "You can only rhyme 'world' with 'unfurled' so many times," he said. Many songwriters today agree that a perfect rhyme is not as important as what the song says. In the past, of course, a professional songwriter's life was far different—songwriters wrote songs for others to perform and needed to impress a publisher with a song to get it pitched to a singer. But when the era of the singer-songwriter arrived, sparked by Dylan and The Beatles and the rest, all of this changed. Time was when a songwriter kept every line in perfect meter and rhyme so that a song would sell. But when a songwriter knows that their song will already be "sold," essentially, because they themselves will perform it, the requirements of song-craft and form diminished. The goal of the songwriter shifted—achieving a perfect rhyme was pushed far down on the list of lyrical requirements, underneath truth, conversational expression, poetic expression, intimacy, and even irony. There are many songwriters who still strive to create perfect rhymes, but there are many more who don't.

"I don't think it's important to rhyme perfectly," Jackson told me. "I used to be pretty obsessed with it. I didn't even want to rhyme a singular with a plural. So it would be perfect. I would go to great lengths to change the line so that it would be. So that it would rhyme with 'time' instead of 'times.' But I'd say that most great music is just fine without that kind of obsessive detail. And I tried to get beyond that."

I asked him if there was something that happened that caused him to change his mind about the need for a perfect rhyme.

"No one thing," he said. "Just appreciating a lot of songs that don't necessarily rhyme very exactly at all—especially blues. And there are songs you don't have to rhyme at all. They don't have to rhyme. It's just something we do. It's almost like a crutch. A song will sound fine if it rhymes, even though it doesn't say a thing. That's the thing about songs. There's a lot of forgiveness in the medium because people are used to hearing stuff that doesn't necessarily mean anything or make a lot of sense. It doesn't have to… You can open up the whole structure and form by choosing to rhyme less often. Sometimes, when I've been writing a song and am kind of aware that I didn't know what the hell I was writing about, I tend to rhyme way too much. Sort of like a stepping stone—like you're going from rhyme to rhyme trying to get something going."

It's not my intention here to suggest that Jackson is wrong. He's a great and legendary songwriter with good reason—he's written countless classic songs. So obviously he's in a good position in which to have ideas on this subject. And many great songwriters—including The Beatles and Dylan—have employed false rhymes repeatedly. Dylan has on occasion used false rhymes over and again even in famous songs. In "Shelter From The Storm," for example, which is one of the many songs he's written in which each verse ends with the title, and so is predicated on the use of a set-up rhyme before the title, uses several false rhymes to set up "storm." Like many of his songs, and my song "What Jesus Meant" that I quoted earlier, "Shelter From The Storm" sets up the title in different ways each time. And Dylan, who is one of the great rhymers of our time, does use real rhymes often to set it up, as in this first verse:

I came in from the wilderness, a creature void of form
Come in, she said, I'll give you shelter from the storm...
—"Shelter From The Storm" by Bob Dylan

That is masterful writing—"a creature void of form" is classic Dylan language—as he told me, his lyrics have a "gallantry," and it's true. They resonate with the timeless beauty of great poetry, and are empowered by an elegant use of language. In the next verse, he also uses a real rhyme:

In a world of steel-eyed death, and men who are fighting to be warm
Come in, she said, I'll give you shelter from the storm.
—"Shelter From the Storm" by Bob Dylan

But by the next verse, he ventures outside of the realm of real rhymes, to match "corn" with "storm." Which works, of course, quite well in terms of meaning and content, but it's not technically a true rhyme:

Hunted like a crocodile, ravaged in the corn
Come in, she said, I'll give you shelter from the storm.
—"Shelter From the Storm" by Bob Dylan

Don't get me wrong—I'm using this example only to show that the world's greatest songwriters do use false rhymes. I don't mean to imply for a second that this isn't a great song—it is. The final lines, though they once again employ a false rhyme, are resonant and beautiful:

If I could only turn back the clock to when God and her were born
Come in, she said, I'll give you shelter from the storm.
> —"Shelter From The Storm" by Bob Dylan

It was hearing The Beatles' use of a false rhyme when I was a kid that made me feel that being a songwriter wasn't such a hard thing to do. It was one of their early songs and one that I loved, "Eight Days A Week." The verse is this:

Love you every day, girl
Always on my mind,
One thing I can say girl,
Love you all the time.
> —"Eight Days A Week" by Lennon and McCartney

I felt that if The Beatles—the ultimate group—could get away with the use of false or almost-rhymes (in this case, rhyming "mind" with "time"), then concocting a song wouldn't be that tough. (Of course, it should be pointed out that on the unstressed lines—the first and third lines of this quatrain—that Lennon and McCartney did have perfect rhymes: "day, girl" with "say, girl.")

But as I started writing songs, I became compelled, as Jackson Browne originally was, and as Sammy Cahn was, to use only perfect rhymes. When Jackson spoke about going to great lengths to avoid rhyming a singular with a plural, I understood, as these are the lengths to which I go everyday. It's a lot of work, it isn't easy, but as Paul Simon said to me, "Whoever said songwriting was easy?" I understand well all the reasons why perfect rhymes aren't obligatory. But I like them. I feel they give a song polish. It holds together better. And I subscribe strongly to Van Dyke Parks' philosophy, which he explained to me: "A song should be sturdy. A song shouldn't fall apart like a cheap watch on the street." I agree. And one sure way of ensuring that sturdiness, that solidity, is by constructing a song with true rhymes. By constructing a song that has, as Sammy Cahn put it, "solid architecture."

Sammy, who wrote his own rhyming dictionary, was a great lyricist who penned some 87 songs that were recorded by Sinatra, as he was proud to inform anyone who would listen. I went over to his Beverly Hills home and was very happy to listen, which was fortunate, as Sammy was much more interested in telling stories than answering questions, as is evident in my interview with him. He was born in 1913 on the lower East Side of Manhattan. ("So low," he liked to say, "that one step backwards would have landed me in the East River.) Sammy wrote the words to countless songs that have since become standards, including "High Hopes," "My Kind of Town (Chicago Is)," "Love and Marriage," "Come Fly With Me," and many others. Sammy was a great rhymer who thought and spoke often in rhymes, and sometime silly ones—when I came into his office, he said, "There's Paul, got a beard, looks a little weird." When he inscribed his songbook to me, he wrote, "Here's one for Paul, a book of songs your parents will recall."

Sammy always strove to use real rhymes. He stressed his opinion that songs must rhyme correctly, because they are meant to be sung, and only a real rhyme sounds right when sung. "Poems are poems," he said. "They read to the eye, to the heart, to the mind. Lyrics you have to sing. They sing to the *ear,* to the mind, to the heart. There's a difference. You can read a poem but you can't sing some poems. Like my joke is that Shakespeare would have been a lousy lyric writer. 'Love can laugh at locksmiths'? You can't sing 'locksmiths.' 'Locksmiths?' Forget it."

I mentioned to him that many songwriters, such as Bob Dylan, tried to incorporate poetry into their lyrics. He would have none of it.

"You see," he said, "most of those writers have no sense of *architecture*...They don't understand it. Those who write today rhyme *sounds.* You know what a pure rhyme is against an impure rhyme? 'Mind' and 'time' is impure. 'Dime' and 'time,' pure. 'Wine' and 'fine,' pure. 'Wine' and 'time,' impure." He then went on to suggest that his need to secure a pure, or true, rhyme at all times was perhaps detrimental to creating the best song he could create. He admitted it was a bit of an unnecessary obsession, but that he was a craftsman with a certain standard and he always rose to that standard. As an example, he mentioned the Number One song in the country at that moment in 1991, which was "Wind Beneath My Wings," sung by Bette Midler and written by Larry Henley and Jeff Silbar. "It's a song beyond," he said. "The meaning and the thought of that song is all so encompassing, it doesn't matter what the words or notes are. I wish I'd written it. But the point is, if I'd written it, I'd probably neaten it up, maybe spoil it."

So even Sammy Cahn, who considered himself a "lyrist" and not a "lyricist" because Oscar Hammerstein did, and who was one of the most adamant lyrical purists who ever wrote a song, admitted that perfect—or pure or true—rhymes are not always necessary. And they're not. But they do go a long way in securing that solidity of which I previously wrote.

It's long been funny and a tad ironic to me that so many songwriters of Sammy's generation who always bemoaned the lack of craft generated by the advent of rock 'n' roll and the evolution of the singer-songwriter, would insist on real rhymes, yet often fudge and twist the language to create these real rhymes. When I told Sammy that I was from Chicago, for example, he said, "Chicago? I know all the rhymes for Chicago—embargo, Wells Fargo…" I said, "Sammy, you've got to be from Brooklyn for those rhymes to work." In his heavy New York accent, which doesn't pronounce Rs, those rhymes are true. He said, "Chic-*ah*-go, em-*bah*-go, Wells *Fah*-go."

There are countless examples of lyricists of the Tin Pan Alley days concocting funny words to ensure a perfect rhyme. One of my favorite examples is from the classic Rodgers and Hart standard "To Keep My Love Alive." The great Larry Hart, who is an astounding rhymer, wrote a brilliant lyric for this song, replete with many clever and original inner rhymes. But even Hart would play around with words sometimes to make his rhyme schemes succeed, still clinging to what was considered a "perfect rhyme":

> *Sir Atherton indulged in fratricide,*
> *He killed his dad and that was patricide*
> *One night I stabbed him by my mattress-side*
> *To keep my love alive*

> —"To Keep My Love Alive"
> Lyrics by Lorenz Hart and music by Richard Rodgers

"Mattress-side"? There's nothing wrong with it. It's funny, and it does rhyme perfectly with "fratricide" and "patricide." But it's exactly the kind of language play that the great lyricists of the Tin Pan Alley era used to solidify their songs. Sure, they employed perfect rhymes. But they often did it in a sneaky way.

Of course, this is an art in itself—toying with the language to effect funny and clever rhymes. The poet Odgen Nash was a master at it, and frequently invented rhyming words for comic effect, as in this famous example from his poem: "Further Reflections on Parsley":

Parsley
Is Gharsley.

—"Further Reflections on Parsley" by Ogden Nash

Another great example is this one:

A bit of talcum
Is always walcum.

—"Ode To A Baby" by Ogden Nash

A lyricist who used this method frequently was the legendary E.Y. "Yip" Harburg, who wrote all the lyrics to Harold Arlen's melodies for the songs in *The Wizard Of Oz,* as well as writing the lyrics for standards such as "Brother, Can You Spare A Dime" (music by Jay Gorney), "(It's Only A) Paper Moon," (music by Arlen), and "April In Paris" (music by Vernon Duke). Harburg was also quite masterful and entertaining in his use of self-invented and twisted words to create a perfect rhyme. A great example is in the famous song performed by Ray Bolger in *The Wizard Of Oz,* "If I Only Had A Brain":

I'd unravel every riddle
For any individle
In trouble or in pain...

—"If I Only Had A Brain" by E.Y. Harburg and Harold Arlen

Even the esteemed Stephen Sondheim has been known to bend words—relying on a New York dialect for example—to effect as rhyme. One of the best and funniest examples of a Sondheim twist is from one of his earliest efforts, In the comic song "Officer Krupke," one of the first songs that informed the Broadway audience of this young man's genius with wordplay, he rhymes 'honor' with 'marijuana.' And it works:

Dear kindly Judge, your Honor
My parents treat me rough,
With all the marijuana,
They won't give me a puff.
They didn't wanna have me,
But somehow I was had.

Leapin' lizards, that's why I'm so bad!
> —"Officer Krupke"
> Lyrics by Stephen Sondheim and music by Leonard Bernstein

Sondheim even pointed to this very method when asked by *Time* magazine about his capacity for constructing great rhymes. "Clever rhyming is easy. To rhyme orange is no trick at all. Anybody can do it. You can say 'an orange, or a porringer.'"

In rap and hip-hop lyrics, it's common to dive into the waters of word play—often uncommon words are rhymed and unusual rhymes are discovered, as in this example by Busta Rhymes:

A microphone fiend, so I'm goin' to see my P.O.
It's August the 1st, so I guess I'm a Leo
My P.O., look like Vanessa Del Rio
She pulled my rap sheet, just like, Neo Geo
> —"Abandon Ship" by Busta Rhymes

Rhyme Schemes

A rhyme scheme is a predetermined pattern of rhymes that is used and repeated in a section of a song or poem. Rhyme schemes are noted by the use of letters, with each letter referring to a line rhyme. A repeating letter in the scheme means there is a rhyme at the end of that line that matches. For example, in an *abcb* rhyme scheme, which is a common one, the *b* lines rhyme, which are the second and fourth lines of the quatrain (a four line verse)—while the *a* and the *c* lines do not rhyme. An example would be:

I went walking down the street (a)
I was feeling sad and blue (b)
The sun was shining down (c)
And I was thinking of you (b)

In that example, the *b* lines rhyme—"blue" and "you."

Or this example from The Beatles:

When I find myself in times of trouble (a)
Mother Mary comes to me (b)
Speaking words of wisdom (c)
Let it be (b)
> —"Let It Be" by John Lennon and Paul McCartney

A slightly more intricate rhyme scheme is the *abab* rhyme scheme, in which the first and third line rhyme, and the second and fourth line also rhyme. It's what I refer to as a Byronic rhyme scheme, as the poet Lord Byron often used it, and I like using the word 'Byronic' whenever I can. Dylan, who loves the work of Byron, also uses this scheme frequently. A classic example of the *abab* rhyme scheme by Lord Byron would be from the poem "She Walks In Beauty," written in 1815, which fits neatly into our purposes here, as it flows so beautifully in terms of content and structure that it was used as the lyric for a song, with music adapted by a traditional Jewish melody by Isaac Nathan.

> *She walks in beauty, like the night*
> *Of cloudless climes and starry skies;*
> *And all that's best of dark and bright*
> *Meet in her aspect and her eyes...*
>
> —"She Walks In Beauty" by Lord Byron

Ralph Waldo Emerson used the *abab* pattern to comment on the art of poetry itself:

> *"Olympian bards who sung,*
> *Divine ideas below,*
> *Which always find us young,*
> *And always keep us so."*

Also quite common is the *aabb* rhyme scheme, which, as you've probably surmised by now, is created by rhyming the first with the second line, and also the third with the fourth word. A good example of that is found in the poem "Lamia," by Keats:

> *It was the custom then to bring away (a)*
> *The bride from home at blushing shut of day, (a)*
> *Veil'd, in a chariot, heralded along (b)*
> *By strewn flowers, torches, and a marriage song. (b)*
>
> —"Lamia, Part II" by John Keats

One of my favorite examples of the *aabb* rhyme scheme was used in a song by one of my favorite songwriters, Randy Newman, in his hilarious and brilliant song "Political Science." Randy is a master at combining humor and commentary, and in this song does just that, ridiculing the prevalent jingoism of Americans by adopting the attitude of an American who feels our best foreign policy involves nuking other nations:

> *We give them money but are they grateful*
> *No, they're spiteful and they're hateful*
> *They don't respect us—so let's surprise them*
> *We'll drop the big one and pulverize them*
> —"Political Science" by Randy Newman

(It's funny to note that, when I asked him about using false rhymes, Randy laughed and told me that because of the way he sings, rarely enunciating well, that nobody notices if he uses real rhymes or not. "I'll rhyme 'girl' with 'world,' you know, if I need to," he told me. It's been reported that Sondheim was upset about Randy using this particular false rhyme.)

Rhyme schemes are beautiful, because they give a songwriter a form within which to work. It's a place to hang your hat. It's a foundation— and building a secure structure necessarily begins with creating a firm foundation. And these structures can lead a writer towards revelatory innovations, as Mark Salerno explained: "From the writer's point of view," Salerno said, "rhyme and other formal structures can free us from 'the fetters of the self,' as Auden put it, because they interrupt our habits. We want to use one word, but it doesn't complete the rhyme, so we're forced to select another. In this way, the form generates the poem, at least in part. This can lead to delightful discoveries that the author had no way of anticipating when he or she sat down to write." Like his poems, Salerno's words on this subject resonate: *The form generates the poem.* It can also generate the song. It's a foundational truth that all songwriters and poets understand. Writing a song or a poem, as I stated earlier, is both a process of following and leading. The writer chooses a rhyme scheme in which to work, and then follows that scheme to assemble a structure.

As previously mentioned, both Dylan and Byron often used the interlocking *abab* rhyme scheme. I call it "interlocking" because the rhymes are intertwined—the first and the third line rhyme, as do the second and the fourth line. Keats also frequently employed the *abab* scheme, as in this quatrain from his beautiful poem "Ode On Melancholy":

But when the melancholy fit shall fall
Sudden from heaven like a weeping cloud,
That fosters the droop-headed flowers all,
And hides the green hill in an April shroud...

—"Ode On Melancholy" by John Keats

William Shakespeare was not only one of the greatest playwrights ever in the history of the English language, but also one of its greatest poets. In his lifetime he wrote 154 beautiful sonnets on the subjects of time, love, death, and life. Though there are several kinds of rhyme schemes that are used in English sonnets, Shakespeare always used the same rhyme scheme in his 14 line sonnets, which is an *abab-cdcd-efef-gg* rhyme scheme. He was not limited by the form—again, as Krishnamurti explained, "Limitations create possibilities." David Ogilvy, who has been called "The Father of Advertising," used the example of the Shakespearean sonnet as evidence of his contention that greatness can be achieved within an exacting form—in this example, a rhymed form. "Shakespeare wrote his sonnets within a strict discipline," he said, "14 lines of iambic pentameter, rhyming in three quatrains and a couplet. Were his sonnets dull?"

As an example, here is my personal favorite Shakespeare sonnet, number 73:

That time of year thou mayst in me behold
When yellow leaves, or none, or few, do hang
Upon those boughs which shake against the cold,
Bare ruined choirs, where late the sweet birds sang.
In me thou see'st the twilight of such day
As after sunset fadeth in the west;
Which by and by black night doth take away,
Death's second self, that seals up all in rest.
In me thou see'st the glowing of such fire,
That on the ashes of his youth doth lie,
As the death-bed, whereon it must expire,
Consum'd with that which it was nourish'd by.
This thou perceiv'st, which makes thy love more strong,
To love that well, which thou must leave ere long.

For other examples of great usages of intricate rhyme schemes in songs, look to Dylan's work. (Many scholars have suggested that Shakespeare didn't write all his own work. I suggested to Dylan that people might think the same about him and his work after he is gone. "People have a hard time accepting anything that overwhelms them," he said. "[People] could look back [at my work] and think nobody produced it." Then, softly, and somewhat wistfully, he added, "It's not to anybody's best interest to think how they will be perceived tomorrow. It hurts you in the long run.") In his classic song, "It's Alright, Ma (I'm Only Bleeding)," he used a rhyme scheme few songwriters have used, since it relies on rhyming five lines in a row, an *aaaaab* rhyme scheme:

> *Darkness at the break of noon*
> *Shadows even the silver spoon*
> *The handmade blade, the child's balloon*
> *Eclipses both the sun and moon*
> *To understand you know too soon*
> *There is no sense in trying.*
> > — "It's Alright, Ma (I'm Only Bleeding)" by Bob Dylan

As mentioned, Dylan often employs interlocking rhyme schemes, such as an *abab* rhyme scheme, in which every line of a quatrain rhymes with another. It's not an easy rhyme scheme to use and still maintain a natural and colloquial flow to a verse, but when it's done well, as Dylan has countless times, it can be sublime. One of my favorite examples of this rhyme scheme is in the song "Isis," which Dylan wrote with the playwright Jacques Levy:

> *She was there in the meadow where the creek used to rise.*
> *Blinded by sleep and in need of a bed,*
> *I came in from the East with the sun in my eyes.*
> *I cursed her one time then I rode on ahead.*
> > —"Isis" by Bob Dylan and Jacques Levy

Cole Porter also used this *abab* rhyme scheme in many songs, including "I've Got You Under My Skin":

> *I'd sacrifice anything come what might*
> *For the sake of having you near*
> *In spite of a warning voice that comes in the night*

And repeats, repeats in my ear
    —"I've Got You Under My Skin" by Cole Porter

Of course, songwriters can devise any rhyme scheme they choose. The goal is to maintain it through the entire song. The aforementioned Leonard Cohen also sometimes concocts intricate rhyme schemes to structure his verses, which are often expansive. In "Democracy," which I quoted from earlier, he employs a ten-line *aabba-cdedd* rhyme scheme (note that the c and e rhymes—"broken" and "open"—are false rhymes which, though false do add structure to the whole):

It's coming to America first,
the cradle of the best and of the worst.
It's here they got the range
and the machinery for change
and it's here they got the spiritual thirst.
It's here the family's broken
and it's here the lonely say
that the heart has got to open
in a fundamental way:
Democracy is coming to the U.S.A.
    —"Democracy" by Leonard Cohen

Stephen Sondheim has also devised many wondrously Byzantine rhyme schemes for his songs but uses them only for characters who are educated and would think in complex terms. That Sondheim would embrace complex rhyme schemes makes sense when you learn that he's a man who adores puzzles of all kinds—and to construct a song with an intricate rhyme scheme that is maintained throughout is not unlike inventing a puzzle. He also devises musical puzzles for himself that he solves in his work. In his beautiful score for *A Little Night Music,* for example, every song is in ¾ or some division of three. But he transforms these puzzles into art, as in the song "Liasons" from *A Little Night Music,* which, like Cohen's "Democracy," has a ten-line pattern, this one being an *abcd-abcd-ee* rhyme scheme:

What was once a rare champagne
Is now just an amiable hock,
What once was a villa at least
Is "digs."

What once was a gown with train
Is now just a simple little frock,
What once was a sumptuous feast
Is figs.
No, no, not even figs—raisins.
Ah, liaisons!

—"Liasons" by Stephen Sondheim

Sondheim, as students of songwriting know, was mentored in the art and craft of writing lyrics by Oscar Hammerstein. In 1971, he shared with *Time* magazine some of the wisdom on this subject that Hammerstein shared with him, specifying that it's not the hard words that are hard to rhyme, it's the easy ones. "Hammerstein said that the really difficult word to rhyme is a word like 'day'," said Sondheim, "because the possibilities are so enormous. One of the things I've learned is that the way to get a laugh in a song is not through the cleverness of the rhyme but by what you're saying. The biggest laugh in *Forum,* is the line in the warriors' song: "I am a parade." That's a brilliant line—and it's not mine, it's Plautus'."

Sondheim is admirably adept at weaving long and elaborate webs of rhyme, which tie together his dazzling wordplay with inventive, funny and inspired verbal links, as in this classic example from the same musical, which sets up the title with an astoundingly capacious rhyme scheme: *aabb-ccdd-eeff-gggg-hhii-jkj*:

Pantaloons and tunics!
Courtesans and eunuchs!
Funerals and chases!
Baritones and basses!
Panderers! Philanderers!
Cupidity! Timidity!
Fakes! Mistakes!
Rhymes! Mimes!
Tumblers! Fumblers! Grumblers! Mumblers!
No royal curse, no Trojan horse,
And a happy ending, of course!
Goodness and badness,
Man in his madness,
This time it all turns out all right.

Tragedy tomorrow!
Comedy Tonight!

—"Comedy Tonight" by Stephen Sondheim

Though songwriters almost always refer to rhyme schemes by their letter names, the following is a list of rhyme schemes and their names:

Chant royal: Five stanzas of *ababccddede* followed by either *ddede* or *ccddede*
Cinquain: *ababb*
Clerihew: *aabb aabb*
Couplet: *aa*, but usually occurs as *aa bb cc dd ...*
Enclosed rhyme (or enclosing rhyme): *abba*
Limerick: *aabba*
Monorhyme: *aaaaa...* an identical rhyme on every line, common in Latin and Arabic
Ottava rima: *ababab cc*
Rhyme royal: *ababbcc*
Rondelet: *abaabba*
Rubaiyat: *aaba*
Sonnets:
    Petrarchan sonnet: *abba abba cde cde* or *abba abba cdc cdc*
    Shakespearean sonnet: *abab cdcd efef gg*
    Simple 4-line: *abcb*
    Spenserian sonnet: *abab bcbc cdcd ee*
    Onegin stanzas: *ababccddeffegg*
Spenserian stanza: "*ababbcbcc*".
Tanaga: traditional Tagalog tanaga is *aaaa*
Terza rima: *aba bcb cdc ...*, ending on *yzy z* or *yzy zz*
Triplet: *aaa*, often repeating like the couplet

Inner or Internal Rhymes

An inner rhyme is, quite simply, a rhyme that occurs within a line, as opposed to at the end of a line. They are not used necessarily to replace the end rhyme but to add extra spice, rhythm, and structure to a line. Scrypt, or text, as it's often known, is a modern style of hip-hop poetry, which often uses inner rhymes. An example is the song "Damage" by Sage Francis, which—though it employs some impure rhymes—comes across with the rhythm and vitality which is at the heart of hip-hop:

I am a nightmare walkin',
psychopath stalkin' Natalie Portman
with a blank tape in my walkman

—"Damage" by Sage Francis

A much older example—this one from a classic Gershwin song— actually, the final song that Ira and George Gershwin ever wrote together, "Our Love Is Here To Stay" is:

It's very clear our love is here to stay
Not for a year, but ever and a day...

—"Our Love Is Here To Stay" by George and Ira Gershwin

In this example, "stay" and "day" are the outer rhymes, while "clear," "here," and "year" are inner rhymes. As with all inner rhymes— especially those that are used well—they might not be noticed at all by the listener as rhymes, but they add an unmistakable cohesion and grace to a lyric.

I use inner rhymes frequently in my work, both because it adds that inner structure which makes the song sturdy, and also because it's fun to find a good one. Here's an example:

The crystal meth, the Sabbath wine
The haunted, wooden ships
The final breath, the seventh sign
Of the apocalypse..."

—"What Jesus Meant" by Paul Zollo

In this example, which is in an *abab* rhyme scheme, the inner rhymes are "meth" and "breath."

As with any of the craft elements of songwriting, not unlike the spices one uses to enhance a dish, the savvy songwriter must know when and how to use them. Inner rhymes, or 'internal rhymes,' as they are also called, can be too overt and call too much attention to the hand and intention of the author, while overwhelming the content and emotion of the lyric. I spoke to Van Dyke Parks about this issue. Parks wrote the lyrics to many of Brian Wilson's greatest songs for the Beach Boys, such as "Heroes and Villains," and also has written both words and music to many solo albums worth of powerful and amazing songs. Not only is he an astounding musician, he's also a very crafty and inspirational lyricist, who embraces many of the values of the past generations, such as the use of inner rhymes. Like Paul Simon, he prefaced his comments on this subject with recognition of just how tough writing a good lyric can be. "Lyrics are hard," he said. "I get the impression, when I'm working on a lyric, for example, because I love internal rhymes and a highly crafted lyric, what some people think of as highly pretentious or overly managed words. At one point, in our songwriting history, this was a prerequisite for a good song. A highly crafted, a heavy internal rhyme scheme. Those things are thought of as elaborate and somehow out of step."

However, I suggested, people do respond to that kind of perfect structure even nowadays, when they have the chance to hear it. "They should be aware of it," he answered. "I'm comforted by such craft. I love it. But there is a time when instinct is the higher teacher. There's a time when internal rhymes—enough of them. There's enough of it. It's like you get to a point of what they say in New Orleans is 'obzakee'—one too many spices in a dish. There gets to be a point when you don't want to have so much internal rhymes."

But when a dish is finely and tastefully seasoned, the result can be transcendent. The same is true with a song. The right blend of inner rhymes with regular rhymes can add a beautiful durability and vigor to a lyric. Many of the great songwriters of the past used inner rhymes abundantly, as in this example from one of Cole Porter's most famous songs:

Some Argentines, without means do it
I hear even Boston beans do it
Let's do it, let's fall in love

—"Let's Do It" by Cole Porter

In that example, Porter uses the inner rhymes of "Argentines," "means," and "beans" to link the lines from the inside rather than from the outside. Another Porter example is in "Love For Sale," with its famous litany of repeated inner rhymes:

Let the poets pipe of love
In their childish ways
I know every type of love
Better far than they

If you want the thrill of love
I've been through the mill of love...

—"Love For Sale" by Cole Porter

In that one, he wondrously links the lines with the inner rhymes of "pipe" and "type," followed by "thrill" and "mill." But as with other songs referenced here, the lines work organically—though they are punctuated by many rhymes, inner and outer, they flow perfectly with the music, and they work perfectly in terms of the lyrical content.

One of my other favorite examples of a great inner rhyme is this one, from Lorenz Hart, which resounds with the comic spirit of an Ogden Nash verse:

Sir Paul was frail, he looked a wreck to me
At night he was a horse's neck to me
So I performed an appendectomy
To keep my love alive

—"To Keep My Love Alive,"
words by Lorenz Hart and music by Richard Rodgers

How To Use This Rhyming Dictionary

This dictionary is designed for easy usage for any songwriter or poet. It is divided into three parts: for one-syllable rhymes, two-syllable rhymes, and three-syllable rhymes.

A one-syllable rhyme—such as "rhyme," "time," "dime," "crime," and "lime"—is also called a masculine rhyme.

A two-syllable rhyme—such as "crabby," "flabby," "gabby," "grabby," "scabby," "shabby," and "tabby"—is also called a feminine rhyme.

A three-syllable rhyme—such as "blabbily," "crabbily," "scabbily" and "shabbily"—is also called a triple rhyme.

Since rhymes are distinguished by their vowel sounds, each section of this dictionary is organized alphabetically according to each vowel sound, with long vowel sounds (such as the long "a" in "game" or the long "i" in "ice"), so marked. When a vowel is not marked as being long, it is a short vowel sound (such as the short "a" in "bat" or the short "e" in "bet").

Part Two:
One-Syllable Rhymes

Long A

a
agape
airway
allay
alleyway
andante
anyway
applique
archway
array
ashtray
assay
astray
attache
ave
away
aweigh
aye
ballet
bay
beltway
beret
betray
bidet
bikeway
birthday
blase
Bombay
bouquet
bray
breakaway
breezeway
Broadway
buffet
byplay
byway
cabaret
cabriolet
cachet

cafe
caraway
carriageway
cartway
castaway
causeway
chalet
hambray
Chevrolet
clay
cliche
communique
consomme
convey
copulae
coupe
cpa
crochet
croquet
crossway
cutaway
dante
daresay
day
decay
deejay
defray
delay
demode
disarray
dismay
disobey
display
DJ
dna
dolce
doomsday
doorway
dossier
douay

downplay
dray
driftway
driveway
emigre
endplay
entendre
entree
entryway
epa
escapeway
essay
estray
everyday
expressway
fairway
faraday
faraway
fay
fda
fha
fiance
fiancee
filet
fillet
flambe
flay
floodway
flyaway
flyway
foldaway
folkway
footway
foray
foreplay
forestay
forte
frappe
fray
freeway

Friday	macrame	overlay
gainsay	Mae	overpay
gangway	mainstay	overplay
gateway	malay	overstay
gay	mammae	overweigh
getaway	manque	padre
giveaway	matinee	papier-mache
glace	may	paraguay
gourmet	mayday	parfait
gray	mba	parkway
grey	melee	parlay
gunplay	midday	parquet
halfway	midway	partway
hallway	milky-way	passageway
hatchway	mislay	passe
hay	misplay	passway
headway	moire	pathway
hearsay	Monday	pay
hey	moray	payday
heyday	naivete	photoplay
hideaway	nay	pique
highway	nebulae	piquet
holiday	negligee	pj
hombre	neigh	play
hooray	noonday	Pompeii
horseplay	Norway	popinjay
hurrah	nosegay	portray
hurray	noway	pray
inlay	NRA	prepay
interplay	NSA	prey
inveigh	obey	protege
jay	offpay	rotegee
KKK	Ojibwa	pupae
kyrie	O.K.	puree
latter-day	okay	purvey
lay	outlay	quay
layaway	outplay	Quixote
layday	outre	raceway
leeway	outstay	railway
lingerie	outweigh	ray

reconvey
reggae
relay
repartee
repay
replay
resume
resurvey
ricochet
risque
RNA
roadway
Rockaway
roue
roundelay
runaway
runway
sachet
safeway
sansei
sashay
Saturday
saute
say
screenplay
seaway
shay
shipway
signore
signorine
skyway
slay
sleigh
sluiceway
sobriquet
soigne
soignee
soiree
someday
someway

soothsay
souffle
spay
speedway
spillway
splay
spray
stairway
stateway
stay
stingray
stowaway
straightaway
straightway
stray
subway
sundae
sunday
superhighway
survey
sway
swordplay
taboret
taipei
taxiway
teleplay
they
throughway
throwaway
thruway
Thursday
tideway
today
tokay
tollway
touche
toupee
trackway
trafficway
tramway

tray
trunkway
Tuesday
UK
umbrae
underlay
underpay
underplay
underway
unsay
USA
valet
vertebrae
vivace
wahine
walkaway
walkway
waterway
way
waylay
Wednesday
weekday
weigh
whey
windway
wordplay
workaday
workaway
workday
x-ray
Yahweh
yea
yesterday
YMCA
YWCA
Zimbabwe

Long AB
Abe
babe

Gabe
Honest Abe
newborn babe

AB
blab
cab
crab
dab
drab
fab
flab
gab
grab
jab
lab
nab
scab
slab
stab
tab
Ahab
backstab
prefab
rehab
sand dab
sand crab
smack-dab
gift of gab
horseshow crab
olive drab
photo lab
taxicab

ACH
batch
catch
hatch
klatsch
latch

match
natch
patch
scratch
snatch
thatch
armpatch
attach
crosspatch
door latch
detach
dogpatch
dispatch
knee patch
love match
mismatch
no match
nuthatch
potlatch
rematch
repatch
unlatch
boxing match
booby hatch
coffee klatsch
cradle-snatch
cabbage patch
down the hatch
elbow patch
escape hatch
mix and match
overmatch
perfect match
polo match
reattach
shouting match
shooting match
tennis match
unattach
up to scratch

strawberry patch
three on a match

Long AD
aid
aide
ade
blade
braid
bayed
brayed
daid
fade
flayed
frayed
grade
glade
grayed
haid
jade
laid
maid
made
made
neighed
paid
played
raid
staid
sleighed
shade
suede
swayed
spade
sprayed
stayed
they'd
trade
wade
weighed

afraid
assayed
air raid
arrayed
abrade
arcade
blockade
barmaid
Band-Aid
brocade
brigade
betrayed
bridesmaid
conveyed
cascade
crusade
charade
crocheted
degrade
downgrade
dissuade
defrayed
displayed
decayed
delayed
dismayed
evade
essayed
fair trade
first aid
grenade
hurrayed
high grade
homemade
housemaid
handmade
inlaid
invade
Kool-Aid
limeade

lampshade
milkmaid
manmade
misplayed
mermaid
nightshade
nursemaid
outweighed
old maid
okayed
obeyed
parlayed
postpaid
parade
pomade
prepaid
persuade
pervade
portrayed
pureed
repaid
remade
relaid
replayed
relayed
stockade
self-made
surveyed
sashayed
sunshade
switchblade
steep grade
tirade
top grade
upgrade
unswayed
unmade
unpaid
upbraid
waylaid

well-made
x-rayed
ace of spade
accolade
appliqued
balustrade
barricade
chambermaid
custom-made
carriage-trade
centigrade
colonnade
cavalcade
disobeyed
disarrayed
dairymaid
escapade
escalade
even trade
everglade
fire brigade
foreign aid
foreign trade
final grade
Gatorade
hand grenade
hearing air
hit parade
lemonade
legal aid
marmalade
masquerade
motorcade
Medicaid
metermaid
Minute Maid
marinade
overpaid
overlaid
overstayed

promenade
palisade
ready-made
retrograde
renegade
Rubbermaid
ricocheted
razor blade
Rose Parade
stock-in-trade
shoulder blade
serenade
tape delayed
teacher's aid
tailormade
ultrasuede
undismayed
unafraid
underlaid
underplayed
welfare aid
Easter Parade
penny arcade
visual aid

AD
add
ad
bad
cad
Chad
clad
dad
fad
gad
grad
had
lad
mad
pad

plaid
sad
shad
tad
Baghdad
cornpad
crash pad
check pad
comrade
Carlsbad
crawdad
doodad
desk pad
egad
footpad
gone mad
granddad
ink pad
launch pad
nomad
note pad
post-grad
Sinbad
skyclad
triad
unclad
want ad
boiling mad
Galahad
heating pad
ivy-clad
ironclad
launching pad
landing pad
Leningrad
Mom and Dad
shoulder pad
steno pad
Trinidad
undergrad

Long AF
chafe
safe
strafe
unsafe
waif

AFF
autograph
barograph
behalf
bioautograph
calf
carafe
cardiograph
chaff
choreograph
cryptograph
digraph
distaff
epigraph
epitaph
ergograph
Flagstaff
gaff
gaffe
giraffe
graph
half
heliograph
holograph
homograph
horselaugh
ideograph
kymograph
laugh
lithograph
mimeograph
monograph
myocardiograph

nomograph
oscillograph
paragraph
paraph
phonograph
photograph
pictograph
pikestaff
pneumograph
polygraph
quaff
quarterstaff
radiograph
iffraff
seismograph
kiagraph
spectrograph
spirograph
staff
staph
stereograph
stethograph
subparagraph
telegraph
thermograph
tipstaff
tomograph

AFT
aft
aircraft
antiaircraft
autographed
campcraft
camshaft
chaffed
choreographed
craft
crankshaft
daft

draft
draught
engraft
graft
graphed
haft
handcraft
handicraft
hovercraft
isograft
kraft
laughed
lithographed
mimeographed
overdraft
paragraphed
photographed
quaffed
raft
seacraft
shaft
spacecraft
staffed
statecraft
taft
telegraphed
understaffed
updraft
waft
watercraft
witchcraft
woodcraft

Long AG
Hague
plague
vague

AG
bag

brag
crag
drag
flag
gag
hag
jag
lag
mag
nag
rag
sag
scrag
shag
slag
snag
stag
swag
tag
wag

Long AJ
age
assuage
backstage
ballastage
cage
disengage
downstage
engage
enrage
front-page
gage
gauge
offstage
onstage
osage
outrage
overage
page

preengage
presage
rage
rampage
reengage
sage
space-age
stage
swage
teenage
underage
upstage
wage

AJ
badge
cadge

Long AK
ache
awake
backache
bake
beefcake
beefsteak
bellyache
betake
brake
break
cake
cheesecake
lambake
coffeecake
cornflake
cupcake
daybreak
drake
earache
earthquake
fake

firebreak
flake
forsake
fruitcake
griddlecake
grubstake
hake
halterbreak
handshake
headache
heartache
heartbreak
hoecake
hotcake
housebreak
intake
jailbreak
jake
johnnycake
keepsake
lake
make
mandrake
mistake
muckrake
namesake
newsbreak
oatcake
offtake
opaque
outbreak
overtake
pancake
partake
patty-cake
quake
rake
rattlesnake
reawake
remake

retake
sake
shake
sheik
sheikh
shortcake
slake
snake
snowflake
spake
stake
steak
stomachache
strake
sweepstake
take
toothache
unawake
undertake
unmake
uptake
wake
wide-awake
windbreak

AK
aback
almanac
ammoniac
amnesiac
amtrac
amtrack
Amtrak
aphasiac
aphrodisiac
applejack
attack
back
backpack
backtrack

bareback
biofeedback
bivouac
black
blackjack
boneblack
bookrack
bootblack
bootjack
bushwack
bushwhack
cadillac
callback
camelback
canvasback
cardiac
clack
claque
claustrophobiac
cleptomaniac
coalsack
coatrack
comeback
cossack
counterattack
crack
crackerjack
cul-de-sac
cutback
demoniac
diamondback
drawback
egomaniac
fastback
fatback
feedback
finback
flack
flak
flapjack

flashback
fullback
gimcrack
greenback
gunnysack
hack
half-track
halfback
hardback
hardhack
hardtack
hatchback
haversack
hayrack
haystack
hemophiliac
hijack
hogback
holdback
hopsack
horseback
humpback
hunchback
hypochondriac
iliac
insomniac
ipecac
jack
jam-pack
kayak
kickback
kleptomaniac
knack
knapsack
knickknack
Kodak
Kodiak
lack
laid-back
leaseback

lilac
lumberjack
mac
macaque
maniac
monomaniac
mossback
mythomaniac
nymphomaniac
offtrack
outback
pack
packsack
paperback
payback
pedophiliac
phobiac
pickaback
piggyback
pitch-black
plaque
playback
pollack
Pontiac
psychoquack
pullback
pyromaniac
quack
quarterback
racetrack
rack
ransack
razorback
repack
rickrack
rollback
rucksack
sac
sack
setback

shack
shellac
shellack
shoeblack
sidetrack
six-pack
skyjack
slack
slapjack
Slovak
smack
smokestack
snack
snowpack
soundtrack
stack
steeplejack
sumac
swayback
swept-back
switchback
tach
tack
tailback
tamarack
tarmac
throwback
thumbtack
thwack
ticktack
tieback
touchback
track
umiak
unpack
wac
wetback
whack
wingback
wisecrack

wrack
yack
yak
zodiac
zwieback

AKS
ajax
almanacs
amnesiacs
anthrax
anticlimax
aphasiacs
aphrodisiacs
attacks
ax
axe
backpacks
backs
backtracks
beeswax
bivouacs
blackjacks
blacks
bootblacks
borax
broadax
bushwhacks
Cadillacs
callbacks
canvasbacks
clacks
climax
comebacks
cossacks
counteracts
counterattacks
crackerjacks
cracks
cutbacks

diamondbacks
drawbacks
earwax
fastbacks
fax
feedbacks
flacks
flapjacks
flashbacks
flax
fullbacks
gimcracks
greenbacks
gunnysacks
hacks
halfbacks
Halifax
hardbacks
hatchbacks
haversacks
haystacks
hemophiliacs
hijacks
hogbacks
humpbacks
hunchbacks
hypochondriacs
impacts
insomniacs
ipecacs
jacks
kayaks
kickbacks
kleptomaniacs
knacks
knapsacks
knickknacks
lacks
lax
lilacs

lumberjacks
macaques
maniacs
max
monomaniacs
mossbacks
overreacts
overtax
packs
paperbacks
parallax
pax
pickax
pickaxe
piggybacks
plaques
pollacks
pullbacks
quacks
quarterbacks
racetracks
racks
ransacks
rax
reacts
refracts
relax
repacks
rollbacks
rucksacks
sacs
sax
shacks
shellacs
sidetracks
skyjacks
slacks
Slovaks
smacks
smilax

smokestacks
snacks
soundtracks
stacks
steeplejacks
storax
styrax
subcompacts
subtracts
sumacs
supertax
surtax
switchbacks
syntax
tachs
tacks
tamaracks
tax
thorax
throwbacks
thumbtacks
thwacks
tiebacks
tracks
umiaks
unpacks
wacs
wax
wetbacks
whacks
wisecracks
wracks
yaks
zodiacs

AKT
abstract
act
artefact
artifact

attacked
attract
backed
backpacked
backtracked
benefact
bivouacked
lacked
blackjacked
bushwhacked
cataract
clacked
coact
compact
contact
contract
counteract
counterattacked
cracked
detract
distract
enact
exact
extract
fact
hacked
hijacked
humpbacked
hunchbacked
impact
inexact
infract
intact
interact
jacked
lacked
overact
overreact
packed
pact

playact
protract
quacked
racked
ransacked
react
redact
reenact
refract
repacked
retract
sacked
shacked
shellacked
sidetracked
skyjacked
slacked
smacked
snacked
stacked
subcompact
subcontract
subtract
swaybacked
tacked
tact
thumbtacked
thwacked
tracked
tract
transact
unbacked
underact
unpacked
whacked
wisecracked
yakked

Long AL
Abigail

ail
airedale
airmail
ale
assail
avail
baal
bail
bale
bewail
blackmail
blacktail
Bloomingdale
bobtail
braille
broadtail
bucktail
Carbondale
cattail
Chippendale
Clydesdale
coattail
cocktail
contrail
cottontail
countervail
curtail
dale
derail
detail
disentail
doornail
dovetail
ducktail
entail
exhale
fail
fantail
female
fingernail

fishscale
fishtail
flail
folktale
foresail
fox-tail
frail
full-scale
gale
ginger-ale
Glendale
grail
guardrail
hail
hale
handrail
hangnail
headsail
hightail
hobnail
horsetail
impale
inhale
jail
kale
mail
mainsail
male
martingale
missmail
monorail
nail
nightingale
oxtail
pail
pale
pass-fail
percale
pigtail
pintail

pinwale
ponytail
prevail
quail
rail
rattail
regale
remail
resale
retail
ringtail
sail
sale
scale
shale
shirttail
snail
stale
swale
swallowtail
taffrail
tail
tale
tattletale
telltale
they'll
thumbnail
toenail
topsail
trail
travail
unveil
upscale
vail
vale
veil
wagtail
wail
wale
wassail

whale
wholesale
yale
yellowtail

AL
cabal
canal
chorale
corral
decal
fatale
gal
locale
mal
mescal
morale
pal
Pascal
paschal
quetzal
shall
tropicale

Long AM
acclaim
aflame
aim
airframe
became
blame
came
claim
dame
defame
disclaim
enflame
exclaim
fame
filename

flame
frame
game
grandame
inflame
kame
lame
maim
mainframe
misname
name
nickname
pregame
prename
proclaim
quitclaim
reclaim
rename
same
selfsame
shame
surname
tame

AM
abscam
anagram
am
Birmingham
buckram
cam
clam
cram
cryptogram
dam
damn
diaphragm
doorjamb
dram
Effingham

engram
exam
flimflam
gram
grandam
ham
hamm
iamb
jam
jamb
lamb
logjam
ma'am
madame
milldam
outswam
pram
program
programme
quondam
ram
Sam
scam
scram
sham
Siam
slam
swam
tram
telegram
wham
yam

AMP
amp
blackdamp
camp
champ
chokedamp
clamp

cramp
damp
decamp
encamp
firedamp
headlamp
lamp
ramp
revamp
scamp
stamp
sunlamp
tamp
tramp
vamp

AIN
abstain
again
airplane
arcane
arraign
astral plane
attain
bane
bestain
biplane
birdbrain
blain
bloodstain
brain
butane
Cain
campaign
cane
chain
champagne
Champaign
chicane
chlordane

chow-mein
cocaine
complain
constrain
contain
coxswain
crane
Dane
deign
deplane
detain
disdain
dogbane
domain
drain
Elaine
emplane
enchain
engrain
enplane
entrain
explain
eyestrain
fain
featherbrain
feign
fleabane
floodplain
forebrain
frangipane
gain
gawain
germane
grain
henbane
hindbrain
hydroplane
humane
inane
ingrain

insane
Jane
lain
lamebrain
lane
main
Maine
maintain
mane
Mark Twain
membrane
methane
midbrain
midpain
midplane
migraine
mortmain
mundane
obtain
octane
ordain
pain
pane
pertain
plain
plane
profane
propane
ptomaine
quatrain
rain
refrain
regain
reign
rein
remain
restrain
retain
retrain
sane

scatterbrain
seaplane
Seine
skein
slain
Spain
sprain
stain
strain
sustain
suzerain
swain
tearstain
terrain
tisane
train
twain
Ukraine
unchain
urbane
vain
vane
vein
vervain
volplane
wain
wane
warplane
wolfsbane
windowpane

AN
adman
afghan
aidman
an
Ann
Anne
bagman
ban

barman
Batman
bedpan
began
brainpan
bran
can
cancan
cayenne
chessman
Cheyenne
clan
corban
Dan
deadman
deadpan
deskman
Diane
dishpan
divan
doorman
dustpan
earthman
fan
flagman
foreran
fran
free-man
frogman
hangman
hardpan
he-man
iceman
Jan
Japan
keyman
Khan
klan
kneepan
Koran

lawman
legman
madman
mailman
man
milkman
newsman
oilcan
outran
overran
packman
pan
pecan
pitchman
plan
postman
preplan
pressman
propman
ran
rattan
reran
sampan
sandman
saran
saucepan
scan
sedan
sideman
snowman
spaceman
span
Spokane
Stan
stockman
strongman
stuntman
Sudan
suntan
Superman

Suzanne
tan
talisman
Tarzan
than
toucan
trackman
unman
van
wingspan
woodman
yardman

ANCH
avalanche
blanch
branch
ranch
rebranch
subbranch

AUNCH
haunch
launch
paunch
stanch
staunch

AND
ampersand
and
backhand
band
bandstand
banned
bland
brand
broadband
cabstand
canned

clubhand
coastland
command
contraband
cowhand
crash-land
cropland
deckhand
demand
disband
dreamland
expand
fanned
farmhand
farmland
fairyland
fatherland
firebrand
firsthand
flatland
forehand
freehand
gangland
gland
grand
grandstand
grassland
hand
handstand
hardstand
hatband
headband
headstand
heartland
homeland
inkstand
inland
kickstand
land
Lapland

left-hand
longhand
Lotus Land
mainland
manned
moorland
motherland
newsstand
nightstand
Oakland
offhand
panned
planned
preplanned
proband
quicksand
rand
rangeland
remand
reprimand
right-hand
Rio Grande
sand
Samarcand
scanned
shorthand
spanned
stagehand
stand
strand
suntanned
swampland
sweatband
tanned
Thailand
tideland
unhand
underhand
understand
unmanned

unplanned
untanned
upland
waistband
washstand
wasteland
watchband
withstand
woodland
workhand
wristband

ANG
bang
boomerang
clang
fang
gang
ginseng
hang
harangue
meringue
mustang
pang
probang
rang
sang
shebang
slang
sprang
tang
twang
yang

Long ANJ
arrange
change
derange
downrange
estrange

exchange
grange
mange
outrange
range
rearrange
shortchange
strange
unchange

Long ANK
ankh
bank
blank
clank
crank
dank
drank
embank
flank
foreshank
franc
frank
Frank
gangplank
hank
lank
mountebank
outflank
outrank
plank
pointblank
prank
rank
sandbank
sank
shank
sheepshank
shrank
snowbank

spank
stank
swank
tank
thank
yank
Yank

Long ANKS
ankhs
banks
blanks
clanks
cranks
embanks
flanks
francs
franks
gangplanks
hanks
manx
outflanks
outranks
phalanx
planks
pranks
ranks
shanks
spanks
tanks
thanks
yanks

ANS
advance
ants
askance
bechance
chance
circumstance

dance
enhance
entrance
expanse
extravagance
finance
France
glance
lance
manse
mischance
pants
perchance
prance
rants
romance
stance
trance

Long ANT
acquaint
ain't
complaint
constraint
faint
greasepaint
housepaint
paint
plaint
quaint
repaint
restraint
saint
taint

ANT
ant
askant
aslant
aunt

can't
cant
chant
decant
descant
disenchant
eggplant
enchant
extant
grandaunt
grant
houseplant
implant
pant
pieplant
plant
rant
recant
regrant
Rembrandt
replant
savant
scant
secant
shan't
slant
supplant
transplant

Long AP
agape
ape
cape
cityscape
crape
crepe
drape
escape
gape
grape

jape
landscape
misshape
moonscape
nape
rape
reshape
scape
scrape
seascape
shape
shipshape
tape
undrape

AP
ASAP
bootstrap
burlap
cap
catnap
chap
clap
claptrap
crap
deathtrap
earflap
entrap
enwrap
firetrap
flap
foolscap
gap
hubcap
icecap
jockstrap
kidnap
kneecap
lap
madcap

mantrap
map
mishap
mousetrap
nap
nape
nightcap
pap
pinesap
rap
rattrap
recap
redcap
rewrap
sap
scrap
skullcap
skycap
slap
snap
snowcap
stopgap
strap
tap
trap
uncap
unsnap
unwrap
whitecap
wiretap
wrap
yap
zap

Long APS
apes
capes
crepes
drapes
escapes

gapes
grapes
jackanapes
japes
landscapes
misshapes
moonscapes
napes
rapes
reshapes
scrapes
seascapes
shapes
tapes
traipse

APS
bootstraps
caps
catnaps
chaps
claps
collapse
craps
deathtraps
earflaps
elapse
entraps
flaps
gaps
haps
hubcaps
icecaps
kidnaps
kneecaps
lapps
laps
lapse
madcaps
mantraps

maps	clapped	billionaire
mishaps	enrapt	bear
mousetraps	entrapped	beware
naps	flapped	blare
nightcaps	inapt	bugbear
perhaps	kidnapped	care
prolapse	lapped	carfare
raps	mapped	chair
rattraps	napped	coheir
recaps	rapped	compare
redcaps	rapt	cookware
relapse	recapped	corsair
rewraps	rewrapped	cudbear
saps	rewrapt	dare
scraps	sapped	day-care
skullcaps	scrapped	debonair
skycaps	slapped	declare
slaps	snapped	despair
snaps	snowcapped	disrepair
stopgaps	strapped	eclair
straps	tapped	elsewhere
synapse	trapped	ensnare
taps	unapt	err
time-lapse	unmapped	fair
traps	unsnapped	faire
unsnaps	untapped	fanfare
unwraps	unwrapped	fare
whitecaps	wiretapped	flair
wiretaps	wrapped	flare
wraps	yapped	flatware
yaps	zapped	footwear
zaps		forbear
	AIR	forebear
APT	affair	foreswear
adapt	air	forswear
apt	airfare	foursquare
bootstrapped	armchair	glare
capped	au pair	glassware
catnapped	aware	hair
chapped	bare	hardware

hare
heir
horsehair
impair
knitwear
lair
legionaire
longhair
mare
menswear
midair
millionaire
mohair
neckwear
nightmare
nightwear
nowhere
outwear
pair
pare
pear
Pierre
plowshare
prayer
prepare
rare
ready-to-wear
repair
scare
share
shorthair
snare
software
somewhere
spare
sportswear
square
stair
stare
stemware

stoneware
swear
tare
tear
their
there
they're
thoroughfare
threadbare
tinware
unaware
unfair
underwear
Voltaire
ware
warfare
wear
welfare
wheelchair
where
wirehair
Zaire

AR
afar
ajar
are
avatar
bar
barre
bazaar
bizarre
boudoir
boxcar
bulbar
car
char
cigar
crossbar
crowbar

czar
debar
disbar
drawbar
drawer
far
feldspar
flatcar
funicular
guitar
handcar
hussar
jaguar
jar
loadstar
lodestar
lumbar
Magyar
mar
memoir
Mylar
our
par
peignoir
plantar
polestar
pourboire
prewar
prowar
pulsar
quare
quasar
radar
registrar
sandbar
savoir
scar
sidecar
sitar
sonar

spar
star
streetcar
tar
tollbar
tsar
tzar
unbar
war
Wordstar

ARB
barb
carb
garb
rhubarb

ARCH
arch
cornstarch
larch
march
outmarch
parch
starch

AIRD
aired
bared
bewared
blared
cared
chaired
compared
dared
dark-haired
declared
despaired
ensnared
erred

fared
flared
glared
haired
impaired
laird
longhaired
paired
pared
prepared
repaired
scared
shared
snared
spared
squared
stared
unaired
unpaired
unshared
wirehaired

ARD
Avant-garde
backyard
bard
barnyard
barred
Bernard
blackguard
blowhard
bombard
brickyard
canard
card
chard
charred
churchyard
courtyard
debarred

diehard
disbarred
discard
disregard
dockyard
dooryard
en garde
farmyard
fireguard
foreyard
foulard
freight-yard
garde
graveyard
guard
hard
jarred
junkyard
lard
lifeguard
mansard
marred
mudguard
nard
on guard
pard
petard
postcard
regard
retard
reward
safeguard
sale-yard
scarred
schoolyard
scorecard
shard
shipyard
sparred
spikenard

starred
steelyard
stockyard
switchyard
tarred
unbarred
unmarred
unscarred
vanguard
ward
yard

ARJ
barge
charge
discharge
enlarge
large
Marge
mischarge
overcharge
recharge
Sarge
surcharge
undercharge

ARK
aardvark
arc
ark
ballpark
bark
birthmark
Bismarck
bookmark
bulwark
Clark
dark
debark
Denmark

disembark
earmark
embark
hallmark
hark
hoofmark
landmark
lark
mark
marque
mintmark
monarch
narc
park
patriarch
Plutarch
pockmark
postmark
pressmark
quark
remark
seamark
shark
skylark
spark
stark
tanbark
tetrarch
trademark

ARL
Arles
carl
Carl
ensnarl
gnarl
marl
snarl
unsnarl

ARM
alarm
arm
charm
disarm
farm
firearm
forearm
gendarme
harm
lukewarm
pre-warm
rearm
schoolmarm
sidearm
swarm
unarm
yardarm

AIRN
bairn
cairn

ARN
barn
darn
forewarn
Marne
tarn
warn
yarn

ARP
cardsharp
carp
harp
scarp
sharp
tarp

ARS
farce
parse
sparse

ARSH
harsh
marsh

ART
apart
art
blackheart
Bogart
cart
chart
counterpart
dart
depart
Descartes
dogcart
fart
flowchart
forepart
handcart
hart
heart
impart
mart
mouthpart
Mozart
outsmart
oxcart
part
pushcart
quart
rampart
rechart
smart
start

swart
sweetheart
tart
upstart

ARV
carve
starve

Long AS
abase
ace
airspace
apace
backspace
base
bass
birthplace
boldface
bookcase
bootlace
brace
braincase
briefcase
case
chaise
chase
commonplace
coupes
crankcase
crawlspace
dace
debase
deface
disgrace
displace
dogface
doughface
efface
embrace

encase
enlace
erase
face
firebase
fireplace
footrace
grace
headrace
headspace
incase
interlace
lace
lactase
lightface
mace
millrace
misplace
notecase
outface
outpace
outrace
pace
paleface
place
plais
race
replace
resting place
retrace
scapegrace
shoelace
showcase
showplace
slipcase
smearcase
someplace
space
staircase
subspace

suitcase
steeplechase
tailrace
Thrace
trace
typeface
ukase
unlace
vase
watchcase
wheelbase
whiteface

ASS
alas
amass
ass
bass
bluegrass
brass
bypass
class
crabgrass
crass
crevasse
demitasse
en masse
eyeglass
gas
glass
grass
harass
hourglass
impasse
jackass
landmass
lass
looking glass
madras
mass

masse
middle class
morass
outclass
overpass
pass
repass
sass
sassafras
spyglass
subclass
sunglass
surpass
sassafras
teargas
trespass
wineglass
working class
wrasse

ASH
abash
ash
backlash
balderdash
bash
brash
cache
calabash
cash
clash
crash
dash
eyelash
flash
gash
gnash
hash
lash
mash

mishmash
moustache
mustache
panache
potash
rash
rehash
sash
slapdash
slash
smash
splash
stash
thrash
tongue-lash
trash
unlash
whiplash

ASK
ask
bask
Basque
cask
casque
flask
mask
task
unmask

ASP
asp
clasp
enclasp
gasp
grasp
handclasp
hasp
rasp
unclasp

Long AST
abased
aced
aftertaste
backspaced
bald-faced
barefaced
based
baste
boldfaced
braced
cased
chased
chaste
debased
defaced
disgraced
displaced
distaste
effaced
embraced
encased
erased
faced
freckle-faced
foretaste
graced
hatchet-faced
haste
incased
laced
lambast
lambaste
lightfaced
misplaced
outfaced
outraced
paced
paste
placed

posthaste
raced
replaced
retraced
self-paced
shamefaced
shirtwaist
showcased
snail-paced
spaced
straight-faced
straight-laced
straitlaced
taste
toothpaste
traced
two-faced
unchaste
unlaced
unplaced
untraced
waist
waste

AST
aghast
amassed
avast
bedfast
Belfast
blast
bombast
broadcast
bypassed
cast
caste
classed
contrast
degassed
downcast

fast
flabbergast
forecast
foremast
gassed
glassed
grassed
handfast
harassed
iconoclast
lambast
lambaste
last
mainmast
massed
mast
miscast
newscast
outcast
outclassed
outlast
overcast
passed
past
recast
repast
roughcast
sandblast
sassed
setfast
sitfast
sportscast
steadfast
surpassed
teargassed
topmast
trespassed
typecast
vast

Long AT

abate
abbreviate
abdicate
abrogate
accelerate
accentuate
acclimate
accommodate
accumulate
acetate
activate
actuate
adjudicate
administrate
adulterate
advocate
aerate
affiliate
agglutinate
aggravate
agitate
airfreight
alienate
alleviate
alliterate
allocate
altercate
alternate
amalgamate
ambulate
ameliorate
amputate
animate
annihilate
annotate
annunciate
antedate
anticipate
antiquate

apartheid
apostate
appreciate
approbate
appropriate
approximate
arbitrate
arrogate
articulate
asphyxiate
aspirate
assassinate
assimilate
associate
ate
attenuate
authenticate
automate
await
backdate
bait
bantamweight
baseplate
bate
bedmate
berate
bicarbonate
bifurcate
billingsgate
birthrate
bodyweight
boilerplate
bookplate
breastplate
calculate
calibrate
candidate
capacitate
capitate
capitulate

capsulate
captivate
carbohydrate
carbonate
carburet
castigate
castrate
celebrate
cheapskate
checkmate
chelate
chlorate
chlorinate
circulate
circumambulate
circumgyrate
circumnavigate
citrate
classmate
coagulate
cogitate
cognate
collaborate
collate
collocate
commemorate
commiserate
communicate
compensate
complicate
concatenate
concentrate
conciliate
confiscate
conflate
congratulate
congregate
conjugate
consecrate
consolidate

consternate
constipate
contaminate
contemplate
contraindicate
cooperate
coordinate
copperplate
copulate
cordate
correlate
corroborate
corrugate
counterweight
crate
create
cremate
criminate
culminate
cultivate
cumulate
cuspidate
cyclamate
date
deactivate
deadweight
deathrate
debate
debilitate
decaffeinate
decapitate
decarbonate
decelerate
decimate
decontaminate
decorate
dedicate
defecate
defibrillate
deflagrate

deflate
defoliate
degenerate
dehydrate
delate
delegate
deliberate
delimitate
delineate
demarcate
demodulate
demonstrate
denigrate
denominate
dentate
denticulate
depilate
depopulate
deprecate
depreciate
depredate
derate
deregulate
derogate
desecrate
desegregate
desiccate
designate
deteriorate
detonate
detoxicate
devaluate
devastate
deviate
dictate
differentiate
digitate
dilapidate
dilate
disaffiliate

disassociate
discombobulate
discriminate
disintegrate
dislocate
disorientate
disseminate
dissimilate
dissipate
dissociate
distillate
divagate
domesticate
dominate
donate
doorplate
downstate
duplicate
educate
eight
ejaculate
elaborate
elate
electroplate
elevate
eliminate
elongate
elucidate
maciate
emanate
mancipate
emasculate
emigrate
emulate
encapsulate
enervate
enumerate
enunciate
equate
equivocate

eradicate
eructate
escalate
estate
estimate
etiolate
evacuate
evaluate
evaporate
eventuate
eviscerate
exacerbate
exaggerate
exasperate
excavate
excommunicate
excruciate
exculpate
execrate
exhilarate
exonerate
expatiate
expectorate
expiate
explicate
expropriate
expurgate
extenuate
exterminate
extrapolate
extricate
fabricate
facilitate
fascinate
fate
featherweight
fecundate
federate
felicitate
fibrillate

filtrate
fixate
flagellate
flocculate
floodgate
fluctuate
fluoridate
flyweight
foliate
folliculate
formulate
fornicate
freight
frustrate
fumigate
gait
gate
gelate
geminate
gemmate
generate
germinate
gestate
gesticulate
gladiate
glutamate
gradate
graduate
granulate
grate
gravitate
great
gyrate
habituate
hallucinate
halogenate
hate
headgate
heavyweight
helpmate

erniate
hesitate
hibernate
homogenate
humate
humiliate
hundredweight
hydrate
hydrogenate
hyperventilate
hyphenate
illuminate
illustrate
imbricate
imitate
immigrate
immolate
impersonate
implicate
imprecate
impregnate
inactivate
inaugurate
incapacitate
incarcerate
incarnate
inchoate
incinerate
incorporate
incriminate
incubate
inculcate
inculpate
indicate
individuate
indoctrinate
indurate
inebriate
infatuate
infiltrate

inflate
infuriate
ingrate
ingratiate
initiate
inmate
innate
innervate
innovate
inoculate
inosculate
inseminate
insensate
insinuate
instate
instigate
insubordinate
insulate
integrate
interdigitate
interpolate
interrelate
interrogate
interstate
intestate
intimate
intimidate
intoxicate
inundate
invalidate
investigate
invigorate
iodate
iodinate
irate
irradiate
irrigate
irritate
isolate
iterate

jailbait
jubilate
Kuwait
lacerate
lactate
laminate
lancinate
lapidate
late
laureate
legate
legislate
levitate
liberate
ligate
lightweight
liquidate
litigate
lobate
locate
loculate
lubricate
lucubrate
luxate
luxuriate
lyrate
lysate
macerate
machinate
maculate
magistrate
magnate
makeweight
mandate
manipulate
marinate
masticate
masturbate
mate
matriculate

maturate
mediate
medicate
meditate
meliorate
menstruate
messmate
metricate
middleweight
migrate
militate
misappropriate
miscalculate
misdate
mismate
mispunctuate
misstate
mistranslate
mithridate
mitigate
moderate
modulate
motivate
muriate
mutate
mutilate
nameplate
narrate
nauseate
navigate
necessitate
negate
negotiate
neonate
nitrate
nodulate
nominate
notate
novate
nucleate

numerate
obfuscate
objurgate
oblate
obligate
obliterate
obviate
officiate
oleate
operate
orate
orchestrate
orientate
originate
ornate
oscillate
osculate
outstate
ovate
overate
overcompensate
overdecorate
overeducate
overestimate
overfreight
overinflate
overpopulate
overrate
overregulate
overstate
overstimulate
overweight
ovulate
oxygenate
paginate
palliate
palmate
palpate
palpitate
paperweight

participate
pate
peculate
penetrate
pennate
pennyweight
perambulate
percolate
perforate
permeate
perpetrate
perpetuate
personate
phonate
phosphate
picrate
pignorate
pileate
pinnate
placate
plait
plate
playmate
plicate
pollinate
pontificate
populate
postdate
postulate
potentate
prate
precalculate
precipitate
predate
predesignate
predestinate
predicate
predominate
preestimate
prefabricate

prelate
premedicate
premeditate
preponderate
prevaricate
primate
probate
procrastinate
procreate
profligate
prognosticate
prolate
proliferate
promulgate
pronate
propagate
propitiate
prorate
prorogate
prostate
prostrate
proximate
pulmonate
pulsate
punctuate
pustulate
quadruplicate
quoit
rabbinate
racemate
radiate
rate
reactivate
rebate
recalculate
recapitulate
reciprocate
recirculate
reconciliate
recreate

recriminate
recuperate
redecorate
rededicate
redesignate
reduplicate
reeducate
reevaluate
reformulate
refrigerate
regenerate
regulate
regurgitate
rehabilitate
rehydrate
reincarnate
reincorporate
reinoculate
reinstate
reintegrate
reinvestigate
reinvigorate
reiterate
rejuvenate
relate
relegate
relocate
remonstrate
remunerate
renegotiate
renominate
renovate
repatriate
replicate
repopulate
reprobate
repudiate
resinate
resituate
resonate

restate
resuscitate
retaliate
reticulate
revaluate
reverberate
roommate
rotate
ruminate
rusticate
saccate
saccharate
salivate
sanitate
satiate
saturate
schoolmate
scintillate
sedate
segregate
sensate
separate
sequestrate
serrate
serrulate
shipmate
sibilate
significate
silicate
simulate
situate
skate
slate
soleplate
somnambulate
sophisticate
spate
speculate
spiculate
spoliate

squamate
stagnate
stalemate
staminate
state
stellate
stimulate
stipulate
straight
strait
strangulate
striate
subdelegate
subjugate
sublimate
subordinate
substantiate
substrate
sucrate
suffocate
sulcate
sulfate
sulfurate
sulphate
sulphurate
sultanate
supersaturate
supinate
supplicate
surrogate
syncopate
syndicate
tabulate
tailgate
tannate
teammate
terminate
titillate
titrate
tolerate

tollgate
trait
translate
transliterate
transmigrate
transubstantiate
triangulate
trifurcate
triloculate
triphosphate
triplicate
truncate
turbinate
ulcerate
ululate
umbellate
umbilicate
umbonate
unadulterate
uncinate
uncrate
underestimate
underrate
understate
underweight
undulate
unsaturate
update
upstate
urinate
vacate
vaccinate
vacillate
vaginate
validate
vallate
valuate
variate
variegate
vegetate

venerate
ventilate
vertebrate
vibrate
vindicate
violate
vitiate
vituperate
vulgate
wait
Watergate
weight
welterweight
zonate

AT

at
acrobat
aristocrat
autocrat
automat
bat
batt
begat
bobcat
brat
brickbat
bureaucrat
cat
chat
chitchat
combat
cravat
defat
democrat
dingbat
diplomat
doormat
drat
fat

flat
format
gnat
hat
hellcat
hepcat
housesat
jurat
landsat
mat
matt
matte
muscat
muskrat
nonfat
pat
photostat
plat
plutocrat
polecat
proletariat
pussycat
rat
rheostat
sat
scat
scatt
secretariat
skat
slat
spat
splat
sprat
stat
tabbycat
tat
that
thereat
thermostat
tigercat

tomcat
vat
whereat
wildcat
wombat

Long ATHE
bathe
lathe
scathe
sunbathe
swathe

Long AITH
faith
wraith

ATH
aftermath
bath
birdbath
bloodbath
bridal path
bypath
footbath
footpath
hath
homeopath
lath
math
path
psychopath
sociopath
towpath
warpath
wrath

Long AV
behave
brave

cave
clave
concave
conclave
crave
deprave
enclave
engrave
enslave
exclave
forgave
gave
grave
knave
lave
margrave
misbehave
nave
outbrave
pave
rave
repave
save
shave
shockwave
shortwave
slave
spokeshave
stave
they've
waive
wave

AV
calve
halve
have
salve

Long AZ
ablaze
agaze
airways
allays
always
amaze
appraise
archways
arrays
ashtrays
assays
baize
ballets
bays
beltways
berets
betrays
bikeways
birthdays
blaze
bouquets
braise
brays
braze
breezeways
buffets
byplays
byways
cachets
cafes
catchphrase
causeways
chaise
chalets
clays
cliches
conveys
craze
crochets

days
daze
decays
deejays
defrays
delays
dismays
displays
doorways
dossiers
drays
driveways
edgeways
endways
entrees
essays
fairways
fays
faze
filets
fillets
flatways
flays
flyways
folkways
forays
fortes
fraise
frappes
frays
freeways
Fridays
gainsays
gangways
gateways
gays
gaze
glaces
glaze
gourmets

grays
graze
hallways
hatchways
Hayes
hays
haze
highways
hoorays
hurrays
inlays
inveighs
jays
lactase
lays
laze
leastways
lengthways
liaise
mainstays
maize
malaise
maltase
mayonnaise
mays
maze
melees
middays
midways
mislays
misplays
Mondays
morays
mores
nays
neighs
nosegays
nowadays
obeys
ok's

okays
outlays
outplays
outstays
outweighs
padres
parfaits
parkways
parlays
pathways
pays
phase
phrase
piques
plays
polonaise
portrays
praise
prays
prepays
preys
purees
purveys
quays
raceways
railways
raise
rase
rays
raze
relays
repays
rephrase
replays
roadways
runways
sanseis
sashays
schooldays
screenplays

seaways
shays
sideways
slantways
slays
sleighs
souffles
spays
speedways
spillways
splays
sprays
stairways
stargaze
stays
strays
subways
sucrase
sundaes
Sundays
surveys
sways
thrombase
throughways
thruways
Thursdays
tokays
toupees

trays
Tuesdays
ukase
upraise
upraised
valets
vase
walkways
waylays
ways
Wednesdays
weekdays
weighs
workdays

AZ
as
has
jazz
pizazz
pizzazz
razz
razzmatazz
snares
topaz
whereas

AZH
barrage
badinage
camouflage
corsage
dislodge
dodge
entourage
garage
hodgepodge
lodge
massage
mirage
persiflage
outdodge

AZM
bioplasm
chasm
ectoplasm
enthusiasm
iconoclasm
metaplasm
protoplasm
sarcasm
spasm
phantasm
plasm

EE

abaci
abalone
abandonee
abashedly
abbey
abc
abdominally
abernathy
aberrancy
aberrantly
abhorrently
abidingly
ability
abjectly
ablatively
ablutionary
ably
abnormality
abnormally
abolitionary
abominably
aboriginally
aborigine
abortively
abrasively
abruptly
absente
absentee
absently
absentmindedly
absolutely
absorbency
absorbingly
abstractly
absurdity
absurdly
abundantly
abusively
abysmally

academically
academy
accentually
acceptability
accessibility
accessory
accidentally
acclivity
accompany
accordingly
accountability
accountably
accountancy
accuracy
accurately
accursedly
accusatively
accusatory
acey-deucey
achy
acidity
acidly
acknowledgedly
acme
acne
acoustically
acquiescently
acquisitively
acridity
acridly
acrimony
acrobatically
actively
activity
actuality
actually
actuary
acuity
acutely
adamantly

adaptability
adaptively
addictively
additionally
addressee
adeptly
adequacy
adequately
adherently
adhesively
adjacency
adjacently
adjectivally
adjudicatory
adjunctly
adjustability
admirably
admiralty
admiringly
admissability
admissibility
admissibly
admittedly
adobe
adolescently
adoptability
adoptee
adoptively
adorably
adroitly
adulterously
adultery
adultly
advantageously
adventurously
adverbially
adversary
adversatively
adversely
adversity

advertently
advisability
advisably
advisatory
advisedly
advisory
advocacy
aerially
aerie
aerobically
aerodynamically
aeronautically
aerotherapy
aesthetically
affability
affably
affectionately
affectively
affinity
affirmably
affirmatively
afflictively
affluently
agelessly
agency
aggressively
agilely
agility
agonizingly
agony
agree
agreeably
agronomy
aimlessly
airily
airlessly
airworthy
airy
alacrity
alarmingly

albany
albuquerque
alchemy
alcoholically
alertly
algae
algebraically
alimentary
alimony
alkalinity
allegedly
Allegheny
allegorically
allegory
allergy
alley
allocatee
allottee
allowedly
alluringly
allusively
almightily
almighty
aloofly
alphabetically
already
alternately
alternatively
altruistically
alumnae
amateurishly
amazedly
amazingly
ambidextrously
ambiguity
ambiguously
ambitiously
ambivalently
ambulatory
amenably

amenity
amiability
amiably
amicability
amicably
amity
amnesty
amoebae
amorality
amorally
amorously
amply
amputee
amusedly
amusingly
Amy
anaerobically
analogically
analogously
analogy
analytically
anarchically
anarchy
anasazi
anatomically
anatomy
ancestrally
ancestry
anchovy
anciently
ancillary
andy
anemone
anesthetically
angelically
angiostomy
angrily
angry
angularity
angularly

animality
animosity
anniversary
annotatively
annoyingly
annually
annuity
annunciatory
anomaly
anomie
anonymity
anonymously
ante
antennae
anteriorly
anthology
anthony
anthropology
anti
antibody
anticipatory
antidotally
antigone
antigravity
antiheroically
antipathy
antiquary
antiquely
antiquity
antiseptically
antislavery
antisocially
antithetically
antsy
anxiety
anxiously
any
anybody
aortae
apache

apathetically
apathy
aphoristically
aphrodite
apiary
apically
aplenty
apocope
apocryphally
apogee
apologetically
apology
apoplectically
apoplexy
apostasy
apostrophe
apothecary
appallingly
apparently
appealingly
appendectomy
appetizingly
applicability
applicably
applicatively
appointee
appositely
appositively
appraisingly
appreciably
appreciatively
appreciatory
apprehensibly
apprehensively
approachability
appropriately
approvingly
approximately
aptly
arbitrarily

arbitrary
archaeologically
archaeology
archaically
archduchy
archenemy
archeology
archery
architecturally
ardently
arduously
areolae
argosy
arguably
argumentatively
aridity
aridly
aristocracy
aristocratically
arithmetically
armlessly
armory
army
aromatically
arrestee
arrivederci
arrogantly
arteriotomy
artery
artfully
articulately
articulatory
artificiality
artificially
artillery
artily
artistically
artistry
artlessly
arty

ascendancy
ascetically
aseptically
asexuality
ashamedly
ashy
asininely
asininity
aspiringly
assembly
assertively
assessee
assiduously
assignee
assisi
assonantly
assuasively
assumably
assumedly
assuredly
asthmatically
astonishingly
astoundingly
astringency
astrology
astronautically
astronomically
astronomy
astutely
asymmetrically
asymmetry
athletically
atmospherically
atomically
atonality
atonally
atrociously
atrocity
atrophy
attackingly

attainability
attainably
attendantly
attentively
attorney
attractively
attributively
atypically
audaciously
audacity
audibly
audiology
auditory
augury
augustly
aurae
aurally
auspiciously
aussie
austerely
austerity
authentically
authenticity
authoritatively
authority
autobiography
autocracy
autocratically
automatically
autopsy
autotherapy
auxiliary
availability
avariciously
avengingly
aversively
aviary
avidly
avoidably
avowedly

avowry
awardee
aweary
awesomely
awfully
awkwardly
axially
axillary
axiomatically
axletree
babbittry
babinski
baby
backwardly
bacteriologically
bacteriology
badly
baggily
baggy
bailee
baily
bailie
bakery
balcony
baldly
balefully
Bali
balky
balladry
ballistically
balmily
balmy
balneotherapy
baloney
banality
banally
banditry
bandy
bankruptcy
banshee

banteringly
banti
baptistery
barbarically
barbarity
barbarously
barberry
barely
bargainee
barky
barley
barometrically
barometry
barony
baselessly
bashfully
basically
bastardly
bastardy
battery
batty
bawdily
bawdry
bawdy
bayberry
be
beachy
beady
beanery
beanie
bearably
bearberry
beastly
beauteously
beautifully
beauty
beckoningly
becomingly
bee
beefy

beery
beggarly
beggary
begrudgingly
belatedly
belfry
believability
believably
bellicosely
bellicosity
belligerency
belligerently
belly
benedictory
beneficently
beneficially
beneficiary
benevolently
benightedly
benignly
benny
beriberi
berkeley
berry
beseechingly
bestiality
bestially
bestiary
betty
bevy
bewilderingly
bewitchery
biannually
biblically
bibliographically
bibliography
bibliotherapy
bicentenary
biconcavity
biconvexity

biddy
biennially
bigamously
bigamy
biggie
bigheartedly
bigotedly
bigotry
bikini
bilaterality
bilaterally
biliary
bilingually
billowy
billy
biloxi
bimonthly
binary
bindery
binocularly
bioactivity
biochemically
biochemistry
biodegradability
bioelectricity
biogeography
biography
biologically
biology
biopsy
biopsychology
biotechnology
biotically
bipolarity
bipotentiality
birdie
bisexuality
bisexually
bitchy
bitingly

bitsy
bitterly
bitty
biweekly
biyearly
bizarrely
blackberry
blackly
blamably
blamelessly
blameworthy
blandly
blankly
blarney
blasphemously
blasphemy
blatancy
blatantly
bleakly
bleary
blenchingly
blessedly
blightingly
blindly
blissfully
blistery
blithely
blocky
bloodily
bloodthirstily
bloodthirsty
bloody
bloomy
blossomy
blotchy
blowsy
blowy
blowzy
blt
blubbery

blueberry
bluey
bluntly
blurry
blushfully
blustery
boastfully
boastingly
bobby
bodily
body
bogey
boggy
bogy
boilary
Boise
boisterously
boldly
bologna
bombastically
bonnie
bonny
bony
booby
boogie
bookie
boorishly
bootee
bootery
bootlessly
booty
boozy
bosky
bosomy
bossily
bossy
botany
botchily
botchy
bottomry

bougie
bouncingly
bouncy
boundary
boundlessly
bounteously
bounty
bourgeoisie
bowery
bowie
boyishly
boysenberry
brainily
brainlessly
brainy
brambly
brandy
brashly
brasserie
brassie
brassy
bratty
bravely
bravery
brawlingly
brawly
brawnily
brawny
brazenly
breathlessly
breathtakingly
breathy
breezily
breezy
brevity
brewery
bribee
bribery
bridally
briefly

briery
brightly
brilliancy
brilliantly
briny
briskly
bristly
broadly
broccoli
brokenly
brokerly
bronchially
bronchopulmonary
bronzy
broody
broomy
brotherly
brothy
brownie
bruskly
brusquely
brutality
brutally
brutishly
bubbly
buckishly
buddy
budgetary
buffoonery
buffy
buggery
buggy
bulgy
bulky
bully
bumblebee
bumpy
bunchy
bunny
buoy

buoyancy
buoyantly
bureaucracy
bureaucratically
burglary
burgundy
burley
burly
burry
bursectomy
burundi
bury
busby
bushy
busily
busty
busy
busybody
butchery
buttery
cabby
cacciatore
cacography
cacophonously
cacophony
cadaverously
caddie
caddishly
caddy
cadency
cadre
cagey
cagily
cajolery
cajolingly
calamity
calculability
calculatedly
calculatingly
calgary

calligraphy
calliope
callously
calmingly
calmly
calorically
calorie
calorimetry
calory
calvary
camaraderie
campi
camporee
campy
canape
canary
cancerously
candidacy
candidly
candy
cannery
cannibalistically
cannily
canny
canonically
canonicity
canonry
canopy
cantankerously
canterbury
cantingly
capability
capably
capaciously
capacity
capillary
capitalistically
capitulatory
capriciously
captaincy

captivity
cardiectomy
cardiography
cardiology
cardiometry
cardiopulmonary
cardiotherapy
carefree
carefully
carelessly
carnality
carnally
carnegie
carnivorously
carny
carousingly
carpentry
Carrie
carroty
carry
cartography
castigatory
casually
casualty
catalytically
catastrophe
catchy
categorically
category
cattery
cattily
catty
causality
causally
caustically
cautionary
cautiously
cavalierly
cavalry
cavernously

cavity
CB
cc
CD
ceaselessly
celebrity
celery
celestially
celibacy
cellularity
cemetery
centeredly
centrality
centrally
century
cephalically
cerebrally
ceremonially
ceremoniously
ceremony
certainly
certainty
certifiably
chairlady
chalky
chamois
chancellery
chancellory
chancy
chandlery
chaplaincy
characteristically
chargee
charitably
charity
charlatanry
Charley
Charlie
charmingly
chassis

chastely
chastity
chattily
chatty
chauvinistically
cheaply
cheatery
checkerberry
cheekily
cheeky
cheerfully
cheerily
cheerlessly
cheery
cheesy
chemically
chemistry
Cherokee
cherry
chesty
chewy
chicanery
chichi
chickadee
chickpea
chiefly
childishly
Chile
chili
chilly
chimney
chimpanzee
chintzy
chippy
chivalrously
chivalry
Chloe
choicely
chokecherry
choky

choosey
choosy
chop-suey
choppily
choppy
chorally
choreographically
choreography
Christianity
Christie
christly
chromotherapy
chronically
chronicity
chronography
chronologically
chronology
chubby
chuffy
chummily
chummy
chunkily
chunky
churlishly
chutney
Cincinnati
cindery
cinematically
cinematography
circuitously
circuitry
circularity
circularly
circulatory
citizenry
city
civically
civility
civilly
clairvoyancy

clairvoyantly
clammy
clamorously
clandestinely
clannishly
clarity
classically
classy
clattery
clayey
cleanly
clearheadedly
clearly
clemency
clemently
clergy
clerkly
cleverly
climatology
clingy
clinically
cliquey
cliquishly
cloddy
cloggy
closely
clotty
cloudberry
cloudily
cloudy
clownishly
clumpy
clumsily
clumsy
clunky
coarsely
coaxingly
cobwebby
cockamamie
cockily

cockney
cocky
coequality
coequally
coercively
coextensively
coffee
cogency
cogently
coherency
coherently
cohesively
coincidentally
coldly
colicky
collectedly
collectively
collectivity
collegiality
collegially
collie
colloquially
colonelcy
colony
colorability
colorably
colorfully
colossally
colostomy
comanche
combatively
combustively
comedy
comely
comfortably
comfy
commemoratively
commendably
commercially
commie

commissary
committee
commodiously
commodity
commonality
commonalty
commonly
communally
communicability
communicably
communicatively
communistically
community
commutatively
compactly
company
comparably
comparatively
compassionately
compatibility
compatibly
compellingly
compensability
compensatively
compensatory
competency
competently
competitively
complacency
complacently
complaisantly
complementary
completely
complexity
compliancy
compliantly
complicatedly
complicity
complimentarily
complimentary

compositely
comprehensibility
comprehensively
compressedly
compressively
compulsively
compulsory
computability
comradely
comradery
concavity
concededly
conceitedly
conceivability
conceivably
concentricity
conceptually
concertedly
conciliatory
concisely
conclusively
concomitantly
concordantly
concretely
concurrently
concussively
condemnatory
condescendingly
conditionality
conditionally
conductivity
coney
confectionery
confederacy
conferee
confessedly
confetti
confidentiality
confidentially
confidently

confirmatory
conformably
conformity
confoundedly
confraternity
confusedly
confusingly
congeniality
congenially
congenitally
congratulatory
congressionally
congruency
congruently
congruity
congruously
conically
conjointly
connectively
Connie
connivery
conscientiously
consciously
consecutively
consensually
consequentially
consequently
conservatively
conservatory
considerably
considerately
consignatary
consignee
consistency
consistently
consolingly
conspicuously
conspiracy
conspiringly
constabulary

constancy
constantly
constituency
constituently
constitutionality
constitutionally
constrainedly
constructively
consultatory
consummately
consumptively
contagiously
contemplatively
contemporaneously
contemporarily
contemporary
contemptibly
contemptuously
contentedly
contentiously
contently
conterminously
contestably
contestee
contextually
contiguity
contiguously
continentally
contingency
contingently
continually
continuity
continuously
contractibility
contractually
contradictively
contradictory
contrarily
contrary
contrastingly

contritely
contrivedly
controllability
controllably
controversially
controversy
conveniently
conventionality
conventionally
convergency
conversationally
conversely
convexity
convincingly
conviviality
convivially
convolutely
convulsively
cony
cookery
cookie
cooley
coolie
coolly
cooperatively
coordinately
cootie
copiously
coppery
copulatively
copulatory
copy
coquetry
coquettishly
cordiality
cordially
cordlessly
corky
corny
corollary

coronary
corporally
corporately
corpulency
corpulently
correctly
correspondingly
corrie
corroboratively
corroboratory
corrodibility
corrosively
corruptibility
corruptibly
corruptly
cosignatory
cosmetically
cosmetology
cosmically
cosmogony
cosmology
costly
coterie
cottony
coulee
counselee
countability
counteractively
counterfeitly
counterinsurgency
counterinsurgently
counterplea
counterproductively
counterrevolutionary
country
county
courageously
courteously
courtesy
courtly

covenantee
covertly
covetously
covey
cowardly
cowrie
cowry
coyly
coyote
cozily
cozy
crabbily
crabby
crackly
craftily
craftsmanly
crafty
craggy
cranberry
cranially
crankily
cranky
cranny
crappie
crappy
crassly
cravenly
cravingly
crawly
crazily
crazy
creakily
creaky
creamery
creamy
creatively
creativity
credibility
credibly
credulity

credulously
cree
creepily
creepy
crematory
crestfallenly
criminality
criminally
criminatory
criminology
crinkly
crisply
crispy
criticality
critically
croakily
croaky
crockery
crony
crookedly
crookery
crosby
crossly
crotchety
croupy
crucially
cruddy
crudely
crudity
cruelly
cruelty
crumbly
crumby
crummy
crunchy
crusty
crybaby
cryptically
cryptographically
cryptography

cryptology
cubby
cuckoldry
cuddly
cuddy
culinary
culpability
culpably
culturally
cumbrously
cumulatively
cunningly
cupidity
curability
curably
curie
curiosity
curiously
curly
currency
currently
curry
cursedly
cursively
cursorily
cursory
curtly
curtsey
curtsy
curvaceously
curvedly
curvy
cushily
cushy
custody
customarily
customary
cutaneously
cutely
cutesy

cutey
cutie
cutlery
cybernetically
cyclically
cylindrically
cynically
cytologically
cytology
daddy
daffy
daftly
daily
daintily
dainty
daiquiri
dairy
daisy
dally
damagingly
damnably
damply
dancingly
dandy
dangerously
dankly
dapperly
daringly
darkly
dashingly
dastardly
datively
daughterly
dauntlessly
dazedly
dazzlingly
ddt
deadly
deafly
deanery

dearie
dearly
deathlessly
deathly
debatably
debauchedly
debauchee
debauchery
Debbie
debility
debonairly
debris
debtee
decadently
deceitfully
deceivingly
decency
decently
deceptively
decidedly
deciduously
decisively
declaratively
declivity
decoratively
decorously
decreasingly
decree
dedicatee
dedicatory
deductively
deeply
defamatory
defamingly
defectively
defenselessly
defensibility
defensibly
defensively
deferentially

defiantly
deficiency
deficiently
defilingly
definably
definitely
definitively
deflationary
deformity
deftly
degeneracy
degenerately
degradedly
degree
deity
dejectedly
delectably
delegacy
delegatory
deleteriously
Delhi
deli
deliberately
deliberatively
delicacy
delicately
deliciously
delightedly
delightfully
delinquency
delinquently
deliriously
delivery
deludingly
delusionary
delusively
delusory
demagoguery
demagogy
dementedly

democracy
democratically
demographically
demography
demonology
demonstrably
demonstratively
dempsey
demurely
dendrology
denigratory
densely
density
dentally
dentistry
deontology
dependability
dependably
dependency
dependently
deplorably
deportee
depositary
depository
depravedly
depravity
deprecatingly
depreciatingly
depressingly
depressively
deputy
derby
derisively
derisory
dermatology
derogatorily
derogatory
descriptively
deservedly
deservingly

desiccatory
desirability
desirably
desolately
despairingly
desperately
despicably
despitefully
despondency
despondently
despotically
destiny
destitutely
destroyingly
destructibility
destructively
detachably
detainee
detectably
determinacy
determinedly
detestably
detrimentally
deuteronomy
devastatingly
developmentally
deviancy
devilishly
devilry
deviltry
deviously
devolutionary
devotedly
devotee
devoutly
dewberry
dewily
dewy
dexterity
dexterously

diabolically
diagnostically
diagonally
diagrammatically
diametrically
diary
dichotomously
dichotomy
dickey
dictatorially
dictatory
dictionary
didactically
dietary
dietetically
differentially
differently
difficultly
difficulty
diffidently
diffusely
digestively
digitally
dignitary
dignity
digressively
dilatorily
dilatory
diligently
dilly
dillydally
dimensionality
dimly
dimply
dinghy
dingily
dingy
dinkey
dinky
diplomacy

diplomatically
dippy
directionally
directly
directory
direfully
direly
dirtily
dirty
disability
disadvantageously
disaffectedly
disagree
disagreeably
disappointedly
disappointingly
disapprovingly
disarmingly
disassembly
disastrously
discerningly
disciplinary
disclamatory
disconcertingly
disconsolately
discontentedly
discontinuity
discontinuously
discordantly
discouragingly
discourteously
discourtesy
discovery
discreetly
discrepancy
discrepantly
discretely
discretionary
discriminately
discriminatory

discursively
disdainfully
disembody
disenchantingly
disgracefully
disgustedly
disgustingly
disharmony
dishearteningly
dishonestly
dishonesty
dishonorably
disinterestedly
disjointedly
disloyally
disloyalty
dismally
Disney
disobediently
disorderly
disparagingly
disparately
disparity
dispassionately
dispensary
disputability
disputably
disquietingly
disreputability
disreputably
disrespectfully
disruptively
dissatisfactory
dissidently
dissimilarity
dissonantly
dissuasively
distally
distantly
distastefully

distillery
distinctively
distinctly
distinguishably
distractedly
distressfully
distressingly
distributively
distrustfully
disturbingly
ditty
diuretically
diurnally
divergently
diversely
diversionary
diversity
divinely
divinity
divisively
divorcee
divvy
dixie
dizzily
dizzy
DMZ
docilely
docility
doctrinally
documentary
doddery
dodgy
doggedly
doggery
doggie
doggy
dogie
doily
Dolby
dolefully

dollishly
dolly
domestically
domesticity
dominantly
Don Quixote
donkey
doohickey
dopey
dormancy
dormitory
dotingly
dotty
doubly
doubtfully
doubtingly
doubtlessly
doughy
dourly
dowdy
downheartedly
downy
dowry
doxy
dozy
drably
draftee
draftily
drafty
draggy
dramatically
drapery
drastically
draughty
drawee
dreadfully
dreamily
dreamy
drearily
dreary

dressy
drifty
drily
drippy
drizzly
dromedary
droopy
dropsy
drossy
drowsily
drowsy
drudgery
druggie
druggy
drunkenly
dryly
duality
dually
dubiously
duchy
ducky
ductility
duddie
duddy
duffy
dully
duly
dumbly
dummy
dumpy
dungaree
duplicity
durability
durably
dusky
dustily
dusty
duteously
dutifully
duty

dynamically
dynasty
dysentery
dystrophy
eagerly
early
earnestly
earthily
earthly
earthy
easily
easterly
eastwardly
easy
eatery
ebony
ebulliently
eccentrically
eccentricity
ecclesiastically
eclectically
ecologically
ecology
economically
economy
ecstacy
ecstasy
ecstatically
ecumenically
edacity
eddy
edgy
edibility
edictally
editorially
educability
educationally
EEG
eely
eerie

eerily
eery
effectively
effeminacy
effeminately
effendi
effervescently
effetely
efficaciously
efficacy
efficiency
efficiently
effigy
effortlessly
effulgently
effusively
egocentricity
egoistically
egotistically
egregiously
eighty
ejaculatory
EKG
elaborately
elastically
elasticity
elatedly
elderberry
elderly
electee
electively
electorally
electrically
electricity
electrolytically
electromagnetically
electronically
electroplexy
electrosurgery
electrotherapy

elegancy
elegantly
elegy
elementally
elementary
elfishly
eligibility
eligibly
eliminatory
elliptically
elocutionary
eloquently
elusively
embarrassedly
embarrassingly
embassy
embody
embracery
embroidery
emcee
emergency
emery
Emily
eminently
emissary
Emmy
emotionally
empathetically
empathy
emphatically
empirically
employee
emptily
empty
enchantingly
encouragingly
endearingly
endlessly
endocrinology
endogamy

endogenously
endomorphy
endorsee
endoscopy
enemy
energetically
energy
engagingly
enigmatically
enjoyably
enlistee
enmity
ennui
enormity
enormously
enquiry
enterostomy
enterprisingly
entertainingly
enthrallingly
enthusiastically
entirely
entirety
entity
entomologically
entomology
entreatingly
entreaty
entropy
entry
enviably
enviously
environmentally
envy
envyingly
epidemically
epigrammatically
epilepsy
epiphany
episodically

epistemology
epitome
epochally
eponymy
epoxy
equably
equality
equally
equanimity
equationally
equerry
equidistantly
equitably
equity
equivalency
equivalently
equivocacy
equivocally
erectly
Erie
erosely
erotically
errancy
errantly
erratically
erroneously
eruditely
eruptively
escapee
escrowee
esoterically
ESP
especially
esprit
essentially
estimably
eternally
eternity
ethereally
ethically

ethnically
ethnicity
ethnology
ethology
etiologically
etiology
etymology
eulogy
euphemistically
euphony
euphorically
eutrophy
evacuee
evanescently
evangelically
evangelistically
evasively
evenly
eventfully
eventuality
eventually
everlastingly
every
everybody
evictee
evidently
evilly
evolutionary
exacerbatingly
exactingly
exactly
exaggeratedly
exceedingly
excellency
excellently
exceptionally
excessively
excitatory
excitedly
exclamatory

exclusively
excretory
excruciatingly
exemplary
exigency
exiguity
exogamy
exorbitantly
exoterically
exotically
expansionary
expansively
expectancy
expectantly
expectedly
expediency
expediently
expeditionary
expeditiously
expensively
experimentally
expertly
explanatory
explicitly
exploratory
explosively
exponentially
expository
expressively
expressly
exquisitely
extemporaneously
extendibility
extensively
exteriority
externally
extorsively
extraneously
extraordinarily
extraordinary

extrasensory
extremely
extremity
extrinsically
exuberantly
exultantly
exultingly
fabulously
facetiously
facially
facilely
facility
facsimile
factory
factually
faculty
failingly
faintheartedly
faintly
fairly
fairy
faithfully
faithlessly
fakery
falconry
fallaciously
fallacy
fallibility
fallibly
falsely
falsie
falsity
falteringly
familiarity
familiarly
family
famously
fanatically
fancifully
fancily

fancy
fancy-free
fanny
fantasie
fantastically
fantasy
farcy
fashionably
fastidiously
fatalistically
fatality
fatally
fatefully
fatherly
fatly
fatty
fatuously
faultily
faultlessly
faulty
favorably
fawningly
FCC
FDIC
fearfully
fearlessly
fearsomely
feasibility
feasibly
feathery
february
fecundity
federally
fee
feeblemindedly
feebly
feelingly
feisty
felicitously
felicity

feloniously
felony
femininely
femininity
ferny
ferociously
ferocity
ferry
fertilely
fertility
fervency
fervently
fervidly
festively
festivity
fetchingly
fettucine
feudally
feverishly
fibulae
fictionally
fictitiously
fidelity
fidgety
fiendishly
fiercely
fieri
fiery
fifty
figuratively
Fiji
filially
filigree
filly
filmy
filthy
finale
finality
finally
financially

finely

finery

finicky

finitely

finny

firmly

firstly

fiscally

fishery

fishy

fitfully

fitly

fittingly

fixity

fizzy

flabbily

flabby

flagrancy

flagrantly

flaky

flamboyancy

flamboyantly

flamingly

flammability

flammably

flappy

flashily

flashy

flatly

flatteringly

flattery

flatulency

flauntingly

flaunty

flavorfully

flawlessly

flaxy

flea

flecky

flee

fleecy

fleetingly

fleetly

fleshly

fleshy

flexibility

flexibly

flighty

flimsily

flimsy

flinchingly

flinty

flippancy

flippantly

flirtatiously

flirtingly

flirty

floatability

floaty

flooey

floosie

floozie

floozy

floppily

floppy

florally

flossy

flouncy

flounderingly

floury

flowery

flowingly

fluency

fluently

fluffy

fluidity

fluidly

fluky

flunkey

flunky

fluoroscopically

flurry

fluttery

fluty

foamy

focally

foggily

foggy

fogy

folksy

folly

fondly

foolery

foolhardily

foolhardy

foolishly

foppery

forbearingly

forbiddingly

forcefully

forcibly

forehandedly

forelady

forensically

foresee

foreseeability

foresightedly

forestry

forgery

forgetfully

forky

forlornly

formalistically

formality

formally

formerly

formidably

formlessly

formulae

forthrightly

fortnightly
fortuitously
fortuity
fortunately
forty
forwardly
foully
foundry
fourpenny
fourthly
foxily
foxy
fragility
fragmentally
fragmentary
fragrancy
fragrantly
frailly
frailty
franchisee
frangibility
frankly
frantically
fraternally
fraternity
fraudulently
freakishly
freaky
freckly
free
freebie
freehandedly
freeheartedly
freely
freemasonry
frenetically
frenzy
frequency
frequently
freshly

fretfully
friary
fricassee
friday
friendly
frighteningly
frightfully
frigidity
frigidly
frilly
frippery
Frisbee
friskily
frisky
frivolity
frivolously
frizzily
frizzly
frizzy
frostily
frosty
frothily
frothy
frowningly
frowsily
frowsy
frowzily
frowzy
frozenly
frugality
frugally
fruitfully
fruitlessly
fruity
frumpy
frustratingly
FTC
fuddy
fuddy-duddy
fully

fumy
functionally
functionary
fundamentally
fundy
funerary
fungicidally
funky
funnily
funny
furiously
furriery
furrowy
furry
furtively
fury
fusee
fussily
fussy
fustily
fusty
futilely
futility
futuristically
fuzzy
fuzzy-wuzzy
gabby
gadgetry
gadgety
gaiety
gaily
gainfully
galaxy
galilee
gallantly
gallantry
gallery
galley
galvanically
gamely

gamesomely
gametically
gamey
gamily
gamy
Gandhi
gangly
gantry
gapingly
garibaldi
garishly
garlicky
garnishee
garrulity
garrulously
gaseously
gassy
gastronomically
gastronomy
gatsby
gaucherie
gaudily
gaudy
gauntly
gauzily
gauzy
gawky
gee
gelatinously
gelidly
geminately
Gemini
gemology
gendarmerie
genealogically
genealogy
generality
generally
generatively
generically

generosity
generously
genetically
geniality
genially
genie
genteelly
gentility
gentlemanly
gently
gentry
genuinely
geocentrically
geochemistry
geodesy
geographically
geography
geologically
geology
geometrically
geometry
germanely
Germany
germfree
germy
gerontology
Gethsemane
ghastly
ghostly
ghosty
ghoulishly
gibbosity
gibbously
gibingly
giddily
giddy
gigantically
gigglingly
giggly
gimcrackery

gimmickry
gimmicky
gimpy
gingerbready
gingerly
gingery
gipsy
glacially
gladioli
gladly
gladsomely
glairy
glamorously
glancingly
glandularly
glaringly
glary
glassily
glassy
gleamy
glcc
gleefully
gleety
glibly
glittery
glitzy
globally
gloomily
gloomy
gloriously
glory
glossary
glossily
glossy
gluey
glumly
glutinously
gluttonously
gluttony
gnarly

gnawingly
GNP
goalie
goatee
Gobi
goby
godlessly
godly
goldenly
golly
goodie
goodly
goody
goody-goody
gooey
goofy
gooseberry
goosey
goosy
gorgeously
gorily
Gorki
gory
gossipy
gothically
gouty
governability
grabby
gracefully
gracelessly
graciously
gradually
graffiti
grainy
grammatically
grammy
granary
grandbaby
grandee
grandiloquently

grandiosely
grandiosity
grandly
grannie
granny
grantee
granularity
granularly
grapey
graphically
graphology
graspingly
grassy
gratefully
gratifyingly
gratingly
gratuitously
gratuity
gravelly
gravely
gravity
gravy
grayly
grazingly
greasily
greasy
greatheartedly
greatly
greedily
greedy
greenery
greenly
gregariously
Gregory
greyly
grievingly
grievously
grimly
grimy
grindingly

grippingly
grippy
gripy
grisly
gristly
gritty
grizzly
grocery
groggily
groggy
groovy
gropingly
grossly
grotesquely
grouchily
grouchy
groundlessly
groupie
growlingly
grubbily
grubby
grudgingly
gruelingly
gruesomely
gruffly
grumbly
grumpily
grumpy
grundy
grungy
gruntingly
guacamole
guarantee
guardedly
Guernsey
Guildry
guilelessly
guiltily
guiltlessly
guilty

guinea	handedly	headily
gullibility	handily	heady
gullibly	handsomely	healthfully
gully	handy	healthily
gummy	hankie	healthy
gunky	hanky	hearteningly
gunnery	hanky-panky	heartily
gunny	haphazardly	heartlessly
guppy	haplessly	hearty
gurney	haply	heatedly
gushily	happily	heathery
gushy	happy	heathy
gussie	harassingly	heavenly
gussy	hardheadedly	heavily
gustatory	hardheartedly	heavy
gustily	hardily	Hebraically
gusty	hardly	hectically
gutsy	hardy	hedonically
gutturally	harlotry	heedfully
gutty	harmfully	heedlessly
gymnastically	harmlessly	hefty
gynecology	harmonically	hegemony
gypsy	harmoniously	heinously
gyroscopically	harmony	heliocentrically
haberdashery	harpy	heliocentricity
habitably	harry	heliotherapy
habitancy	harshly	heliotropically
habitually	hastily	hellishly
hackberry	hasty	helpfully
hackie	hatchery	helplessly
hackly	hatefully	Helsinki
hackney	haughtily	hematology
haggardly	haughty	Henry
hairy	hauntingly	heraldry
Haiti	Hawaii	herbicidally
halfheartedly	hazardously	herbivorously
halfpenny	hazily	Herby
hallucinatory	hazy	hereditarily
haltingly	he	hereditary
hammy	headachy	heredity

heresy
heretically
heritability
heritably
hermeneutically
hermetically
heroically
herpetology
Hershey
hesitancy
hesitantly
hesitatingly
heterodoxy
heterosexuality
heterosexually
heterotrophically
heuristically
hibachi
hickey
hickory
hideously
hierarchically
hierarchy
hieratically
highhandedly
highly
hilariously
hilarity
Hillary
hillbilly
hilly
Hindi
Hindostani
Hindustani
hippie
histologically
histology
historically
historicity
history

hitchy
hoagie
hoagy
hoarsely
hoary
hobby
hockey
hoggishly
hokey
hokeypokey
hoky-poky
holandry
holey
holistically
holly
holographically
holography
hologyny
holy
homebody
homely
homeopathy
homey
homicidally
homily
hominy
homogamy
homogeneity
homogeny
homology
homonymy
homosexuality
homosexually
homozygously
honestly
honesty
honey
honeybee
honkey
honkie

honky
honorably
honorarily
honorary
honoree
hooey
hookey
hooky
hootenanny
hopefully
hopelessly
Hopi
horizontally
hormonally
horny
horology
horrendously
horribly
horridly
horsey
horsy
hortatory
hosiery
hospitably
hospitality
hostelry
hostilely
hostility
hotheadedly
hotly
hourly
housewifely
housewifery
howdy
hubby
huckleberry
huffily
huffy
hugely
hulky

humanely
humanistically
humanity
humanly
humbly
humidity
humidly
humiliatingly
humility
humorlessly
humorously
Hungary
hungrily
hungry
hunky
hunky-dory
Huntley
hurriedly
hurry
hurry-scurry
hurtfully
husbandly
husbandry
huskily
husky
hussy
hydraulically
hydrology
hydrotherapy
hydrothermally
hydroxy
hygienically
hymnody
hyperacidity
hyperactivity
hyperbole
hyperbolically
hypercritically
hypersensitivity
hypersexuality

hypnotherapy
hypnotically
hypoacidity
hypocrisy
hypocritically
hypodermically
hyposensitivity
hypothetically
hypotonically
hysterectomy
hysterically
hysterology
ichthyology
icily
icky
icy
idealistically
ideally
idealogy
identically
identifiability
identifiably
identity
ideologically
ideology
idiocrasy
idiocy
idiomatically
idiosyncracy
idiosyncrasy
idiosyncratically
idiotically
idly
idolatry
iffy
ignobility
ignobly
ignominiously
ignominy
ignorantly

ileostomy
illegality
illegally
illegibly
illegitimacy
illegitimately
illicitly
illiteracy
illiterately
illogically
illuminatingly
illusory
illustratively
illustriously
imagery
imaginably
imaginarily
imaginary
imaginatively
imbecility
imitatee
imitatively
immaculately
immanency
immanently
immaterially
immaturely
immaturity
immeasurably
immediacy
immediately
immemorially
immensely
immensity
imminently
immobility
immoderately
immodestly
immodesty
immorality

immorally
immortality
immortally
immovably
immunity
immunology
immunotherapy
immutability
immutably
impalpability
impalpably
impartiality
impartially
impassability
impassibility
impassibly
impassively
impassivity
impatiently
impeccability
impeccably
impecuniously
impenetrably
impenitently
imperatively
imperceptibility
imperceptibly
imperfectly
imperially
imperiously
imperishably
impermanently
impermeably
impersonally
impertinently
imperturbably
imperviously
impetuously
impiety
impiously

impishly
implacability
implacably
implausibly
implicitly
impliedly
imploringly
impolitely
imponderably
importantly
importee
imposingly
impossibility
impossibly
impotency
impotently
impracticality
imprecisely
impregnability
impregnably
impressibility
impressionably
impressively
improbability
improbably
improperly
impropriety
improvidently
imprudently
impudently
impulsively
impunity
impurely
impurity
inability
inaccessibility
inaccuracy
inaccurately
inactively
inactivity

inadequacy
inadequately
inadmissibly
inadvertently
inadvisably
inalienably
inalterably
inanely
inanimately
inanity
inapplicably
inappropriately
inarticulately
inartistically
inattentively
inaudibly
inauspiciously
incalculably
incandescently
incapability
incapably
incapacity
incautiously
incendiary
incessantly
incestuously
inchoately
incidentally
incidently
incipiency
incisively
incitingly
inclemency
inclusively
incoherently
incomparably
incompatibility
incompatibly
incompetency
incompetently

incompletely
incomputably
inconceivably
inconclusively
incongruently
incongruity
incongruously
inconsiderately
inconsistency
inconsistently
inconsolably
inconspicuously
incontestably
incontinency
incontinently
incontrovertibly
inconveniently
incorrectly
incorrigibly
incorruptibility
incorruptibly
incorruptly
increasingly
incredibility
incredibly
incredulity
incredulously
incriminatory
inculpability
incumbency
incumbently
incurably
indecency
indecently
indecisively
indecorously
indefatigably
indefensibly
indefinitely
indelibly

indelicacy
indelicately
indemnitee
indemnity
independently
indescribably
indeterminacy
indeterminately
indicatively
indictably
indictee
indifferently
indigently
indignantly
indignity
indirectly
indiscreetly
indiscriminately
indisputably
indistinctly
indistinguishably
individuality
individually
indivisibility
indivisibly
indolently
indomitably
indorsee
indubitably
inductee
inductively
indulgently
industrially
industriously
industry
inebriety
ineffably
ineffectively
ineffectually
inefficaciously

inefficacy
inefficiency
inefficiently
inelegantly
ineligibility
ineligibly
ineloquently
ineptly
inequality
inequitably
inequity
inertly
inescapably
inestimably
inevitability
inevitably
inexactly
inexcusably
inexhaustibly
inexorably
inexpensively
inexpertly
inexplicably
inexplicit
inexpressibly
inextinguishably
inextricably
infallibility
infallibly
infamously
infamy
infancy
infantry
infectiously
infelicity
inferentially
inferiority
infernally
infertilely
infertility

infidelity
infinitely
infinitesimally
infinity
infirmary
infirmity
infirmly
inflammatory
inflationary
inflexibility
inflexibly
informality
informally
informatively
infrequency
infrequently
infuriatingly
infusibility
ingeniously
ingenuity
ingenuously
ingloriously
inhabitability
inherently
inheritably
inhospitably
inhumanely
inhumanity
inhumanly
inimically
inimitably
iniquitously
iniquity
initially
initiatory
injudiciously
injuriously
injury
inky
innately

innocency
innocently
innocuously
inoffensively
inopportunely
inordinately
inorganically
inquiringly
inquiry
inquisitively
insalubrity
insanely
insanitary
insanity
insatiably
inscrutably
insecurely
insecurity
insensately
insensibility
insensibly
insensitively
insensitivity
inseparably
insidiously
insignificantly
insincerely
insincerity
insipidity
insipidly
insistency
insistently
insistingly
insobriety
insolently
insolubly
insolvency
instability
instantaneously
instantly

instinctively
instrumentality
instrumentally
insubordinately
insufferably
insufficiency
insufficiently
insularity
insultingly
insurgency
insurmountably
intangibly
integrally
integrity
intellectually
intelligently
intelligibility
intelligibly
intemperately
intensely
intensity
intensively
intentionally
intently
interactively
interagency
intercessory
intercity
interdependency
interdictory
interdisciplinary
interestingly
interiority
interjectory
interlibrary
intermarry
interminably
intermittently
internally
interplanetary

interpretatively
interrogatively
interrogatory
interrogee
interviewee
intimacy
intimately
intolerably
intracity
intramurally
intransigently
intransitively
intravenously
intrepidly
intricacy
intricately
intriguingly
intrinsically
introductory
introspectively
intrudingly
intrusively
intuitively
invalidity
invalidly
invaluably
invariability
invariably
inventively
inventory
inversely
investigatory
inveterately
invidiously
invincibly
inviolably
inviolately
invisibility
invisibly
invitee

involuntarily
involuntary
inwardly
irately
irefully
irksomely
ironically
irony
irrationality
irrationally
irregularity
irregularly
irrelevancy
irrelevantly
irreligiously
irreparably
irresistibly
irresolutely
irrespectively
irresponsibly
irretrievably
irreverently
irreversibly
irrevocably
irritability
irritably
irritancy
irritatingly
isogony
isometrically
isotonically
isotopically
Israeli
Italy
itchy
itinerary
itsy-bitsy
itty-bitty
ivory
ivy

jabberwocky
jabbingly
jaborandi
Jackie
jacuzzi
jadedly
jaggedly
jaggy
jalopy
jalousie
jamboree
jangly
January
japery
jauntily
jaunty
jaycee
jayvee
jazzily
jazzy
jealously
jealousy
jeeringly
jelly
Jenny
jeopardy
jerkily
jerky
Jerry
jersey
Jesse
jetty
jewelry
jewry
jiffy
jiggly
Jimmy
jingly
jinni
jitney

jittery
jobbery
jockey
jocosely
jocosity
jocularity
jocundity
jocundly
Joey
Johnny
jointly
jokingly
jollily
jolly
jolty
jouncy
journalistically
journey
joviality
jovially
jowly
joyfully
joyously
jubilantly
jubilee
judgmatically
judicatory
judicially
judiciary
judiciously
judy
jugglery
jugglingly
juicily
juicy
jumpily
jumpingly
jumpy
junkie
junky

jurally
juratory
juristically
jury
justifiably
justly
juttingly
juvenility
Kabuki
kaleidoscopically
kamikaze
karate
keenly
Kelly
kennedy
kentucky
kewpie
key
KGB
khaki
kicky
kiddy
kidnapee
kidney
kimchee
kinaesthetically
kindheartedly
kindly
kinematically
kinesiology
kingly
kinky
kitschy
kittenishly
kitty
kiwi
klutzy
knavery
knavishly
knee

knightly
knobby
knock-knee
knottily
knotty
knowingly
knowledgeably
kohlrabi
kookie
kooky
kremlinology
kymography
labially
laboratory
laboredly
laboringly
laboriously
lackadaisically
lackey
laconically
lacy
laddie
lady
laggardly
lamasery
lambency
lambently
lamely
lamentably
lampoonery
landlady
landlordly
languidly
languorously
lankily
lanky
lapidary
larcenously
larceny
lardy

largely
larvae
laryngeally
laryngectomy
lasciviously
lassie
lastingly
lastly
latchkey
lately
latency
latently
laterality
laterally
lathery
laudability
laudably
laudatory
laughably
laughingly
laundry
lavatory
lavishly
lawfully
lawlessly
lawny
laxity
laxly
lazily
lazy
leadenly
leafy
leaky
leanly
leathery
lecherously
lechery
lee
leeringly
leery

leewardly
lefty
legacy
legalistically
legality
legally
legatee
legendarily
legendary
leggy
legibility
legibly
legionary
legislatively
legitimacy
legitimately
leisurely
lemony
lengthily
lengthy
leniency
leniently
lenity
leprosy
lessee
lethality
lethally
lethargically
lethargy
levee
levelly
levi
levity
levorotary
levy
lewdly
lexically
lexicography
lexicology
liability

libationary
libelee
libellee
libellously
liberality
liberally
liberty
libidinally
library
licensee
licentiously
licitly
lickety
lieutenancy
lifelessly
lightheartedly
lightly
likability
likely
lily
limberly
limitedly
limitlessly
limpidity
limpidly
limply
limy
lindy
linearly
lineny
lingeringly
lingually
linguine
linguistically
linty
lippy
liquidity
lispingly
lissomely
listlessly

litany
literacy
literally
literary
literately
lithely
lithographically
lithography
lithology
lithotomy
littery
liturgically
liturgy
lively
livery
lividly
loamy
loathsomely
lobby
lobotomy
locality
locally
loftily
lofty
loganberry
logically
logistically
logy
loiteringly
lonely
lonesomely
longevity
longingly
loony
loopy
loosely
lopsidedly
loquaciously
loquacity
lordly

lorry
lottery
lottie
loudly
lousily
lousy
loutishly
lovably
loveably
lovelessly
lovely
lovingly
lowly
loyally
loyalty
LP
LSD
ltd
lubberly
lubricity
lucidity
lucidly
luckily
lucky
lucratively
Lucy
ludicrously
lugubriously
lukewarmly
lullingly
luminary
luminosity
luminously
lumpily
lumpy
lunacy
lunatically
luny
luridly
luringly

lusciously
lustfully
lustily
lusty
luxuriantly
luxuriously
luxury
lymphatically
lyrically
macaroni
machete
machiavellianly
machinability
machinery
Macy
madcaply
maddeningly
madly
mafiosi
Maggie
maggoty
magically
magistery
magnanimity
magnanimously
magnetically
magnificently
maharanee
maharishi
mahogany
maidenly
mainly
majestically
majesty
majority
maladroitly
malady
malagasy
malapertly
malarkey

maledictory
maleficently
malevolently
malfeasantly
maliciously
malignancy
malignantly
malignity
malleability
malleably
malodorously
malty
mammae
mammary
mammography
manageably
mandatee
mandatorily
mandatory
maneuverability
manfully
mangily
mangy
maniacally
manically
manifestly
manifoldly
manipulatively
manipulatory
manly
mannerly
mannishly
manually
manufactory
many
maori
marconi
mardi
marginality
marginally

mariachi
markedly
marquee
marquetry
marquis
marry
marshalcy
marshy
martially
martini
martyry
marvelously
masculinely
masculinity
masochistically
masonry
massively
mastectomy
masterfully
masterly
mastery
matchlessly
materialistically
materially
maternally
maternity
matey
mathematically
matriarchy
matrimony
matronly
maturely
maturity
matutinally
maudlinly
mawkishly
maxi
maxillary
maximally
maybe

mazy
MC
MD
me
meadowy
meagerly
mealie
mealy
meaningfully
meanly
meany
measly
measurably
meaty
mechanically
mechanistically
meddlesomely
medially
medically
medicinally
medievally
mediocrity
meditatively
medley
meekly
meetly
melancholically
melancholy
melanie
mellifluously
mellowly
melodically
melodiously
melodramatically
melody
meltingly
membranously
memorably
memory
menacingly

menagerie	microbiology	miscellaneously
mendaciously	microscopy	miscellany
mendacity	microsurgery	mischievously
mendicancy	midbody	miscibility
menially	middlingly	miscopy
mentality	middy	miscreancy
mentally	midweekly	miserably
mercenarily	midwifery	miserly
mercenary	mightily	misery
merchantry	mighty	misguidedly
mercifully	migratory	misleadingly
mercilessly	mildewy	misogamy
mercury	mildly	misogyny
mercy	miliary	misology
merely	militancy	misrepresentee
meretriciously	militantly	missilery
meristically	militarily	missionary
meritoriously	military	Mississippi
merrily	milky	mistakenly
merry	millinery	mistily
mesentery	Milwaukee	mistrustfully
meshy	mimicry	mistrustingly
mesomorphy	minatory	misty
messily	mindedly	misunderstandingly
messy	mindfully	mitigatory
metabolically	mindlessly	mnemonically
metallically	mineralogy	mobility
metallurgically	minestrone	mobocracy
metallurgy	mini	mockery
metaphorically	minimally	mockingly
metaphysically	ministry	modality
meteorically	Minnie	moderately
meteorology	minority	modernly
methodically	minty	modestly
methodology	minutely	modesty
meticulously	miraculously	modishly
metonymy	mirthfully	modularity
metrically	misanthropically	modulatory
Miami	misanthropy	moistly
Mickey	miscarry	moldy

molecularly	mopey	movie
molly	morae	movingly
moltenly	moralistically	moxie
momentarily	morality	MP
momentary	morally	mpg
momentously	moratory	mucky
mommy	morbidity	muddy
monarchy	morbidly	muggily
monastery	mordancy	muggy
monastically	mordantly	mulberry
monaurally	moribundity	muliebrity
monday	moribundly	mulishly
monetarily	moronically	mulligatawny
monetary	morosely	multi
money	morphemically	multifariously
monkey	morphologically	multiparty
monkishly	morphology	multiplicity
monochromatically	mortality	multisensory
monochromaticity	mortally	multiversity
monocularly	mortgagee	mummery
monogamously	mortifyingly	mummy
monogamy	mortuary	munchy
monogyny	mosey	mundanely
monopolistically	mossy	municipality
monopoly	mostly	municipally
monosyllabically	motherly	munificently
monotonously	motility	murderee
monotony	motionlessly	murderously
monsignori	motley	murkily
monstrosity	mouldy	murky
monstrously	mountie	muscularity
monte	mounty	muscularly
Montessori	mournfully	mushy
Montgomery	mousey	musically
monthly	mousy	musicology
monumentally	mouthily	musingly
moodily	mouthy	musketry
moody	movability	musky
Moonie	movably	mussily
moony	moveability	mussy

mustily	nationalistically	negotiatory
musty	nationality	neighborly
mutability	nationally	neoclassically
mutably	nativity	neology
mutely	nattily	neoteny
mutinously	natty	nepotistically
mutiny	naturally	nervelessly
muttony	naturedly	nervily
mutually	naturopathy	nervosity
MVP	naughtily	nervously
myopically	naughty	nervy
mysteriously	nauseatingly	neurally
mystery	nauseously	neurologically
mystically	nautically	neurology
mystifyingly	navigability	neurotically
mythologically	navigably	neutrality
mythology	navy	neutrally
Nairobi	Nazi	newly
naively	nearly	newsworthy
naivety	nearsightedly	newsy
nakedly	neatly	nextly
namelessly	nebulae	nicely
namely	nebulously	nicety
Nancy	necessarily	nietzsche
nannie	necessary	nifty
nanny	necessitously	niggardly
napery	necessity	nigglingly
nappy	necrology	nightie
narcissi	necromancy	nightly
narcissistically	necropsy	nighty
narcolepsy	needily	nihilistically
narcotically	needlessly	nimbi
narrowly	needy	nimbly
nary	nefariously	ninety
nasality	negatively	ninny
nasally	negativity	nippy
nascency	neglectfully	nitty
nastily	negligently	nitty-gritty
nasty	negligibly	nixie
natally	negotiability	nixy

nobility	northeastwardly	nuttily
nobly	northerly	nutty
nobody	northwardly	nympholepsy
nocturnally	northwesterly	oafishly
nocuously	northwestwardly	obduracy
nodally	nosey	obediently
noddy	nosily	obesity
noiselessly	nosology	obfuscatory
noisily	nosy	obituary
noisomely	notability	objectee
noisy	notably	objectively
nomadically	notary	objectivity
nominally	notchy	oblately
nominatively	notedly	obligatory
nominee	noteworthily	obligee
nonassertively	noteworthy	obligingly
nonchalantly	noticeably	obliquely
nonconformity	notionally	obliviously
nonconstructively	notoriety	oblongly
noncontiguously	notoriously	obloquy
noncontrollably	novelly	obnoxiety
nondestructively	novelty	obnoxiously
nondisciplinary	noxiously	obscenely
nondiscriminatory	nubby	obscenity
nonethically	nudely	obscurely
nonmilitary	nudity	obscurity
nonpolitically	nugatory	obsequiously
nonpredatory	nuggety	obsequy
nonreciprocally	numbingly	observably
nonsecretly	numbly	observatory
nonsensically	numerably	observingly
nontechnically	numerically	obsessingly
nonviolently	numerology	obsessively
nonvisually	numerously	obsolescently
normalcy	nunnery	obsoletely
normality	nuptially	obstinacy
normally	nursery	obstinately
normandy	nutritionally	obstreperously
normatively	nutritiously	obstructively
northeasterly	nutritively	obtrusively

obtusely
obviously
occasionally
occupancy
oceanography
oceanology
octagonally
ocularly
OD
oddity
oddly
odiously
odoriferously
odorously
odyssey
off-key
offensively
offeree
offertory
offhandedly
officially
officiary
officiously
oily
okey
okey-dokey
okeydokey
okie
oldie
olfactory
oligarchy
oligopoly
ominously
omnipotently
omnisciently
omnivorously
oncology
onerosity
onerously
only

ontogenetically
ontogeny
ontology
oozy
opacity
opaquely
openhandedly
openheartedly
openly
operability
operably
operatically
operationally
operatively
ophthalmology
opinionatedly
opportunely
opportunity
oppositely
oppressively
optically
optimally
optimistically
optionally
optionee
optometry
opulently
oracularly
orally
orangery
oratorically
oratory
orchestrally
orderly
ordinarily
ordinary
organdy
organically
orgy
origami

originality
originally
ornately
ornery
ornithology
orogeny
orotundity
orthodoxy
orthoepy
orthographically
orthography
orthopedically
oscillatory
osmotically
osseously
ossuary
ostensibly
ostensively
ostentatiously
osteology
osteopathy
ostomy
otherworldly
oui
ouija
outlandishly
outlawry
outrageously
outspokenly
outstandingly
outwardly
ovary
overactivity
overambitiously
overapprehensively
overassertively
overattentively
overbearingly
overcapacity
overcomplacency

overdiligently
overfamiliarity
overhastily
overhasty
overinsistently
overintensely
overly
overmodestly
overpromptly
oversee
overtly
overwhelmingly
owlishly
oystery
pacifically
paddy
padre
pageantry
painfully
painlessly
painstakingly
paisley
pakistani
palatability
palatably
paleography
paleontology
palfrey
palimony
palliatively
palmistry
palmy
palpability
palpably
palsy
paltrily
paltry
pandowdy
panicky
panoply

panoramically
pansy
pantie
pantingly
pantry
panty
papacy
papally
papery
pappy
paradisiacally
paradoxically
parapsychology
pardonably
parenthetically
parity
parlay
parley
parliamentary
parlously
parochially
parody
parolee
parquetry
parry
parsimoniously
parsimony
parsley
partiality
partially
participatory
particularly
partly
party
passably
passingly
passionately
passively
passivity
passkey

pastrami
pastry
pasty
patchy
patellectomy
patency
patentee
patently
paternally
paternity
pathetically
pathologically
pathology
patiently
patriarchy
patrimonially
patrimony
patriotically
patronymically
patsy
Patty
patulously
paucity
paultry
paunchy
pawnee
payability
payee
PC
PCB
PCP
pea
peabody
peaceably
peacefully
peachy
pearly
peasantry
peaty
peavey

pebbly
peccary
pectinously
peculiarity
peculiarly
pecuniary
pedagogically
pedagogy
pedantically
pedantry
pederastically
pederasty
pedigree
pedology
pee
peerlessly
peevishly
peewee
pejoratively
penally
penalty
Penelope
penetrably
penetratingly
penitentiary
penitently
Penney
penny
penny-ante
penology
pensionary
pensively
pentagonally
pentalogy
penuche
penuriously
penury
peony
pepperoni
peppertree

peppery
peppy
Pepsi
perceivably
perceptibility
perceptibly
perceptively
perceptivity
perceptually
percutaneously
peremptory
perennially
perfectibility
perfectly
perfidiously
perfidy
perfumery
perfunctory
perigee
perilously
periodically
peripherally
periphery
perishability
perishably
perjury
perky
perlingually
permanency
permanently
permeability
permeably
permissibility
permissibly
permissively
permittee
perniciously
pernickety
perorally
perpetually

perpetuities
perpetuity
perplexedly
perplexity
persecutee
persistency
persistently
persnickety
personably
personality
personally
personalty
perspicaciously
perspicacity
perspicuity
perspicuously
perspiratory
persuadably
persuasively
pertinacity
pertinency
pertinently
pertly
pervasively
perversely
perversity
pervertedly
pesky
pessary
pessimistically
pestiferously
petitionee
petri
petrochemistry
petrologically
petrology
pettifoggery
pettily
pettishly
petty

petulantly
peyote
phallically
phantasy
pharisaically
pharisee
pharmaceutically
pharmacologically
pharmacology
pharmacy
phenotypically
philanthropy
philately
philology
philosophically
philosophy
phlebotomy
phlegmatically
Phoebe
phonemically
phonetically
phoney
phonically
phonographically
phonologically
phonology
phony
phooey
phosphorescently
photochemically
photochemistry
photocopy
photoelectrically
photogenically
photographically
photography
photolytically
photometry
photostability
photosynthetically

phototactically
phototherapy
phraseology
phrenology
phylactery
phylogeny
physically
physiognomy
physiologically
physiology
pianoforte
piccalilli
pickaninny
picky
pictorially
picturesquely
piercingly
piety
piggery
piggy
pillory
pillowy
pimply
pinery
pinkie
pinky
pinnately
piously
pipingly
piquancy
piquantly
piracy
piscary
pitchy
piteously
pithily
pithy
pitiably
pitifully
pitilessly

pituitary
pity
pityingly
pivotally
pixie
pixy
placability
placidity
placidly
plainly
plaintively
planetary
planetology
plangency
plastery
plasticity
platonically
plausibility
plausibly
playfully
plea
pleasantly
pleasantry
pleasingly
pleasurably
pledgee
pledgery
plenary
plentifully
plenty
pleurisy
pliability
pliably
pliancy
pliantly
plicately
ploddingly
ploidy
pluckily
plucky

plumply
plumy
plurality
plurally
plushly
plushy
plutocracy
pneumatically
pneumography
podgy
podiatry
poesy
poetically
poetry
poignancy
poignantly
pointedly
pointlessly
pointy
poisonously
pokey
pokily
poky
polarity
polemically
policy
politely
politically
polity
poly
polyandry
polygamy
polygonally
polygraphically
polygyny
polymorphously
polypectomy
polyphagy
polyphonically
polyphony

pomposity
pompously
ponderously
pongee
pontifically
pony
poorly
poppy
popularity
popularly
porgy
porky
pornographically
pornography
porosity
porously
portability
portentously
portly
poshly
posingly
positively
posse
possessively
possessory
possibility
possibly
posteriority
posterity
posthumously
postnatally
posy
potability
potbelly
potency
potentially
potently
potpourri
pottery
potty

poultry
poverty
powdery
powerfully
powerlessly
practicably
practicality
practically
pragmatically
prairie
praiseworthily
praiseworthy
prancingly
prayerfully
prayingly
preachy
preassembly
precariously
precautionary
preciously
precipitately
precipitously
precis
precisely
preclusively
precociously
precocity
preconsciously
precursory
predacity
predatory
predicatory
predictability
predictably
predictively
predominantly
predominately
preemie
preeminently
preemptively

preemptory
prefatory
preferability
preferably
preferentially
pregnability
pregnancy
pregnantly
prehistorically
prehistory
prejudicedly
prejudicially
preliminarily
preliminary
prematurely
prematurity
premenstrually
prenatally
preoperatively
preparatory
preponderantly
preposterously
preppie
preppy
presentably
presently
presidency
presley
pressingly
prestigiously
presumably
presumptively
presumptuously
pretentiously
prettily
pretty
prevalently
preventively
previously
prexy

prickly
pridefully
priestly
priggery
priggishly
primacy
primarily
primary
primevally
primitively
primly
princely
principality
principally
priori
priority
prissily
prissy
prithee
privacy
privately
privily
privity
privy
prix
probability
probably
probationary
procedurally
proclivity
procreativity
proctology
prodigally
prodigiously
prodigy
productively
productivity
profanely
profanity
professedly

professionally
proficiency
proficiently
profitability
profitably
profligacy
profligately
profoundly
profundity
profusely
progeny
progressively
prohibitively
prohibitory
proliferously
prolificacy
prolifically
prolixity
prolixly
promilitary
prominently
promiscuity
promiscuously
promisee
promisingly
promissory
promontory
promptly
pronely
pronouncedly
propensity
properly
property
prophecy
prophetically
prophylactically
propinquity
propitiatory
proportionably
proportionally

proportionately
proprietary
propriety
prosaically
prosody
prospectively
prosperity
prosperously
prosthetically
prosy
protectively
protozoology
proudly
provability
providentially
providently
provinciality
provincially
provisionally
provocatively
provokingly
provolone
proximally
proximately
proximity
proxy
prudentially
prudently
prudery
pruriently
pryingly
psalmody
pseudolegendary
pseudoliterary
pseudopregnancy
psyche
psychedelically
psychiatrically
psychiatry
psychically

psychoanalytically
psychodynamically
psycholepsy
psychologically
psychology
psychometrically
psychometry
psychopathically
psychophysically
psychoquackery
psychosocially
psychosomatically
psychosurgery
psychotherapeutically
psychotherapy
psychotically
ptolemy
puberty
publicity
publicly
puccini
puddly
pudgy
puerilely
puerility
puffy
puggy
pugnaciously
pugnacity
puisne
puissantly
pulley
pulmonary
pulpally
pulpy
pulsatory
punchy
punctiliously
punctuality
punctually

pungency
pungently
punily
punishability
punishably
punitively
punitory
Punjabi
puny
puppetry
puppy
puree
purely
purgatively
purgatory
puritanically
purity
purportedly
purposefully
purposely
purulency
purulently
pushily
pushy
pusillanimously
pussy
putatively
putridity
puttee
putty
puzzlingly
PVC
pygmy
pyxie
quackery
quackishly
quacky
quaintly
quakingly
quaky

qualitatively	radiancy	rationalistically
quality	radiantly	rationality
qualmishly	radically	rationally
quandary	radioactively	rattly
quantitatively	radioactivity	ratty
quantity	radiochemistry	raucously
quarry	radiographically	raunchy
quarterly	radiography	ravenously
quaternary	radiology	ravingly
quaveringly	radioscopy	ravioli
quavery	raffishly	ravishingly
queasily	raggedly	rawly
queasy	rainey	reactionary
queazy	rainy	reactively
queenly	rakishly	reactivity
queerly	rally	readily
querulously	ramie	ready
query	rancidity	reagency
questionably	rancorously	realistically
quickie	randomly	reality
quickly	randy	really
quiescency	rangy	realty
quiescently	ranklingly	reasonably
quietly	rankly	reassembly
quinsy	rantingly	reassuringly
quirky	rapaciously	rebelliously
quiveringly	rapacity	rebukingly
quivery	rapidity	recantingly
quixote	rapidly	recency
quixotically	raptly	recently
quizzically	rapturously	receptively
rabbinically	rarely	receptivity
rabbitry	rarity	recessively
rabidity	rascality	recipe
rabidly	rascally	reciprocally
racially	rashly	reciprocity
racily	raspberry	recklessly
rackety	raspingly	recognizably
racy	raspy	reconcilably
radially	rateably	reconditely

recopy
recovery
recreantly
rectally
rectory
recumbency
recurrently
redemptory
rediscovery
redly
redolency
redolently
reducibly
redundancy
redundantly
reedy
reefy
reeky
reembody
reentry
referee
refinery
reflectively
reflexively
reflexology
reformatory
refractory
refreshingly
refugee
refulgently
refutably
regally
regency
regeneracy
regimentally
regionally
registry
regnancy
regressively
regretfully

regrettably
regularity
regularly
regulatively
regulatory
rehabilitee
relatively
relativity
releasee
relentlessly
relevancy
relevantly
reliably
reliantly
religiously
reluctancy
reluctantly
remarkably
remarry
remedially
remedy
reminiscently
remissly
remittee
remittently
remonstrantly
remorsefully
remorselessly
remotely
remuneratively
repartee
repeatedly
repellently
repertory
repetitiously
repetitively
replevy
reportedly
repository
reprehensibly

representatively
representee
repressively
reproachfully
reproachingly
reproductively
reprography
reprovingly
repugnancy
repugnantly
repulsively
reputably
reputedly
requisitely
rescissory
resentfully
reservedly
residency
residentially
resignedly
resiliency
resiliently
resistably
resistantly
resolutely
resonantly
resoundingly
resourcefully
respectability
respectably
respectfully
respectively
respiratory
resplendency
resplendently
respondency
responsibility
responsibly
responsively
restfully

restively
restlessly
restoratively
restrainedly
restrictively
rete
reticently
retiree
retiringly
retroactively
retroactivity
retrospectively
returnee
reveille
revelatory
revelry
revengefully
reverently
reverie
reversely
revery
revisionary
revoltingly
revolutionarily
revolutionary
rfd
rhapsody
rhetorically
rheumatically
rheumatology
rhythmically
ribaldly
ribaldry
richly
rickety
ridgy
ridiculously
righteously
rightfully
rightly

rigidity
rigidly
rigorously
riotously
ripely
ripply
risky
ritualistically
ritually
ritzily
ritzy
rivalry
roadie
robbery
Robby
robustly
rockery
rocketry
rocky
roguery
roguishly
roily
rollickingly
romantically
romany
rooftree
rookery
rookie
roomily
roomy
rooty
rosary
Rosemary
Rosie
rosily
rosy
rotary
rotc
rotisserie
rottenly

rotundly
rough-and-ready
roughly
roundly
routinely
rowdily
rowdy
royally
royalty
rsvp
rubbery
rubbishy
rubbly
rubicundity
ruby
ruddily
ruddy
rudely
rudimentary
ruefully
ruffianly
ruffly
rugby
ruggedly
ruinously
rumblingly
rumbly
rummy
rumply
runny
runty
rupee
rurally
rushingly
rushy
rustically
rusticity
rusty
ruthlessly
rutty

RV
saccharinity
sacerdotally
sacramentally
sacredly
sacrificially
sacrilegiously
sacrosanctity
saddletree
sadducee
sadistically
sadly
safari
safely
safety
sagaciously
sagacity
sagely
saggy
saintly
saki
salability
salaciously
salami
salary
saleslady
saliency
saliently
salinity
salisbury
salivary
sally
salmagundi
salty
salubriously
salubrity
salutarily
salutary
salutatory
sanatory

sanctimony
sanctity
sanctuary
sandy
sanely
sanguinary
sanguinely
sanitary
sanity
sapiently
sappy
sarcastically
sardonically
saree
sari
sassy
satanically
satiety
satiny
satirically
satisfactory
satisfyingly
saturday
saucily
saucy
savagely
savagery
savory
savoury
savvy
saxony
sayee
scabbily
scabby
scabrously
scaloppine
scaly
scammony
scampi
scandalously

scantily
scantly
scanty
scarcely
scarcity
scarily
scary
scathingly
scatology
scenery
scenically
schematically
schismatically
schmaltzy
scholarly
scholastically
scientifically
scintillatingly
scoffingly
scoldingly
scorchingly
scornfully
scot-free
scowlingly
scraggly
scraggy
scrappily
scrappy
scratchily
scratchy
scrawly
scrawny
screaky
screamingly
screechy
screwy
scrimpy
scripturally
scrubby
scruffy

scrumptiously
scrupulosity
scrupulously
scrutinizingly
scrutiny
sculduggery
scullduggery
scullery
scummy
scurrility
scurrilously
scurry
scurvily
scurvy
sea
seamanly
seamy
searchingly
seasonably
seasonality
seasonally
seaworthy
secludedly
secondarily
secondary
secondly
secrecy
secretary
secretively
secretly
secretory
sectary
sectility
sectionally
secularity
secularly
securely
security
sedately
sedentary

sedgy
sedimentary
seditionary
seducee
seducingly
seductively
sedulously
see
seedily
seedy
seemingly
seemly
seethingly
segmentary
seismically
seismicity
seismography
seismology
seismometry
selectee
selectively
selectivity
self-flattery
self-pity
selfishly
selflessly
semantically
semiconsciously
semimonthly
seminary
seminudity
semiology
semiweekly
sendee
senilely
senility
seniority
sensationally
senselessly
sensibility

sensibly
sensitively
sensitivity
sensory
sensuality
sensually
sensuously
sententiously
sentiently
sentimentality
sentimentally
sentry
separability
separably
separately
sepulchrally
sequentially
seraphically
serendipity
serenely
serenity
sergeancy
serially
seriously
serjeancy
serology
serosity
serpiginously
serviceably
servilely
servility
sesame
setaceously
settee
seventy
severally
severely
severity
sexily
sexlessly

sexology
sexuality
sexually
sexy
shabbily
shabby
shadily
shadowy
shady
shaggily
shaggy
shakily
shaky
shamefacedly
shamefully
shamelessly
shanty
shapelessly
shapely
sharpey
sharpie
sharply
shatteringly
shawnee
she
sheeny
sheepishly
sheerly
Shelley
Shelly
sheriffcy
sherry
shiftily
shiftlessly
shifty
shillalah
shillelagh
shimmeringly
shimmery
shimmy

shinily
shiningly
shinney
shinny
shiny
shivaree
shiveringly
shivery
shoaly
shockingly
shoddily
shoddy
shoetree
shootee
shortly
shortsightedly
shorty
shoshone
shoshoni
showery
showily
showy
shrewdly
shrievalty
shrilly
shrubbery
shrubby
shudderingly
shyly
sibilantly
Sicily
sickeningly
sickly
sidlingly
sidney
sightly
sightsee
signally
signatary
signatory

signee
significantly
silently
silkily
silky
silly
silty
silvery
similarity
similarly
simile
simony
simperingly
simplemindedly
simplicity
simplistically
simply
sincerely
sincerity
sinewy
sinfully
singlehandedly
singletree
singly
singularity
singularly
sinisterly
sinlessly
sinuously
sippy
sissy
sisterly
sitology
sixpenny
sixty
sizably
skeletally
skeptically
sketchily
sketchy

ski	sloppy	snarlingly
skiagraphy	sloshy	snarly
skiascopy	slouchingly	snazzy
skiddy	slouchy	sneakily
skillfully	sloughy	sneakingly
skimpily	slovenly	sneaky
skimpy	slowly	sneeringly
skinny	sludgy	sneezy
skittishly	sluggishly	snickeringly
skivvy	sluggy	sniffily
skulduggery	slummy	sniffingly
skullduggery	slurry	sniffy
slackly	slushy	sniggeringly
slanderously	slyly	snippety
slangy	smartie	snippily
slantingly	smartingly	snippy
slaphappy	smartly	snobbery
slashingly	smarty	snobbishly
slatternly	smashingly	snobby
slaty	smeary	snoopy
slavery	smelly	snootily
slavishly	smeltery	snooty
sleazily	smilingly	snoozy
sleazy	smirkingly	snorty
sleekly	smithy	snotty
sleepily	smoggy	snowy
sleeplessly	smokey	snubby
sleepy	smoky	snuffly
sleety	smoochy	snuffy
slenderly	smoothly	snugly
slickly	smothery	soaky
slightly	smudgy	soapily
slimly	smugly	soapy
slimsy	smutchy	sobbingly
slimy	smutty	soberly
slinky	snaggy	sobriety
slippery	snakily	sociability
slithery	snaky	sociably
slobbery	snappily	socially
sloppily	snappy	society

sociology
sociometry
soddenly
sodomy
softheartedly
softie
softly
softy
soggily
soggy
soldierly
soldiery
solely
solemnity
solemnly
solicitously
solidarity
solidary
solidity
solidly
soliloquy
solitary
solubility
solubly
solvency
solvently
somali
somberly
somebody
somniferously
somniloquy
somnolency
somnolently
songfully
sonny
sonority
sonorously
soothingly
sooty
sophistry

sophomorically
soppy
sorcery
sordidly
sorely
sorority
sorrily
sorrowfully
sorry
sortie
sottishly
soulfully
soundlessly
soundly
soupy
sourly
southeasterly
southeastwardly
southerly
southwardly
southwesterly
southwestwardly
sovereignly
sovereignty
spaciously
spaghetti
spangly
sparely
sparingly
sparsely
sparsity
spastically
spatially
spatteringly
speakeasy
specially
specialty
specie
specifically
specificity

speciosity
speciously
spectacularly
spectrally
spectrography
spectroscopy
speculatively
speechlessly
speedily
speedy
speleology
spendthrifty
spermaceti
spermary
spermatically
spherically
spicily
spicy
spidery
spiffily
spiffy
spiky
spinally
spindly
spinosely
spiny
spirally
spiritedly
spiritlessly
spirituality
spiritually
spiry
spitefully
spivery
spivvery
splashily
splashy
splendidly
splintery
splotchy

spondee	stammeringly	stimulatory
spongy	standee	stimuli
spontaneity	stanley	stingily
spontaneously	stannary	stingingly
spooky	starchy	stingy
spoony	starkly	stinky
sporadically	starry	stintingly
sportively	startlingly	stipulatory
sporty	stately	stir-crazy
spotlessly	statically	stirringly
spottily	stationary	stitchery
spotty	stationery	stockily
spree	statistically	stocky
sprightly	statuary	stodgily
springy	statutably	stodgy
spryly	statutory	stogie
spumoni	staunchly	stoically
spunky	steadfastly	stolidity
spuriously	steadily	stolidly
squabby	steady	stonily
squalidly	stealthily	stony
squally	stealthy	stoopingly
squarely	steamy	stormily
squashy	steely	stormy
squatty	steeply	story
squeaky	stellately	stoutly
squeamishly	stenographically	STP
squeegee	stenography	straggly
squiggly	stephanie	straightforwardly
squinty	stereometry	straightly
squirmy	stereoscopy	straitly
squishy	stereotypy	strangely
stability	sterilely	strangury
stably	sterility	strategically
staggeringly	sternly	strategy
stagnancy	stickily	stratigraphy
stagnantly	sticky	stravinsky
stagy	stiffly	strawberry
staidly	stilly	strawy
stalwartly	stimulatingly	streaky

streamy
strenuously
stretchy
striae
strickenly
strictly
stridency
stridently
strikingly
stringency
stringently
stringy
strobili
stroboscopically
strongly
strophe
structurally
strumae
stubbly
stubbornly
stubby
studiedly
studiously
study
stuffily
stuffy
stumblingly
stumpy
stupendously
stupidity
stupidly
sturdily
sturdy
stutteringly
stylishly
stylistically
stymie
suably
suasively
suavely

suavity
subcategory
subclinically
subcommittee
subconsciously
subcortically
subcutaneously
subentry
subfamily
subjacency
subjacently
subjectively
subjectivity
sublessee
sublimely
subliminally
sublimity
sublunary
submissively
subnormality
subnormally
subordinately
subsequently
subserviency
subserviently
subsidiary
subsidy
substantially
substantively
subtenancy
subtlety
subtly
subtreasury
subvariety
subversively
successfully
successively
succinctly
succulency
succulently

suddenly
sudsy
suety
suey
sufferingly
sufficiency
sufficiently
suffocatingly
sugary
suggestibility
suggestively
sui
suicidally
suitability
suitably
sukiyaki
sulkily
sulky
sullenly
sully
sultry
summarily
summary
summery
summitry
sumptuously
Sunday
sundry
sunnily
sunny
sunshiny
superbly
superficially
superfluity
superiority
superlatively
supernally
supersonically
superstitiously
supervisee

supervisory	swiftly	tactically
supinely	swimmingly	tactility
supplementally	swingy	tactlessly
supplementary	swirly	taffy
supposedly	swishy	tahini
suppository	swooningly	Tahiti
supremacy	sycophancy	talkatively
supremely	sydney	talkie
surely	syllogistically	talky
surety	symbiotically	tallahassee
surgery	symbolically	tallowy
surgically	symmetrically	tally
surlily	symmetry	tamale
surly	sympathetically	tamely
surpassingly	sympathy	tangentially
surprisingly	symphony	tangibility
surrealistically	synaptically	tangibly
surrenderee	synchronously	tangy
surreptitiously	synchrony	tannery
surrey	syncope	tansy
surrogacy	synecdoche	tantalizingly
susceptibly	synergically	taperingly
suspensory	synergistically	tapestry
suspiciously	synergy	tardily
suttee	syngamy	tardy
Swahili	synonymy	tarry
swami	synthetically	tartly
swampy	syphilology	tastefully
swanky	syrupy	tastelessly
swarthy	systematically	tastily
swashy	systemically	tasty
swazi	systole	tauntingly
sweaty	syzygy	tautly
sweeney	tabby	tautologically
sweeny	tabularly	tautology
sweepingly	tacitly	tawdry
sweepy	taciturnity	tawny
sweetie	taciturnly	taxi
sweetly	tacky	taxidermy
swelteringly	tactfully	taxonomy

Tchaikovsky
tea
teachability
tearfully
teary
teasingly
technicality
technically
technocracy
technologically
technology
teddy
tediously
tee
teeny
teeny-weeny
telegraphically
telegraphy
teleology
telepathically
telepathy
telephonically
telescopically
teletherapy
tellingly
temerity
temperamentally
temperately
tempestuously
temporality
temporally
temporarily
temporary
temptingly
tenably
tenaciously
tenacity
tenancy
tenantry
tendency

tendentiously
tenderheartedly
tenderly
tenency
tennessee
tensely
tensity
tentatively
tenuously
tepee
tepidity
tepidly
teriyaki
terminally
terminologically
terminology
ternary
terrestrially
terribly
terrifically
terrifyingly
territory
terry
tersely
tertiary
testability
testacy
teste
testee
testily
testimony
testy
tetchy
tetralogy
textually
thankfully
thanklessly
theatrically
thee
theistically

thematically
theocracy
theocratically
theologically
theology
theoretically
theory
theosophically
theosophy
therapeutically
therapy
thermally
thermochemistry
thermostatically
thermotherapy
thickety
thickly
thievery
thinkably
thinly
thirdly
thirstily
thirsty
thirty
thistly
thorny
thoroughly
thoughtfully
thoughtlessly
thready
threateningly
three
threnody
thriftily
thrifty
thrillingly
throatily
throaty
thuddingly
thuggee

thuggery
thunderingly
thunderously
ticklishly
ticky-tacky
tidally
tidily
tidy
tiffany
tightly
timelessly
timely
timeously
timidity
timidly
timorously
timothy
timpani
tingly
tinnily
tinny
tiny
tippee
tipsily
tipsy
tiredly
tirelessly
tiresomely
titillatingly
titteringly
tizzy
tlc
tnt
toady
toby
toddy
toffee
toggery
toiletry
tolerably

tolerantly
tomfoolery
tomography
tonality
tonally
tonically
tonicity
tonsillectomy
tony
toothily
toothy
topicality
topically
topographically
topography
topologically
topology
toponymy
topsy
tori
tormentedly
tormentingly
torpidity
torpidly
torridity
torridly
torsionally
tortiously
tortuously
torturedly
torturously
tory
totality
totally
tottery
touchily
touchingly
touchy
toughie
toughly

tourney
towability
toweringly
towery
towhee
townie
towny
toxically
toxicity
toxicology
traceability
traceably
tracery
tracheoscopy
tracheostomy
tracheotomy
tractability
tractably
Tracy
traditionally
tragedy
tragically
tragicomedy
trainee
traitorously
trajectory
tranquility
tranquillity
transcendency
transcendentally
transcendently
transferee
transiency
transiently
transitively
transitivity
transitorily
transitory
translucency
translucently

transparency
transparently
transportability
transportee
transversely
trashy
traumatically
travesty
treacherously
treachery
treacly
treasonably
treasury
treaty
tree
tremblingly
trembly
tremendously
tremulously
trenchancy
trenchantly
trendy
triangularly
tributary
trickery
trickily
trickingly
trickishly
tricksy
tricky
triennially
triflingly
trigamy
trigger-happy
trigonally
trigonometry
trilogy
trimly
trimonthly
trinity

triply
tritely
triumphantly
trivalency
triviality
trivially
triweekly
troche
trochee
trolley
trophy
tropically
troublesomely
truancy
truantry
truculency
truculently
truly
trumpery
trustability
trustee
trustfully
trustworthily
trustworthy
trusty
truthfully
tryingly
tsetse
tubby
tubectomy
tuberculously
tubularly
tuesday
tumidity
tummy
tunably
tunefully
tunelessly
tunney
tunny

turbary
turbidity
turbidly
turbulency
turbulently
turfy
turgidity
turgidly
turkey
turnkey
turvy
tussocky
tutti
TV
twangy
tweedy
twenty
twiggy
twitchingly
twitchy
twittery
tympani
tympany
typicality
typically
typographically
typography
tyrannically
tyrannously
tyranny
ubiquitously
ubiquity
ugly
ukelele
ukulele
ulteriorly
ultimacy
ultimately
ultrasonically
unabashedly

unacceptably
unaccountably
unadvisedly
unaffectedly
unalterably
unanimity
unanimously
unappealingly
unapproachably
unarguably
unartfully
unashamedly
unassailably
unassertively
unassumingly
unattractively
unavailingly
unavoidably
unbearably
unbeatably
unbecomingly
unbelievably
unbiasedly
unblinkingly
unblushingly
uncannily
uncanny
unceasingly
uncertainly
uncertainty
uncharitably
unchastely
unchastity
uncheerfully
uncivilly
unclarity
uncomfortably
uncommonly
uncomplainingly
unconditionally

unconquerably
unconscionably
unconsciously
uncontrollably
unconvincingly
uncouthly
uncritically
unctuously
undauntedly
undemocratically
undeniably
underbelly
underhandedly
undersea
understandably
understudy
undiscernibly
undoubtedly
undulatory
unduly
undutifully
undyingly
unearthly
uneasily
uneasy
unendingly
unendurably
unenviously
unequally
unequivocally
unerringly
unescapably
unethically
unevenly
uneventfully
unexcusably
unexpectedly
unexplainably
unfailingly
unfairly

unfaithfully
unfalteringly
unfashionably
unfavorably
unfeelingly
unfitly
unfittingly
unflaggingly
unflappably
unflinchingly
unforgettably
unforgivably
unfortunately
unfree
unfriendly
unfunny
ungainly
ungodly
ungracefully
ungraciously
ungrammatically
ungratefully
ungrudgingly
unguiltily
unguilty
unhandy
unhappily
unhappy
unhealthy
unhelpfully
unholy
unhurriedly
unidiomatically
uniformity
uniformly
unimpressively
uniquely
unitary
unitedly
unity

universally
university
unjudicially
unjustly
unkindly
unkingly
unknowingly
unlawfully
unlikely
unluckily
unlucky
unmanly
unmannerly
unmercifully
unmilitary
unmistakably
unmorality
unnaturally
unnecessarily
unnecessary
unneedfully
unneighborly
unnervingly
unnewsworthy
unnoticeably
unobtrusively
unoffensively
unofficially
unofficiously
unorthodoxly
unorthodoxy
unpalatably
unperceptively
unpersuasively
unperturbably
unpleasantly
unpoetically
unpossessively
unpredictably
unpretentiously

unproductively
unprofitably
unpropitiously
unquestionably
unquietly
unready
unrealistically
unreality
unreasonably
unreceptively
unreliably
unremorsefully
unresponsively
unrighteously
unromantically
unruly
unsafely
unsatiably
unsatisfactorily
unsatisfactory
unsavory
unscholarly
unscientifically
unscrupulously
unseasonably
unseaworthy
unseemly
unselfishly
unshakably
unshapely
unsightly
unskillfully
unsmilingly
unsociably
unsocially
unsoundly
unsparingly
unspeakably
unspecifically
unstably

unsteadily
unsteady
unstintingly
unsubtly
unsuccessfully
unsuitably
unsurely
unsurmountably
unsurpassably
unsuspiciously
unswervingly
unsympathetically
untactfully
untastefully
unthinkably
unthinkingly
unthrifty
untidily
untidy
untimely
untiringly
untouchably
untruly
untrustworthy
untruthfully
untypically
unusually
unvaryingly
unwarily
unwary
unwaveringly
unweary
unwholesomely
unwieldy
unwifely
unwillingly
unwisely
unwittingly
unwomanly
unwontedly

unworkably	validity	verbally
unworldly	validly	verbosely
unworthily	valley	verbosity
unworthy	valorously	verdantly
unyieldingly	vanity	verdi
unzealously	vapidity	verily
upcountry	vapidly	veritably
upholstery	vaporously	verity
uppity	vapory	verminously
uprightly	variably	vernally
uproariously	varicosity	versatility
upwardly	variety	vertebrae
urbanely	variously	vertically
urbanity	varsity	very
urgency	vary	vestee
urgently	vascularity	vestry
urinary	vascularly	veterinary
urology	vasectomy	vexatiously
usability	vastly	viability
usee	vaulty	viably
usefully	veeringly	vibrancy
uselessly	veery	vibrantly
usually	vehemency	vibratory
usury	vehemently	vicariously
utility	veiny	viceroyalty
utterly	velocity	vicinity
uvularly	velvety	viciously
uxoriously	venality	victoriously
vacancy	venally	victory
vacantly	vendee	viduity
vacuity	venerably	vigilante
vacuously	venery	vigilantly
vagary	vengefully	vigorously
vagrancy	venially	villainously
vagrantly	venomously	villainy
vaguely	ventrally	villously
vainly	ventriloquy	vindicatory
valedictory	venturously	vindictively
valiancy	veraciously	vinegary
valiantly	veracity	violably

violently	voluptuously	weakly
virginity	voraciously	wealthy
virility	voracity	weaponry
virology	votary	wearily
virtually	vouchee	wearisomely
virtuosity	vulgarity	weary
virtuously	vulgarly	webby
virulency	vulnerably	Wednesday
virulently	vulnerary	wee
viscerally	wacky	weedily
viscidity	waggery	weedy
viscidly	waggly	weekly
viscosity	wailfully	weeny
viscously	walkie	weepy
visibility	walkie-talkie	weevilly
visibly	wallaby	weevily
visionary	wanly	weightily
visually	wantonly	weightlessly
vitality	wapiti	weighty
vitally	warily	weirdly
vivaciously	warmheartedly	westerly
vivacity	warmly	westwardly
vividly	warningly	wetly
viviparity	warrantee	whammy
viviparously	warranty	wheelie
vixenishly	warty	wheezy
vocabulary	wary	wherry
vocally	washability	whiffletree
vocatively	washy	whiggery
vociferously	waspishly	whimperingly
voicelessly	waspy	whimsicality
volatility	wastefully	whimsically
volcanically	watchfully	whimsy
volley	waterworthy	whiningly
volubility	watery	whinny
volubly	waveringly	whirry
voluminously	wavy	whiskey
voluntarily	waxy	whisky
voluntary	waywardly	whitey
voluptuary	we	whitsunday

wholeheartedly	wobbly	xenically
wholely	woefully	xenobiology
wholesomely	womanly	xerography
wholly	wonderfully	Yangtze
whoopee	wonderingly	yankee
wickedly	wondrously	yanqui
widely	wonky	yarely
wiener	woodenly	ye
wienie	woodsy	yearly
wifely	woody	yearningly
wiggly	woolly	yeasty
wildly	wooly	yeomanly
wilfully	woozily	yeomanry
willfully	woozy	yesterday
willingly	wordily	yeti
willowy	wordlessly	yippee
willy-nilly	wordy	yippie
wily	workability	yogi
windily	worldly	yolky
windy	wormy	Yosemite
winery	worriedly	youthfully
winningly	worrisomely	yucky
winsomely	worry	yummy
wintery	worshipfully	zanily
wintry	worthily	zany
winy	worthlessly	zealotry
wiry	worthy	zealously
wisely	woundingly	zestfully
wishfully	wrathfully	zesty
wishy	wreathy	zingy
wispy	wretchedly	zippy
wistfully	wriggly	zloty
witchery	wrigley	zombie
witchy	wrinkly	zonally
witheringly	writhingly	zonary
witlessly	wrongfully	zoologically
wittily	wrongheadedly	zoology
wittingly	wrongly	zootherapy
witty	wryly	zucchini
wizardry	xanthippe	Zuni

zygosity
zygotically
zymology
zymotically
zymurgy

Long EB
glebe
grebe
plebe

EB
cobweb
Deb
ebb
subdeb
web

Long ECH
beach
beech
beseech
bleach
breach
breech
each
forereach
impeach
leach
leech
outreach
peach
preach
reach
reteach
screech
speech
teach
unteach

ECH
backstretch
etch
fetch
homestretch
ketch
kvetch
outstretch
retch
sketch
stretch
vetch
wretch

Long ED
accede
acned
agreed
airspeed
anteed
babied
bandied
bead
bellied
berried
birdseed
bleed
bloodied
bodied
brandied
breast-feed
breed
bullied
buried
busied
caddied
candied
carried
cede
centipede

chickweed
concede
copied
creed
crossbreed
curried
curtseyed
curtsied
dallied
decreed
deed
dirtied
divvied
dizzied
duckweed
eddied
emceed
emptied
envied
exceed
fancied
feed
ferried
flaxseed
flurried
formfeed
freed
frenzied
Ganymede
glede
gleed
gloried
godspeed
greed
gussied
hackneyed
half-breed
harried
hayseed
he'd

heed
high-speed
honeyed
hurried
impede
implead
inbreed
indeed
interbreed
intercede
ivied
jellied
jewelweed
jimmied
jockeyed
jollied
journeyed
keyed
knead
kneed
lead
levied
linefeed
linseed
lip-read
lobbied
married
mead
meed
milkweed
misdeed
mislead
misread
moneyed
monied
monkeyed
moseyed
muddied
mutinied
need

nosebleed
oilseed
palsied
parlayed
parleyed
parried
partied
pigweed
pitied
plead
precede
prettied
proceed
proofread
pureed
puttied
quarried
queried
ragweed
rallied
rapeseed
read
readied
recede
reed
reread
reseed
Runnymede
sallied
savvied
screed
scurried
seaweed
secede
seed
sentried
serried
she'd
shimmied
shinnied

sight-read
skied
snakeweed
speed
speed-read
spoon-feed
stampede
steadied
steed
stinkweed
storied
studied
stymied
subbreed
succeed
sullied
supercede
swede
tallied
tarried
taxied
teed
ten-speed
tidied
toadied
treed
trusteed
tweed
varied
velocipede
volleyed
we'd
wearied
weed
whinnied
wormseed
worried

ED
aforesaid

ahead
airhead
beachhead
bed
bedspread
bedstead
behead
bighead
billhead
biped
blackhead
bled
blockhead
blood-red
bloodshed
bobsled
bonehead
bread
bred
bridgehead
bulkhead
bullhead
childbed
chucklehead
coed
copperhead
cornbread
cowshed
crossbred
daybed
dead
deadhead
deathbed
delead
dog-sled
dread
drumhead
dumbhead
dunderhead
egghead

embed
farmstead
fathead
featherbed
featherhead
fed
flatbed
flathead
figurehead
fled
flowerbed
forehead
foresaid
fountainhead
Fred
gainsaid
gingerbread
go-ahead
godhead
half-bred
hardhead
head
highbred
hogshead
homebred
homestead
hophead
hotbed
hothead
imbed
impled
inbred
instead
lead
led
lunkhead
masthead
meathead
misled
misread

moped
nonsked
outspread
overfed
overspread
packthread
ped
pinhead
pled
pothead
premed
proofread
purebred
quadruped
railhead
read
red
redd
redhead
reread
retread
riverbed
roadbed
roadstead
said
seabed
seedbed
shed
shewbread
shortbread
shred
sickbed
skinhead
sled
snowshed
sorehead
spearhead
sped
spread
stead

subhead
sweetbread
swellhead
thickhead
thoroughbred
thread
thunderhead
toolshed
towhead
tread
unbred
unfed
underfed
unsaid
unshed
unwed
warhead
wed
well-read
wellhead
whitehead
widespread
wingspread
woodshed
zed

Long EF
beef
belief
brief
chief
debrief
disbelief
flyleaf
greenleaf
grief
kerchief
leaf
lief
loose-leaf

massif
motif
reef
relief
sheaf
subchief
thief

EFT
eft
bereft
cleft
deft
heft
left
theft
weft

Long EG
blitzkrieg
colleague
fatigue
intrigue
league

EG
beg
blackleg
bootleg
bowleg
dogleg
egg
foreleg
jackleg
keg
leg
muskeg
nutmeg
peg
proleg

renege
unpeg
yegg

Long EJ
besiege
liege
prestige
siege

EJ
allege
dredge
edge
hedge
kedge
ledge
pledge
sedge
sledge
straightedge
swage
wedge

Long EK
antique
batik
beak
bespeak
bleak
boutique
cacique
cheek
chic
clique
creak
creek
critique
eke
freak

geek	wreak	xebec
gleek		
greek	**EK**	**EKS**
grosbeak	Aztec	annex
hairstreak	beck	apex
hide-and-seek	bedeck	Aztecs
leak	breakneck	bedecks
leek	check	checks
Martinique	cheque	circumflex
meek	crookneck	codex
midweek	cross-check	complex
Mozambique	Czech	convex
mystique	deck	corrects
newspeak	fleck	cortex
Newsweek	flyspeck	crooknecks
oblique	foredeck	Czechs
peak	gooseneck	decks
peek	heck	deflects
perique	henpeck	desex
physique	kopeck	duplex
pipsqueak	kopek	effects
pique	leatherneck	flecks
reek	neck	flex
seek	opec	flyspecks
sheik	paycheck	henpecks
sheikh	peck	hex
shriek	Quebec	ibex
sikh	recheck	index
sleek	reck	infects
sneak	redneck	inflects
speak	ringneck	injects
squeak	roughneck	Kleenex
streak	shipwreck	kopecks
teak	spec	kopeks
technique	speck	lastex
tweak	tech	latex
unique	trek	lex
weak	Uzbek	Middlesex
week	wreck	narthex
workweek	wryneck	necks

neglects	flexed	elect
objects	hexed	erect
paychecks	indexed	expect
pecks	next	flecked
perplex	perplexed	genuflect
pollex	pretext	henpecked
protects	reflexed	incorrect
pyrex	sexed	infect
rechecks	sext	inflect
rednecks	telexed	indirect
reflects	text	inject
reflex	unvexed	insect
rex	vexed	inspect
Rollieflex		intellect
roughnecks	**EKT**	interject
scolex	abject	misdirect
sex	affect	necked
shipwrecks	architect	neglect
silex	aspect	object
simplex	bedecked	pecked
spandex	bisect	perfect
specks	bullnecked	prefect
specs	checked	project
telex	circumspect	prosect
tex	collect	prospect
treks	connect	protect
triplex	convect	rechecked
unsex	correct	recollect
unisex	decked	reflect
vertex	defect	reject
vex	deflect	resect
vortex	deject	respect
wrecks	detect	sect
wrynecks	direct	select
xebecs	disconnect	self-respect
	disinfect	shipwrecked
EKST	disrespect	specked
annexed	dissect	subject
bisexed	effect	suspect
context	eject	transect

trekked
trisect
unchecked
v-necked
wrecked

Long EL
anneal
appeal
automobile
bastille
cartwheel
castile
Castille
cogwheel
conceal
congeal
cornmeal
creel
deal
eel
feel
flywheel
freewheel
gearwheel
genteel
handwheel
he'll
heal
heel
ideal
keel
kneel
Lucille
meal
misdeal
mobile
newsreel
nosewheel
oatmeal

ordeal
pastille
peal
peel
piecemeal
pinwheel
privy seal
real
reel
reheel
repeal
reveal
schlemiel
seal
she'll
speel
spiel
squeal
stabile
steal
steel
surreal
teal
thunderpeal
unreal
unseal
veal
we'll
wheel
zeal

EL
bagatelle
barbell
béchamel
befell
bell
belle
bluebell
bombshell

bridewell
brinell
carrousel
caravel
Carmel
cartel
cell
citadel
clamshell
clientele
cockerel
cockle-shell
compel
Cornell
cowbell
Cromwell
dell
delle
demoiselle
dinnerbell
dispel
doggerel
doorbell
dumbbell
dwell
eggshell
ell
excel
expel
farewell
fell
foretell
gazelle
gel
groundswell
harebell
hell
hotel
impel
indwell

infidel
inkwell
jell
Jezebel
knell
lapel
mademoiselle
Michelle
misspell
morel
motel
nacelle
Nobel
Noel
Noelle
novell
nutshell
Orwell
outsell
outspell
outyell
passing bell
pastel
pell
pell-mell
personnel
pimpernel
propel
quell
Ravel
rebel
repel
resell
retell
riel
sell
sentinel
shell
shrapnel
shrapnell

smell
southern belle
speedwell
spell
stairwell
subcell
swell
tell
undersell
unwell
vesper bell
well
yell

ELCH
belch
squelch
welch

Long ELD
afield
airfield
annealed
appealed
backfield
battlefield
Chesterfield
coalfield
concealed
congealed
cornfield
downfield
field
four-wheeled
Garfield
goldfield
grainfield
hayfield
healed
heeled

infield
keeled
kneeled
lancefield
midfield
outfield
pealed
peeled
reeled
reheeled
repealed
resealed
revealed
sealed
shield
snowfield
Springfield
squealed
steeled
unhealed
unsealed
well-heeled
wheeled
wield
windshield
yield

ELD
beheld
belled
celled
compelled
dispelled
dwelled
excelled
expelled
felled
geld
gelled
held

impelled
jelled
knelled
lapeled
lapelled
meld
misspelled
outspelled
outyelled
propelled
quelled
rebelled
repelled
shelled
smelled
spelled
swelled
unshelled
upheld
weld
withheld
yelled

ELF
bookshelf
elf
Guelph
herself
himself
itself
mantle
shelf
myself
oneself
ourself
self
shelf
thyself
yourself

ELM
elm
helm
overwhelm
realm
whelm

ELP
help
kelp
whelp
yelp

ELT
belt
Celt
dealt
dwelt
felt
flybelt
gelt
greenbelt
heartfelt
indwelt
kelt
knelt
melt
misdealt
misspelt
pelt
smelt
snowbelt
spelled
spelt
sunbelt
svelte
unfelt
veldt
welt

ELTH
commonwealth
health
stealth
wealth

ELV
delve
helve
shelve
twelve

Long EM
agleam
airstream
beam
beseem
blaspheme
bloodstream
bream
centime
cream
creme
crossbeam
daydream
deem
downstream
dream
esteem
extreme
gleam
inseam
mainstream
midstream
millstream
moonbeam
morpheme
phoneme
pipedream
raceme

ream
redeem
regime
scheme
scream
seam
self-esteem
seem
steam
stream
sunbeam
supreme
team
teem
theme
upstream

EM
ahem
apothegm
Bethlehem
condemn
femme
flem
fm
gem
hem
idem
mayhem
phlegm
pm
poem
rehem
requiem
schlemm
stem
stratagem
them
theorem

EMT
attempt
contempt
dreamt
exempt
kempt
preempt
tempt
undreamt
unkempt

EMZ
condemns
gems
hems
poems
rehems
stems
Thames

Long EN
Aberdeen
Abilene
acetylene
almandine
amphetamine
antihistamine
aquamarine
Argentine
Augustine
bean
been
benzedrine
benzene
berberine
between
brilliantine
buckbean
byzantine
caffeine

canteen
carbine
careen
carotene
chlorine
christine
clean
codeine
contravene
convene
creatine
crystalline
cuisine
cystine
damascene
dauphin
dean
demean
dentin
dentine
dramamine
eighteen
elephantine
epicene
epinephrine
ergotamine
ethylene
evergreen
fifteen
figurine
florentine
fluorene
fluorine
foreseen
gabardine
gaberdine
gallein
gangrene
gasoline
gene

glean
green
grenadine
guillotine
halloween
histamine
holstein
houseclean
hygiene
incarnadine
intervene
Jean
Jeanne
jellybean
keen
kerosene
kerosine
latrine
lean
legatine
libertine
lien
limousine
lipoprotein
lysine
machine
magazine
magdalene
marine
mean
melamine
mescaline
mesne
mezzanine
mien
morphine
murine
muscarine
nankeen
nectarine

neoprene
newsmagazine
nicotine
nineteen
obscene
olivine
opaline
overseen
paleocene
peen
philippine
philistine
phosphene
phosphine
pleistocene
pliocene
polyethylene
praline
preen
preteen
pristine
proline
propylene
protein
putrescine
quarantine
queen
quinidine
ravine
reconvene
routine
saccharine
saline
saltine
sardine
sateen
scene
screen
seen
serene

serpentine
seventeen
sheen
sibylline
silkscreen
sistine
sixteen
soybean
sparteine
spleen
strychnine
styrene
submachine
submarine
subroutine
subteen
sunscreen
supergene
supervene
synephrine
tambourine
tangerine
taurine
teen
terpene
thiamine
thirteen
thyroxine
tontine
trampoline
travertine
tureen
tween
ultramarine
umpteen
unclean
unforeseen
unforseen
unseen
vaccine

vaseline
velveteen
vitelline
wean
windscreen
wintergreen
wolverine
xanthine
xylene

EN
again
aidmen
airmen
amen
badmen
bagmen
bailsmen
bandsmen
barmen
batmen
bellmen
Ben
boatmen
bondmen
bondsmen
bowmen
brakemen
bullpen
bushmen
chainmen
chairmen
chessmen
churchmen
citizen
clansmen
coachmen
comedienne
corpsmen
cowmen

craftsmen
crewmen
den
denizen
doormen
dutchmen
earthmen
fen
firemen
footmen
fountain pen
freemen
frenchmen
freshmen
frogmen
glen
goodmen
halogen
helmsmen
hen
henchmen
herdsmen
horsemen
housemen
huntsmen
hydrogen
icemen
Ken
kinsmen
lawmen
linemen
linesmen
madmen
Magdelene
magsmen
mailmen
marksmen
men
mermen
milkmen

newsmen
nightmen
norsemen
oarsmen
oxygen
Parisienne
peahen
pen
penmen
pigpen
pitchmen
plainsmen
playpen
plowmen
postmen
pressmen
ranchmen
regimen
RN
scotsmen
seamen
Seine
shiftmen
showmen
sidemen
snowmen
spacemen
specimen
spoilsmen
spokesmen
sportsmen
statesmen
steersmen
stockmen
strongmen
switchmen
swordsmen
tacksmen
talesmen
ten

then
tollmen
topmen
townsmen
trackmen
tradesmen
trainmen
tribesmen
truckmen
when
workmen
wren
yachtsmen
yardmen
yeggmen
yen
yeomen
Zen

END
amend
append
apprehend
ascend
attend
backbend
bartend
befriend
bend
blend
bookend
boyfriend
commend
comprehend
condescend
contend
defend
depend
descend
distend

dividend
downtrend
emend
end
expend
extend
fend
friend
girlfriend
godsend
impend
intend
kenned
lend
mend
minuend
misapprehend
misspend
offend
outspend
overextend
overspend
pend
penned
pitchblende
portend
pretend
reascend
recommend
rend
reprehend
resend
send
spend
stipend
subtend
subtrahend
superintend
suspend
tend

transcend
trend
unbend
underspend
upend
uptrend
vend
weekend
wend

ENGTH
length
strength
tenth

ENJ
avenge
revenge
Stonehenge

ENS
commence
condense
consequence
defence
defense
dense
dispense
expense
fence
frankincense
hence
immense
incense
intense
mense
missense
nonsense
offence
offense

overintense
pence
pense
prepense
pretence
pretense
recompense
sense
sequence
sixpence
suspense
tense
thence
whence

ENST
against
condensed
commenced
dispensed
fenced
incensed
pretensed
sensed
tensed
unfenced

ENT
accent
advent
ascent
assent
augment
bent
cement
cent
circumvent
comment
complement
compliment

consent
consequent
content
convent
dent
descent
discontent
disorient
document
event
extent
ferment
foment
forwent
fragment
gent
hellbent
indent
intent
invent
lament
leant
lent
malcontent
meant
misrepresent
misspent
orient
overspent
pent
percent
portent
present
prevent
reascent
reinvent
relent
rent
reorient
repent

represent
resent
scent
sent
spent
supplement
tent
torment
trident
unbent
underspent
underwent
unmeant
unsent
unspent
vent
went

ENZ
amens
bullpens
cleanse
dens
fens
glens
hens
lens
men's
parens
peahens
pens
pigpens
playpens
tens
weekends
wrens
yens

Long EP
asleep

barkeep
beauty sleep
beep
bleep
cheap
cheep
creep
deep
dustheap
heap
housekeep
jeep
keep
knee-deep
leap
neap
outleap
overleap
oversleep
peep
reap
seep
sheep
skin-deep
sleep
steep
sweep
upkeep
upsweep
veep
weep

EP
doorstep
footstep
hep
instep
misstep
overstep
pep

prep
quickstep
schlep
sidestep
step
steppe
strep

EPT
accept
adept
backswept
concept
crept
except
inept
intercept
kept
leapt
outleapt
overstepped
pepped
percept
precept
prepped
sept
sidestepped
slept
stepped
swept
unkept
unwept
upswept
wept
windswept

EER
adhere

appear
arrear
astrosphere
atmosphere
auctioneer
austere
balladeer
bandoleer
bandolier
bathysphere
beer
belvedere
besmear
bier
biosphere
blear
bombardier
boutonniere
brassiere
brigadier
buccaneer
budgeteer
cannoneer
career
cashier
cashmere
cavalier
chandelier
charioteer
cheer
chromosphere
circuiteer
clear
cohere
commandeer
conventioneer
dear
deer
disappear
dogear

domineer
drear
ear
electioneer
elixir
emir
endear
engineer
exosphere
fakir
fear
financier
fleer
footgear
frontier
gadgeteer
gazetteer
gear
gondolier
goodyear
grenadier
headgear
hear
hemisphere
here
hydrosphere
inhere
insincere
interfere
ionosphere
jeer
junketeer
kefir
killdeer
lavaliere
leer
lithosphere
marketeer
mere
midyear

mishear
mountaineer
muleteer
musketeer
mutineer
nadir
near
overhear
peer
persevere
photosphere
pier
pioneer
premier
premiere
privateer
profiteer
puppeteer
queer
racketeer
reappear
rear
rehear
reindeer
revere
sear
seer
severe
shakespeare
shear
sheer
sincere
smear
sneer
souvenir
spear
sphere
steer
stratosphere
tear

thermosphere
tier
transfrontier
unclear
veer
veneer
vizier
volunteer
we're
year
yesteryear
Zaire

ERD
adhered
appeared
beard
besmeared
bleared
bluebeard
careered
cashiered
cheered
cohered
dog-eared
eared
endeared
feared
fleered
geared
Graybeard
inhered
jeered
leered
neared
peered
premiered
queered
reared
revered

seared
sheared
sheered
smeared
sneered
speared
steered
tiered
uncleared
unfeared
veered
weird

EERS
fierce
pierce

Long ES
bailpiece
caprice
cease
crease
crosspiece
decrease
earpiece
eyepiece
fieldpiece
fowling piece
frontispiece
fleece
geese
grandniece
grease
Greece
hairpiece
handpiece
headpiece
increase
lease
mantelpiece

masterpiece
mouthpiece
niece
nosepiece
obese
peace
pelisse
piece
police
predecease
release
showpiece
sidepiece
sublease
surcease
tailpiece
timepiece
valise

ES
abidingness
abscess
access
acquiesce
address
assess
bareness
bless
broadness
bs
caress
cbs
chattiness
cheekiness
chess
clothespress
coalesce
compress
confess
convalesce

cps
cress
decompress
depress
digress
dispossess
distress
dress
duress
effervesce
effloresce
egress
evanesce
excess
express
finesse
fluoresce
guess
headdress
headmistress
impress
incandesce
ingress
irs
jess
largess
largesse
less
letterpress
luminesce
mess
nevertheless
nightdress
noblesse
nonetheless
obsess
oppress
outguess
overdress
overimpress

politesse
possess
prepossess
press
princess
process
profess
progress
readdress
reassess
recess
recrudesce
redress
regress
repossess
repress
reprocess
retrogress
shirtdress
SOS
stress
subprocess
success
sundress
suppress
transgress
tress
underdress
undress
unless
wardress
watercress
winepress
yes

Long ESH
affiche
fiche
leash
quiche

schottische
unleash

ESH
afresh
crèche
enmesh
flesh
fresh
gooseflesh
horseflesh
mesh
refresh
secesh
thresh

ESK
burlesque
desk
grotesque
picaresque
picturesque
statuesque

Long EST
artiste
beast
ceased
creased
deceased
decreased
east
feast
fleeced
greased
increased
leased
least
mideast
northeast

pieced
policed
priest
released
southeast
subleased
unleased
yeast

EST
abreast
abscessed
addressed
armrest
arrest
assessed
attest
backrest
bequest
best
blessed
blest
bloodtest
breast
Bucharest
caressed
celeste
chest
compressed
confessed
congest
conquest
contest
crest
depressed
detest
devest
digest
digressed
distressed

divest
dressed
expressed
finessed
fluoresced
footrest
gabfest
geste
guessed
guest
headrest
houseguest
impressed
incest
infest
ingest
inquest
invest
jest
lest
manifest
messed
midwest
molest
nest
northwest
obsessed
overdressed
oppressed
outguessed
pest
possessed
pressed
prestressed
pretest
processed
professed
progressed
protest
quest

recessed
redbreast
redressed
regressed
repressed
request
rest
retest
second best
songfest
southwest
stressed
suggest
suppressed
test
transgressed
Trieste
unblessed
underdressed
undressed
unexpressed
unguessed
unpressed
unrest
unstressed
vest
west
wrest
zest

Long ET
aesthete
Antoinette, Marie
athlete
bassinet
bayonet
beat
beet
bittersweet
blackfeet

bleat
browbeat
buckwheat
bystreet
cabinet
castanet
chansonette
cheat
clarinet
cleat
clipsheet
clubfeet
compete
complete
conceit
concrete
coronet
Crete
deadbeat
deceit
defeat
delete
deplete
discreet
discrete
dopesheet
downbeat
drawsheet
drumbeat
eat
effete
elite
entreat
escheat
excrete
feat
feet
fete
flatfeet
fleet

forefeet
foresheet
gamete
greet
heartbeat
heat
helpmeet
hoofbeat
incomplete
indiscrete
maltreat
meat
meet
mesquite
mete
mincemeat
mistreat
neat
nutmeat
obsolete
offbeat
overeat
peat
Pete
petite
pleat
preheat
receipt
reheat
repeat
replete
retreat
seat
secrete
self-deceit
sheet
skeet
sleet
splayfeet
spreadsheet

street
suite
sweet
sweetmeat
teat
treat
tweet
unseat
upbeat
wheat
wholewheat

ET
abet
alphabet
amulet
anisette
Annette
asset
beget
beset
bet
briquette
brochette
brunette
cadet
cadette
calumet
cassette
cigarette
coquet
coquette
cornet
Corvette
coverlet
croquette
crystal set
debt
dinette
diskette

dragnet
duet
etiquette
fanjet
farmerette
fishnet
forget
fret
gazette
get
handset
headset
inset
Jeannette
jet
Joliet
Juliet
Juliette
kismet
layette
let
lorgnette
lucheonette
lunette
marionette
marmoset
martinet
mignonette
minaret
met
musette
net
novelette
octet
offset
omelet
onset
oubliette
outlet
outset

parapet
pet
pirouette
pipette
planchette
preset
propjet
quartet
quartette
quickset
quintet
quintette
ramjet
regret
reset
rivulet
roomette
rosette
roulette
set
sestet
sextet
silhouette
somerset
Somerset
soubrette
statuette
sublet
subset
suffragette
sunset
sweat
thickset
threat
Tibet
typeset
unmet
upset
vet
vignette

vinaigrette
well-met
wet
whet
yet

Long ETH
beneath
bequeath
buckteeth
dogteeth
ensheathe
eyeteeth
heath
'neath
sheath
teeth
underneath
unsheathe
wreath

ETH
Beth
breath
death
Elizabeth
Macbeth
shibboleth

Long EV
achieve
believe
bereave
breve
Christmas Eve
cleave
conceive
deceive
disbelieve
eave

eve
greave
grieve
heave
interweave
khedive
leave
misconceive
naive
New Year's Eve
peeve
perceive
preconceive
receive
recitative
reeve
relieve
reprieve
retrieve
sheave
shirtsleeve
sleeve
Steve
thieve
unweave
wayleave
we've
weave

Long EZ
abalones
abbeys
abcs
abilities
abnormalities
aborigines
absentees
absorbencies
absurdities
academies

accessaries
accompanies
accuracies
achilles
activities
actualities
actuaries
acuities
addressees
adequacies
adobes
adoptabilities
adulteries
adversaries
adversities
advisories
advocacies
aeries
aerotherapies
affinities
agencies
agonies
agrees
alimonies
allegories
allergies
alleys
ambergrease
ambiguities
amenities
amputees
analogies
analyses
anarchies
ancestries
anchovies
ancillaries
Andes
anemones
angiostomies

angularities
animalities
animosities
anniversaries
annuities
anomalies
anomies
anonymities
anthologies
antibodies
antifreeze
antilles
antipathies
antiquaries
antiquities
antitheses
anureses
anxieties
anybodies
Apaches
apathies
apiaries
apogees
apologies
apoplexies
apostasies
apostrophes
apothecaries
appease
appendectomies
appointees
archdiocese
ares
argosies
aries
aristocracies
armies
armories
arteries
artilleries

assemblies
assignees
asymmetries
atrocities
atrophies
attorneys
auguries
auspices
Aussies
authenticities
authorities
autopsies
auxiliaries
availabilities
aviaries
avowries
axillaries
axletrees
babies
bacteriologies
bakeries
balconies
banalities
bandies
banditries
bankruptcies
baptisteries
barbarities
barberries
barleys
bastardies
batteries
bayberries
beaneries
beanies
bearberries
beauties
bees
belfries
bellicosities

bellies
belligerencies
beneficiaries
berries
bestialities
bevies
bibliographies
biddies
bigamies
biggies
bigotries
bikinis
bilateralities
bimonthlies
binaries
binderies
biographies
biologies
biopsies
biotechnologies
birdies
biweeklies
blackberries
blasphemies
bloodies
blueberries
bobbies
bodies
bogeys
boilaries
boobies
bookies
bootees
booteries
booties
bottomries
boundaries
bounties
boysenberries
brandies

brasseries
brassies
braveries
breeze
breweries
briberies
brilliancies
brownies
brutalities
buddies
buggeries
buggies
bullies
bumblebees
bunnies
buoys
bureaucracies
bureaucratese
burglaries
burgundies
buries
burleys
burmese
busbies
busies
busybodies
butcheries
butteries
cabbies
cacophonies
caddies
cadencies
cadres
cajoleries
calamities
calliopes
calories
calorimetries
camporees
canapes

canaries
candidacies
candies
canneries
canonries
canopies
cantonese
capabilities
capacities
capillaries
captaincies
captivities
cardiographies
carnalities
carnies
carries
cartographies
casualties
catastrophes
categories
causalities
cavalries
cavities
celebrities
celeries
cemeteries
centralities
centuries
ceremonies
certainties
ceylonese
chairladies
chancellories
chaplaincies
charities
chastities
cheateries
checkerberries
cheese
chemise

chemistries
Cherokees
cherries
chicaneries
chickadees
chickpeas
chilies
chimneys
chimpanzees
Chinese
chippies
chronologies
cities
citizenries
civilities
civvies
clairvoyancies
clemencies
clergies
cockneys
coffees
cogencies
colonies
comanches
comedies
commentaries
commissaries
committees
commodities
commonalities
communities
companies
compatibilities
competencies
complexities
compliancies
complicities
concavities
conditionalities
coneys

confectioneries
confederacies
conferees
confidentialities
conformities
confraternities
congeries
Congolese
congruencies
congruities
conniveries
conservatories
consignataries
consignees
consistencies
conspiracies
constabularies
constituencies
contemporaries
contiguities
contingencies
continuities
contractibilities
contraries
controversies
convexities
cookies
coolies
cooties
coparties
copies
coronaries
corpulencies
corruptibilities
cosignatories
coteries
coulees
counterinsurgencies
counties
countries

courtesies
coveys
cowries
coyotes
cozies
cranberries
crannies
crappies
crazies
creameries
credibilities
crees
crematories
criminalities
crises
cronies
crookeries
crudities
cruelties
crybabies
cubbies
curies
curiosities
currencies
curries
curtesies
curtseys
curtsies
custodies
cyclopes
cytologies
daddies
dailies
dainties
daiquiris
dairies
daisies
damocles
dandies
deaneries

debauchees
debaucheries
debilities
decease
decencies
declivities
decrees
deep-freeze
deficiencies
deformities
degeneracies
degrees
deities
delegacies
delicacies
delinquencies
deliveries
democracies
demographies
demonologies
densities
dentistries
deontologies
dependabilities
dependencies
depositaries
depositories
depravities
deputies
derbies
despondencies
destinies
deviancies
deviltries
devotees
dewberries
diabetes
diagnoses
dialyses
diaries

dichotomies
dickeys
dictionaries
dietaries
difficulties
dignitaries
dignities
dillies
dillydallies
dinghies
diocese
diplomacies
directories
dirties
disabilities
disagrees
discontinuities
discourtesies
discoveries
discrepancies
disease
disembodies
disharmonies
dishonesties
disloyalties
disparities
dispensaries
displease
dissimilarities
distilleries
ditties
diureses
diversities
divinities
divorcees
divvies
documentaries
doggies
dogies
doilies

dollies
domesticities
donkeys
dormancies
dormitories
dowries
draftees
draperies
dromedaries
dropsies
drudgeries
dualities
duchies
ductilities
dummies
dungarees
duplicities
durabilities
duties
dynasties
dysenteries
dystrophies
ease
eateries
ebonies
eccentricities
ecologies
economies
ecstacies
ecstasies
eddies
effendis
efficiencies
effigies
egocentricities
eighties
elasticities
elderberries
electees
electrosurgeries

electrotherapies
elegies
ellipses
embassies
embodies
embroideries
emcees
emergencies
emissaries
emmies
Emmys
empathies
emphases
employees
empties
enemies
energies
enlistees
enmities
enormities
enquiries
entireties
entities
entomologies
entreaties
entries
envies
epilepsies
epiphanies
epitomes
epoxies
equalities
equerries
equities
equivalencies
equivocacies
eries
errancies
escapees
eternities

ethologies
etiologies
etymologies
eulogies
euphonies
euphrates
euripides
evacuees
eventualities
excellencies
exegeses
exigencies
exiguities
exogamies
expectancies
expediencies
expertise
extremities
facilities
facsimiles
factories
faculties
fairies
fallacies
falsies
falsities
familiarities
families
fancies
fannies
fantasies
farcies
fatalities
feces
fees
felicities
felonies
ferries
fertilities
festivities

fidelities
fifties
filigrees
fillies
finales
finalities
fineries
fisheries
flatteries
fleas
flees
flippancies
floozies
floppies
flunkies
flurries
fogies
follies
fooleries
foreladies
foresees
forgeries
formalities
forties
fortuities
foundries
fragilities
frailties
franchisees
fraternities
freebies
frees
freeze
frenzies
frequencies
friaries
fricassees
Fridays
frigidities
fripperies

Frisbees
frivolities
frugalities
functionaries
funnies
furies
furious
furrieries
fusees
gaieties
galaxies
gallantries
galleries
galleys
gantries
garnishees
gaucheries
geminis
genealogies
generalities
generosities
genies
geographies
geologies
geometries
germanies
giardiases
gibbosities
gipsies
glees
glories
glossaries
goalies
goatees
goodies
gooseberries
grammies
granaries
grandees
grannies

grantees
graphologies
gratuities
gravities
grease
grizzlies
groceries
groupies
guernseys
guildries
guineas
gullies
guppies
gurneys
gussies
guyanese
gypsies
haberdasheries
habitancies
hackneys
hades
hankies
harlotries
harmonies
harpies
harries
hatcheries
he's
headcheese
hearties
heavies
hegemonies
heliotherapies
henries
henrys
heracles
heraldries
Hercules
heresies
Hermes

herpes
hesitancies
heterodoxies
heterosexualities
hibachis
hickeys
hickories
hierarchies
hilarities
hillbillies
hippies
hippocrates
histologies
histories
hoagies
hobbies
holandries
hollies
homebodies
homilies
homologies
honeybees
honeys
honkeys
honkies
honorees
hootenannies
Hopis
hostelries
hostilities
hubbies
huckleberries
humanities
humidities
hurries
huskies
hussies
hyperacidities
hyperactivities
hyperboles

hypersensitivities
hypersexualities
hypoacidities
hyposensitivities
hypotheses
hysterectomies
idealogies
identities
ideologies
idiocies
idiocrasies
idiosyncrasies
idolatries
ignominies
illegalities
illegitimacies
illiteracies
imageries
imbecilities
immaturities
immensities
immoralities
immunities
impieties
impossibilities
impracticalities
improbabilities
improprieties
impurities
inabilities
inaccuracies
inactivities
inadequacies
inanities
incapabilities
incapacities
incendiaries
incipiencies
incompatibilities
incompetencies

incongruities
inconsistencies
incontinencies
indecencies
indemnities
indices
indignities
individualities
indochinese
inductees
industries
inefficiencies
inequalities
inequities
infamies
infancies
infantries
inferiorities
infertilities
infidelities
infinities
infirmaries
infirmities
informalities
iniquities
injuries
inquiries
insecurities
insensitivities
insincerities
insolvencies
integrities
intensities
intermarries
interviewees
intimacies
intricacies
inventories
ironies
irrationalities

irregularities
irrelevancies
irritancies
israelis
itineraries
ivies
ivories
jalopies
jamborees
Japanese
japeries
javanese
jaycees
jayvees
jealousies
jellies
jennies
jeopardies
Jesses
jetties
jiffies
jimmies
jitneys
jobberies
jockeys
jocundities
jollies
journalese
journeys
jubilees
judiciaries
junkies
juries
juvenilities
kamikazes
keys
khakis
kiddies
kidneys
kineses

kitties	liquidities	masculinities
kiwis	litanies	masonries
knaveries	liturgies	masteries
knees	liveries	maternities
krispies	lobbies	matriarchies
laboratories	lobotomies	meanies
lackeys	localities	mediocrities
laddies	loganberries	medleys
ladies	longevities	melancholies
landladies	lorries	melodies
lapidaries	lotteries	memories
larcenies	louise	menageries
lassies	lovelies	mendacities
latchkeys	loyalties	menses
latencies	lucidities	mentalities
laundries	lues	mephistopheles
lavatories	luminaries	mercenaries
Lebanese	lunacies	mercies
lecheries	luxuries	mercuries
lees	machetes	mesenteries
lefties	machineries	metatheses
legacies	magisteries	methodologies
legalese	magistracies	microsurgeries
legalities	maharanees	middies
legatees	maharishis	midwiferies
legionaries	mahoganies	militaries
legitimacies	majesties	mimicries
leniencies	majorities	miniseries
leprosies	maladies	ministries
lessees	malignancies	minorities
lethargies	malignities	misanthropies
levees	maltese	miscarries
levies	maneuverabilities	miscellanies
levities	manganese	miscopies
liabilities	maoris	miscreancies
liberalities	mariachis	miseries
liberties	marquees	misogamies
libraries	marquise	misogynies
licensees	marries	missionaries
lilies	martinis	modalities

mommies
monarchies
monasteries
Mondays
moneys
monies
monkeys
monogamies
monogynies
monopolies
monstrosities
montes
monthlies
morbidities
moribundities
morphologies
mortalities
mortgagees
mortuaries
moseys
mounties
movies
muddies
mulberries
multiplicities
multiversities
mummies
munchies
municipalities
mutinies
mysteries
mythologies
nannies
nationalities
nativities
navies
Nazis
necessaries
necessities
Nepalese

neurologies
neutralities
niceties
nighties
nineties
ninnies
nipponese
nixies
nobilities
nobodies
noddies
nominees
normalcies
normalities
notabilities
notaries
notorieties
novelties
nunneries
nurseries
oases
obesities
obituaries
obloquies
obscenities
obscurities
observatories
obstinacies
occupancies
oddities
odysseys
oldies
oligarchies
oligopolies
onerosities
opacities
operabilities
opportunities
oratories
orderlies

orgies
originalities
orthodoxies
outlawries
ovaries
overseas
oversees
oysteries
paddies
padres
paisleys
Pakistanis
palfreys
palsies
pandowdies
panoplies
pansies
panties
pantries
papacies
parentheses
pareses
parities
parlays
parleys
parodies
parolees
parries
parsleys
partialities
parties
passkeys
pastries
patellectomies
patencies
patentees
paternities
pathologies
patrimonies
patsies

patties
pawnees
payees
peas
pease
peccaries
peculiarities
pedigrees
pedologies
peewees
pekinese
pekingese
penalties
pennies
penuches
peonies
perfidies
perfumeries
pericles
perigees
peripheries
perjuries
permanencies
perpetuities
perplexities
personalities
personalties
pertinencies
perversities
phantasies
pharisees
pharmacies
pharmacologies
philanthropies
philosophies
phoebes
phonies
phonologies
photochemistries
photocopies

physiologies
pianofortes
pickaninnies
pieties
piggies
pillories
pinkies
piracies
piscaries
pisces
pities
pixies
plasticities
pleas
pleasantries
please
plenties
pluralities
plutocracies
poetries
policies
polyandries
polygamies
polygynies
ponies
poppies
porgies
pornographies
portuguese
posies
posses
possibilities
potbellies
potencies
potpourris
potteries
poverties
prairies
preemies
pregnancies

preliminaries
prematurities
preppies
presidencies
pretties
prexies
primacies
primaries
principalities
priorities
privacies
privies
privities
proclivities
proctologies
prodigies
profanities
profundities
progenies
promiscuities
propensities
properties
prophecies
prophylaxes
protheses
proxies
psyches
psychiatries
psychogeneses
psychologies
psychoquackeries
psychoses
psychosurgeries
psychotherapies
pubes
puerilities
pulleys
puppies
purees
purgatories

purulencies
puttees
putties
pygmies
quackeries
qualities
quandaries
quantities
quarries
quarterlies
queries
quick-freeze
quickies
rabies
radiancies
radioactivities
radiochemistries
rallies
rarities
raspberries
rationalities
reactionaries
readies
reagencies
realities
realties
reassemblies
reciprocities
recopies
recoveries
rediscoveries
redundancies
reembodies
reentries
referees
refineries
reformatories
refugees
registries
regnancies

regularities
relevancies
remarries
remedies
repertories
repositories
residencies
respondencies
retirees
returnees
reveilles
reveries
revolutionaries
rigidities
rivalries
robberies
rockies
rogueries
rooftrees
rookeries
rookies
rotaries
rotisseries
rowdies
royalties
rubies
rupees
safeties
salesladies
salubrities
sanctities
sanctuaries
sanies
sanities
satieties
saturdays
savvies
scabies
scammonies
scarcities

scatologies
sceneries
scrutinies
sculduggeries
scullduggeries
sculleries
scurries
scurrilities
scurvies
seas
secondaries
secrecies
secretaries
securities
sees
seize
sentries
series
seventies
sexologies
shanties
sharpies
shawnees
she's
sherries
shillalahs
shillelaghs
shimmies
shinnies
shoddies
shoetrees
shoshones
shrubberies
siamese
signataries
signatories
similarities
similes
simonies
simplicities

singhalese	stabilities	sweenies
singletrees	standees	sycoses
singularities	stannaries	symmetries
sinhalese	stapes	sympathies
sissies	stases	symphonies
sixties	stationeries	synapses
skiagraphies	statuaries	synchronies
skis	steadies	syncopes
skivvies	sterilities	synergies
skulduggeries	stories	syngamies
skullduggeries	strategies	synopses
sleaze	strawberries	syntheses
slurries	striptease	syzygies
smarties	strophes	tabbies
smelteries	studies	tactilities
smithies	sturdies	Taiwanese
sneeze	stymies	talkies
societies	subcategories	tallies
socrates	subcommittees	tamales
sodomies	subentries	tanneries
softies	sublimities	tansies
soliloquies	subseries	tapestries
somebodies	subsidiaries	tarries
sonnies	subsidies	tautologies
sonorities	subspecies	taxies
sophistries	subtleties	taxonomies
sophocles	subvarieties	tease
sorceries	sudanese	technicalities
sorties	sufficiencies	technologies
sovereignties	sullies	teddies
speakeasies	summaries	tees
specialties	sundays	temporalities
species	sundries	tenacities
specificities	suppositories	tenancies
speciosities	sureties	tenantries
spiveries	surgeries	tendencies
spivveries	surreys	tepees
sprees	surrogacies	terminologies
squeegees	swamis	testes
squeeze	sweeneys	testimonies

theocracies
theologies
theories
therapies
these
theses
thieveries
thirties
threes
threnodies
thuggeries
tidies
tizzies
toadies
toddies
toffees
toiletries
tomographies
tonalities
tonsillectomies
topographies
topologies
tories
totalities
toties
tourneys
towhees
toxicities
traceries
tracheostomies
tracheotomies
tragedies
tragicomedies
trainees
trajectories
translucencies
transparencies
trapeze
travesties
treacheries

treasuries
treaties
trees
tributaries
trickeries
trilogies
trinities
trivalencies
trochees
trolleys
trollies
trophies
truancies
trustees
trusties
tsetses
tuberculoses
tuesdays
tummies
tunnies
turbidities
turgidities
turkeys
turnkeys
TVs
tweeze
twenties
tympanies
typographies
tyrannies
ukeleles
ukuleles
ultimacies
Ulysses
umbones
unanimities
uncertainties
underbellies
underseas
understudies

unfreeze
unities
universities
upholsteries
urgencies
utilities
vacancies
vanities
varicosities
varies
varieties
varsities
vendees
veracities
verities
vestees
veterinaries
viabilities
vicinities
victories
Viennese
Vietnamese
vigilantes
villainies
virilities
virtuosities
virulencies
viscidities
viscosities
visionaries
viviparities
vocabularies
volleys
vollies
vulgarities
waggeries
wallabies
wapitis
warranties
Wednesdays

weeklies
whammies
wheaties
wheeze
wherries
whiffletrees
whimsies
whinnies
whiskeys
willies
wineries
witcheries
woollies
worries
worthies
yankees
yanquis
yesterdays
yetis
yippies
yogis
zanies
zlotys
zombies
zoologies
zootherapies
zucchinis

Long I
abaci
acidify
alibi
alkali
ally
alumni
amplify
anti
apply
awry
aye
b'nai
banzai
barfly
beautify
belie
bird'seye
blowfly
bonsai
botfly
buckeye
butterfly
buy
by
bye
cacti
calcify
certify
chi
citify
clarify
classify
cockeye
codify
comply
counterspy
crucify
cry
damnify

damselfly
dandify
decalcify
declassify
decry
deerfly
defy
dehumidify
deify
deny
detoxify
die
dignify
disqualify
dissatisfy
diversify
dragonfly
dry
dy
dye
edify
electrify
emulsify
espy
esterify
exemplify
eye
falsify
fbi
firefly
fisheye
fly
flyby
foci
fortify
fructify
fry
fungi
gadfly
gemini

gladioli
glorify
goodby
goodbye
gratify
guy
hawkeye
hereby
hi
high
hog-tie
hogtie
horrify
horsefly
housefly
humidify
I
identify
imply
indemnify
intensify
July
justify
lanai
levi
lie
lignify
liquefy
lullaby
lye
magi
magnify
magpie
malachi
mayfly
misapply
misclassify
modify
mollify
mortify

multi
multiply
mummify
my
mystify
nearby
necktie
nigh
nisi
nitrify
notify
nuclei
nullify
occupy
octopi
operandi
ossify
outbye
outcry
overbuy
overcertify
overdiversify
overfly
overlie
oversimplify
oversupply
pacify
papyri
passerby
passersby
personify
petrify
phi
pie
pigsty
pinkeye
ply
popeye
potpie
preoccupy

prettify
prophesy
pry
psi
purify
putrefy
qualify
quantify
quasi
rabbi
rarefy
rarify
ratify
rbi
recertify
reclassify
rectify
redry
redye
refortify
refry
rely
remodify
renotify
reoccupy
reply
reunify
reverify
revivify
rye
saccharify
samurai
sanctify
sandfly
saponify
satisfy
scarify
shanghai
shuteye
shy

sigh
signify
simplify
sinai
sky
sly
solidify
specify
spry
spy
standby
stimuli
stratify
stultify
stupefy
sty
subclassify
supply
syllabi
syllabify
terrify
testify
Thai
thereby
thigh
thy
tie
tigereye
torrify
toxify
triumviri
try
typify
ultrahigh
underlie
undersupply
unify
untie
verify
versify

vie
vilify
vitrify
vivify
walleye
whereby
why
wry

Long IB

ascribe
bribe
circumscribe
describe
diatribe
gibe
imbibe
inscribe
jibe
prescribe
proscribe
scribe
subscribe
transcribe
tribe

IB

ad lib
bib
corncrib
crib
fib
glib
jib
lib
nib
rib
sahib
squib

Long ID

abide
aborticide
alibied
allied
almond-eyed
alongside
amplified
applied
aside
astride
backside
backslide
bactericide
beautified
bedside
belied
beside
bestride
betide
bichloride
bide
bleary-eyed
bona-fide
bride
broadside
bromide
calcified
carbide
certified
chide
chloride
christmastide
citified
citywide
clarified
classified
cockeyed
codified
coincide

collide
complied
confide
countrified
countryside
countrywide
cowhide
cried
crucified
curbside
cyanide
damnified
dandified
decalcified
decide
declassified
decried
defied
dehumidified
deified
denied
deride
descried
detoxified
dewy-eyed
died
dignified
dioxide
disqualified
dissatisfied
diversified
divide
dockside
downside
dried
dyed
eastertide
edified
electrified
elide

emulsified
espied
esterified
eventide
exemplified
eyed
falsified
feticide
fireside
flied
fluoride
formaldehyde
fortified
fratricide
freeze-dried
fried
fungicide
genocide
germicide
glass-eyed
glide
glorified
glyceride
gratified
guide
guyed
hayride
hearthside
herbicide
hexachloride
hide
hillside
hogtied
homicide
horrified
horsehide
humidified
hyde
hydroxide
I'd

identified
implied
indemnified
infanticide
insecticide
inside
intensified
iodide
ironside
joyride
justified
landslide
larvacide
larvicide
lied
lignified
lipide
liquefied
magnified
matricide
misapplied
misguide
misty-eyed
modified
mollified
monoxide
mortified
mountainside
multiplied
mummified
mystified
nationwide
naugahyde
nitride
noontide
notified
nucleoside
nuclide
nullified
occupied

oceanside
offside
ossified
outside
overdiversified
overqualified
override
oversimplified
overstride
oversupplied
oxide
ozonide
pacified
paraldehyde
parricide
patricide
peptide
peroxide
personified
pesticide
petrified
phosphide
pied
plied
polypeptide
poolside
popeyed
preoccupied
preside
pride
pried
prophesied
provide
purified
putrefied
qualified
quantified
railside
ramified
rarefied

rarified
ratified
rawhide
recertified
reclassified
rectified
redyed
refortified
refried
relied
remodified
renotified
reoccupied
replied
reside
reunified
revivified
ride
ringside
riptide
riverside
roadside
saccharide
sanctified
saponified
satisfied
scarified
seaside
shanghaied
shipside
side
sighed
signified
simplified
sissified
skyed
slide
snide
snowslide
solidified

specified
spermatocide
spermicide
spied
sporicide
starry-eyed
stateside
statewide
storewide
stride
stultified
stupefied
subclassified
subdivide
subside
suicide
sulfide
sulphide
supplied
supply-side
syllabified
terrified
testified
thalidomide
tide
tied
topside
torrified
toxified
tried
triglyceride
trioxide
typified
unallied
unamplified
unapplied
uncertified
unclarified
unclassified
undenied

underside
undignified
undyed
unfortified
unidentified
unified
unjustified
unmagnified
unmodified
unmollified
unoccupied
unpacified
unpurified
unqualified
unrectified
unsanctified
unsatisfied
unspecified
unterrified
untied
untried
unverified
upside
verified
vermicide
versified
vied
vilified
viricide
vitrified
vivified
walleyed
waterside
wayside
whitsuntide
wide
worldwide
yuletide

ID
acrid
amid
backslid
bid
did
El Cid
eyelid
forbid
grid
hid
id
invalid
katydid
kid
lid
Madrid
mid
misdid
nonskid
overdid
outbid
outdid
pyramid
quid
rid
sid
skid
slid
squid
undid

Long IF
afterlife
alewife
fife
fishwife
goodwife
halflife
housewife

jackknife
knife
life
lowlife
midwife
nightlife
penknife
rife
strife
wife
wildlife

IF
bailiff
cliff
griff
handkerchief
hieroglyph
if
jiff
kerchief
midriff
miff
neckerchief
Pecksniff
plaintiff
pontiff
riff
schiff
skiff
sniff
spiff
stiff
tiff
whiff

IFT
adrift
airlift
biffed

downshift
drift
facelift
festschrift
floorshift
foregift
forklift
gearshift
gift
grift
lift
makeshift
miffed
presift
riffed
rift
shift
shoplift
shrift
sift
sniffed
snowdrift
spendthrift
spindrift
swift
thrift
uplift
upshift
whiffed

IG
big
bigwig
brig
dig
earwig
fig
gig
guinea pig
jig

Ludwig
mig
pig
prig
renege
rig
shindig
sprig
swig
thingamajig
trig
twig
Whig
whirligig
wig

IJ
abridge
adage
baggage
bainbridge
bandage
blockage
bondage
boomage
brakeage
breakage
brewage
bridge
brokage
cabbage
Cambridge
carnage
carriage
cartridge
cleavage
college
Coolidge
cordage
cottage

courage
cribbage
damage
dockage
dosage
dotage
drainage
drawbridge
drayage
dunnage
floatage
floorage
flotage
flowage
foliage
footage
footbridge
forage
freightage
fridge
frontage
frottage
fruitage
garbage
groundage
haulage
herbage
homage
hostage
image
knowledge
language
leafage
leakage
linage
lineage
linkage
lockage
luggage
manage

marriage	seepage	voltage
message	sewage	voyage
midge	shippage	warpage
mileage	shortage	wastage
millage	shrinkage	wattage
mintage	silage	weighage
moorage	slackage	wharfage
mortgage	slippage	windage
outage	soakage	wordage
package	socage	wreckage
partridge	spillage	yardage
passage	splintage	
pawnage	spoilage	**Long IK**
peerage	stealage	alike
pickage	steerage	antlike
pierage	stoppage	apelike
pillage	storage	beaklike
plottage	stowage	beanlike
plumage	stumpage	beelike
porridge	suffrage	bike
portage	sullage	bowlike
postage	tallage	boxlike
pottage	tankage	branchlike
poundage	teethridge	brushlike
presage	tillage	budlike
privilege	tollage	catlike
quayage	tonnage	chainlike
raftage	towage	childlike
railage	trackage	Christlike
ravage	truckage	deathlike
rentage	tubage	dike
ridge	ullage	dislike
roughage	umbrage	doglike
rummage	usage	dreamlike
salvage	vantage	fernlike
sausage	verbiage	flintlike
savage	vestige	folklike
scalage	village	forklike
schoolage	vintage	fringelike
scrimmage	visage	frostlike

gemlike	starlike	citric
ghostlike	strike	civic
gladelike	suchlike	classic
gnomelike	turnpike	cleric
godlike	tyke	click
grasslike	unlike	clinic
gumlike	warlike	clique
gutlike	wavelike	colic
hairlike		comic
handspike	**IK**	conic
harelike	airsick	coptic
heathlike	antic	cosmic
hike	arctic	cowlick
hitchhike	arithmetic	creek
homelike	arsenic	crick
hornlike	aspic	critic
knifelike	attic	cryptic
lacelike	bailiwick	cubic
lawlike	Baltic	cultic
lifelike	bardic	cyclic
like	basic	cymric
manlike	beatnik	cynic
mike	bootlick	cystic
nestlike	boric	deictic
netlike	brainsick	dermic
pike	bric	derrick
psych	brick	dick
ringlike	broomstick	dipstick
rocklike	Brunswick	double-quick
rootlike	Buick	drastic
ruglike	cambric	dropkick
scalelike	candlestick	drumstick
seedlike	carsick	epic
sheaflike	Catholic	Eric
sheetlike	caustic	ethic
shrike	Celtic	ethnic
shunpike	centric	fabric
snaillike	chick	finnic
snakelike	chopstick	firebrick
spike	chronic	flick

folic	lubric	picric
frantic	lunatic	pinprick
Frederick	lyric	plasmic
frolic	lytic	plastic
Gaelic	magic	plumbic
gallic	manic	pogo stick
gamic	mastic	politic
garlic	maverick	pontic
gastric	medic	prick
gimmick	metric	psychic
gnomic	mimic	ptarmic
gnostic	Munich	pubic
goldbrick	music	public
gothic	myrrhic	punic
graphic	mystic	pyrrhic
handpick	mythic	quick
hayrick	nick	relic
heartsick	nightstick	rhythmic
hectic	nitpick	rick
Heimlich	nitric	rollick
hemic	nordic	rubric
herdic	nutpick	runic
heretic	ohmic	rustic
hick	optic	Sapphic
homesick	orphic	scenic
humic	osmic	Schick
impolitic	otic	seasick
indic	paddock	seismic
isthmic	panic	septic
karmic	pectic	shtick
keltic	pelvic	sic
kick	peptic	sick
lactic	phallic	sidekick
lick	phasic	skeptic
limbic	phobic	slapstick
limerick	phonic	Slavic
lipstick	photic	slick
lithic	physic	sonic
logic	pick	sorbic
lovesick	picnic	spastic

spick

Sputnik

stannic

static

stick

stoic

stomach

strophic

styptic

syndic

tactic

tannic

technic

thermic

thick

thymic

tic

tick

tonic

toothpick

topic

toxic

traffic

traffick

tragic

trainsick

trick

triple-quick

trophic

tropic

tunic

turkic

unpick

unstick

vatic

vedic

walking stock

wick

xanthic

xenic

xeric

yardstick

zoic

IKS

acrobatics

admix

affix

antics

Arctics

aspics

attics

aviatrix

basics

beatniks

bootlicks

bricks

broomsticks

Buicks

calix

cervix

chicks

chopsticks

cicatrix

civics

classics

clerics

clicks

clinics

cliques

comics

convicts

cowlicks

cricks

critics

crucifix

cynics

deep-six

derricks

dicks

dipsticks

drumsticks

epics

ethics

ethnics

executrix

fabrics

Felix

fiddlesticks

fix

flicks

frolics

garlics

gimmicks

goldbricks

gothics

graphics

handpicks

helix

hicks

infix

inflicts

intermix

kicks

licks

limericks

lipsticks

lyrics

mathematics

matrix

mavericks

medics

metrics

mimics

mix

mystics

nicks

nitpicks

nix

nutpicks

onyx
optics
osmics
paddocks
panics
phoenix
phonics
physics
picks
picnics
pics
pinpricks
pix
plastics
politics
predicts
prefix
prelix
premix
pricks
prix
prolix
psychics
publics
radix
relics
restricts
rhythmics
ricks
rollicks
rubrics
rustics
shticks
sidekicks
six
skeptics
slapsticks
slicks
spadix
spastics

sputniks
sticks
stoics
Styx
suffix
Sussex
tactics
ticks
tics
tonics
toothpicks
topics
trafficks
traffics
transfix
tricks
tropics
tunics
unfix
unpicks
wicks
yardsticks

IKST
admixed
affixed
betwixt
deep-sixed
fixed
mixed
nixed
prefixed
premixed
sixed
suffixed
transfixed
transfixt
twixt
unfixed
unmixed

well-fixed

IKT
addict
afflict
bootlicked
bricked
clicked
conflict
constrict
contradict
convict
depict
derelict
district
edict
evict
flicked
frolicked
handpicked
inflict
kicked
licked
mimicked
nicked
nitpicked
object
panicked
perfect
picked
picnicked
predict
pricked
restrict
rollicked
sicced
sicked
slicked
strict
subject

ticked
trafficked
tricked
unpicked
verdict

Long IL
aisle
anglophile
argyle
argyll
audiophile
awhile
axile
beguile
bibliophile
bile
compile
crocodile
defile
domicile
erectile
erstwhile
exile
file
francophile
freestyle
gentile
guile
hairstyle
halophile
hemophile
I'll
infantile
isle
juvenile
labile
lifestyle
meanwhile
mile

misfile
mobile
motile
necrophile
nile
nubile
pedophile
penile
percentile
peristyle
photophile
pile
presenile
profile
projectile
protractile
reconcile
refile
reptile
retractile
revile
rile
sandpile
sectile
senile
servile
sessile
smile
stabile
stile
stockpile
strobile
style
tactile
tensile
textile
tile
turnstile
unpile
vile

virile
while
wile
woodpile
worthwhile

IL
anthill
axil
bill
bluegill
Brazil
brill
Catskill
chenille
chill
Churchill
codicil
daffodil
dill
distil
distill
doorsill
downhill
drill
duckbill
dunghill
escadrille
fill
foothill
freewill
frill
fulfil
fulfill
gill
goodwill
grill
gristmill
handbill
hill

imbecile
ill
ill will
instill
Jill
kill
Knoxville
landfill
limekiln
Melville
mill
molehill
Nashville
nil
pastil
Phil
pill
playbill
prechill
quadrille
quill
refill
rill
sawmill
shill
shoebill
shrill
sidehill
sill
skill
spill
spoonbill
squill
stabile
standstill
still
swill
thrill
till
treadmill

trill
twill
until
uphill
volatile
waybill
whippoorwill
will
windchill
windmill
windowsill

ILCH
filch
milch
pilch
zilch

Long ILD
beguiled
brainchild
child
compiled
defiled
dialed
dialled
exiled
filed
godchild
grandchild
mild
misfiled
piled
profiled
refiled
reviled
riled
schoolchild
smiled
stepchild

stockpiled
styled
tiled
unpiled
whiled
wild
wiled

ILD
billed
build
chilled
distilled
drilled
filled
fulfilled
gild
grilled
guild
instilled
killed
milled
nonskilled
prechilled
rebuild
refilled
shrilled
skilled
spilled
stilled
swilled
thrilled
tilled
trilled
unchilled
unfilled
unmilled
unskilled
untilled
willed

ILK
bilk
ilk
milk
silk

ILT
atilt
bed quilt
built
gilt
guilt
hilt
jilt
kilt
lilt
milt
quilt
rebuilt
silt
spilt
stilt
tilt
Vanderbilt
wilt
yilt

Long ILZ
aisles
argyles
beguiles
compiles
defiles
exiles
files
gentiles
hairstyles
isles
lifestyles
miles

misfiles
piles
profiles
refiles
reptiles
reviles
riles
smiles
stiles
stockpiles
styles
textiles
tiles
turnstiles
unpiles
whiles
wiles
woodpiles

Long IM
bedtime
begrime
birdlime
chime
climb
clime
crime
daytime
dime
downtime
enzyme
grime
halftime
I'm
lifetime
lime
longtime
lunchtime
maritime
mealtime

meantime
mime
mistime
nighttime
noontime
onetime
overtime
pastime
pantomime
peacetime
playtime
prime
quicklime
ragtime
rhyme
rime
schooltime
slime
sometime
springtime
sublime
summertime
teatime
thyme
time
wartime

IM
antonym
baalim
bedim
brim
cherubim
dim
forelimb
grim
gym
him
hymn
Jim

limb
limn
outswim
passim
prim
pseudonym
Purim
rim
scrim
seraphim
shim
skim
slim
synonym
swim
tim
trim
vim
whim

Long IN
airline
align
alkaline
alpine
anodyne
aquiline
argentine
asinine
assign
bahrain
baseline
beeline
benign
bloodline
borderline
bovine
bowline
brine
bromine

byline
calamine
calcimine
canine
carbine
caroline
centerline
clandestine
clementine
clothesline
coastline
columbine
combine
concubine
confine
consign
copyline
cosine
countermine
countersign
dateline
deadline
decline
define
design
dine
divine
dyne
einstein
elephantine
enshrine
ensign
entwine
epstein
equine
feline
fine
florentine
Frankenstein
grapevine

guideline
hairline
headline
hemline
hipline
hyaline
incarnadine
incline
intertwine
iodine
jawline
kine
liechtenstein
lifeline
line
mainline
malign
midline
mine
misdefine
monkeyshine
moonshine
neckline
nine
opaline
opine
outline
outshine
overrefine
palatine
palestine
pine
pipeline
platyrhine
porcine
porcupine
preassign
predefine
quinine
ranine

realign
reassign
recline
recombine
redefine
redesign
redline
refine
repine
resign
rhine
saccharine
saline
saturnine
serpentine
shine
shoreline
shrine
sibylline
sideline
sign
sine
skyline
spine
stein
streamline
strychnine
sunshine
supine
swine
syncline
thine
timberline
tine
truckline
turbine
turpentine
twine
underline
undermine

undersign
valentine
vine
viperine
vulpine
waistline
whine
wine
woodbine

IN

akin
backspin
bacteriotoxin
bearskin
bedouin
been
begin
berlin
bin
bodkin
breastpin
buckskin
bufotoxin
bumpkin
calfskin
candlepin
capeskin
chagrin
chin
clothespin
coonskin
deerskin
din
discipline
doeskin
duckpin
fin
finn
fishskin

foreskin
gin
goatskin
grin
hairpin
headpin
herein
in
inn
jinn
kidskin
kin
kingpin
lambkin
lambskin
lenin
linchpin
love-in
mandolin
mannikin
moleskin
napkin
oilskin
onionskin
pigskin
pin
pumpkin
redskin
rin-tin-tin
rumpelstiltskin
saccharin
scarfskin
sealskin
sharkskin
sheepskin
shin
sin
skin
spin
stickpin

subdiscipline
tailspin
tenpin
therein
thin
tholepin
thoroughpin
tin
trade-in
turn-in
twin
underpin
unpin
violin
weigh-in
wherein
win
wineskin
within
yin
zeppelin
zinn

INCH
bullfinch
chinch
cinch
clinch
finch
flinch
goldfinch
inch
lynch
pinch
winch

IND
chagrined
chagrinned
chinned

crosswind
disciplined
dinned
downwind
finned
ginned
grinned
pinned
rescind
sea-wind
shinned
sinned
skinned
tamarind
thick-skinned
thin-skinned
thinned
tinned
twinned
unpinned
upwind
whirlwind
wind
woodwind

ING
abandoning
abashing
abasing
abating
abbreviating
abdicating
abducting
abetting
abhorring
abiding
abolishing
aborting
abounding
abridging

abrogating
abscessing
absconding
absenting
absolving
absorbing
abusing
acceding
accenting
accessing
accompanying
according
accosting
accounting
accrediting
accruing
accumulating
accusing
achieving
aching
acing
acknowledging
acquainting
acquiescing
acquiring
acquitting
acting
actualizing
actuating
adapting
addicting
adding
addressing
adducing
adhering
adjoining
adjourning
adjudging
adjudicating
adjuring

adjusting
administrating
admiring
admitting
admixing
admonishing
adopting
adoring
adorning
adulterating
advancing
advantaging
adventuring
adverting
advertising
advertizing
advising
advocating
aerating
affecting
affiliating
affirming
affixing
afflicting
affording
affronting
ageing
agglutinating
aggrandizing
aggravating
aggregating
aging
agitating
agonizing
agreeing
aiding
ailing
aiming
airbrushing
airdropping

airing
airlifting
airmailing
alarming
alerting
alibiing
alienating
alighting
aligning
alkalinizing
alkalizing
all-embracing
allaying
alleging
alleviating
alliterating
allocating
allotting
allowing
alloying
alluding
alluring
allying
almsgiving
alphabetizing
altering
alternating
amalgamating
amassing
amazing
ambling
ambulating
ambushing
ameliorating
amending
amortising
amortizing
amounting
amplifying
amputating

amusing
anaesthetizing
analyzing
anathematizing
anatomizing
anchoring
anesthetizing
angering
anglicizing
angling
anguishing
animating
annealing
annexing
annihilating
annotating
announcing
annoying
annulling
annunciating
anodizing
anointing
answering
antagonizing
antedating
anteing
anthologizing
antibusing
anticipating
antiquating
antiquing
anything
aping
apologizing
apostatizing
appalling
appareling
apparelling
appealing
appearing

appeasing
appending
appertaining
appetizing
applauding
appliqueing
applying
appointing
apportioning
apposing
appraising
appreciating
apprehending
apprenticing
apprising
apprizing
approaching
approbating
appropriating
approving
approximating
aquaplaning
arbitrating
arborizing
arching
arguing
arising
arming
armoring
arousing
arraigning
arranging
arraying
arresting
arriving
arrogating
articulating
ascending
ascertaining
ascribing

asking
aspersing
asphyxiating
aspirating
aspiring
assailing
assassinating
assaulting
assaying
assembling
assenting
asserting
assessing
assigning
assimilating
assisting
associating
assorting
assuaging
assuming
assuring
astonishing
astounding
atomizing
atrophying
attaching
attacking
attaining
attempting
attending
attenuating
attesting
attiring
attracting
attributing
attuning
auctioning
auditing
auditioning
augmenting

authenticating
authorizing
autographing
automating
availing
avenging
averaging
averring
averting
avoiding
avouching
avowing
avulsing
awaiting
awakening
awaking
awarding
awing
awning
axing
baaing
babbling
babying
backbearing
backbiting
backbreaking
backdating
backfiring
backhanding
backing
backlogging
backpacking
backslapping
backsliding
backspacing
backstitching
backstroking
backtracking
badgering
badmouthing

baffling
bagging
bailing
baiting
baking
balancing
baling
balking
ballasting
ballooning
balloting
ballyhooing
bamboozling
bandaging
banding
bandying
banging
banishing
banking
bankrolling
bankrupting
banning
banqueting
bantering
banting
baptizing
barbarizing
barbecuing
barbering
barbing
bargaining
barging
barking
barnstorming
barraging
barreling
barricading
barring
bartering
bashing

basing
basking
bastardizing
basting
bathing
bating
battening
battering
batting
battling
baying
bayoneting
bayonetting
beaching
beading
beaming
beaning
bearding
bearing
beating
beautifying
beckoning
beclouding
becoming
bedaubing
bedazzling
bedding
bedecking
bedewing
bedimming
bedraggling
bedspring
beefing
beekeeping
beeping
befalling
befitting
befogging
befouling
befriending

befuddling
begetting
beggaring
begging
beginning
begrudging
beguiling
behaving
beheading
beholding
behooving
being
belaboring
belching
beleaguering
believing
belittling
bellowing
bellyaching
bellying
belonging
belting
belying
bemiring
bemoaning
bemusing
benching
bending
benefiting
benefitting
benumbing
bequeathing
berating
bereaving
berrying
berthing
beseeching
beseeming
besetting
besieging

besmearing
besmirching
bespangling
bespattering
bespeaking
bestirring
bestowing
bestrewing
betaking
bethinking
betiding
betokening
betraying
betrothing
bettering
betting
beveling
bevelling
bewailing
bewaring
bewildering
bewitching
biasing
biassing
bibbing
bickering
bicycling
bidding
bifurcating
bigamizing
biking
bilging
bilking
billeting
billing
billowing
binding
bing
biodegrading
bioengineering

birching
bisecting
bitewing
biting
bivouacking
blabbing
blackballing
blackening
blacking
blackjacking
blacklisting
blackmailing
blacktopping
blaming
blanching
blandishing
blanketing
blanking
blaring
blaspheming
blasting
blazing
blazoning
bleaching
blearing
bleating
bleeding
bleeping
blemishing
blenching
blending
blessing
blighting
blindfolding
blinding
blinking
blipping
blistering
blitzing
blitzkrieging

bloating
blobbing
blockading
blockbusting
blocking
bloodcurdling
bloodletting
bloodshedding
bloodsucking
bloodying
blooming
blossoming
blotching
blotting
blousing
blowing
blubbering
bludgeoning
blueing
blueprinting
bluestocking
bluffing
bluing
blundering
blunting
blurring
blurting
blushing
blustering
boarding
boasting
boating
bobbing
bobbling
bobsledding
boding
bodybuilding
boeing
bogging
boggling

boiling
boldfacing
bolstering
bolting
bombarding
bombing
bonding
bonging
boning
boodling
booing
bookbinding
booking
bookkeeping
bookmaking
booming
boondoggling
boosting
booting
bootlegging
bootlicking
bootstrapping
boozing
bopping
bordering
boring
borrowing
bossing
botching
bothering
bottling
bottoming
bouncing
bounding
bowing
bowling
bowstring
boxing
boycotting
bracing

bracketing
bragging
braiding
brain-picking
braining
brainstorming
brainwashing
braising
braking
branching
branding
brandishing
brandying
braving
brawling
braying
brazing
breaching
breading
breadwinning
breakfasting
breaking
breasting
breathing
breathtaking
breeding
breezing
brewing
bribing
bricking
bricklaying
bridging
bridling
briefing
brightening
brimming
bring
bringing
brisling
bristling

broaching
broadcasting
broadening
brocading
broidering
broiling
bronzing
brooding
brooking
browbeating
browning
browsing
bruising
brushing
brutalizing
bubbling
bucketing
bucking
buckling
budding
budgeting
budging
buffaloing
buffering
buffeting
buffing
bugging
bugling
building
bulging
bulking
bulldogging
bulldozing
bulletproofing
bullfighting
bulling
bullring
bullying
bumbling
bumming

bumping
bunching
bundling
bungling
bunking
bunting
buoying
burdening
burgeoning
burglarizing
burgling
burlesquing
burning
burnishing
burping
burring
burrowing
bursting
burying
bushing
bushwhacking
busing
bussing
busting
bustling
busying
butchering
buttering
butting
buttonholing
buttoning
buttressing
buying
buzzing
bypassing
caballing
cabinetmaking
cabling
cacheting
cackling

caddying
cadging
cageling
cajoling
caking
calcifying
calculating
calendaring
calibrating
calipering
calling
callousing
callusing
calming
calving
cambering
camouflaging
campaigning
camping
canceling
cancelling
candling
candying
cankering
cannibalizing
canning
cannonading
cannonballing
canoeing
canonizing
canopying
cantering
cantilevering
canting
canvasing
canvassing
capacitating
capering
capitalising
capitalizing

capitulating
capping
capsizing
capsuling
captaining
captioning
captivating
capturing
caramelizing
carbonating
carbonizing
carbureting
carding
careening
careering
caressing
caretaking
caring
caroling
carousing
carpetbagging
carpeting
carping
carrying
carting
cartooning
carving
cascading
casehardening
cashiering
cashing
casing
castigating
casting
castling
castrating
cataloging
cataloguing
catapulting
catcalling

catching
categorizing
catering
catheterizing
catnapping
catting
caucusing
caulking
causing
cauterizing
cautioning
caving
cavorting
cawing
ceasing
ceiling
celebrating
cementing
censoring
censuring
centering
centralizing
centrifuging
certifying
chaffing
chagrining
chagrinning
chaining
chairing
chairmaning
chairmanning
chalking
challenging
chambering
chamfering
championing
chancing
changing
channeling
channelizing

channelling
chanting
chaperoning
chapping
characterizing
charbroiling
charging
charming
charring
chartering
charting
chasing
chastening
chastising
chattering
chatting
chauffeuring
cheapening
cheating
checkering
checking
checkmating
checkpointing
cheeping
cheering
cherishing
chickening
chiding
childbearing
chilling
chiming
chinking
chinning
chipping
chirping
chiseling
chiselling
chloroforming
chocking
choking

chomping
choosing
chopping
choreographing
chortling
chorusing
christening
christianizing
chroming
chucking
chuckling
chugging
chumming
chungking
churchgoing
churning
cinching
ciphering
circling
circuiting
circulating
circumcising
circumscribing
circumventing
citing
civilizing
clacking
cladding
claiming
clamming
clamoring
clamping
clanging
clanking
clapping
clarifying
clashing
clasping
classifying
classing

clattering
clawing
cleaning
cleansing
clearing
cleaving
clenching
clerking
clicking
cliffhanging
climaxing
climbing
clinching
cling
clinging
clinkering
clinking
clipping
cloaking
clobbering
clocking
clodhopping
clogging
cloistering
cloning
closefitting
closeting
closing
clothing
clotting
cloturing
clouding
clouting
clowning
clubbing
clucking
clueing
cluing
clumping
clustering

clutching
cluttering
coaching
coagulating
coalescing
coarsening
coasting
coating
coaxing
cobbling
cock-fighting
cockfighting
cocking
coddling
codifying
coding
codling
coercing
coexisting
cogitating
cohabiting
cohering
coiling
coinciding
coining
collaborating
collapsing
collaring
collecting
collectivizing
colliding
collocating
colonizing
colorcasting
coloring
combating
combatting
combing
combining
comforting

coming
commandeering
commanding
commemorating
commencing
commending
commercializing
commingling
commiserating
commissioning
committing
communalizing
communicating
communing
commuting
compacting
comparing
compassing
compelling
compensating
competing
compiling
complaining
complementing
completing
complicating
complimenting
complying
composing
compounding
comprehending
compressing
comprising
compromising
computerizing
computing
concatenating
concealing
conceding
conceiving

concentrating
concerning
conciliating
concluding
concocting
concurring
condemning
condensing
condescending
conditioning
condoling
condoning
conducing
conducting
confabbing
confederating
conferring
confessing
confiding
configuring
confining
confirming
confiscating
conflicting
conforming
confounding
confronting
confusing
congealing
congesting
conglomerating
congratulating
congregating
conjecturing
conjoining
conjugating
conjuring
conking
connecting
conning

conniving
connoting
conquering
conscripting
consecrating
consenting
conserving
considering
consigning
consisting
consolidating
consoling
consorting
conspiring
constipating
constituting
constraining
constricting
constructing
construing
consulting
consuming
consummating
contacting
containerizing
containing
contaminating
contemplating
contending
contenting
contesting
continuing
contouring
contracting
contradicting
contraindicating
contrasting
contravening
contributing
contriving

controlling
controverting
convalescing
convecting
convening
conventionalizing
converging
conversing
converting
conveyancing
conveying
convicting
convincing
convoking
convoluting
convoying
convulsing
cooing
cooking
cooling
cooperating
cooping
coopting
coordinating
coping
copping
copulating
copying
copyrighting
coquetting
cording
cordoning
coring
corking
corkscrewing
cornering
corning
corralling
correcting
correlating

corresponding
corroborating
corroding
corrugating
corrupting
cosponsoring
cotton-picking
cottoning
couching
coughing
counseling
counselling
countenancing
counteracting
counterattacking
counterbalancing
counterclaiming
counterconditioning
counterfeiting
countering
countermanding
counteropening
counterplotting
counterpointing
counterpoising
countersigning
countersinking
countervailing
counting
coupling
coursing
courting
covenanting
covering
coveting
cowering
cowing
cowling
crabbing
cracking

crackling
cradling
crafting
cramming
cramping
cranking
crashing
crating
craving
crawling
crazing
creaking
creaming
creasing
creating
crediting
creeping
cremating
cresting
cretinizing
cribbing
criminating
crimping
crimsoning
cringing
crinkling
crippling
crisscrossing
criticizing
croaking
crocheting
crooking
crooning
cropping
crossbreeding
crosscutting
crosshatching
crossing
crouching
crowding

crowing
crowning
crucifying
cruising
crumbing
crumbling
crumpling
crunching
crusading
crushing
crusting
crying
crystallizing
cubing
cuckolding
cuddling
cudgeling
cudgelling
cuffing
cuing
culling
culminating
cultivating
culturing
cumbering
cumulating
cunning
cupping
curbing
curdling
curfewing
curing
curling
currycombing
currying
cursing
curtailing
curtaining
curtseying
curtsying

curving
cushing
cushioning
cussing
customizing
cutting
cycling
dabbing
dabbling
dairying
dallying
damaging
damascening
damming
damnifying
damning
dampening
damping
dancing
dandifying
dandling
dangling
dappling
daring
darkening
darkling
darling
darning
darting
dashing
dating
daubing
daunting
dawdling
dawning
daydreaming
dazing
dazzling
deactivating
deadening

deadlocking
deafening
dealing
debarking
debarring
debasing
debating
debauching
debilitating
debiting
debouching
debriefing
debugging
debunking
decaffeinating
decalcifying
decamping
decanting
decapitating
decarbonizing
decaying
deceasing
deceiving
decelerating
decentralizing
deciding
decimating
deciphering
decking
declaring
declassifying
declining
decoding
decomposing
decompressing
decongesting
decontaminating
decontrolling
decorating
decoying

decreasing
decreeing
decriminalizing
decrying
dedicating
deducing
deducting
deeding
deeming
deepening
defacing
defaming
defatting
defaulting
defeating
defecating
defecting
defeminizing
defending
deferring
defibrillating
defiling
defining
deflagrating
deflating
deflecting
deflowering
defogging
defoliating
deforcing
deforesting
deforming
defrauding
defraying
defrocking
defrosting
defusing
defuzing
defying
degassing

degenerating
degrading
dehorning
dehumanizing
dehumidifying
dehydrating
deicing
deifying
deigning
delating
delaying
delegating
deleting
deliberating
delighting
delimitating
delimiting
delineating
delivering
delousing
deluding
deluging
delving
demagnetizing
demanding
demarcating
demasculinizing
demeaning
demilitarizing
demineralizing
demobilizing
democratizing
demodulating
demolishing
demonetizing
demonstrating
demoralizing
demoting
demounting
demurring

denationalizing
denaturalizing
denaturing
denigrating
denominating
denoting
denouncing
denting
denuding
denying
deodorizing
deoxidizing
departing
depending
depersonalizing
depicting
depilating
deplaning
depleting
deploring
deploying
depopulating
deporting
deposing
depositing
depraving
deprecating
depreciating
depredating
depressing
depriving
deprogramming
deputizing
derailing
deranging
derating
deregulating
deriding
deriving
derogating

desalting
descanting
descending
describing
desecrating
desegregating
desensitizing
deserting
deserving
desiccating
designating
designing
desiring
desisting
desolating
despairing
despatching
despising
despoiling
destroying
destructing
detaching
detailing
detaining
detecting
deteriorating
determining
deterring
detesting
dethroning
detonating
detouring
detoxicating
detoxifying
detracting
devaluating
devaluing
devastating
developing
deviating

deviling
devilling
devising
devitalizing
devolving
devoting
devouring
diagnosing
diagraming
diagramming
dialing
dialling
diapering
dicing
dickering
dictating
diddling
dieting
differentiating
differing
diffusing
digesting
digging
digitalizing
dignifying
digressing
dilapidating
dilating
dillydallying
diminishing
dimming
dimpling
ding
dining
dinning
dipping
directing
dirtying
disabling
disabusing

disaffecting
disaffiliating
disagreeing
disallowing
disappearing
disappointing
disapproving
disarming
disarranging
disarraying
disassembling
disavowing
disbanding
disbarring
disbelieving
disburdening
disbursing
discarding
discerning
discharging
disciplining
disclaiming
disclosing
discoloring
discombobulating
discomfiting
discomforting
discommoding
discomposing
disconcerting
disconnecting
discontinuing
discounting
discouraging
discoursing
discovering
discrediting
discriminating
discussing
disdaining

disembarking
disembodying
disemboweling
disembowelling
disenchanting
disencumbering
disengaging
disentangling
disfiguring
disgorging
disgracing
disgruntling
disguising
disgusting
disheartening
disheveling
dishevelling
dishing
dishonoring
disillusioning
disinfecting
disintegrating
disjoining
disjointing
disliking
dislocating
dislodging
dismantling
dismaying
dismembering
dismissing
dismounting
disobeying
disordering
disorganizing
disorientating
disorienting
disowning
disparaging
dispatching

dispelling	diving	dragging
dispensing	divining	dragooning
dispersing	divorcing	draining
displacing	divulging	dramatizing
displaying	divvying	drawing
displeasing	dizzying	drawling
disposing	docketing	drawstring
disproving	docking	dreading
disputing	doctoring	dreaming
disqualifying	documenting	dredging
disquieting	doddering	drenching
disregarding	dodging	dressing
disrobing	doffing	dressmaking
disrupting	dogging	dribbling
dissatisfying	doing	drifting
dissecting	dolling	drilling
disseminating	domesticating	drinking
dissenting	dominating	dripping
dissevering	domineering	driveling
dissimilating	donating	drivelling
dissipating	donning	driving
dissociating	doodling	drizzling
dissolving	dooming	droning
dissuading	doping	drooling
distancing	doting	drooping
distending	dotting	dropping
distilling	double-dealing	drowning
distinguishing	doubling	drowsing
distorting	doubting	drudging
distracting	douching	drugging
distressing	dousing	drumming
distributing	dovetailing	drying
distrusting	doweling	dubbing
disturbing	downgrading	ducking
ditching	downshifting	duckling
diverging	downsizing	ducting
diversifying	downswing	dueling
diverting	dowsing	duelling
divesting	dozing	dulling
dividing	drafting	dumbfounding

dumfounding
dumping
dumpling
dunking
dunning
duping
duplicating
during
dusting
dwarfing
dwelling
dwindling
dyeing
dying
dynamiting
earmarking
earning
earring
earsplitting
earthling
earthmoving
earthshaking
easing
easygoing
eating
eavesdropping
ebbing
echoing
eclipsing
economizing
eddying
edging
edifying
editing
editorializing
educating
educing
effacing
effecting
effective

effervescing
efflorescing
egging
ejaculating
ejecting
elaborating
elapsing
elasticizing
elating
elbowing
electing
electioneering
electrifying
electrocuting
electrolyzing
electroplating
elegizing
elevating
eliciting
eliding
eliminating
elongating
eloping
elucidating
eluding
emaciating
emanating
emancipating
emasculating
embalming
embanking
embargoing
embarking
embarrassing
embedding
embellishing
embezzling
embittering
emblazoning
embodying

emboldening
embossing
embracing
embroidering
embroiling
emceeing
emending
emerging
emigrating
emitting
emoting
empaneling
empathizing
emphasizing
employing
empowering
emptying
emulating
emulsifying
enabling
enacting
enameling
enamoring
encamping
encapsulating
encapsuling
encasing
enchaining
enchanting
enciphering
encircling
enclosing
encoding
encompassing
encountering
encouraging
encroaching
encumbering
endangering
endearing

endeavoring
ending
endorsing
endowing
enduring
energizing
enervating
enfeebling
enfolding
enforcing
enfranchising
engaging
engendering
engineering
engorging
engrafting
engraving
engrossing
engulfing
enhancing
enjoining
enjoying
enlarging
enlightening
enlisting
enlivening
enmeshing
ennobling
enplaning
enquiring
enraging
enrapturing
enriching
enrolling
ensconcing
ensheathing
enshrining
enshrouding
enslaving
ensnaring

ensuing
ensuring
entailing
entangling
entering
enterprising
entertaining
enthralling
enthroning
enthusing
enticing
entitling
entombing
entraining
entrancing
entrapping
entreating
entrenching
entrusting
entwining
enumerating
enunciating
enveloping
envisaging
envisioning
envying
epitomizing
equaling
equalizing
equalling
equating
equipping
equivocating
eradicating
erasing
erecting
eroding
eroticizing
erring
eructating

eructing
erupting
escalating
escalloping
escaping
eschewing
escorting
espousing
espying
essaying
establishing
esteeming
esterifying
estimating
estranging
etching
eulogizing
evacuating
evading
evaluating
evangelizing
evaporating
evening
everblooming
everlasting
everything
evicting
evidencing
evildoing
evincing
evoking
evolving
ewing
exacerbating
exacting
exaggerating
exalting
examining
exasperating
excavating

exceeding
excelling
excepting
excerpting
exchanging
excising
exciting
exclaiming
excluding
excommunicating
excreting
excruciating
exculpating
excusing
execrating
executing
exemplifying
exempting
exercising
exerting
exhaling
exhausting
exhibiting
exhilarating
exhorting
exhuming
exiling
existing
exiting
exonerating
exorcising
expanding
expatiating
expatriating
expecting
expectorating
expediting
expelling
expending
experiencing

experimenting
expiating
expiring
explaining
explicating
exploding
exploiting
exploring
exporting
exposing
expounding
expressing
expropriating
expunging
expurgating
extending
extenuating
exterminating
extinguishing
extolling
extorting
extracting
extraditing
extrapolating
extricating
extruding
exuding
exulting
eyeing
eying
fabricating
faceting
facilitating
facing
factoring
factorizing
fading
fagging
fagoting
failing

fainting
faking
falling
falsifying
faltering
familiarizing
famishing
fanaticizing
fancying
fanning
fantasizing
faring
farming
farrowing
farseeing
farthing
fascinating
fashioning
fastening
fasting
fathering
fathoming
fatiguing
fatling
fattening
fatting
faultfinding
faulting
favoring
fawning
fazing
fearing
feasting
featherbedding
feathering
featuring
federalizing
federating
feeding
feeing

feeling
feigning
felicitating
felling
feminizing
fenagling
fence-sitting
fencing
fending
fermenting
ferreting
ferrying
festering
festooning
fetching
fettering
feuding
fibbing
fibrillating
fictionalizing
fiddling
fidgeting
fielding
fighting
figuring
filching
filibustering
filigreeing
filing
filling
filming
filtering
filtrating
finagling
finalizing
financing
finding
finessing
fingering
fingerling

fingerprinting
fining
finishing
finking
finning
firing
firming
firstling
fishing
fissuring
fitting
fixating
fixing
fizzing
fizzling
flabbergasting
flagging
flailing
flaking
flaming
flanking
flapping
flaring
flashing
flatling
flattening
flattering
flatting
flaunting
flavoring
flaying
flecking
fledgling
fleecing
fleeing
fleering
fleeting
fleming
fleshing
fletcherizing

flexing
flickering
flicking
flinching
fling
flinging
flipping
flirting
flitting
floating
floccing
flocculating
flocking
flogging
flooding
floodlighting
flooring
flopping
flossing
flouncing
floundering
flouring
flourishing
flouting
flowering
flowing
flubbing
fluctuating
fluffing
flunking
fluorescing
fluoridating
flurrying
flushing
flustering
fluting
fluttering
fluxing
flying
foaling

foaming
fobbing
focalizing
focusing
focussing
fogging
foiling
foisting
folding
following
fomenting
fondling
fooling
footing
footnoting
foraging
foraying
forbearing
forbidding
forcing
fording
forearming
forebearing
foreboding
forecasting
foreclosing
foredooming
foregoing
foreknowing
foreordaining
foreseeing
foreshadowing
forestalling
foreswearing
foretasting
foretelling
foretokening
forewarning
forfeiting
forgetting

forging
forgiving
forgoing
forking
formalizing
formatting
formfitting
forming
formulating
fornicating
forsaking
forswearing
forthcoming
fortifying
fortunetelling
forwarding
fossilizing
fostering
fosterling
fouling
foundering
founding
foundling
fowling
foxing
fracturing
fragging
fragmenting
framing
franchising
franking
fraternizing
fraying
frazzling
freaking
freckling
freeing
freeloading
freestanding
freethinking

freewheeling
freezing
freighting
frequenting
freshening
fretting
fricasseeing
frightening
fringing
frisking
frittering
frizzing
frizzling
frolicking
fronting
frostbiting
frosting
frothing
frowning
fructifying
fruiting
frustrating
frying
fuddling
fudging
fueling
fulfilling
fumbling
fumigating
fuming
functioning
fund-raising
funding
funneling
funnelling
furbishing
furling
furloughing
furnishing
furring

furrowing	gazing	gliding
furthering	gearing	glimmering
fussing	gelatinizing	glimpsing
fuzing	gelding	glinting
fuzzing	gelling	glistening
gabbing	geminating	glittering
gabbling	gendering	gloaming
gadding	generalizing	gloating
gagging	generating	globalizing
gaging	genuflecting	globetrotting
gaining	germinating	glorifying
gainsaying	gerrymandering	glorying
gallivanting	gestating	glossing
galloping	gesticulating	glowering
galvanizing	gesturing	glowing
gambling	getting	gluing
gaming	ghettoizing	glutting
gangling	ghosting	gnarling
gaping	ghostwriting	gnashing
garaging	gibbering	gnawing
garbing	gibbeting	goading
garbling	gibing	gobbling
gardening	giggling	goggling
gargling	gilding	going
garlanding	ginning	golfing
garnering	girding	good-looking
garnisheeing	girdling	goofing
garnishing	girting	goosing
garrisoning	giving	gorging
garroting	glaceing	goring
gartering	gladdening	gormandizing
gashing	glamorizing	gosling
gasping	glancing	gossiping
gassing	glaring	gouging
gathering	glassblowing	governing
gauging	glassing	grabbing
gaveling	glassmaking	gracing
gavelling	glazing	grading
gawking	gleaming	graduating
gazetting	gleaning	grafting

graining
granting
granulating
graphing
grappling
grasping
gratifying
grating
graveling
gravitating
graying
grayling
grazing
greasing
greenling
greeting
greying
grieving
grilling
grimacing
grinding
grinning
griping
gripping
gritting
grizzling
groaning
grooming
grooving
groping
grossing
grouching
grounding
groundling
grouping
grousing
groveling
grovelling
growing
growling

grubbing
grubstaking
grudging
grueling
gruelling
grumbling
grunting
guarding
guessing
guffawing
guiding
guillotining
gulling
gulping
gumming
gunning
gunrunning
gunslinging
gurgling
gushing
gussying
gutting
guying
guzzling
gypping
gyrating
gyving
habit-forming
habituating
hacking
hackling
haggling
hailing
hair-raising
haircutting
hairdressing
hairsplitting
hairspring
hairstyling
hairweaving

hallowing
hallucinating
halogenating
haltering
halting
halving
hammering
hamming
hampering
hamstring
hamstringing
handcrafting
handicapping
handing
handling
handpicking
handshaking
handspring
handwriting
hanging
hankering
happening
haranguing
harassing
harboring
hard-hitting
hardening
hardworking
harkening
harking
harming
harmonizing
harnessing
harping
harpooning
harrowing
harrying
harshening
harvesting
hashing

hassling
hastening
hatching
hatchling
hatemongering
hating
hauling
haunting
havocking
hawing
hawking
haying
hazarding
hazing
headhunting
heading
headlining
healing
heaping
hearing
hearkening
heartbreaking
heartening
heartrending
heartstring
heartwarming
heating
heaving
heckling
hectoring
hedgehopping
hedging
heeding
heeling
hefting
heightening
heisting
hell-raising
helping
hemming

hemorrhaging
hemstitching
hennaing
henpecking
heralding
herding
herniating
herring
hesitating
hewing
hexing
hibernating
hiccuping
hiccupping
hiding
highlighting
hightailing
hijacking
hiking
hindering
hinging
hinting
hireling
hirelings
hiring
hissing
hitchhiking
hitching
hitting
hiving
hoarding
hoarsening
hoaxing
hobbling
hobnobbing
hocking
hoeing
hogging
hogtying
hoising

hoisting
hoking
holding
holing
hollering
hollowing
homebuilding
homecoming
homemaking
homing
homogenizing
homologizing
honeymooning
honing
honking
honoring
hoodwinking
hoofing
hooking
hooraying
hooting
hoping
hopping
hopsacking
hording
horning
hornswoggling
horrifying
horsewhipping
horsing
hosing
hospitalizing
hosting
hounding
house-raising
housebreaking
housecleaning
housekeeping
housesitting
housewarming

housing
hovering
howling
huckstering
huddling
huffing
hugging
hulking
hulling
humanizing
humbling
humbugging
humidifying
humiliating
humming
humoring
humping
hunching
hungering
hunkering
hunting
hurdling
hurling
hurrahing
hurraying
hurrying
hurting
hurtling
husbanding
hushing
husking
hustling
hybridizing
hydrating
hydrogenating
hydrolyzing
hydroplaning
hypersensitizing
hyphenating
hyping

hypnotising
hypnotizing
hypothesizing
hysterectomizing
icing
idealizing
identifying
ideologizing
idling
idolizing
igniting
ignoring
ill-being
illuminating
illumining
illustrating
imaging
imagining
imbargoing
imbedding
imbibing
imbricating
imbuing
imitating
immersing
immigrating
immobilizing
immolating
immortalizing
immunizing
immuring
impacting
impairing
impaling
impaneling
impanelling
imparting
impassioning
impeaching
impearling

impeding
impelling
impending
imperiling
imperilling
impersonating
impinging
implanting
impleading
implementing
implicating
imploding
imploring
implying
importing
importuning
imposing
impounding
impoverishing
imprecating
impregnating
impressing
imprinting
imprisoning
improving
improvising
impugning
imputing
inactivating
inbreeding
incapacitating
incarcerating
incarnating
incasing
incensing
inching
incinerating
incising
inciting
inclining

inclosing
including
incoming
inconveniencing
incorporating
increasing
incrementing
incriminating
incubating
inculcating
inculpating
incumbering
incurring
indemnifying
indenting
indenturing
indexing
indicating
indicting
indiscriminating
inditing
individualizing
individuating
indoctrinating
indorsing
inducing
inducting
indulging
industrializing
indwelling
inebriating
infatuating
infecting
inferring
infesting
infighting
infiltrating
inflaming
inflating
inflecting

inflicting
influencing
infolding
informing
infringing
infuriating
infusing
ingesting
ingraining
ingratiating
ingrowing
inhabiting
inhaling
inhering
inheriting
inhibiting
initialing
initialling
initiating
injecting
injuring
inking
inkling
inlaying
innerspring
innervating
inning
innovating
inoculating
inosculating
inquiring
inrushing
inscribing
inseminating
inserting
insetting
insinuating
insisting
inspecting
inspiring

installing
instancing
instating
instigating
instilling
instituting
instructing
instrumenting
insulating
insulting
insuring
integrating
intellectualizing
intending
intensifying
interacting
interbreeding
interceding
intercepting
interchanging
interdicting
interdigitating
interesting
interfacing
interfering
interjecting
interlacing
interlarding
interleaving
interlocking
interloping
intermarrying
intermeshing
intermingling
intermitting
intermixing
internalizing
interning
interpolating
interpreting

interrelating
interrogating
interrupting
intersecting
interspersing
intertwining
intervening
interviewing
interweaving
intimating
intimidating
intoning
intoxicating
intriguing
introducing
intruding
intrusting
intuiting
inundating
inuring
invading
invalidating
inveighing
inveigling
inventing
inverting
investigating
investing
invigorating
inviting
invoicing
invoking
involving
iodinating
iodizing
ionizing
irking
ironing
irradiating
irrigating

irritating
irrupting
isolating
issuing
italicizing
itching
itemizing
iterating
jabbering
jabbing
jacking
jackknifing
jading
jailing
jamming
jangling
japing
jargonizing
jarring
jaundicing
jaunting
jawboning
jawing
jaywalking
jazzing
jeering
jelling
jellying
jeopardizing
jeopardying
jerking
jesting
jetting
jettisoning
jeweling
jibbing
jibing
jigging
jiggling
jilting

jimmying
jingling
jinxing
jitterbugging
jittering
jiving
jobbing
jockeying
jogging
joggling
joining
jointing
joking
jollying
jolting
joshing
jostling
jotting
jouncing
journalizing
journeying
jousting
joypopping
joyriding
judging
juggling
juicing
jumbling
jumping
junketing
junking
juring
justifying
jutting
juxtaposing
kayoing
kedging
keeling
keening
keeping

kenning
keratinizing
kerning
keying
keynoting
keypunching
kibbling
kibitzing
kicking
kidding
kidnaping
kidnapping
killing
kindling
king
kinking
kippering
kissing
kithing
kiting
kneading
kneeing
kneeling
knelling
knifing
knighting
knitting
knocking
knotting
knowing
knuckling
kowtowing
labeling
labelling
laboring
laborsaving
lacerating
lacing
lacking
lacquering

lactating
ladening
lading
ladling
lagging
laking
lallygagging
lambasting
lambing
lamenting
laminating
laming
lampooning
lancinating
lancing
landholding
landing
landowning
landscaping
languishing
lapping
lapsing
lapwing
larding
larking
larruping
lashing
lassoing
lasting
latching
latchstring
lathering
lathing
latticing
lauding
laughing
launching
laundering
lavishing
lawbreaking

lawgiving
lawmaking
lawyering
layering
laying
lazing
leaching
leading
leafing
leaguing
leaking
leaning
leapfrogging
leaping
learning
leashing
leasing
leavening
leaving
lecturing
leeching
leering
legalizing
legating
legging
legislating
legitimating
legitimatizing
legitimizing
lemming
lending
lengthening
lessening
lettering
letting
leveling
levelling
leveraging
levering
levitating

levying
liaising
libbing
libeling
libelling
liberalizing
liberating
libidinizing
licencing
licensing
licking
lifesaving
lifting
ligating
lightening
lighting
lightning
lignifying
likening
liking
limbering
limiting
limning
limping
lingering
lining
linking
lionizing
lipreading
liquefying
liquidating
liquidizing
lisping
listening
listerizing
listing
lithographing
litigating
littering
livening

living
loading
loafing
loaning
loathing
lobbing
lobbying
lobotomizing
localizing
locating
locking
lodging
logging
logrolling
loitering
lolling
lollygagging
longing
longstanding
looking
looming
looping
loosening
loosing
looting
loping
lopping
lording
losing
lounging
lousing
lovemaking
loving
lowering
lowing
lubricating
lucking
lucubrating
luffing
lugging

lulling
lumbering
luminescing
lumping
lunching
lunging
lurching
luring
lurking
lusting
luteinizing
luxating
luxuriating
lying
lynching
lysing
macadamizing
macerating
machinating
machining
maculating
maddening
magnetizing
magnifying
mailing
maiming
mainlining
mainspring
maintaining
majoring
making
maladministering
malfunctioning
maligning
malingering
malpracticing
maltreating
manacling
managing
mandating

maneuvering
mangling
manhandling
manicuring
manifesting
manifolding
manipulating
manning
manoeuvering
mantling
manufacturing
manuring
mapping
marauding
marbleizing
marbling
marching
marinading
marinating
marketing
marking
marooning
marring
marrying
marshaling
marshalling
martialing
martialling
martyring
marveling
marvelling
masculinizing
mashing
masking
masquerading
massacring
massaging
massing
mastering
masterminding

masticating
masturbating
matching
matchmaking
materializing
mating
matriculating
matrixing
mattering
matting
maturating
maturing
mauling
maundering
maximizing
mayheming
mayhemming
meandering
meaning
measuring
mechanizing
meddling
mediating
medicating
meditating
meeting
melanizing
melding
meliorating
mellowing
melting
memorializing
memorizing
menacing
mending
menstruating
mentioning
meowing
mercerizing
merchandising

merchandizing
merging
meriting
merrymaking
meshing
mesmerizing
messing
metabolizing
metalworking
metastasizing
metering
methodizing
metricating
metricizing
mewing
mewling
miaowing
microfilming
microspacing
middling
midmorning
midwifing
midwiving
miffing
migrating
mildewing
militarizing
militating
milking
milling
mimeographing
mimeoing
mimicking
miming
mincing
mind-blowing
minding
mineralizing
minesweeping
Ming

mingling
miniaturizing
minimizing
mining
ministering
minting
miring
mirroring
misadvising
misapplying
misapprehending
misappropriating
misarranging
misbehaving
miscalculating
miscarrying
miscasting
mischarging
misclassifying
misconceiving
misconstruing
miscopying
miscounting
miscuing
misdating
misdealing
misdefining
misdiagnosing
misdirecting
misdoing
misfiling
misfiring
misgiving
misgoverning
misguiding
mishandling
mishearing
misinforming
misinstructing
misinterpreting

misjudging
mislabeling
mislabelling
mislaying
misleading
mismanaging
mismatching
mismating
misnaming
misnumbering
misplacing
misplaying
misprinting
mispronouncing
misquoting
misreading
misrepresenting
misruling
misshaping
missing
missorting
misspelling
misspending
misstating
mistaking
mistiming
misting
mistranslating
mistreating
mistrusting
mistuning
mistyping
misunderstanding
misusing
mitigating
mixing
moaning
mobbing
mobilizing
mocking

modeling
modelling
moderating
modernizing
modifying
modulating
moiling
moistening
moisturizing
moldering
molding
molesting
mollifying
mollycoddling
molting
monetizing
moneying
moneymaking
monitoring
monkeying
monogramming
monopolizing
mooching
mooing
mooning
moonlighting
moonshining
mooring
mooting
moping
mopping
moralizing
morning
mortaring
mortgaging
mortifying
moseying
mothering
motioning
motivating

motoring
motorizing
mottling
mounding
mountaineering
mounting
mourning
mousing
mouthing
moviegoing
moving
mowing
mucking
muckraking
muddling
muddying
mudslinging
muffing
muffling
muggering
mugging
mulching
mulcting
mulling
multiplying
mumbling
mummifying
munching
murdering
murmuring
muscling
mushing
mushrooming
musing
mussing
mustering
mutating
mutilating
muting
mutinying

muttering
muzzling
mystifying
nabbing
nagging
nailing
naming
napping
narcotizing
narrating
narrowing
nasalizing
nationalizing
naturalizing
nauseating
navigating
nearing
nebulizing
necessitating
necking
necropsying
necrotizing
needing
needling
negating
negativing
neglecting
negotiating
neighboring
neighing
nerving
nesslerizing
nesting
nestling
netting
nettling
networking
neurologizing
neutering
neutralizing

newscasting
newswriting
nibbling
nickering
nicking
nicknaming
nicotinizing
niggling
nipping
nitpicking
nitrating
nitrifying
nitrogenizing
nixing
nodding
nodulating
noising
nominating
nonaddicting
noncomplying
nonconfining
nonconflicting
nonconforming
nonconsenting
noncontributing
noncorroding
nondiscriminating
nonexisting
nonfreezing
nonincriminating
nonirritating
nonparticipating
nonpaying
nonplusing
nonspeaking
nonthinking
nonvoting
normalizing
nosing
notarizing

notating
notching
nothing
noticing
notifying
noting
notwithstanding
nourishing
novating
novelizing
nucleating
nudging
nullifying
numbering
numbing
numerating
nurseling
nursing
nursling
nurturing
nuzzling
obeying
obfuscating
objecting
objurgating
obligating
obliging
obliterating
obscuring
observing
obsessing
obstructing
obtaining
obtruding
obviating
occasioning
occluding
occupying
occurring
oceangoing

octroying
offending
offering
officiating
offing
offsetting
offspring
ogling
oilheating
oiling
oinking
ok'ing
okaying
omitting
oncoming
ongoing
onlooking
onrushing
oozing
opening
operating
opining
opposing
oppressing
opting
orating
orbiting
orchestrating
ordaining
ordering
organizing
orientating
orienting
originating
ornamenting
orphaning
oscillating
osculating
osmosing
ossifying

ostracizing
ousting
outbalancing
outbargaining
outbidding
outbluffing
outboarding
outboasting
outboxing
outbuilding
outclassing
outcropping
outdistancing
outdodging
outdoing
outfacing
outfielding
outfighting
outfitting
outflanking
outfoxing
outgoing
outgrowing
outguessing
outgunning
outhitting
outing
outlasting
outlawing
outleaping
outlining
outliving
outlying
outmaneuvering
outmarching
outnumbering
outperforming
outplaying
outpocketing
outpouring

outproducing
outracing
outraging
outranging
outranking
outreaching
outreasoning
outrunning
outscoring
outselling
outshining
outshouting
outsmarting
outspelling
outspreading
outstanding
outstaying
outstretching
outstripping
outswimming
outvoting
outwalking
outwearing
outweighing
outwitting
outworking
outyelling
overabounding
overachieving
overacting
overanalyzing
overawing
overbalancing
overbearing
overbidding
overburdening
overbuying
overcapitalizing
overcasting
overcharging

overclouding
overcoming
overcompensating
overcooking
overcooling
overcrowding
overdecorating
overdeveloping
overdiversifying
overdoing
overdosing
overdramatizing
overdrawing
overdressing
overdrinking
overeating
overeducating
overembellishing
overestimating
overexciting
overexercising
overexerting
overexpanding
overexposing
overextending
overfatiguing
overfeeding
overfilling
overflowing
overflying
overfurnishing
overgeneralizing
overgrazing
overgrowing
overhanging
overhauling
overhearing
overheating
overimpressing
overindulging

overindustrializing
overinflating
overinsuring
overinvesting
overjoying
overlapping
overlaying
overloading
overlooking
overlying
overpaying
overplaying
overpopulating
overpowering
overpricing
overprinting
overprotecting
overrating
overreaching
overreacting
overriding
overroasting
overruling
oversalting
overseeing
overselling
overshadowing
overshooting
oversimplifying
oversleeping
overspecializing
overspending
overspreading
overstating
overstaying
overstepping
overstimulating
overstocking
overstriking
oversubscribing

oversupplying
overtaking
overtaxing
overthrowing
overtiring
overtopping
overtraining
overturning
overusing
overvaluing
overweighing
overwhelming
overworking
overwriting
ovulating
owing
owning
oxidizing
oxygenating
oystering
ozonizing
pacemaking
pacesetting
pacifying
pacing
packaging
packing
padding
paddling
padlocking
paginating
paging
paining
painkilling
painstaking
painting
pairing
palavering
paling
palliating

palming
palpating
palpitating
paltering
pampering
pandering
paneling
panelling
panhandling
panicking
panning
panting
pantomiming
paperhanging
papering
parachuting
parading
paragraphing
paralleling
parallelling
paralysing
paralyzing
paraphrasing
parboiling
parceling
parcelling
parching
pardoning
paring
parking
parlaying
parleying
parodying
paroling
parqueting
parring
parroting
parrying
parsing
partaking

participating
particularizing
parting
partitioning
partying
passing
pasteurizing
pasting
pasturing
patching
patenting
pathfinding
patrolling
patronizing
pattering
patterning
patting
pauperizing
pausing
paving
pawing
pawnbroking
pawning
paying
peacekeeping
peacemaking
peaking
pealing
pebbling
pecking
peculating
pedaling
pedalling
peddling
peeking
peeling
peeping
peering
peeving
pegging

peking
pelletizing
pelting
penalizing
penciling
pencilling
pending
penetrating
penning
pensioning
peopling
peppering
pepping
peptonizing
perambulating
perceiving
perching
percolating
perfecting
perforating
performing
perfuming
perfusing
periling
perishing
peritonizing
perjuring
perking
permeating
permitting
perpetrating
perpetuating
perplexing
persecuting
persevering
persisting
personalizing
personifying
perspiring
persuading

pertaining
perturbing
perusing
pervading
perverting
pestering
petering
petitioning
petnapping
petrifying
pettifogging
petting
phasing
philandering
philosophizing
phlebotomizing
phonating
phoning
phosphating
photocopying
photoengraving
photographing
photolyzing
photosynthesizing
phrasing
picketing
picking
pickling
picnicking
picturing
piddling
piecing
piercing
piffling
pigeonholing
pignorating
pilfering
piling
pillaging
pillorying

pillowing
piloting
pimping
pimpling
pinching
ping
pinging
pining
pinioning
pinking
pinnacling
pinning
pinpointing
pioneering
piping
piquing
pirating
pirouetting
pitching
pitting
pitying
pivoting
placarding
placating
placing
plagiarizing
plaguing
plaiting
planing
planking
planning
planting
plastering
plating
platting
playacting
playing
plaything
pleading
pleasing

pleating
pledging
plighting
plodding
plopping
plotting
plowing
plucking
plugging
plumbing
pluming
plummeting
plumping
plundering
plunging
plunking
pluralizing
plying
poaching
pocketing
poinding
pointing
poising
poisoning
poking
polarizing
policing
poling
polishing
politicizing
politicking
pollinating
polling
polluting
polymerizing
pommeling
pommelling
pondering
pontificating
pooling

pooping
popping
popularizing
populating
poring
portaging
portending
porting
portioning
portraying
posing
positing
positioning
possessing
postdating
posting
postmarking
postponing
postulating
posturing
pottering
potting
pouching
poulticing
pouncing
pounding
pouring
pouting
powdering
powering
practicing
praising
prancing
prattling
praying
preaching
preappointing
prearranging
preassembling
preassigning

preboiling
precalculating
precanceling
preceding
prechilling
precipitating
precluding
preconcealing
preconceiving
precondemning
preconditioning
preconstructing
precooking
predating
predefining
predestinating
predestining
predetermining
predicating
predicting
predigesting
predisposing
predominating
preempting
preengaging
preening
preestablishing
preestimating
preexamining
preexisting
preexposing
prefabricating
prefacing
preferring
prefiguring
prefixing
preforming
preheating
preinserting
preinstructing

prejudging
prejudicing
prelimiting
premedicating
premeditating
premiering
premising
premixing
preoccupying
preordaining
prepackaging
preparing
prepaying
preplanning
preponderating
prepossessing
prepping
prerecording
preregistering
presaging
prescoring
prescribing
preselecting
presenting
preserving
presetting
presiding
presifting
presoaking
pressing
pressuring
pressurizing
presuming
presupposing
pretending
pretesting
prettifying
prettying
prevailing
prevaricating

preventing
previewing
prewarming
prewashing
preying
pricing
pricking
prickling
priding
priming
primping
prinking
printing
privatizing
privileging
prizefighting
prizewinning
prizing
probating
probing
proceeding
processing
proclaiming
procrastinating
procreating
proctoring
procuring
prodding
producing
profaning
professing
proffering
profiling
profiteering
profiting
prognosticating
programing
programming
progressing
prohibiting

projecting
prolapsing
proliferating
prolonging
promenading
promising
promoting
prompting
promulgating
pronating
pronouncing
proofing
proofreading
propagandizing
propagating
propelling
prophesying
propitiating
proportioning
proposing
propounding
propping
prorating
proscribing
prosecuting
proselyting
proselytizing
prospecting
prospering
prostituting
prostrating
protecting
protesting
protracting
protruding
providing
proving
provoking
prowling
pruning

prying
psyching
psychoanalyzing
psychologizing
publicizing
publishing
puckering
pudding
puddling
puffing
puking
pulling
pulping
pulsating
pulsing
pulverizing
pummeling
pummelling
pumping
punching
punctuating
puncturing
punishing
punning
punting
purchasing
pureeing
purging
purifying
purling
purloining
purporting
purposing
purring
pursing
pursuing
purveying
pushing
pussyfooting
pustulating

putrefying
puttering
putting
puttying
puzzling
quacking
quacksalving
quadruplicating
quadrupling
quaffing
quailing
quaking
qualifying
quantifying
quarantining
quarreling
quarrelling
quarrying
quartering
quashing
quavering
queening
queering
quelling
quenching
querying
questioning
queueing
queuing
quibbling
quickening
quieting
quilting
quipping
quisling
quitclaiming
quitting
quivering
quizzing
quoting

rabbeting
racing
racketeering
racking
radiating
radicalizing
radioing
raffling
rafting
ragging
raging
raiding
railing
railroading
raining
rainmaking
raising
raking
rallying
rambling
ramifying
ramming
rampaging
ranching
randomizing
ranging
ranking
rankling
ransacking
ransoming
ranting
raping
rapping
rarefying
rarifying
raring
rasing
rasping
ratifying
rating

rationalizing
rationing
rattening
ratting
rattling
ravaging
raveling
ravelling
ravening
raving
ravishing
razing
razzing
reabandoning
reabsorbing
reaching
reacquainting
reacquiring
reacting
reactivating
readapting
readdressing
reading
readjourning
readjusting
readmitting
readopting
readying
reaffirming
realigning
realizing
reaming
reaping
reappearing
reapportioning
rearing
rearming
rearousing
rearranging
reascending

reasoning
reassembling
reasserting
reassessing
reassigning
reassuring
reattaining
reavowing
reawakening
reawaking
rebaptizing
rebating
rebelling
rebinding
reboiling
rebounding
rebroadcasting
rebuffing
rebuilding
rebuking
rebutting
rebuttoning
recalculating
recalling
recanting
recapitulating
recapping
recapturing
recasting
receding
receipting
receiving
recertifying
recessing
rechartering
recharting
rechecking
rechristening
reciprocating
recirculating

reciting
reckoning
reclaiming
reclassifying
reclining
recognizing
recoiling
recoining
recoloring
recombing
recombining
recommending
recommitting
recompensing
reconciliating
reconciling
reconditioning
reconnecting
reconnoitering
reconquering
reconsidering
reconstituting
reconstructing
reconvening
reconverting
reconveying
recooking
recopying
recording
recounting
recouping
recovering
recreating
recriminating
recrudescing
recruiting
rectifying
recuperating
recurring
recycling

reddening
redecorating
rededicating
redeeming
redefining
redeploying
redesignating
redesigning
redeveloping
redirecting
rediscovering
redissolving
redistributing
redlining
redoing
redoubling
redressing
redrying
reducing
reduplicating
redwing
redyeing
reechoing
reediting
reeducating
reefing
reeking
reelecting
reeling
reembarking
reembodying
reemerging
reemphasizing
reemploying
reenacting
reendowing
reenforcing
reengaging
reenjoying
reenlarging

reenlightening
reenlisting
reenslaving
reentering
reestablishing
reevaluating
reeving
reexamining
refashioning
refastening
refereeing
referencing
referring
refiling
refilling
refilming
refiltering
refinancing
refining
refinishing
refiring
refitting
reflecting
refocusing
refocussing
refolding
reforesting
reforging
reformatting
reforming
reformulating
refortifying
refracting
refraining
refreshing
refrigerating
refrying
refueling
refunding
refurbishing

refurnishing
refusing
refuting
regaining
regarding
regenerating
regimenting
registering
regressing
regretting
regrouping
regularizing
regulating
regurgitating
rehabilitating
rehashing
rehearsing
reheating
reheeling
rehemming
rehiring
rehydrating
reigning
reigniting
reimbursing
reimposing
reincarnating
reinforcing
reinforming
reining
reinscribing
reinserting
reinspecting
reinstalling
reinstating
reinsuring
reintegrating
reinventing
reinvoking
reissuing

reiterating
rejecting
rejoicing
rejoining
rejuvenating
rekindling
relabeling
relabelling
relapsing
relating
relaxing
relaying
relearning
releasing
relegating
relenting
relieving
relinquishing
relishing
reliving
reloading
reloaning
relocating
relying
remailing
remaindering
remaining
remaking
remanding
remarking
remarrying
rematching
remedying
remembering
remilitarizing
reminding
reminiscing
remising
remitting
remodeling

remodelling
remodifying
remolding
remonetizing
remonstrating
remortgaging
removing
remunerating
renaming
rendering
rendezvousing
rending
renegading
reneging
renegotiating
renewing
renominating
renotifying
renouncing
renovating
renting
renumbering
reoccupying
reoccurring
reopening
reordering
reorganizing
reorienting
repackaging
repacking
repainting
repairing
repatriating
repaving
repaying
repealing
repeating
repelling
repenting
rephrasing

repining
replacing
replanting
replaying
replenishing
replicating
replying
repopulating
reporting
reposing
repositioning
repossessing
reprehending
representing
repressing
reprieving
reprimanding
reprinting
reprising
reproaching
reprobating
reproducing
reprogramming
reproving
republishing
repudiating
repulsing
reputing
requesting
requiring
requisitioning
requiting
rereading
rerunning
rescheduling
rescinding
rescuing
resealing
researching
reseeding

reselling
resembling
resenting
reserving
resetting
resettling
reshaping
resharpening
reshuffling
residing
resigning
resisting
resituating
resoling
resolving
resonating
resorting
resounding
respecting
respirating
responding
restating
resting
restituting
restoring
restraining
restricting
resubmitting
resulting
resuming
resurfacing
resurrecting
resurveying
resuscitating
retailing
retaining
retaking
retaliating
retarding
retching

retelling
retesting
rethinking
retiring
retorting
retouching
retracing
retracting
retraining
retreading
retreating
retrenching
retrieving
retrofiring
retrogressing
returning
retyping
reunifying
reuniting
reupholstering
reusing
reutilizing
revaluating
revaluing
revamping
revarnishing
revealing
reveling
revelling
revenging
reverberating
reverifying
reverting
reviewing
reviling
revising
revisiting
revitalizing
revivifying
reviving

revoking
revolting
revolutionizing
revolving
revving
rewarding
rewinding
rewiring
rewording
reworking
rewrapping
rewriting
rezoning
rhapsodizing
rhyming
ribbing
ricocheting
ridding
riddling
ridgeling
ridging
ridgling
ridiculing
riding
riffing
riffling
rifling
rifting
rigging
righting
riling
rimming
ring
ringing
rinsing
rioting
rip-roaring
ripening
ripping
rippling

rising
risking
rivaling
riveting
rivetting
riving
roaming
roaring
roasting
robbing
robing
rocketing
rocking
roiling
rollicking
rolling
romancing
romanticizing
romping
roofing
rooking
rooming
roosting
rooting
roping
rosining
rotating
rotting
roughening
roughhewing
roughhousing
roughing
rounding
rousing
routing
routinizing
roving
rowing
rubberizing
rubbernecking

rubbing
ruffing
ruffling
ruing
ruining
ruling
rumbling
ruminating
rummaging
rumoring
rumpling
rumrunning
running
rupturing
rushing
rusticating
rusting
rustling
rutting
sabotaging
sacking
sacrificing
saddening
safecracking
safeguarding
safekeeping
sagging
sailboating
sailing
salaaming
salarying
salivating
sallying
salting
salvaging
salving
sampling
sanctifying
sanctioning
sandbagging

sandblasting
sanding
sandpapering
sanitating
sanitizing
sapling
saponifying
sapping
sashaying
sassing
satiating
satirizing
satisfying
saturating
saucerizing
saucing
sauntering
sauteing
saving
savoring
savvying
sawing
saying
scabbing
scaffolding
scalding
scaling
scalloping
scalping
scampering
scandalizing
scanning
scanting
scantling
scaring
scarring
scathing
scattering
scatting
scavenging

scenting
scheduling
scheming
schilling
schismatizing
schooling
schoolteaching
schussing
scintillating
scissoring
sclerosing
scoffing
scolding
scooping
scooting
scoping
scorching
scoring
scorning
scotching
scourging
scouring
scouting
scowling
scrabbling
scrambling
scramming
scraping
scrapping
scratching
scrawling
screaming
screeching
screening
screwing
scribbling
scrimmaging
scrimping
scrolling
scrounging

scrubbing
scrunching
scrutinising
scrutinizing
scudding
scuffing
scuffling
sculling
sculpting
sculpturing
scurrying
scuttling
seafaring
seagoing
seakeeping
sealing
seaming
searching
searing
seasoning
seating
seceding
secluding
seconding
secreting
sectioning
sectionizing
sectoring
secularizing
securing
sedating
seducing
seeding
seedling
seeing
seeking
seeming
seeping
seesawing
seething

segmenting
segregating
seining
seizing
selecting
self-revealing
self-sealing
self-supporting
self-winding
selling
sembling
sending
sensing
sensitizing
sentencing
sentimentalizing
sentrying
separating
sepulchering
sepulchring
sequencing
sequestering
serenading
serializing
sermonizing
servicing
serving
setting
settling
severing
sewing
sexualizing
shacking
shackling
shading
shadowboxing
shadowing
shafting
shaking
shambling

shaming
shamming
shampooing
shanghaiing
shaping
sharecropping
sharing
sharpening
sharping
sharpshooting
shattering
shaving
shearing
sheathing
shedding
sheepherding
sheepshearing
sheering
sheeting
shellacking
shelling
sheltering
shelving
shepherding
shielding
shifting
shilling
shimmering
shimmying
shingling
shining
shinning
shinnying
shipbreaking
shipbuilding
shipping
shipwrecking
shirking
shirring
shirting

shivering
shocking
shoeing
shoestring
shooing
shooting
shoplifting
shopping
shoring
shortchanging
shortcoming
shortening
shorting
shouldering
shouting
shoveling
shovelling
shoving
showcasing
showering
showing
shredding
shrieking
shrilling
shrimping
shrinking
shriveling
shrivelling
shrouding
shrugging
shucking
shuddering
shuffling
shunning
shunpiking
shunting
shushing
shuttering
shutting
shuttling

shying
sibilating
sibling
siccing
sickening
sicking
sickling
sideling
sideslipping
sidesplitting
sidestepping
sideswiping
sidetracking
siding
sidling
sieving
sifting
sighing
sighting
sightseeing
signaling
signalizing
signalling
signifying
signing
silencing
silhouetting
silkscreening
silting
silvering
simmering
simonizing
simpering
simplifying
simulating
simulcasting
sing
singeing
singing
singling

sinking
sinning
siphoning
sipping
siring
sitting
situating
sixing
sizing
sizzling
skateboarding
skating
sketching
skewering
skewing
skidding
skiing
skimming
skimping
skindiving
skinning
skipping
skirmishing
skirting
skittering
skulking
skunking
skydiving
skying
skyjacking
skylarking
skyrocketing
skywriting
slackening
slacking
slaking
slamming
slandering
slanting
slapping

slashing
slathering
slating
slatting
slaughtering
slavering
slaving
slaying
sledding
sledging
sleeping
sleepwalking
sleeting
sleighing
slenderizing
slicing
slicking
sliding
slighting
slimming
sling
slinging
slinking
slipping
slithering
slitting
slivering
slobbering
slogging
sloping
slopping
sloshing
slotting
slouching
sloughing
slowing
slugging
sluicing
sluing
slumbering

slumming
slumping
slurping
slurring
smacking
smartening
smarting
smashing
smattering
smearing
smelling
smelting
smiling
smirching
smirking
smiting
smocking
smoking
smoldering
smooching
smoothing
smothering
smudging
smuggling
snacking
snagging
snaking
snapping
snaring
snarling
snatching
sneaking
sneering
sneezing
snickering
sniffing
sniffling
sniggering
sniping
snipping

snitching
sniveling
snivelling
snooping
snoozing
snoring
snorkeling
snorting
snowballing
snowing
snowmobiling
snowshoeing
snubbing
snuffing
snuffling
snuggling
soaking
soaping
soapmaking
soaring
sobbing
sobering
socializing
socking
sodding
softening
soiling
sojourning
solacing
solarizing
soldering
soldiering
solemnizing
soliciting
solidifying
soliloquizing
soling
soloing
solving
somersaulting

something
somnambulating
soothing
soothsaying
sopping
sorrowing
sorting
soughing
sounding
soundproofing
souping
souring
sousing
sovietizing
sowing
spacewalking
spacing
spading
spangling
spanking
spanning
sparing
sparking
sparkling
sparring
spattering
spatting
spawning
spaying
speaking
spearheading
spearing
specializing
specifying
specking
speckling
speculating
speedboating
speeding
spellbinding

spelling
spelunking
spending
spewing
spicing
spiking
spilling
spinning
spiraling
spiralling
spiriting
spiting
spitting
splashing
splattering
splaying
splicing
splintering
splinting
splitting
splotching
splurging
spluttering
spoiling
spoliating
sponging
sponsoring
spoofing
spooking
spooning
sporting
sportswriting
spotting
spouting
spragging
spraining
sprawling
spraying
spreading
spring

springing
sprinkling
sprinting
sprouting
sprucing
spurning
spurring
spurting
sputtering
spying
squabbling
squalling
squandering
squaring
squashing
squatting
squawking
squeaking
squealing
squeezing
squelching
squiggling
squinting
squiring
squirming
squirting
stabbing
stabilizing
stabling
stacking
staffing
staggering
staging
stagnating
staining
staking
stalemating
stalking
stalling
stammering

stampeding
stamping
stanching
standardizing
standing
stapling
starching
stargazing
staring
starling
starring
starting
startling
starveling
starving
stashing
stating
stationing
staving
staying
steading
steadying
stealing
steaming
steamrollering
steeling
steepening
steeping
steering
stemming
stenciling
stencilling
stepping
stereotyping
sterilizing
sterling
stetting
stevedoring
stewing
sticking

stiffening
stifling
stigmatizing
stilling
stimulating
sting
stinging
stinking
stinting
stippling
stipulating
stirring
stitching
stockading
stockbroking
stockholding
stocking
stockjobbing
stockpiling
stocktaking
stoking
stomping
stonecutting
stonewalling
stoning
stooping
stopping
stoppling
storing
storming
storytelling
stowing
straddling
strafing
straggling
straightening
straining
straitening
stranding
strangling

strangulating
strapping
stratifying
straying
streaking
streaming
streamlining
streetwalking
strengthening
stressing
stretching
strewing
striding
strikebreaking
striking
string
stringing
striping
stripling
stripping
stripteasing
striving
stroking
strolling
structuring
struggling
strumming
strutting
stubbing
stuccoing
studding
studying
stuffing
stultifying
stumbling
stumping
stunning
stunting
stupefying
stuttering

styling
stylizing
stymieing
subbing
subclassifying
subcontracting
subdelegating
subdividing
subduing
subfreezing
subheading
subjecting
subjoining
subjugating
subleasing
subletting
sublimating
submerging
submersing
submitting
subordinating
suborning
subpoenaing
subscribing
subscripting
subsidizing
subsisting
substantiating
substituting
subsuming
subtending
subtitling
subtotaling
subtotalling
subtracting
subverting
succeeding
succoring
succumbing
sucking

suckling
suffering
sufficing
suffixing
suffocating
suffusing
sugarcoating
sugaring
suggesting
suing
suiting
sulfating
sulfuring
sulfurizing
sulking
sullying
sulphating
sulphurating
sulphuring
sulphurizing
summarizing
summering
summing
summoning
summonsing
sunbathing
sunburning
sundering
sunning
supercharging
superimposing
superposing
superscribing
superscripting
superseding
supervening
supervising
supinating
supping
supplanting

supplementing
supplicating
supplying
supporting
supposing
suppressing
surcharging
surfacing
surfeiting
surfing
surging
surmising
surmounting
surnaming
surpassing
surprising
surrebutting
surrendering
surrounding
surveying
surviving
suspecting
suspending
sustaining
suturing
swabbing
swaddling
swaggering
swallowing
swamping
swapping
swarming
swashbuckling
swashing
swathing
swatting
swaying
swearing
sweating
sweeping

sweetening
swelling
sweltering
swerving
swigging
swilling
swimming
swindling
swing
swinging
swiping
swirling
swishing
switching
swiveling
swivelling
swooning
swooping
swopping
syllabifying
symbolizing
sympathizing
synapsing
synchronizing
syncing
syncopating
syndicating
synthesizing
syphilizing
syphoning
syringing
systematizing
systemizing
tabbing
tabling
tabooing
tabulating
tacking
tackling
tagging

tailgating
tailing
tailoring
tainting
taking
talebearing
talking
tallying
taming
tampering
tamping
tangling
tangoing
tanning
tantalizing
tapering
taping
tapping
targeting
tarnishing
tarring
tarrying
tasking
tasseling
tasselling
tasting
tattering
tatting
tattling
tattooing
taunting
taxiing
taxing
taxpaying
teaching
teaming
teargassing
tearing
teasing
teeing

teeming
teetering
teething
telecasting
telegraphing
telephoning
telescoping
televising
telexing
telling
tempering
temporizing
tempting
tendering
tenderizing
tending
tensing
tenting
terminating
terming
terracing
terrifying
terrorizing
testifying
testing
tethering
thanking
thanksgiving
thatching
thawing
theorizing
thickening
thieving
thing
thinking
thinning
thirsting
thoroughgoing
thrashing
threading

threatening
threshing
thrilling
thriving
throbbing
thronging
throttling
throwing
thrumming
thrusting
thudding
thumbing
thumbtacking
thumping
thundering
thwacking
thwarting
ticketing
ticking
tickling
tiding
tidying
tieing
tightening
tiling
tilling
tilting
timbering
timekeeping
timesaving
timeserving
timesharing
timing
tincturing
tingeing
tingling
tinkering
tinkling
tinning
tinting

tipping
tippling
tiptoeing
tiring
tithing
titillating
titling
titrating
tittering
toadying
toasting
toddling
toeing
togging
toggling
toiling
tolerating
tolling
toning
tooling
toolmaking
tooting
toping
topping
toppling
tormenting
torpedoing
torquing
torrifying
torturing
tossing
totaling
totalizing
totalling
toting
tottering
totting
touching
toughening
touring

tousling
touting
toweling
towering
towing
toxifying
toying
tracheotomizing
tracing
tracking
trading
traducing
trafficking
trailblazing
trailing
training
traipsing
trammeling
trammelling
tramping
trampling
tranquilizing
tranquillizing
transacting
transcending
transcribing
transducing
transferring
transfiguring
transfixing
transforming
transfusing
transgressing
transistorizing
translating
transliterating
transmigrating
transmitting
transmuting
transpiring

transplanting
transporting
transposing
transubstantiating
transuding
trapping
trapshooting
trashing
traumatizing
travailing
traveling
travelling
traversing
travestying
trawling
treading
treasuring
treating
trebling
treeing
trekking
trembling
trenching
trespassing
triangulating
tricking
trickling
trifling
trifurcating
triggering
trilling
trimming
triplicating
tripling
tripping
trisecting
trithing
triumphing
trolling
tromping

trooping
trotting
troubleshooting
troubling
trouncing
trucking
truckling
trudging
trueing
truing
trumpeting
trumping
truncating
trundling
trussing
trustbusting
trusteeing
trusting
trying
tubing
tucking
tufting
tugging
tumbling
tuning
tunneling
tunnelling
turfing
turning
tussling
tutoring
twaddling
twanging
tweaking
tweeting
tweezing
twiddling
twingeing
twinging
twinkling

twinning
twirling
twisting
twitching
twittering
twitting
tying
typecasting
typesetting
typewriting
typifying
typing
tyrannizing
ulcerating
ulcering
ululating
umpiring
unacknowledging
unalarming
unamusing
unappealing
unappetizing
unapproving
unaspiring
unassisting
unassuming
unavailing
unbalancing
unbarring
unbecoming
unbefitting
unbelieving
unbending
unbinding
unblinking
unblocking
unblushing
unbolting
unbuckling
unbudging

unburdening
unbuttoning
uncaring
unceasing
unchaining
unchallenging
unchanging
unclasping
unclenching
uncloaking
unclogging
uncoiling
uncomforting
uncomplaining
uncompromising
unconsenting
unconvincing
uncorking
uncoupling
uncovering
uncrating
uncrossing
uncurling
undemanding
underachieving
underacting
undercharging
underclothing
undercoating
undercooking
undercutting
underdrawing
underdressing
underestimating
underexposing
underfeeding
undergirding
undergoing
underlaying
underling

underlining
underlying
undermining
underpaying
underpinning
underplaying
underrating
underscoring
underselling
undershooting
understanding
understating
understudying
undertaking
undervaluing
underwriting
undeserving
undeviating
undiscerning
undoing
undoubting
undraping
undressing
undulating
undying
unearthing
unedifying
unending
unenduring
unerring
unexciting
unfading
unfailing
unfaltering
unfastening
unfearing
unfeeling
unfitting
unfixing
unflagging

unflattering
unflinching
unfolding
unforbidding
unforgiving
unfreezing
unfrocking
unfurling
ungratifying
ungrudging
unharnessing
unheeding
unhesitating
unhinging
unhitching
unhooking
unhorsing
unifying
unimposing
uninspiring
uninviting
unionizing
uniting
unknowing
unlacing
unlatching
unlearning
unleashing
unloading
unlocking
unloosening
unloosing
unloving
unmasking
unmeaning
unmerging
unmoving
unmuffling
unmuzzling
unnerving

unobliging
unobserving
unpacking
unpaying
unpegging
unperceiving
unpicking
unpiling
unpinning
unpitying
unpleasing
unplugging
unpretending
unpromising
unprotesting
unquestioning
unraveling
unravelling
unreasoning
unreflecting
unrelenting
unremitting
unrepenting
unresisting
unrewarding
unrolling
unscrambling
unscrewing
unsealing
unseating
unseeing
unsettling
unshackling
unsling
unsmiling
unsnapping
unsnarling
unsparing
unsporting
unsticking

unstinting
unstopping
unstring
unsurprising
unsuspecting
unswerving
untangling
untempting
unthinking
untiring
untwisting
untying
unvarying
unveiling
unwavering
unweaving
unwilling
unwinding
unwitting
unwrapping
unwrinkling
unyielding
unyoking
unzipping
upbraiding
upbringing
upchucking
upcoming
updating
upending
upgrading
upholding
upholstering
uplifting
upraising
uprising
uprooting
upsetting
upshifting
upstaging

upstanding	venturing	vouchsafing
upswing	verbalizing	vowing
upturning	verging	voyaging
upzoning	verifying	vulcanizing
urbanizing	vernalizing	vulgarizing
urging	versifying	vying
urinating	vesting	wadding
ushering	vetoing	waddling
using	vexing	wading
usurping	vibrating	waffling
utilizing	victimizing	wafting
uttering	victualing	wagering
vacating	videotaping	wagging
vacationing	viewing	waggling
vaccinating	vignetting	waging
vacillating	viking	wailing
vacuuming	vilifying	wainscoting
validating	vindicating	waiting
valorizing	violating	waiving
valuating	virilizing	wakening
valuing	visioning	waking
vamoosing	visiting	waling
vamping	visualizing	walking
vandalizing	vitalizing	walling
vanishing	vitaminizing	walloping
vanquishing	vitiating	wallowing
vaporizing	vitrifying	wallpapering
variegating	vivifying	waltzing
varnishing	vivisecting	wandering
varying	vocalizing	wangling
vaulting	vociferating	waning
vaunting	voicing	wanting
veering	voiding	wantoning
vegetating	volatilizing	warbling
veiling	volleying	warding
veining	volplaning	warehousing
vending	volunteering	warming
venerating	vomiting	warmongering
ventilating	voting	warning
venting	vouching	warping

warranting
warring
washing
wasting
watching
watchmaking
watering
waterlogging
watermarking
waterproofing
waterskiing
wavering
waving
waxing
waxwing
wayfaring
waylaying
weakening
weakling
weaning
weanling
wearing
wearying
weaseling
weathering
weatherproofing
weatherstripping
weaving
webbing
wedding
wedging
weeding
weeping
weighing
welcoming
welding
well-being
wellspring
welshing
weltering

welting
wending
westernizing
wetting
whacking
whaling
whamming
wheedling
wheeling
wheezing
whelming
whelping
whetting
whiffing
whiffling
whiling
whimpering
whining
whinnying
whipping
whipsawing
whirling
whirring
whisking
whispering
whistle-blowing
whistling
whitecapping
whitening
whitewashing
whittling
whizzing
wholesaling
whooping
whooshing
whopping
whoring
wide-spreading
widening
wielding

wifing
wigging
wiggling
wigwagging
wildcatting
wiling
willing
wilting
winching
wincing
winding
windowing
wing
wingding
winging
wining
winking
winning
winnowing
wintering
winterizing
winterkilling
wiping
wirepulling
wiretapping
wiring
wisecracking
wishing
witching
withdrawing
withering
withholding
withstanding
witnessing
witting
wiving
wobbling
womanizing
wondering
woodcarving

woodcutting
woodgraining
woodworking
wooing
woolgathering
wording
working
worldling
worming
worrying
worsening
worshiping
worshipping
worsting
wounding
wowing
wracking
wrangling
wrapping
wreaking
wreathing
wrecking
wrenching
wresting
wrestling
wriggling
wring
wringing
wrinkling
writhing
writing
wrongdoing
wronging
wyoming
xeroxing
yachting
yakking
yammering
yanking
yapping

yawing
yawning
yawping
yearling
yearning
yelling
yellowing
yelping
yielding
yipping
yodeling
yodelling
yoking
youngling
yowling
zapping
zeroing
zigzagging
zincking
zing
zinging
zipping
zoning
zooming

INKT
blinked
chinked
clinked
distinct
extinct
finked
hoodwinked
indistinct
inked
instinct
kinked
linked
pinked
precinct

prinked
succinct
synced
unlinked
winked
zincked

INJ
astringe
binge
cringe
fringe
hinge
impinge
infringe
singe
syringe
tinge
twinge
unhinge

INK
bethink
blink
bobolink
brink
chink
clink
countersink
doublethink
drink
fink
hoodwink
Humperdinck
ink
interlink
kink
link
mink
overdrink

pink
prink
rethink
rink
shrink
sink
slink
stink
sync
think
tiddlywink
wink
zinc

INS
blintz
blintze
blueprints
chintz
dints
fingerprints
flints
footprints
forints
glints
hints
imprints
lints
mince
mints
misprints
offprints
overprints
peppermints
prince
prints
province
quince
quints
reprints

rinse
shinsplints
since
skinflints
spearmints
splints
sprints
squints
stints
tints
voiceprints
wince

INT
blueprint
dint
fingerprint
flint
footprint
forint
glint
gunflint
hint
hoofprint
imprint
lint
mint
misprint
newsprint
offprint
overprint
peppermint
print
quint
reprint
skinflint
soleprint
spearmint
splint
sprint

squint
stint
suint
thumbprint
tint
voiceprint

INTH
hyacinth
labyrinth
plinth

INTS
blintz
blintze
blueprints
chintz
dints
fingerprints
flints
footprints
forints
glints
hints
imprints
lints
mince
mints
misprints
offprints
overprints
peppermints
prince
prints
province
quince
quints
reprints
rinse
shinsplints

since
skinflints
spearmints
splints
sprints
squints
stints
tints
voiceprints
wince

Long IP
archetype
bagpipe
biotype
blowpipe
daguerreotype
drainpipe
genotype
gripe
guttersnipe
hornpipe
hype
karyotype
linotype
logotype
mistype
overripe
phenotype
pinstripe
pipe
prototype
retype
ripe
sideswipe
snipe
standpipe
stereotype
stovepipe
stripe

subtype
swipe
tailpipe
teletype
tintype
tripe
type
underripe
unripe
windpipe
wipe

IP
accountantship
acquaintanceship
admiralship
airmanship
airship
airstrip
apostleship
apprenticeship
assessorship
authorship
battleship
bipartisanship
blip
brinkmanship
bullwhip
bursarship
cadetship
captainship
catnip
censorship
chairmanship
championship
chancellorship
chieftainship
chip
citizenship
clerkship

clip
colonelship
commissionership
companionship
comradeship
conservatorship
consulship
containership
copartnership
cosponsorship
courtship
coverslip
cowslip
craftsmanship
custodianship
dealership
deanship
dictatorship
dip
directorship
discipleship
doctorship
draftsmanship
drip
editorship
entrepreneurship
equip
executorship
fellowship
filmstrip
fingertip
flagship
flip
friendship
gamesmanship
generalship
governorship
grip
gyp
handgrip

hardship
harelip
heirship
hip
horsemanship
horsewhip
internship
judgeship
kindredship
kingship
kinship
kinsmanship
kip
ladyship
leadership
lightship
lip
lordship
marksmanship
mayorship
membership
motorship
nip
oarsmanship
outstrip
ownership
parsnip
partnership
pastorship
penmanship
pillowslip
pip
premiership
professorship
proprietorship
quip
readership
receivership
relationship
rip

saintship
scholarship
scrip
seamanship
ship
showmanship
sideslip
sip
skip
slip
snip
spaceship
sponsorship
sportsmanship
starship
statesmanship
steamship
stewardship
strip
subpartnership
successorship
swordsmanship
tellership
tenantship
tip
township
trip
troopship
trusteeship
tutorship
underlip
unzip
upmanship
wardship
warship
weatherstrip
whip
workmanship
yachtsmanship
yip

zip

IPS
acquaintanceships
admiralships
airships
airstrips
apocalypse
apostleships
apprenticeships
battleships
blips
catnips
chairmanships
championships
chips
clips
colonelships
conscripts
consulships
cosponsorships
courtships
cowslips
dealerships
deanships
dictatorships
dips
directorships
drips
eclipse
editorships
ellipse
equips
fellowships
filmstrips
fingertips
flagships
flips
friendships
generalships

grips
gyps
hardships
harelips
hips
horsewhips
judgeships
kingships
kinships
kips
lightships
lips
lordships
manuscripts
mayorships
midships
motorships
outstrips
parsnips
partnerships
pillowslips
pips
premierships
professorships
quips
readerships
rips
scrips
ships
sips
skips
slips
snips
spaceships
sponsorships
steamships
strips
subscripts
tips
townships

trips
troopships
trusteeships
underlips
unzips
warships
weatherstrips
whips
yips
zips

IPT
blipped
chipped
clipped
conscript
crypt
dipped
dripped
dript
Egypt
equipped
flipped
gripped
gypped
harelipped
hipped
horsewhipped
manuscript
nipped
nondescript
outstripped
postscript
quipped
ripped
script
shipped
sideslipped
sipped
skipped

slipped
snipped
stripped
subscript
superscript
tipped
transcript
tripped
typescript
unequipped
unzipped
weatherstripped
whipped
yipped
zipped

Long IRE
acquire
admire
afire
antechoir
aspire
attire
backfire
barbwire
bemire
bonfire
briar
brushfire
campfire
choir
conspire
desire
dire
empire
enquire
entire
esquire
expire
eyre

fire
foxfire
grassfire
greenbrier
gunfire
gyre
haywire
hellfire
hire
hot-wire
inspire
ire
lyre
mire
misfire
overtire
perspire
pismire
quagmire
quire
reacquire
refire
rehire
require
retire
retrofire
rewire
sapphire
satire
shellfire
shire
sire
spire
spitfire
squire
surefire
tightwire
tire
transpire
umpire

vampire
wildfire
wire

Long IS
advice
allspice
cockatrice
concise
deice
device
dice
edelweiss
entice
excise
gneiss
ice
imprecise
lice
lyse
merchandise
mice
nice
overnice
overprecise
overprice
paradise
precise
price
rice
sacrifice
slice
spice
splice
suffice
thrice
titmice
trice
twice
vice

vise

IS
abyss
acropolis
ambergis
amiss
analysis
antithesis
anuresis
armistice
artifice
biogenesis
bliss
bodice
cannabis
cicatrice
cowardice
dentrifice
dialysis
dismiss
edifice
emphasis
epiglottis
genesis
hiss
hypothesis
kiss
koumiss
kumiss
licorice
metamorphosis
metatastasis
metropolis
miss
necropolis
nemesis
orifice
paralysis
parenthesis

precipice
prejudice
reminisce
remiss
sui generis
Swiss
sythesis
this
verdigris

ISH
abolish
accomplish
admonish
amateurish
Amish
Angelfish
anguish
astonish
baboonish
babyish
banish
biggish
blackish
blandish
bleakish
blemish
blockish
blowfish
bluefish
bluish
boarish
bonefish
bookish
boorish
boyish
brackish
brandish
brattish
British

broguish
brownish
brutish
buckish
buffoonish
bugbearish
bullish
bumpkinish
burnish
butterfish
caddish
catfish
cherish
childish
churlish
clannish
clayish
cleverish
cliquish
cloddish
clownish
codfish
coltish
coolish
coquettish
crawfish
crayfish
cuttlefish
Danish
darkish
demolish
dervish
devilish
dilettantish
diminish
dish
distinguish
dogfish
doggish
dollish

donnish
dovish
dudish
dumpish
dwarfish
elfish
embellish
English
establish
extinguish
faddish
famish
fattish
fetich
fetish
feverish
fiendish
finish
Finnish
fish
flatfish
flattish
Flemish
flourish
fogyish
foolish
foppish
freakish
frumpish
furbish
furnish
garfish
garish
garnish
gawkish
ghoulish
gibberish
girlish
gnomish
goldfish

goodish
grayfish
grayish
greenish
grumpish
haggish
hashish
hawkish
heathenish
hellish
hoggish
horseradish
hunnish
impish
impoverish
Irish
jadish
jellyfish
Jewish
jingoish
kaddish
kiddish
kittenish
knavish
languish
lappish
largish
latish
lavish
licorice
liquorice
littlish
liverish
longish
loutish
lumpish
mannish
mawkish
minxish
modish

monish
monkish
moonish
moorish
mopish
mulish
narrowish
nightmarish
nourish
oafish
oblongish
offish
oldish
outlandish
overembellish
overfurnish
overlavish
owlish
paganish
panfish
parish
peevish
perish
pettish
picayunish
piggish
pinkish
pipefish
plumpish
polish
poorish
preestablish
premonish
priggish
prudish
publish
puckish
puggish
punish
purplish

quackish
qualmish
radish
raffish
rakish
ravish
reddish
reestablish
refinish
refurbish
refurnish
relinquish
relish
replenish
republish
revarnish
roguish
roundish
rowdyish
rubbish
ruttish
sailfish
schoolgirlish
Scottish
selfish
sheepish
shellfish
shish
shrewish
sickish
silverfish
skirmish
skittish
slavish
sluggish
sluttish
smallish
snappish
snobbish
sottish

Spanish
spearfish
squarish
squeamish
squish
standoffish
starfish
strongish
stylish
sunfish
Swedish
sweetish
swinish
swish
swordfish
tarnish
thievish
ticklish
tigerish
trickish
Turkish
unselfish
unstylish
uppish
vanish
vanquish
vaporish
varnish
vixenish
voguish
waggish
wannish
warmish
waspish
weakfish
weakish
whiggish
whitefish
whitish
whorish

wish
wolfish
womanish
yellowish
Yiddish
youngish

ISK
asterisk
basilisk
brisk
disc
disk
fisk
frisk
obelisk
odelisk
risk
videodisc
whisk

ISP
crisp
lisp
wisp

IST
ablest
abolitionist
abortionist
absolutist
absurdist
accompanist
accordionist
achiest
activist
acupuncturist
acutest
adjust
aerialist
agriculturist

agronomist
airiest
airworthiest
alarmist
alchemist
alcoholist
allegorist
allergist
altruist
Americanist
amethyst
amplest
anaesthetist
analyst
anarchist
anatomist
anecdotist
anesthetist
angriest
animist
annalist
antagonist
anthologist
anthropologist
antiabortionist
anticommunist
antitrust
apiarist
apologist
apprenticed
aptest
archaeologist
archaist
archeologist
archivist
arsonist
artiest
artillerist
artist
ashiest

astrophysicist
atheist
atomist
audiologist
august
autonomist
aviarist
bacteriologist
baggiest
baldest
balkiest
ballast
balloonist
balmiest
banjoist
barest
bassist
bassoonist
battiest
bawdiest
beadiest
beastliest
beefiest
behaviorist
biased
biassed
bicyclist
bigamist
biggest
bimetallist
biochemist
biologist
biophysicist
bioscientist
bitterest
blackest
blandest
blankest
bleakest
bleariest

blindest
blithest
blondest
bloodiest
bloodthirstiest
bloomiest
blotchiest
blowiest
blowziest
bluest
bluntest
blurriest
boggiest
boldest
bolshevist
boniest
bonniest
booziest
boskiest
bossiest
botanist
botchiest
bounciest
brahmanist
brahminist
brainiest
brambliest
brashest
brassiest
brattiest
bravest
brawniest
breakfast
breathiest
breeziest
briefest
brightest
briniest
briskest
bristliest

broadest
broodiest
broomiest
brothiest
brownest
bruskest
bubbliest
buddhist
bulgiest
bulkiest
bummest
bumpiest
bunchiest
burliest
bused
bushiest
busiest
bussed
buttressed
caesarist
cagiest
calloused
callused
calmest
calvinist
cameralist
campiest
canniest
canoeist
canonist
canvased
canvassed
capitalist
cardiologist
cartoonist
catalyst
catchiest
cattiest
caucused
cellist

centralist
centrist
ceramicist
ceramist
ceremonialist
chalkiest
chanciest
chattiest
chauvinist
cheapest
cheekiest
cheeriest
cheesiest
chemist
chewiest
chilliest
chintziest
choicest
choosiest
choppiest
chorused
chronologist
chubbiest
chummiest
chunkiest
civilest
clammiest
clarinetist
clarinettist
classicist
classiest
clavichordist
cleanest
cleanliest
clearest
cleverest
climatologist
clingiest
cliquiest
cloddiest

cloggiest
closest
cloudiest
clumpiest
clumsiest
coalitionist
coarsest
cockiest
coldest
collectivist
colonialist
colonist
colorist
columnist
comeliest
comfiest
commercialist
commonest
communalist
communist
compassed
completest
conformist
congregationalist
conservationist
constructionist
contortionist
contrabandist
conversationalist
coolest
copyist
corkiest
cornetist
corniest
corruptionist
cosmetologist
cosmologist
costliest
courtliest
coyest

coziest
crabbiest
crackliest
craftiest
craggiest
crankiest
crappiest
crassest
crawliest
crayonist
craziest
creakiest
creamiest
creepiest
criminologist
crinkliest
crispest
crispiest
croakiest
crossest
croupiest
crudest
cruelest
cruellest
crummiest
crunchiest
crust
crustiest
cubist
cuddliest
curliest
curtest
curviest
cushiest
cussed
cutest
cyberneticist
cyclist
cymbalist
cytologist

czarist
dadaist
daffiest
daftest
daintiest
dampest
dandiest
dankest
darkest
darwinist
deadest
deadliest
deafest
dearest
decentralist
deepest
defeatist
deforest
deftest
deist
delusionist
demolitionist
demonstrationist
demurest
dendrologist
densest
dentist
dermatologist
determinist
dewiest
diarist
diciest
dimmest
dingiest
dinkiest
dippiest
dirtiest
dishonest
disinterest
diversionist

dizziest
doest
dogmatist
dopiest
dottiest
doughiest
dowdiest
drabbest
draftiest
draggiest
dramatist
dreamiest
dreariest
dressiest
driest
droopiest
drowsiest
druggist
drunkest
dualist
duckiest
duelist
dullest
dumbest
dumpiest
duskiest
dusticst
dynamist
earliest
earnest
earthiest
earthliest
easiest
ecologist
economist
edgiest
editorialist
eeriest
egoist
egotist

eldest
elitist
elocutionist
embarrassed
embryologist
emotionalist
empiricist
emptiest
encompassed
encrust
endocrinologist
enthusiast
entomologist
entrust
environmentalist
epigrammatist
ergonomist
Ernest
eroticist
escapist
essayist
ethnologist
ethologist
etymologist
Eucharist
eugenicist
eulogist
evangelist
everest
evolutionist
excursionist
exhibitionist
existentialist
exorcist
expansionist
experimentalist
expressionist
extortionist
extremist
faddist

faintest	flippest	fussiest
fairest	floppiest	fustiest
falsest	florist	futurist
fanciest	flossiest	fuzziest
fantasist	fluffiest	gabbiest
farthest	flukiest	gamest
fascist	flutist	gamiest
fastest	foamiest	gassiest
fatalist	foggiest	gastronomist
fattest	folklorist	gaudiest
fattiest	folksiest	gauntest
faultiest	fondest	gauziest
federalist	foolhardiest	gawkiest
feeblest	forest	gayest
feistiest	formalist	gemmologist
feminist	foulest	gemologist
feudalist	foxiest	genealogist
feudist	frailest	geneticist
fewest	frankest	gentlest
fiercest	freakiest	geochemist
filmiest	freest	geodesist
filthiest	frescoist	geologist
finalist	freshest	germiest
finest	friendliest	ghastliest
finniest	friskiest	giddiest
firmest	frizziest	gimpiest
fishiest	frostiest	gladdest
fittest	frothiest	glassiest
fizziest	frowsiest	gleamiest
flabbiest	frowziest	glibbest
flakiest	fruitiest	globalist
flashiest	frumpiest	gloomiest
flattest	fullest	glossiest
fleeciest	fumiest	gluiest
fleetest	functionalist	glummest
fleshiest	fundamentalist	godliest
fleshliest	funkiest	goodliest
flightiest	funniest	goofiest
flimsiest	furriest	gooiest
flintiest	furthest	goriest

gothicist	hairiest	homeliest
goutiest	hairstylist	homiest
grabbiest	hammiest	honest
grainiest	handiest	horniest
grandest	handsomest	horologist
graphologist	happiest	horsiest
grassiest	harassed	horticulturist
gravest	hardest	hottest
grayest	hardiest	huffiest
greasiest	harnessed	hugest
greatest	harpist	humanist
greediest	harpsichordist	humblest
greenest	harshest	humorist
greyest	harvest	hungriest
grimaced	hastiest	huskiest
grimiest	haughtiest	hydrologist
grimmest	haziest	hydrotherapist
gripiest	headiest	hygienist
grippiest	healthiest	hypnotist
grisliest	heartiest	hypothesist
grittiest	heaviest	ichthyologist
grizzliest	hebraist	iciest
groggiest	hedonist	ickiest
grooviest	heftiest	idealist
grossest	Hellenist	ideologist
grouchiest	hematologist	idlest
grubbiest	heraldist	illusionist
gruffest	herbalist	immodest
grumpiest	herbst	immunist
grungiest	herpetologist	immunologist
guiltiest	highest	imperialist
guitarist	hilliest	impressionist
gummiest	hippest	incendiarist
gushiest	histologist	individualist
gust	hoariest	industrialist
gustiest	hoarsest	inflationist
gutsiest	hobbyist	inkiest
guttiest	hokiest	instrumentalist
gymnast	holiest	integrationist
gynecologist	holist	interest

internationalist
internist
interventionist
intrust
isolationist
itchiest
jaundiced
jauntiest
jazziest
jerkiest
jingoist
jointist
jolliest
jounciest
journalist
judoist
juiciest
jumpiest
jurist
keenest
kickiest
kindest
kindliest
kingliest
kinkiest
knobbiest
knottiest
kookiest
kremlinologist
laciest
lakiest
lamest
lampoonist
landscapist
lankiest
larcenist
lardiest
largest
latest
latticed

laxest
laziest
leafiest
leakiest
leanest
leeriest
leftist
legalist
leggiest
lengthiest
leninist
lewdest
libelist
liberationist
librettist
lightest
likeliest
limiest
linguist
lintiest
lithest
littlest
liturgist
liveliest
loamiest
lobbyist
locust
loftiest
logiest
loneliest
longest
looniest
loosest
lordliest
loudest
lousiest
loveliest
lowest
lowliest
loyalist

luckiest
lumpiest
lustiest
lutanists
lutist
lyricist
lyrist
machinist
maddest
mainmast
malpracticed
mandolinist
mangiest
manicurist
manliest
maoist
marshiest
martialist
marxist
masochist
massagist
massiest
materialist
maturest
mayest
mealiest
meanest
measliest
meatiest
mechanist
medalist
medievalist
meekest
mellowest
melodramatist
memorialist
menaced
mendelist
mentalist
merriest

mesmerist
messiest
metallurgist
meteorologist
methodist
microbiologist
mightiest
mildest
militarist
milkiest
mineralogist
miniaturist
minimalist
mintiest
minutest
miriest
misanthropist
misogamist
misogynist
misoneist
mistiest
mistrust
modernist
modest
moistest
moldiest
monarchist
monetarist
monist
monogamist
monologist
monologuist
monopolist
monotheist
moodiest
mopiest
moralist
morphologist
mossiest
motorcyclist

motorist
mouldiest
mousiest
mouthiest
muckiest
muddiest
muggiest
muralist
murkiest
mushiest
musicologist
muskiest
mussed
must
mustiest
mutualist
mythologist
naivest
narcissist
narrowest
nastiest
nationalist
nattiest
naturalist
naughtiest
nearest
neatest
neediest
neoclassicist
nepotist
nerviest
neurologist
neutralist
newest
newsiest
nicest
niftiest
nighest
nihilist
nimblest

nippiest
nobelist
noblest
noisiest
nonconformist
nonsexist
nonspecialist
nosiest
noticed
novelist
nudest
nudist
numbest
numerologist
numismatist
nutritionist
nuttiest
oboist
obscurest
obstructionist
occultist
oceanologist
oculist
oddest
oiliest
oldest
oligopolist
onanist
oocyst
ooziest
ophthalmologist
opportunist
oppositionist
optimist
optometrist
orchardist
organist
orientalist
ornithologist
orthodontist

orthoepist
orthopedist
osteologist
overearnest
overmodest
pacifist
paleontologist
passivist
pastiest
pastoralist
patchiest
pathologist
pearliest
peatiest
pebbliest
pediatrist
pedicurist
pedologist
penologist
peppiest
percussionist
perfectionist
perkiest
permutationist
pertest
peskiest
pessimist
petrologist
pettiest
pharmaceutist
pharmacist
pharmacologist
philanthropist
philatelist
philologist
phoniest
phonologist
photochemist
phrenologist
physicist

physiologist
pianist
pickiest
piggiest
pimpliest
pinkest
pithiest
plagiarist
plainest
planetologist
pluckiest
plumiest
plumpest
plushest
podiatrist
pointiest
pokiest
polemicist
politest
polyandrist
polygamist
polygynist
polytheist
poorest
populist
porkiest
portliest
portraitist
poshest
poulticed
practiced
pragmatist
precipiced
prefaced
prejudiced
prissiest
procommunist
proctologist
profascist
profeminist

premised
prettiest
prickliest
primmest
professionalist
profoundest
progressionist
prohibitionist
projectionist
promised
pronationalist
propagandist
protagonist
protectionist
protist
protozoologist
proudest
psalmist
psychiatrist
psychoanalyst
psychologist
psychophysicist
psychotherapist
publicist
pudgiest
puffiest
pugilist
pulpiest
punchiest
puniest
purchased
purest
purist
purposed
pushiest
pussiest
quackiest
quaintest
quakiest
quarterfinalist

queasiest
queerest
quickest
quietest
quirkiest
racialist
raciest
racist
radiochemist
radiologist
rainiest
randiest
rangiest
rankest
rapist
rarest
raspiest
rationalist
rattiest
raunchiest
rawest
readiest
readjust
realest
realist
receptionist
recidivist
recitalist
reconstructionist
recordist
reddest
reediest
refocused
refocussed
reforest
refractionist
reincarnationist
religionist
remotest
reservist

resurfaced
resurrectionist
reversionist
revisionist
revivalist
rightist
ripest
riskiest
ritualist
ritziest
robust
rockiest
romanist
romanticist
roomiest
rosiest
rottenest
roughest
rowdiest
royalist
ruddiest
rudest
runniest
runtiest
revolutionist
richest
rightist
ripest
riskiest
ritualist
ritziest
robust
rockiest
romanist
romanticist
roomiest
rosiest
rottenest
roughest
rowdiest

royalist
ruddiest
rudest
runniest
runtiest
rust
rustiest
ruttiest
saddest
sadist
safest
saggiest
saintliest
saltiest
sandiest
sanest
sappiest
sassiest
satanist
satirist
sauciest
saxophonist
sayest
scabbiest
scaliest
scantiest
scarcest
scariest
scenarist
schmaltziest
scientist
scraggliest
scrappiest
scratchiest
scrawniest
screechiest
screwiest
scrimpiest
scrubbiest
scruffiest

scummiest	showiest	smoggiest
scurviest	shrewdest	smokiest
seamiest	shrillest	smoothest
secessionist	shyest	smudgiest
seclusionist	sickest	smuggest
secularist	sickliest	smuttiest
securest	sightliest	snakiest
seditionist	silkiest	snappiest
seediest	silliest	snarliest
seemliest	siltiest	snazziest
segregationist	simplest	sneakiest
seismologist	sincerest	sneeziest
semanticist	sketchiest	snidest
semifinalist	skimpiest	snippiest
sensualist	skinniest	snobbiest
sentimentalist	slangiest	snoopiest
separatist	slaphappiest	snootiest
serialist	sleaziest	snottiest
serologist	sleekest	snowiest
serologist	sleepiest	snuggest
serviced	sleetiest	soapiest
severest	slenderest	soberest
sexiest	slickest	socialist
sexist	sliest	sociologist
sexologist	slightest	softest
shabbiest	slimiest	soggiest
shadiest	slimmest	solaced
shaggiest	slinkiest	solidest
shakiest	slipperiest	soliloquist
shallowest	sloppiest	solipsist
shapeliest	sloshiest	soloist
sharpest	slouchiest	somnambulist
sheeniest	slowest	somniloquist
shiest	sludgiest	soonest
shiftiest	slushiest	sootiest
shiniest	slyest	sophist
shintoist	smallest	soppiest
shoddiest	smartest	sorest
shortest	smeariest	sorriest
shouldest	smelliest	soundest

soupiest	steadiest	supremacist
sourest	stealthiest	surest
sparest	steamiest	surfaced
sparsest	steeliest	surliest
specialist	steepest	surrealist
speediest	sternest	survivalist
speleologist	stickiest	sveltest
spiciest	stiffest	swampiest
spiffiest	stillest	swankiest
spikiest	stingiest	swarthiest
spindliest	stinkiest	sweatiest
spiniest	stockiest	sweetest
spiritualist	stodgiest	swiftest
splashiest	stoniest	synergist
splotchiest	stormiest	syphilologist
spongiest	stoutest	tackiest
spookiest	straggliest	talkiest
sportiest	straightest	tallest
spottiest	strangest	talmudist
spriest	strategist	tamest
sprightliest	streakiest	tangiest
springiest	streamiest	tannest
sprucest	stretchiest	taoist
spryest	strictest	tardiest
spunkiest	stringiest	tarriest
squabbiest	strongest	tartest
squarest	stubbiest	tastiest
squashiest	stubbornest	tattooist
squattiest	stuffiest	tautest
squeakiest	stumpiest	tawdriest
squirmiest	stupidest	tawniest
stagiest	sturdiest	taxidermist
staidest	stylist	taxonomist
stalest	subtlest	teariest
stalinist	sudsiest	technologist
starchiest	suffragist	teeniest
starkest	sulkiest	telegraphist
starriest	sultriest	telephonist
stateliest	sunniest	teletypist
statist	supplest	tempest

tensest	trickiest	voodooist
terminologist	trigamist	wackiest
terraced	trimmest	wannest
terrorist	tritest	wariest
tersest	trombonist	warmest
testiest	truest	wartiest
tetchiest	trussed	washiest
theist	trust	wastiest
theorist	trustiest	waviest
theosophist	tubbiest	waxiest
therapeutist	twangiest	weakest
therapist	tweediest	weakliest
thickest	typist	wealthiest
thinnest	ugliest	weariest
thirstiest	ultraist	weediest
thorniest	unbiased	weeniest
threadiest	unharnessed	weepiest
thriftiest	unhealthiest	weightiest
throatiest	unicyclist	weirdest
thrust	unionist	wettest
tidiest	universalist	wheeziest
tightest	unjust	whiniest
timpanist	unnoticed	whitest
tiniest	unpracticed	widest
tinniest	unprejudiced	wildest
tipsiest	unruliest	wiliest
titlist	unwitnessed	windiest
tobogganist	upthrust	winiest
toothiest	urologist	wintriest
topmast	vacationist	wiriest
touchiest	vaguest	wisest
toughest	ventriloquist	wispiest
tourist	vignettist	witnessed
toxicologist	vilest	wittiest
traditionalist	violinist	wobbliest
trampolinist	violist	woodiest
transcendentalist	virologist	woodsiest
trashiest	vitalist	woolliest
trendiest	viticulturist	wooziest
trespassed	vocalist	wordiest

worldliest
wormiest
worthiest
wouldest
wriggliest
wrongest
xylophonist
yahwist
yeastiest
youngest
yummiest
zaniest
zestiest
zionist
zippiest
zitherist
zoologist

Long IT
affright
airtight
alight
alright
ammonite
anthracite
apartheid
appetite
aright
athrocyte
axite
backbite
backlight
bentonite
bight
biosatellite
bipartite
birthright
bite
blacklight
blight

bobwhite
bombsight
bright
bullfight
byte
calcite
campsite
canaanite
candlelight
Carmelite
checkbite
chlorite
chromocyte
chrysolite
cite
cockfight
contrite
copyright
cordite
crystallite
Darwinite
daylight
delight
dendrite
despite
dogfight
dolomite
downright
dwight
dynamite
ebonite
electrolyte
eremite
erudite
excite
expedite
extradite
eyebright
eyesight
Fahrenheit

fanlight
favorite
ferrite
fight
finite
firelight
fistfight
flashlight
fleabite
flight
floodlight
fluorite
fly-by-night
footlight
foresight
forthright
fortnight
fright
frostbite
gaslight
gelignite
gesundheit
ghostwrite
glycerite
goodnight
graphite
gunfight
handwrite
headlight
headright
height
hellgrammite
hermaphrodite
highlight
hindsight
Hitlerite
hittite
homesite
ignite
impolite

in-flight
incite
indict
indite
insight
invite
Israelite
Jacobite
jadeite
kite
knight
krait
labradorite
lamplight
landright
levite
light
lignite
lily-white
limelight
limonite
lintwhite
lite
lucite
lymphocyte
magnetite
malachite
megabyte
mennonite
meteorite
midnight
might
millwright
miswrite
mite
moonlight
multipartite
muscovite
neophyte
nephrite

night
night-light
nitrite
off-white
on-site
oocyte
outfight
outright
overbite
overexcite
overflight
overnight
oversight
overwrite
parasite
partite
pegmatite
penlight
phagocyte
phosphite
playwright
plebescite
plebiscite
plight
polite
prizefight
proselyte
pseudoparasite
pyrite
quartzite
quite
recite
recondite
reignite
reindict
requite
respite
reunite
rewrite
right

rite
safelight
satellite
scattersite
searchlight
semite
shemite
Shiite
shipwright
sidelight
siderite
sight
site
skintight
skylight
skywrite
sleight
slight
smite
snakebite
snow-white
socialite
sodomite
somite
spaceflight
spermatocyte
spite
spotlight
spright
sprite
stalactite
stalagmite
starlight
stoplight
streetlight
suburbanite
sulfite
sulphite
sunlight
sybarite

taconite
taillight
tektite
termite
tight
Tokyoite
tonight
topflight
torchlight
townsite
transvestite
trilobite
tripartite
trite
trotskyite
twilight
twinight
typewrite
underwrite
unite
upright
uptight
urbanite
vulcanite
wainwright
water-sprite
watertight
weathertight
weeknight
wheelwright
white
wright
write
wyomingite
zeolite

IT
acquit
admit
armpit

baby-sit
backbit
bandit
befit
benefit
bit
bowsprit
Brit
chit
close-knit
cockpit
commit
counterfeit
credit
culprit
dimwit
emit
favorite
fit
flit
floodlit
frostbit
grit
half-wit
hit
housesit
hypocrite
infinite
it
Jesuit
kit
knit
legit
lit
misfit
mit
mitt
moonlit
nit
nitwit

obit
omit
outfit
outhit
outsit
outwit
permit
pinch-hit
pit
preterite
quit
readmit
recommit
refit
remit
resubmit
retrofit
Sanskrit
sit
skit
slit
spit
split
sprit
starlit
submit
sunlit
tidbit
tit
tomtit
transmit
twilit
twit
unfit
unknit
unlit
whit
wit
writ
zit

Long ITH
blithe
kithe
lithe
scythe
tithe
withe
writhe

ITH
b'rith
blacksmith
coppersmith
cryptolith
forthwith
goldsmith
gunsmith
herewith
kith
locksmith
megalith
monolith
myth
neolith
paleolith
pith
silversmith
smith
therewith
tinsmith
wherewith
with
wordsmith
xenolith

Long IV
alive
archive
arrive
beehive

chive
connive
contrive
deprive
derive
dive
drive
endive
five
gyve
hive
I've
jive
live
nosedive
overdrive
power-dive
revive
rive
shrive
skindive
skydive
strive
survive
test-drive
thrive
wive

IV
ablative
abortive
abrasive
abstractive
abusive
accumulative
accusative
acquisitive
active
adaptive
addictive

additive
adhesive
adjective
adjudicative
adjunctive
administrative
admissive
adoptive
adversative
affective
affirmative
afflictive
agglutinative
aggressive
alleviative
alliterative
allusive
alternative
ameliorative
annotative
anticipative
antidepressive
applicative
appointive
appositive
appreciative
apprehensive
approbative
argumentative
argumentive
ascriptive
assaultive
assertive
assimilative
associative
assuasive
assumptive
attentive
attractive
attributive

authoritative
automotive
aversive
benefactive
calculative
capacitative
captive
causative
circulative
circumventive
coercive
coextensive
cognitive
cohesive
collaborative
collective
collusive
combative
combustive
commemorative
commissive
communicative
commutative
comparative
compensative
competitive
comprehensive
compressive
compulsive
conceptive
concessive
conclusive
concussive
conducive
conductive
confederative
configurative
conflictive
congestive
conjunctive

connective
connotative
consecrative
consecutive
conservative
constitutive
constrictive
constructive
consultative
consultive
consumptive
contaminative
contemplative
contortive
contraceptive
contractive
contradictive
contradistinctive
contraindicative
convective
convulsive
cooperative
copulative
corporative
corrective
correlative
corroborative
corrosive
corruptive
counteractive
counteroffensive
counterproductive
creative
cumulative
cursive
dative
debilitative
deceptive
decisive
declarative

decompressive
decongestive
decorative
deductive
defective
defensive
definitive
deflective
deformative
defunctive
degenerative
deliberative
delimitative
delineative
delusive
demonstrative
denotative
denotive
depletive
deprecative
depressive
derisive
derivative
descriptive
desiccative
destructive
detective
detractive
devastative
diffusive
digestive
digressive
diminutive
directive
discriminative
discursive
disintegrative
disjunctive
disruptive
dissociative

dissuasive	festive	indecisive
distinctive	fictive	indicative
distractive	figurative	indigestive
distributive	fixative	inductive
divisive	forgive	ineffective
educative	formative	inexpensive
effective	frequentative	inexpressive
effusive	fugitive	infective
elective	furtive	infinitive
electromotive	generative	infirmative
electropositive	genitive	inflammative
eliminative	give	inflictive
elusive	gustative	informative
emanative	hallucinative	ingestive
emissive	hortative	ingressive
emotive	hyperactive	inhibitive
emulsive	hypersensitive	initiative
erosive	hypertensive	injunctive
eruptive	hyposensitive	innovative
evaporative	hypotensive	inoffensive
evasive	illuminative	inoperative
evocative	illusive	inquisitive
exaggerative	illustrative	insensitive
excessive	imaginative	instinctive
exclusive	imitative	instructive
executive	impassive	integrative
exhaustive	imperative	intensive
exhibitive	imperceptive	interactive
exhilarative	implosive	interceptive
expansive	impressive	interdictive
expensive	impulsive	interpretative
expletive	inactive	interpretive
explicative	inattentive	interrogative
explorative	incentive	interruptive
explosive	inceptive	intransitive
expressive	incisive	introductive
extensive	incitive	introspective
extorsive	inclusive	introversive
extraversive	inconclusive	intrusive
extrusive	inconsecutive	intuitive

invective
inventive
inversive
investigative
irrespective
irritative
irruptive
jurisdictive
lacerative
laxative
legislative
lenitive
liquefactive
live
locative
locomotive
lucrative
maladaptive
maladjustive
maledictive
manipulative
massive
meditative
meliorative
misgive
misrepresentative
missive
mitigative
modulative
motive
mutative
mutilative
narrative
native
negative
nominative
nonaddictive
nonadhesive
nonaggressive
nonassertive

nonconsecutive
nonconstructive
noncorrosive
noncreative
nondescriptive
nondestructive
nondirective
nonexclusive
nonexplosive
noninclusive
nonnative
nonobjective
nonproductive
nonreactive
nonrestrictive
nonselective
nonsensitive
normative
nutritive
objective
obliterative
obsessive
obstructive
obtrusive
occlusive
octave
offensive
olive
operative
oppressive
optative
optive
outlive
overactive
overaggressive
overapprehensive
overassertive
overattentive
overcompetitive
overconservative

overdefensive
overimaginative
overprotective
oversensitive
palliative
partitive
passive
pejorative
penetrative
pensive
perceptive
percussive
perfective
permissive
perspective
persuasive
pervasive
perversive
petrifactive
photopositive
photosensitive
plaintive
positive
possessive
postdigestive
preclusive
precognitive
predicative
predictive
preemptive
premeditative
preoperative
preperceptive
prerogative
prescriptive
preservative
presumptive
preventative
preventive
primitive

proactive
probative
procreative
productive
progressive
prohibitive
proliferative
promotive
propagative
propulsive
prospective
protective
protrusive
provocative
psychoactive
punitive
purgative
purposive
putative
putrefactive
qualitative
quantitative
radiative
radioactive
reactive
receptive
recessive
reciprocative
reclusive
recompensive
reconstructive
recriminative
recuperative
redemptive
reductive
reduplicative
reflective
reflexive
reformative
refractive

regenerative
regressive
regulative
regurgitative
reintegrative
reiterative
relative
relive
remonstrative
remunerative
reparative
repercussive
repetitive
replicative
reprehensive
representative
repressive
reproductive
repulsive
resistive
respective
responsive
restitutive
restive
restorative
restrictive
resuscitative
retentive
retroactive
retrogressive
retrospective
retrusive
revulsive
ruminative
sanative
seclusive
secretive
sedative
seductive
segregative

selective
semiactive
sensitive
separative
shiv
siccative
sieve
significative
simulative
speculative
spiv
sportive
stimulative
stupefactive
suasive
subjective
subjunctive
submissive
substantive
subversive
successive
suggestive
superlative
supersensitive
supportive
suppositive
suppressive
suspensive
talkative
tentative
titillative
tolerative
transgressive
transitive
translative
transmissive
ulcerative
unassertive
unattractive
uncompetitive

uncreative
unexpressive
unfestive
unimpressive
uninventive
unobtrusive
unoffensive
unperceptive
unpermissive
unpersuasive
unpossessive
unproductive
unreactive
unreceptive
unreflective
unresponsive
unrestrictive
unsensitive
unsubmissive
usurpative
valuative
variative
vegetative
vindicative
vindictive
vituperative
vocative
vomitive
votive

Long IS
acclimatize
actualize
advertise
advertize
advise
aggrandize
agonize
alibies

alibis
alkalies
alkalinize
alkalize
allies
alphabetize
americanize
amortise
amortize
amplifies
anaesthetize
analogize
analyze
anathematize
anatomize
anesthetize
anglicize
anodize
antagonize
anthologize
anywise
apologize
apostatize
applies
apprise
apprize
arborize
arise
assize
atomize
authorize
ayes
banzais
baptize
barbarize
barflies
bastardize
beautifies
belies
bigamize

blowflies
botflies
brutalize
buckeyes
burglarize
butterflies
buys
byes
calcifies
cannibalize
canonize
capitalise
capitalize
capsize
capsulize
caramelize
carbonize
catalyze
categorize
catheterize
cauterize
centralize
certifies
channelize
characterize
chastise
christianize
circularize
circumcise
citifies
civilize
clarifies
classifies
clockwise
coastwise
cockeyes
codifies
collectivize
colonize
commercialize

communalize
compartmentalize
complies
comprise
compromise
computerize
conceptualize
containerize
contrariwise
conventionalize
counterclockwise
counterspies
cretinize
cries
criticize
crosswise
crucifies
crystalize
crystallize
customize
damselflies
dandifies
decalcifies
decarbonize
decentralize
declassifies
decries
decriminalize
defeminize
defies
dehumanize
dehumidifies
deifies
delegalize
demagnetize
demasculinize
demilitarize
demineralize
demise
demobilize

democratize
demonetize
demoralize
denationalize
denaturalize
denies
deodorize
deoxidize
depersonalize
deputize
descries
desensitize
despise
detoxifies
devise
devitalize
dies
digitalize
digitize
dignifies
disenfranchise
disguise
disorganize
disqualifies
dissatisfies
diversifies
downsize
dragonflies
dramatize
dries
drys
dyes
ebonize
economize
edgewise
edifies
editorialize
elasticize
electrifies
electrolyze

elegize
empathize
emphasize
emulsifies
endwise
energize
enfranchise
enterprise
enterprize
epitomize
equalize
eroticize
espies
etherize
eulogize
evangelize
excise
exemplifies
exercise
exorcise
externalize
eyes
factorize
falsifies
familiarize
fanaticize
fantasize
federalize
feminize
fertilize
fictionalize
finalize
fireflies
fisheyes
fletcherize
flies
flybys
focalize
formalize
fortifies

fossilize
franchise
fraternize
fries
fructifies
full-size
gadflies
galvanize
gelatinize
Geminis
generalize
ghettoize
glamorize
glamourize
globalize
glorifies
goodbyes
goodbys
gormandize
gothicize
gratifies
guise
guys
harmonize
high-rise
highs
hogties
homogenize
homologize
horrifies
horseflies
hospitalize
houseflies
humanize
humidifies
hybridize
hydrolyze
hypersensitize
hypnotise
hypnotize

hyposensitize
hypothesize
hysterectomize
idealize
identifies
ideologize
idolize
immobilize
immortalize
immunize
impersonalize
implies
improvise
incise
indemnifies
individualize
industrialize
initialize
intellectualize
intensifies
internalize
iodize
ionize
italicize
itemize
jargonize
jeopardize
journalize
justifies
keratinize
lanais
leastwise
legalize
legitimatize
legitimize
lengthwise
Levis
liberalize
libidinize
lies

life-size
lignifies
likewise
lionize
liquefies
liquidize
listerize
lobotomize
localize
lullabies
luteinize
lyes
lyse
macadamize
magis
magnetize
magnifies
magpies
marbleize
marketwise
masculinize
materialize
maximize
mayflies
mechanize
melanize
memorialize
memorize
mercerize
merchandise
merchandize
mesmerize
metabolize
metastasize
methodize
metricize
midsize
militarize
mineralize
miniaturize

minimize	ostracize	photolyze
misadvise	otherwise	photosensitize
misapplies	outcries	photosynthesize
mobilize	outsize	pies
modernize	overanalyze	pigsties
modifies	overbuys	plagiarize
moisturize	overcapitalize	plasticize
mollifies	overdiversifies	plies
monetize	overdramatize	pluralize
monopolize	overemphasize	polarize
moonrise	overexercise	politicize
moralize	overflies	polymerize
mortifies	overgeneralize	popularize
motorize	overindustrialize	potpies
multiplies	overlies	preoccupies
mummifies	oversimplifies	pressurize
mystifies	oversize	pries
narcotize	overspecialize	privatize
nasalize	oversupplies	prize
nationalize	oxidize	professionalize
naturalize	ozonize	propagandize
nebulize	pacifies	prophesies
neckties	paganize	proselytize
necrotize	pagesize	psychoanalyze
nesslerize	paralyse	psychologize
neurologize	paralyze	publicize
neutralize	parenthesize	pulverize
nicotinize	particularize	purifies
nitrogenize	pasteurize	putrefies
normalize	patronize	qualifies
notarize	pauperize	quantifies
notifies	pelletize	rabbis
novelize	penalize	radicalize
nowise	penny-wise	ramifies
nullifies	peptonize	randomize
occupies	peritonize	rarefies
opsonize	personalize	rationalize
optimize	personifies	realize
organize	petrifies	rebaptize
ossifies	philosophize	reclassifies

recognize
recolonize
rectifies
redyes
reemphasize
refortifies
refries
regularize
reharmonize
relies
remilitarize
remise
remodifies
remonetize
renotifies
reoccupies
reorganize
replies
reprise
reunifies
reutilize
revise
revitalize
revivifies
revolutionize
rhapsodize
rise
ritualize
robotize
romanize
romanticize
routinize
rubberize
sacrifice
sanctifies
sanitize
satirize
satisfies
saucerize
scandalize

schismatize
scrutinise
scrutinize
sectionize
secularize
sensationalize
sensitize
sensualize
sentimentalize
serialize
sermonize
sexualize
shanghais
shies
sighs
signalize
signifies
simonize
simplifies
size
skies
slantwise
slenderize
socialize
sodomize
solarize
solemnize
solidifies
soliloquize
Sovietize
specialize
specifies
spies
stabilize
standardize
standbys
sterilize
sties
stigmatize
stratifies

streetwise
stultifies
stupefies
stylize
subclassifies
subsidize
sulfurize
sulphurize
summarize
sunrise
supervise
supplies
surmise
surprise
syllabifies
symbolize
sympathize
synchronize
synopsize
synthesize
syphilize
systematize
systemize
tantalize
televise
temporize
tenderize
terrifies
terrorize
testifies
theorize
thighs
ties
totalize
tracheotomize
traditionalize
tranquilize
tranquillize
transistorize
traumatize

tries
typifies
tyrannize
underlies
undersize
unifies
unionize
unitize
unties
unwise
urbanize
utilize
valorize
vandalize
vaporize
vasectomize
verbalize
verifies
vernalize
versifies
victimize
vilifies
virilize
visualize
vitalize
vitaminize
vitrifies
vivifies
vocalize
volatilize
vulcanize
vulgarize
walleyes
weatherize
weatherwise
westernize
whys
winterize
wise
womanize

IS
biz
Cadiz
fizz
gin fizz
friz
his
is
Liz
ms
phiz
quiz
show biz
'tis
whiz

ISM
abolitionism
absenteeism
absolutism
abstractionism
accustom
activism
ad-infinitum
ad-nauseum
Adam
addendum
adventuresome
agendum
agnosticism
alarmism
albinoism
album
alcoholism
algorithm
altruism
alum
aluminum
amalgam
amateurism

Anabaptism
anabolism
anachronism
anarchism
aneurism
aneurysm
angiospasm
Anglicanism
Anglicism
angstrom
animalism
animism
antagonism
antebellum
antemortem
anthem
anum
aphorism
aquarium
arboretum
archaism
asceticism
ashram
asphaltum
astigmatism
asylum
atheism
atom
atomism
atrium
auditorium
authoritarianism
autism
autumn
awesome
axiom
baalim
bacterium
balsam
bantam

baptism
barbarianism
barbarism
barium
basidium
bdellium
become
bedlam
behaviorism
Belgium
benumb
betacism
biculturalism
biennium
bioplasm
biorhythm
biracialism
birchism
bisexualism
blithesome
blossom
bolshevism
bonum
boredom
bosom
bossism
bothersome
bottom
botulism
Brahmanism
Brahminism
briticism
brougham
Buddhism
bum
burdensome
bureaucratism
buxom
Byzantium
cabalism

cadmium
Caesarism
calcium
Calvinism
cameralism
canadianism
candelabrum
cannibalism
cannonism
capitalism
capsicum
cardamom
cardiospasm
cartelism
cartesianism
cataclysm
Catholicism
centralism
centroplasm
centrum
cerebellum
cerebrum
ceremonialism
chasm
chauvinism
cherubim
chiasm
chloralism
Christendom
chromium
chrysanthemum
chum
circum
classicalism
classicism
coliseum
collectivism
colloquialism
colloquium
colonialism

colosseum
colostrum
column
come
commercialism
communalism
communism
compendium
condom
condominium
conformism
Confucianism
congregationalism
conservationism
conservatism
consortium
constructionism
consumerism
continuum
conundrum
conventionalism
cosmopolitanism
cranium
crematorium
cretinism
criminalism
criterium
criticism
crowism
crumb
cubism
cuddlesome
cultism
cumbersome
curriculum
custom
cynicism
cytoplasm
czardom
czarism

Dadaism
dandyism
darksome
Darwinism
datum
decentralism
decorum
defeatism
defluvium
deism
delightsome
delirium
democratism
denim
desideratum
despotism
determinism
dictum
didacticism
diem
dilettantism
dimorphism
dogmatism
dorsum
druidism
drum
dualism
dukedom
dumb
dumdum
dwarfism
dynamism
eardrum
earldom
eclecticism
ecosystem
ecumenicalism
Ecumenicism
ecumenism
edam

effluvium
egalitarianism
egocentrism
egoism
egotism
ejaculum
electromagnetism
elitism
elysium
emblem
emotionalism
empiricism
emporium
endomorphism
enthusiasm
environmentalism
epsom
equestrianism
equilibrium
ergotism
eroticism
erotism
erratum
escapism
eunuchism
euphemism
evangelicalism
evangelism
evolutionism
exhibitionism
existentialism
exorcism
exoticism
expansionism
expressionism
externalism
extremism
fabianism
factionalism
factum

fanaticism
fandom
fantom
fascism
fastidium
fatalism
fathom
favoritism
fearsome
federalism
feminism
fetichism
fetishism
feudalism
filesystem
filmdom
flavorsome
fletcherism
flotsam
formalism
forum
foursome
fraternalism
freedom
freudianism
frolicsome
fulcrum
fundamentalism
futurism
gallicism
gallium
galvanism
gamesome
gangsterism
gargoylism
geomagnetism
geranium
giantism
gigantism
gingham

gladsome	hooliganism	labialism
gleesome	hum	labium
globalism	humanism	labrum
glum	humanitarianism	lamaism
gothicism	humdrum	landlordism
graham	hybridism	leftism
grandam	hypnotism	legalism
grewsome	hypochondrium	leninism
gruesome	hypothyroidism	lesbianism
gum	iconoclasm	liberalism
gymnasium	idealism	libertarianism
gypsum	idiom	lightsome
handsome	ileum	lignum
hansom	ilium	linoleum
harem	imperialism	lissome
harlem	imperium	literalism
harmonium	impressionism	lithesome
Hasidim	income	lithium
Hasidism	indecorum	loathsome
heathendom	individualism	lobbyism
heathenism	industrialism	localism
hebraism	infantilism	locoism
hedonism	infinitum	logarithm
heliotropism	interim	lonesome
helium	internationalism	Lutheranism
hellenism	invalidism	lyceum
herbarium	iotacism	lyricism
heroinism	irksome	ma'am
heroism	ism	macadam
hierarchism	isomorphism	Machiavellianism
Hinduism	item	macrocosm
hippiedom	Jerusalem	madam
Hitlerism	jetsam	madame
ho-hum	jingoism	maelstrom
hobbism	journalism	magnesium
hokum	judaism	magnetism
holism	jugulum	magnum
hominem	kettledrum	malapropism
honorarium	kingdom	mannerism
hoodlum	klanism	manubrium

maoism
marjoram
martialism
martyrdom
marxism
masochism
materialism
maternalism
mausoleum
maxim
maximum
mechanism
meddlesome
medievalism
medium
melanism
memorandum
Mendelism
mesmerism
metabolism
metamorphism
meteorism
methodism
mettlesome
miasm
microcosm
middlebrowism
militarism
milium
millennium
minimum
misoneism
modem
modernism
modicum
momentum
monarchism
mongolianism
mongolism
monism

monochromatism
monomorphism
monosodium
monotheism
moralism
moratorium
mormonism
mortem
moslem
mum
museum
Muslim
mutism
mutualism
myocardium
mysticism
narcism
narcissism
nasturtium
nationalism
nativism
naturalism
nauseam
naziism
necessarium
necrophilism
negativism
neoclassicism
neologism
neoplasm
nepotism
neptunium
nettlesome
neutralism
nicotinism
nihilism
nobelium
noisome
nostrum
nudism

numb
oakum
obstructionism
occultism
odium
officialdom
officialism
oleum
olibanum
onanism
opium
opossum
opportunism
optimism
optimum
orem
organism
orgasm
osseum
ostium
ostracism
outcome
outswum
overburdensome
overcome
overoptimism
ovum
pablum
pacifism
paganism
palladium
paludism
pandemonium
panderism
panjandrum
pantheism
parallelism
paralogism
paramecium
parochialism

pastoralism
paternalism
patriotism
pauperism
pedestrianism
perfectionism
pessimism
petrolatum
petroleum
phantasm
phantom
phobism
phylum
pilgrim
plagiarism
planetarium
plasm
platinum
plenum
plum
plumb
pluralism
plutonium
pneumatism
podium
poem
pogrom
polymorphism
polytheism
positivism
possum
postmortem
postpartum
potassium
pragmatism
premium
prepartum
presbyterianism
presidium
prism

privatism
problem
professionalism
promethium
protectionism
protestantism
protoplasm
provincialism
psalterium
pseudoclassicism
psyllium
pugilism
purim
purism
Puritanism
quackism
quadrennium
quakerism
quantum
quarrelsome
quondam
quorum
racialism
racism
radicalism
radium
random
ransom
rationalism
realism
rebaptism
recidivism
rectum
referendum
relativism
republicanism
requiem
revisionism
rheumatism
rhotacism

rhumb
rhythm
robotism
romanticism
rostrum
rotacism
rowdyism
rum
ruralism
sachem
sacrum
sadism
saintdom
salem
sanatarium
sanatorium
sanctum
sanitarium
sanitorium
sapphism
sarcasm
satanism
Saturnism
scandium
schism
scrotum
scum
secularism
seldom
semitism
separatism
septum
serfdom
serum
sexism
shahdom
sheikdom
sheikhdom
sheriffdom
shintoism

signum	subsystem	tourism
sikhism	succumb	traditionalism
skepticism	sugarplum	traitorism
slalom	sum	transcendentalism
slum	summum	transom
socialism	superstardom	transvestism
sodium	surrealism	trillium
sodom	swum	trinitarianism
solarium	syllogism	trivium
solecism	symbolism	trophism
solemn	symposium	tropism
solipsism	symptom	troublesome
some	synchronism	truism
somnambulism	synergism	twosome
sophism	system	tympanum
sorghum	talcum	ultimatum
spasm	tandem	ultimum
specialism	tantalum	ultraism
spectrum	tantrum	unionism
speculum	Taoism	unsolemn
sphagnum	Tarantism	unwelcome
spiculum	tedium	unwholesome
spirillum	teetotalism	uranium
spoonerism	tenaculum	urbanism
sputum	terrarium	utopianism
stadium	terrorism	vagabondism
stagnum	theism	Valium
stalinism	theorem	vampirism
stardom	thraldom	vanadium
sternum	thralldom	vandalism
stigmatism	threesome	veganism
stoicism	thrum	vegetarianism
stratagem	thumb	velum
stratum	tiresome	venom
striatum	titanium	venturesome
strum	toilsome	verbatim
strychninism	tokenism	victim
subkingdom	toothsome	vinculum
subphylum	totalitarianism	virilism
substratum	totem	volcanism

volume

voodooism

voyeurism

vulcanism

vulgarism

wampum

wearisome

welcome

wholesome

whoredom

winsome

wisdom

witticism

wolfram

workaholism

worrisome

xiphisternum

xylem

yankeeism

yttrium

yum-yum

zionism

zirconium

Zoroastrianism

Long O

adagio

aero

aficionado

afro

afterglow

aglow

ago

airflow

Alamo

albino

allegro

aloe

alpenglow

also

although

alto

amigo

amino

ammo

andantino

Anglo

antihero

Apollo

apropos

Arapaho

archipelago

argot

armadillo

arpeggio

arrow

audio

auto

autogiro

avocado

backhoe

bandeau

banjo

barrow

basso

beau

bedfellow

beefalo

bellow

below

bestow

billow

bingo

bistro

blow

Boccaccio

bolero

bolo

bongo

Bordeaux

bordello

Borneo

borough

borrow

bow

bozo

braggadocio

Brando

bravado

bravo

bromo

bronco

bucko

buffalo

bunco

bungalow

bunko

bureau

burrito

burro

burrow

caballero

cacao

Cairo

calico

callow	deco	foe
calypso	depot	folio
cameo	desperado	follow
canto	dido	forego
cargo	Diego	foreknow
casino	diminuendo	foreshadow
Castro	dingo	forgo
cello	disco	fortissimo
centavo	ditto	Francisco
chateau	dodo	Franco
cheerio	doe	fresco
Chicago	domino	Fresno
Chicano	dough	Frisco
Chico	duo	fro
chino	dynamo	furlough
cigarillo	echo	furrow
cockcrow	ego	garbanzo
coco	elbow	Garbo
cocoa	embargo	gaucho
Colorado	embryo	gazebo
combo	ergo	gecko
commando	escargot	generalissimo
concerto	escrow	Gestapo
condo	escudo	ghetto
Congo	Eskimo	gigolo
contralto	Esperanto	ginkgo
cornrow	espresso	gizmo
cosmo	expo	glow
counterblow	fallow	go
counterflow	falsetto	gogo
credo	fandango	graffito
crescendo	farrow	grotto
crossbow	fellow	Groucho
crow	fiasco	grow
Crusoe	Filipino	gumbo
curio	flambeau	gung-ho
dado	flamenco	gusto
day-glo	flamingo	gyro
De-Soto	floe	hallo
deathblow	flow	hallow

halo	judo	manifesto
hammertoe	jumbo	Mao
handbarrow	Juneau	maraschino
Harpo	Juno	marrow
harrow	Junto	marshmallow
haymow	kayo	matzo
heave-ho	keno	mayo
hedgerow	kilo	meadow
heigh-ho	know	medico
hello	Kongo	mellow
hereinbelow	Kyoto	memento
hero	largo	memo
hippo	lasso	merino
ho	lavabo	mestizo
hobo	Leonardo	metro
hoe	libido	Mexico
hollow	libretto	Michelangelo
homo	lido	micro
honcho	limbo	Mikado
Hugo	limo	mimeo
hypo	lingo	minnow
Idaho	loco	mistletoe
imago	logo	Monaco
imbargo	longbow	mongo
impetigo	lotto	mono
impresario	low	Monroe
incognito	lumbago	Morocco
incommunicado	machismo	morrow
indigo	macho	mosquito
inferno	macro	motto
inflow	maestro	mow
info	Mafioso	mulatto
innuendo	magneto	mumbo
intermezzo	magnifico	mumbo-jumbo
jabot	maillot	mustachio
jato	malapropos	narrow
jell-o	mallow	nato
jingo	mambo	Navaho
joe	mango	Navajo

Negrito	piano	psycho
negro	Picasso	pueblo
Nero	piccolo	punctilio
no	picot	quo
no-no	pillow	radio
no-show	pimento	rainbow
nolo	pinko	ratio
nouveau	Pinocchio	reecho
nuncio	pinto	reflow
obbligato	pistachio	regrow
oboe	pizzicato	Reno
octavo	placebo	rhino
oh	Plano	Rio
Ohio	plateau	rococo
oleo	Plato	rodeo
Ontario	playfellow	roe
oratorio	plo	Romeo
oregano	plumbago	rouleau
Orlando	Pluto	Rousseau
Oslo	poco	row
Othello	Poe	Sacramento
outflow	polio	saddlebow
outgo	politburo	saguaro
outgrow	politico	sallow
overflow	polo	salvo
overgrow	pompano	Santiago
overshadow	poncho	scarecrow
overthrow	porno	scenario
owe	portfolio	scherzo
oxbow	portico	schizo
palmetto	portmanteau	schmo
palomino	potato	schmoe
patio	presidio	schoolfellow
pekoe	presto	Scirocco
perfecto	pro	Scorpio
peso	pronto	semipro
Peugeot	proviso	seraglio
pharaoh	provo	sew
photo	Proximo	shadow
pianissimo	pseudo	shako

shakos
shallow
shew
shinto
show
sideshow
silo
simpatico
sirocco
sloe
sloppy-joe
slow
snow
so
so-and-so
so-so
solfeggio
solidago
solo
sombrero
soprano
sorrow
sotto
sourdough
sow
sparrow
Speedo
staccato
status-quo
steno
stereo
stiletto
stoccado
stow
stucco
studio
subdepot
sumo
superego
swallow

tabasco
tableau
taco
tallow
tallyho
tangelo
tango
taro
telephoto
tempo
terrazzo
testudo
Texaco
tho
thorough
though
throe
throw
tick-tack-toe
tiptoe
tit-tat-toe
TKO
tobacco
toe
Tokyo
Toledo
tomato
tomorrow
tornado
Toronto
torpedo
torso
Toto
tow
tremolo
tricot
trio
trousseau
Trudeau
turbo

tuxedo
typo
tyro
UFO
ultimo
umbo
undergo
undertoe
undertow
unesco
uno
velcro
vertigo
veto
vibrato
video
virago
vireo
Virgo
virtuoso
volcano
wacko
wallow
weirdo
wheelbarrow
whoa
whoso
widow
willow
window
windrow
winnow
wino
wirephoto
woe
yellow
yo
yo-yo
zero
zucchetto

O (AH)

Arkansas
awe
blaw
bucksaw
bylaw
cat's-paw
caw
chaw
Chickasaw
claw
coleslaw
craw
draw
flaw
forepaw
foresaw
gewgaw
gnaw
grandma
grandpa
guffaw
hacksaw
handsaw
haw
heehaw
hurrah
jackdaw
jackstraw
jaw
jigsaw
jinrikisha
kickshaw
kumshaw
law
lockjaw
macaw
mackinaw
maw
outlaw

overawe
overdraw
oversaw
papaw
paw
pipsissewa
prelaw
pshaw
rah
raw
ricksha
rickshaw
ripsaw
saw
scofflaw
scrimshaw
seesaw
shah
shaw
slaw
southpaw
squaw
straw
taw
thaw
underdraw
unlaw
warsaw
whipsaw
williwaw
withdraw
yaw

Long OB

aerobe
anglophobe
bathrobe
claustrophobe
disrobe
earlobe

globe
heliophobe
lobe
microbe
probe
robe
strobe
wardrobe
xenophobe

OB

bedaub
blob
bob
cob
corncob
daub
doorknob
fob
glob
gob
heartthrob
hob
hobnob
job
kabob
kebab
knob
lob
macabre
mob
nabob
rob
slob
snob
sob
squab
swab
thingamabob
throb

Long OCH
approach
broach
brooch
coach
cockroach
encroach
loach
poach
reproach
roach
skycoach
stagecoach

OCH
blotch
botch
butterscotch
crotch
deathwatch
debauch
hopscotch
hotch
hotchpotch
klatch
klatsch
notch
Sasquatch
scotch
splotch
stopwatch
swatch
topnotch
watch
wristwatch

Long OD
a-la-mode
abode
anode

armload
bellowed
bestowed
billowed
bode
borrowed
bowed
buffaloed
burrowed
byroad
carload
caseload
cathode
code
commode
corrode
crossroad
crowed
decode
diode
discommode
echoed
eisteddfod
elbowed
electrode
embargoed
encode
episode
erode
explode
farrowed
flowed
followed
forbode
forebode
foreshadowed
freeload
furloughed
furrowed
geode

glowed
goad
hallowed
harrowed
highroad
hoed
hollowed
imbargoed
implode
incommode
inroad
joyrode
kayoed
lassoed
load
locoed
lode
lowed
manifestoed
mellowed
mimeoed
mode
mowed
mustachioed
narrowed
nematode
node
ode
off-load
outmode
overflowed
overload
overrode
overshadowed
owed
palinode
payload
pigeon-toed
pillowed
planeload

porticoed
radioed
railroad
reechoed
reflowed
reload
road
rode
rowed
sewed
shadowed
shewed
shipload
showed
slowed
snowed
soloed
sorrowed
sowed
spode
stowed
strode
stuccoed
swallowed
tangoed
tiptoed
toad
toed
torpedoed
towed
trainload
tramroad
trematode
triode
truckload
underload
unhallowed
unload
vetoed
wallowed

widowed
windowed
winnowed
woad
workload
yellowed
yod
zeroed

OD
abroad
applaud
arthropod
awed
baaed
bawd
broad
cawed
clawed
clod
cod
decapod
defraud
demigod
esplanade
facade
flawed
fraud
gnawed
god
goldenrod
guffawed
hawed
hexapod
hod
hotrod
hurrahed
jawed
jihad
laud

maraud
mod
nimrod
nod
odd
outlawed
overawed
pawed
plod
pod
pomade
prod
promenade
quad
quod
ramrod
riyadh
rod
roughshod
sawed
scrod
seedpod
seesawed
shod
slipshod
sod
squad
thawed
tie-rod
tightwad
tod
tripod
trod
unshod
untrod
wad
whipsawed
yawed

OFF
blastoff
boff
brush-off
castoff
Chekhov
coif
cough
cutoff
die-off
doff
drop-off
face-off
falloff
far-off
goof-off
handoff
hands-off
kickoff
knock-off
Korsakoff
layoff
liftoff
off
payoff
pick-off
pilaf
playoff
quaff
rip-off
runoff
scoff
sendoff
showoff
shutoff
spinoff
standoff
stroganoff
takeoff
tipoff

tradeoff
tough
turnoff
well-off
write-off

OFT
aloft
coughed
doffed
hayloft
loft
Microsoft
oft
quaffed
scoffed
soft
toft
waft

Long OG
brogue
drogue
pirogue
prorogue
rogue
vogue
yogh

OG
analog
analogue
apologue
backlog
befog
bird-dog
bog
bulldog
bullfrog
catalog

catalogue
clog
cog
decalogue
defog
demagogue
dialogue
dog
eggnog
epilogue
firedog
flog
fog
frog
grog
groundhog
hangdog
hedgehog
hog
homologue
hot-dog
jog
lapdog
leapfrog
log
Magog
monologue
nog
pedagogue
pettifog
polliwog
pollywog
Prague
prologue
sandhog
sheepdog
slog
smog
synagog
synagogue

tog
travelogue
unclog
underdog
watchdog
waterlog

OY

ahoy
alloy
annoy
bellboy
boy
buoy
busboy
carboy
choirboy
convoy
copyboy
corduroy
cowboy
coy
decoy
deploy
destroy
doughboy
employ
enjoy
envoy
Hanoi
highboy
hobbledehoy
houseboy
Illinois
Iroquois
joy
killjoy
lowboy
newsboy
octroy

overjoy
pageboy
paperboy
playboy
ploughboy
plowboy
ploy
poi
redeploy
reemploy
reenjoy
schoolboy
sepoy
soy
stableboy
Tinkertoy
Tolstoy
tomboy
toy
troy
viceroy

OID

adenoid
alkaloid
alloyed
android
annoyed
anthropoid
asteroid
avoid
bacteroid
buoyed
cancroid
carcinoid
cardioid
caucasoid
celluloid
conoid
convoyed

cretinoid
decoyed
dendroid
deployed
destroyed
devoid
discoid
ellipsoid
embryoid
employed
enjoyed
eunuchoid
Freud
hemorrhoid
hominoid
humanoid
hypothyroid
hysteroid
keloid
lymphoid
mastoid
metalloid
meteoroid
mongoloid
negroid
octroyed
overjoyed
paranoid
pellagroid
polaroid
redeployed
reemployed
reenjoyed
rheumatoid
sarcoid
schizoid
sesamoid
sigmoid
sinusoid
solenoid

sphenoid
spheroid
steroid
syphiloid
tabloid
thyroid
toxoid
toyed
trapezoid
tuberculoid
typhoid
unemployed
void
zincoid

OIL
airfoil
boil
boyle
broil
charbroil
coil
counterfoil
despoil
embroil
fencing foil
foil
gargoyle
gumboil
Hoyle
hydrofoil
moil
oil
parboil
preboil
quatrefoil
reboil
recoil
roil
soil

spoil
subsoil
tinfoil
toil
topsoil
trefoil
turmoil
uncoil

OIN
adjoin
coin
conjoin
Des Moines
disjoin
enjoin
essoin
groin
join
loin
purloin
quoin
recoin
rejoin
sirloin
subjoin
surrejoin
tenderloin

OINT
anoint
appoint
ballpoint
bluepoint
breakpoint
checkpoint
conjoint
counterpoint
disappoint
disjoint

endpoint
gunpoint
joint
midpoint
needlepoint
pinpoint
point
preappoint
standpoint
viewpoint

OIS
choice
devoice
invoice
Joyce
pro-choice
rejoice
unvoice
voice

OIST
foist
hoist
invoiced
joist
moist
rejoiced
unvoiced
voiced

OIT
adroit
Detroit
droit
exploit
maladroit
quoit

OIZ

alloys
annoys
bellboys
boys
buoys
busboys
carboys
convoys
copyboys
corduroys
counterpoise
cowboys
decoys
deploys
destroys
doughboys
employs
enjoys
envoys
equipoise
highboys
hobbledehoys
hoise
houseboys
joys
killjoys
lowboys
newsboys
noise
overjoys
pageboys
playboys
ploys
poise
redeploys
reemploys
reenjoys
schoolboys
tomboys

toys
turquoise
viceroys

OG (OZH, ODG)

barrage
camouflage
corsage
dislodge
dodge
garage
hodgepodge
lodge
massage
outdodge
sabotage
thermomassage

Long OK

artichoke
awoke
backstroke
baroque
bespoke
bloke
breaststroke
broke
chain-smoke
choke
cloak
coke
convoke
counterstroke
cowpoke
croak
downstroke
evoke
folk
gentlefolk
heartbroke

heatstroke
homefolk
housebroke
in-joke
invoke
joke
keystroke
kinfolk
kinsfolk
menfolk
oak
okeydoke
outspoke
outstroke
poke
polk
presoak
provoke
reawoke
reinvoke
revoke
sidestroke
slowpoke
smoke
soak
spoke
stoke
stroke
sunstroke
toque
townsfolk
tradesfolk
uncloak
unyoke
upstroke
woke
womenfolk
workfolk
yoke
yolk

OK
aftershock
airlock
alpenstock
antiknock
Babcock
bach
balk
Bangkok
beanstalk
bedrock
blalock
bloc
block
boardwalk
bock
burdock
buttstock
cakewalk
calk
catwalk
caulk
cellblock
chalk
chock
clock
cock
cognac
cornstalk
countershock
crock
crosswalk
deadlock
defrock
doc
dock
electroshock
epoch
fetlock
firelock

flintlock
floc
flock
forelock
frock
gamecock
gawk
goshawk
gridlock
gunlock
hammerlock
hawk
haycock
headlock
headstock
hemlock
hitchcock
hoc
hock
hollyhock
interlock
jaywalk
jock
kapok
knock
kulak
laughingstock
leafstalk
livestock
lock
locke
macaque
mach
matchlock
mock
mohawk
moonwalk
nighthawk
o'clock
oarlock

outwalk
overstock
padlock
peacock
penstock
petcock
photoshock
pibroch
pock
polack
poppycock
relock
rimrock
roadblock
rock
rootstock
rorschach
schlock
shamrock
sheepwalk
sheetrock
sherlock
shock
shoptalk
shuttlecock
shylock
sidewalk
skywalk
sleepwalk
Slovak
smock
sock
spacewalk
squawk
stalk
stock
stopcock
talk
ticktock
tomahawk

unblock
undock
unfrock
unlock
walk
warlock
weathercock
wedlock
windsock
wok
woodblock
woodcock

Long OKS
artichokes
backstrokes
blokes
breaststrokes
chokes
cloaks
coax
Cokes
convokes
cowpokes
croaks
downstrokes
evokes
folks
gentlefolks
heatstrokes
hoax
invokes
jokes
keystrokes
kinfolks
menfolks
oaks
pokes
presoaks
provokes

reinvokes
revokes
smokes
soaks
spokes
stokes
strokes
sunstrokes
toques
uncloaks
unyokes
upstrokes
yokes
yolks

OKS
alpenstocks
auks
balks
bandbox
beanstalks
blocks
blocs
boardwalks
boondocks
box
burdocks
cakewalks
catwalks
caulks
cellblocks
chalks
chatterbox
chocks
clocks
cocks
cognacs
cornstalks
cowpox
cox

crocks
crosswalks
deadlocks
deedbox
defrocks
docks
docs
electroshocks
equinox
fetlocks
firebox
flintlocks
flocks
forelocks
fox
frocks
gamecocks
gearbox
gunlocks
hammerlocks
hatbox
haycocks
headlocks
hemlocks
heterodox
hocks
hollyhocks
horsepox
hotbox
icebox
interlocks
jack-in-the-box
jocks
jukebox
knocks
knox
kulaks
laughingstocks
locks
lox

macaques
mailbox
matchlocks
mocks
mousepox
nonorthodox
oarlocks
orthodox
outbox
outfox
overstocks
ox
padlocks
paradox
peacocks
penstocks
pepperbox
phlox
pibrochs
pillbox
pocks
postbox
pox
roadblocks
rocks
rootstocks
saltbox
sandbox
shadowbox
shamrocks
shocks
shuttlecocks
shylocks
Slovaks
smallpox
smocks
snuffbox
soapbox
socks
sox

stocks
strongbox
sweatbox
ticktocks
tinderbox
toolbox
unfrocks
unlocks
unorthodox
vox
warlocks
weathercocks
windsocks
woks
woodblocks
woodcocks
Xerox

OKT
blocked
chocked
clocked
cocked
concoct
crocked
deadlocked
defrocked
docked
flocced
flocked
hocked
interlocked
knocked
landlocked
locked
mocked
overstocked
padlocked
pocked
rocked

shell-shocked
shocked
smocked
socked
stocked
unblocked
unfrocked
unlocked

Long OL
armhole
aureole
bankroll
bedroll
bowl
buttonhole
cajole
camisole
casserole
catchpole
charcoal
chuckhole
coal
Cole
condole
console
control
Creole
creosol
cresol
cubbyhole
decontrol
dole
enroll
escarole
extol
eyehole
fishbowl
flagpole
foal

foxhole
glycol
goal
hellhole
hole
indole
innersole
insole
jackroll
keyhole
kneehole
knoll
knothole
loophole
manhole
maypole
mole
mongol
oriole
parole
patrol
payroll
peephole
phenol
pigeonhole
pinhole
pistole
pole
poll
porthole
pothole
resole
ridgepole
rigmarole
role
roll
scroll
Seminole
shoal
sinkhole

sole
soul
steamroll
stole
stroll
tadpole
thumbhole
toll
troll
unroll
washbowl
whole
wormhole
Xylol

OL (ALL)
aerosol
alcohol
all
appall
awl
awol
ball
barbital
baseball
basketball
bawl
befall
biventral
blackball
brawl
call
camisole
cannonball
carryall
catcall
catchall
cholesterol
cobol
confrontal

cornball
coverall
crawl
cure-all
disenthrall
doll
downfall
drawl
drywall
enthrall
ethanol
eyeball
fall
fireball
football
footfall
forestall
gall
gasohol
gaul
Gaulle
goofball
hairball
hall
handball
hardball
haul
highball
icefall
install
knuckleball
landfall
loll
mal
mall
mannitol
maul
meatball
menthol
methanol

mistral

moll

Montreal

mothball

narwhal

Neanderthal

Nepal

nightfall

oddball

overall

overhaul

pall

parasol

pastorale

Paul

pawl

phenobarbital

pinball

pitfall

pratfall

protocol

Provencal

puffball

quetzal

racquetball

rainfall

recall

reinstall

riyal

rockfall

Saul

scrawl

screwball

seawall

shawl

shortfall

sidewall

small

snowball

snowfall

softball

sol

Sorbitol

spall

speedball

spitball

sprawl

squall

stall

stonewall

tall

tetherball

therewithal

thrall

trawl

volleyball

wall

waterfall

wherewithal

whitehall

whitewall

windfall

windgall

Xylitol

yawl

Long OLD

bankrolled

behold

billfold

blindfold

bold

bowled

buttonholed

cajoled

centerfold

cold

condoled

consoled

controlled

copyhold

decontrolled

doled

enfold

enrolled

extolled

fanfold

fivefold

foaled

fold

foothold

foretold

fourfold

freehold

gold

handhold

hold

holed

household

hundredfold

ice-cold

infold

leasehold

manifold

manyfold

marigold

mold

mould

old

outsold

overbold

oversold

paroled

patrolled

pigeonholed

pinfold

poled

polled

potholed

remold

resold
resoled
rolled
scold
scrolled
sheepfold
sold
soled
stone-cold
strolled
stronghold
tenfold
threefold
threshold
toehold
told
tolled
trolled
twofold
unconsoled
uncontrolled
undersold
unenrolled
unfold
unforetold
unpolled
unrolled
unsold
untold
uphold
withhold
wold

OLD
appalled
archibald
auld
bald
bawled
blackballed

brawled
called
cannonballed
catcalled
crawled
dolled
drawled
enthralled
forestalled
galled
hauled
installed
kobold
lolled
mauled
overhauled
palled
piebald
recalled
reinstalled
scald
scrawled
snowballed
so-called
sprawled
squalled
stalled
stonewalled
trawled
uncalled
walled

Long OLT
bolt
colt
dolt
holt
jolt
millivolt
molt

moult
poult
revolt
smolt
thunderbolt
unbolt
volt

OLTZ
assaults
defaults
desalts
exalts
faults
gestalts
halts
malts
oversalts
salts
schmaltz
schmalz
somersaults
vaults
waltz

OLVE
absolve
devolve
dissolve
evolve
involve
redissolve
reinvolve
resolve
revolve
solve

Long OM
aerodrome
airdrome

astrodome
catacomb
chrome
chromosome
cockscomb
comb
currycomb
dome
fluorochrome
foam
gastronome
genome
gnome
hippodrome
home
honeycomb
loam
lysosome
mercurochrome
metronome
monochrome
motordrome
myotome
nome
ohm
palindrome
prodrome
radome
recomb
roam
rome
shalom
styrofoam
syndrome
tome
whitecomb

OM
alm
aplomb

balm
becalm
bomb
calm
embalm
firebomb
from
genome
Guam
imam
intercom
Islam
maelstrom
mom
napalm
noncom
palm
pogrom
prom
psalm
qualm
salaam
sitcom
therefrom
Tom
Vietnam
wherefrom
wigwam
yom

OLM
alm
aplomb
balm
becalm
bomb
calm
embalm
firebomb
from

genome
guam
imam
intercom
islam
maelstrom
mom
napalm
noncom
palm
pogrom
prom
psalm
qualm
salaam
sitcom
therefrom
tom
vietnam
wherefrom
wigwam
yom

OMP
chomp
clomp
comp
pomp
romp
stomp
swamp
tromp
whomp

OMPT
chomp
clomp
pomp
romp
stomp

swamp
tromp
whomp

Long ON
acetone
aitchbone
allophone
alone
anklebone
atone
axone
backbone
baritone
bemoan
birthstone
bloodstone
blown
bone
breakbone
breastbone
brimstone
brownstone
capstone
chaperon
cheekbone
cherrystone
chinbone
clingstone
clone
cobblestone
collarbone
cologne
condone
cone
cornerstone
cortisone
crone
curbstone
cuttlebone

cyclone
depone
dethrone
dictaphone
disown
drone
earphone
enthrone
estrone
evzone
fieldstone
flagstone
flown
flyblown
foreknown
freestone
gallstone
gemstone
gladstone
gramophone
gravestone
grindstone
groan
grown
hailstone
halazone
halftone
headphone
headstone
hearthstone
herringbone
hipbone
holystone
homegrown
homophone
hone
hormone
hotzone
hydrazone
hydrophone

ingrown
intone
jawbone
joan
ketone
keystone
known
knucklebone
lactone
limestone
loadstone
loan
lone
marrowbone
megaphone
methadone
microphone
milestone
millstone
moan
monotone
moonstone
mown
oilstone
outgrown
outshone
overblown
overflown
overgrown
overthrown
overtone
own
ozone
peptone
phone
picturephone
pinbone
pone
postpone
progesterone

prone
pulpstone
radiophone
reloan
rezone
rhinestone
ringbone
roan
rotenone
sandstone
saxophone
scone
sewn
shinbone
shone
shown
silicone
soapstone
soupcon
sown
steppingstone
stone
tailbone
telephone
testosterone
thighbone
throne
thrown
tombstone
tone
touchstone
trombone
unbeknown
undertone
unknown
unmown
unsewn
vibraphone
whalebone
whetstone

windblown
wishbone
xanthone
xylophone
yellowstone
zone

ON
aeon
agamemnon
aileron
amazon
anon
argon
autobahn
awn
axon
Babylon
baton
begone
biathlon
biotron
bon
bonbon
bonn
bouillon
brawn
bygone
cabochon
caisson
canton
carillon
ceylon
chevron
chiffon
con
conn
coupon
crayon
cretonne

croissant
crouton
cyclotron
dacron
darvon
dawn
dead-on
decagon
decathlon
demijohn
denouement
divan
doggone
drawn
echelon
electron
eon
epsilon
Exxon
faun
fawn
foregone
forgone
freon
gone
heptagon
hereon
hereupon
hexagon
huron
icon
ion
John
Kahn
khan
krypton
lawn
leprechaun
lexicon
liaison

macron
marathon
marzipan
mastodon
merman
micron
millimicron
moron
neon
neuron
neutron
nucleon
nylon
octagon
omicron
on
orlon
overdrawn
oxymoron
pantheon
paragon
parmesan
Parthenon
pawn
pecan
pentagon
pentathlon
peon
phenomenon
photon
pion
piton
pluton
polygon
pompon
positron
prawn
predawn
prolegomenon
proton

pylon
python
radon
rayon
rubicon
Saigon
salon
sawn
schwann
scone
silicon
solon
soupcon
spawn
swan
symbion
Taiwan
talkathon
tampon
tarragon
taxon
teflon
telethon
thereon
thereupon
tisane
toucan
trigon
Tucson
underdrawn
undergone
upon
upsilon
walkathon
wan
whereon
whereupon
whipsawn
withdrawn
woebegone

xenon
yawn
yon
yuan
yukon
zircon

ONCH
conch
haunch
launch
paunch
stanch
staunch

OND
abscond
awned
beyond
blond
blonde
bond
conned
correspond
dawned
despond
doggoned
donned
fawned
fishpond
fond
frond
millpond
overfond
pawned
pond
respond
spawned
vagabond
wand

yawned

ONG
along
belong
bong
cong
cradlesong
ding-dong
diphthong
dong
erelong
furlong
gong
headlong
headstrong
hong
Hong Kong
King Kong
kong
lifelong
livelong
long
mahjongg
Mekong
nightlong
oblong
overlong
ping-pong
pong
prolong
prong
sarong
sidelong
sing-along
singsong
song
strong
tagalong
thong

throng
tong
Vietcong
wrong
yearlong

ONK
clonk
conk
honk
honky-tonk
plonk
tonk
zonk

ONS
Afrikaans
aunts
commandants
confidants
daunts
debutantes
detentes
dilettantes
flaunts
fonts
gallants
Hans
haunts
jaunts
nonce
nonchalance
nuance
omnipotence
reconnaissance
renaissance
response
restaurants
sconce
seance

subdebutantes
taunts
vaunts
vivants
wants

Long ONT
don't
won't
wont

ONT
avaunt
daunt
flaunt
gaunt
haunt
jaunt
taunt
vaunt
wont

Long ONZ
anklebones
atones
backbones
bemoans
birthstones
bloodstones
bones
breastbones
brownstones
capstones
chaperons
cheekbones
cherrystones
clingstones
clones
cobblestones
collarbones

colognes
condones
cones
cornerstones
crones
crossbones
curbstones
cuttlebones
cyclones
dethrones
dictaphones
disowns
drones
earphones
enthrones
evzones
flagstones
freestones
gallstones
gemstones
gramophones
gravestones
grindstones
groans
hailstones
halftones
headphones
headstones
hearthstones
herringbones
hipbones
holystones
homophones
hones
hormones
hydrophones
intones
jawbones
Jones
keystones

knucklebones
lazybones
limestones
loadstones
loans
marrowbones
megaphones
microphones
milestones
millstones
moans
monotones
moonstones
overtones
owns
phones
picturephones
pones
postpones
radiophones
reloans
rezones
sawbones
shinbones
silicones
soapstones
soupcons
steppingstones
stones
telephones
thighbones
thrones
tombstones
tones
touchstones
trombones
undertones
unknowns
vibraphones
whalebones

whetstones
wishbones
xylophones
zones

ONZ
aeons
Afrikaans
ailerons
amazons
autobahns
axons
biathlons
bonbons
bonze
bronze
bygones
cabochons
caissons
cantons
chevrons
cons
coupons
crayons
croissants
croutons
cyclotrons
dawns
decathlons
demijohns
divans
echelons
electrons
eons
fauns
fawns
hexagons
hurons
icons
ions

johns
khans
lawns
leprechauns
lexicons
liaisons
long-johns
macrons
marathons
mastodons
microns
morons
neurons
neutrons
nylons
octagons
pantheons
paragons
pecans
pentagons
pentathlons
peons
phenomenons
photons
pitons
polygons
pompons
pons
positrons
protons
pylons
pythons
rayons
soupcons
swans
tampons
telethons
toucans
zircons

ODD
adulthood
babyhood
bachelorhood
basswood
bentwood
boxwood
boyhood
brotherhood
brushwood
cedarwood
childhood
cottonwood
could
deadwood
dogwood
driftwood
falsehood
fatherhood
firewood
girlhood
glenwood
godhood
good
greasewood
gumwood
hardwood
heartwood
Hollywood
hood
ironwood
knighthood
likelihood
livelihood
lopwood
maidenhood
maidhood
manhood
misunderstood
monkshood

motherhood
nationhood
neighborhood
orphanhood
parenthood
pinewood
plywood
priesthood
pulpwood
redwood
rosewood
sainthood
sandalwood
sappanwood
sapwood
satinwood
selfhood
should
sisterhood
softwood
spinsterhood
statehood
stinkwood
stood
Talmud
unclehood
understood
unlikelihood
widowerhood
widowhood
wifehood
withstood
womanhood
wood
wormwood
would

OOD (as in feud, See *UD*)

OOK (as in uke, *See UK*)

OOK
book
bankbook
betook
bluebook
book
brook
buttonhook
caoutchouc
casebook
cashbook
chapbook
checkbook
chinook
cook
cookbook
copybook
crook
daybook
fishhook
forsook
gobbledygook
gook
guidebook
handbook
hook
hornbook
hymnbook
lawbook
logbook
look
matchbook
mistook
nainsook
nook
notebook
outlook

overbook
overcook
overlook
overtook
partook
passbook
playbook
pocketbook
pollbook
pothook
precook
promptbook
recook
redbook
rook
schnook
schoolbook
scrapbook
shook
sketchbook
songbook
storybook
studbook
stylebook
tenterhook
textbook
took
undercook
undertook
unhook
wordbook
workbook
yearbook

OOL (as in cool)
barstool
campstool
car-pool
cesspool
cool

cruel
drool
fool
footstool
fuel
ghoul
globule
gruel
ligule
Liverpool
lunule
macule
majuscule
mewl
minuscule
module
molecule
mule
nodule
overcool
overrule
pilule
pool
preschool
refuel
retool
ridicule
rule
saccule
school
spicule
spool
stool
subrule
synfuel
toadstool
tool
uncool
vestibule

virgule
water-cool
whirlpool
you'll
yule

OOT
acre-foot
afoot
barefoot
bigfoot
blackfoot
bloodroot
clubfoot
crowfoot
crows-foot
flatfoot
foot
forefoot
hotfoot
input
kaput
output
pussyfoot
put
root
snakeroot
soot
splayfoot
tenderfoot
throughput
thruput
underfoot
uproot
webfoot

Long OP
antelope
biomicroscope

bronchoscope
cantaloupe
chromoscope
cope
dope
electroscope
elope
envelope
fiberscope
fluoroscope
grope
gyroscope
heliotrope
hope
horoscope
interlope
isotope
kaleidoscope
kinescope
lope
microscope
misanthrope
mope
myope
nope
oscilloscope
periscope
pope
proctoscope
radarscope
radioisotope
radioscope
rope
scop
scope
skiascope
slope
sniperscope
soap
spectroscope

stereoscope
stethoscope
stope
stroboscope
taupe
telescope
thermoscope
tightrope
tope
towrope
trope
zootrope

OP
aesop
airdrop
atop
backdrop
backstop
bakeshop
barbershop
bellhop
blacktop
bookshop
bop
bricktop
bubbletop
carhop
cartop
chop
chop-chop
clip-clop
co-op
coin-op
cop
crop
dewdrop
doorstop
drop
eardrop

eavesdrop
flattop
flip-flop
flop
fop
gumdrop
hardtop
hedgehop
hilltop
hockshop
hop
housetop
joypop
lollipop
lollypop
lop
maintop
malaprop
milksop
mop
mountaintop
nonstop
outcrop
overtop
pawnshop
plop
pop
prop
raindrop
rooftop
scop
sharecrop
shop
shortstop
slop
snowdrop
sop
stop
strop
swap

sweatshop
sweet-shop
swop
table-hop
tabletop
tabstop
teardrop
tiptop
toedrop
top
treetop
turboprop
unstop
whistle-stop
whop
window-shop
wop
workshop
yawp

OR

abhor
adore
ambassador
amour
antiwar
anymore
ashore
bailor
Baltimore
bedsore
before
boar
bookstore
boor
bore
boudoir
brochure
brontosaur
carnivore

centaur
claymore
cocksure
coinsure
commodore
condor
conquistador
contour
core
corps
corridor
cure
cuspidor
decor
deplore
dinosaur
door
door-to-door
downpour
drawer
drugstore
eleanor
encore
entrepreneur
evermore
exospore
explore
eyesore
Fillmore
floor
fluor
folklore
footsore
for
fore
foreshore
foreswore
forevermore
forswore
four

fourscore
furthermore
galore
gore
hardcore
heartsore
hellebore
herbivore
hereinbefore
heretofore
hoar
ignore
implore
indoor
inshore
Labrador
lessor
lore
matador
mentor
metaphor
meteor
minotaur
moor
more
nevermore
nor
o'er
oar
obligor
offshore
onshore
oospore
or
ore
outdoor
outpour
outscore
outwore
overbore

overinsure
pinafore
pompadour
poor
pore
postwar
pour
prescore
prewar
promisor
provacateur
prowar
rancor
rapport
reassure
reservoir
restore
roar
Salvador
savior
saviour
score
seashore
semaphore
senor
servitor
shore
signor
Singapore
snore
soar
sophomore
sopor
sore
spoor
spore
stegosaur
stentor
stevedore
store

stridor
subfloor
sublessor
sure
swore
sycamore
therefor
therefore
thereinbefore
theretofore
thor
threescore
tore
toreador
tour
troubadour
two-by-four
tyrannosaur
underscore
uproar
war
wherefor
wherefore
whore
wore
yore
zoospore
zygospore

ORB
absorb
orb
reabsorb

ORCH
blowtorch
porch
scorch
torch

ORD
abhorred
aboard
aboveboard
accord
adored
afford
backboard
baseboard
billboard
blackboard
board
bored
breadboard
broadsword
buckboard
cardboard
centerboard
chalkboard
checkerboard
chessboard
chipboard
chord
clavichord
clipboard
coinsured
concord
contoured
cord
cored
corkboard
cured
dashboard
deplored
discord
duckboard
explored
fiberboard
fingerboard
fiord

fjord
floorboard
floored
footboard
ford
freeboard
gored
gourd
gourde
hardboard
harpsichord
headboard
highboard
hoard
hord
horde
ignored
implored
inboard
keyboard
landlord
lapboard
lord
moldboard
moored
mortarboard
notochord
oared
outboard
outscored
overassured
overboard
overinsured
overlord
paperboard
particleboard
pasteboard
pegboard
pinafored
plasterboard

pompadoured
pored
poured
prerecord
prescored
rancored
reassured
record
restored
roared
scoreboard
scored
seaboard
shipboard
shored
shuffleboard
sideboard
signboard
skateboard
slumlord
smorgasbord
snored
soared
soundboard
springboard
stevedored
stored
surfboard
switchboard
sword
tagboard
toured
toward
underscored
unexplored
unrestored
untoward
wallboard
warlord
warred

washboard
weatherboard
whipcord
whored

ORF
Orff
dwarf
wharf

ORJ
disgorge
engorge
forge
George
gorge
reforge

ORK
cork
fork
hayfork
pitchfork
pork
stork
torque
uncork
york

ORM
barnstorm
brainstorm
chloroform
conform
cruciform
cuneiform
deform
dendriform
dentiform
dorm

ensiform
firestorm
form
freeform
hailstorm
inform
landform
linguiform
lukewarm
microform
misinform
misperform
multiform
norm
outperform
perform
pisiform
platform
preform
prewarm
puriform
rainstorm
reform
reinform
reniform
sandstorm
scutiform
snowstorm
stelliform
storm
styliform
swarm
thunderstorm
transform
uniform
warm
whipworm
windstorm

ORN
acorn
adorn
airborne
alpenhorn
baseborn
bighorn
blackthorn
born
borne
buckthorn
bullhorn
Capricorn
careworn
corn
Dearborn
dehorn
firstborn
foghorn
forborne
foreign-born
foresworn
forewarn
forlorn
forsworn
forworn
freeborn
greenhorn
hawthorn
Hawthorne
highborn
horn
inborn
inkhorn
leghorn
longhorn
lorn
lovelorn
lowborn
morn

mourn
newborn
outworn
overborne
peppercorn
popcorn
porn
pronghorn
reborn
scorn
seaborne
shoehorn
shopworn
shorn
shorthorn
soilborne
stillborn
suborn
sworn
thorn
timeworn
tinhorn
torn
tricorn
twinborn
unborn
unicorn
unshorn
unsworn
unworn
warn
waterborne
wayworn
weatherworn
well-worn
wellborn
worn

ORPS
corpse

thorps
warps

ORS
charley-horse
clotheshorse
coarse
cockhorse
concourse
course
deforce
discourse
divorce
endorse
enforce
force
gorse
hoarse
hobbyhorse
horse
indorse
intercourse
morse
norse
packhorse
perforce
racecourse
racehorse
recourse
reenforce
reinforce
remorse
resource
sawhorse
seahorse
source
telecourse
unhorse
warhorse
watercourse

whitehorse
workhorse

ORT
abort
airport
assort
backcourt
beaufort
bort
bridgeport
carport
cavort
cohort
consort
contort
court
davenport
deport
distort
escort
exhort
export
extort
forecourt
fort
heliport
import
jetport
lawcourt
missort
Newport
passport
port
purport
quart
report
resort
retort
seaport

short
snort
sort
spaceport
spoilsport
sport
support
swart
thwart
tort
torte
transport
wart
worrywart

ORTH
forth
fourth
henceforth
north
orth
thenceforth

ORTS
aborts
airports
assorts
carports
cavorts
cohorts
consorts
contorts
courts
davenports
deports
distorts
escorts
exhorts
exports
extorts

forts
heliports
imports
jetports
missorts
passports
ports
purports
quarts
quartz
reports
resorts
retorts
seaports
shorts
snorts
sorts
spoilsports
sports
supports
thwarts
torts
transports
undershorts
warts
worrywarts

ORZ
abhors
adores
bailors
bedsores
boars
bookstores
boors
boudoirs
brontosaurs
carnivores
centaurs
claymores

commodores
condors
conquistadors
contours
cores
corridors
cuspidors
deplores
dinosaurs
doors
downpours
drawers
drugstores
encores
explores
eyesores
floors
fours
gores
hellebores
herbivores
ignores
implores
indoors
lessors
matadors
memoir
memoirs
mentors
metaphors
moors
oars
ores
outdoors
outscores
overinsures
pinafores
pompadours
pores
prescores

reassures
restores
roars
seashores
semaphores
shores
snores
soars
sophomores
sores
spoors
spores
stegosaurs
stevedores
stores
subfloors
sycamores
toreadors
tours
troubadours
tyrannosaurs
underscores
uproars
wars
whores
yours

Long OS
adios
Barbados
bellicose
boroughs
cellulose
close
comatose
cosmos
dextrose
diagnose
dose
engross

eros
erose
fructose
glucose
grandiose
gross
jocose
ketose
kudos
lactose
Laos
logos
maltose
megadose
misdiagnose
morose
nodose
overdose
pappose
pathos
plumose
raffinose
ramose
rimose
saccharose
sclerose
spinose
sucrose
tiros
varicose
verbose
viscose
xylose

OS
across
albatross
applesauce
backcross
boss

crisscross
cross
dos
doss
double-cross
dross
emboss
ethos
floss
gloss
lacrosse
logos
loss
madras
moss
motocross
pathos
recross
rhinoceros
ringtoss
sauce
semigloss
toss
uncross

OSH
bosh
frosh
galosh
gosh
goulash
Josh
kibosh
mackintosh
panache
posh
quash
slosh
squash

OSK
bosk
kiosk
mosque

Long OST
aftermost
almost
bedpost
boast
bottommost
centermost
coast
coast-to-coast
compost
diagnosed
doorpost
dosed
easternmost
endmost
engrossed
farthermost
fencepost
foremost
furthermost
gatepost
ghost
goalpost
grossed
guidepost
headmost
hindmost
hithermost
host
inmost
innermost
lamppost
lowermost
middlemost
midmost

milepost
milquetoast
misdiagnosed
most
nethermost
northernmost
outboast
outermost
outpost
overdosed
overroast
post
provost
rearmost
riposte
roast
sclerosed
seacoast
signpost
southernmost
toast
topmost
undermost
upmost
uppermost
utmost
uttermost
varicosed
westernmost

OST
accost
bossed
cost
crisscrossed
crossed
defrost
embossed
exhaust
flossed

frost
glossed
hoarfrost
holocaust
lost
pentecost
permafrost
sauced
star-crossed
tossed
uncrossed

Long OT
afloat
anecdote
antidote
banknote
bareboat
billy-goat
bloat
boat
canalboat
coat
connote
cote
coyote
creosote
cutthroat
demote
denote
devote
dote
dreamboat
emote
endnote
ferryboat
fireboat
flatboat
float
foldboat

footnote
garrote
ghostwrote
gloat
goat
groat
gunboat
handwrote
headnote
homozygote
houseboat
housecoat
iceboat
keynote
lifeboat
longboat
misquote
moat
mote
motorboat
note
oat
outvote
overcoat
petticoat
powerboat
promote
quote
raincoat
redcoat
remote
rewrote
rote
rowboat
sailboat
scapegoat
shoat
showboat
smote
speedboat

steamboat
stoat
sugarcoat
sukkoth
surcoat
tailcoat
throat
topcoat
tote
towboat
tugboat
turncoat
typewrote
undercoat
underwrote
unquote
vote
wainscot
waistcoat
whaleboat
woodnote
wrote
zygote

OT

aeronaut
aforethought
afterthought
allot
apricot
aquanaut
ascot
astronaut
aught
begot
besot
besought
bethought
big-shot
bloodshot

blot
bought
bowknot
boycott
brought
buckshot
bullshot
cachepot
camelot
cannot
carlot
caught
clot
coffeepot
cosmonaut
cot
counterplot
crackpot
culotte
dashpot
dogtrot
dot
earshot
eyeshot
feedlot
fiat
fleshpot
flowerpot
forethought
forget-me-not
forgot
fought
foxtrot
fusspot
garrote
gavotte
ghat
got
grapeshot
grassplot

grot
gunshot
handwrought
hardbought
have-not
hot
hotchpot
hotshot
hottentot
huguenot
inkblot
jackpot
jot
kilowatt
knot
kumquat
Lancelot
lot
marplot
mascot
moonshot
naught
nightspot
not
nought
oceanaut
ocelot
ought
outfought
outlot
overshot
peridot
plot
polka-dot
polyglot
pot
potshot
pott
reallot
robot

rot
sandlot
scot
scott
sexpot
shallot
shot
slingshot
slipknot
slot
snapshot
snot
somewhat
sot
sought
spot
squat
stinkpot
subplot
sunspot
swat
teapot
thought
tommyrot
topknot
tot
trot
troubleshot
undershot
unsought
unthought
upshot
wainscot
watt
whatnot
woodlot
yacht

Long OTHE
betroth

clothe
loath
loathe
unclothe

Long OTH
betroth
both
growth
ingrowth
loath
oath
outgrowth
overgrowth
quoth
troth
undergrowth

OTH
Behemoth
betroth
breechcloth
broadcloth
broth
cheesecloth
cloth
dishcloth
doth
froth
goth
haircloth
loincloth
moth
oilcloth
Ostrogoth
sackcloth
saddlecloth
sailcloth
sloth
swath

tablecloth
troth
Visigoth
washcloth
wroth

OU
allow
anyhow
avow
bough
bow
bowwow
brow
cacao
carabao
chow
ciao
cow
disallow
disavow
dow
endow
eyebrow
Foochow
frau
Hankow
hausfrau
highbrow
hoosegow
how
know-how
kowtow
landau
lowbrow
luau
meow
miaow
middlebrow
Moscow

nohow
now
plough
plow
pow
powwow
prow
reavow
reendow
row
scow
slough
snowplow
somehow
Soochow
sough
sow
Tao
thou
vow
wow

OUCH
avouch
couch
crouch
debouch
grouch
ouch
pouch
slouch
vouch

OUD
allowed
aloud
avowed
becloud
bowed
cloud

cowed
crowd
disallowed
disavowed
endowed
enshroud
kowtowed
loud
meowed
miaowed
overcloud
overcrowd
overproud
plowed
proud
reavowed
reendowed
rowed
shroud
soughed
thundercloud
unallowed
unavowed
unplowed
unvowed
vowed
wowed

OUND
abound
aboveground
aground
around
astound
background
battleground
bloodhound
bound
browned
buckhound

campground
chowhound
clothbound
clowned
compound
confound
coonhound
crowned
deerhound
downed
drowned
dumbfound
dumfound
earthbound
eastbound
elkhound
expound
fairground
fogbound
foreground
found
foxhound
frowned
go-around
greyhound
ground
hardbound
hellhound
hidebound
homebound
hoofbound
horehound
hound
housebound
icebound
impound
inbound
ironbound
merry-go-round
mound

musclebound
newfound
northbound
outbound
overabound
playground
pound
profound
propound
rebound
renowned
resound
rewound
rock-bound
round
runaround
runround
snowbound
softbound
sound
southbound
spellbound
stone-ground
stormbound
surround
turnaround
ultrasound
unbound
uncrowned
underground
unrenowned
unsound
weatherbound
well-found
westbound
wolfhound
wound
wraparound

OUNJ
lounge
scrounge

OUNS
announce
bounce
denounce
enounce
flounce
fluidounce
jounce
mispronounce
ounce
pounce
preannounce
pronounce
renounce
trounce

OUNT
account
amount
count
demount
discount
dismount
fount
miscount
mount
paramount
recount
remount
surmount
tantamount
viscount

OUR
devour
dour

dower
flower
hour
our
passionflower
scour
sour
sweet-and-sour
wildflower

OUS
alehouse
almshouse
backhouse
bathhouse
birdhouse
blockhouse
blouse
boardinghouse
bunkhouse
cathouse
chophouse
clearinghouse
clubhouse
coffeehouse
courthouse
customhouse
customshouse
delouse
doghouse
dollhouse
dormouse
douse
espouse
farmhouse
firehouse
flophouse
gashouse
glasshouse
greenhouse

grouse
guardhouse
henhouse
hothouse
house
icehouse
jailhouse
lighthouse
louse
madhouse
meetinghouse
mouse
nuthouse
outhouse
packinghouse
penthouse
pilothouse
playhouse
poorhouse
porterhouse
powerhouse
roadhouse
roughhouse
roundhouse
schoolhouse
slaughterhouse
smokehouse
souse
spouse
statehouse
storehouse
Strauss
sugarhouse
summerhouse
teahouse
titmouse
tollhouse
toolhouse
warehouse
waterhouse

westinghouse
whorehouse
workhouse

OUST
bloused
deloused
doused
Faust
groused
joust
loused
moused
oust
roust
soused

OUT
about
bailout
blackout
blowout
bout
breakout
brownout
burn-out
burnout
carryout
checkout
closeout
clout
cookout
copout
cutout
devout
doubt
dropout
drought
dugout
fade-out

fallout
far-out
farmout
flameout
flout
foldout
force-out
freakout
gadabout
gout
grayout
grout
handout
hangout
hereabout
hideout
holdout
knockabout
knockout
knout
kraut
layout
lights-out
lockout
lookout
lout
out
outshout
payout
phaseout
pitchout
pout
printout
pullout
punch-out
putout
readout
rollout
roundabout
roustabout

rout
route
runabout
sauerkraut
scout
sellout
shareout
shootout
shout
shutout
sickout
snout
spout
sprout
stakeout
standout
stout
strikeout
takeout
thereabout
thereout
throughout
timeout
tout
trout
tryout
turnabout
turnout
walkabout
walkout
washout
waterspout
whereabout
whiteout
wipeout
without
workout
worn-out

Long OV
alcove
By Jove
clove
cove
drove
grove
interwove
Jove
mangrove
mauve
rewove
rove
stove
strove
throve
trove
unwove
wove

OWL
afoul
befoul
cowl
disembowel
dishtowel
foul
fowl
growl
howl
jowl
owl
peafowl
prowl
scowl
vowel
waterfowl
wildfowl
yowl

OWN
acetone
aitchbone
allophone
alone
anklebone
atone
axone
backbone
baritone
bemoan
birthstone
bloodstone
blown
bone
breakbone
breastbone
brimstone
brownstone
capstone
chaperon
cheekbone
cherrystone
chinbone
clingstone
clone
cobblestone
collarbone
Cologne
condone
cone
cornerstone
cortisone
crone
curbstone
cuttlebone
cyclone
depone
dethrone
dictaphone

disown
drone
earphone
enthrone
estrone
evzone
fieldstone
flagstone
flown
flyblown
foreknown
freestone
gallstone
gemstone
gladstone
gramophone
gravestone
grindstone
groan
grown
hailstone
halazone
halftone
headphone
headstone
hearthstone
herringbone
hipbone
holystone
homegrown
homophone
hone
hormone
hotzone
hydrazone
hydrophone
ingrown
intone
jawbone
Joan

ketone
keystone
known
knucklebone
lactone
limestone
loadstone
loan
lone
marrowbone
megaphone
methadone
microphone
milestone
millstone
moan
monotone
moonstone
mown
oilstone
outgrown
outshone
overblown
overflown
overgrown
overthrown
overtone
own
ozone
peptone
phone
picturephone
pinbone
pone
postpone
progesterone
prone
pulpstone
radiophone
reloan

rezone
rhinestone
ringbone
roan
rotenone
sandstone
saxophone
scone
sewn
shinbone
shone
shown
silicone
soapstone
soupcon
sown
steppingstone
stone
tailbone
telephone
testosterone
thighbone
throne
thrown
tombstone
tone
touchstone
trombone
unbeknown
undertone
unknown
unmown
unsewn
vibraphone
whalebone
whetstone
windblown
wishbone
xanthone
xylophone

yellowstone
zone

Long OZ
adagios
aficionados
afros
afterglows
airflows
albinos
allegros
allhallows
aloes
altos
amigos
Anglos
antiheroes
appose
Arapahos
archipelagoes
archipelagos
argots
armadillos
arose
arpeggios
arrows
autogiros
autos
avocadoes
avocados
banjoes
banjos
barrows
beaus
bedclothes
bedfellows
bellows
bestows
billows
bingos

bistros
blows
bluenose
boleros
bongoes
bongos
bordellos
boroughs
borrows
bows
braggadocios
bravadoes
bravados
bravos
broncos
brownnose
buffaloes
buffalos
bulldoze
bullnose
buncos
bungalows
bureaus
burros
burroughs
burrows
caballeros
calicoes
calicos
calypsos
cameos
cantos
cargoes
cargos
casinos
cellos
chateaus
Chicanos
chose
cigarillos

close
combos
commandoes
commandos
compose
concertos
condos
contraltos
cornrows
credos
crescendos
crossbows
crows
curios
dadoes
dados
deathblows
decompose
demos
depose
depots
desperadoes
desperados
didoes
didos
diminuendos
dingoes
disclose
discompose
discos
dispose
dittoes
dittos
dodoes
dodos
dominoes
dominos
doze
duos
dynamos

echoes
egos
elbows
embargoes
embryos
enclose
escargots
escrows
escudos
Eskimos
espressos
expos
expose
falsettos
fandangos
farrows
fellows
fiascoes
fiascos
Filipinos
flambeaus
flamingoes
flamingos
floes
flows
foes
folios
follows
foreclose
foreknows
foreshadows
forgoes
frescoes
frescos
froze
furloughs
furrows
gallows
garbanzos
gauchos

gazeboes
gazebos
ghettoes
ghettos
gigolos
ginkgoes
gizmos
glows
goes
grottoes
grottos
grows
gumbos
gyros
hallos
hallows
haloes
halos
hammertoes
handbarrows
harrows
haymows
hellos
heroes
heros
hippos
hoboes
hobos
hoes
hollows
homos
honchos
hose
imagoes
imbargoes
impetigos
impose
impresarios
inclose
incognitos

indigoes
indigos
indispose
infernos
inflows
innuendoes
innuendos
intermezzos
jabots
jatos
jingoes
jumbos
juntos
juxtapose
kayos
ketose
kilos
knows
kudos
largos
lassoes
lassos
lavaboes
libidos
librettos
limbos
limos
lingoes
locoes
locos
lows
lumbagos
machos
maestros
magnetos
magnificoes
maillots
mallows
maltose
mambos

mangoes
mangos
manifestoes
manifestos
maraschinos
marrows
marshmallows
matzos
meadows
mellows
mementoes
mementos
memos
merinos
mestizoes
mestizos
mikados
mimeos
minnows
mistletoes
morrows
mosquitoes
mosquitos
mottoes
mottos
mows
mulattoes
mulattos
narrows
Navahoes
Navahos
Navajos
negroes
nightclothes
nodose
nose
nuncios
obbligatos
oboes
octavos

ohs
oppose
oratorios
oreganos
osmose
outflows
outgoes
outgrows
overexpose
overflows
overgrows
overshadows
overthrows
owes
oxbows
palmettoes
palmettos
palominos
pantyhose
patios
perfectos
pesos
pharaohs
photos
pianos
piccolos
picots
pillows
pimentos
pinkos
pintoes
pintos
pistachios
placebos
plainclothes
plateaus
playfellows
plumbagos
politicos
pompanos

ponchos
portfolios
porticoes
porticos
portmanteaus
pose
potatoes
predispose
preexpose
presuppose
primrose
propose
prose
provisoes
provisos
psychos
pueblos
radios
raffinose
rainbows
ratios
reechoes
refroze
reimpose
repose
rodeos
rose
rows
saccharose
salvos
scherzos
schizos
schmoes
sclerose
sews
shakos
shallows
shows
sideshows
silos

siroccos
slows
snows
solos
sombreros
sopranos
sorrows
sourdoughs
sows
sparrows
staccatos
stereos
stilettoes
stilettos
stows
stuccoes
stuccos
studios
subdepots
sucrose
superegos
superimpose
superpose
suppose
swallows
tableaus
tableaux
tacos
tangelos
tangos
taros
tempos
those
throes
throws
tiptoes
tobaccoes
tobaccos
toes
tomatoes

tornadoes
tornados
torpedoes
torsoes
torsos
tows
transpose
tremolos
tricots
trousseaus
tuxedos
typos
UFOs
underclothes
underexpose
undergoes
undertows
unfroze
vertigoes
vertigos
vetoes
vibratos
videos
viragoes
viragos
vireos
Virgos
virtuosos
viscose
volcanoes
wallows
weirdos
widows
willows
windows
windrows
winnows
winos
wirephotos
woes

xylose
yellows
zeroes
zeros
zucchettos

OZ
alohas
applause
awes
babas
because
blahs
bras
bucksaws
bylaws
cause
caws
chickasaws
chihuahuas
chippewas
choctaws
claus
clause
claws
craws
denouements
draws
flaws
forepaws
gauze
gewgaws
gnaws
grandmas
grandpas
guffaws
hacksaws
handsaws
haws
hooplas

hurrahs
jacarandas
jackdaws
jackstraws
jaws
jinrikishas
kickshaws
korunas
lamaze
laws
macaws
mackinaws
maws
menopause
omahas
outlaws
overawes
overdraws
Oz
papaws
pashas
pause
paws
rickshas
rickshaw
rickshaws
ripsaws
santa-claus
saws
seesaws
shahs
southpaws
spas
squaws
straws
subclause
taws
thaws
twas
vase

was
whipsaws
yaws

Long U

accrue	coup	hue
ACLU	crew	hugh
adieu	cuckoo	hullabaloo
ado	cue	igloo
ainu	curfew	imbue
Andrew	curlicue	impromptu
anew	debut	interview
argue	devalue	into
askew	dew	IOU
avenue	discontinue	issue
ballyhoo	do	jackscrew
bamboo	drew	Jew
bantu	due	jujitsu
barbecue	ensue	kangaroo
bayou	eschew	kazoo
beaucoup	ewe	kinkajou
bedew	few	knew
Bellevue	flew	kudzu
bestrew	flu	kung-fu
bijou	flue	lean-to
blew	fondue	lieu
blue	glue	lulu
boo	gnu	make-do
breakthrough	goo	Manchu
brew	grew	Manitou
btu	gumshoe	Mantoux
buckaroo	guru	marabou
bugaboo	haiku	menu
byu	hairdo	mew
canoe	hebrew	mildew
caribou	hereto	milieu
cashew	hereunto	misconstrue
chew	hew	miscue
clue	hindu	misdo
cockatoo	hitherto	moo
construe	honeydew	muumuu
continue	honolulu	nehru
coo	hoodoo	nephew
corkscrew	horseshoe	new
	how-to	onto

outdo
outgrew
overdo
overdrew
overdue
overflew
overgrew
overshoe
overthrew
overvalue
overview
pdq
peekaboo
Peru
pew
pooh
preview
purlieu
pursue
purview
queue
ragout
redo
reissue
rendezvous
renew
rescue
residue
retinue
revalue
revenue
review
revue
roughhew
rue
screw
see-through
shampoo
shoe
shoo

shrew
sinew
Sioux
skew
skiddoo
slew
slough
slue
snafu
snowshoe
spew
sprue
statue
stew
strew
subdue
sue
switcheroo
taboo
tatoo
tattoo
teleview
therethrough
thereto
thereunto
threw
through
thumbscrew
Timbuktu
tissue
to
tofu
too
true
tutu
two
undervalue
undo
undue
unglue

unscrew
unto
untrue
value
vendue
venue
view
virtu
virtue
Vshnu
voodoo
wahoo
waterloo
wherethrough
whereto
whereunto
whew
who
withdrew
woo
yahoo
yew
you
zebu
zoo
Zulu

Long UB
boob
cube
Danube
flashcube
flashtube
jujube
lube
rube
tube

UB
bathtub

Beelzebub
carob
cherub
chub
club
cub
drub
dub
flub
grub
grubb
hub
hubbub
Jacob
nightclub
nub
pub
rub
scrub
shrub
snub
stub
sub
tub
washtub

Long UCH
brooch
cooch
gooch
hooch
hootch
mooch
pooch
smooch

UCH
clutch
crutch
Dutch

hutch
inasmuch
insomuch
much
nonesuch
retouch
such
touch

Long UD
accrued
allude
altitude
amplitude
aptitude
argued
attitude
ballyhooed
barbecued
beatitude
bedewed
bestrewed
blued
booed
brewed
brood
canoed
certitude
chewed
clued
collude
conclude
construed
continued
cooed
corkscrewed
crude
cued
curfewed
definitude

delude
denude
devalued
discontinued
disquietude
dude
elude
ensued
eschewed
etude
exactitude
exclude
extrude
exude
feud
food
fortitude
glued
gratitude
hewed
hued
imbued
inaptitude
incertitude
include
ineptitude
infinitude
ingratitude
interlude
interviewed
intrude
issued
Jude
lassitude
latitude
lewd
longitude
magnitude
mewed
mildewed

misconstrued
miscued
mood
mooed
multitude
negritude
nude
obtrude
occlude
overvalued
platitude
plenitude
postlude
preclude
prelude
previewed
promptitude
protrude
prude
pulchritude
pursued
queued
quietude
rectitude
reissued
rendezvoused
renewed
rescued
retinued
retrude
revalued
revenued
reviewed
rood
roughhewed
rude
rued
screwed
seafood
seclude

seminude
servitude
shampooed
shoed
shooed
shrewd
similitude
skewed
sloughed
slued
snowshoed
solicitude
solitude
spewed
stewed
strewed
subdued
sued
tabooed
tattooed
transude
trued
turpitude
unaccrued
undervalued
unglued
unrenewed
unreviewed
unscrewed
unsubdued
unvalued
valued
verisimilitude
vicissitude
viewed
who'd
wooed
you'd

UD
blood
bud
cud
dud
flood
mud
scud
spud
stud
thud

UDZ
aphids
ballads
bloods
buds
cuds
duds
floods
methods
myriads
periods
rosebuds
scuds
soapsuds
spuds
studs
suds
thuds

Long UF
aloof
bombproof
bulletproof
burglarproof
childproof
crushproof
disproof
fireproof

flameproof
foolproof
germproof
goof
heatproof
holeproof
moistureproof
mothproof
poof
proof
rainproof
reproof
roof
rustproof
shatterproof
shockproof
soundproof
spoof
sunroof
theftproof
waterproof
weatherproof
wetproof
windproof
woof

UF
bluff
breadstuff
buff
cuff
dandruff
dyestuff
earmuff
enough
feedstuff
fisticuff
fluff
foodstuff
gruff

handcuff
huff
luff
muff
outbluff
overstuff
powder puff
puff
rebuff
rough
ruff
scruff
scuff
slough
sluff
snuff
sough
stuff
tough
tuff

UFT
bluffed
buffed
cuffed
fluffed
huffed
luffed
muffed
outbluffed
overstuffed
puffed
rebuffed
roughed
ruffed
scuffed
sloughed
snuffed
soughed
stuffed

tuft

UG
bedbug
bug
chug
debug
Doug
drug
dug
earplug
firebug
fireplug
hug
humbug
jitterbug
jug
ladybug
litterbug
lug
mealybug
mug
plug
pug
rug
shrug
shutterbug
slug
smug
snug
sparkplug
thug
tug
ugh
unplug

Long UJ
centrifuge
deluge

huge
refuge
rouge
scrooge
scrouge
stooge
subterfuge

UJ
adjudge
begrudge
budge
carnage
carriage
cleavage
coinage
drudge
forejudge
fudge
grudge
judge
misjudge
nudge
prejudge
sludge
smudge
trudge

Long UK
archduke
caoutchouc
duke
fluke
gobbledegook
gobbledygook
gook
Hexateauch
kook
luke
nuke

Pentateuch
puke
rebuke
spook
tuque
uke

UK
amok
amuck
awestruck
bannock
barrack
buck
bullock
buttock
Canuck
chuck
cluck
Donald Duck
duck
dumbstruck
epoch
eunuch
guck
habakkuk
haddock
hammock
hassock
havoc
hillock
horror-struck
huck
hummock
lame-duck
lubbock
luck
mattock
megabuck
moonstruck

motortruck
muck
mukluk
pluck
pollack
potluck
puck
roebuck
sawbuck
schmuck
shuck
snuck
stagestruck
struck
stuck
suck
sunstruck
thunderstruck
truck
tuck
tussock
unstuck
upchuck
woodchuck
yuck

UKS
aw-shucks
barracks
bucks
bullocks
buttocks
chucks
clucks
conflux
crux
deluxe
ducks
eunuchs
flux

haddocks
hammocks
hassocks
hillocks
hummocks
influx
instructs
knucks
lucks
lummox
lux
mattocks
misinstructs
motortrucks
mucks
mukluks
paddocks
plucks
pollacks
preinstructs
pucks
reconstructs
reflux
roebucks
shucks
stomachs
sucks
trucks
tucks
tussocks
tux
upchucks
woodchucks

UKT
abduct
aqueduct
bucked
byproduct
chucked

clucked
conduct
construct
deduct
destruct
ducked
duct
eruct
havocked
induct
instruct
lucked
malconduct
misconduct
misinstruct
mucked
obstruct
oviduct
plucked
preconstruct
preinstruct
product
reconstruct
shucked
subduct
sucked
tucked
untucked
upchucked
viaduct

Long UL
abacterial
abatable
abdicable
abdominal
abel
aberrational
able
abnormal

abolishable
abominable
aboriginal
abortional
abusable
abysmal
accentual
acceptable
accessible
accidental
accomplishable
accountable
accruable
accrual
accusable
accusal
accusatorial
achievable
acknowledgeable
acoustical
acquirable
acquittal
actable
actionable
actual
actuarial
adaptable
addable
addible
additional
adduceable
adducible
adenoidal
adhesional
adjectival
adjournal
adjustable
admirable
admiral
admissable

admissible
adoptable
adorable
adrenal
adverbial
advisable
aerial
aerodynamical
aeronautical
aesthetical
affable
affirmable
affixal
affordable
afunctional
agile
agreeable
agricultural
aisle
alchemical
allegeable
allegorical
allocable
allottable
allowable
alluvial
alphabetical
alterable
ambassadorial
ambisexual
amble
ambrosial
amenable
amendable
amiable
amicable
amoral
ample
amplifiable
anal

analogical
analytical
analyzable
anarchical
anatomical
ancestral
anecdotal
aneurismal
angel
angelical
anginal
angle
animal
ankle
annual
annul
answerable
antenatal
antennal
anthropical
anticlerical
antidotal
antisocial
antithetical
anvil
aortal
apical
apocalyptical
apocryphal
apolitical
apostle
apparel
appealable
appeasable
applaudable
apple
applicable
apposable
appraisal
appreciable

apprehensible
approachable
appropriable
approvable
approval
arable
arbitrable
arbitrational
arboreal
archaeological
archangel
archetypal
archetypical
architectural
areal
arguable
aristotle
arithmetical
armorial
arousal
arrayal
arrival
arsenal
arterial
artful
article
artificial
ascendable
ascertainable
ascribable
asexual
asocial
asphyxial
assailable
assemble
assessable
assignable
assimilable
assumable
asteroidal

astraddle
astronautical
astronomical
astrophysical
asymmetrical
atmospherical
atonal
atoneable
attachable
attainable
attemptable
attestable
attitudinal
attractable
attributable
attritional
atypical
audible
audiovisual
aural
auroral
austral
autumnal
available
avocational
avoidable
avowal
awful
axal
axial
axil
axle
axonal
babble
babel
bacterial
bactericidal
bacteriocidal
bacteriological
bacteroidal

baffle
bagel
bailable
baleful
ballottable
bamboozle
banal
baneful
bangle
bankable
baptismal
bare-knuckle
bargainable
barnacle
barometrical
baronial
barrel
basal
bashful
battle
bauble
beadle
beagle
bearable
beatable
beautiful
bedazzle
bedevil
bedraggle
beetle
befuddle
behavioral
bejewel
believable
belittle
bendable
beneficial
bengal
bequeathal
beryl

bespangle
besprinkle
bestial
bestowal
bethel
betrayal
betrothal
bevel
bi-level
biannual
bible
biblical
bibliographical
bicameral
bicaudal
bicentennial
bicipital
bicorporal
bicultural
bicycle
biddable
biennial
bifacial
bifocal
bilateral
bilingual
billable
bimanual
bimodal
binational
bindable
binomial
biochemical
biodegradable
bioelectrical
bioenvironmental
biogeographical
biographical
biological
biomaterial

biomedical
biophysical
biorbital
biotechnological
biparental
biparietal
bipedal
biracial
bisectional
bisexual
bitemporal
blamable
blameable
blameful
blissful
bluebottle
blushful
boastful
boatable
bobble
boggle
bondable
boodle
boondoggle
boreal
botanical
bottle
bountiful
bowel
bramble
brattle
breakable
breathable
bribable
bribeable
brickle
bridal
bridgeable
bridle
brindle

bristle
bristol
brittle
bronchial
brothel
brutal
bubble
buccal
buckle
bugle
bundle
bungle
burble
burgle
burial
burnable
bursal
bushel
bustle
cable
caboodle
cackle
cacuminal
caesural
calculable
calorimetrical
camel
cameral
Campbell
cancel
cancelable
cancellable
candle
cannibal
canonical
canticle
cantorial
capable
capital
capitol

capsule
caramel
carbuncle
cardinal
cardiological
careful
carnal
carnival
carol
carousel
carrel
cartable
carvel
castle
casual
cataclysmal
catechismal
categorical
cathedral
cattle
caudal
caudle
causal
celestial
censorable
censorial
censurable
centennial
central
centrifugal
cereal
cerebral
ceremonial
certifiable
cervical
changeable
channel
chapel
chargeable
charitable

chasmal
chattel
checkable
cheerful
chemical
chewable
chicle
chisel
chloral
choral
chordal
chortle
chronicle
chronological
chuckle
circle
circumstantial
circumventable
cisternal
citadel
civil
claimable
clarifiable
classical
classifiable
clausal
clavicle
cleanable
clearable
clerical
cliental
climatological
climbable
clinical
clitoral
cloistral
closeable
coachable
coalitional
coastal

coaxial
cobble
cockerel
cockle
coddle
coeducational
coequal
coercible
cognitional
coincidental
coital
collapsible
collateral
collectable
collectible
collegial
colloquial
colonel
colonial
colorable
colorful
colossal
combustible
comfortable
comical
commandable
commendable
commensurable
commercial
commingle
committable
committal
communal
communicable
commutable
companionable
comparable
compartmental
compatible
compensable

compilable
complemental
complexional
componential
compoundable
comprehendible
comprehensible
compressible
compressional
compromisable
computable
computational
concealable
conceivable
conceptional
conceptual
condemnable
condensable
conditional
condonable
conductible
conferral
confessable
confessional
confidential
configurational
confirmable
conformable
confutable
congealable
congenial
congenital
congregational
congressional
conical
conjecturable
conjectural
conjugal
conjugational
connubial

conoidal
conquerable
consensual
consequential
conservable
conservational
considerable
consonantal
constable
Constantinople
constitutional
constrainable
construable
consul
consumable
containable
contemptible
contentional
contestable
contextual
continental
continuable
continual
contractible
contractual
contralateral
contrapuntal
contrastable
controllable
controversial
controvertible
convectional
conventicle
conventional
conversational
convertible
conveyable
convivial
copyrightable
coracle

coral
cordial
corneal
coronal
corporal
corporeal
corpuscle
correctable
correctional
correlatable
corrigible
corrodible
corruptible
cortical
cosmical
cosmological
council
counsel
counselable
counsellable
countable
couple
crabapple
crackle
cradle
cranial
credential
credible
creditable
crewel
criminal
crinkle
cripple
critical
criticizable
cross-sectional
crucial
crucible
cruel
crumble

crumple
crushable
crystal
cubical
cubicle
cubital
cuddle
cudgel
cul
culpable
cultivable
cultivatable
cultural
curable
curdle
custodial
cuticle
cybernetical
cycle
cyclical
cylindrical
cymbal
cynical
cytological
dabble
dactyl
damageable
damnable
damsel
danceable
dandle
dangle
Daniel
dapple
daredevil
darnel
datable
dateable
dawdle
dazzle

debacle
debatable
debateable
debitable
decasyllable
decayable
deceitful
deceivable
decidable
decimal
decipherable
decisional
declarable
declinable
declinational
decomposable
decouple
dedicational
deducible
deductible
defeasible
defendable
defensible
deferable
deferential
deferrable
deferral
definable
deflectable
deformable
defrayable
defrayal
degradable
delectable
delegable
delightful
deliverable
delusional
demandable
democratical

demoniacal
demonical
demonstrable
demonstrational
demountable
demurrable
demurral
deniable
denial
denominational
dental
denticle
dentilabial
dentilingual
dentinal
departmental
dependable
depletable
deplorable
deportable
deposal
depositional
depreciable
depressible
depressional
deputational
derisible
dermal
descendible
describable
desirable
desireable
despicable
despiteful
destroyable
destructible
detachable
detectable
detectible
determinable

detestable
detonable
detrimental
developmental
deviational
devisable
devotional
dextral
diabolical
diacritical
diadermal
diagnoseable
diagonal
diagrammable
diagrammatical
dial
dialectal
dialectical
diametrical
diarrheal
dibble
dictatorial
diddle
diesel
differential
diffusible
digestible
digital
dimensional
dimple
dingle
diphtherial
directional
direful
dirigible
dirndl
disable
disagreeable
disannul
disapproval

disassemble
disavowal
disbursal
discernable
discernible
dischargeable
disciple
discoidal
discountable
discoverable
discretional
discriminational
disdainful
disembowel
disenable
disentangle
disgraceful
disgruntle
dishevel
dishonorable
dishtowel
disloyal
dismal
dismantle
dismissal
dismountable
dispensable
dispersal
displayable
disposable
disposal
disproportional
disprovable
disputable
disregardful
disreputable
disrespectable
disrespectful
dissemble
dissolvable

dissuadable
distal
distasteful
distillable
distinguishable
distortable
distortional
distressful
distrustful
diurnal
dividable
divisible
divisional
doable
docile
doctoral
doctrinal
documentable
documental
doggerel
doleful
doodle
dorsal
dottle
double
doubtable
doubtful
dowel
draftable
drapable
drapeable
dreadful
dribble
drinkable
drivel
drizzle
dropsical
dryable
dual
ducal

ductal
ductile
duel
duffel
duffle
dull
duple
durational
dutiful
dwindle
dynamical
dysfunctional
dyspeptical
eagle
earnable
easel
eatable
ecclesiastical
ecological
economical
ecumenical
edible
edictal
editorial
educable
educational
educible
effaceable
effectual
effluvial
egoistical
egotistical
Eiffel
ejectable
electoral
electorial
electrical
elemental
eligible
ellipsoidal

elliptical
embattle
embezzle
emblematical
embraceable
embrittle
emendable
emigrational
emotional
empanel
empirical
employable
emulsible
emulsifiable
enable
enamel
encapsule
encircle
enclosable
encyclical
endorsable
endurable
enfeeble
enforceable
enigmatical
enjoyable
enkindle
ennoble
ensemble
entangle
enterable
entitle
entomological
entrepreneurial
enumerable
enviable
environmental
epicentral
epiglottal
epigrammatical

epigraphical
episcopal
episodical
epistle
epochal
equable
equal
equational
equatorial
equilateral
equitable
equivocal
eradicable
erasable
erectable
erodible
erosional
erotical
eruptional
escapable
escheatable
eschewal
esophagal
esophageal
especial
espousal
essential
establishable
estimable
eternal
Ethel
ethereal
ethical
ethnological
ethological
etiological
etymological
eucharistical
evangel
evangelical

eventful
eventual
evidential
evil
evincible
evocable
example
exceptionable
exceptional
exchangeable
excisable
excitable
excremental
excusable
executable
executional
exercisable
exhaustible
exigible
existential
expandable
expansible
expectable
expellable
expendable
experiential
experimental
explainable
explicable
exploitable
exponential
exportable
expressible
extendable
extendible
extensible
external
extinguishable
extractable
extramarital

extramural
extraterrestrial
extricable
Ezekiel
fable
facial
facile
factful
factional
factorable
factorial
factual
faddle
faithful
falafel
fallible
falsifiable
familial
fanatical
fanciful
fantastical
farcical
farmable
fascicle
fashionable
fatal
fateful
fathomable
favorable
fearful
feasible
federal
federational
feeble
feedable
fellable
femoral
fenagle
fennel
feral

fermentable
ferrule
fertile
ferule
festival
fetal
feticidal
fettle
feudal
fibril
fickle
fictional
fiddle
fileable
fillable
filterable
finable
finagle
final
financial
fineable
finial
fiscal
fitful
fixable
fizzle
flammable
flannel
flappable
flavorful
flexible
floatable
floral
fluctuational
flushable
flyable
focal
foible
follicle
fondle

fontal
forceful
forcible
fordable
forecastle
foreseeable
forethoughtful
forfeitable
forgetful
forgettable
forgivable
formal
formidable
fossil
foundational
fractional
fragile
fragmental
frangible
fraternal
fratricidal
frazzle
freckle
freezable
fretful
friable
frictional
frightful
frivol
frizzle
frontal
frugal
fruitful
fuddle
fuel
fugal
fugle
fumble
functional
fundamental

funeral
fungal
fungicidal
funnel
fusional
futile
gabble
gable
gaggle
gainful
gamble
gambol
gambrel
ganglial
garble
gargle
garnishable
gastral
gastronomical
gaugeable
gavel
genealogical
general
generational
genial
genital
genocidal
gentle
geochemical
geographical
geological
geometrical
geopolitical
geothermal
gerbil
gerbille
germicidal
germinal
giggle
gingival

girdle
giveable
glacial
gleanable
gleeful
global
glossal
glottal
glycerol
gobble
goggle
gonadal
gonorrheal
gospel
governable
governmental
grabble
graceful
grackle
gradational
gradual
grammatical
granule
graphical
graphological
grapple
graspable
grateful
gravel
gravitational
griddle
grippal
gristle
grizzle
grovel
gruel
grumble
gubernatorial
guidable
guileful

gull
gullible
gunbarrel
gunmetal
gunnel
gunwale
gurgle
gustatorial
guttural
guzzle
habitable
habitual
hackle
haggle
hallucinational
Handel
handle
handsel
hangable
Hansel
harmful
harvestable
hassle
hatchable
hateful
hazel
healable
healthful
heatable
heckle
heedful
helical
helpful
hemal
hemispherical
hemorrhoidal
heptagonal
herbal
herbicidal
heretical

heritable
hermeneutical
hermetical
hernial
heroical
heterosexual
hexagonal
hexahedral
hiatal
hibernal
hierarchal
hierarchial
hierarchical
histological
historical
hobble
homicidal
homosexual
honeysuckle
honorable
hopeful
horizonal
horizontal
hormonal
hornswoggle
horological
horrible
horticultural
hospitable
hospital
hostel
hostile
hovel
hoyle
huckle
huddle
huggable
hull
humble
humeral

humoral
hurdle
hurtful
hurtle
hustle
hydrological
hydrostatical
hydrothermal
hygienical
hymenal
hymeneal
hymnal
hyperbolical
hypercritical
hyperexcitable
hyperirritable
hypersexual
hypnotizable
hypocritical
hypodermal
hypothermal
hypothetical
hysterical
hysteroidal
iatrical
icicle
ideal
ideational
identical
identifiable
ideological
idiotical
idle
idol
idyll
ignitable
ignitible
ignoble
ileal
illegal

illegible
illogical
illusional
imaginable
imaginal
imbecile
imitational
immanuel
immaterial
immeasurable
immemorial
immobile
immoral
immortal
immovable
immoveable
immunological
immutable
impalpable
impanel
impartial
impassable
impassible
impeachable
impeccable
impenetrable
imperceivable
imperceptible
imperial
imperil
imperishable
impermeable
impermissible
impersonal
imperturbable
implacable
implausible
imponderable
importable
impossible

impoundable
impracticable
impractical
impregnable
impressible
impressionable
improbable
improvable
improvisational
impugnable
imputable
inaccessible
inadmissable
inadmissible
inadvisable
inalienable
inalterable
inapplicable
inaudible
inaugural
incalculable
incapable
incidental
incivil
inclinable
incomparable
incompatible
incomprehensible
incomputable
inconceivable
inconsequential
inconsiderable
inconsolable
incontestable
incontrovertible
incorrigible
incorruptible
increasable
incredible
incremental

incubational
inculpable
incurable
indefatigable
indefensible
indefinable
indelible
indescribable
indestructible
indeterminable
indexable
indictable
indigestible
indiscernible
indispensable
indisputable
indistinguishable
individual
indivisible
indomitable
indubitable
inducible
industrial
inedible
ineducable
ineffable
ineffectual
ineligible
inequable
inequitable
inertial
inescapable
inessential
inestimable
inevitable
inexcusable
inexhaustible
inexorable
inexpiable
inexplainable

inexplicable
inexpressible
inextinguishable
inextricable
infallible
infanticidal
infantile
infeasible
inferable
inferential
infernal
infertile
infidel
infinitesimal
infirmable
inflammable
inflatable
inflectional
inflexible
inflictable
influenceable
influential
informal
informational
infractible
infusible
ingestible
inguinal
inhabitable
inheritable
inhibitable
inhospitable
inimicable
inimical
inimitable
initial
injectable
innumerable
inoperable
inquisitional

insatiable	intolerable	janitorial
inscrutable	intractable	jekyll
insecticidal	intramural	jewel
insensible	introducible	jiggle
inseparable	invadable	jingle
insightful	invaluable	Joel
insoluble	invariable	joggle
insolvable	inveigle	jonquil
inspirational	invertible	jostle
instable	investable	joule
institutional	investible	journal
instructional	inviable	jovial
instrumental	invincible	jowl
insubstantial	inviolable	joyful
insufferable	invisible	judaical
insurable	invitational	judgmatical
insurmountable	irascible	judgmental
intangible	ireful	judicial
integral	ironical	juggle
intellectual	irrational	jumble
intelligible	irreducible	jumpable
intentional	irreparable	junctional
intercerebral	irreplaceable	jungle
intercessional	irrepressible	jural
interdental	irresistible	jurisdictional
interfacial	irresponsible	justifiable
interglacial	irretrievable	justle
interjectional	irreversible	karakul
interminable	irrevocable	karyotypical
intermingle	irrigable	keloidal
intermural	irritable	kennel
internal	isobutyl	kernel
international	isometrical	kestrel
interpersonal	isopropyl	kettle
interpretable	isothermal	kibble
interpretational	Israel	kilocycle
interracial	issuable	kindle
intertribal	it'll	kinematical
interval	jackal	kinspeople
intestinal	jangle	kirtle

kissable
kittle
knowable
knowledgeable
knuckle
label
labial
labile
labiodental
labiogingival
labiomental
labionasal
lackadaisical
lactational
lacteal
ladle
lagoonal
lamentable
larval
laryngeal
lateral
latitudinal
laudable
laughable
laurel
lavational
lawful
learnable
leasable
legal
legible
lendable
lentil
lethal
level
leviable
levitical
lexical
lexicographical
liable

libel
liberal
libidinal
licensable
lickspittle
lienable
lienal
likable
likeable
liminal
limitable
lineal
lingual
linguistical
lintel
liquefiable
lisle
literal
little
liturgical
livable
liveable
loadable
local
logarithmical
logical
logistical
longitudinal
lovable
loveable
loyal
lull
lumenal
luminal
lunule
lustful
luteal
lyrical
machinable
machineable

mackerel
madrigal
magical
magisterial
magistral
magnetizable
mailable
maintainable
majestical
malarial
malleable
mammal
manacle
manageable
managerial
mandible
mandrel
mandril
mandrill
maneuverable
manful
mangle
manhandle
maniacal
manifestable
maniple
manipulable
manipulatable
manorial
mantel
mantle
manual
manubrial
maple
mappable
marble
marginal
marital
marketable
marmoreal

marriageable
marshal
marshall
marsupial
martial
marvel
maskable
masterful
mastoidal
matchable
material
maternal
mathematical
matriarchal
matricidal
matrilineal
matrimonial
maturational
matutinal
maximal
mayoral
meaningful
measle
measurable
mechanical
medal
meddle
medial
mediational
medical
medicinable
medicinal
medicolegal
medieval
megacycle
meltable
memorable
memorial
menial
menopausal

menstrual
mensurable
mensural
mental
menthyl
mentionable
mephitical
merciful
mercurial
meritable
merkel
mesodermal
metabolical
metacarpal
metal
metalloidal
metallurgical
metaphorical
metaphysical
metatarsal
meteorological
methodical
methodological
methyl
metonymical
metrical
mettle
mewl
miasmal
michael
microbial
microcosmical
microscopical
microsurgical
midcarpal
midchannel
middle
migrational
millennial
minable

mindful
mineral
mingle
minimal
ministerial
minstrel
miracle
mirthful
misanthropical
miscible
miserable
mishandle
mislabel
missal
missile
mistakable
mistitle
mistral
mistrial
mistrustful
mitchell
mitochondrial
mitral
mixable
mnemonical
mobil
mobile
modal
model
modifiable
module
mogul
molal
moldable
mollycoddle
monarchial
monarchical
monasterial
monastical
monaural

Mongol
mongrel
monistical
monocle
monolingual
monomaniacal
monomial
monosexual
monosyllable
monsoonal
monumental
moral
morphological
morsel
mortal
mortgageable
motile
motivational
motorcycle
mottle
mountable
mournful
movable
moveable
muddle
muffle
mull
multidimensional
multidirectional
multilingual
multinational
multiple
multiplicational
multiracial
mumble
municipal
mural
muscle
musical
musicological

mussel
mutable
mutational
mutual
muzzle
myocardial
myrtle
mystical
mythical
mythological
nahuatl
nameable
narwhal
nasal
natal
national
natural
nautical
naval
navel
navigable
navigational
needful
needle
neglectful
negligible
negotiable
neoclassical
neocolonial
neonatal
nepotistical
nestle
nettable
nettle
neural
neurological
neutral
Newcastle
newel
nibble

nickel
niggle
nimble
nipple
nitrile
noble
nocturnal
nodal
noddle
nodule
nominal
nonbreakable
noncommittal
noncontestable
noncontrollable
noncontroversial
nonconventional
nonconvertible
noncritical
nondeductible
nondetachable
nondirectional
nondivisible
nonessential
nonethical
nonfatal
nonfictional
nonflammable
nonfunctional
nonindustrial
noninflectional
nonlethal
nonmetal
nonphysical
nonpolitical
nonpredictable
nonprejudicial
nonpreservable
nonprofessional
nonprofitable

nonproportional
nonpunishable
nonracial
nonradical
nonrational
nonreciprocal
nonrecoverable
nonreimbursable
nonresidential
nonreturnable
nonseasonal
nonsensical
nonsexual
nonsinkable
nonsocial
nonspiritual
nontechnical
nontemporal
nontheatrical
nontraditional
nontransferable
nontropical
nontypical
nonverbal
nonviable
nonvisible
nonvocal
nonvocational
noodle
normal
nostril
notable
notarial
notational
noticeable
notifiable
notional
notochordal
novel
nozzle

nubile
nuchal
null
numberable
numbskull
numerable
numeral
numerical
numskull
nuptial
nutational
nutrimental
nutritional
nuzzle
obeyable
obfuscable
objectionable
objectional
oblational
obligational
observable
observational
obsessional
obstacle
obstetrical
obtainable
occasional
occidental
occipital
occupational
octagonal
octahedral
octal
octuple
oedipal
offal
offerable
official
ogle
oligarchical

omissible
ontological
opal
operable
operational
opposable
oppositional
optical
optimal
optimistical
optional
oracle
oral
oratorical
orbital
orchestral
ordeal
ordinal
organismal
organizational
oriel
oriental
orificial
original
oriole
ornamental
ornithological
ossicle
osteal
ostensible
oval
overcareful
overcasual
overcritical
overemotional
overfanciful
overpowerful
oversimple
overtechnical
overthrowal

pachydermial
pacifiable
packable
packsaddle
paddle
painful
palatable
palatal
palatial
paleographical
pallial
palpable
paludal
panel
panhandle
panicle
pantheistical
papal
parable
paradisal
paradisiacal
paradoxical
paralegal
paralytical
paramedical
paranormal
paraphrasable
parasitical
parcel
pardonable
parental
parenthetical
parietal
parochial
parolable
partial
partible
participial
participle
particle

passable
passel
passible
pastoral
patchable
paternal
pathological
patriarchal
patrilineal
patrimonial
payable
peaceable
peaceful
pebble
pectoral
pedagogical
pedal
peddle
pedestal
pedicle
peduncle
penal
pencil
penetrable
pensionable
pentacle
pentadactyl
pentagonal
pentateuchal
pentecostal
people
perceivable
perceptible
perceptual
percussional
perennial
perfectible
performable
peridental
peridermal

perihelial
periodical
periodontal
peripheral
perishable
periwinkle
perlingual
permeable
permissible
permutational
peroral
perpetual
personable
personal
persuadable
persuasible
perturbable
perusal
pesticidal
pestilential
pestle
petal
petitional
petrel
petrochemical
petrol
petrological
pharisaical
pharmacal
pharmaceutical
pharmacological
pharyngeal
phenomenal
phenotypical
phenyl
phial
philanthropical
philological
philosophical
phlegmatical

phonal
phonological
photochemical
photomural
photostable
photothermal
phrasal
physical
physiological
pial
pickerel
pickle
pictorial
piddle
piffle
pilule
pimple
pineal
pineapple
pinnacle
pinochle
piratical
piscatorial
pistil
pistol
pitiable
pitiful
pivotal
placable
placeable
placental
plasmal
plausible
playable
playful
pleadable
pleasurable
pleasureful
plentiful
pleural

pliable
plical
plowable
plumbable
plunderable
plural
podagral
poetical
polemical
political
pollical
polydactyl
polygonal
polyhedral
polynomial
polysyllable
pommel
ponderable
pontifical
poodle
popple
popsicle
portable
portal
portrayal
Portugal
positional
possessable
possessible
possible
postal
postcentral
postclassical
postdoctoral
postglacial
postmortal
postnasal
postnatal
postnuptial
postpartal

postseasonal
postural
potable
potential
pourable
powerful
practicable
practical
pragmatical
prattle
prayerful
preamble
preassemble
precancel
preclinical
predatorial
predial
predicable
predictable
preferable
preferential
prefixal
prefrontal
preglacial
pregnable
prehistorical
preinaugural
preindustrial
prejudicial
prelegal
premarital
premedical
premenstrual
premortal
prenatal
prenuptial
prepalatal
prepartal
preplacental
prepositional

prepuberal
prescribable
presentable
preservable
presidential
prestigeful
presumable
pretemporal
preterminal
pretrial
pretzel
preventable
preventible
prevocational
prickle
prideful
primal
primeval
primordial
principal
principle
printable
probable
probational
problematical
procedural
processional
proconsul
proctological
proctorial
prodigal
producible
professional
professorial
profitable
programmable
progressional
projectable
projectile
promotable

promotional
pronominal
pronounceable
propagational
prophetical
proportionable
proportional
proposal
propositional
prosecutable
protectional
protestable
protoplasmal
protozoal
protractile
provable
proverbial
providential
provincial
proviral
provisional
proximal
prudential
psalterial
pseudobiographical
pseudoclassical
pseudohistorical
pseudointellectual
pseudoliberal
pseudophilosophical
pseudoprofessional
psychiatrical
psychical
psychoanalytical
psychological
psychophysical
psychosexual
psychosocial
psychosurgical
pterodactyl

puberal
pubertal
publishable
puddle
puerile
pulpal
pummel
pumpernickel
punctual
punishable
pupal
pupil
purchasable
purgatorial
puritanical
purl
purple
purposeful
pursuable
pursual
pustule
puzzle
pyramidal
pyrotechnical
quadrangle
quadrennial
quadricentennial
quadrupedal
quadruple
qualifiable
quarrel
quarterfinal
quenchable
questionable
quibble
quintal
quintessential
quintuple
quizzical
quotable

rabbinical
rabble
racial
radial
radical
radicle
radiocarpal
raffle
ramble
ramshackle
rankle
ransomable
rascal
ratable
rateable
rational
rattle
ravel
razzle-dazzle
reachable
readable
readjustable
real
reappraisal
rearousal
reasonable
reassemble
rebel
rebuttal
recallable
recappable
receivable
receptacle
recessional
rechargeable
reciprocal
recital
reclaimable
recognizable
recommendable

recommittal
recompensable
reconcilable
reconstructible
recordable
recoverable
recreational
rectal
rectangle
rectifiable
recycle
redeemable
redouble
reducible
referable
referential
referral
reformable
reformational
refractile
refundable
refusal
refutable
regal
regardful
regimental
regional
registrable
regnal
regretful
regrettable
rehearsal
reheatable
reimbursable
rejectable
rekindle
relabel
relatable
relational
releasable

reliable
relishable
remarkable
remedial
rememberable
remindful
remittable
remittal
remodel
remorseful
removable
removal
remunerable
renal
renderable
renewable
renewal
renounceable
rentable
rental
repairable
reparable
repayable
repealable
repeatable
replaceable
replicable
reportable
reposeful
reprehensible
representable
representational
repressible
reprieval
reprisal
reproachable
reproachful
reproducible
reptile
reputable

requital
resalable
rescindable
rescissible
resectable
resemble
resentful
resettle
reshuffle
residential
residual
resistible
resolvable
resourceful
respectable
respectful
respirable
respirational
responsible
restful
restorable
restrainable
retable
retainable
retinal
retouchable
retraceable
retractable
retractile
retrainable
retrial
retrievable
retrieval
returnable
reusable
revealable
revel
revelational
revengeful
reverential

reversal
reversible
reviewable
reviewal
revival
revocable
revokable
revolvable
rhetorical
rhinal
rhythmical
rictal
riddle
riffle
rifle
rightful
ripple
ritual
rival
rotatable
rotational
rouble
royal
rubble
ruble
ruddle
rueful
ruffle
rulable
rumble
rumple
runnel
rural
rustle
ruthful
sabbatical
sable
sacerdotal
sacral
sacramental

sacrificial
saddle
sagittal
sailable
salable
saleable
salespeople
salvable
salvageable
salvational
sample
samuel
sandal
sanicle
sartorial
satanical
satchel
satiable
satirical
satisfiable
saturable
savable
saveable
sayable
scalpel
scatological
schedule
schlemiel
schnitzel
schnozzle
scleral
scornful
scoundrel
scrabble
scramble
scrapple
scribble
scriptural
scrotal
scruple

scrutable
scuffle
scull
sculptural
scurrile
scuttle
sealable
searchable
seasonable
seasonal
Seattle
secretarial
sectile
sectional
sectoral
sectorial
securable
seduceable
seducible
seeable
segmental
seismological
selectional
sellable
semantical
semble
semiannual
semicircle
semifinal
semiformal
seminal
seminormal
semiofficial
semitropical
semivowel
senatorial
senegal
sensational
senseful
sensible

sensorial
sensual
sentimental
sentinel
seoul
sepal
separable
septal
septuple
sepulchral
sequel
sequential
serial
serviceable
servile
sessile
sessional
setal
settle
severable
several
sewable
sexological
sextuple
sexual
shackle
shakable
shakeable
shamble
shameful
shapable
shapeable
sharable
shareable
shavable
shaveable
shiftable
shingle
shippable
shovel

shrapnel
shrapnell
shrieval
shrinkable
shrivel
shuffle
shuttle
sibyl
sickle
sidereal
sidesaddle
sidle
sigmoidal
signable
signal
simple
sincipital
sinful
single
sinistral
sinkable
sinusoidal
situational
sizable
sizeable
sizzle
skedaddle
skeletal
skeptical
skiable
skilful
skillful
skittle
skull
sliceable
slothful
smashable
smokable
smuggle
snaffle

sneerful
sniffle
snivel
snorkel
snuffle
snuggle
sociable
social
societal
sociological
sociopolitical
solstitial
soluble
solvable
songful
sophistical
soremuzzle
sorrel
sorrowful
soulful
spacial
spackle
spangle
spaniel
spareable
sparkle
spasmatical
spatial
speakable
special
speckle
spectacle
spectral
spendable
spermicidal
spherical
spheroidal
sphincteral
spillable
spinal

spindle
spiracle
spiral
spiritual
spirochetal
spital
spiteful
spittle
split-level
spoilable
sponsorial
sporicidal
spousal
spreadable
sprinkle
squabble
squiggle
squirrel
stable
stackable
stainable
standardizable
staphylococcal
staple
startle
statable
statal
stateable
statistical
statutable
stealable
steeple
steerable
stencil
stenothermal
sterile
sternal
steroidal
stifle
stigmal

stipple
stipulable
stoical
stomal
stopple
storable
straddle
straggle
strangle
streptococcal
stressful
stretchable
streusel
striatal
strobil
strobile
stromal
structural
strudel
struggle
stubble
stumble
suable
suasible
subclinical
subcontinental
subcortical
subcouncil
subcranial
subcritical
subdermal
subdividable
subdivisible
subdorsal
subgingival
subglacial
subjectional
subliminal
sublingual
submental

submergible
submersible
submittal
subnasal
subneural
subnormal
subpectoral
subpoenal
subprincipal
subsequential
substantial
substantival
substitutable
subsumable
subterminal
subtitle
subtle
subtotal
subtropical
subvertible
subviral
subvocal
successful
successional
suckle
suctional
suctorial
sufferable
suffixal
suggestible
suicidal
suitable
sundial
superficial
supernal
supernatural
supernormal
supple
supplemental
supportable

supposable
suppositional
suppressible
supraglottal
supraliminal
supramental
supranasal
supranational
supraspinal
sural
surcingle
surgical
surmisable
surmountable
surpassable
surreal
surrebuttal
surveyable
surveyal
survivable
survival
susceptible
suspectable
suspenseful
sustainable
swaddle
swimmable
swindle
switchable
swivel
syllable
symbiotical
symbol
symbolical
symmetrical
synaptical
syncopal
syndactyl
syndactyle
syndical

synergical
synergistical
synodal
synodical
synoptical
synovial
syntactical
synthetical
systematical
syzygial
tabernacle
table
tackle
tactful
tactical
tactile
taffrail
takable
takeable
tameable
tamil
tangential
tangible
tangle
tarnishable
tarsal
tassel
tasteful
tattersall
tattle
tautological
taxable
teachable
teakettle
tearable
tearful
teasel
technical
technological
televisional

tellable
temperamental
temple
temporal
temptable
tenable
tendril
tensile
tensional
tentacle
terminable
terminal
terminological
terrestrial
terrible
territorial
testable
testicle
testimonial
tetanal
tetrahedral
textile
textual
thankful
theatrical
theistical
theological
theoretical
theosophical
therapeutical
thermal
thermocouple
thermometrical
thimble
thinkable
thistle
thoughtful
threatful
throttle
thyroidal

tibial
tickle
tidal
tillable
timbale
timetable
tingle
tinkle
tinsel
tipple
tithable
title
tittle
tittle-tattle
toddle
toggle
toil
tolerable
tonal
tonsil
topical
topographical
topological
topple
torrential
torsional
total
tottle
touchable
tousle
towable
towel
townspeople
toxicological
traceable
tracheal
trackable
tractable
tractional
tradable

tradeable
tradespeople
traditional
trafficable
tragical
tragicomical
trainable
trammel
trample
tranquil
transactional
transcendental
transcontinental
transcutaneal
transferable
transferal
transferrable
transferral
transfusable
transfusible
transfusional
transitional
translatable
transmissible
transmittable
transmittal
transmittible
transmural
transmutable
transorbital
transportable
transportal
transportational
transsexual
trapezial
trapezoidal
travel
travelable
travellable
traversable

traversal
treacle
treadle
treasonable
treasurable
treatable
treble
tremble
trestle
triable
trial
triangle
tribal
tribunal
tricentennial
trickle
tricycle
tridactyl
triennial
trifacial
trifle
trifocal
trigonal
trilateral
triliteral
triple
triumphal
triumviral
trivial
trommel
tropical
trouble
trowel
truckle
truffle
truncal
trundle
trustable
trustful
truthful

tubal
tubercle
tumble
tumbrel
tumoral
tunable
tuneable
tuneful
tunnel
turbinal
turnbuckle
turntable
turtle
tussle
tutorial
twaddle
twattle
twiddle
twinkle
twistable
typhoidal
typical
typographical
typological
tyrannical
ultraliberal
umbel
umbilical
umbonal
umbral
unable
unacceptable
unaccessible
unaccountable
unaccusable
unadaptable
unadvisable
unaffordable
unallowable
unalterable

unamenable
unamendable
unanswerable
unappeasable
unapplicable
unapproachable
unarguable
unartful
unassailable
unattainable
unavailable
unavoidable
unbearable
unbeatable
unbelievable
unbreakable
unbribable
unbuckle
unchangeable
uncharitable
uncheerful
uncial
uncivil
unclassifiable
uncle
uncomfortable
unconditional
unconquerable
unconscionable
uncontestable
uncontrollable
unconventional
unconvertible
uncountable
uncouple
uncritical
undatable
undefensible
undeniable
understandable

undesirable	ungraceful	unnavigable
undetectable	ungrammatical	unneedful
undiscernible	ungrateful	unnegotiable
undrinkable	unhabitable	unnoticeable
undubitable	unharmful	unobtainable
undutiful	unhealthful	unofficial
uneatable	unheedful	unoriginal
uneducable	unhelpful	unpalatable
unemotional	unicameral	unpardonable
unemployable	unicycle	unpayable
unendurable	unidentifiable	unperturbable
unenforceable	unidirectional	unplayable
unenjoyable	unilateral	unpoetical
unenviable	uninsurable	unpolitical
unequal	unintentional	unpractical
unequitable	unisexual	unpredictable
unequivocal	universal	unpresentable
unescapable	univocal	unpreventable
unessential	unjudicial	unprintable
unethical	unknowable	unprofessional
uneventful	unlawful	unprofitable
unexceptional	unlegal	unpronounceable
unexcitable	unlikable	unprovable
unexcusable	unlivable	unpunctual
unexplainable	unlovable	unpunishable
unfaithful	unmailable	unquenchable
unfashionable	unmanageable	unquestionable
unfathomable	unmeasurable	unquotable
unfavorable	unmentionable	unratable
unfeasible	unmerciful	unravel
unfertile	unmethodical	unreachable
unfilial	unmindful	unreadable
unflappable	unmistakable	unreal
unforeseeable	unmoral	unreasonable
unforgettable	unmovable	unredeemable
unforgivable	unmuffle	unrefutable
unfruitful	unmusical	unreliable
unfulfillable	unmuzzle	unremorseful
ungentle	unnameable	unremovable
ungovernable	unnatural	unrepeatable

unresentful
unresolvable
unreturnable
unsaddle
unsalable
unsatiable
unsatisfiable
unscramble
unscriptural
unseasonable
unsensible
unsentimental
unserviceable
unsettle
unshackle
unshakable
unshrinkable
unsinful
unsinkable
unskillful
unsnarl
unsociable
unsocial
unsolvable
unspeakable
unspiritual
unstable
unsterile
unstoppable
unsubstantial
unsubtle
unsuccessful
unsuitable
unsuppressible
unsurmountable
unsurpassable
unsustainable
unsymmetrical
untactful
untasteful

unteachable
untenable
unthankful
unthinkable
unthoughtful
untillable
untouchable
untraceable
untractable
untraditional
untransferable
untranslatable
untrustful
untruthful
untypical
unusable
unusual
unutterable
unwearable
unworkable
unwrinkle
updatable
upheaval
ural
urinal
usable
useable
useful
usual
utensil
utilizable
uveal
uxorial
vacatable
vaginal
valuable
valuational
vandal
variable
variational

varietal
vassal
vatical
vectorial
vegetable
vegetal
vehicle
venal
vendable
vendible
venerable
venereal
vengeful
venial
ventral
ventricle
verbal
verifiable
veritable
vermeil
vernal
versatile
versional
vertebral
vertical
vesical
vesicle
vessel
vestal
vestibule
vestigial
viable
vial
vicarial
vicinal
victual
viewable
vigil
vincible
vindicable

vinyl
violable
viral
virgil
virginal
viricidal
virile
virological
virtual
visceral
visible
visitable
visual
vital
vitrifiable
vocable
vocal
vocational
voidable
volitional
voluble
vortical
vowel
vulnerable
vulval
wadable
waddle
wadeable
waffle
waggle
wail
wailful
wakeful
wangle
wankel
warble
washable
wassail
wasteful
wastrel

watchful
wattle
wearable
weasel
weevil
wheedle
whiffle
whimsical
whistle
whittle
whorl
wiener schnitzel
wiggle
wildfowl
wilful
willable
willful
wimble
wimple
winkle
winnable
wishful
wistful
withdrawable
withdrawal
witnessable
wobble
woeful
wonderful
workable
worktable
worshipful
worthful
wrangle
wrathful
wrestle
wriggle
wrinkle
writable
wrongful

xiphisternal
yankee-doodle
yodel
yokel
youthful
yowl
zenithal
zestful
zodiacal
zonal
zoological

ULCH
gulch
mulch

ULJ
bulge
divulge
indulge
overindulge

ULK
bulk
hulk
skulk
sulk

ULKT
bulked
mulct
skulked
sulked

ULP
gulp
pulp

ULS
avulse

barnacles
carrels
convulse
flannels
hospitals
impulse
mollycoddles
pulse
repulse
staples
trifles

ULT
adult
catapult
consult
cult
difficult
exult
insult
nonadult
occult
result
tumult

Long UM
abloom
anteroom
assume
ballroom
barroom
bathroom
bedroom
bloom
board-room
boom
bridegroom
broadloom
broom
cardroom

checkroom
classroom
cloakroom
coatroom
consume
costume
courtroom
darkroom
day-room
doom
elbowroom
entomb
exhume
flume
foredoom
fume
gloom
glume
headroom
heirloom
homeroom
jibboom
Khartoum
legroom
legume
loom
lunchroom
mushroom
newsroom
perfume
playroom
plume
poolroom
pressroom
presume
resume
rheum
room
saleroom
salesroom

schoolroom
showroom
sickroom
spume
stateroom
stockroom
storeroom
strongroom
subsume
taproom
targum
tomb
toolroom
vacuum
volume
vroom
wardroom
washroom
whom
womb
workroom
zoom

UM
abolitionism
absenteeism
absolutism
abstractionism
accustom
activism
ad-infinitum
ad-nauseum
Adam
addendum
adventuresome
agendum
agnosticism
alarmism
albinoism
album

alcoholism
algorithm
altruism
alum
aluminum
amalgam
amateurism
anabaptism
anabolism
anachronism
anarchism
aneurism
aneurysm
angiospasm
anglicanism
anglicism
angstrom
animalism
animism
antagonism
antebellum
antemortem
anthem
anum
aphorism
aquarium
arboretum
archaism
asceticism
ashram
asphaltum
astigmatism
asylum
atheism
atom
atomism
atrium
auditorium
authoritarianism
autism

autumn
awesome
axiom
baalim
bacterium
balsam
bantam
baptism
barbarianism
barbarism
barium
basidium
bdellium
become
bedlam
behaviorism
belgium
benumb
betacism
biculturalism
biennium
bioplasm
biorhythm
biracialism
birchism
bisexualism
blithesome
blossom
bolshevism
bonum
boredom
bosom
bossism
bothersome
bottom
botulism
brahmanism
brahminism
briticism
brougham

Buddhism
bum
burdensome
bureaucratism
buxom
Byzantium
cabalism
cadmium
caesarism
calcium
calvinism
cameralism
canadianism
candelabrum
cannibalism
cannonism
capitalism
capsicum
cardamom
cardiospasm
cartelism
cartesianism
cataclysm
catholicism
centralism
centroplasm
centrum
cerebellum
cerebrum
ceremonialism
chasm
chauvinism
chiasm
chloralism
christendom
chromium
chrysanthemum
chum
circum
classicalism

classicism
coliseum
collectivism
colloquialism
colloquium
colonialism
colosseum
colostrum
column
come
commercialism
communalism
communism
compendium
condom
condominium
conformism
confucianism
congregationalism
conservationism
conservatism
consortium
constructionism
consumerism
continuum
conundrum
conventionalism
cosmopolitanism
cranium
crematorium
cretinism
criminalism
criterium
criticism
crowism
crumb
cubism
cuddlesome
cultism
cumbersome

curriculum
custom
cynicism
cytoplasm
czardom
czarism
dadaism
dandyism
darksome
Darwinism
datum
decentralism
decorum
defeatism
defluvium
deism
delightsome
delirium
democratism
denim
desideratum
despotism
determinism
dictum
didacticism
diem
dilettantism
dimorphism
dogmatism
dorsum
druidism
drum
dualism
dukedom
dumb
dumdum
dwarfism
dynamism
eardrum
earldom

eclecticism
ecosystem
ecumenicalism
ecumenicism
ecumenism
edam
effluvium
egalitarianism
egocentrism
egoism
egotism
ejaculum
electromagnetism
elitism
elysium
emblem
emotionalism
empiricism
emporium
endomorphism
enthusiasm
environmentalism
epsom
equestrianism
equilibrium
ergotism
eroticism
erotism
erratum
escapism
eunuchism
euphemism
evangelicalism
evangelism
evolutionism
exhibitionism
existentialism
exorcism
exoticism
expansionism

expressionism	gargoylism	hobbism
externalism	geomagnetism	hokum
extremism	geranium	holism
fabianism	giantism	hominem
factionalism	gigantism	honorarium
factum	gingham	hoodlum
fanaticism	gladsome	hooliganism
fandom	gleesome	hum
fantom	globalism	humanism
fascism	glum	humanitarianism
fastidium	gothicism	humdrum
fatalism	graham	hybridism
fathom	grandam	hypnotism
favoritism	grewsome	hypochondrium
fearsome	gruesome	hypothyroidism
federalism	gum	iconoclasm
feminism	gymnasium	idealism
fetichism	gypsum	idiom
fetishism	handsome	ileum
feudalism	hansom	ilium
filesystem	harem	imperialism
filmdom	Harlem	imperium
flavorsome	harmonium	impressionism
fletcherism	hasidim	income
flotsam	hasidism	indecorum
formalism	heathendom	individualism
forum	heathenism	industrialism
foursome	hebraism	infantilism
fraternalism	hedonism	infinitum
freedom	heliotropism	interim
freudianism	helium	internationalism
frolicsome	Hellenism	invalidism
fulcrum	herbarium	iotacism
fundamentalism	heroinism	irksome
futurism	heroism	ism
gallicism	hierarchism	isomorphism
gallium	Hinduism	item
galvanism	hippiedom	Jerusalem
gamesome	Hitlerism	jetsam
gangsterism	ho-hum	jingoism

journalism
Judaism
jugulum
kettledrum
kingdom
klanism
labialism
labium
labrum
lamaism
landlordism
leftism
legalism
leninism
lesbianism
liberalism
libertarianism
lightsome
lignum
linoleum
lissome
literalism
lithesome
lithium
loathsome
lobbyism
localism
locoism
logarithm
lonesome
lutheranism
lyceum
lyricism
ma'am
macadam
Machiavellianism
macrocosm
madam
madame
maelstrom

magnesium
magnetism
magnum
malapropism
mannerism
manubrium
maoism
marjoram
martialism
martyrdom
marxism
masochism
materialism
maternalism
mausoleum
maxim
maximum
mechanism
meddlesome
medievalism
medium
melanism
memorandum
mendelism
mesmerism
metabolism
metamorphism
meteorism
methodism
mettlesome
miasm
microcosm
middlebrowism
militarism
milium
millennium
minimum
misoneism
modem
modernism

modicum
momentum
monarchism
mongolianism
mongolism
monism
monochromatism
monomorphism
monosodium
monotheism
moralism
moratorium
mormonism
mortem
moslem
mum
museum
Muslim
mutism
mutualism
myocardium
mysticism
narcism
narcissism
nasturtium
nationalism
nativism
naturalism
nauseam
Naziism
necessarium
necrophilism
negativism
neoclassicism
neologism
neoplasm
nepotism
neptunium
nettlesome
neutralism

nicotinism	panjandrum	postpartum
nihilism	pantheism	potassium
nobelium	parallelism	pragmatism
noisome	paralogism	premium
nostrum	paramecium	prepartum
nudism	parochialism	presbyterianism
numb	passim	presidium
oakum	pastoralism	prism
obstructionism	paternalism	privatism
occultism	patriotism	problem
odium	pauperism	professionalism
officialdom	pedestrianism	promethium
officialism	pendulum	protectionism
oleum	perfectionism	protestantism
olibanum	pessimism	protoplasm
onanism	petrolatum	provincialism
opium	petroleum	psalterium
opossum	phantasm	pseudoclassicism
opportunism	phantom	psyllium
optimism	phobism	pugilism
optimum	phylum	purim
orem	pilgrim	purism
organism	plagiarism	puritanism
orgasm	planetarium	quackism
osseum	plasm	quadrennium
ostium	platinum	quakerism
ostracism	plenum	quantum
outcome	plum	quarrelsome
outswum	plumb	quondam
overburdensome	pluralism	quorum
overcome	plutonium	racialism
overoptimism	pneumatism	racism
ovum	podium	radicalism
pablum	poem	radium
pacifism	pogrom	random
paganism	polymorphism	ransom
palladium	polytheism	rationalism
paludism	positivism	realism
pandemonium	possum	rebaptism
panderism	postmortem	recidivism

rectum
referendum
relativism
republicanism
requiem
revisionism
rheumatism
rhotacism
rhumb
rhythm
robotism
romanticism
rostrum
rotacism
rowdyism
rum
ruralism
sachem
sacrum
sadism
saintdom
salem
sanatarium
sanatorium
sanctum
sanitarium
sanitorium
sapphism
sarcasm
satanism
saturnism
scandium
schism
scrotum
scum
secularism
seldom
semitism
separatism
septum

serfdom
serum
sexism
shahdom
sheikdom
sheikhdom
sheriffdom
shintoism
signum
sikhism
skepticism
slalom
slum
socialism
sodium
sodom
solarium
solecism
solemn
solipsism
some
somnambulism
sophism
sorghum
spasm
specialism
spectrum
speculum
sphagnum
spiculum
spirillum
spoonerism
sputum
stadium
stagnum
stalinism
stardom
sternum
stigmatism
stoicism

stratagem
stratum
striatum
strum
strychninism
subkingdom
subphylum
substratum
subsystem
succumb
sugarplum
sum
summum
superstardom
surrealism
swum
syllogism
symbolism
symposium
symptom
synchronism
synergism
system
talcum
tandem
tantalum
tantrum
Taoism
tarantism
tedium
teetotalism
tenaculum
terrarium
terrorism
theism
theorem
thraldom
thralldom
threesome
thrum

thumb
tiresome
titanium
toilsome
tokenism
toothsome
totalitarianism
totem
tourism
traditionalism
traitorism
transcendentalism
transom
transvestism
trillium
trinitarianism
trivium
trophism
tropism
troublesome
truism
twosome
tympanum
ultimatum
ultimum
ultraism
unionism
unsolemn
unwelcome
unwholesome
uranium
urbanism
utopianism
vagabondism
Valium
vampirism
vanadium
vandalism
veganism
vegetarianism

velum
venom
venturesome
verbatim
victim
vinculum
virilism
volcanism
volume
voodooism
voyeurism
vulcanism
vulgarism
wampum
wearisome
welcome
wholesome
whoredom
winsome
wisdom
witticism
wolfram
workaholism
worrisome
xiphisternum
xylem
yankeeism
yttrium
yum-yum
zionism
zirconium
Zoroastrianism

UMP
bump
chump
clump
dump
frump
grump

hump
jump
lump
mugwump
plump
pump
rump
slump
stump
thump
trump
ump

UMPS
bumps
chumps
clumps
dumps
frumps
humps
jumps
lumps
mugwumps
mumps
plumps
pumps
rumps
slumps
stumps
thumps
trumps
umps

Long UN
afternoon
attune
baboon
balloon
bassoon
bestrewn

boon
buffoon
cameroon
cartoon
cocoon
commune
coon
croon
doubloon
dragoon
dune
festoon
forenoon
goon
harpoon
hewn
honeymoon
immune
importune
impugn
inopportune
jejune
june
lagoon
lampoon
loon
lune
macaroon
maroon
mistune
monsoon
moon
neptune
noon
octoroon
opportune
oppugn
pantaloon
picaroon
picayune

platoon
poltroon
pontoon
prune
quadroon
raccoon
racoon
rangoon
roughhewn
rune
saloon
Saskatoon
shogun
soon
spittoon
spoon
strewn
swoon
tablespoon
teaspoon
tribune
triune
tune
tycoon
typhoon
walloon

UN
Aaron
abandon
abbreviation
abdication
abdomen
abduction
aberration
abjection
ablution
abolition
abomination
abortion

abrasion
abrogation
absolution
absorption
abstension
abstention
abstraction
academician
acceleration
accentuation
acclamation
accommodation
accordion
accreditation
accretion
acculturation
accumulation
accusation
acquisition
action
activation
actualization
actuation
acumen
adamson
adaptation
adaption
addiction
addison
addisonian
addition
adhesion
adjudication
adjunction
administration
admiration
admission
admonition
adoption
adoration

adulteration
advocation
Aegean
aeration
aeroplankton
Aesopian
affectation
affection
affiliation
affirmation
affixation
affliction
afterimpression
aftersensation
agglutination
aggravation
aggregation
aggression
agitation
agrarian
Alabaman
Alan
Alaskan
Albanian
Albertan
albumen
albumin
alderman
alderwoman
alderwomen
Aleutian
Alexandrian
Algerian
Algonquian
Algonquin
alien
alienation
alkaline
allegation
allen

alleviation
alligation
alliteration
allocation
allusion
almsman
alteration
altercation
alternation
amalgamation
Amazonian
ambition
ambulation
amelioration
Amerasian
American
Amerindian
ammon
ammunition
amortization
amphibian
ampicillin
amplification
amputation
anatoxin
anchorwoman
andean
anderson
anglian
anglican
Angolan
animation
annexation
annihilation
annotation
annunciation
anodization
antediluvian
antiabortion
anticipation

antigen
antihistamine
antiquarian
antiquation
antitoxin
anyone
Appalachian
apparition
application
apportion
apposition
appreciation
apprehension
approbation
appropriation
approximation
apron
aquarian
aquiline
Arabian
arbitration
arcadian
archdeacon
Argentinean
argumentation
arisen
Aristotelian
Arizonan
Arizonian
Armageddon
Armenian
arrogation
arson
Arthurian
articulation
artilleryman
artisan
Aryan
ascension
ascription

ashen
Ashton
Asian
Aspen
aspersion
asphyxiation
aspiration
aspirin
assassin
assassination
assemblyman
assemblywoman
assemblywomen
assertion
assignation
assimilation
association
assumption
assyrian
athapaskan
athenian
attention
attenuation
attestation
attraction
attribution
attrition
auction
audition
augmentation
Augustan
Augustinian
Australian
Austrian
austronesian
authentication
authoritarian
authorization
automation
automaton

autoregulation
autosuggestion
aversion
avian
aviation
avocation
avulsion
awaken
awestricken
babylonian
backbitten
backgammon
backslidden
backwoodsman
bacon
badminton
bahamian
bailsman
balkan
Baltimorean
bandsman
bandwagon
banyan
barbarian
barbarization
bargain
baron
barren
baseman
basin
bastardization
bastian
bastion
batsman
battalion
batten
battlewagon
batwoman
batwomen
bavarian

beacon
beaten
beautician
beautification
beckon
bedlington
bedouin
bedridden
beechen
Beethoven
befallen
begotten
begun
beholden
Belgian
bellybutton
benediction
benefaction
Benjamin
Bergman
Bermudian
bespoken
betaken
betoken
bidden
bifurcation
bilirubin
billion
biomedicine
biometrician
biotransformation
bipartisan
bipartition
bipartizan
birchen
birotation
bisection
bison
bitten
bitumen

blacken	brutalization	canyon
blazon	Bulgarian	capacitation
blowgun	bullion	capitalization
bludgeon	bun	capitation
boatman	bunion	capitulation
boatswain	bunsen	capstan
bobbin	bunyan	capsulation
bodkin	burden	captain
Bohemian	burgeon	caption
Bolivian	burton	captivation
bondman	burundian	carbonation
bondsman	bushman	carbonization
bondwoman	businessman	carcinogen
bondwomen	businesswoman	cardamon
Boston	businesswomen	cardigan
Bostonian	button	Caribbean
boughten	byelorussian	carnation
bourbon	byron	Caroline
bowman	cabin	Carolinian
bracken	caesarean	Carson
brahman	caesarian	cartesian
brahmin	caisson	carton
brainchildren	Cajun	caseharden
brakeman	calculation	Caspian
brazen	caldron	castigation
Brazilian	calibration	castration
break-even	Californian	categorization
brethren	Calvin	cattleman
breton	Cambodian	caucasian
Brian	cambrian	cauldron
brighten	Cameroonian	causation
Brisbane	canaan	caution
Britain	Canadian	cavalryman
briton	canalization	celebration
broaden	cancelation	cementation
brogan	cancellation	centenarian
broken	cannibalization	centillion
Brooklyn	cannon	centralization
browbeaten	canon	centurion
bruin	canonization	certain

certification
cesarean
chadian
chainman
chairman
chairperson
chairwoman
chairwomen
chamberlain
chameleon
champion
chaplain
characterization
charlatan
Charleston
charwoman
charwomen
chasten
chaucerian
cheapen
chelation
chevron
Chicagoan
chicken
chieftain
chlorination
chosen
christen
Christian
Christianization
churchman
churchwarden
churchwoman
churchwomen
cinnamon
circadian
circulation
circumcision
circumlocution
circumnavigation

circumscription
circumspection
circumvention
citation
citizen
citron
civilian
civilization
clansman
clanswoman
clanswomen
clarification
clarion
classification
clergyman
clergywoman
clergywomen
clinician
cloven
coachman
coaction
coagulation
coalition
coarsen
coastguardsman
coeducation
coffin
cogitation
cognition
cohabitation
cohen
cohesion
collaboration
collagen
collection
collegian
collision
collocation
collusion
Colombian

colon
colonization
coloration
columbian
combination
combustion
comedian
commemoration
commendation
commercialization
commiseration
commission
committeeman
committeewoman
committeewomen
common
commotion
communication
communion
commutation
compaction
companion
comparison
compassion
compensation
competition
compilation
complementation
completion
complexion
complication
composition
comprehension
compression
compulsion
compunction
computation
computerization
concatenation
concentration

conception
conceptualization
concession
conciliation
concision
conclusion
concoction
concretion
concussion
condemnation
condensation
condescension
condition
conduction
confection
confederation
confession
configuration
confirmation
confiscation
conflagration
conflation
conformation
confrontation
confucian
confusion
congestion
conglomeration
congratulation
congregation
congressman
congresswoman
congresswomen
conjugation
conjunction
connection
conniption
connotation
consanguine
conscription

consecration
conservation
consideration
consolation
consolidation
constellation
consternation
constipation
constitution
constriction
construction
consultation
consummation
consumption
contagion
containerization
contamination
contemplation
contention
continuation
contortion
contraception
contraction
contradiction
contradistinction
contraindication
contraption
contravention
contribution
contrition
contusion
convection
convention
conversation
conversion
conviction
convocation
convolution
convulsion
cooperation

coordination
Copenhagen
copernican
copulation
cordon
cordovan
corinthian
cornucopian
coronation
corporation
corpsman
correction
correlation
corroboration
corrosion
corrugation
corruption
cosmetician
cosmopolitan
cotillion
cotton
councilman
councilwoman
councilwomen
counteraction
counterirritation
counterman
counterrevolution
countertraction
countryman
countrywoman
countrywomen
courtesan
cracksman
craftsman
craven
crayon
creation
cremation
crestfallen

cretin
crewman
crimean
crimination
crimson
criterion
croton
crucifixion
crustacean
crystallization
Cuban
culmination
cultivation
cumin
curmudgeon
curtain
cushion
custodian
cybernation
cybernetician
cytoskeleton
cytotoxin
Czechoslovakian
dairyman
Dakotan
dalmatian
damnation
damnification
dampen
damson
dandelion
darken
Darwinian
Datsun
Dayton
deacon
deactivation
deaden
deafen
debarkation

debilitation
decahedron
decalcification
decapitation
decarbonation
deceleration
decentralization
deception
decimation
decision
declaration
declassification
declension
declination
decoction
decomposition
decompression
decondition
decongestion
decontamination
decoration
dedication
deduction
deepen
defamation
defecation
defection
defibrillation
definition
deflagration
deflation
deflection
defloration
defoliation
deforestation
deformation
degeneration
degradation
dehumanization
dehydration

deification
dejection
delawarean
delegation
deletion
deliberation
delicatessen
delimitation
delineation
delusion
demagnification
demarcation
demarkation
demilitarization
demobilization
democratization
demodulation
demolition
demon
demonstration
demoralization
demotion
denaturalization
denigration
denizen
denomination
denotation
dentation
dentin
dentition
denunciation
depiction
depilation
depletion
depopulation
deportation
deposition
depravation
deprecation
depreciation

depredation
depression
deprivation
deputation
deregulation
dereliction
derision
derivation
derogation
description
desecration
desegregation
desertion
desiccation
designation
desolation
desperation
destination
destine
destitution
destruction
detection
detention
deterioration
determination
determine
detestation
detonation
detoxication
detoxification
detraction
devaluation
devastation
deviation
devolution
devon
devonian
devotion
diagnostician
dictation

diction
dietician
dietitian
differentiation
diffusion
digestion
digitation
digression
dilapidation
dilation
dimension
diminution
Dionysian
dioxin
diphtherian
direction
disaffection
disaffiliation
disburden
disciplinarian
discipline
discoloration
disconnection
discontinuation
discretion
discrimination
discursion
discussion
disembarkation
disfunction
dishearten
disillusion
disinfection
disintegration
dislocation
disorganization
disorientation
dispassion
dispensation
dispersion

disposition
disproportion
disputation
disqualification
disruption
dissatisfaction
dissection
dissemination
dissension
dissention
dissertation
dissimilation
dissipation
dissociation
dissuasion
distension
distention
distillation
distinction
distortion
distraction
distribution
diversification
diversion
divination
division
doberman
documentation
dolman
dolmen
domestication
domination
dominican
dominion
donation
done
doorman
downfallen
downtrodden
dozen

draconian
draftsman
dragon
dramatization
driven
drunken
dublin
dudgeon
dun
dungeon
duplication
duration
dutchman
dysfunction
earthen
earthman
Eastman
eaten
echolocation
eden
edification
edison
edition
Edmonton
education
Edwardian
effusion
egalitarian
Egyptian
ejaculation
ejection
elaboration
elation
election
electrician
electrification
electrocution
elevation
eleven
elfin

elicitation
elimination
elision
Elizabethan
Ellen
elocution
elongation
elucidation
Elysian
emaciation
emanation
emancipation
emasculation
embarkation
emblazon
embolden
emendation
emersion
Emerson
emission
emotion
emulation
emulsification
emulsion
encapsulation
encrustation
endocrine
endoskeleton
enervation
engine
englishman
englishwoman
englishwomen
enlighten
enliven
ensign
entryman
enumeration
enunciation
envision

epicurean
epinephrine
episcopalian
equalization
equation
equestrian
equitation
equivocation
eradication
erection
Erin
ermine
erosion
eructation
erudition
eruption
escalation
escutcheon
estimation
Estonian
estrogen
ethiopian
etruscan
euclidean
euclidian
euphonium
Eurasian
European
eustachian
evacuation
evaluation
evaporation
evasion
even
eversion
everyone
eviction
evocation
evolution
evulsion

exacerbation
exaction
exaggeration
exaltation
examination
examine
exasperation
excavation
exception
excision
excitation
exclamation
exclusion
excommunication
excretion
exculpation
excursion
execration
execution
exemption
exertion
exhalation
exhaustion
exhibition
exhilaration
exhortation
exoneration
exoskeleton
exotoxin
expansion
expatiation
expatriation
expectation
expectoration
expedition
experimentation
expiation
expiration
explanation
explication

exploitation
exploration
explosion
exportation
exposition
expression
expropriation
expulsion
expurgation
extension
extenuation
extermination
extinction
extorsion
extortion
extraction
extradition
extrapolation
extraversion
extrication
extroversion
extrusion
exultation
Fabian
fabrication
facilitation
faction
falcon
fallen
fallopian
falsification
familiarization
famine
fascination
fashion
fasten
fatten
Faustian
federation
felicitation

felon
feminine
feminization
fermentation
ferryman
fertilization
festschriften
fibrillation
fiction
figuration
filtration
finalization
finespun
fireman
fisherman
fission
fixation
flacon
flagellation
flagon
flatten
flaxen
flection
flexion
flirtation
floatation
flocculation
floorman
flotation
fluctuation
fluoridation
fluorocarbon
foeman
foliation
fomentation
footman
forbidden
foreign
foreman
foreordination

forerun
foreshorten
forestation
foretoken
forgiven
forgotten
formalization
formation
formulation
fornication
forsaken
fortification
fortune
fossilization
foundation
fountain
fraction
fragmentation
Franciscan
freeman
freemartin
freemason
Frenchman
Frenchwoman
Frenchwomen
freshen
freshman
Freudian
friction
frighten
frisian
frontiersman
frostbitten
frozen
fruition
frustration
fumigation
fun
function
fusion

galactan
galilean
gallein
galleon
gallon
galvanization
gamin
gammon
ganglion
garden
gargantuan
garrison
gawain
gemination
gemmation
generalization
generation
Genevan
gentleman
gentlewoman
gentlewomen
genuflection
geomedicine
geometrician
geriatrician
German
germination
gestation
gesticulation
gherkin
ghostwritten
gibbon
Gibson
gladden
glamorization
glisten
globulin
glorification
gluten
glutton

gnomon
goblin
godchildren
godson
golden
goodman
gordon
gorgon
goshen
gotten
gownsman
gradation
graduation
grammarian
grandchildren
grandson
grantsman
granulation
gratification
gratin
graven
gravitation
grecian
Gregorian
gremlin
griffin
grunion
guardian
guardsman
Guatemalan
gudgeon
Guinean
gulden
gumption
gun
guncotton
gunman
gustation
gyration
habitation

habituation
hackman
Haitian
halcyon
hallucination
hallucinogen
halogen
Hamilton
Hamiltonian
handgun
handmaiden
handwoven
handwritten
hangman
happen
harden
harken
harlequin
harmonization
harshen
hasten
haven
Hawaiian
Haydn
headsman
hearken
heartbroken
hearten
heathen
heaven
heighten
Helen
heliozoan
hellion
helmsman
hemiglobin
hemin
hemoglobin
hempen
henchman

herculean
herdsman
herdswoman
herdswomen
herniation
heron
hesitation
hexahedron
hibernation
hidden
highfalutin
highwayman
Himalayan
histamine
historian
hoarsen
hobbesian
hobgoblin
Hodgkin
holden
homespun
honduran
hooligan
horatian
horizon
horseman
horsewoman
horsewomen
housebroken
houseman
houston
hoyden
hudson
human
humanitarian
humanization
humiliation
hun
Hungarian
Huntington

huntsman
huron
husbandman
hyaline
hybridization
hydration
hydrogen
hydrogenation
hygeian
hymen
hyperextension
hyperinflation
hypertension
hyperventilation
hyphen
hyphenation
hypotension
Iberian
Ibsen
Idahoan
idealization
ideation
identification
ignition
illumination
illusion
illustration
imagination
imagine
imbrication
imitation
immersion
immigration
immobilization
immolation
immunization
impaction
impassion
imperception
imperfection

impersonation
implantation
implementation
implication
implosion
importation
imposition
imprecation
imprecision
impregnation
impression
imprison
improvisation
impulsion
imputation
inaction
inactivation
inattention
inauguration
incantation
incapacitation
incarceration
incarnation
inception
incineration
incision
incitation
inclination
inclusion
incorporation
incorruption
incrimination
incrustation
incubation
inculcation
incursion
indecision
indemnification
indentation
indention

indexation
Indian
Indianan
indication
indigestion
indignation
indirection
indiscretion
individuation
indoctrination
indonesian
induction
induration
industrialization
inebriation
infantryman
infarction
infatuation
infection
infestation
infiltration
infirmation
inflammation
inflation
inflection
infliction
information
infraction
infusion
ingestion
ingratiation
ingression
inhabitation
inhalation
inhibition
inhuman
initiation
injection
injunction
innervation

innovation
inoculation
inosculation
inquisition
insanitation
inscription
insemination
insertion
insinuation
inspection
inspiration
installation
instigation
institution
instruction
instrumentation
insubordination
insulation
insulin
insurrection
integration
intensification
intention
interaction
interception
intercession
interconnection
interdiction
interdigitation
interferon
interjection
interlocution
intermission
interpolation
interpretation
interrelation
interrogation
interruption
intersection
intersession

interspersion
intervention
interwoven
intestine
intimation
intimidation
intonation
intoxication
introduction
introspection
introversion
intrusion
intuition
inunction
inundation
invalidation
invasion
invention
inversion
investigation
invigoration
invitation
invocation
involution
iodination
ion
Iowan
Irishman
Irishwoman
Irishwomen
iroquoian
irradiation
irresolution
irrigation
irritation
irruption
isolation
isthmian
Italian
itemization

iteration
Jackson
Jacksonian
jacobean
jacobin
Jamaican
jargon
jasmine
Jason
javelin
Jefferson
Jeffersonian
jerkin
jettison
jimpson
Johnson
Jonathan
Jordan
Jordanian
journeyman
joyridden
jubilation
junction
jungian
juration
jurisdiction
juryman
jurywoman
jurywomen
justification
juxtaposition
kantian
keratin
kiloton
kindergarten
kinsman
kinswoman
kitchen
kitten
klansman

Korean
Kremlin
kuchen
laceration
lacrimation
lactation
lactovegetarian
laden
lamentation
lamination
laotian
lapidation
Latin
latvian
laundryman
laundrywoman
lavation
layman
laywoman
leaden
leaven
lecithin
lederhosen
legalization
legation
legion
legislation
lemon
lengthen
lenin
lenten
lesbian
lesion
lessen
lesson
letterman
leukotoxin
leviathan
levitation
levorotation

libation
liberalization
liberation
Liberian
libertarian
librarian
Libyan
lichen
licitation
ligan
ligation
lighten
lignification
lignin
liken
lilliputian
limen
limitation
Lincoln
linden
lineman
linen
linesman
linin
lion
liquefaction
liquidation
Lisbon
listen
Lithuanian
litigation
liven
localization
location
locomotion
loculation
locution
logan
logician
London

longshoreman
longshoremen
loosen
lotion
Louisianan
lowerclassman
lubrication
lucubration
lumberman
lumen
luncheon
lupine
lutein
luteinization
lutheran
luxation
Lyon
lysin
Macedonian
maceration
Machiavellian
machination
macron
maculation
madden
madison
madwoman
madwomen
Magellan
magician
magnesian
magnetization
magnification
magsman
mahican
maiden
mailwoman
mailwomen
malarian
Malayan

Malaysian
malediction
malefaction
malformation
malfunction
malnutrition
malocclusion
malposition
malrotation
malthusian
malversation
mammalian
mammon
manchurian
mandarin
mandrin
Manhattan
manifestation
manikin
manipulation
mannequin
mansion
manuscript
margarine
margin
marksman
markswoman
markswomen
marlin
marten
martian
Martin
Marxian
masculine
mason
mastication
masturbation
mathematician
matriculation
matron

maturation	midden	moderation
maudlin	midsection	modification
mauritanian	midshipman	modulation
maximization	migration	Mohegan
Mayan	militiaman	Mohican
meccan	million	moisten
mechanization	Milton	molestation
medallion	miniaturization	mollification
mediation	minion	molluscan
medication	ministration	molluskan
medicine	minnesotan	molten
meditation	misapplication	monarchian
mediterranean	misapprehension	Mongolian
megaton	misappropriation	monition
megavitamin	misbegotten	monopolization
melanesian	miscalculation	montanan
melanization	miscommunication	Mormon
melioration	misconception	Moroccan
mellon	misdirection	mortician
melon	misdone	mortification
Melvin	misfortune	Morton
memorization	misinformation	motion
menhaden	misinstruction	motivation
menstruation	misinterpretation	motorization
mention	misprision	motorman
merchantman	mispronunciation	mountain
meridian	misproportion	muffin
merlin	misquotation	mullein
merman	misrepresentation	mulligan
mesmerization	misshapen	mullion
Mesopotamian	mission	multimillion
mesozoan	Mississippian	mummification
metaphysician	mistaken	munition
metrication	mistranslation	murrain
metropolitan	mitigation	musician
Mexican	mitochondrion	muskmelon
Michigan	mitten	muslin
microbian	mizzen	mutagen
micronesian	mobilization	mutation
microsurgeon	moccasin	mutilation

mutton	noggin	obfuscation
myelin	nomen	objection
myelination	nomination	objuration
myosin	nonaggression	objurgation
mystification	nondirection	oblation
Napoleon	nondiscrimination	obligation
narration	none	obliteration
nasalization	nonfiction	oblivion
nation	nonhuman	observation
nationalization	nonintervention	obsession
naturalization	nonparticipation	obsidian
nauseation	nonpartisan	obstetrician
navigation	nonproduction	obstruction
Neapolitan	nonproliferation	obtrusion
neaten	nonrecognition	obviation
nebulization	nonregistration	occasion
negation	nonregulation	occlusion
negotiation	nonsectarian	occupation
Neptunian	nonviolation	ocean
nervation	normalization	oedipean
neutralization	norman	officiation
newsman	Norseman	often
newswoman	Norton	Ohioan
newswomen	Norwegian	Oklahoman
newton	notarization	olden
Newtonian	notation	olefin
niacin	notification	olein
Nicaraguan	notion	oleomargarine
nickelodeon	novation	olfaction
Nigerian	nubbin	olympian
nightman	nucleation	ombudsman
Nippon	nullification	omen
nitration	numeration	omission
nitrogen	nun	one
nitroglycerin	nurseryman	onion
nitroglycerine	nutation	opalescent
nobleman	nutrition	open
noblewoman	oaken	operation
noblewomen	oarsman	opinion
nodulation	oaten	opposition

oppression	overburden	pancreatin
opsin	overcommon	panic-stricken
opsonin	overcompensation	papain
optician	overcorrection	papuan
option	overdiversification	Paraguayan
oration	overdone	paramedian
oratorian	overestimation	pardon
orchardman	overexertion	Parisian
orchestration	overexpansion	Parkinson
ordination	overextension	Parkinsonian
Oregon	overnutrition	parliamentarian
Oregonian	overpopulation	parson
organ	overprotection	partaken
organization	overreaction	participation
orientation	overregulation	partisan
origin	overridden	partition
orion	overrun	partizan
orison	oversimplification	passion
ornamentation	oversubscription	pathogen
orphan	overtaken	patrolman
Orwellian	overwritten	patrolwoman
oscillation	ovulation	patrolwomen
osculation	oxen	patron
ossein	oxidation	patten
ossification	oxonian	pavilion
ostentation	oxygen	pavlovian
ottoman	oxygenation	pecten
ouabain	oysterman	pectin
outbargain	oysterwoman	peculation
outbidden	oysterwomen	pedestrian
outdone	pacification	pediatrician
outgun	paean	pelican
outreason	pagan	pellagrin
outrun	pagination	penalization
outspoken	paladin	penetration
outstation	palestinian	penguin
ovarian	palliation	penicillin
ovation	palpation	penman
oven	palpitation	pension
overbidden	Panamanian	pepsin

perambulation
perception
percolation
percussion
perdition
peregrination
peremption
perfection
perforation
perfusion
perihelion
permeation
permian
permission
permutation
peroration
perpetration
perpetuation
persecution
Persian
persimmon
person
personation
personification
perspiration
persuasion
perturbation
Peruvian
pervasion
perversion
Peterson
petition
petrifaction
petrification
phenomenon
Philadelphian
philodendron
Phoenician
phonation
phonetician

physician
pickwickian
picrotoxin
pidgin
pigeon
pigmentation
pillion
pincushion
pinion
pinon
pippin
piston
pitchman
placation
plainclothesman
plainsman
plainspoken
plankton
plantation
platen
plebeian
plenum
plication
ploughman
plowman
pluralization
pogonion
poison
polarization
policeman
policewoman
policewomen
politician
pollen
pollination
pollution
polyhedron
Polynesian
pomeranian
popgun

poplin
population
porcelain
portion
poseidon
position
possession
postilion
postman
postseason
postulation
potation
potion
poverty-stricken
precalculation
precambrian
precaution
precipitation
precision
preclusion
precognition
preconception
preconcession
precondemnation
precondition
preconsideration
preconstruction
predation
predestination
predestine
predetermination
predetermine
predication
prediction
predigestion
predilection
predisposition
predomination
preelection
preemption

preexamine
prefabrication
prehension
prehuman
preinduction
preinstruction
prekindergarten
premedication
premeditation
premonition
premunition
preoccupation
preordination
preparation
preperception
preposition
prepossession
preregistration
presbyterian
prescription
preseason
presentation
preservation
pressman
prestidigitation
presumption
presupposition
pretension
pretention
prevarication
prevention
princeton
prison
privation
privatization
probation
procession
proclamation
proconservation
procrastination

procreation
procrustean
production
profession
profusion
progestin
prognostication
progression
prohibition
prointegration
prointervention
projection
prolactin
prolegomenon
proletarian
proliferation
prolongation
promethean
promotion
promulgation
pronation
pronunciation
propagation
propitiation
proportion
proposition
propulsion
proration
proscription
prosection
prosecution
prostitution
prostration
protean
protection
protein
protestation
protozoan
protraction
protrusion

prounion
proven
provision
provocation
prussian
pseudocopulation
psychosurgeon
ptarmigan
publican
publication
puffin
pullman
pulsation
pulverization
pun
punctuation
purgation
purification
puritan
purpurin
purslane
pustulation
putrefaction
pygmalion
pylon
pyrotoxin
pythagorean
python
quadrillion
quadruplication
qualification
question
quicken
quickfrozen
quintan
quintillion
quotation
quotidian
radian
radiation

radiocarbon
radioman
ragamuffin
raglan
raisin
ramekin
ramification
ramsden
ranchman
randomization
rapine
rapscallion
rarefaction
ratification
ration
rationalization
ratline
raven
reabandon
reaccreditation
reacquisition
reaction
reactivation
readaptation
readmission
readoption
reaffirmation
reagan
realization
reapportion
reason
reassertion
reawaken
rebellion
rebutton
recalculation
recantation
recapitulation
recaption
reception

recession
rechristen
reciprocation
recirculation
recision
recitation
reckon
reclamation
reclusion
recognition
recollection
recoloration
recombination
recommendation
reconciliation
recondition
reconstitution
reconstruction
reconversion
reconviction
recreation
recrimination
rectification
recuperation
redden
redecoration
rededication
redefinition
redemption
redesignation
redirection
redistribution
redone
reduction
reduplication
reeducation
reelection
reenlighten
reevaluation
reexamine

refashion
refasten
reflection
reforestation
reformation
reformulation
refraction
refrigeration
refrozen
refutation
regeneration
regimen
regimentation
region
registration
regression
regularization
regulation
regurgitation
rehabilitation
rehydration
reimposition
reimprison
reincarnation
reinfusion
reinsertion
reinsman
reinspection
reinstallation
reintegration
reiteration
rejection
rejuvenation
relation
relaxation
relegation
reliction
religion
relocation
remission

remonstration
remuneration
rendition
renegotiation
renomination
renotification
renovation
renunciation
reopen
reorientation
repairman
reparation
repatriation
repercussion
repetition
replantation
repletion
replication
repopulation
reposition
repossession
reprehension
representation
repression
reprobation
reproduction
reptilian
republican
republication
repudiation
repulsion
reputation
requisition
rerun
rescission
resection
reservation
resharpen
resignation
resolution

resonation
resorption
respiration
restitution
restoration
restriction
resubmission
resumption
resurrection
resuscitation
retaken
retaliation
retardation
retention
reticulation
retortion
retraction
retribution
retroflection
retroflexion
retrogression
retrospection
retroversion
reunion
revaluation
revelation
reverberation
reversion
revision
revocation
revolution
revulsion
rewoven
rewritten
rhetorician
Rhodesian
rhododendron
ribbon
riboflavin
richen

ridden
rifleman
riparian
ripen
risen
riven
Robertson
robin
Robinson
robotization
roentgen
Roman
rotation
rotten
roughen
round-robin
rubefaction
ruffian
ruin
ruination
rumination
run
ruskin
Russian
rustication
sabin
saccharin
saccharine
sacristan
sadden
sadducean
saffron
Sagittarian
Saharan
salesman
salesperson
saleswoman
salivation
salmon
salutation

salvation
Samaritan
Samoan
sanctification
sanction
sanguine
sanitarian
sanitation
saponin
saracen
Sardinian
Satan
satiation
satin
satisfaction
saturation
sauerbraten
Saxon
Saxton
scaleman
scallion
Scandinavian
scansion
schoolchildren
scintillation
scion
scission
scorpion
Scotchman
scotian
Scotsman
scrubwoman
scullion
scutcheon
seaman
season
secession
seclusion
secretin
secretion

sectarian
section
sedation
sedimentation
sedition
seduction
segmentation
segregation
seisin
selection
semen
semicolon
seminarian
senatorian
sensation
separation
sequestration
sequin
serbian
sermon
serration
serrulation
serviceman
session
seven
sexton
shaken
Shakespearean
Shakespearian
shaman
sharpen
shaven
shavian
shenanigan
Shetland
shiftman
shipman
shogun
shorten
Shoshonean

shotgun
shovelman
showman
shrunken
shun
Siberian
sibilation
Sicilian
sicken
signalman
signification
silicon
silken
silurian
simian
simoleon
Simon
simpleton
simplification
simulation
singleton
siphon
siren
situation
skeleton
skinnerian
slacken
Slavonian
sleeken
slogan
sloven
slow-motion
smarten
smidgen
smidgeon
smidgin
Smithsonian
smitten
snapdragon
socialization

sodden	stagflation	stun
soften	stagnation	stupefaction
solarization	stalin	sturgeon
solicitation	stallion	Stygian
Solomon	stamen	suasion
solon	stanchion	subclavian
solution	standardization	subcommission
someone	starvation	subdeacon
somnambulation	staten	subdefinition
son	statesman	subdelegation
sophistication	stateswoman	subdistinction
Sophoclean	stateswomen	subdivision
sovereign	station	subduction
spaceman	statistician	subfunction
spacewoman	steapsin	subfunctions
spacewomen	steepen	subhuman
spartan	steersman	subjection
sparteine	stentorian	subjugation
spavin	stepchildren	sublation
specialization	stephen	sublimation
specification	stepson	submersion
specimen	sterilization	submission
speculation	Stetson	subordination
spiculation	Steven	subornation
spoilsman	stiffen	subregion
spoken	stimulation	subscription
spokesman	stipulation	subsection
spokeswoman	stockman	substantiation
spokeswomen	stolen	substation
spoliation	straighten	substitution
spongin	straiten	subterranean
sponsion	strangulation	subtraction
sporozoan	stratification	suburban
sportsman	strengthen	subvention
sportswoman	striation	subversion
sportswomen	stricken	succession
spun	stridden	succussion
squadron	striven	suction
stabilization	strychnine	sudden
stableman	stultification	suffixation

suffocation
suffragan
suffusion
suggestion
sullen
sultan
summation
summon
sun
sunken
superhuman
superposition
superscription
superstition
supervention
supervision
supination
supplementation
supplication
supposition
suppression
surgeon
suspension
suspicion
suzerain
Swahilian
sweden
sweeten
swiftian
switchman
swollen
swordsman
symbolization
sympathin
syncopation
syndication
synephrine
syphon
Syrian
tabulation

tacksman
tactician
taction
tahitian
taken
talesman
talisman
tallyman
talon
tannin
Tanzanian
tarpaulin
tarragon
tartan
Tarzan
tauten
taxation
taximan
technician
telecommunication
teledendron
television
temptation
tendon
Tennyson
tension
termination
terpin
terrapin
tertian
testation
tetrahedron
teuton
Texan
theologian
theoretician
thespian
thiamin
thiamine
thicken

Thompson
threaten
thriven
thyroxin
tibetan
tighten
titan
titillation
titration
toboggan
token
toleration
tollman
ton
torsion
totalitarian
toughen
townsman
townswoman
townswomen
toxin
trackman
traction
tradesman
tradition
tragedian
trainman
transaction
transcription
transduction
transection
transfiguration
transfixion
transformation
transfusion
transgression
transition
translation
transliteration
translocation

transmigration
transmission
transmutation
transocean
transpiration
transplantation
transportation
transposition
transubstantiation
transversion
treason
Trenton
trepidation
triangulation
tribesman
tribeswoman
tribeswomen
tribulation
trifurcation
triggerman
trillion
trinitarian
triplication
trisection
trodden
Trojan
truckman
Truman
truncation
truncheon
trunnion
trypsin
tuition
tungsten
turban
turbine
tuscan
typewritten
Ugandan
Ukrainian

ulceration
ultimation
ululation
umbilication
un
unawakened
unbeaten
unbeholden
unbidden
unbroken
unburden
unbutton
uncertain
unchosen
unchristian
uncommon
unction
underclassman
underestimation
undertaken
underwritten
undone
undulation
uneaten
uneven
unfasten
unfeminine
unforbidden
unforgiven
unforgotten
unforsaken
unfrozen
unification
union
unionization
unison
Unitarian
unladen
unloosen
unmistaken

unperson
unprison
unproven
unshaken
unshaven
unspoken
untrodden
unwoven
unwritten
upperclassman
urban
urbanization
urchin
urination
urine
usurpation
utahan
uterine
utilization
utopian
vacation
vaccination
vacillation
valediction
validation
valorization
valuation
vanillin
vaporization
variation
variegation
vatican
vaudevillian
vegan
vegetarian
vegetation
venation
vendition
veneration
Venetian

venison
ventilation
Venusian
verboten
verification
vermilion
vermillion
vermin
vermination
versification
version
vestryman
veteran
veterinarian
vexation
vibration
Victorian
vilification
villain
vindication
violation
virgin
vision
visitation
vitalization
vitamin
vitellin
vitiation
vitrification
vituperation
vivification
vivisection
vixen
vocalization
vocation
vociferation
volition
Volkswagen
vulcan
vulgarian

vulgarization
Wagnerian
wagon
waken
wanton
warden
washerwoman
Washington
Washingtonian
washwoman
watchman
watchwoman
watermelon
waxen
weaken
weapon
weighman
Wellington
Welshman
welshwomen
wheaten
whiten
whoreson
widen
widgeon
winterization
wireman
wizen
woken
wolffian
wollaston
woman
women
won
wonton
wooden
woodman
woodsman
woolen
woollen

workingwoman
workingwomen
workman
workwoman
workwomen
wormian
worsen
woven
written
xanthin
yachtsman
yachtswoman
yachtswomen
yardman
yeggman
yeoman
yuan
yucatecan
Yugoslavian
Zambian
zeeman
zein
zeppelin
zillion
zion
zonation
zoroastrian
zunian

UNCH
brunch
bunch
crunch
hunch
keypunch
lunch
munch
punch
scrunch

UND

abandoned
aforementioned
almond
apportioned
auctioned
auditioned
awakened
bargained
bastioned
beckoned
betokened
blackened
blazoned
bludgeoned
brightened
broadened
burdened
burgeoned
buttoned
captained
captioned
casehardened
cautioned
chairmaned
chairmanned
chamberland
championed
chastened
cheapened
chickened
christened
Cleveland
coarsened
commissioned
complexioned
conditioned
cordoned
cottoned
crimsoned

cummerbund
curtained
cushioned
dachshund
dampened
darkened
deadened
deafened
deepened
destined
determined
diamond
disburdened
disciplined
disheartened
disillusioned
dunned
emblazoned
emboldened
England
enlightened
enlivened
envisioned
errand
evened
exhusband
fashioned
fastened
fattened
fecund
Finland
flattened
foretokened
freshened
frightened
functioned
fund
gardened
garland
garrisoned

gerund
gladdened
glistened
Greenland
gunned
happened
hardened
harkened
harshened
hastened
hearkened
heartened
heightened
highland
hoarsened
Holland
househusband
husband
Iceland
illumined
imagined
impassioned
imprisoned
intentioned
jettisoned
jocund
leavened
legend
lengthened
lessened
lightened
likened
listened
loosened
maddened
malfunctioned
mentioned
microsecond
midland
millisecond

moistened
moorland
moribund
motioned
nanosecond
New Zealand
noncommissioned
Oakland
occasioned
omened
opened
orotund
orphaned
outbargained
outgunned
outreasoned
overburdened
pardoned
partitioned
pensioned
petitioned
picosecond
pinioned
poisoned
Poland
portioned
Portland
positioned
preconditioned
predestined
predetermined
preexamined
proportioned
punned
questioned
quickened
rationed
reabandoned
reapportioned
reasoned

reawakened
rebuttoned
rechristened
reckoned
reconditioned
reddened
reenlightened
reexamined
refashioned
refastened
refund
reimprisoned
reopened
repositioned
requisitioned
resharpened
reverend
ripened
rotund
roughened
rubicund
ruined
saddened
sanctioned
Scotland
seasoned
second
sectioned
sequined
sharpened
shetland
shortened
shunned
sickened
siphoned
slackened
smartened
softened
spavined
stationed

steepened
stiffened
stipend
straightened
straitened
strengthened
stunned
summoned
sunned
sweetened
Switzerland
syphoned
thickened
thousand
threatened
tightened
toughened
unapportioned
unburdened
unbuttoned
unchastened
unchristened
uncommissioned
unconditioned
underripened
undetermined
unenlightened
unexamined
unfastened
unhardened
unleavened
unloosened
unmentioned
unopened
unpardoned
unquestioned
unreckoned
unripened
unsanctioned
unseasoned

unsharpened
unsweetened
unweakened
visioned
wakened
wantoned
weakened
whitened
widened
wizened
woodland
worsened
Zealand

UNG
among
bluetongue
clung
double-tongue
dung
far-flung
flung
gung
hamstrung
high-strung
hung
kung
lung
overhung
overstrung
rehung
rung
slung
sprung
strung
stung
sung
swung
thereamong
tongue

triple-tongue
underslung
unhung
unsprung
unstrung
unsung
wrung
young

UNJ
expunge
lozenge
lunge
muskellunge
orange
plunge
scavenge
sponge

UNK
bunk
chipmunk
chunk
clunk
countersunk
debunk
drunk
dunk
flunk
funk
gunk
hunk
junk
monk
plunk
podunk
preshrunk
punch-drunk
punk
shrunk

skunk
slunk
spunk
stunk
sunk
trunk

UNKT
adjunct
bunked
conjunct
debunked
defunct
disjunct
dunked
funked
flunked
injunct
junked
plunked
skunked

UNS
abeyance
abhorrence
abidance
abscondence
absence
abundance
accedence
acceptance
accidence
accordance
acquaintance
acquiescence
acquittance
adherence
admittance
adolescence
advertence

affirmance
affluence
africans
allegiance
alliance
allowance
ambiance
ambience
ambivalence
ambulance
annoyance
antecedence
appearance
appliance
arrogance
ascendance
ascendence
assistance
assonance
assurance
attendance
audience
avoidance
balance
belligerence
beneficence
benevolence
bioscience
brilliance
cadence
candescence
circumference
clairvoyance
clearance
coalescence
coexistence
cogence
cognizance
coherence
coincidence

coinsurance
comeuppance
competence
complacence
complaisance
compliance
concomitance
concordance
concurrence
condescendence
condolence
conductance
conference
confidence
confluence
congruence
connivance
conscience
consistence
consonance
constance
continence
contingence
continuance
contrivance
convalescence
convenience
convergence
conveyance
corpulence
correspondence
countenance
counterbalance
counterintelligence
countertransference
credence
dalliance
decadence
defeasance
deference

defiance
deflorescence
deliverance
dependance
dependence
descendance
descendence
desistance
despondence
deterrence
deviance
difference
diffidence
diligence
disallowance
disappearance
discontinuance
discordance
disobedience
dissidence
dissonance
distance
disturbance
divergence
dominance
dunce
ebullience
effervescence
efflorescence
effluence
elegance
eloquence
emergence
eminence
encumbrance
endurance
equidistance
equivalence
essence
evanescence

evidence
excellence
exigence
existence
exorbitance
expedience
experience
exuberance
flagrance
flamboyance
flatulence
florescence
fluorescence
forbearance
forbiddance
fragrance
fraudulence
furtherance
governance
grandiloquence
grievance
guidance
halfpence
hinderance
hindrance
ignorance
imbalance
immanence
imminence
impatience
impatiens
impedance
impenitence
impermanence
impertinence
importance
impotence
improvidence
imprudence
impudence

inadvertence
incandescence
incidence
incipience
incoherence
incompetence
incompliance
incongruence
inconsistence
incontinence
inconvenience
incumbrance
independence
independents
indifference
indigence
indolence
inductance
indulgence
inelegance
inexperience
inference
influence
infrequence
inhabitance
inherence
inheritance
innocence
insentience
insignificance
insistence
insolence
instance
insurance
insurgence
intelligence
intemperance
interdependence
interference
intermittence

intolerance
intransigence
intumescence
iridescence
irrelevance
irreverence
issuance
joyance
jurisprudence
lenience
licence
license
luminance
luminescence
luxuriance
magnificence
magniloquence
maintenance
maleficence
malevolence
malfeasance
malignance
mergence
misalliance
misfeasance
misguidance
monstrance
munificence
nascence
negligence
nescience
nonacceptance
noncompliance
nonexistence
nonfeasance
nonviolence
nuisance
obedience
obeisance
obeyance

observance
obsolescence
occupance
occurrence
omittance
omnipotence
omnipresence
omniscience
once
opalescence
operance
opulence
ordinance
ordnance
outbalance
outdistance
overabundance
overbalance
overconfidence
overindulgence
overinsistence
overinsurance
parlance
patience
penance
penitence
percipience
performance
permanence
perseverance
persistence
pertinence
pestilence
petulance
phosphorescence
pittance
pleasance
potence
precedence
predominance

preeminence
preexistence
preference
prelicense
preponderance
prescience
presence
presentence
prevalence
prominence
protuberance
provenance
providence
prudence
prurience
pubescence
puissance
pursuance
purulence
purveyance
putrescence
quiescence
quintessence
quittance
radiance
reacquaintance
reactance
readmittance
reappearance
reassurance
recalcitrance
recognizance
reconnaissance
reconveyance
recreance
recrudescence
recurrence
redolence
redundance
reemergence

reentrance
reference
relevance
reliance
reluctance
remembrance
reminiscence
remittance
remonstrance
renascence
reoccurrence
repentance
repugnance
residence
residents
resilience
resistance
resonance
resplendence
respondence
resurgence
reticence
reverence
riddance
rubescence
salience
sapience
science
securance
self-confidence
semblance
senescence
sentence
sentience
severance
significance
silence
sixpence
somnolence
stridence

sublicense
submergence
submittance
subprovince
subservience
subsistence
substance
subventions
succorance
succulence
sufferance
supersedence
suppliance
surveillance
surveyance
survivance
sustenance
temperance
teutons
tolerance
transcendence
transference
transience
transients
translucence
transmittance
transparence
trivalence
truculence
tumescence
turbulence
unacceptance
unbalance
undulance
unimportance
utterance
vagrance
valance
valence
valiance

variance
vehemence
vengeance
vigilance
violence
virulence
voidance

UNT
abandonment
abasement
abashment
abatement
aberrant
abetment
abeyant
abhorrent
abolishment
abridgement
abridgment
absent
absorbent
abstinent
abundant
accident
accompaniment
accomplishment
accordant
accountant
accouterment
accruement
achievement
acknowledgement
acknowledgment
acquiescent
adamant
adherent
adjacent
adjournment
adjustment

adjutant
admonishment
adolescent
adornment
adulterant
advancement
advertent
advertisement
advertizement
advisement
affluent
affront
agent
agglutinant
aggrandizement
agreement
ailment
alignment
allegement
allegiant
allotment
allurement
amazement
ambient
ambivalent
ambulant
ambushment
amendment
amortizement
amusement
ancient
announcement
annulment
anointment
anorexiant
antecedent
anticipant
antidepressant
antiperspirant
apartment

apparent
appeasement
appellant
applicant
appointment
apportionment
appraisement
approvement
ardent
argument
armament
arraignment
arrangement
arrant
arrestment
arrogant
ascendant
ascendent
ascertainment
asphyxiant
aspirant
assailant
assailment
assessment
assignment
assistant
assonant
assortment
assuagement
astonishment
astringent
atonement
attachment
attainment
attendant
attestant
attractant
averment
avoidant
avowant

bafflement
bailment
bammoozlement
banishment
basement
battlefront
battlement
bedazzlement
bedevilment
befuddlement
beguilement
belittlement
belligerent
beneficent
benevolent
bequeathment
bereavement
besetment
besiegement
betrothment
betterment
bewilderment
bewitchment
blandishment
blatant
blunt
bombardment
brilliant
brunt
bunt
buoyant
cajolement
candescent
cantonment
casement
celebrant
chastisement
claimant
clairvoyant
clement

client
coalescent
codefendant
coefficient
coexistent
cogent
cognizant
cohabitant
coherent
coincident
combatant
combattant
commandment
commencement
commitment
communicant
compartment
competent
complacent
complainant
complaisant
complement
compliant
compliment
component
concealment
concernment
concomitant
concordant
concurrent
condiment
conferment
confident
confinement
confluent
confront
congealment
congruent
consequent
consignment

consistent
consonant
constant
constituent
constrainment
constringent
consultant
containment
contaminant
contentment
contestant
continent
contingent
continuant
contrastimulant
convalescent
convenient
convergent
conversant
convulsant
coolant
corespondent
corpulent
correspondent
cotangent
counteragent
countercurrent
counterinsurgent
counterirritant
covenant
crescent
crosscurrent
currant
current
curtailment
dachshund
debarment
debasement
debilitant
decadent

decampment
decedent
decent
decongestant
defacement
defendant
deferent
deferment
defiant
deficient
defilement
definement
defoliant
deforcement
defrayment
dehydrant
delinquent
denaturant
denouncement
deodorant
department
dependant
dependent
deployment
deponent
deportment
depravement
depressant
derailment
derangement
descendant
descendent
desiccant
designment
despoilment
despondent
detachment
detainment
detergent
determent

determinant
deterrent
dethronement
detoxicant
detriment
development
deviant
devilment
devolvement
didn't
different
diffident
digestant
diligent
diminishment
disablement
disagreement
disappointment
disarmament
disarrangement
disbandment
disbarment
disbursement
discernment
discontentment
discordant
discouragement
discrepant
discussant
disembodiment
disembowelment
disenchantment
disenfranchisement
disengagement
disentailment
disentanglement
disfigurement
disguisement
dishevelment
disillusionment

disinfectant
dismantlement
dismemberment
disobedient
disparagement
dispersant
dispersement
displacement
disputant
dissident
dissonant
distant
divalent
divergent
divorcement
docent
document
doesn't
dominant
dormant
easement
ebullient
effacement
effervescent
efficient
efflorescent
effluent
effulgence
effulgent
elegant
element
elephant
elopement
eloquent
embankment
embarkment
embarrassment
embellishment
embezzlement
embitterment

emblazonment
embodiment
embossment
embracement
embroilment
emergent
emigrant
eminent
emollient
emplacement
employment
empowerment
enactment
encampment
encapsulant
encasement
enchainment
enchantment
encipherment
encirclement
encompassment
encouragement
encroachment
endamagement
endangerment
endearment
endorsement
endowment
enfant
enfeeblement
enforcement
enfranchisement
engagement
engorgement
engrossment
engulfment
enhancement
enjambment
enjoyment
enlacement

enlargement
enlightenment
enlistment
enlivenment
enmeshment
ennoblement
enrichment
enrollment
enshrinement
enslavement
ensnarement
entailment
entanglement
entertainment
enthrallment
enthronement
enticement
entitlement
entombment
entrancement
entrant
entrapment
entrenchment
entrustment
envelopment
environment
equidistant
equipment
equipotent
equivalent
errant
escapement
escarpment
establishment
estrangement
euphoriant
evanescent
evident
evolvement
examinant

excellent
excipient
excitant
excitement
excrement
exhalant
exhalent
exhibitant
exhilarant
exigent
existent
exorbitant
expectant
expectorant
expedient
experiment
exponent
extant
extinguishment
exuberant
exultant
fervent
figment
filament
firmament
flagellant
flagrant
flamboyant
flatulent
flippant
flocculent
florescent
fluctuant
fluent
fluorescent
foment
fondant
forefront
forejudgment
foreordainment

forestallment
fragment
fragrant
fraudulent
frequent
front
fulfillment
fumigant
fundament
gallant
garment
garnishment
giant
godparent
government
gradient
grandiloquent
grandparent
grievant
grunt
habitant
hadn't
harassment
hasn't
hatchment
haven't
hesitant
humectant
hunt
hydrant
ignorant
immanent
immigrant
imminent
immunosuppressant
impairment
impalement
impatient
impeachment
impediment

impenitent
imperilment
impermanent
impertinent
impingement
implement
important
impotent
impoundment
impoverishment
impressment
imprisonment
improvement
improvident
imprudent
impudent
impugnment
inadvertent
incandescent
incapacitant
incessant
incident
incipient
incitement
inclement
incognizant
incoherent
incompetent
incompliant
incongruent
inconsequent
inconsistent
inconsonant
incontinent
inconvenient
increment
incumbent
indecent
independent
indicant

indictment
indifferent
indigent
indignant
indolent
indorsement
inducement
indulgent
inebriant
inefficient
inelegant
ineloquent
inexpedient
infant
informant
infrequent
infringement
ingestant
ingredient
inhabitant
inhalant
inherent
injectant
innocent
inoculant
inpatient
insentient
insignificant
insistent
insolent
insolvent
installment
instant
instatement
instrument
insufficient
insurgent
intelligent
interactant
interagent

interdependent
interment
intermittent
internment
intertwinement
intolerant
intoxicant
intransigent
intumescent
inurement
invariant
inveiglement
investment
involvement
iridescent
irrelevant
irreverent
irritant
itinerant
jostlement
jubilant
judgement
judgment
jurisprudent
lactescent
lambent
latent
lenient
libelant
libellant
lieutenant
ligament
lineament
liniment
liquescent
litigant
lodgement
lodgment
lubricant
lucent

luminescent
luxuriant
magnificent
magniloquent
maidservant
maladjustment
maleficent
malevolent
malfeasant
malignant
malnourishment
maltreatment
management
manhunt
manservant
measurement
mellifluent
mendicant
merchant
merriment
migrant
militant
ministrant
misalignment
misarrangement
miscreant
misgovernment
misjudgment
mismanagement
misplacement
misstatement
mistreatment
mitigant
moment
monofilament
monument
mordant
movement
munificent
muniment

mustn't	occident	patient
mutafacient	occupant	pavement
mutant	occurrent	payment
nascent	oceanfront	peasant
needn't	oddment	peccant
negligent	odorant	pedant
negotiant	officiant	pediment
nonabsorbent	ointment	penchant
nonalignment	omnipotent	pendant
nonbelligerent	omnipresent	penitent
noncombatant	omniscient	pennant
nonconvergent	operant	peppermint
nonconversant	opponent	percipient
nondevelopment	opulent	permanent
nonequivalent	ordainment	persistent
nonexistent	orient	pertinent
nonfulfillment	ornament	pestilent
nonirritant	outpatient	petulant
nonmalignant	outpayment	pheasant
nonmilitant	overabundant	phosphorescent
nonparticipant	overassessment	pigment
nonpayment	overcomplacent	piquant
nonpregnant	overconfident	placement
nonresident	overdependent	plangent
nonsignificant	overdevelopment	pleasant
nontransparent	overdiligent	pliant
nonviolent	overgarment	poignant
nonvirulent	overindulgent	pollutant
nourishment	overinsistent	postponement
nutrient	overpayment	postulant
nutriment	overrefinement	potent
obedient	overstatement	preachment
obeisant	overviolent	prearrangement
obligant	pageant	precedent
obscurant	parchment	precipitant
obscurement	parent	preconcealment
observant	parliament	predicament
obsolescent	participant	predominant
obstruent	passant	preeminent
obtainment	patent	preenlistment

preexistent
preferment
pregnant
prejudgment
prepayment
preponderant
present
president
prevalent
procurement
proficient
progovernment
prominent
pronouncement
propellant
propellent
proponent
protestant
protuberant
provident
prudent
prurient
pseudopregnant
pubescent
puissant
pungent
punishment
punt
pursuant
purulent
pustulant
putrescent
puzzlement
quadrant
querulant
quiescent
quotient
radiant
radiolucent
raiment

rampant
ravishment
reactant
readjournment
readjustment
reagent
realignment
reallotment
reapportionment
reappraisement
rearmament
rearrangement
reassessment
reassignment
reattachment
reattainment
rebatement
rebutment
recalcitrant
recent
recipient
reclaimant
recombinant
recommitment
reconcilement
recoupment
recreant
recrudescent
recruitment
recumbent
recurrent
redevelopment
redolent
redundant
reemployment
reenactment
reenforcement
reenlargement
reenlistment
reestablishment

referent
refinement
refreshment
refrigerant
refulgent
refurbishment
regalement
regent
regiment
registrant
regnant
regroupment
regurgitant
rehabilitant
reimbursement
reinforcement
reinstallment
reinstatement
reinvolvement
relaxant
relevant
reliant
reluctant
remanent
reminiscent
remitment
remittent
remnant
remonstrant
renascent
renouncement
repayment
repellant
repellent
repentant
replacement
replenishment
repugnant
requirement
rescindment

resentment	segment	subbasement
resettlement	segregant	subcontinent
resident	self-effacement	subjacent
resilient	senescent	subsegment
resistant	sentient	subsequent
resistent	sentiment	subservient
resolvent	septuagint	subtenant
resonant	sequent	succorant
resplendent	sergeant	succulent
respondent	serjeant	sufficient
restatement	serpent	suint
restaurant	servant	supergiant
resultant	settlement	superintendent
resurgent	sextant	superpotent
retainment	shipment	supplement
retardant	shirtfront	suppliant
reticent	shouldn't	supplicant
retirement	shunt	suppressant
reverberant	sibilant	surveillant
reverent	signalment	sustainment
revilement	significant	sustenant
riverfront	silent	sycophant
rodent	sojournment	talent
rubefacient	solicitant	tangent
rubescent	solvent	temperament
rudiment	somnambulant	tenant
runt	somnifacient	tenement
sacrament	somnolent	testament
salient	spearmint	tetravalent
sapient	stagnant	tolerant
savant	statement	torrent
scient	stepparent	tournament
scintillant	stimulant	toxicant
seafront	storefront	traducement
sealant	strewment	transcendent
secant	strident	transient
secernent	stringent	translucent
securement	student	transparent
sediment	stunt	treatment
seducement	stupefacient	trenchant

trepidant
triumphant
trivalent
truant
truculent
tumescent
turbulent
turgescent
tyrant
unabsorbent
unapparent
uncompliant
undercurrent
underdevelopment
undergarment
undernourishment
underpayment
understatement
undulant
unemployment
unfulfillment
unimportant
univalent
unobservant
unpleasant
unrepentant
unresistant
unsettlement
upliftment
urgent
vacant
vagrant
valiant
variant
varmint
vehement
verdant
vesicant
vestment
vibrant

vigilant
violent
viridescent
virulent
visitant
warrant
waterfront
weighment
wonderment
worriment
worsement
wouldn't

Long UP
age-group
bloop
coop
coupe
croup
droop
drupe
dupe
goop
group
hoop
in-group
loop
loupe
nincompoop
paratroop
poop
recoup
regroup
scoop
sloop
snoop
soup
stoop
stupe
subgroup

swoop
troop
troupe
whoop

UP
archbishop
backup
bishop
blowup
breakup
buildup
buttercup
catchup
catsup
checkup
cleanup
closeup
coverup
crackup
cup
cutup
develop
develope
dollop
envelop
escallop
europe
eyecup
faceup
gallop
gallup
getup
gossip
grownup
hiccough
hiccup
holdup
hookup
hyssop

julep
ketchup
kickup
larrup
letup
lineup
linkup
lockup
lollop
makeup
markup
mixup
mockup
overdevelop
Philip
pickup
pileup
pinup
polyp
pup
pushup
redevelop
roundup
scallop
scollop
setup
shakeup
shallop
shapeup
showup
situp
slipup
smashup
speedup
stickup
stirrup
sunup
sup
syrup
teacup

tossup
trollop
tulip
tuneup
turnip
turnup
up
walkup
wallop
warmup
wickiup
windup
workup
worship

UPT
abrupt
bankrupt
corrupt
cupped
developed
disrupt
enveloped
erupt
escalloped
galloped
gossiped
hiccuped
hiccupped
incorrupt
interrupt
irrupt
larruped
overdeveloped
redeveloped
scalloped
supped
underdeveloped
undeveloped
upped

walloped

UR
adjure
allure
amateur
amour
assure
azure
boor
brochure
carillonneur
cocksure
coinsure
connoisseur
couture
cure
demure
detour
embouchure
endure
ensure
entrepreneur
epicure
fluor
grandeur
immature
immure
impure
insecure
insure
inure
investiture
kippur
ligature
liqueur
literature
lure
manicure
manure

mature
miniature
moor
obscure
outpour
overinsure
overture
paramour
pedicure
pompadour
poor
pour
premature
procure
provacateur
pure
reassure
reinsure
saboteur
saviour
secure
sinecure
spoor
sure
tablature
tambour
tenure
tour
troubadour
unsure
velour
you're
your

URB
adverb
blurb
curb
disturb
herb

perturb
proverb
Serb
suburb
superb
verb

URCH
besmirch
bioresearch
birch
church
lurch
perch
prochurch
research
search
smirch
unchurch

URD
absurd
acquired
administered
adventured
afterward
altered
anchored
angered
answered
armored
augured
averred
awkward
backward
badgered
bantered
barbered
bartered
bastard

battered
bedford
beggared
belabored
beleaguered
bespattered
bestirred
bettered
bewildered
billiard
biohazard
bird
blackbird
blistered
blizzard
blubbered
bluebird
blundered
blurred
blustered
bolstered
bordered
bothered
bradford
broidered
burred
butchered
buttered
butterfingered
buzzard
buzzword
byword
calendared
calipered
cambered
cankered
cantered
cantilevered
capered
captured

caricatured
catbird
catchword
catered
censored
censured
centered
chambered
chamfered
chartered
chattered
chauffeured
checkered
ciphered
clamored
clapboard
clattered
clobbered
cloistered
closured
clotured
clustered
cluttered
coastward
codeword
collard
collared
colored
concurred
conferred
configured
conjectured
conjured
conquered
considered
cornered
cosponsored
countered
covered
coward

cowbird
cowered
crossword
cultured
cumbered
cupboard
curd
custard
dastard
deciphered
deferred
deflowered
delivered
demurred
denatured
deterred
diapered
dickered
differed
discolored
discovered
disencumbered
disfigured
dishonored
dismembered
disordered
dissevered
doctored
doddered
downward
drunkard
dullard
earthward
eastward
Edward
embittered
embroidered
empowered
enamored
enciphered

encountered
encumbered
endangered
endeavored
endeavoured
engendered
enraptured
entered
erred
euchred
factored
faltered
fathered
favored
feathered
featured
festered
fettered
fevered
figured
filibustered
filtered
fingered
fissured
flattered
flavored
flickered
floundered
floured
flowered
flustered
fluttered
foreword
forward
fostered
foundered
fractured
frittered
furred
furthered

garnered
gartered
gathered
gerrymandered
gestured
gibbered
gird
gizzard
glaciered
glimmered
glittered
glowered
goatherd
guttered
haggard
halberd
haltered
halyard
hammered
hampered
hankered
haphazard
harbored
hartford
Harvard
hayward
hazard
headquartered
headword
heard
heathered
heavenward
hectored
henceforward
herd
hereford
hindered
hired
hollered
homeward

honored
hovered
hummingbird
humored
hungered
hunkered
incumbered
incurred
indentured
inferred
injured
inquired
interred
inward
jabbered
jailbird
jaybird
jeopard
jittered
kippered
labored
lacquered
ladybird
laggard
landward
lanyard
lathered
laundered
layered
lectured
leeward
leopard
lettered
levered
limbered
lingered
littered
livered
lizard
loanword

loitered
louvered
lovebird
lowered
lumbered
majored
maladministered
malingered
mallard
maneuvered
mannered
manoeuvered
manufactured
martyred
massacred
mastered
mattered
maundered
meandered
measured
metered
ministered
mirrored
misheard
misnumbered
mockingbird
moldered
monitored
mortared
mothered
motored
muggered
multicolored
murdered
murmured
mustard
mustered
muttered
natured
neighbored

nerd
neutered
nickered
niggard
nonregistered
nonstandard
northeastward
northward
northwestward
numbered
nurtured
occurred
offered
onward
orchard
ordered
outmaneuvered
outnumbered
outward
overheard
overpowered
oxford
paltered
pampered
pandered
papered
password
pastured
pattered
peppered
perjured
pestered
petered
philandered
pictured
pilastered
pilchard
pilfered
pillared
placard

plastered
plundered
pondered
poniard
postured
potsherd
powdered
powered
preferred
prefigured
preregistered
pressured
proffered
prospered
puckered
punctured
purred
puttered
quartered
quavered
quivered
rancored
rapiered
rearward
recaptured
rechartered
recolored
reconnoitered
reconquered
reconsidered
record
recovered
recurred
rediscovered
reentered
referred
refiltered
registered
reheard
remaindered

remembered
rendered
renumbered
reoccurred
reordered
reupholstered
reword
round-shouldered
rumored
ruptured
sandpapered
sauntered
savored
scabbard
scampered
scattered
scissored
scoured
sculptured
seabird
seaward
sepulchered
sepulchred
sequestered
shattered
sheltered
shepherd
shimmered
shirred
shivered
shorebird
shoreward
shouldered
showered
shuddered
shuttered
signatured
silvered
simmered
simpered

skewered
skittered
skyward
slandered
slathered
slaughtered
slavered
slickered
slithered
slivered
slobbered
sluggard
slumbered
slurred
smoldered
smothered
snickered
sniggered
snowbird
sobered
soldered
soldiered
songbird
soured
southeastward
southward
southwestward
spaceward
Spaniard
spattered
splattered
splintered
spluttered
sponsored
spurred
sputtered
squandered
staggered
stammered
standard

Stanford
starboard
steamrollered
steward
stirred
straightforward
strictured
structured
stuttered
substandard
succored
suffered
sugared
sulfured
sulphured
summered
sundered
surrendered
sutured
swaggered
swearword
sweltered
tabard
tailored
tampered
tankard
tapered
tarpapered
tattered
teetered
tempered
tendered
tenured
tethered
textured
third
thitherward
thunderbird
thundered
timbered

tinctured
tinkered
tittered
tortured
tottered
towered
transferred
transfigured
treasured
triggered
twittered
ulcered
umpired
unaltered
unanchored
unanswered
unarmored
unblurred
uncensored
uncensured
unchartered
uncluttered
uncolored
unconquered
unconsidered
uncovered
uncultured
uncumbered
undergird
undeterred
undiscovered
undowered
unencumbered
unentered
unexpired
unfavored
unfettered
unfiltered
unflavored
unhampered

unheard
unhindered
unhonored
unincumbered
uninjured
unlettered
unmeasured
unnumbered
unoffered
unordered
unperjured
unpressured
unregistered
unsheltered
unstructured
untired
untransferred
untutored
unuttered
upholstered
upward
ushered
uttered
varicolored
ventured
versicolored
vineyard
visored
vizard
wagered
wallpapered
wandered
watchword
watered
wavered
wayward
weathered
weltered
westered
westward

whimpered
whirlybird
whirred
whiskered
whispered
widowered
willard
windward
wintered
withered
wizard
wondered
woodward
word
yammered
yardbird
zippered

URF
astroturf
bodysurf
serf
surf
turf

URJ
converge
dirge
diverge
emerge
immerge
merge
purge
reemerge
scourge
serge
splurge
spurge
submerge
surge

unmerge
upsurge
urge
verge

URK
artwork
basketwork
beadwork
berserk
brainwork
breastwork
brickwork
bridgework
brushwork
bulwark
busywork
cabinetwork
casework
circ
cirque
clerk
clockwork
coachwork
crewelwork
dirk
earthwork
enamelwork
fancywork
feltwork
fieldwork
firework
flatwork
footwork
framework
frostwork
glasswork
grillework
grillwork
groundwork

guesswork
hackwork
handiwork
handwork
headwork
homework
housework
irk
ironwork
jerk
kirk
knee-jerk
lacework
latticework
legwork
lifework
lurk
masonwork
masterwork
meshwork
metalwork
millwork
murk
needlework
network
openwork
outwork
overwork
paperwork
patchwork
perk
piecework
plasterwork
presswork
quirk
rework
roadwork
salesclerk
schoolwork
scrollwork

shirk
smirk
spadework
steelwork
stonework
stuccowork
taskwork
teamwork
timework
Turk
waxwork
wickerwork
woodwork
work

URL
awhirl
burl
churl
cowgirl
curl
Earl
furl
girl
hurl
impearl
knurl
newsgirl
pearl
playgirl
purl
salesgirl
schoolgirl
squirrel
swirl
twirl
uncurl
unfurl
whirl

URLD
burled
curled
dream-world
furled
hurled
impearled
knurled
netherworld
purled
swirled
twirled
uncurled
underworld
unfurled
whirled
world

URM
affirm
angiosperm
angleworm
armyworm
berm
blastoderm
bloodworm
bookworm
cankerworm
confirm
cutworm
deworm
disaffirm
disconfirm
dynatherm
earthworm
firm
flatworm
fullterm
gapeworm
germ

glowworm
hairworm
heartworm
hookworm
hypoderm
inchworm
infirm
isotherm
long-term
lungworm
mesoderm
midterm
misterm
oosperm
pachyderm
periderm
perm
pinworm
poikilotherm
reaffirm
reconfirm
ringworm
roundworm
screwworm
seatworm
silkworm
sperm
squirm
stenotherm
tapeworm
term
therm
threadworm
woodworm
worm
zygosperm

URN
adjourn
andiron

auburn
bern
burn
cavern
churn
cistern
concern
discern
downturn
earn
eastern
fern
flatiron
govern
gridiron
heartburn
intern
iron
lantern
learn
leathern
lectern
midwestern
misgovern
modern
nocturn
nocturne
northeastern
northern
northwestern
overconcern
overturn
pattern
postern
promodern
pseudomodern
radioiron
readjourn
relearn
return

sadiron
saturn
secern
sideburn
slattern
sojourn
southeastern
southern
southwestern
spurn
stern
stubborn
sunburn
taciturn
tavern
tern
turn
u-turn
ultramodern
unconcern
unlearn
upturn
urn
western
windburn
yearn

URNT
burnt
earnt
learnt
relearnt
sunburnt
unburnt
weren't

URP
Antwerp
burp
chirp

slurp
twerp
twirp
usurp

URPT
burped
chirped
excerpt
slurped
usurped

URS
accurse
adverse
asperse
averse
breathers
coerce
commerce
converse
curse
cutpurse
detectors
disburse
disperse
diverse
guiders
hearse
imburse
immerse
intersperse
inverse
nurse
obverse
perverse
producers
purse
rehearse
reimburse

reverse
submerse
terce
terse
transverse
traverse
universe
verse
worse

URST
accursed
accurst
airburst
aspersed
athirst
bratwurst
burst
cloudburst
coerced
conversed
cursed
curst
disbursed
dispersed
durst
emersed
erst
feetfirst
first
headfirst
immersed
interspersed
knackwurst
knockwurst
liverwurst
nursed
outburst
pursed
rehearsed

reimbursed
reversed
submersed
sunburst
thirst
traversed
unrehearsed
untraversed
unversed
versed
verst
worst
wurst

URT
advert
Albert
alert
assert
avert
blurt
braggart
comfort
concert
controvert
convert
covert
culvert
curt
desert
dessert
dirt
discomfort
disconcert
divert
effort
exert
expert
extravert
extrovert

filbert
flirt
Frankfort
Frankfurt
Gilbert
girt
Herbert
hoopskirt
hurt
inert
inexpert
insert
introvert
invert
malapert
miniskirt
nightshirt
nonexpert
overexert
overskirt
overt
pert
pervert
preinsert
quirt
reassert
reconvert
reinsert
revert
Robert
roquefort
Schubert
sherbet
shirt
skirt
spurt
squirt
stalwart
Stewart
Stuart

subvert
sweatshirt
undershirt
underskirt
unhurt
vert
wert
yoghurt
yogurt
yurt

URTH
afterbirth
berth
birth
childbirth
dearth
earth
firth
girth
mirth
rebirth
stillbirth
unearth
woolworth
wordsworth
worth

URV
conserve
curve
deserve
mirv
nerve
observe
preserve
reserve
serve
swerve
unnerve

verve

Long US
abuse
adduce
Bruce
caboose
calaboose
chartreuse
cruse
deduce
deuce
diffuse
disuse
duce
educe
effuse
excuse
footloose
goose
induce
introduce
juice
loose
mass-produce
misuse
mongoose
moose
mousse
nonuse
noose
obtuse
outproduce
overproduce
papoose
perfuse
produce
profuse
puce
recluse

reduce
refuse
reinduce
reproduce
ruse
schuss
seduce
self-abuse
sluice
spruce
traduce
transduce
truce
underproduce
unloose
use
vamoose
Zeus

US
abacus
abjectness
abortiveness
abrasiveness
abruptness
absentmindedness
absoluteness
abstractness
absurdness
abusiveness
accomplice
accountableness
accurateness
accursedness
accusativeness
acquisitiveness
acridness
acrimonious
acropolis
activeness

actless
actress
acuteness
adaptableness
adaptiveness
addictiveness
adeptness
adequateness
adhesiveness
Adonis
adorableness
adroitness
adulteress
adulterous
adulterousness
adultness
advantageous
advantageousness
adventuress
adventurous
adventurousness
adverseness
advisedness
aegis
Aeschylus
affectedness
affectionless
affirmativeness
ageless
agelessness
aggressiveness
agileness
agreeableness
agribusiness
aimless
aimlessness
airiness
airless
airlessness
airsickness

airworthiness
alertness
alias
Alice
alikeness
aliveness
allusiveness
almightiness
aloneness
aloofness
alumnus
amateurishness
ambidextrous
ambiguous
ambiguousness
ambitious
ambitiousness
amiableness
amicableness
amorous
amorousness
amorphous
Amos
amphibious
ampleness
analogous
analogousness
analysis
ancestress
anchorless
ancientness
Angeles
angularness
Angus
anise
anomalous
anonymous
anonymousness
anticancerous
antiqueness

antithesis
antonymous
anuresis
anus
anxious
anxiousness
apparatus
appendicitis
appositeness
appreciativeness
apprehensiveness
apprentice
appropriateness
aptness
Aquarius
Aquinas
arbitrariness
archdiocese
archduchess
arduous
arduousness
armistice
armless
armlessness
arsonous
arteriosclerosis
artfulness
arthritis
articulateness
artifice
artificialness
artiness
artless
artlessness
asbestos
asbestosis
asbestus
asepsis
ashiness
asparagus

assertiveness
assiduous
assiduousness
assuasiveness
assumptiveness
astuteness
atlas
atrocious
atrociousness
attentiveness
attractiveness
audacious
audaciousness
augustness
Augustus
auspice
auspicious
auspiciousness
austereness
authoress
authoritativeness
autohypnosis
autonomous
avarice
avaricious
avis
awareness
aweless
awesomeness
awfulness
awkwardness
axis
azygous
Bacchus
backless
backwardness
bacteriosis
bacteriostasis
badness
bagginess

baldness
balefulness
balkiness
balminess
bandboxes
Barabbas
barbarious
barbarous
barbarousness
bareness
baritosis
baroness
barotaxis
barotitis
barrenness
baseless
baselessness
baseness
bashfulness
basis
basses
battiness
bawdiness
beaconless
beardless
beastliness
beauteous
beggarliness
bellicoseness
Benedictus
benefactress
beneficialness
benightedness
benumbedness
bias
bigamous
bigness
bilious
biliousness
biosynthesis

bitterness
bituminous
bizarreness
blackness
blamableness
blameless
blamelessness
blameworthiness
blandness
blankness
blasphemous
bleakness
blessedness
blindness
blissfulness
blitheness
blockhouses
blondness
bloodedness
bloodiness
bloodless
bloodthirstiness
blouses
blowiness
blueness
blunderbuss
bluntness
boastfulness
bodacious
bodice
bodiless
bogus
boisterous
boisterousness
boldness
bondless
boneless
boniness
bonniness
bonus

boorishness
bootless
bootyless
borealis
Boris
bossiness
bottomless
boundless
bounteous
bounteousness
bountyless
bowedness
boyishness
brackishness
braininess
brainless
brainlessness
brakeless
braless
branchless
brashness
brattiness
braveness
brawniness
brazenness
breadless
breathless
breeziness
briefless
briefness
brightness
brimless
brininess
briskness
brittleness
broadness
brokenness
bronchiolitis
bronchitis
brontosaurus

brotherliness
bruskness
brusqueness
brutalness
buckleless
bulbous
bullheadedness
bumpiness
burgess
burliness
bursitis
bus
business
buss
busyness
buttress
buxomness
cacogenesis
cacophonous
cactus
cactuses
cadaverous
caddishness
cageyness
caginess
calamitous
calculus
caliginous
callous
callousness
callowness
callus
calmness
campiness
campus
cancerous
candidness
cankerous
canniness
cantankerous

cantankerousness
canvas
canvass
capableness
capacious
capaciousness
capricious
capriciousness
captious
captress
Caracas
carbonless
carcass
carcinosis
carefulness
careless
carelessness
carnivorous
carnivorousness
carsickness
casteless
casualness
catharsis
cattiness
Caucasus
caucus
causeless
cautious
cautiousness
cavalierness
cavernous
ceaseless
ceaselessness
Celsius
census
centeredness
Cephaelis
ceremonious
ceremoniousness
certainness

chalice
chalkiness
challis
changeless
chaoticness
characterless
charitableness
chasteness
chattiness
cheapness
checkless
cheekiness
cheerfulness
cheeriness
cheerless
cheerlessness
cheesiness
chiasmas
chicness
childishness
childless
childlessness
chilliness
chillness
chinless
chitinous
chivalrous
chivalrousness
choiceness
choosiness
choppiness
chorus
Christmas
chrysalis
chubbiness
chumminess
chunkiness
churchless
churlishness
cinderous

circuitous
circularness
circulus
circus
cirrhosis
cirrocumulus
cirrostratus
cirrus
citrus
civilness
claimless
clamminess
clamorous
clamorousness
clannishness
classless
classlessness
cleanliness
cleanness
clearheadedness
clearness
cleverness
clientless
cliquishness
cloddishness
closeness
cloudiness
cloudless
clownishness
clumsiness
coarseness
cockatrice
cockiness
coconscious
coconsciousness
codeless
coerciveness
coheiress
cohesiveness
coitus

coldness
coleus
colitis
collarless
colorfastness
colorfulness
colorless
colossus
Columbus
combativeness
comeliness
comfortableness
comfortless
commodious
commodiousness
commonness
communicableness
communicativeness
compactness
companionless
comparativeness
compass
compatibleness
competitiveness
completeness
complexness
complicatedness
composedness
comprehensiveness
compulsiveness
concaveness
conceitedness
conceivableness
conciseness
conclusiveness
concreteness
concuss
conduciveness
confidentialness
Confucius

congress
congruous
coniferous
conjunctivitis
consanguineous
conscienceless
conscientious
conscientiousness
conscious
consciousness
consecutiveness
consensus
conspicuous
conspicuousness
constructiveness
consumptiveness
contagious
contagiousness
contemporaneous
contemptuous
contemptuousness
contentedness
contentious
contentiousness
conterminous
conterminousness
contiguous
contiguousness
continuous
continuousness
contrariness
contriteness
conus
coolness
cooperativeness
Copernicus
copious
copiousness
coppice
cordialness

corditis
cordless
corneous
cornice
corniness
corpus
correctness
corrosiveness
corruptibleness
corruptness
cosmopolis
cost-plus
costless
costliness
coterminous
counteractiveness
counterfeitness
countess
countless
courageous
courageousness
courteous
courteousness
courtliness
covertness
covetous
covetousness
cowardice
cowardliness
coyness
coziness
crabbiness
craftiness
cragginess
crankiness
crappiness
crapulous
crassness
cravenness
craziness

creakiness
creaminess
creativeness
credibleness
creditableness
credulous
creepiness
crestless
cretaceous
cretinous
crevice
crewless
crimeless
criminalness
crinkliness
crisis
crispiness
crispness
criticalness
croakiness
crocus
crookedness
crossness
crotchetiness
crowdedness
crucialness
crudeness
cruelness
crumbliness
culpableness
cumbersomeness
cumbrous
cumulonimbus
cumulus
cunningness
curableness
cureless
curious
curiousness
curliness

currentness
cursedness
cursiveness
cursoriness
curtness
curvaceous
curvaceousness
curviness
cushiness
cuss
cutaneous
cuteness
cutlass
cypress
Cyprus
daffiness
daftness
daintiness
dais
Dallas
Damascus
damnableness
dampness
dangerous
dangerousness
dankness
dapperness
daringness
darkness
dastardliness
datedness
dateless
dauntless
dauntlessness
davis
dazedness
deaconess
deadliness
deadness
deafness

dearness
deathless
deathlessness
debauchedness
debonairness
decayedness
deceitfulness
deceptiveness
deciduous
deciduousness
decisiveness
decorativeness
decorous
decorousness
deepness
defectiveness
defenseless
defenselessness
defensiveness
definiteness
definitiveness
deftness
defunctness
degenerateness
degradedness
dejectedness
deleterious
deleteriousness
deliberateness
deliberativeness
delicateness
delicious
deliciousness
delightfulness
delirious
deliriousness
delusiveness
demonstrativeness
demureness
dennis

denseness
dentifrice
dentigerous
dentulous
dependableness
deplorableness
depravedness
derisiveness
dermatitis
dermis
derogatoriness
derris
descriptiveness
desirous
desolateness
desperateness
destituteness
destructiveness
determinedness
detrimentalness
devilishness
devious
deviousness
devoutness
dewiness
dexterous
dexterousness
diabetes
diagnoses
diagnosis
dialysis
dichotomous
dictatorialness
diffuseness
digestiveness
digitalis
dilatoriness
dimness
dimorphous
dimwittedness

dinginess
dingus
diocese
directness
direness
dirtiness
disadvantageous
disagreeableness
disastrous
disconsolateness
discontentedness
discontinuous
discourteous
discreetness
discursiveness
discus
discuss
disgracefulness
disharmonious
dishonorableness
disjointedness
dismalness
disorderliness
disputatious
disruptiveness
disservice
dissuasiveness
distantness
distastefulness
distinctiveness
distinctness
distrustfulness
ditchless
diuresis
diverseness
diverticulitis
diverticulosis
divisiveness
dizziness
doggedness

dolefulness
doneness
dopiness
Doris
doubleness
doubtfulness
doubtless
douglas
dowdiness
dowryless
drabness
draftiness
dreadfulness
dreaminess
dreamless
dreariness
dressiness
dripless
driverless
droopiness
drossiness
drowsiness
drunkenness
dryness
dubious
dubiousness
duchess
ductless
dullness
dulness
dumbness
dumpiness
duplicitous
durableness
duskiness
dustiness
dustless
duteous
dutifulness
eagerness

earless
earliness
earnestness
earthiness
earthliness
earwitness
easiness
easygoingness
echoless
edginess
edibleness
edifice
eeriness
effectiveness
effeteness
efficacious
effortless
effortlessness
effusiveness
egregious
egregiousness
elaborateness
electrolysis
electrotaxis
elfishness
ellipsis
elusiveness
Elvis
embarrass
emeritus
emotionless
emotionlessness
emphasis
empress
emptiness
encephalitis
enchantress
enchantresses
encompass
endless

endlessness
endogamous
endogenous
engineless
enormous
enormousness
enteritis
entireness
envious
enviousness
epidermis
epiglottis
equivocalness
Erasmus
erectness
erogenous
eros
erosiveness
erroneous
erroneousness
errorless
esophagus
esthesis
estrous
estrus
eternalness
etherealness
ethicalness
eucalyptus
euphonious
evasiveness
evenness
eventfulness
exactingness
exactness
excessiveness
exclusiveness
excusableness
exegesis
exhaustless

exiguous
exitus
exodus
exogamous
expanses
expansiveness
expeditious
expeditiousness
expertness
explicitness
explosiveness
expressionless
expressiveness
exquisiteness
extemporaneous
extensiveness
extraneous
extraneousness
extraneus
extremeness
eyedness
eyeless
eyewitness
fabulous
faceless
facelessness
facetious
facetiousness
facileness
fadeless
faintheartedness
faintness
fairness
faithfulness
faithless
faithlessness
fallacious
fallibleness
falseness
familiarness

famous
fancifulness
fanciness
fantabulous
farsightedness
fashionableness
fastidious
fastidiousness
fastness
fatalness
fatefulness
fatherless
fatherliness
fathomless
fatigueless
fatness
fatuous
fatuousness
faultiness
faultless
faultlessness
Faustus
favorableness
fearfulness
fearless
fearlessness
feasibleness
featheriness
featherless
featureless
feeblemindedness
feebleness
feistiness
felicitous
fellness
felonious
feloniousness
femaleness
fenceless
ferocious

ferociousness
Ferris
ferrous
fertileness
fervidness
festiveness
fetus
feverishness
feverous
fewness
fibrous
fickleness
fictitious
fidgetiness
fiendishness
fierceness
fieriness
figurativeness
filminess
filthiness
fineness
finiteness
fireless
firmness
fishiness
fitfulness
fitness
fittingness
flabbiness
flakiness
flashiness
flatness
flavorless
flawless
flawlessness
fleeciness
fleetingness
fleetness
fleshiness
flightiness

flightless
flimsiness
flirtatious
floppiness
floweriness
flowerless
fluffiness
fluidness
flushness
foaminess
focus
fogginess
fogless
foliaceous
fondness
foolhardiness
foolishness
footless
footlessness
footsoreness
forcefulness
forceless
forcibleness
foreconscious
forehandedness
foreignness
forenotice
foresightedness
forgetfulness
forgiveness
formless
formlessness
forthrightness
fortress
fortuitous
fortunateness
forwardness
foulness
foundress
foxiness

fracas
fragileness
frailness
frankness
fraudulentness
freakishness
freeness
frequentness
freshness
fretfulness
friableness
frictionless
friendless
friendlessness
friendliness
frightfulness
frilliness
fringeless
friskiness
frivolous
frizziness
frostiness
frothiness
frowsiness
frowziness
frozenness
fruitfulness
fruitiness
fruitless
fruitlessness
fullness
functionless
fungous
fungus
funniness
furious
furnace
furriness
furtiveness
fuseless

fuss
fussiness
fustiness
futileness
futureless
fuzziness
gabbiness
gainfulness
gainless
gallinaceous
gameness
gaminess
gangrenous
garishness
garrulous
garrulousness
gaseous
gaseousness
gassiness
gastritis
gaucheness
gaudiness
gauntness
gauziness
gayness
gearless
gelatinous
geminous
generous
generousness
genesis
Genghis
genius
genteelness
gentleness
genuineness
genus
germaneness
ghastliness
ghostliness

ghoulishness
giantess
giardiasis
gibbous
gibbousness
giddiness
gingivitis
girlishness
glabrous
gladiolus
gladness
glamorous
glamorousness
glamourous
glassiness
gleefulness
glibness
gloominess
glorious
gloriousness
glossiness
glottis
glumness
gluteus
glutinous
gluttonous
goddess
godless
godlessness
godliness
goodness
goofiness
gorgeous
gorgeousness
goriness
gouges
goutiness
governableness
governess
gracefulness

graceless
gracelessness
gracious
graciousness
graininess
grampus
grandioseness
grandness
granivorous
graspingness
gratefulness
gratis
gratuitous
gratuitousness
graveless
graveness
grayness
greasiness
greatheartedness
greatness
greediness
greenishness
greenness
gregarious
gregariousness
greyness
grievous
grievousness
grimace
griminess
grimness
grittiness
grogginess
grossness
grotesqueness
grouchiness
groundless
groundlessness
grubbiness
gruesomeness

gruffness
grumpiness
guileless
guilelessness
guiltiness
guiltless
guiltlessness
gustless
gutless
gutlessness
gyrocompass
habeas
habitableness
habitualness
hairiness
hairless
hairlessness
haleness
halfheartedness
halitosis
halogenous
hammerless
handedness
handiness
handless
handsomeness
haphazardness
hapless
haplessness
happiness
harass
harborless
hardhandedness
hardheadedness
hardheartedness
hardiness
hardness
harmfulness
harmless
harmlessness

harmonious
harmoniousness
harness
harshness
hastiness
hatefulness
hatless
haughtiness
hazardless
hazardous
hazardousness
haziness
headiness
headless
healthfulness
healthiness
heartiness
heartless
heartlessness
heartsickness
heatless
heaviness
heavyheartedness
heedfulness
heedless
heedlessness
heelless
heftiness
heinous
heinousness
heiress
heirless
heliotaxis
hellishness
helpfulness
helpless
helplessness
hemostasis
hepatitis
herbaceous

herbivorous
hereditariness
herpesvirus
heteromorphous
hiatus
hibiscus
hideous
hideousness
highhandedness
highness
hilarious
hilariousness
hilliness
hingeless
hippopotamus
hoariness
hoarseness
hocus
hocus-pocus
hoggishness
holiness
hollowness
homeless
homeliness
homeostasis
homesickness
homeyness
homogamous
homogeneous
homogenous
homologous
homonomous
homonymous
homozygous
Honduras
honestness
honorableness
honorless
hoopless
hopefulness

hopeless
hopelessness
horace
hornless
horrendous
horribleness
horridness
horseless
hospice
hospitableness
hostess
hotheadedness
hotness
houseless
housewifeliness
hubris
huffiness
hugeness
humaneness
humanness
humbleness
humerus
humongous
humorless
humorlessness
humorous
humorousness
humus
hungerless
hunnishness
huntress
hurriedness
hurtfulness
huskiness
hybris
hydrolysis
hydrous
hypersensitiveness
hypnosis
hypodermis

hypothesis
iambus
ibis
ichthyosis
iciness
ictus
identicalness
idleness
idolatrous
igneous
ignominious
ignoramus
ignorantness
illicitness
illness
illusiveness
illustrious
illustriousness
immaculateness
immaterialness
immediateness
immoderateness
immutableness
impartialness
impassiveness
impecunious
impecuniousness
impenetrableness
imperceptibleness
imperceptiveness
imperfectness
imperialness
imperious
imperiousness
impervious
imperviousness
impetiginous
impetuous
impetuousness
impetus

impious
impishness
implausibleness
implicitness
impoliteness
imponderableness
impossibleness
impreciseness
impressiveness
imprimis
improperness
impulsiveness
impureness
inadequateness
inaneness
inanimateness
inappropriateness
inaptness
inarticulateness
inattentiveness
inauspicious
inauspiciousness
incalculableness
incautious
incestuous
incestuousness
incidentless
incisiveness
inclusiveness
incomeless
incommodious
incompleteness
inconceivableness
inconclusiveness
incongruous
incongruousness
inconsiderableness
inconsiderateness
inconsistentness
inconspicuous

inconspicuousness
incorrectness
incorrigibleness
incorruptibleness
incredibleness
incredulous
incubus
incurious
indebtedness
indecisiveness
indecorous
indecorousness
indefiniteness
indeterminateness
indianapolis
indigenous
indirectness
indiscreetness
indiscriminateness
indisputableness
indistinctness
inductiveness
industrious
industriousness
inebrious
ineffectiveness
ineffectualness
inefficacious
inefficaciousness
ineptness
inequitableness
inertness
inevitableness
inexactness
inexcusableness
inexpressiveness
infallibleness
infamous
infectious
infectiousness

infelicitous
infiniteness
infirmness
inflexibleness
ingenious
ingeniousness
ingenuous
ingenuousness
inglorious
inhabitress
inharmonious
inheritress
iniquitous
injudicious
injudiciousness
injurious
injuriousness
injustice
inkiness
innateness
innocuous
innocuousness
inoffensiveness
inquisitiveness
insalubrious
insaneness
inscrutableness
insectivorous
insecureness
insensateness
insidious
insidiousness
instantaneous
instantaneousness
intactness
intemperateness
intenseness
intensiveness
intentness
interrelatedness

intimateness	jerkiness	knavishness
intransitiveness	Jesus	knobbiness
intravenous	Jewess	knottiness
intricateness	jobless	knowingness
introspectiveness	joblessness	knowledgeless
intrusiveness	jocoseness	kookiness
intuitiveness	jointress	koumiss
invalidness	jolliness	kumiss
inventiveness	joyfulness	kyphosis
invidious	joyless	laborious
invidiousness	joylessness	laciness
inviolateness	joyous	lactiferous
invisibleness	joyousness	laggardness
involuntariness	Judas	lameness
irateness	judicious	landless
iris	judiciousness	landlessness
irksomeness	juiceless	languidness
irrationalness	juiciness	languorous
irreligious	jumpiness	languorousness
irrevocableness	juryless	lankiness
irritableness	justice	larcenous
Isis	justness	largeness
isomerous	Kansas	laryngitis
isomorphous	katharsis	lascivious
issueless	keelless	lasciviousness
isthmus	keenness	lastingness
itchiness	keratinous	lateness
jacketless	ketosis	lattice
jadedness	keyless	laundress
jaggedness	kindheartedness	lavishness
janitress	kindliness	lawfulness
janitresses	kindness	lawless
Janus	kindredless	lawlessness
jaundice	kindredness	laxness
jauntiness	kinesis	laziness
jawless	kinesthesis	leaderless
jazziness	kingless	leafless
jealous	kingliness	leakiness
jealousness	kinkiness	leanness
jeopardous	kinless	learnedness

leaseless
leatheriness
lecherous
lecherousness
ledgeless
leeriness
legalness
legibleness
legitimateness
legless
leguminous
leisureless
leprous
lettuce
leucosis
leukosis
levelheadedness
levelness
Leviticus
lewdness
Lewis
libellous
libelous
liberalness
libidinous
licenseless
licentious
licentiousness
lichenous
lifeless
lifelessness
lightheartedness
lightness
ligneous
likableness
likeness
limberness
limbless
limbus
limitedness

limitless
limpidness
limpness
lineless
lioness
lipless
lippiness
lissomeness
listless
listlessness
literalness
literariness
litheness
litmus
littleness
liveliness
liverishness
lividness
loathness
lockless
loculus
locus
loftiness
loftless
loginess
loneliness
loneness
lonesomeness
looniness
looseness
lopsidedness
loquacious
loquaciousness
lordliness
loris
lotus
loudness
Louis
lousiness
lovableness

loveless
lovelessness
loveliness
lovesickness
lowliness
lowness
loyalness
lubricous
lucidness
luckiness
luckless
lucrativeness
ludicrous
ludicrousness
lugubrious
lugubriousness
lukewarmness
luminiferous
luminous
lumpiness
lupus
luridness
luscious
lusciousness
lushness
lusterless
lustfulness
lustiness
lustrous
luxurious
luxuriousness
lysis
madness
madras
Maecenas
magnanimous
magnanimousness
magus
maidenliness
maimedness

maladroitness
malapertness
malarious
malefactress
maleness
malice
malicious
maliciousness
malleableness
malodorous
malodorousness
malpractice
manageress
manfulness
manganous
manginess
manifoldness
manless
manliness
mannerless
mannerliness
mannishness
mantis
marshiness
marvelous
marvelousness
masculineness
massiness
massiveness
massless
masterfulness
mastitis
matchless
matronliness
mattress
matureness
mawkishness
mayoress
meagerness
meandrous

meaningless
meanness
measureless
meatiness
meatless
meatus
medius
meekness
megalopolis
melanous
mellifluous
mellowness
melodious
melodiousness
membranous
memorableness
Memphis
menace
mendacious
meningitis
meniscus
menstruous
mercenariness
mercifulness
merciless
mercurous
meretricious
meretriciousness
meritorious
meritoriousness
merriness
messiness
metamorphosis
metastasis
metatarsus
metathesis
meticulous
meticulousness
metropolis
miasmas

Michaelis
microbus
Midas
mightiness
mildness
militantness
milkiness
millionaress
mindedness
mindfulness
mindless
mindlessness
minibus
Minneapolis
minus
minuteness
miraculous
miraculousness
mirthfulness
mirthless
miscellaneous
miscellaneousness
mischievous
mischievousness
misdiagnosis
miserableness
miserliness
misogynous
mistiness
mistress
mistrustfulness
mitosis
mittimus
modalis
modeless
moderateness
modernness
modifiableness
modishness
modus

moistness
moldiness
momentariness
momentous
momentousness
monkishness
monogamous
monogamousness
monogenesis
monogynous
monomorphous
mononucleosis
monotonous
monotonousness
monstrous
monstrousness
moodiness
moonless
morbidness
moroseness
Morris
mortarless
mortis
mortise
Moses
mossiness
motherless
motherliness
motionless
motionlessness
motiveless
mountainous
mournfulness
mousiness
movableness
mucous
muddiness
mugginess
mulishness
multifarious

multifariousness
multipurpose
multitudinous
murderess
murderous
murderousness
murkiness
murmurous
mushiness
muskiness
muss
mussiness
mustiness
mutandis
mutatis
muteness
mutinous
mutinousness
myelitis
myocarditis
myocardosis
myopsychosis
myosis
myositis
mysterious
mysteriousness
nacreous
nacrous
naiveness
nakedness
nameless
napless
Narcissus
narcosis
narcous
naris
narrowness
nastiness
nationless
nattiness

naturalness
naughtiness
nauseous
nautilus
nearness
nearsightedness
neatness
nebulous
necessariness
necessitous
necklace
necrophilous
necropolis
necrosis
needless
needlessness
nefarious
nefariousness
negativeness
neglectfulness
negotiatress
neighborliness
nemesis
nephritis
nephrosis
nerveless
nervelessness
nerviness
nervous
nervousness
neuritis
neurosis
newness
newsiness
nexus
niceness
Nicholas
niggardliness
nimbleness
nimbus

nisus
nitrous
nobleness
nocuous
nodulous
noiseless
noiselessness
noisiness
noncancerous
noncontagious
noncontentious
noncontiguous
nondestructiveness
nonethicalness
nonferrous
noninfectious
nonplus
nonpoisonous
nonporous
nonprecious
nonreligious
normativeness
Norris
nosiness
noteworthiness
nothingness
notice
notorious
novas
novice
noxious
noxiousness
nucleus
nudeness
numberless
numbness
numerous
numerousness
nutritious
nutritiousness

nuttiness
nystagmus
oafishness
oasis
objectiveness
obliqueness
oblivious
obliviousness
oblongness
obnoxious
obnoxiousness
obsequious
obsequiousness
obsessiveness
obstinateness
obstreperous
obstreperousness
obstructiveness
obtrusiveness
obtuseness
obvious
obviousness
octopus
oddness
odious
odiousness
odoriferous
odoriferousness
odorless
odorous
Oedipus
offenseless
offensiveness
offhandedness
office
officious
officiousness
offishness
oftenness
ogress

oiliness
oldness
oleaginous
Olympus
ominous
ominousness
omnibus
omnivorous
omnivorousness
oneness
onerous
onerousness
ontogenesis
onus
oogenesis
ooziness
opaqueness
openhandedness
openheartedness
openness
oppositeness
oppressiveness
opus
orderliness
ordinariness
orifice
oris
ornateness
orneriness
ornice
ornithosis
Orpheus
orris
orthogenesis
osmosis
osseus
osteitis
ostentatious
otherworldliness
otitis

outlandishness
outrageous
outrageousness
outrightness
outspokenness
overambitious
overanxious
overapprehensiveness
overassertiveness
overattentiveness
overcautious
overconscientious
overcurious
overdesirous
overdramatizes
overemphasis
overfastidious
overgenerous
overhastiness
overrighteous
oversolicitous
oversuspicious
overzealous
ownerless
pachydermatous
painfulness
painless
painlessness
palace
paleness
paltriness
pancreas
pancreatitis
pappose
pappous
pappus
papyrus
parakinesis
paralysis
parenthesis

paresis
Paris
parlous
parsimonious
parvis
passionless
passiveness
pastiness
patchiness
pathless
patroness
patulous
paunchiness
peacefulness
peakedness
pearliness
pectinous
peeress
peerless
peevishness
Pegasus
pellagrous
pelvis
pendulous
penis
penniless
pennilessness
pensionless
pensiveness
penurious
penuriousness
pepperiness
peppiness
perceptiveness
percuss
percutaneous
perfectness
perfidious
perilous
perilousness

perishableness
peristalsis
peritonitis
perkiness
permissibleness
permissiveness
pernicious
perniciousness
perosis
perpetualness
persnicketiness
personableness
perspicacious
perspicaciousness
perspicuous
perspicuousness
persuasiveness
pertinacious
pertness
pertussis
pervasiveness
perverseness
pervertedness
pervious
perviousness
peskiness
pestiferous
pettiness
pettishness
phallus
phlebitis
phoniness
phosphorous
photokinesis
photolysis
photophilous
photosynthesis
Phyllis
piceous
picturesqueness

piggishness
pigheadedness
pilotless
pinheadedness
pinkishness
pinnace
pious
piousness
pipeless
piteous
piteousness
pitiableness
pitifulness
pitiless
pitilessness
Pius
placeless
placidness
plainness
plainspokenness
planless
platinous
platitudinous
platypodia
plausibleness
playfulness
pleasantness
pleasingness
plenteous
plenteousness
plentifulness
pleuritis
plexus
plicateness
pluckiness
plumpness
pluribus
plus
pocus
podagrous

poetess
pointedness
pointless
pointlessness
poisonous
pokiness
Polaris
poliovirus
politeness
pollinosis
polonius
polyandrous
polyestrous
polygamous
polygynous
polyhidrosis
polymorphous
polyphagous
polypus
pompous
pompousness
ponderous
populace
populous
populousness
porous
porousness
porpoise
portcullis
portentous
portionless
portliness
poshness
positiveness
possessiveness
posthumous
postoffice
poultice
powerfulness
powerless

poxvirus
practice
praiseworthiness
prayerfulness
precancerous
precarious
precariousness
precedentless
precious
preciousness
precipice
precipitateness
precipitous
precipitousness
preciseness
precocious
precociousness
preconscious
predaceous
predaceousness
predacious
predaciousness
predatoriness
predictiveness
preface
prejudice
prematureness
premise
preparedness
preposterous
preposterousness
pressingness
prestigious
prestigiousness
presumptuous
presumptuousness
pretentious
pretentiousness
prettiness
preventiveness

previous
priapus
priceless
pricelessness
prickliness
priestess
priestliness
priggishness
primariness
primitiveness
primness
princeliness
princess
prissiness
privateness
probusiness
prodigious
prodigiousness
productiveness
profaneness
profitableness
profitless
profoundness
profuseness
proglottis
prognosis
progress
progressiveness
prolepsis
proliferous
prolificness
proligerous
Prometheus
promiscuous
promiscuousness
promise
promptness
proneness
properness
prophetess

prophylaxis
propitious
propmistress
proprietress
prospectus
prosperous
prosperousness
prosthesis
protectiveness
protectress
proteus
prothesis
proudness
prowess
prudishness
pseudocirrhosis
pseudonymous
pseudoparalysis
psoriasis
psychoanalysis
psychogenesis
psychokinesis
psychoneurosis
psychosis
psychosynthesis
ptosis
publicus
pudginess
puffiness
pugnacious
pugnaciousness
pulchritudinous
pumice
punctilious
punctiliousness
punctualness
puniness
purblindness
purchase
pureness

purpose
purposeless
pus
pushiness
pusillanimous
putridness
pythagoras
quackishness
quaintness
qualmishness
queasiness
queenliness
queerness
quenchless
querulous
querulousness
quickness
quietness
quirkiness
quizzicalness
rabidness
raciness
radiances
radicalness
radius
raffishness
raggedness
raininess
rakishness
rambunctious
rambunctiousness
rampageous
rancidness
rancorous
randomness
ranginess
rankness
rapacious
rapaciousness
rapidness

raptness
rapturous
rapturousness
rareness
rashness
rationalness
raucous
raucousness
raunchiness
ravenous
ravenousness
rawness
readiness
realness
reasonableness
reasonless
rebellious
rebelliousness
rebus
recentness
receptiveness
recessiveness
reckless
recklessness
recoilless
reconditeness
rectus
reddishness
redness
reediness
reemphasis
reflexiveness
refocus
refractiveness
regardless
regressiveness
regretfulness
reinless
relatedness
relativeness

relentless
relentlessness
reliableness
religious
religiousness
remarkableness
remediless
remissness
remorsefulness
remorseless
remorselessness
remoteness
remunerativeness
repercussiveness
repetitious
repetitiousness
repetitiveness
repleteness
repressiveness
reproachfulness
reproductiveness
repulsiveness
requisiteness
resentfulness
reservedness
resinous
resistless
resoluteness
resourcefulness
respectfulness
responsibleness
responsiveness
restfulness
restiveness
restless
restlessness
restorativeness
restrictiveness
resurface
retentiveness

rhesus
rhinoceros
rhombus
richness
ricketiness
rictus
riderless
ridiculous
ridiculousness
rifeness
righteous
righteousness
rightfulness
rightness
rigidness
rigorous
rigorousness
rimless
rimous
riotous
riotousness
ripeness
riskiness
ritziness
robustness
rockiness
rodless
roguishness
roofless
roominess
rootless
rosiness
rottenness
rotundness
roughness
roundness
rowdiness
rubiginous
rubus
ruckus

rudderless
ruddiness
rudeness
ruefulness
rufous
ruggedness
ruinous
ruinousness
ruleless
rumpus
rungless
runless
runtiness
rustiness
ruthless
ruthlessness
ruttiness
sabulous
sacchariferous
sacredness
sacrilegious
sacrilegiousness
sacrosanctness
sadness
safeness
sagacious
sageness
Sagittarius
Saint Nicholas
saintliness
salacious
salaciousness
sallowness
saltiness
saltless
salubrious
salubriousness
salutariness
sameness
sanctimonios

sanctimonious
sandiness
saneness
sanguineness
sanguineous
sapless
sappiness
sarcophagus
sarcous
sauciness
savageness
savoriness
savorless
scabbiness
scabious
scabrous
scabrousness
scaleless
scandalous
scandalousness
scantiness
scantness
scarceness
scariness
scarless
scentless
schizogenesis
scholarliness
schoolmistress
scirrhous
scirrhus
sclerosis
sclerous
scoliosis
scoreless
scornfulness
scrappiness
scratchiness
scrawniness
scrumptious

scrumptiousness
scrupulous
scrupulousness
sculptress
scurrilous
seaminess
seamless
seamstress
seasickness
seasonableness
seasonless
seaworthiness
sebaceous
secludedness
secretiveness
secretness
secureness
sedateness
seditious
seditiousness
seductiveness
seductress
sedulous
sedulousness
seediness
seedless
seemingness
seemliness
seeress
seldomness
selectiveness
selectness
selfishness
selfless
selflessness
semiconscious
semiconsciousness
semiprecious
senseless
senselessness

sensibleness
sensitiveness
sensualness
sensuous
sensuousness
sententious
sententiousness
separableness
separateness
sepsis
serendipitous
sereneness
serious
seriousness
serous
serpiginous
service
setaceous
severeness
sexiness
sexless
sexlessness
shabbiness
shadeless
shadiness
shadowiness
shadowless
shagginess
shakiness
shallowness
shamefacedness
shamefulness
shameless
shamelessness
shapeless
shapelessness
shapeliness
sharpness
sheepishness
sheerness

shelterless
shepherdess
shiftiness
shiftless
shiftlessness
shininess
shoddiness
shoeless
shoreless
shortness
shortsightedness
showiness
shrewdness
shrewishness
shrillness
shyness
sickliness
sickness
sidedness
sightless
sightlessness
sightliness
signatureless
silentness
siliceous
silicious
silicosis
silkiness
silliness
silveriness
simplemindedness
simpleness
simultaneous
sinfulness
singleness
sinistrous
sinless
sinlessness
sinuous
sinus

sinusitis
sireless
situs
sketchiness
skewness
skillfulness
skimpiness
skinless
skinniness
skittishness
slackness
slanderous
slanginess
slavishness
sleaziness
sleekness
sleepiness
sleepless
sleeplessness
sleeveless
slenderness
slickness
slightness
slimness
slipperiness
slipshoddiness
slipshodness
sloppiness
slothfulness
slovenliness
slowness
sluggishness
slumberous
slumbrous
slushiness
sluttishness
slyness
smallness
smartness
smelliness

smokeless
smokiness
smoothness
smugness
smuttiness
snappiness
sneakiness
snideness
snippiness
snobbishness
snootiness
snugness
soapiness
soberness
soddenness
softheartedness
softness
sogginess
soilless
solace
solemnness
solicitous
solicitousness
solicitress
solidness
solitariness
solstice
solstices
somberness
somniferous
songstress
sonorous
soporiferous
sorceress
sordidness
soreness
sorriness
sorrowfulness
soulfulness
soulless

soullessness
soundless
soundness
sourness
spaceless
spacious
spaciousness
spareness
sparseness
specious
speciousness
speechless
speechlessness
speediness
spiciness
spineless
spinelessness
spinous
spiritedness
spiritless
spirituous
spitefulness
splashiness
splendorous
spondylitis
spontaneous
spontaneousness
spookiness
spotless
spotlessness
spottiness
spouseless
sprightliness
springiness
spryness
spunkiness
spurious
spuriousness
squalidness
squareness

squatness
squeamishness
stableness
stainless
staleness
stalkless
stannous
staphylococcus
starchiness
starkness
starless
stasis
stateless
statelessness
stateliness
status
statutableness
staunchness
steadfastness
steadiness
stealthiness
steepness
stegosaurus
stemless
stenosis
sternness
stewardess
stickiness
stiffness
stillness
stimulus
stinginess
stockiness
stodginess
stoniness
storminess
stoutness
straightforwardness
straightness
strandedness

strangeness
strapless
stratocumulus
stratus
streakiness
strenuous
strenuousness
streptobacillus
streptococcus
strictness
stridulous
stringiness
stringless
stripeless
strobilus
strumous
stubbiness
stubbornness
studious
studiousness
stuffiness
stuntedness
stupendous
stuporous
sturdiness
styleless
stylishness
stylus
stypsis
suasiveness
suaveness
subclavius
subconscious
subconsciousness
subcutaneous
subcutis
subgenus
subjectiveness
sublimeness
submissiveness

substanceless
substantialness
substantiveness
subsurface
subterraneous
subtleness
succinctness
suddenness
sudoriferous
sugariness
sugarless
suggestiveness
suitableness
Sukkoth
sulcus
sulfurous
sulkiness
sullenness
sulphurous
sultriness
sumptuous
sumptuousness
sunless
sunniness
supercilious
superficialness
superfluous
superlativeness
superstitious
supperless
suppleness
supportless
supremeness
surefootedness
sureness
surface
surliness
surplice
surplus
surreptitious

surreptitiousness
suspicious
suspiciousness
swampiness
swarthiness
sweetness
swiftness
sycosis
syllabus
syllepsis
symbiosis
symphonious
symphysis
symptomless
synapsis
synchronous
syndesis
syneresis
syngenesis
synonymous
synopsis
synovitis
syntaxis
synthesis
syphilis
systemless
tacitness
tackiness
tactfulness
tactless
tactlessness
tailless
tailoress
talkativeness
tallness
tameless
tameness
tangibleness
tardiness
tariffless

tarriness
tarsus
tartness
tasteless
tastelessness
tastiness
Taurus
tautness
tautologous
tawdriness
tawniness
taxless
tearless
tedious
tediousness
telekinesis
temperateness
tempestuous
tempestuousness
temporariness
temptress
tenableness
tenacious
tenantless
tendentious
tendentiousness
tenderheartedness
tenderness
tendinitis
tendinous
tendonitis
tennis
tenseness
tensionless
tentativeness
tenuous
tenuousness
tepidness
terminus
termless

terrace
terribleness
terseness
testiness
Texas
thankfulness
thankless
thanklessness
thermotaxis
thesaurus
thesis
thetis
thickness
thinness
thirstiness
thomas
thoroughness
thoughtfulness
thoughtless
thoughtlessness
thriftiness
thriftless
thriftlessness
throatiness
thrombosis
thrombus
thunderous
thus
thymus
ticklishness
tideless
tidiness
tightness
tigress
tigris
timeless
timelessness
timeliness
timeous
timidness

timorous
timorousness
tininess
tinniness
tinnitus
tintless
tipsiness
tiredness
tireless
tirelessness
tiresomeness
Titus
toastmistress
togetherness
tolerances
toneless
tongueless
tonsillitis
tonus
toothless
toothsomeness
topless
toplessness
torridness
tortious
tortoise
tortuous
tortuousness
torturous
torus
touchiness
toughness
toxiferous
traceableness
traceless
trackless
tractless
traditionless
trainsickness
traitoress

traitorous
traitorousness
traitress
transcutaneous
transfixes
transitiveness
transitoriness
treacherous
treacherousness
treasonous
treatise
treeless
trellis
tremendous
tremendousness
tremulous
tremulousness
trespass
trichiasis
trichinosis
trichinous
trickiness
trickishness
trimness
trimorphous
trismus
triteness
troublous
trueness
truss
trustfulness
trustworthiness
truthfulness
truthless
tubbiness
tubeless
tuberculosis
tuberculous
tuberous
tumorous

tumultuous
tunefulness
tuneless
turbidness
turgidness
tympanous
typhous
typhus
typicalness
tyrannosaurus
tyrannous
ubiquitous
ubiquitousness
ugliness
ulcerous
ultimateness
umbrageous
unadvantageous
unadventurous
unaffectedness
unambiguous
unambitious
unanimous
unartfulness
unauspicious
unawareness
uncanniness
unceremonious
uncharitableness
unchasteness
unchivalrous
uncleanliness
uncleanness
uncomfortableness
uncommonness
unconscious
unconsciousness
uncourteous
uncouthness
unctuous

uncurious
underhandedness
uneasiness
unenvious
unevenness
unexpectedness
unfailingness
unfairness
unfaithfulness
unfitness
unfortunateness
unfriendliness
ungainliness
ungodliness
ungracious
ungraciousness
ungratefulness
unhappiness
unharmonious
unharness
unhealthiness
unholiness
uniformness
uninjurious
uniqueness
unjudicious
unjustness
unkindness
unlawfulness
unlikeliness
unlikeness
unluckiness
unmanliness
unmelodious
unnaturalness
unnecessariness
unobnoxious
unobtrusiveness
unofficious
unpleasantness

unpreparedness
unpretentious
unpretentiousness
unproductiveness
unpropitious
unprosperous
unreadiness
unresponsiveness
unrighteous
unrighteousness
unruliness
unsavoriness
unscrupulous
unscrupulousness
unseemliness
unselfishness
unsightliness
unsolicitous
unsoundness
unsparingness
unstableness
unsteadiness
unsureness
unsuspicious
untidiness
untimeliness
untruthfulness
unwariness
unwholesomeness
unwieldiness
unwillingness
unwontedness
unworthiness
unzealous
uprightness
uproarious
uproariousness
uptightness
upwardness
us

usableness
usefulness
useless
uselessness
uterus
utterances
uxorious
uxoriousness
vacuous
vacuousness
vagarious
vagueness
vainness
validness
valorous
valueless
valveless
vapidness
vaporishness
vaporous
vaporousness
variableness
various
variousness
vastness
Vegas
venalness
vengefulness
Venice
venomous
venous
venturous
venturousness
venus
veracious
veraciousness
verbless
verboseness
verminosis
verminous

versatileness
verticalness
vertiginous
vesuvius
vexatious
vexatiousness
vicarious
vicariousness
vicious
viciousness
victimless
victorious
victoriousness
viewless
vigilantness
vigorous
vigorousness
vileness
villainess
villainous
villainousness
villous
vindictiveness
vinous
violaceous
viperous
viraginous
virosis
virtuous
virtuousness
virus
viscountess
viscous
viscousness
viscus
visorless
vitreous
vivacious
vivaciousness
vividness

viviparous
vociferous
vociferousness
voicedness
voiceless
voicelessness
voidableness
voidness
voluminous
voluminousness
voluptuous
voluptuousness
vomitus
voracious
voraciousness
voteless
vulgarness
vulturous
wackiness
wageless
waitress
wakefulness
walrus
wanness
wantonness
wariness
warless
warmheartedness
warrantless
washiness
waspishness
wastefulness
watchfulness
waveless
waviness
waywardness
weakness
wealthless
weaponless
weariless

weariness
wearisomeness
weediness
weightiness
weightless
weightlessness
weirdness
wetness
wheelless
wheeziness
whiteness
whitishness
wholeheartedness
wholeness
wholesomeness
wickedness
wideness
wifeless
wilderness
wildness
wilfulness
wiliness
willfulness
willingness
windiness
windlass
windless
windowless
wingless
winless
winsomeness
wireless
wiriness
wishfulness
wistfulness
witless
witlessness
witness
wittedness
wittiness

wobbliness
woefulness
womanliness
wonderfulness
wondrous
wondrousness
woodenness
woodiness
woolliness
wooziness
wordiness
wordless
workableness
workless
worldliness
worthiness
worthless
worthlessness
woundless
wrathfulness
wretchedness
wrongfulness
wrongheadedness
wrongness
wryness
xanthomatous
Xmas
yeastiness
youthfulness
Zacharias
zaniness
zealous
zealousness
zestfulness
zoogenous
zymosis

Long USH
douche
ruche

scaramouch
swoosh
whoosh

UHSH
airbrush
blush
brush
bulrush
crush
flush
gush
hairbrush
hush
inrush
lush
mush
onrush
paintbrush
plush
rush
sagebrush
shush
slush
thrush
toothbrush
tush
underbrush

USH
ambush
bramblebush
bush
debouch
push
rosebush
saltbush
thornbush
whoosh

USK
brusk
brusque
damask
dusk
husk
mollusc
mollusk
musk
rusk
tusk

Long UST
adduced
boost
deduced
educed
goosed
induced
introduced
juiced
loosed
outproduced
overproduced
perfused
produced
reduced
reinduced
reproduced
roost
schussed
seduced
sluiced
spruced
traduced
transduced
unloosed
unproduced
unreduced
unseduced

vamoosed

UST
abolitionist
abortionist
absolutist
absurdist
accompanist
accordionist
achiest
activist
acupuncturist
acutest
adjust
aerialist
agriculturist
agronomist
airiest
airworthiest
alarmist
alchemist
alcoholist
allegorist
allergist
altruist
americanist
amethyst
amplest
anaesthetist
analyst
anarchist
anatomist
anecdotist
anesthetist
angriest
animist
annalist
antagonist
anthologist
anthropologist

antiabortionist
anticommunist
antitrust
apiarist
apologist
apprenticed
aptest
archaeologist
archaist
archeologist
archivist
arsonist
artiest
artillerist
artist
ashiest
astrophysicist
atheist
atomist
audiologist
august
autonomist
aviarist
bacteriologist
baggiest
baldest
balkiest
ballast
balloonist
balmiest
banjoist
barest
bassist
bassoonist
battiest
bawdiest
beadiest
beastliest
beefiest
behaviorist

biased
biassed
bicyclist
bigamist
biggest
bimetallist
biochemist
biologist
biophysicist
bioscientist
bitterest
blackest
blandest
blankest
bleakest
bleariest
blindest
blithest
blondest
bloodiest
bloodthirstiest
bloomiest
blotchiest
blowiest
blowziest
bluest
bluntest
blurriest
boggiest
boldest
bolshevist
boniest
bonniest
booziest
boskiest
bossiest
botanist
botchiest
bounciest
brahmanist

brahminist
brainiest
brambliest
brashest
brassiest
brattiest
bravest
brawniest
breakfast
breathiest
breeziest
briefest
brightest
briniest
briskest
bristliest
broadest
broodiest
broomiest
brothiest
brownest
bruskest
bubbliest
buddhist
bulgiest
bulkiest
bummest
bumpiest
bunchiest
burliest
bused
bushiest
busiest
bussed
bust
buttressed
Caesarist
cagiest
calloused
callused

calmest
calvinist
cameralist
campiest
canniest
canoeist
canonist
canvased
canvassed
capitalist
cardiologist
cartoonist
catalyst
catchiest
cattiest
caucused
cellist
centralist
centrist
ceramicist
ceramist
ceremonialist
chalkiest
chanciest
chattiest
chauvinist
cheapest
cheekiest
cheeriest
cheesiest
chemist
chewiest
chilliest
chintziest
choicest
choosiest
choppiest
chorused
chronologist
chubbiest

chummiest
chunkiest
civilest
clammiest
clarinetist
clarinettist
classicist
classiest
clavichordist
cleanest
cleanliest
clearest
cleverest
climatologist
clingiest
cliquiest
cloddiest
cloggiest
closest
cloudiest
clumpiest
clumsiest
coalitionist
coarsest
cockiest
coldest
collectivist
colonialist
colonist
colorist
columnist
comeliest
comfiest
commercialist
commonest
communalist
communist
compassed
completest
conformist

congregationalist
conservationist
constructionist
contortionist
contrabandist
conversationalist
coolest
copyist
corkiest
cornetist
corniest
corruptionist
cosmetologist
cosmologist
costliest
courtliest
coyest
coziest
crabbiest
crackliest
craftiest
craggiest
crankiest
crappiest
crassest
crawliest
crayonist
craziest
creakiest
creamiest
creepiest
criminologist
crinkliest
crispest
crispiest
croakiest
crossest
croupiest
crudest
cruelest

cruellest
crummiest
crunchiest
crust
crustiest
cubist
cuddliest
curliest
curtest
curviest
cushiest
cussed
cutest
cyberneticist
cyclist
cymbalist
cytologist
czarist
dadaist
daffiest
daftest
daintiest
dampest
dandiest
dankest
darkest
darwinist
deadest
deadliest
deafest
dearest
decentralist
deepest
defeatist
deforest
deftest
deist
delusionist
demolitionist
demonstrationist

demurest
dendrologist
densest
dentist
dermatologist
determinist
dewiest
diarist
diciest
dimmest
dingiest
dinkiest
dippiest
dirtiest
discussed
disgust
dishonest
disinterest
distrust
diversionist
dizziest
doest
dogmatist
dopiest
dottiest
doughiest
dowdiest
drabbest
draftiest
draggiest
dramatist
dreamiest
dreariest
dressiest
driest
droopiest
drowsiest
druggist
drunkest
dualist

duckiest
duelist
dullest
dumbest
dumpiest
duskiest
dust
dustiest
dynamist
earliest
earnest
earthiest
earthliest
easiest
ecologist
economist
edgiest
editorialist
eeriest
egoist
egotist
eldest
elitist
elocutionist
embarrassed
embryologist
emotionalist
empiricist
emptiest
encompassed
encrust
endocrinologist
enthusiast
entomologist
entrust
environmentalist
epigrammatist
ergonomist
ernest
eroticist

escapist
essayist
ethnologist
ethologist
etymologist
Eucharist
eugenicist
eulogist
evangelist
Everest
evolutionist
excursionist
exhibitionist
existentialist
exorcist
expansionist
experimentalist
expressionist
extortionist
extremist
faddist
faintest
fairest
falsest
fanciest
fantasist
farthest
fascist
fastest
fatalist
fattest
fattiest
faultiest
federalist
feeblest
feistiest
feminist
feudalist
feudist
fewest

fiercest
filmiest
filthiest
finalist
finest
finniest
firmest
fishiest
fittest
fizziest
flabbiest
flakiest
flashiest
flattest
fleeciest
fleetest
fleshiest
fleshliest
flightiest
flimsiest
flintiest
flippest
floppiest
florist
flossiest
fluffiest
flukiest
flutist
foamiest
focused
focussed
foggiest
folklorist
folksiest
fondest
foolhardiest
forest
formalist
foulest
foxiest

frailest
frankest
freakiest
freest
frescoist
freshest
friendliest
friskiest
frizziest
frostiest
frothiest
frowsiest
frowziest
fruitiest
frumpiest
fullest
fumiest
functionalist
fundamentalist
funkiest
funniest
furriest
furthest
fussed
fussiest
fustiest
futurist
fuzziest
gabbiest
gamest
gamiest
gassiest
gastronomist
gaudiest
gauntest
gauziest
gawkiest
gayest
gemmologist
gemologist

genealogist	grimmest	haziest
geneticist	gripiest	headiest
gentlest	grippiest	healthiest
geochemist	grisliest	heartiest
geodesist	grittiest	heaviest
geologist	grizzliest	hebraist
germiest	groggiest	hedonist
ghastliest	grooviest	heftiest
giddiest	grossest	Hellenist
gimpiest	grouchiest	hematologist
gladdest	grubbiest	heraldist
glassiest	gruffest	herbalist
gleamiest	grumpiest	herbst
glibbest	grungiest	herpetologist
globalist	guiltiest	highest
gloomiest	guitarist	hilliest
glossiest	gummiest	hippest
gluiest	gushiest	histologist
glummest	gust	hoariest
godliest	gustiest	hoarsest
goodliest	gutsiest	hobbyist
goofiest	guttiest	hokiest
gooiest	gymnast	holiest
goriest	gynecologist	holist
gothicist	hairiest	homeliest
goutiest	hairstylist	homiest
grabbiest	hammiest	honest
grainiest	handiest	horniest
grandest	handsomest	horologist
graphologist	happiest	horsiest
grassiest	harassed	horticulturist
gravest	hardest	hottest
grayest	hardiest	huffiest
greasiest	harnessed	hugest
greatest	harpist	humanist
greediest	harpsichordist	humblest
greenest	harshest	humorist
greyest	harvest	hungriest
grimaced	hastiest	huskiest
grimiest	haughtiest	hydrologist

hydrotherapist
hygienist
hypnotist
hypothesist
ichthyologist
iciest
ickiest
idealist
ideologist
idlest
illusionist
immodest
immunist
immunologist
imperialist
impressionist
incendiarist
individualist
industrialist
inflationist
inkiest
instrumentalist
integrationist
interest
internationalist
internist
interventionist
intrust
isolationist
itchiest
jaundiced
jauntiest
jazziest
jerkiest
jingoist
jointist
jolliest
jounciest
journalist
judoist

juiciest
jumpiest
jurist
just
keenest
kickiest
kindest
kindliest
kingliest
kinkiest
knobbiest
knottiest
kookiest
kremlinologist
laciest
lakiest
lamest
lampoonist
landscapist
lankiest
larcenist
lardiest
largest
latest
latticed
laxest
laziest
leafiest
leakiest
leanest
leeriest
leftist
legalist
leggiest
lengthiest
leninist
lewdest
libelist
liberationist
librettist

lightest
likeliest
limiest
linguist
lintiest
lithest
littlest
liturgist
liveliest
loamiest
lobbyist
locust
loftiest
logiest
loneliest
longest
looniest
loosest
lordliest
loudest
lousiest
loveliest
lowest
lowliest
loyalist
luckiest
lumpiest
lust
lustiest
lutanists
lutist
lyricist
lyrist
machinist
maddest
mainmast
malpracticed
mandolinist
mandolinists
mangiest

manicurist
manliest
Maoist
marshiest
martialist
Marxist
masochist
massagist
massiest
materialist
maturest
mayest
mealiest
meanest
measliest
meatiest
mechanist
medalist
medievalist
meekest
mellowest
melodramatist
memorialist
menaced
mendelist
mentalist
merriest
mesmerist
messiest
metallurgist
meteorologist
methodist
microbiologist
mightiest
mildest
militarist
milkiest
mineralogist
miniaturist
minimalist

mintiest
minutest
miriest
misanthropist
misogamist
misogynist
misoneist
mistiest
mistrust
modernist
modest
moistest
moldiest
monarchist
monetarist
monist
monogamist
monologist
monologuist
monopolist
monotheist
moodiest
mopiest
moralist
morphologist
mossiest
motorcyclist
motorist
mouldiest
mousiest
mouthiest
muckiest
muddiest
muggiest
muralist
murkiest
mushiest
musicologist
muskiest
mussed

must
mustiest
mutualist
mythologist
naivest
narcissist
narrowest
nastiest
nationalist
nattiest
naturalist
naughtiest
nearest
neatest
neediest
neoclassicist
nepotist
nerviest
neurologist
neutralist
newest
newsiest
nicest
niftiest
nighest
nihilist
nimblest
nippiest
nobelist
noblest
noisiest
nonconformist
nonplused
nonplussed
nonsexist
nonspecialist
nosiest
noticed
novelist
nudest

nudist

numbest

numerologist

numismatist

nutritionist

nuttiest

oboist

obscurest

obstructionist

occultist

oceanologist

oculist

oddest

oiliest

oldest

oligopolist

onanist

oocyst

ooziest

ophthalmologist

opportunist

oppositionist

optimist

optometrist

orchardist

organist

orientalist

ornithologist

orthodontist

orthoepist

orthopedist

osteologist

overearnest

overmodest

pacifist

paleontologist

palest

palmiest

palmist

paltriest

panelist

pantheist

pantomimist

papist

parachutist

parodist

passivist

pastiest

pastoralist

patchiest

pathologist

pearliest

peatiest

pebbliest

pediatrist

pedicurist

pedologist

penologist

peppiest

percussionist

perfectionist

perkiest

permutationist

pertest

peskiest

pessimist

petrologist

pettiest

pharmaceutist

pharmacist

pharmacologist

philanthropist

philatelist

philologist

phoniest

phonologist

photochemist

phrenologist

physicist

physiologist

pianist

pickiest

piggiest

pimpliest

pinkest

pithiest

plagiarist

plainest

planetologist

pluckiest

plumiest

plumpest

plushest

podiatrist

pointiest

pokiest

polemicist

politest

polyandrist

polygamist

polygynist

polytheist

poorest

populist

porkiest

portliest

portraitist

poshest

poulticed

practiced

pragmatist

precipiced

prefaced

prejudiced

premised

prettiest

prickliest

primmest

prissiest

procommunist

proctologist
profascist
profeminist
professionalist
profoundest
progressionist
prohibitionist
projectionist
promised
pronationalist
propagandist
protagonist
protectionist
protist
protozoologist
proudest
psalmist
psychiatrist
psychoanalyst
psychologist
psychophysicist
psychotherapist
publicist
pudgiest
puffiest
pugilist
pulpiest
punchiest
puniest
purchased
purest
purist
purposed
pushiest
pussiest
quackiest
quaintest
quakiest
quarterfinalist
queasiest

queerest
quickest
quietest
quirkiest
racialist
raciest
racist
radiochemist
radiologist
rainiest
randiest
rangiest
rankest
rapist
rarest
raspiest
rationalist
rattiest
raunchiest
rawest
readiest
readjust
realest
realist
receptionist
recidivist
recitalist
reconstructionist
recordist
reddest
reediest
refocused
refocussed
reforest
refractionist
reincarnationist
religionist
remotest
reservist
resurfaced

resurrectionist
reversionist
revisionist
revivalist
revolutionist
richest
rightist
ripest
riskiest
ritualist
ritziest
robust
rockiest
romanist
romanticist
roomiest
rosiest
rottenest
roughest
rowdiest
royalist
ruddiest
rudest
runniest
runtiest
rust
rustiest
ruttiest
saddest
sadist
safest
saggiest
saintliest
saltiest
sandiest
sanest
sappiest
sassiest
satanist
satirist

sauciest
sawdust
saxophonist
sayest
scabbiest
scaliest
scantiest
scarcest
scariest
scenarist
schmaltziest
scientist
scraggliest
scrappiest
scratchiest
scrawniest
screechiest
screwiest
scrimpiest
scrubbiest
scruffiest
scummiest
scurviest
seamiest
secessionist
seclusionist
secularist
securest
seditionist
seediest
seemliest
segregationist
seismologist
semanticist
semifinalist
sensualist
sentimentalist
separatist
serialist
serologist

serviced
severest
sexiest
sexist
sexologist
shabbiest
shadiest
shaggiest
shakiest
shallowest
shapeliest
sharpest
sheeniest
shiest
shiftiest
shiniest
shintoist
shoddiest
shortest
shouldest
showiest
shrewdest
shrillest
shyest
sickest
sickliest
sightliest
silkiest
silliest
siltiest
simplest
sincerest
sketchiest
skimpiest
skinniest
slangiest
slaphappiest
sleaziest
sleekest
sleepiest

sleetiest
slenderest
slickest
sliest
slightest
slimiest
slimmest
slinkiest
slipperiest
sloppiest
sloshiest
slouchiest
slowest
sludgiest
slushiest
slyest
smallest
smartest
smeariest
smelliest
smoggiest
smokiest
smoothest
smudgiest
smuggest
smuttiest
snakiest
snappiest
snarliest
snazziest
sneakiest
sneeziest
snidest
snippiest
snobbiest
snoopiest
snootiest
snottiest
snowiest
snuggest

soapiest
soberest
socialist
sociologist
softest
soggiest
solaced
solidest
soliloquist
solipsist
soloist
somnambulist
somniloquist
soonest
sootiest
sophist
soppiest
sorest
sorriest
soundest
soupiest
sourest
sparest
sparsest
specialist
speediest
speleologist
spiciest
spiffiest
spikiest
spindliest
spiniest
spiritualist
splashiest
splotchiest
spongiest
spookiest
sportiest
spottiest
spriest

sprightliest
springiest
sprucest
spryest
spunkiest
squabbiest
squarest
squashiest
squattiest
squeakiest
squirmiest
stagiest
staidest
stalest
Stalinist
starchiest
starkest
starriest
stateliest
statist
steadiest
stealthiest
steamiest
steeliest
steepest
sternest
stickiest
stiffest
stillest
stingiest
stinkiest
stockiest
stodgiest
stoniest
stormiest
stoutest
straggliest
straightest
strangest
strategist

streakiest
streamiest
stretchiest
strictest
stringiest
strongest
stubbiest
stubbornest
stuffiest
stumpiest
stupidest
sturdiest
stylist
subtlest
sudsiest
suffragist
sulkiest
sultriest
sunniest
supplest
supremacist
surest
surfaced
surliest
surrealist
survivalist
sveltest
swampiest
swankiest
swarthiest
sweatiest
sweetest
swiftest
synergist
syphilologist
tackiest
talkiest
tallest
talmudist
tamest

tangiest
tannest
taoist
tardiest
tarriest
tartest
tastiest
tattooist
tautest
tawdriest
tawniest
taxidermist
taxonomist
teariest
technologist
teeniest
telegraphist
telephonist
teletypist
tempest
tensest
terminologist
terraced
terrorist
tersest
testiest
tetchiest
theist
theorist
theosophist
therapeutist
therapist
thickest
thinnest
thirstiest
thorniest
threadiest
thriftiest
throatiest
thrust

tidiest
tightest
timpanist
tiniest
tinniest
tipsiest
titlist
tobogganist
toothiest
topmast
touchiest
toughest
tourist
toxicologist
traditionalist
trampolinist
transcendentalist
trashiest
trendiest
trespassed
trickiest
trigamist
trimmest
tritest
trombonist
truest
trussed
trust
trustiest
tubbiest
twangiest
tweediest
typist
ugliest
ultraist
unbiased
unharnessed
unhealthiest
unicyclist
unionist

universalist
unjust
unnoticed
unpracticed
unprejudiced
unruliest
unwitnessed
upthrust
urologist
vacationist
vaguest
ventriloquist
vignettist
vilest
violinist
violist
virologist
vitalist
viticulturist
vocalist
voodooist
wackiest
wanderlust
wannest
wariest
warmest
wartiest
washiest
wastiest
waviest
waxiest
weakest
weakliest
wealthiest
weariest
weediest
weeniest
weepiest
weightiest
weirdest

wettest	**Long UT**	institute
wheeziest	absolute	involute
whiniest	acute	irresolute
whitest	aleut	jackboot
widest	arrowroot	jute
wildest	astute	kaput
wiliest	attribute	kiwi-fruit
windiest	beaut	knout
winiest	beirut	lawsuit
wintriest	bloodroot	loot
wiriest	bodysuit	lute
wisest	boot	malamute
wispiest	breadfruit	moot
witnessed	brut	mute
wittiest	brute	offshoot
wobbliest	butte	orrisroot
woodiest	cahoot	outshoot
woodsiest	caput	overshoot
woolliest	chute	pantsuit
wooziest	commute	parachute
wordiest	compute	persecute
worldliest	consolute	playsuit
wormiest	constitute	pollute
worthiest	contribute	prosecute
wouldest	convolute	prostitute
wriggliest	coot	pursuit
wrongest	cute	recompute
xylophonist	depute	reconstitute
yahwist	destitute	recruit
yeastiest	dilute	redistribute
youngest	dispute	refute
yummiest	disrepute	repute
zaniest	distribute	resolute
zestiest	electrocute	restitute
zionist	execute	revolute
zippiest	flute	root
zitherist	fruit	route
zoologist	grapefruit	salute
	hoot	scoot
	impute	shoot

snakeroot
snoot
snowsuit
solute
soot
spacesuit
statute
substitute
suit
sunsuit
swimsuit
taproot
toot
transmute
tribute
troubleshoot
undershoot
uproot
ute
volute
wetsuit

UT
abbot
acclimate
accredit
accurate
adequate
affectionate
affidavit
affricate
aftermarket
agate
agglutinate
aggregate
albeit
alternate
amulet
animate
anklet

appellate
apposite
appropriate
approximate
argot
armlet
ascot
associate
attenuate
audit
autopilot
babbitt
baccalaureate
ballot
bandit
banquet
barbiturate
bartlett
basket
basset
beechnut
bicarbonate
bigot
billet
biscuit
blanket
bluebonnet
bluejacket
bonelet
bonnet
booklet
bracelet
bracket
branchlet
breadbasket
brisket
brooklet
bucket
budget
buffet

bullet
but
butt
butternut
cabinet
cabot
candidate
carat
carpet
carrot
casket
catgut
caveat
celibate
certificate
chariot
charlotte
chestnut
chocolate
circlet
circuit
climate
closet
cloudlet
coconut
cohabit
collegiate
comet
commissariat
compassionate
compatriot
composite
conduit
confederate
conglomerate
connecticut
considerate
consulate
consummate
coordinate

copilot	discomfit	fagot
copy-edit	disconsolate	faucet
corporate	discredit	favorite
corset	disinherit	ferret
cosset	disparate	fidget
couplet	dispassionate	fillet
coverlet	disproportionate	flibbertigibbet
covet	disquiet	foregut
credit	distillate	forfeit
crewcut	divot	fortunate
cricket	docket	frigate
crosscut	doctorate	frontlet
crotchet	donut	fussbudget
cruet	double-digit	gadget
crumpet	doublet	gambit
cubit	doughnut	gamut
culprit	driblet	gannet
cut	droplet	garnet
cutlet	ducat	garret
cypriot	eaglet	gasket
davit	edit	gauntlet
debit	effeminate	geminate
decrepit	elaborate	gibbet
deficit	electorate	giblet
definite	electromagnet	gimlet
degenerate	elicit	glut
delegate	emirate	gobbet
deliberate	epaulet	goblet
delicate	epithet	graduate
delimit	ergot	granite
demerit	estimate	greenlet
denticulate	etiquette	grommet
deposit	exhibit	guesstimate
desolate	exit	gullet
desperate	expatriate	gusset
despot	explicit	gut
determinate	exquisite	habit
diet	eyelet	haircut
digit	facet	halibut
directorate	faggot	hamlet

harlot
hatchet
hazelnut
helmet
helot
heriot
hermit
hobbit
hooklet
hornet
howbeit
hut
idiot
illegitimate
illicit
illiterate
illuminate
immaculate
immediate
immoderate
implicit
inaccurate
inadequate
inanimate
inappropriate
inarticulate
inchoate
inconsiderate
indefinite
indelicate
indeterminate
indiscriminate
indurate
inexplicit
infinite
ingot
inhabit
inherit
inhibit
inlet

inordinate
insatiate
inspirit
insubordinate
intemperate
intercollegiate
intermediate
interpret
intricate
intuit
invertebrate
inveterate
inviolate
iscariot
islet
jacket
jackrabbit
Janet
jesuit
junket
jut
karat
kinglet
kismet
lancet
lariat
latchet
laureate
leaflet
legate
legitimate
levirate
licentiate
licit
limit
limpet
linnet
literate
locket
maculate

maggot
magnet
mallet
mantelet
market
marmot
merit
midget
midgut
millet
minute
misinterpret
moppet
mullet
muscat
musket
mutt
Nantucket
noncredit
nonprofit
nonsecret
nougat
novitiate
nugget
nut
obdurate
obit
obstinate
offcut
omelet
omelette
opiate
opposite
orbit
ordinate
osselet
overconsiderate
overdelicate
overexplicit
owlet

packet
palate
palette
pallet
pamphlet
pamphlets
parapet
parrot
particulate
passionate
patellate
patriot
pawtucket
peanut
pellet
penultimate
picket
pickpocket
piglet
pilate
pilot
pirate
pivot
placket
planet
platelet
plaudit
playlet
pledget
plummet
pocket
poet
pomegranate
poppet
portrait
posit
postgraduate
postulate
precollegiate
precut

predicate
preestimate
prelate
prelimit
preliterate
prerequisite
preterit
private
privet
proconsulate
professorate
professoriate
profit
profligate
prohibit
proletariat
prophet
proportionate
protectorate
proximate
pullet
pulpit
pundit
puppet
pustulate
putt
quadruplet
quiet
quintuplet
quixote
quonset
rabbet
rabbinate
rabbit
rachet
racket
racquet
ratchet
reaccredit
rebut

redeposit
reedit
reinterpret
requisite
respite
reticulate
retrorocket
revisit
ringlet
riot
rivet
rivulet
rocket
roseate
russet
rut
saccharate
scarlet
scuttlebutt
secret
secretariat
secrete
semiprivate
senate
separate
septuplet
serrulate
sextuplet
sherbet
shortcut
shut
signet
silicate
skillet
skyrocket
slut
smut
snippet
socket
solicit

somewhat
sonnet
soot
sorbet
spatulate
spigot
spinet
spirit
sprocket
starlet
straightjacket
straitjacket
streamlet
striate
strumpet
strut
stylet
subdelegate
sublimate
subordinate
suet
sultanate
summit
sunbonnet
supermarket
supersecret
surfeit
surrebut
surrogate
syndicate
tablet
tacit
tappet
target
tartlet
temperate
template
templet
tenet
thicket

ticket
tippet
toilet
tourniquet
transit
tricot
trinket
triplet
triplicate
triumvirate
trivet
trumpet
turbot
turret
ultimate
ultraviolet
unaffectionate
unarticulate
uncompassionate
uncut
undercut
undergraduate
undeterminate
unexplicit
unfortunate
unit
unproportionate
unquiet
uppercut
valet
velvet
vertebrate
violet
visit
vomit
vulgate
wainscot
wallet
walnut
war-bonnet

wastebasket
wavelet
weskit
what
whatchamacallit
whippet
whodunit
wicket
widget
wiglet
woodcut
workbasket
zealot

Long UTH
booth
bucktooth
dogtooth
Duluth
eyetooth
forsooth
half-truth
ruth
sawtooth
sleuth
sooth
tollbooth
tooth
truth
uncouth
untruth
vermouth
youth

Long UTS
absolutes
arrowroots
attributes
beauts
bloodroots

boots
breadfruits
brutes
buttes
cahoots
chutes
commutes
computes
constitutes
contributes
coots
deputes
disputes
distributes
electrocutes
executes
firstfruits
flutes
fruits
grapefruits
grassroots
hoots
imputes
institutes
jackboots
kibbutz
knouts
lawsuits
loots
malamutes
moots
mutes
offshoots
overshoots
pantsuits
parachutes
persecutes
playsuits
pollutes
pursuits

reconstitutes
recruits
redistributes
refutes
reputes
roots
routes
saluting
scoots
shoots
snoots
spacesuits
statutes
substitutes
suits
taproots
toots
transmutes
tributes
troubleshoots
uproots

Long UV
approve
behoove
disapprove
disprove
groove
improve
move
prove
remove
reprove
you've

UV
above
dove
foxglove
glove

hereinabove
ladylove
love
of
shove
turtledove

Long UZ
abuse
accrues
accuse
adieus
amuse
argues
avenues
ballyhoos
bamboos
Bantus
barbecues
bayous
bedews
bemuse
bestrews
blues
boos
booze
breakthroughs
brews
bruise
canoes
caribous
cashews
chews
choose
clues
cockatoos
confuse
construes
continues
corkscrews

coups
crews
cruise
cruse
cuckoos
cues
curfews
curlicues
debuts
defuse
defuze
devalues
diffuse
disabuse
discontinues
dues
effuse
ensues
enthuse
eschews
ewes
excuse
flues
fuse
fuze
glues
gnus
gumshoes
gurus
hairdos
Hebrews
hews
Hindus
honeydews
hoodoos
horseshoes
hues
igloos
imbues
infuse

interviews
issues
jackscrews
Jews
kangaroos
kazoos
kinkajous
kudzus
lose
marabous
masseuse
menus
mews
mildews
misconstrues
miscues
misuse
moos
muse
muumuus
nephews
news
ooze
overshoes
overuse
overvalues
overviews
perfuse
peruse
pews
poohs
previews
purlieus
pursues
purviews
queues
refuse
reissues
rendezvouses
rescues

residues
retinues
reuse
revalues
revenues
reviews
revues
roughhews
rues
ruse
screws
shampoos
shoes
shoos
shrews
sinews
skews
slews
sloughs
slues
snooze
snowshoes
spews
statues
stews
strews
subdues
sues
suffuse
Syracuse
taboos
tatoos
tattoos
thews
thumbscrews
tissues
transfuse
trues
tutus
twos

undervalues
unscrews
use
values
venues
views
virtues
voodoos
wahoos
whose
woos
yahoos
yews
zoos
Zulus

UZ

abacuses
abases
abashes
abeyances
abhorrences
abolishes
abridges
abscesses
absences
abundances
abuses
acceptances
accomplices
accuses
aces
acknowledges
acquaintances
acquiesces
actresses
actualizes
adages
addresses
adduces

adjudges
admittances
admixes
admonishes
adulteresses
advances
advantages
adventuresses
advertises
advises
adzes
affixes
afterimages
agendas
ages
aggrandizes
agonizes
airbrushes
airspaces
albatrosses
alehouses
alfalfas
algebras
aliases
alkalinizes
alkalizes
alleges
allegiances
alliances
allowances
allspices
almshouses
alpacas
alphabetizes
altarpieces
amasses
amazes
ambiances
ambiences
ambulances

ambushes
amebas
americas
amnesias
amoebas
amortizes
amperages
amuses
anacondas
analyzes
anathemas
anathematizes
anatomizes
anchorages
anesthetizes
angelfishes
angelicas
anginas
anglicizes
angoras
anguishes
anguses
anises
annexes
announces
annoyances
anodizes
antagonizes
antennas
anthologizes
anticlimaxes
antifreezes
antihelixes
anuses
aortas
apexes
apocalypses
apologizes
apostatizes
appaloosas

apparatuses
appearances
appeases
appendages
appendixes
appliances
apposes
appraises
apprentices
apprises
approaches
archduchesses
arches
arenas
areolas
arias
arises
armadas
armistices
aromas
arouses
arranges
artifices
ashes
asparaguses
asperses
assemblages
asses
assesses
assizes
assonances
assuages
assurances
astonishes
atlases
atomizes
attaches
attendances
audiences
auras

auroras
auspices
authorizes
avalanches
avenges
averages
aviatrixes
avoidances
avouches
axes
axillas
ayahs
ayatollahs
azaleas
babas
babushkas
backlashes
backspaces
backstretches
backwashes
badges
baggages
Bahamas
balalaikas
balances
balboas
ballerinas
bananas
bandages
bandannas
banishes
baptizes
barbarizes
barges
baronesses
barracudas
barrages
bases
bashes
basilicas

basses
bastardizes
batches
bathhouses
battle-axes
bazookas
beaches
beeches
begonias
begrudges
belches
bemuses
benches
benefactresses
beseeches
besieges
besmirches
beverages
bewitches
biases
bilges
binges
biosciences
birches
birdhouses
birthplaces
bitches
blanches
blandishes
blazes
bleaches
blemishes
blenches
blesses
blintzes
blitzes
blockages
blockhouses
blotches
blouses

blowtorches
bluefishes
bluenoses
blunderbusses
blushes
boardinghouses
boas
bodices
bolas
bonanzas
bonefishes
bonuses
bookcases
boozes
bosses
botches
bounces
boxes
braces
brainwashes
braises
branches
brandishes
brazes
breaches
breakages
breeches
breezes
bridges
briefcases
britches
broaches
brokerages
bronzes
brooches
browses
bruises
brunches
brushes
brutalizes

budges
bulges
bulldozes
bullfinches
bulrushes
bunches
bunkhouses
burgesses
burglarizes
burnishes
buses
bushes
businesses
busses
butches
butterfishes
buttresses
buzz
buzzes
bwanas
bypasses
cabalas
cabanas
cabbages
cabooses
caches
cadences
cadenzas
caesuras
cafeterias
cages
calabashes
calabooses
calculuses
callouses
calluses
camellias
cameras
camouflages
campuses

cannibalizes
canonizes
cantatas
canvases
canvasses
capitalizes
caprices
capsizes
captresses
caramelizes
carcasses
carcinomas
cardias
caresses
carolinas
carouses
carriages
cartilages
cartridges
carwashes
cases
cashes
catches
categorizes
catfishes
catheterizes
caucuses
causes
cauterizes
ceases
cedillas
censuses
centerpieces
centralizes
centrifuges
cervices
cervixes
chaises
chalices
challenges

chances
changes
characterizes
charges
chases
chatterboxes
cheeses
cheetahs
chemises
cherishes
Chihuahuas
chinchillas
choices
chooses
chophouses
choruses
Christianizes
Christmases
chrysalises
chukkas
churches
cinches
cinemas
circumcises
circumferences
circumflexes
circumstances
circuses
citruses
civilizes
clashes
classes
clauses
cleanses
clearances
clearinghouses
cleavages
clenches
climaxes
clinches

closes
clotheshorses
clothespresses
clubhouses
clutches
coaches
coalesces
coaxes
cobras
cockatrices
cockhorses
cockroaches
codfishes
coerces
coincidences
colas
coleuses
collapses
collectivizes
colleges
colonizes
colossuses
comas
comeuppances
commas
commercializes
commonplaces
compasses
complexes
compliances
composes
compresses
comprises
compromises
computerizes
concertinas
concordances
concourses
concurrences
condenses

condolences
conduces
conferences
confesses
confidences
confluences
confuses
congresses
congruences
consciences
consensuses
consequences
consistences
consonances
containerizes
continuances
contrivances
convalesces
conveniences
conventionalizes
converges
converses
conveyances
convinces
convulses
coppices
copses
copulas
cordobas
corneas
cornices
cornucopias
corollas
corpses
corpulences
correspondences
corsages
corteges
cortexes
cosmoses

cottages
couches
countenances
counterbalances
counterpoises
countesses
courses
courthouses
crankcases
crashes
crawfishes
crayfishes
crazes
creases
credenzas
cresses
crevasses
crevices
cringes
crisscrosses
criticizes
crocuses
crosses
crosshatches
crosspatches
crosspieces
crotches
crouches
crucifixes
cruises
crunches
crushes
crutches
cruxes
crystallizes
cupolas
curses
cusses
customhouses
customizes

cutlasses
cuttlefishes
cyclopedias
cypresses
czarinas
daces
dachas
dahlias
daises
dakotas
dalliances
damages
dances
dashes
databases
dazes
deaconesses
deathwatches
debases
debauches
debouches
deceases
decentralizes
decomposes
decompresses
decreases
decriminalizes
deduces
defaces
defenses
defuses
degasses
dehumanizes
deices
delouses
deltas
deluges
demagnetizes
demilitarizes
demineralizes

demises
demitasses
demobilizes
democratizes
demolishes
demonetizes
demoralizes
demurrages
denounces
dentifrices
deodorizes
deoxidizes
depersonalizes
deposes
depresses
deputizes
deranges
derrises
dervishes
desensitizes
despatches
despises
detaches
deuces
deviances
devices
devises
devitalizes
diarrheas
differences
diffuses
digresses
dilemmas
diminishes
dinguses
dioramas
diplomas
dirges
disabuses
disadvantages

disallowances
disappearances
disarranges
disburses
discharges
discloses
discomposes
discontinuances
discourages
discourses
discuses
discusses
diseases
disengages
disgorges
disgraces
disguises
dishes
dislodges
dismisses
disorganizes
disparages
dispatches
dispatchs
dispenses
disperses
displaces
displeases
disposes
dissonances
distances
distinguishes
distresses
disturbances
ditches
divas
divergences
diverges
divorces
divulges

dodges
does
doges
dogfaces
dogfishes
doghouses
dogmas
dosages
douches
douses
downsizes
dowses
dozes
dramas
dramatizes
drawbridges
dredges
drenches
dresses
drowses
drudges
duces
duchesses
dunces
duplexes
eases
eclipses
economizes
edelweisses
edemas
edges
edifices
editorializes
educes
effaces
effervesces
effluences
effluvias
effulgences
egresses

elapses
elasticizes
elegances
elegizes
embarrasses
embellishes
embosses
embraces
emerges
eminences
empathizes
emphasizes
empresses
encases
enchiladas
encloses
encompasses
encourages
encroaches
encumbrances
encyclopedias
enemas
energizes
enforces
enfranchises
engages
engrosses
enhances
enigmas
enlarges
enmeshes
enrages
enriches
ensconces
enterprises
enthuses
entices
entourages
entrances
entrenches

envisages
epiglottises
epitomizes
equalizes
equinoxes
equipoises
equivalences
eras
erases
espouses
essences
estranges
etches
eucalyptuses
eulogizes
evangelizes
evidences
evinces
excellences
excesses
exchanges
excises
excuses
executrixes
exercises
existences
exorcises
expediences
expenses
experiences
exposes
expresses
expunges
extinguishes
extras
extravaganzas
eyeglasses
eyelashes
eyepieces
eyewitnesses

faces
familiarizes
famishes
fantasias
fantasizes
farces
farmhouses
fazes
featheredges
federalizes
fellahs
fences
fertilizes
fetches
fetishes
fetuses
fezes
fezzes
fibulas
fiches
fictionalizes
fieldpieces
fiestas
filches
finalizes
finances
finches
finesses
finishes
firebases
fireboxes
fireplaces
fishes
fixes
fizzes
flanges
flashes
flatfishes
flaxes
fleeces

fleshes
flexes
flinches
flitches
flophouses
floras
flosses
flotillas
flounces
flourishes
fluoresces
flushes
fluxes
focuses
focusses
footbridges
forages
forcepses
forces
forecloses
forges
formalizes
formulas
forsythias
fortresses
fossilizes
foxes
fracases
fragrances
Frances
franchises
fraternizes
freezes
fringes
frizzes
fuchsias
fudges
funguses
furbishes
furnaces

furnishes
fuselages
fuses
fusses
fuzes
fuzz
fuzzes
gages
galas
galoshes
galvanizes
garages
garbages
gardenias
garfishes
garnishes
gases
gashes
gasses
gauges
gazes
gearboxes
geishas
generalizes
genius
geniuses
genres
genuses
ghettoizes
giantesses
gladioluses
glances
glasses
glazes
glimpses
glitches
glosses
glottises
gnashes
goddesses

goldfinches
goldfishes
gondolas
gonzales
gooses
gorges
gorillas
gormandizes
gouges
goulashes
governesses
graces
granges
grasses
grazes
greases
greenhouses
grievances
grimaces
grosses
grouches
grouses
grudges
guardhouses
guavas
guerrillas
guesses
guises
gulches
gummas
gushes
gyrocompasses
haciendas
hairbrushes
hairpieces
hallelujahs
harasses
harmonicas
harmonizes
harnesses

hashes
hatches
haunches
hazes
headdresses
headmistresses
headpieces
hearses
hedges
hegiras
heiresses
helixes
hematomas
hemistiches
hemstitches
henhouses
hennas
hepaticas
heritages
hermitages
hernias
hexes
hiatuses
hibiscuses
highnesses
Himalayas
hindrances
hinges
hippopotamuses
hisses
hitches
hoaxes
hobbyhorses
hodgepodges
homages
homestretches
homogenizes
hookahs
horseradishes
horses

hosannahs
hosannas
hoses
hospices
hospitalizes
hostages
hostesses
hotboxes
hothouses
hourglasses
houses
hulas
humanizes
hunches
huntresses
hushes
hutches
hybridizes
hyenas
hypnotizes
hypothesizes
hysterectomizes
hysterias
iambuses
ibexes
ibises
iceboxes
ices
ictuses
idealizes
ideas
idolizes
ignoramuses
iguanas
illnesses
images
imbalances
immerses
immobilizes
immortalizes

immunizes
impalas
impasses
impeaches
impedances
impetuses
impinges
imposes
impoverishes
impresses
improvises
impulses
incas
incases
incenses
inches
incises
incoherences
inconveniences
increases
incubuses
indexes
individualizes
induces
indulgences
indulges
industrializes
inertias
inferences
influences
influenzas
influxes
infringes
infuses
inheritances
injustices
inrushes
insignias
instances
intellectualizes

intelligences
interchanges
interfaces
interferences
interlaces
intermarriages
intermeshes
intermixes
intersperses
introduces
inverses
invoices
iodizes
ionizes
iotas
irises
irrelevances
issuances
isthmuses
italicizes
itches
itemizes
jacarandas
jackasses
jaundices
jazzes
jellyfishes
jeopardizes
jinxes
Jonahs
Joneses
joshes
jounces
judases
judges
juices
jukeboxes
juntas
justices
juxtaposes

kaddishes
kappas
karmas
kedges
ketches
keypunches
kibitzes
kimonos
kindnesses
kisses
koalas
laces
laches
lamas
lances
landmasses
languages
languishes
lapses
larvas
larynxes
lashes
lasses
latches
latexes
lattices
launches
laundresses
lavas
lavishes
lazes
leaches
leakages
leases
leashes
ledges
leeches
legalizes
legitimizes
lenses

lettuces
leverages
liberalizes
licenses
lieges
lightfaces
lighthouses
likenesses
limas
lineages
linkages
lionesses
lionizes
lipomas
liquidizes
liras
llamas
localizes
lodges
looses
loses
losses
lotuses
lounges
louses
lozenges
lummoxes
lunches
lunges
lurches
lushes
lymphomas
lynches
lynxes
macadamizes
maces
mackintoshes
maculas
madeiras
madhouses

madonnas
magnetizes
magnolias
maharajahs
mahatmas
mailboxes
maintenances
malaises
malefactresses
mamas
mambas
manages
mananas
manias
mantelpieces
mantillas
mantises
mantissas
mantlepieces
maracas
marbleizes
marches
marimbas
marinas
marketplaces
marquises
marriages
marshes
mascaras
mashes
massages
masses
masseuses
masterpieces
matches
materializes
matrixes
mattresses
matzos
maximizes

mayas
mayoresses
mazes
mazurkas
meccas
mechanizes
medias
melanges
melanomas
melodramas
memorializes
memorizes
menaces
meniscuses
menorahs
mercerizes
merchandises
merges
mesas
meshes
mesmerizes
messages
messes
messiahs
mestizas
metabolizes
metastasizes
methodizes
metricizes
microfiches
midges
militarizes
millraces
minces
mineralizes
miniaturizes
minibuses
minimizes
minuses
minxes

mirages
misadvises
misalliances
misarranges
miscarriages
mischances
mischarges
misdoes
misfeasances
mishmashes
misjudges
mismanages
mismatches
misplaces
mispronounces
misses
mistresses
mittimuses
mixes
mobilizes
modernizes
moisturizes
molasses
mongooses
monomanias
monopolizes
monstrances
montages
mooches
moralizes
moras
morasses
mortgages
mortises
mosses
motorizes
mouses
mousses
moustaches
mouthpieces

mouthwashes
Mrs.
mulches
mullahs
munches
murderesses
muses
mushes
musses
mustaches
mynas
myomas
myosarcomas
narcissuses
narcotizes
nasalizes
nationalizes
naturalizes
nebulas
nebulizes
necklaces
neuralgias
neutralizes
nexuses
niches
nieces
nimbuses
nixes
noises
nonpluses
nooses
normalizes
noses
notarizes
notches
notices
nourishes
novas
novelizes
novellas

novenas
novices
nuances
nudges
nuisances
nurses
nuthatches
nutrias
obliges
observances
obsesses
occurrences
octopuses
Oedipuses
offenses
offices
ogresses
okras
omnibuses
Oneidas
oozes
operas
operettas
opposes
oppresses
opuses
oranges
orchestras
ordinances
organizes
orifices
orphanages
orrises
osages
ostracizes
ostriches
ounces
outages
outbalances
outboxes

outclasses
outdodges
outdoes
outfaces
outfoxes
outguesses
outhouses
outmarches
outproduces
outraces
outrages
outranges
outreaches
outstretches
overages
overanalyzes
overbalances
overcapitalizes
overcharges
overdoes
overdoses
overdramatizes
overdresses
overembellishes
overemphasizes
overexercises
overexposes
overfurnishes
overgeneralizes
overglazes
overgrazes
overimpresses
overindulges
overindustrializes
overpasses
overpraises
overprices
overproduces
overreaches
overspecializes

overtaxes
overuses
oxidizes
paces
pachysandras
packages
packhorses
pages
pagodas
paintbrushes
pajamas
palaces
palefaces
panaceas
panatellas
pancreases
pandas
panoramas
papayas
papooses
papyruses
parabolas
paradises
paradoxes
parallaxes
paralyzes
paraphrases
parches
parishes
parkas
parses
parsonages
particularizes
partridges
pashas
passages
passes
pastas
pasteurizes
patches

patellas
patinas
patronesses
patronizes
paunches
pauperizes
pauses
peaches
peeresses
pelletizes
penalizes
peninsulas
penises
penthouses
percentages
perches
performances
perishes
perplexes
personages
personalizes
peruses
pestilences
petunias
phalluses
pharynxes
phases
philosophizes
phobias
phoenixes
photosynthesizes
phrases
piazzas
pickaxes
pieces
pierces
pilgrimages
pillages
pillboxes
pillowcases

pilothouses
pinches
piranhas
pitches
pittances
pizzas
pizzerias
placentas
places
plagiarizes
plasmas
playhouses
plazas
pleases
pledges
plexuses
plunges
pluralizes
pluses
poaches
poetesses
Poincianas
poinsettias
poises
polarizes
polices
polishes
politicizes
polkas
polonaises
polymerizes
pooches
poorhouses
popularizes
porches
porpoises
portages
poses
possesses
potlatches

pouches
poultices
pounces
powerhouses
poxes
practices
praises
prances
preaches
prearranges
precipices
predisposes
preengages
preestablishes
preexposes
prefaces
preferences
prefixes
prejudges
prejudices
premises
premixes
prepackages
prepossesses
presages
presences
presses
pressurizes
presupposes
pretenses
prewashes
prices
priestesses
primroses
princes
privileges
prizes
processes
produces
professes

progresses
pronounces
proposes
protectresses
protuberances
provenances
provinces
provirus
psychoanalyzes
psychodramas
publicizes
publishes
pulses
pulverizes
pumas
punches
punishes
pupas
purchases
purges
purposes
purses
purulences
pushes
putsches
quashes
quenches
quinces
quittances
quizzes
quotas
racecourses
racehorses
races
radicalizes
radishes
radiuses
rages
raises
rajahs

rampages
ranches
randomizes
ranges
rashes
rationalizes
ravages
ravishes
razes
razzes
reaches
readdresses
reappearances
reappraises
rearouses
rearranges
reassesses
reassurances
reattaches
rebaptizes
rebuses
recesses
recharges
recluses
recognizes
recolonizes
recolors
recompenses
reconnaissances
recurrences
redoes
redresses
reduces
redundances
reemerges
reemphasizes
reenforces
reengages
reenlarges
reestablishes

references
refinances
refinishes
reflexes
refocuses
reforges
refreshes
refuges
refurbishes
refurnishes
regresses
regularizes
rehashes
rehearses
reimburses
reimposes
reinduces
reinforces
rejoices
relapses
relaxes
releases
relevances
relinquishes
relishes
remarriages
rematches
remilitarizes
reminiscences
reminisces
remittances
remonetizes
remonstrances
remortgages
reoccurrences
reorganizes
repackages
rephrases
replaces
replenishes

replicas
reposes
repossesses
represses
reprises
reproaches
reprocesses
reproduces
republishes
repulses
researches
resemblances
residences
resistances
resonances
resorters
resources
respondences
responses
resurfaces
retches
retinas
retouches
retraces
retrenches
retrogresses
reuses
reutilizes
revarnishes
revenges
reverses
revises
revitalizes
revolutionizes
rhapsodizes
rhinoceroses
rices
riches
rictuses
ridges

rinses
rises
roaches
romances
romanticizes
rosebushes
roses
rotundas
roughhouses
roughnesses
roundhouses
rouses
routinizes
rubberizes
ruckuses
rumbas
rummages
rumpuses
ruses
rushes
rutabagas
sabotages
sabras
sandboxes
sandwiches
sashes
sasses
sauces
scandalizes
scorches
scourges
scratches
screeches
scrimmages
scrooges
scrounges
scrunches
scrutinizes
scubas
sculptresses

seamstresses
seances
searches
secularizes
sedges
seductresses
semblances
sentimentalizes
sermonizes
sexes
shellfishes
shepherdesses
sherpas
shoelaces
shortages
shortchanges
showcases
showpieces
showplaces
shrinkages
shushes
sicknesses
sidepieces
sierras
siestas
signalizes
signoras
signorinas
silences
silverfishes
simonizes
singes
sinuses
sixes
sizes
sketches
skirmishes
slashes
slaughterhouses
sledges

slenderizes
slices
sloshes
slouches
sluices
smashes
smilaxes
smirches
smokehouses
smooches
smudges
snatches
sneezes
snitches
snoozes
soapboxes
socializes
sodas
sofas
solemnizes
soliloquizes
solstices
sonatas
songstresses
sorceresses
sources
sourpusses
souses
Sovietizes
spaces
spatulas
specializes
speeches
sphinxes
spices
splashes
splices
splotches
splurges
sponges

spouses
spruces
spyglasses
squashes
squeezes
squelches
stabilizes
stagecoaches
stages
staircases
stances
stanches
standardizes
stanzas
starches
starfishes
stargazes
stashes
statehouses
statuses
steeplechases
stenches
sterilizes
stewardesses
stigmas
stigmatizes
stitches
stooges
stoppages
stopwatches
storehouses
straightedges
stresses
stretches
stripteases
strongboxes
strumas
stylizes
styluses
subbranches

subclasses
subclauses
subleases
submerges
submerses
subpoenas
subprovinces
subsidizes
substances
subsurfaces
subterfuges
successes
suffices
suffixes
suffrages
suffuses
suitcases
sultanas
summarizes
summerhouses
summonses
sunfishes
sunglasses
sunrises
supercharges
superimposes
supernovas
superposes
supervises
supposes
suppresses
surceases
surcharges
surfaces
surges
surmises
surpasses
surplices
surpluses
surprises

surtaxes
sutras
swages
swashes
swastikas
swatches
swishes
switches
swordfishes
syllabuses
symbolizes
sympathizes
synchronizes
syntaxes
synthesizes
syphilomas
syringes
syrinxes
systematizes
systemizes
tantalizes
tarantulas
tarnishes
taxes
teaches
teases
televises
telexes
temporizes
temptresses
tenderizes
tenses
terminuses
terraces
terrorizes
thatches
theorizes
thesauruses
thicknesses
thoraxes

thrashes
threshes
thrushes
thymuses
tiaras
tibias
tigresses
tildes
timepieces
tinderboxes
tinges
toastmistresses
tobaccoes
togas
tolerances
tonnages
toothbrushes
topazes
torahs
torches
tortillas
tortoises
tosses
touches
Toyotas
traces
tracheas
traduces
traipses
traitresses
trances
tranquilizes
transfuses
transgresses
transistorizes
transmittances
transposes
transverses
trapezes
trashes

traumas
traverses
treatises
trellises
trenches
trespasses
tresses
triplexes
trivalences
troikas
trounces
truces
trudges
trusses
tsarinas
tubas
tunas
turquoises
tuxes
tweezes
twinges
twitches
typefaces
tyrannizes
tzarinas
umbras
umbrellas
unclenches
uncrosses
undercarriages
undercharges
underdresses
underexposes
underpasses
undoes
undresses
unfixes
unfreezes
unhinges
unhitches

unionizes
universes
unlaces
unlatches
unleashes
unlooses
upraises
upstages
upsurges
urbanizes
urges
uses
utilizes
utopias
utterances
uvulas
valences
valorizes
valses
vamooses
vandalizes
vanillas
vanishes
vanquishes
vaporizes
variances
varnishes
vendettas
verbalizes
vernalizes
verses
versus
vertebras
vertexes
vestiges
vexes
vicarages
vices
victimizes

villages
villainesses
villas
vintages
violas
virulences
viruses
visages
visas
vistas
visualizes
vitalizes
vocalizes
vodkas
voices
volatilizes
voltages
vortexes
vouches
voyages
vulcanizes
vulgarizes
vulvas
wages
waitresses
walruses
waltzes
warehouses
warhorses
was
washes
watches
watercourses
waxes
weaknesses
weatherglasses
wedges
Welshes
wenches

westernizes
wheelbases
wheezes
whiplashes
whitefishes
whitewashes
whizzes
whooshes
winces
winches
windlasses
winterizes
wishes
wisterias
witches
witnesses
womanizes
workbenches
workhorses
workhouses
wrasses
wrenches
wretches
wristwatches
xanthomas
Xeroxes
Xmases
yarmelkes
yarmulkes
yeses
yeshivahs
yeshivas
yuccas
zebras
zenanas
zinnias
zonas
zoysias

Part Three:
Two Syllable, or
Feminine Rhymes

Long A-ANS
abeyance
conveyance
obeyance
purveyance
reconveyance
surveyance

Long A-BY
baby
crybaby
grandbaby
maybe

A-BY
abbey
cabby
crabby
flabby
gabby
grabby
scabby
shabby
tabby

A-BID
rabid
tabid

AB-ING
blabbing
cabbing
confabbing
crabbing
dabbing
gabbing
grabbing
jabbing
nabbing
scabbing

stabbing
tabbing
taxicabbing

AB-IT
abbot
babbitt
cabot
cohabit
grab it
habit
inhabit
jackrabbit
rabbet
rabbit

Long A-BL
Abel
able
cable
disable
disenable
enable
fable
gable
instable
label
labile
mislabel
photostable
retable
sable
stable
table
timetable
turntable
unable
unstable
worktable

AB-L
babble
Babel
dabble
gabble
grabble
rabble
scrabble

AB-LING
babbling
dabbling
gabbling
scrabbling

AB-LUR
babbler
dabbler
gabbler
scrabbler

A-BOT
abbot
cabot
habit

Long A-BUR
antilabor
labor
neighbor
prolabor
saber
sabre
tabor

AB-UR
blabber
bonnyclabber
clabber
crabber

dabber
drabber
gabber
grabber
jabber
slabber
stabber

AB-URD
blabbered
clapboard
jabbered
scabbard
tabard

ACH-ET
hatchet
latchet
rachet
ratchet

ACH-EZ
attaches
batches
catches
crosshatches
crosspatches
despatches
detaches
dispatches
dispatchs
hatches
laches
latches
matches
mismatches
Natchez
nuthatches
patches
potlatches

reattaches
rematches
scratches
snatches
thatches
unlatches

ACH-I
Apache
catchy
patchy
scratchy

ACH-ING
attaching
catching
crosshatching
despatching
detaching
dispatching
hatching
latching
matching
mismatching
patching
rematching
scratching
snatching
thatching
unlatching

ACH-LESS
matchless
patchless
scratchless
thatchless

ACH-MENT
attachment
catchment

detachment
hatchment
reattachment

ACH-UR
attacher
back scratcher
body-snatcher
catcher
cowcatcher
despatcher
dispatcher
dogcatcher
eye-catcher
flycatcher
hatcher
matcher
patcher
scratcher
snatcher
stature
thatcher

ACH-WURK
catchwork
patchwork

Long A-DAY
gray day
heyday
layday
Mayday
payday
play day

AD-AM
Adam
Macadam
MacAdam
madam

madame

Long A-DED
aided
ambuscaded
barricaded
blockaded
brocaded
cannonaded
crusaded
degraded
dissuaded
downgraded
evaded
faded
graded
haded
invaded
jaded
laded
marinaded
masqueraded
paraded
pervaded
serenaded
shaded
unaided
unfaded
ungraded
unshaded

A-DED
added
gadded
padded
plaided

Long A-DEN
Aden

handmaiden
heavy-laden
laden
maiden
menhaden
overladen
unladen

AD-EN
gladden
madden
sadden

AD-EST
baddest
faddist
gladdest
maddest
saddest

Long AD-I
chairlady
forelady
glady
lady
saleslady
shady

AD-I
baddy
caddie
caddy
daddy
finnan haddie
laddie
paddy
sugar daddy

AD-IK
dyadic

haggadic
maenadic
monadic
nomadic
paddock
sporadic
triadic

Long A-DING
aiding
barricading
biodegrading
blockading
braiding
brocading
cannonading
cascading
crusading
degrading
dissuading
downgrading
evading
fading
grading
invading
jading
lading
marinading
masquerading
parading
persuading
pervading
promenading
raiding
renegading
serenading
shading
spading
stockading
trading

unfading
upbraiding
upgrading
wading

AD-ING
adding
cladding
gadding
madding
padding

AD-ISH
baddish
caddish
faddish
gladdish
horseradish
radish
saddish

Long A-DL
cradle
ladle

AD-L
addle
astraddle
bestraddle
faddle
fiddle-faddle
gonadal
packsaddle
paddle
saddle
sidesaddle
skedaddle
straddle
unsaddle

Long AD-LESS
bladeless
braidless
fadeless
gradeless
maidless
shadeless
tradeless

Long AD-LI
gradely
retrogradely
staidly

AD-LI
badly
comradely
gladly
madly
sadly

Long AD-LING
cradling
ladling

AD-LING
Addling
daddling
paddling
skedaddling
spraddling
straddling
unsaddling

AD-LUR
addler
paddler
saddler
skedaddler
straddler

AD-NESS
badness
gladness
madness
sadness

Long A-DO
bastinado
dado
Laredo
Play-dough
tornado

AD-O
foreshadow
overshadow
shadow

AH-DO
aficionado
amontillado
avocado
bravado
Colorado
desperado
El Dorado
incommunicado
Mikado
stoccado
strappado

AD-OK
haddock
paddock

AD-POL
tadpole
sad Pole

AD-SUM
gladsome
madsome

Long A-DUR
aider
barricader
blockader
braider
crusader
evader
grader
parader
persuader
promenader
raider
Seder
trader
upbraider
wader

AD-UR
adder
bladder
gadder
gallbladder
gladder
ladder
madder
sadder
stepladder

Long A-EST
archaist
essayist
gayest
grayest
greyest
Hebraist
mayest

sayest

Long A-FAIR
Mayfair
Playfair

AF-I
daffy
taffy

AF-IK
autobiographic
autographic
barographic
bibliographic
bioautographic
biographic
calligraphic
cardiographic
cartographic
choreographic
cryptographic
demographic
epigraphic
ergographic
geographic
graphic
holographic
homographic
ichnographic
lexicographic
lithographic
oceanographic
orthographic
oscillographic
paleographic
phonographic
photographic
pictographic
pneumographic

polarographic
polygraphic
pornographic
radiographic
Sapphic
seismographic
seraphic
spectrographic
spirographic
stenographic
stethographic
stratigraphic
telegraphic
thermographic
tomographic
topographic
traffic
traffick
typographic
xerographic

AF-ING
autographing
chaffing
choreographing
graphing
laughing
lithographing
mimeographing
paragraphing
photographing
quaffing
staffing
strafing
telegraphing

AF-L
baffle
raffle
snaffle

AF-LING
baffling
raffling
snaffling

AF-OLD
baffled
raffled
scaffold

AF-TED
crafted
drafted
engrafted
grafted
handcrafted
rafted
shafted
wafted

AF-TI
crafty
draftee
drafty
draughty

AF-TING
crafting
drafting
engrafting
grafting
handcrafting
rafting
shafting
wafting

AFT-LESS
craftless
draftless
raftless

shaftless

AFTS-MAN
craftsman
draftsman
handicraftsman
raftsman

AF-TUR
after
dafter
drafter
grafter
hereafter
hereinafter
laughter
rafter
thereafter
thereinafter
whereafter

Long A-FUL
playful
trayful

Long A-FUR
chafer
safer
strafer
wafer

A-FUR
chaffer
gaffer
laugher
lithographer
quaffer
staffer

Long A-GA
omega
rutabaga

AH-GA
raga
saga

Long A-GAN
Fagin
pagan
ray gun
Ronald Reagan

AG-ARD
haggard
laggard
staggard
staggered
swaggered

AG-UT
agate
faggot
fagot
maggot

AG-ED
jagged
ragged

AG-I
aggie
baggy
craggy
draggy
jaggy
Maggie
saggy
scraggy

shaggy
slaggy
snaggy
swaggy
waggy

AG-ING
bagging
bragging
carpetbagging
dragging
fagging
flagging
fragging
gagging
lagging
lallygagging
lollygagging
nagging
ragging
sagging
sandbagging
snagging
spragging
tagging
unflagging
wagging
wigwagging
zigzagging

AG-L
bedraggle
draggle
gaggle
haggle
straggle
waggle

AG-LING
bedraggling

draggling
haggling
straggling
waggling

AG-LUR
bedraggler
draggler
haggler
straggler
waggler

AG-MAN
bagman
dragman
flagman
gagman
ragman

AG-NAT
magnate
stagnate

Long A-GO
Diego
imago
lumbago
plumbago
San Diego
solidago

AH-GO
Chicago
Iago
Santiago

AG-ON
bandwagon
battlewagon
dragon

flagon
snapdragon
Volkswagen
Wagon

AG-OT
agate
faggot
fagot
maggot

Long AG-RANS
flagrance
fragrance
vagrance
vagrants

AG-RANT
flagrant
fragrant
vagrant

AG-UR
bragger
carpetbagger
dagger
dragger
Jagger
nagger
sandbagger
stagger
swagger
tagger
three-bagger
two-bagger

AH-HOO
wahoo
Yahoo

AH-MI
balmy
mommy
palmy
salami
swami
Tommy

Long A-IK
algebraic
altaic
Aramaic
archaic
deltaic
formulaic
Hebraic
Judaic
linoleic
mishnaic
mosaic
nucleic
oleic
Passaic
Pharisaic
prosaic
Ptolemaic
spondaic
stanzaic
trochaic
voltaic

Long A-ING
allaying
appliqueing
arraying
assaying
baying
betraying
braying
bricklaying

cacheting
conveying
crocheting
decaying
defraying
delaying
disarraying
dismaying
disobeying
displaying
enplaning
essaying
flaying
foraying
fraying
gainsaying
glaceing
graying
greying
haying
hooraying
hurrahing
hurraying
inlaying
inveighing
laying
mislaying
misplaying
neighing
nonpaying
obeying
ok'ing
okaying
outplaying
outstaying
outweighing
overlaying
overpaying
overplaying
overstaying

overweighing
parlaying
parqueting
paying
playing
portraying
praying
prepaying
preying
pureeing
purveying
reconveying
relaying
repaying
replaying
resurveying
ricocheting
sashaying
sauteing
saying
slaying
sleighing
soothsaying
spaying
splaying
spraying
staying
straying
surveying
swaying
taxpaying
underlaying
underpaying
underplaying
unpaying
waylaying
weighing

AH-ING
awing

cawing
clawing
drawing
gnawing
guffawing
hawing
hurrahing
jawing
outlawing
overawing
overdrawing
pawing
sawing
seesawing
thawing
underdrawing
whipsawing
withdrawing
yawing

AH-TA
regatta
ricotta
sonata
stigmata

Long A-ISH
cayish
gayish
grayish

Long A-JEZ
Ages
assuages
cages
disengages
enrages
gages
gauges
outrages

pages
presages
rampages
stages
wages

Long A-JI
cagey
EKG
stagy

AJ-IK
magic
pelagic
tragic

AJ-IL
agile
fragile

Long A-JING
ageing
aging
assuaging
disengaging
engaging
enraging
gaging
gauging
outraging
paging
preengaging
presaging
raging
rampaging
reengaging
staging
upstaging
waging

AJ-ING
badging
cadging

Long AJ-LESS
ageless
cageless
pageless
rageless
sageless
stageless
wageless

Long AJ-MENT
assuagement
disengagement
encagement
engagement

Long AJ-UR
assuager
cager
engager
gauger
major
pager
sergeant major
stager
teenager
wager

AJ-UR
badger
cadger

A-JUS
advantageous
contagious
courageous
disadvantageous

noncontagious
outrageous
rampageous
umbrageous
unadvantageous

AK-A
alpaca
Malacca

Long AK-DOWN
breakdown
shakedown
takedown

Long A-KEN
awaken
bacon
Jamaican
forsaken
makin'
mistaken
overtaken
partaken
shaken
undertaken
unshaken
taken
waken

AK-EN
blacken
bracken
flacon
slacken

AK-EST
blackest
slackest

AK-ET
bluejacket
bracket
jacket
packet
placket
racket
racquet
straightjacket
straitjacket

Long A-KI
achy
caky
fakey
flaky
headachy
quaky
shaky
snaky

AK-I
by cracky
hackie
Jackie
lackey
quacky
tacky
ticky-tacky
wacky

AK-IJ
package
prepackage
repackage
slackage
trackage

Long A-KING
aching

awaking
backbreaking
baking
bellyaching
betaking
bookmaking
braking
breaking
breathtaking
cabinetmaking
caking
caretaking
dressmaking
earthshaking
faking
flaking
forsaking
glassmaking
grubstaking
handshaking
heartbreaking
homemaking
housebreaking
laking
lawbreaking
lawmaking
lovemaking
making
matchmaking
merrymaking
mistaking
moneymaking
muckraking
overtaking
pacemaking
painstaking
partaking
peacemaking
quaking
rainmaking

raking
reawaking
remaking
retaking
shaking
shipbreaking
slaking
snaking
soapmaking
staking
stocktaking
strikebreaking
taking
toolmaking
undertaking
unmaking
waking
watchmaking

AK-ING
attacking
backing
backpacking
backtracking
bivouacking
blacking
blackjacking
bushwhacking
clacking
counterattacking
cracking
hacking
hijacking
hopsacking
jacking
lacking
packing
quacking
racking
ransacking

repacking
sacking
safecracking
shacking
shellacking
sidetracking
skyjacking
slacking
smacking
snacking
stacking
tacking
thumbtacking
thwacking
tracking
unpacking
whacking
wisecracking
wracking
yacking
yakking

AK-ISH
blackish
brackish
quackish

AK-L
cackle
crackle
grackle
hackle
jackal
ramshackle
shackle
spackle
tabernacle
tackle
unshackle

AK-LING
cackling
crackling
hackling
shackling
tackling
unshackling

AK-LUR
cackler
hackler
shackler
tackler

AK-MAN
black man
jackman
packman
Pakman
trackman

AK-NESS
blackness
inexactness
slackness

AK-NI
acne
hackney

Long A-KOFF
break off
make off
rake-off
takeoff

A-KON
bacon
Jamaican
Macon

mistaken
waken

AK-OUT
Blackout

AK-POT
crackpot
jackpot

AK-RON
Akron
Dacron
macron

AK-RUM
sacrum
simalacrum

AK-SEZ
anticlimaxes
axes
battle-axes
climaxes
flaxes
overtaxes
parallaxes
pickaxes
relaxes
smilaxes
surtaxes
syntaxes
taxes
thoraxes
waxes

AK-SHUN
abstraction
action
attraction

benefaction
coaction
compaction
contraction
counteraction
countertraction
detraction
dissatisfaction
distraction
exaction
extraction
faction
fraction
impaction
inaction
infraction
interaction
liquefaction
malefaction
olfaction
overreaction
petrifaction
protraction
putrefaction
rarefaction
reaction
refraction
retraction
rubefaction
satisfaction
stupefaction
subtraction
taction
traction
transaction

AK-SHUS
factious
fractious

AKS-SING
axing
climaxing
overtaxing
relaxing
taxing
waxing

AKS-MAN
axman
cracksman
sax man
tacksman
tax man

AK-SON
Anglo-Saxon
flaxen
Jackson
klaxon
retraction
Saxon
waxen

AK-TED
abstracted
acted
attracted
compacted
contacted
contracted
counteracted
detracted
distracted
enacted
exacted
extracted
impacted
interacted
overacted

overreacted
playacted
protracted
reacted
reenacted
refracted
retracted
subcontracted
subtracted
transacted
unattracted
underacted
undistracted

AK-TIC
anticlimactic
chiropractic
climactic
didactic
galactic
intergalactic
lactic
phototactic
prophylactic
syntactic
tactic
thermotactic

AK-TIL
dactyl
pentadactyl
polydactyl
protractile
pterodactyl
refractile
retractile
syndactyl
syndactyle
tactile
tractile

tridactyl

AK-TING
acting
attracting
compacting
contacting
contracting
counteracting
detracting
distracting
enacting
exacting
extracting
impacting
interacting
overacting
overreacting
playacting
protracting
reacting
reenacting
refracting
retracting
subcontracting
subtracting
transacting
underacting

AK-TIV
abstractive
active
attractive
benefactive
contractive
counteractive
detractive
distractive
hyperactive
inactive

interactive
liquefactive
nonreactive
overactive
petrifactive
proactive
psychoactive
putrefactive
radioactive
reactive
refractive
retroactive
semiactive
stupefactive
unattractive
unreactive

AKT-LESS
actless
factless
tactless
tractless

AKT-LI
abstractly
compactly
exactly
inexactly
matter-of-factly

AKT-NESS
abstractness
compactness
exactness
inexactness
intactness

AK-TRESS
actress
benefactress

malefactress

AK-CHUR
contracture
fracture
manufacture

AK-TUR
abstractor
actor
benefactor
chiropractor
co-contractor
cofactor
compactor
contractor
detractor
enactor
exacter
extractor
factor
infractor
malefactor
protractor
reactor
refractor
subcontractor
tractor
transactor

Long A-KUP
breakup
makeup
shake-up
wake up

AK-UP
backup
crackup
jack up

pack up
rack up
shack up
smack-up
stack up

Long A-KUR
acre
baker
breaker
dressmaker
faker
fakir
heartbreaker
maker
moneymaker
muckraker
nacre
noisemaker
partaker
Quaker
shopbreaker
strikebreaker
toolmaker
troublemaker
undertaker
watchmaker

AK-UR
attacker
backer
backpacker
blacker
bushwacker
bushwhacker
clacker
cracker
firecracker
hacker
hijacker

jacker
knacker
lacquer
linebacker
nutcracker
packer
ransacker
sacker
safecracker
shacker
shellacker
skyjacker
slacker
smacker
stacker
tacker
thwacker
tracker
whacker
wisecracker

Long A-KURZ
bakers
boilermakers
bookmakers
breakers
cabinetmakers
caretakers
dressmakers
fakers
haymakers
homemakers
housebreakers
icebreakers
jawbreakers
lawbreakers
lawmakers
makers
matchmakers
merrymakers

muckrakers
partakers
peacemakers
quakers
rainmakers
rakers
retakers
shakers
shoemakers
strikebreakers
takers
undertakers
wiseacres

AL-UD
ballad
invalid
pallid
salad
valid

AL-ANS
balance
counterbalance
imbalance
outbalance
overbalance
unbalance
valance

Long A-LANT
assailant
divalent
exhalant
exhalent
inhalant
surveillant
tetravalent
trivalent
univalent

AL-AS
Alice
borealis
callous
callus
cephaelis
chalice
Dallas
digitalis
malice
modalis
palace
phallus

Long A-LBURD
jailbird
railbird

AL-ENT
gallant
talent
topgallant
ungallant

AL-ET
ballot
mallet
palate
palette
pallet
valet

Long A-LFUL
baleful
pailful
wailful

Long A-LI
bailey
daily

gaily
grayly
greyly
Israeli
scaly
shillelagh
ukelele
ukulele

AL-I
alley
dally
dillydally
galley
pally
rally
sally
shally
shilly-shally
tally
valley

A-LIF
bailiff
Caliph

AL-IK
bimetallic
brachycephalic
cephalic
encephalic
Gallic
hydrocephalic
intervocalic
italic
macrocephalic
metallic
nonmetallic
oxalic
phallic

salic
uralic
vandalic

Long A-LING
ailing
airmailing
assailing
availing
bailing
baling
bewailing
blackmailing
countervailing
curtailing
derailing
detailing
dovetailing
entailing
exhaling
failing
flailing
grayling
hailing
hightailing
impaling
inhaling
jailing
mailing
nailing
paling
prevailing
quailing
railing
remailing
retailing
sailing
scaling
tailing
trailing

travailing
unavailing
unfailing
unveiling
veiling
wailing
waling
whaling
wholesaling

AL-IS
Alice
borealis
callous
callus
cephaelis
chalice
Dallas
digitalis
malice
modalis
palace
phallus

AL-JIK
myalgic
neuralgic
nostalgic

Long AL-MENT
ailment
assailment
bailment
curtailment
derailment
detailment
disentailment
empalement
entailment
impalement

regalement

Long AL-NESS
femaleness
frailness
haleness
maleness
paleness
staleness

A-LO
aloe
callow
fallow
hallow
mallow
marshmallow
sallow
shallow
tallow

AH-LO
Apollo
follow
hollow
swallow
wallow

AL-ON
Alan
Allen
gallon
talon

AL-OP
escallop
gallop
gallup
scallop
shallop

AL-OT
ballot
mallet
palate
palette
pallet
valet

AL-OZ
allhallows
aloes
gallows
hallows
mallows
marshmallows
shallows

AL-TO
alto
contralto
Palo Alto
rialto

Long A-lur
bailor
entailer
impaler
inhaler
jailer
jailor
mailer
malar
nailer
prevailer
railer
retailer
sailor
semitrailer
tailor
wailer

waler
wassailer
whaler
wholesaler

AL-UR
pallor
valor

Long A-LYA
Australia
azalea
Bacchanalia
glossolalia
mammalia
paraphernalia
regalia
Saturnalia

Long A-LYAN
accordion
Addisonian
Aegean
Aesopian
agrarian
Albanian
Alexandrian
Algerian
Algonquian
alien
Amazonian
Amerindian
amphibian
Andean
Anglian
antiquarian
Appalachian
Aquarian
Arabian
Arcadian

Argentinean
Aristotelian
Arizonian
Armenian
Arthurian
Aryan
Assyrian
Athenian
Augustinian
Australian
Austrian
authoritarian
avian
Babylonian
Bahamian
Baltimorean
barbarian
Bavarian
Bermudian
bohemian
Bolivian
Bostonian
Bulgarian
Burundian
caesarean
caesarian
Californian
Cambodian
Cambrian
Cameroonian
Canadian
Caribbean
Carolinian
Caspian
centenarian
centurion
cesarean
chadian
champion
Chaucerian

Chilean
circadian
clarion
Colombian
Columbian
comedian
Corinthian
cornucopian
crimean
criterion
custodian
Czechoslovakian
Darwinian
Delawarean
Devonian
Dionysian
diphtherian
disciplinarian
draconian
Edwardian
egalitarian
epicurean
Episcopalian
equestrian
Estonian
Ethiopian
Euclidean
Euclidian
euphonium
European
Fabian
fallopian
Faustian
Freudian
galilean
gallein
galleon
ganglion
grammarian
Gregorian

guardian
Guinean
halcyon
Hamiltonian
Herculean
historian
Hobbesian
humanitarian
Hungarian
hygeian
Iberian
Indian
isthmian
Jacksonian
Jacobean
Jeffersonian
Jordanian
Jungian
kantian
Korean
lactovegetarian
Latvian
lesbian
liberian
libertarian
librarian
Libyan
Lithuanian
lutein
Macedonian
Machiavellian
Malarian
mammalian
Manchurian
Marxian
Mauritanian
Mediterranean
meridian
Mesopotamian
microbian

Mississippian
mitochondrion
monarchian
Mongolian
napoleon
Neptunian
Newtonian
nickelodeon
Nigerian
nonsectarian
oblivion
obsidian
Oedipean
olein
Olympian
oratorian
Oregonian
Orwellian
ossein
ovarian
oxonian
Palestinian
Panamanian
Paramedian
Parkinsonian
parliamentarian
Pavlovian
pedestrian
permian
Peruvian
Philadelphian
Pickwickian
plebeian
pogonion
Pomeranian
Precambrian
Presbyterian
procrustean
proletarian
promethean

protean
protein
Pygmalion
Pythagorean
quotidian
radian
reptilian
riparian
ruffian
Sadducean
Sagittarian
sanitarian
Sardinian
Scandinavian
scorpion
sectarian
seminarian
Senatorian
Serbian
Shakespearean
Shakespearian
Shavian
Shoshonean
Siberian
Silurian
simian
simoleon
Skinnerian
Slavonian
Smithsonian
Sophoclean
sparteine
stentorian
stygian
subclavian
subterranean
Swahilian
Swiftian
Syrian
Tanzanian

thespian
totalitarian
tragedian
Trinitarian
Ukrainian
Unitarian
utopian
vegetarian
veterinarian
Victorian
vulgarian
Wagnerian
Washingtonian
wolffian
wormian
Yugoslavian
zambian
zein
Zoroastrian
zunian

AL-YUN
battalion
Italian
medallion
rapscallion
scallion
stallion

AH-MA
Bahama
comma
cyclorama
Dalia Lama
diorama
drama
Fujiyama
lama
llama
melodrama

pajama
panorama
psychodrama
Yokohama

Long A-MAN
dayman
highwayman
layman
shaman
stamen
weighman

AM-BIT
ambit
damn bit
gambit

AM-BLE
amble
bramble
Campbell
gamble
gambol
preamble
ramble
scramble
shamble
unscramble

AM-BLING
ambling
gambling
rambling
scrambling
shambling
unscrambling

AM-BLUR
ambler

gambler
rambler
scrambler
unscrambler

AM-BUR
amber
camber
clamber
timbre

AM-EL
camel
enamel
mammal
trammel

AM-ELD
enameled
enamelled
trammeled
trammelled
untrammeled

Long A-MEN
amen
daymen
draymen
highwaymen
laymen
stamen

Long A-MENT
claimant
defrayment
nonpayment
outpayment
overpayment
payment
prepayment

raiment
repayment
underpayment
weighment

Long AM-FUL
blameful
shameful

Long A-MI
Amy
cockamamie
gamey
gamy
ramie

AM-I
chamois
clammy
Grammy
hammy
mammy
Miami
ramie
shammy
tammy
whammy

AM-IK
Abrahamic
adamic
aerodynamic
biodynamic
ceramic
dioramic
dynamic
gamic
hyperdynamic
monogamic
panoramic

polygamic
psychodynamic
thermodynamic

AM-IN
Alabaman
ammon
backgammon
examine
famine
gamin
gammon
mammon
preexamine
reexamine
salmon

Long A-MING
aiming
blaming
claiming
counterclaiming
defaming
disclaiming
exclaiming
flaming
framing
gaming
inflaming
laming
maiming
misnaming
naming
nicknaming
proclaiming
quitclaiming
reclaiming
renaming
shaming
taming

AM-ING
clamming
cramming
damming
damning
deprogramming
diagraming
diagramming
hamming
jamming
lambing
monogramming
programing
programming
ramming
reprogramming
scramming
shamming
slamming
whamming

A-MING
balming
bombing
calming
embalming
palming
salaaming

Long AM-LESS
aimless
blameless
claimless
nameless
shameless
tameless

Long AM-LI
gamely
lamely

namely
tamely

Long AM-NESS
gameness
lameness
sameness
tameness

AM-ON
alabaman
ammon
backgammon
examine
famine
gamin
gammon
mammon
preexamine
reexamine
salmon

AMP-ING
camping
clamping
cramping
damping
decamping
encamping
revamping
stamping
tamping
tramping
vamping

AMP-EL
ample
example
sample
trample

AM-PLING
sampling
trampling

AM-PLUR
ampler
sampler
trampler

AM-PUR
ampere
camper
damper
hamper
pamper
scamper
stamper
tamper
tramper

AM-PUS
campus
grampus

Long A-MUR
acclaimer
blamer
claimer
declaimer
defamer
disclaimer
exclaimer
framer
gamer
lamer
maimer
proclaimer
tamer

AM-UR
clamor
crammer
deprogrammer
diagrammer
flimflammer
gammer
glamor
glamour
grammar
hammer
jackhammer
jammer
katzenjammer
programer
programmer
shammer
slammer
sledgehammer
stammer
trammer
windjammer
yammer

Long A-MUS
famous
mandamus
ignoramus
ramus
squamous

AN-A
Americana
banana
bandanna
cabana
Diana
Guyana
Hannah
Havana

hosanna
hosannah
Indiana
Louisiana
manna
Montana
poinciana
Polyanna
savanna
Savannah
sultana
Susquehanna
Urbana
vox humana

A-NA
Americana
Donna
iguana
Madonna
manana
Nirvana
piranha
zenana

AN-AL
annal
channel
empanel
flannel
impanel
midchannel
panel

AN-ALZ
annals
channels
flannels
impanels
panels

AN-CHEZ
avalanches
blanches
branches
ranches

AN-CHING
blanching
branching
ranching

AN-DA
jacaranda
memoranda
panda
propaganda
veranda

AND-BAG
handbag
sandbag

AND-BALL
grand ball
handball
sand ball

AND-BOKS
bandbox
sandbox

AND-ED
backhanded
banded
barehanded
branded
candid
commanded
countermanded
demanded

disbanded
evenhanded
expanded
forehanded
freehanded
handed
hardhanded
highhanded
landed
left-handed
offhanded
openhanded
overexpanded
overhanded
redhanded
remanded
reprimanded
sanded
shorthanded
stranded
two-handed
unbranded
underhanded
unhanded

AN-DEST
blandest
contrabandist
grandest
propagandist

AN-DI
Andy
bandy
brandy
candy
dandy
grandee
handy
randy

sandy
standee
unhandy

AN-DEED
bandied
brandied
candied

AND-ING
backhanding
banding
branding
commanding
countermanding
demanding
disbanding
expanding
freestanding
handing
landing
longstanding
misunderstanding
notwithstanding
outstanding
overexpanding
remanding
reprimanding
sanding
standing
stranding
undemanding
understanding
upstanding
withstanding

AND-ISH
blandish
brandish
grandish

outlandish

AND-IST
blandest
contrabandist
grandest
propagandist

AND-DEEZ
Andes
bandies
brandies
candies
dandies
grandees
standees

AND-EL
candle
dandle
handel
handle
manhandle
mishandle
panhandle
sandal
vandal

AND-LESS
bandless
brandless
glandless
handless
landless
sandles

AND-LI
blandly
grandly

AND-LUR
candler
chandler
handler
panhandler

AND-MAID
handmade
handmaid

AND-MARK
brand mark
hand mark
landmark

AND-MENT
commandment
disbandment

AND-NESS
blandness
grandness

AND-O
bandeau
Brando
commando
Fernando
Orlando
parlando
San Fernando

AND-RIL
band drill
hand drill
mandrel
mandril
mandrill

AND-STAND
bandstand
grandstand
handstand

AND-UM
fandom
grandam
memorandum
random
tandem

AND-UR
Afrikander
Alexander
bander
blander
brander
bystander
candor
commander
coriander
dander
demander
expander
gander
gerrymander
goosey-gander
grander
grandstander
lander
Laplander
Michigander
meander
oleander
outlander
pander
pandor
philander
salamander

sander
slander
subcommander
Uitlander
woodlander

AHN-DUR
launder
maunder

AND-URD
gerrymandered
meandered
nonstandard
pandered
philandered
slandered
standard
substandard

ANDZ-MAN
bandsman
landsman

Long A-NESS
anus
gayness
grayness
greyness
heinous
janus
membranous

Long A-NEST
humanist
inanenest
insanest
plainest
sanest
urbanest

vainest

AN-ET
gannet
granite
Janet
planet
pomegranate
sultanate

Long AN-FUL
baneful
disdainful
gainful
painful

Long AN-GLE
angle
bangle
bespangle
dangle
disentangle
entangle
jangle
mangle
quadrangle
rectangle
spangle
strangle
tangle
triangle
untangle
wangle
wrangle

Long AN-GLED
angled
bespangled
dangled
disentangled

entangled
jangled
mangled
newfangled
oldfangled
spangled
star-spangled
strangled
tangled
unentangled
untangled
wangled
wrangled

Long ANG-LING
angling
dangling
disentangling
entangling
gangling
jangling
mangling
spangling
strangling
tangling
wrangling

Long ANG-LER
angler
entangler
jangler
mangler
strangler
wangler
wrangler

Long ANG-GO
fandango
mango
tango

Long AN-GUR
anger
clangor
languor

Long ANG-WISH
anguish
languish

Long ANG-EY
bangy
slangy
tangy
twangy

Long ANG-ING
banging
clanging
cliffhanging
hanging
haranguing
overhanging
paperhanging
twanging

Long AN-KEST
blankest
dankest
frankest
rankest

Long AN-KFUL
tankfull
thankful
unthankful

Long AN-KEY
cranky
hankie
hanky

hanky-panky
lanky
swanky
Yankee
Yanqui

Long AN-KING
banking
blanking
clanking
cranking
embanking
flanking
franking
outflanking
outranking
planking
ranking
spanking
thanking
yanking

Long ANK-EL
ankle
rankle
wankel

Long AN-KLESS
bankless
prankless
rankless
thankless

Long AN-KLY
blankly
dankly
frankly
rankly

Long ANK-NESS
blankness
dankness
frankness
rankness
sacrosanctness

Long AN-KUR
anchor
banker
blanker
canker
danker
flanker
hanker
outflanker
rancor
ranker
spanker
supertanker
tanker
thanker

Long AN-KURD
anchored
cankered
hankered
rancored
tankard
unanchored

Long ANG-UR
anger
banger
clangor
cliffhanger
doppelganger
hangar
hanger
haranguer

languor
paperhanger

Long A-NI
brainy
detainee
grainy
rainey
veiny

AN-I
canny
fanny
nannie
nanny

AN-IK
bioorganic
botanic
Britannic
galvanic
Germanic
Hispanic
homorganic
Indo-Germanic
inorganic
manganic
manic
mechanic
melanic
messianic
oceanic
organic
panic
psychogalvanic
Puritanic
satanic
stannic
subtetanic
tannic

tetanic
titanic
transoceanic
tympanic
tyrannic
volcanic

Long A-NING
appertaining
aquaplaning
arraigning
ascertaining
hattaining
braining
campaigning
chaining
complaining
constraining
containing
deigning
deplaning
detaining
disdaining
draining
enchaining
entertaining
entraining
explaining
feigning
foreordaining
gaining
graining
hydroplaning
ingraining
maintaining
obtaining
ordaining
overtraining
paining
pertaining

preordaining
profaning
raining
reattaining
refraining
regaining
reigning
reining
remaining
restraining
retaining
retraining
seining
spraining
staining
straining
sustaining
training
unchaining
uncomplaining
veining
volplaning
waning
woodgraining

AN-ING
banning
canning
fanning
manning
panning
planing
planning
preplanning
scanning
spanning
tanning
trepanning

AN-ISH
banish
clannish
mannish
Spanish
vanish

AN-JENT
cotangent
plangent
tangent

Long AN-JEZ
arranges
changes
deranges
estranges
exchanges
granges
interchanges
outranges
ranges
shortchanges

Long AN-JEE
mangy
rangy

Long AN-JING
arranging
changing
deranging
disarranging
estranging
exchanging
interchanging
misarranging
outranging
prearranging
ranging

rearranging
shortchanging
unchanging

Long ANJ-LESS
changeless
rangeless

Long ANJ-MENT
arrangement
changement
exchangement
derangement
disarrangement
estrangement
interchangement
misarrangement
prearrangement
rearrangement

Long AN-JUR
arranger
changer
danger
endanger
exchanger
manger
moneychanger
ranger
shortchanger
stranger

Long AN-LESS
brainless
gainless
painless
reinless
stainless

AN-LESS
clanless
fanless
manless
planless
tanless

Long AN-LY
germanely
humanely
inanely
inhumanely
insanely
mainly
mundanely
plainly
profanely
sanely
ungainly
urbanely
vainly

AN-LEE
manly
Stanley
unmanly

Long AN-MENT
arraignment
ascertainment
attainment
constrainment
containment
detainment
enchainment
entertainment
foreordainment
obtainment
ordainment
reattainment

retainment
sustainment

Long A-NESS
germaneness
humaneness
inaneness
insaneness
plainness
profaneness
saneness
vainness

Long A-NO
Draino
Plano
volcano

A-NO
anno
piano
soprano

AN-ON
cannon
canon
Indianan
Louisianan
Montanan
tannin

AN-SEZ
advances
chances
circumstances
dances
enhances
entrances
finances
frances

glances
lances
mischances
prances
refinances
romances
stances
trances

AN-SHUL
circumstantial
financial
insubstantial
substantial
unsubstantial

AN-SHUN
expansion
mansion
overexpansion
scansion

AN-SI
chancy
fancy
Nancy
necromancy

AN-SING
advancing
chancing
dancing
enhancing
entrancing
financing
glancing
lancing
prancing
refinancing
romancing

ANS-MENT
advancement
enhancement
entrancement

AN-SUM
handsome
hansom
ransom
transom

AN-SUR
advancer
answer
anticancer
cancer
chancer
dancer
free-lancer
lancer
merganser
prancer
romancer

AN-TA
Atlanta
infanta
Santa
Vedanta

AN-TAM
bantam
fantom
phantom

Long AN-TED
acquainted
fainted
painted
reacquainted

repainted
sainted
tainted
unacquainted
unpainted
untainted

AN-TED
canted
chanted
decanted
descanted
disenchanted
enchanted
gallivanted
granted
implanted
panted
planted
ranted
recanted
replanted
scanted
slanted
supplanted
transplanted
ungranted
unplanted

Long AN-TEST
faintest
quaintest

AN-TEE
ante
anti
banti
grantee
pantie
panty

penny-ante
shanty

AN-TIK
antic
Atlantic
frantic
gigantic
pedantic
romantic
semantic
transatlantic
unromantic

ANT-INE
Argentine
brilliantine
Byzantine
elephantine
florentine
quarantine
serpentine
seventeen

Long ANT-ING
acquainting
fainting
painting
reacquainting
repainting
tainting

ANT-ING
banting
canting
chanting
decanting
descanting
disenchanting
enchanting

gallivanting
granting
implanting
panting
planting
ranting
recanting
replanting
scanting
slanting
supplanting
transplanting

AN-TIS
Atlantis
mantis

ANT-EL
dismantle
mantel
mantle

Long AN-TLEE
faintly
quaintly
saintly

ANT-LUR
antler
dismantler

Long ANT-NESS
faintness
quaintness

ANT-OR
banter
canter
cantor
chanter

decanter
enchanter
gallivanter
granter
grantor
implanter
plantar
planter
ranter
recanter
supplanter
transplanter

ANT-REE
gantry
pantry

Long ANT-TUR
fainter
painter
quainter

ANT-UR
banter
canter
cantor
chanter
decanter
enchanter
gallivanter
granter
grantor
implanter
plantar
planter
ranter
recanter
supplanter
transplanter

Long A-NUR
abstainer
arraigner
campaigner
chainer
complainer
container
detainer
drainer
enchainer
entertainer
explainer
feigner
gainer
maintainer
obtainer
retainer
stainer
strainer
sustainer
trainer

AN-UR
banner
canner
manner
manor
planner
scanner
spanner
tanner

AN-URD
bannered
mannered
ill-mannered
unmannered
well-mannered

Long A-NUS
anus
gayness
grayness
greyness
heinous
janus
membranous

Long AN-WURK
brainwork
canework
chain work

AN-YUN
banyan
canyon
companion

AN-YEL
Daniel
spaniel

AN-ZA
bonanza
extravaganza
organza
stanza

A-ON
crayon
rayon

AP-EE
crappie
crappy
flappy
happy
kidnapee
nappy

sappy
scrappy
slaphappy
snappy
trigger-happy
unhappy

AP-ID
rapid
sapid
vapid

A-PING
aping
escaping
gaping
japing
landscaping
misshaping
raping
reshaping
scraping
shaping
taping
undraping
videotaping

AP-ING
backslapping
bootstrapping
capping
catnapping
chapping
clapping
entrapping
flapping
handicapping
kidnaping
kidnapping
lapping

mapping
napping
overlapping
petnapping
rapping
recapping
rewrapping
sapping
scrapping
slapping
snapping
strapping
tapping
trapping
unsnapping
unwrapping
whitecapping
wiretapping
wrapping
yapping
zapping

Long A-PIST
escapist
landscapist
papist
rapist

Long A-PEL
maple
papal
staple

A-PEL
apple
chapel
crabapple
dapple
grapple
pineapple

scrapple

Long AP-LESS
capeless
scrapeless
shapeless
tapeless

AP-LESS
hapless
napless
sapless
strapless

AP-LING
dappling
grappling
sapling

Long A-PELS
maples
Naples
staples

AP-NEL
grapnel
shrapnel
shrapnell

AP-SHUN
adaption
caption
contraption
recaption

AP-TIV
adaptive
captive
maladaptive

APT-LEE
aptly
raptly

APT-NESS
aptness
inaptness
raptness

AP-TUR
adapter
adaptor
apter
captor
chapter
recaptor
subchapter

AP-TURE
capture
enrapture
rapture
recapture

Long A-PUR
caper
draper
landscaper
raper
sandpaper
scraper
skyscraper
taper

A-PUR
backslapper
capper
clapper
dapper
flapper

handicapper
kidnapper
lapper
mapper
napper
rapper
scrapper
slapper
snapper
tapper
trapper
whippersnapper
whitecapper
wiretapper
wrapper
yapper

AR-A
aura
Clara
Sayonara
Theda Bara
Tiara

AR-AB
Arab
carob
cherub

AR-AK
arrack
barrack

AR-ANS
aberrance
appearance
forbearance
transparence

AR-ANT
aberrant
adulterant
antiperspirant
aspirant
belligerent
deferent
denaturant
deodorant
different
exhilarant
expectorant
exuberant
ignorant
indifferent
intolerant
irreverent
itinerant
nonbelligerent
odorant
operant
preponderant
protuberant
referent
refrigerant
reverberant
reverent
succorant
tolerant

AR-BEL
garble
marble

AR-BORD
barbered
harbored
larboard
starboard

AR-BUR
arbor
barber
harbor

ARCH-EZ
arches
marches
outmarches
parches
starches

ARCH-ING
arching
marching
outmarching
overarching
parching
starching

ARCH-UR
archer
departure
marcher

ARD-ED
bombarded
carded
interlarded
regarded
retarded
safeguarded
unguarded

ARD-EN
garden
harden
pardon

ARD-END
gardened
hardened
pardoned
unhardened
unpardoned

ARD-EY
foolhardy
hardy
lardy
mardi
party
smarty
tardy

ARD-ING
bombarding
carding
discarding
disregarding
guarding
interlarding
larding
regarding
retarding
rewarding
safeguarding

ARD-UR
ardor
guarder
harder
larder

AR-EL
apparel
barrel
beryl
carol

carrel
feral
ferrule
ferule
gunbarrel
imperil
peril
scleral
sterile
unsterile

AR-ENS
adherence
appearance
clearance
coherence
disappearance
incoherence
inherence
interference
perseverance
reappearance

AR-ENT
apparent
arrant
godparent
grandparent
parent
stepparent
transparent
unapparent

AR-EST
apiarist
barest
embarrassed
fairest
incendiarist
rarest

scenarist
sparest
squarest
terraced

AR-ET
carat
carrot
demerit
disinherit
ferret
garret
inherit
merit
parrot

AR-FOR
therefor
therefore
wherefor
wherefore

AR-GO
argot
cargo
embargo
escargot
imbargo
Key Largo
largo
Wells Fargo

AR-GON
argon
bargain
jargon
outbargain

AR-EY
ablutionary

abolitionary	consignatary	hackberry
actuary	constabulary	hairy
adversary	contemporary	hereditary
aerie	contrary	honorary
airy	corollary	huckleberry
ancillary	coronary	imaginary
antiquary	counterrevolutionary	incendiary
apiary	cranberry	inflationary
apothecary	culinary	interdisciplinary
arbitrary	customary	interlibrary
aviary	dairy	interplanetary
axillary	deflationary	involuntary
barberry	delusionary	itinerary
bayberry	depositary	January
bearberry	devolutionary	jerry
beriberi	dewberry	lamasery
berry	dictionary	lapidary
bestiary	dietary	legendary
biliary	dignitary	legionary
binary	disciplinary	libationary
blackberry	discretionary	library
blueberry	diversionary	literary
boysenberry	dromedary	loganberry
bronchopulmonary	dysentery	luminary
budgetary	elderberry	marry
bury	elocutionary	maxillary
canary	emissary	mercenary
canterbury	evolutionary	merry
capillary	expansionary	mesentery
cardiopulmonary	expeditionary	military
carrie	extraordinary	millinery
carry	fairy	miscarry
cautionary	February	missionary
cemetery	ferry	momentary
checkerberry	fragmentary	monastery
cherry	functionary	monetary
chokecherry	funerary	mortuary
cloudberry	glairy	mulberry
commissary	glary	nary
confectionery	gooseberry	necessary

nondisciplinary
nonmilitary
obituary
officiary
ordinary
ossuary
parry
pecuniary
pensionary
pituitary
planetary
prairie
precautionary
preliminary
primary
probationary
promilitary
pseudolegendary
pseudoliterary
pulmonary
quaternary
raspberry
reactionary
revisionary
revolutionary
rosemary
salisbury
salivary
salutary
sanctuary
sanguinary
sanitary
scary
secondary
secretary
sedentary
seditionary
segmentary
seminary
sherry

signatary
solidary
solitary
stationary
stationery
statuary
strawberry
subsidiary
temporary
terry
tertiary
tributary
unitary
unmilitary
unnecessary
unwary
urinary
vary
very
veterinary
visionary
vocabulary
voluntary
voluptuary
vulnerary
wary
wherry

ARR-EY
aurae
nary
safari
saree
sari
starry
tarry

AR-IJ
carriage
marriage

miscarriage
undercarriage

AR-ING
airing
backbearing
bearing
bewaring
blaring
caring
chairing
childbearing
comparing
daring
declaring
despairing
erring
faring
flaring
forbearing
forebearing
foreswearing
forswearing
glaring
herring
impairing
inhering
outwearing
overbearing
pairing
paring
parring
preparing
raring
repairing
scaring
seafaring
sharing
snaring
sparing

squaring
staring
swearing
talebearing
tearing
timesharing
uncaring
unerring
unsparing
wearing

ARR-ING
barring
charring
debarring
disbarring
jarring
marring
scarring
sparring
starring
tarring

AR-INKS
larynx
pharynx

AR-IS
coheiress
derris
embarrass
eros
ferris
ferrous
heiress
millionaress
naris
nonferrous
Paris
polaris

sclerous
terrace

AR-ISH
bearish
bugbearish
cherish
fairish
garish
nightmarish
parish
perish
squarish

AR-JENT
argent
sergeant

AR-JEZ
barges
charges
discharges
enlarges
mischarges
recharges
reenlarges
supercharges
surcharges
undercharges

AR-JING
barging
charging
discharging
enlarging
mischarging
overcharging
reenlarging
supercharging
surcharging

undercharging

ARJ-UR
charger
discharger
enlarger
larger
recharger
supercharger
surcharger

ARK-EN
darken
harken
hearken

ARK-EST
anarchist
darkest
monarchist
starkest

ARK-EY
barky
hierarchy
malarkey
marquee
marquis
matriarchy
oligarchy
patriarchy

ARK-IK
anarchic
hierarchic
heptarchic
monarchic
oligarchic
patriarchic

ARK-ING
barking
debarking
disembarking
earmarking
embarking
harking
larking
marking
parking
postmarking
reembarking
remarking
skylarking
sparking
watermarking

ARK-LEY
darkly
starkly

ARK-LING
darkling
sparkling

ARK-ER
barker
darker
marker
parker
skylarker

AR-LAND
garland
engarland

AIR-LESS
airless
careless
hairless

heirless

ARR-LESS
carless
parlous
scarless
starless

AR-LET
charlotte
harlot
scarlet
starlet

AIR-LEY
barely
debonairly
fairly
rarely
sparely
squarely
unfairly

AR-LEY
barley
bizarrely
Charley
Charlie
gnarly
parlay
parley
snarly
yarely

AR-LINE
airline
hairline

AR-LING
darling

gnarling
snarling
starling
unsnarling

AR-LOT
Charlotte
harlot
scarlet
starlet

AR-MAN
airman
chairman
repairman

AR-MENT
debarment
disbarment
garment
overgarment
undergarment
varmint

ARM-FUL
armful
charmful
harmful
unharmful

AR-MEY
army
smarmy

ARM-ING
alarming
arming
charming
disarming
farming

forearming
harming
heartwarming
housewarming
prewarming
rearming
swarming
unalarming

ARM-LESS
armless
harmless

ARM-LET
armlet
charmlet

AR-MUR
armor
charmer
farmer
harmer
strongarmer

AR-NAL
carnal
charnel
darnel

AR-NESS
awareness
bareness
debonairness
fairness
rareness
spareness
squareness
unawareness
unfairness

AR-NESS
bizarreness
harness
unharness

AR-NEY
Barney
blarney
carny
chili con carne
Killarney

AR-NISH
garnish
revarnish
tarnish
varnish

AR-NISHED
garnished
revarnished
tarnished
ungarnished
untarnished
unvarnished
varnished

AR-O
aero
arrow
barrow
bolero
caballero
farrow
handbarrow
narrow
pharaoh
sombrero
sparrow
taro

AR-OLD
appareled
apparelled
barreled
barrelled
caroled
Harold
herald
imperiled
imperilled
periled

AR-ON
Aaron
baron
barren
Erin
heron
interferon
Saharan

ARP-ING
carping
harping
sharping
warping

ARP-UR
cardsharper
carper
harper
scarper
sharper

ARSH-AL
impartial
marshal
marshall
martial
partial

ARS-NESS
scarceness
sparseness

AR-SON
arson
Carson
parson

ART-ED
bighearted
brokenhearted
carted
charted
chicken-hearted
coldhearted
darted
departed
downhearted
fainthearted
freehearted
good-hearted
greathearted
halfhearted
hardhearted
hearted
heavyhearted
imparted
kindhearted
lighthearted
lionhearted
openhearted
outsmarted
parted
recharted
smarted
softhearted
started
stouthearted
tenderhearted

thwarted
uncharted
warmhearted
weakhearted
wholehearted

ART-EN
carton
dishearten
freemartin
hearten
kindergarten
marten
martin
prekindergarten
smarten
tartan

ART-FUL
artful
cartful
heart full

ART-TEY
arty
hearty
multiparty
party
repartee
smartie

ART-ING
carting
charting
darting
departing
imparting
outsmarting
parting
recharting

smarting
starting
thwarting

ART-IST
artist
smartest
tartest

ART-LESS
artless
heartless

ART-LEY
partly
smartly
tartly

ART-MENT
apartment
compartment
department

ART-NESS
smartness
tartness

ART-RIDJ
cartridge
partridge

ART-UR
barter
carter
charter
darter
garter
martyr
recharter
smarter

starter
tartar
tarter
thwarter

AR-UM
carrom
harem
harum-scarum
serum

AR-UR
barer
bearer
carer
comparer
coswearer
crossbearer
cupbearer
darer
declarer
error
fairer
forbearer
pallbearer
preparer
rarer
repairer
seafarer
sharer
snarer
sparer
squarer
standard-bearer
starer
swearer
talebearer
terror
torchbearer
wayfarer

wearer

AR-VAL
carvel
larval
marvel

AR-VING
carving
starving
woodcarving

AR-WEL
farewell
stairwell

AR-WORN
careworn
prayerworn

Long A-SENS
obeisance
adjacense
renascence
complacense

Long A-SENT
adjacent
complacent
complaisant
nascent
obeisant
subjacent

AS-ET
basset
facet
tacit

Long A-SEZ
abases
aces
airspaces
backspaces
bases
basses
birthplaces
bookcases
braces
briefcases
cases
chaises
chases
commonplaces
crankcases
daces
databases
debases
defaces
disgraces
displaces
dogfaces
effaces
encases
erases
faces
firebases
fireplaces
graces
incases
interfaces
interlaces
laces
lightfaces
maces
marketplaces
millraces
misplaces
outraces

paces
palefaces
pillowcases
places
races
replaces
retraces
shoelaces
showcases
showplaces
spaces
staircases
steeplechases
suitcases
traces
typefaces
unlaces
wheelbases

AS-EZ
amasses
asses
bypasses
classes
crevasses
degasses
eyeglasses
gases
gasses
glasses
grasses
harasses
hourglasses
impasses
jackasses
landmasses
lasses
masses
molasses
morasses

outclasses
overpasses
passes
sasses
spyglasses
subclasses
sunglasses
surpasses
trespasses
underpasses
weatherglasses
wrasses

Long AS-FUL
disgraceful
graceful
ungraceful

ASH-AY
cachet
sachet
sashay

Long A-SHAL
bifacial
biracial
facial
glacial
interfacial
interglacial
interracial
multiracial
palatial
racial
spacial
spatial
subglacial

ASH-BORD
dashboard

splashboard

ASH-EZ
abashes
ashes
backlashes
calabashes
cashes
clashes
crashes
dashes
eyelashes
flashes
gashes
gnashes
hashes
lashes
mashes
mishmashes
moustaches
mustaches
rashes
rehashes
sashes
slashes
smashes
splashes
stashes
thrashes
trashes
whiplashes

ASH-EY
ashy
flashy
splashy
trashy

ASH-ING
abashing

bashing
cashing
clashing
crashing
dashing
flashing
gashing
gnashing
hashing
lashing
mashing
rehashing
slashing
smashing
splashing
stashing
thrashing
trashing

Long A-SHUN
abbreviation
abdication
aberration
abomination
abrogation
acceleration
accentuation
acclamation
accommodation
accreditation
acculturation
accumulation
accusation
activation
actualization
actuation
adaptation
adjudication
administration
admiration

adoration
adulteration
advocation
aeration
affectation
affiliation
affirmation
affixation
aftersensation
agglutination
aggravation
aggregation
agitation
alienation
allegation
alleviation
alligation
alliteration
allocation
alteration
altercation
alternation
amalgamation
ambulation
amelioration
amortization
amplification
amputation
animation
annexation
annihilation
annotation
annunciation
anodization
anticipation
antiquation
appalachian
application
appreciation
approbation

appropriation
approximation
arbitration
argumentation
arrogation
articulation
asphyxiation
aspiration
assassination
assignation
assimilation
association
attenuation
attestation
augmentation
authentication
authorization
automation
autoregulation
aviation
avocation
barbarization
bastardization
beautification
bifurcation
biotransformation
brutalization
calculation
calibration
canalization
cancelation
cancellation
cannibalization
canonization
capacitation
capitalization
capitation
capitulation
capsulation
captivation

carbonation
carbonization
carnation
castigation
castration
categorization
causation
celebration
cementation
centralization
certification
characterization
chelation
chlorination
christianization
circulation
circumnavigation
citation
civilization
clarification
classification
coagulation
coeducation
cogitation
cohabitation
collaboration
collocation
colonization
coloration
combination
commemoration
commendation
commercialization
commiseration
communication
commutation
compensation
compilation
complementation
complication

computation
computerization
concatenation
concentration
conceptualization
conciliation
condemnation
condensation
confederation
configuration
confirmation
confiscation
conflagration
conflation
conformation
confrontation
conglomeration
congratulation
congregation
conjugation
connotation
consecration
conservation
consideration
consolation
consolidation
constellation
consternation
constipation
consultation
consummation
containerization
contamination
contemplation
continuation
contraindication
conversation
convocation
cooperation
coordination

copulation
coronation
corporation
correlation
corroboration
corrugation
counterirritation
creation
cremation
crimination
crustacean
crystallization
culmination
cultivation
cybernation
dalmatian
damnation
damnification
deactivation
debarkation
debilitation
decalcification
decapitation
decarbonation
deceleration
decentralization
decimation
declaration
declassification
declination
decontamination
decoration
dedication
defamation
defecation
defibrillation
deflagration
deflation
defloration
defoliation

deforestation
deformation
degeneration
degradation
dehumanization
dehydration
deification
delegation
deliberation
delimitation
delineation
demagnification
demarcation
demarkation
demilitarization
demobilization
democratization
demodulation
demonstration
demoralization
denaturalization
denigration
denomination
denotation
dentation
denunciation
depilation
depopulation
deportation
depravation
deprecation
depreciation
depredation
deprivation
deputation
deregulation
derivation
derogation
desecration
desegregation

desiccation
designation
desolation
desperation
destination
deterioration
determination
detestation
detonation
detoxication
detoxification
devaluation
devastation
deviation
dictation
differentiation
digitation
dilapidation
dilation
disaffiliation
discoloration
discontinuation
discrimination
disembarkation
disintegration
dislocation
disorganization
disorientation
dispensation
disputation
disqualification
dissemination
dissertation
dissimilation
dissipation
dissociation
distillation
diversification
divination
documentation

domestication
domination
donation
dramatization
duplication
duration
echolocation
edification
education
ejaculation
elaboration
elation
electrification
elevation
licitation
elimination
elongation
elucidation
emaciation
emanation
emancipation
emasculation
embarkation
emendation
emigration
emulation
emulsification
encapsulation
encrustation
enervation
enumeration
enunciation
equalization
equitation
equivocation
eradication
escalation
estimation
eustachian
evacuation

evaluation
evaporation
evocation
exacerbation
exaggeration
exaltation
examination
exasperation
excavation
excitation
exclamation
excommunication
exculpation
execration
exhalation
exhilaration
exhortation
exoneration
expatiation
expatriation
expectation
expectoration
experimentation
expiation
expiration
explanation
explication
exploitation
exploration
exportation
expropriation
expurgation
extenuation
extermination
extrapolation
extrication
exultation
fabrication
facilitation
falsification

familiarization
fascination
federation
felicitation
feminization
fermentation
fertilization
fibrillation
figuration
filtration
finalization
fixation
flagellation
flirtation
floatation
flocculation
flotation
fluctuation
fluoridation
foliation
fomentation
foreordination
forestation
formalization
formation
formulation
fornication
fortification
fossilization
foundation
fragmentation
frustration
fumigation
galvanization
gemination
gemmation
generalization
generation
germination
gestation

gesticulation
glamorization
glorification
gradation
graduation
granulation
gratification
gravitation
gustation
gyration
habitation
habituation
Haitian
hallucination
harmonization
herniation
hesitation
hibernation
horatian
humanization
humiliation
hybridization
hydration
hydrogenation
hyperinflation
hyperventilation
hyphenation
idealization
ideation
identification
illumination
illustration
imagination
imbrication
imitation
immigration
immobilization
immolation
immunization
impersonation

implantation
implementation
implication
importation
imprecation
impregnation
improvisation
imputation
inactivation
inauguration
incantation
incapacitation
incarceration
incarnation
incineration
incitation
inclination
incorporation
incrimination
incrustation
incubation
inculcation
indemnification
indentation
indexation
indication
indignation
individuation
indoctrination
induration
industrialization
inebriation
infatuation
infestation
infiltration
infirmation
inflammation
inflation
information
ingratiation

inhabitation
inhalation
initiation
innervation
innovation
inoculation
inosculation
insanitation
insemination
insinuation
inspiration
installation
instigation
instrumentation
insubordination
insulation
integration
intensification
interdigitation
interpolation
interpretation
interrelation
interrogation
intimation
intimidation
intonation
intoxication
inundation
invalidation
investigation
invigoration
invitation
invocation
iodination
irradiation
irrigation
irritation
isolation
itemization
iteration

jubilation
juration
justification
laceration
lacrimation
lactation
lamentation
lamination
lapidation
lavation
legalization
legation
legislation
levitation
levorotation
libation
liberalization
liberation
licitation
ligation
lignification
limitation
liquidation
litigation
localization
location
loculation
lubrication
lucubration
luteinization
luxation
maceration
machination
maculation
magnetization
magnification
malformation
malrotation
malversation
manifestation

manipulation
mastication
masturbation
matriculation
maturation
maximization
mechanization
mediation
medication
meditation
melanization
melioration
memorization
menstruation
mesmerization
metrication
migration
miniaturization
ministration
misapplication
misappropriation
miscalculation
miscommunication
misinformation
misinterpretation
mispronunciation
misquotation
misrepresentation
mistranslation
mitigation
mobilization
moderation
modification
modulation
molestation
mollification
monopolization
mortification
motivation
motorization

multiplication
mummification
mutation
mutilation
myelination
mystification
narration
nasalization
nation
nationalization
naturalization
nauseation
navigation
nebulization
negation
negotiation
nervation
neutralization
nitration
nodulation
nomination
nondiscrimination
nonparticipation
nonproliferation
nonregistration
nonregulation
nonviolation
normalization
notarization
notation
notification
novation
nucleation
nullification
numeration
nutation
obfuscation
objuration
objurgation
oblation

obligation
obliteration
observation
obviation
occupation
officiation
operation
oration
orchestration
ordination
organization
orientation
origination
ornamentation
oscillation
osculation
ossification
ostentation
outstation
ovation
overcompensation
overdiversification
overestimation
overpopulation
overregulation
oversimplification
ovulation
oxidation
oxygenation
pacification
pagination
palliation
palpation
palpitation
participation
peculation
penalization
penetration
perambulation
percolation

peregrination
perforation
permeation
permutation
peroration
perpetration
perpetuation
personation
personification
perspiration
perturbation
petrification
phonation
pigmentation
placation
plantation
plication
pluralization
polarization
pollination
population
postulation
potation
precalculation
precipitation
precondemnation
preconsideration
predation
predestination
predetermination
predication
predomination
prefabrication
premedication
premeditation
preoccupation
preordination
preparation
preregistration
presentation

preservation
prestidigitation
prevarication
privation
privatization
probation
proclamation
proconservation
procrastination
procreation
prognostication
prointegration
proliferation
prolongation
promulgation
pronation
pronunciation
propagation
propitiation
proration
prostration
protestation
provocation
pseudocopulation
publication
pulsation
pulverization
punctuation
purgation
purification
pustulation
quadruplication
qualification
quotation
radiation
ramification
randomization
ratification
ration
rationalization

reaccreditation
reactivation
readaptation
reaffirmation
realization
recalculation
recantation
recapitulation
reciprocation
recirculation
recitation
reclamation
recoloration
recombination
recommendation
reconciliation
recreation
recrimination
rectification
recuperation
redecoration
rededication
redesignation
reduplication
reeducation
reevaluation
reforestation
reformation
reformulation
refrigeration
refutation
regeneration
regimentation
registration
regularization
regulation
regurgitation
rehabilitation
rehydration
reincarnation

reinstallation
reintegration
reiteration
rejuvenation
relation
relaxation
relegation
relocation
remonstration
remuneration
renegotiation
renomination
renotification
renovation
renunciation
reorientation
reparation
repatriation
replantation
replication
repopulation
representation
reprobation
republication
repudiation
reputation
reservation
resignation
resonation
respiration
restoration
resuscitation
retaliation
retardation
reticulation
revaluation
revelation
reverberation
revocation
robotization

rotation
ruination
rumination
rustication
salivation
salutation
salvation
sanctification
sanitation
satiation
saturation
scintillation
sedation
sedimentation
segmentation
segregation
sensation
separation
sequestration
serration
serrulation
sibilation
signification
simplification
simulation
situation
socialization
solarization
solicitation
somnambulation
sophistication
specialization
specification
speculation
spiculation
spoliation
stabilization
stagflation
stagnation
standardization

starvation
station
sterilization
stimulation
stipulation
strangulation
stratification
striation
stultification
subdelegation
subjugation
sublation
sublimation
subordination
subornation
substantiation
substation
suffixation
suffocation
summation
supination
supplementation
supplication
symbolization
syncopation
syndication
tabulation
taxation
telecommunication
temptation
termination
testation
titillation
titration
toleration
transfiguration
transformation
translation
transliteration
translocation

transmigration
transmutation
transpiration
transplantation
transportation
transubstantiation
trepidation
triangulation
tribulation
trifurcation
triplication
truncation
ulceration
ultimation
ululation
umbilication
underestimation
undulation
unification
unionization
urbanization
urination
usurpation
utilization
vacation
vaccination
vacillation
validation
valorization
valuation
vaporization
variation
variegation
vegetation
venation
veneration
ventilation
verification
vermination
versification

vexation
vibration
vilification
vindication
violation
visitation
vitalization
vitiation
vitrification
vituperation
vivification
vocalization
vocation
vociferation
vulgarization
winterization
zonation

ASH-UN
ashen
compassion
dispassion
fashion
impassion
passion
ration
refashion

ASH-UND
fashioned
impassioned
rationed
refashioned

ASH-UR
asher
brasher
casher
clasher
crasher

dasher
flasher
gatecrasher
haberdasher
lasher
masher
rasher
slasher
smasher
splasher
thrasher

Long A-SHUS
audacious
bodacious
cretaceous
curvaceous
disputatious
efficacious
fallacious
flirtatious
foliaceous
gallinaceous
gracious
herbaceous
inefficacious
loquacious
mendacious
ostentatious
perspicacious
pertinacious
predaceous
predacious
pugnacious
rapacious
sagacious
salacious
sebaceous
setaceous
spacious

tenacious
ungracious
veracious
vexatious
violaceous
vivacious
voracious

AS-EY
brassie
brassy
classy
gassy
glassy
grassy
lassie
malagasy
sassy
Tallahassee

AS-ID
acid
antacid
hasid
hyperacid
placid

AS-IK
boracic
classic
Jurassic
neoclassic
potassic
pseudoclassic
thoracic
Triassic

Long A-SIN
basin
caisson

chasten
hasten
Jason
mason
washbasin

AS-IN
assassin
fasten
refasten
unfasten

Long A-SING
abasing
acing
all-embracing
backspacing
basing
boldfacing
bracing
casing
chasing
debasing
defacing
disgracing
displacing
effacing
embracing
encasing
erasing
facing
gracing
incasing
interfacing
interlacing
lacing
microspacing
misplacing
outfacing
outracing

pacing
placing
racing
replacing
retracing
showcasing
spacing
tracing
unlacing

AS-ING
amassing
bypassing
classing
degassing
gassing
glassing
harassing
massing
outclassing
passing
sassing
surpassing
teargassing
trespassing

Long A-SIS
basis
bacteriostasis
homeostasis
oasis
stasis

Long A-SIV
abrasive
assuasive
dissuasive
evasive
persuasive
pervasive

suasive
unpersuasive

AS-IVE
impassive
massive
passive

AS-KET
ascot
basket
breadbasket
gasket
wastebasket
workbasket

AS-KING
asking
basking
masking
tasking
unmasking

AS-KO
Belasco
fiasco
tabasco

AS-KUR
asker
basker
Madagascar
Masker

AS-EL
basil
castle
forecastle
hassle
Newcastle

passel
tassel
vassal

Long AS-LESS
baseless
faceless
graceless
placeless
spaceless
traceless

AS-MAN
classman
lowerclassman
underclassman
upperclassman

Long AS-MENT
abasement
basement
casement
debasement
defacement
displacement
effacement
embracement
emplacement
encasement
enlacement
misplacement
placement
replacement
self-effacement
subbasement

AS-O
basso
lasso
Sargasso

AS-OK
cassock
hassock
Masoch

AS-PING
clasping
gasping
grasping
rasping
unclasping

AS-PUR
Casper
clasper
gasper
grasper
jasper
rasper

Long AS-TED
basted
foretasted
lambasted
pasted
tasted
untasted
wasted

AS-TED
blasted
broadcasted
casted
contrasted
fasted
flabbergasted
forecasted
lambasted
lasted
masted

outlasted
plastid
rebroadcasted
sandblasted
simulcasted
telecasted

AST-EST
fastest
vastest

Long AST-FUL
distasteful
tasteful
untasteful
wasteful

Long A-STEY
hasty
overhasty
pasty
tasty

AS-TIK
angiospastic
bombastic
cardiospastic
drastic
dynastic
ecclesiastic
elastic
enthusiastic
fantastic
gymnastic
hypoblastic
iconoclastic
interscholastic
mastic
metaplastic
monastic

neoplastic
nonscholastic
onomastic
orgastic
orgiastic
overenthusiastic
pederastic
plastic
sarcastic
scholastic
spastic

Long AS-TING
basting
foretasting
lambasting
pasting
tasting
wasting

AST-ING
blasting
broadcasting
casting
colorcasting
contrasting
everlasting
fasting
flabbergasting
forecasting
lambasting
lasting
miscasting
newscasting
outlasting
overcasting
rebroadcasting
recasting
sandblasting
simulcasting

telecasting
typecasting

Long A-STLESS
hasteless
tasteless
waistless
wasteless

AST-LEY
fastly
ghastly
lastly
steadfastly
vastly

AST-NESS
colorfastness
fastness
steadfastness
vastness

Long AS-TUR
chaster
taster
waster

AST-UR
alabaster
bandmaster
broadcaster
bushmaster
cadastre
caster
castor
choirmaster
concertmaster
disaster
drillmaster
faster

forecaster
grandmaster
headmaster
laster
master
mintmaster
newscaster
pastor
paymaster
piaster
pilaster
plaster
poetaster
postmaster
quartermaster
radiobroadcaster
radiocaster
raster
ringmaster
sandblaster
schoolmaster
scoutmaster
shipmaster
sportscaster
stationmaster
taskmaster
telecaster
toastmaster
trainmaster
truckmaster
weighmaster
wharfmaster
whoremaster
workmaster
yardmaster
zoroaster

AS-TURD
bastard
dastard

mastered
pilastered
plastered

Long A-SUR
abaser
bracer
chaser
debaser
defacer
disgracer
effacer
embracer
eraser
facer
lacer
pacer
placer
racer
replacer
spacer
steeplechaser
tracer

AS-UR
amasser
crasser
glasser
harasser
passer
trespasser

AT-A
data
errata
pro rata
regatta
ultimata
strata

Long A-TAL
fatal
hiatal
natal
neonatal
nonfatal
postnatal
prenatal
statal

Long A-TANT
blatant
latent

Long A-TED
abated
abbreviated
abdicated
abrogated
accentuated
accommodated
accumulated
actuated
administrated
adulterated
advocated
aerated
affiliated
agglutinated
aggravated
aggregated
agitated
alienated
alleviated
alliterated
allocated
alternated
amalgamated
ambulated
amputated

animated
annihilated
annotated
annunciated
antedated
anticipated
antiquated
appreciated
approbated
appropriated
approximated
arbitrated
arrogated
articulated
asphyxiated
aspirated
assassinated
assimilated
associated
attenuated
authenticated
automated
awaited
backdated
baited
bated
belated
berated
bifurcated
calculated
calibrated
capacitated
capitulated
capsulated
captivated
carbonated
carbureted
castigated
castrated
celebrated

checkmated
chlorinated
circulated
circumnavigated
coagulated
cogitated
collaborated
collocated
commemorated
commiserated
communicated
compensated
complicated
concatenated
concentrated
conciliated
confederated
confiscated
congratulated
congregated
conjugated
consecrated
consolidated
constipated
consummated
contaminated
contemplated
contraindicated
cooperated
coordinated
copulated
correlated
corroborated
corrugated
crated
created
cremated
criminated
culminated
cultivated

cumulated
cuspidated
cybernated
dated
deactivated
debated
debilitated
decaffeinated
decapitated
decelerated
decimated
decontaminated
decorated
dedicated
defecated
defibrillated
deflagrated
deflated
defoliated
degenerated
dehydrated
delated
delegated
deliberated
delimitated
delineated
demarcated
demodulated
demonstrated
denigrated
denominated
dentated
denticulated
depilated
depopulated
deprecated
depreciated
depredated
derated
deregulated

derogated
desecrated
desegregated
desiccated
designated
desolated
detonated
detoxicated
devaluated
devastated
deviated
dictated
differentiated
digitated
dilapidated
dilated
disaffiliated
discombobulated
discriminated
disintegrated
dislocated
disorientated
disseminated
dissimilated
dissipated
dissociated
domesticated
dominated
donated
duplicated
educated
ejaculated
elaborated
elated
electroplated
elevated
eliminated
elongated
elucidated
emaciated

emanated
emancipated
emasculated
emigrated
emulated
encapsulated
enervated
enumerated
equated
equivocated
eradicated
eructated
escalated
estimated
evacuated
evaluated
evaporated
exacerbated
exaggerated
exasperated
excavated
excommunicated
exculpated
execrated
exhilarated
exonerated
expatiated
expatriated
expectorated
expiated
explicated
expropriated
expurgated
extenuated
exterminated
extrapolated
extricated
fabricated
facilitated
fascinated

fated
federated
felicitated
fibrillated
filtrated
fixated
flagellated
flocculated
fluctuated
fluoridated
foliated
folliculated
formulated
fornicated
freighted
frustrated
fumigated
gaited
gelated
geminated
generated
germinated
gestated
gesticulated
graduated
granulated
grated
gravitated
gyrated
habituated
hallucinated
halogenated
hated
herniated
hesitated
hibernated
humiliated
hydrated
hydrogenated
hyphenated

illuminated
illustrated
imbricated
imitated
immigrated
immolated
impersonated
implicated
imprecated
impregnated
inactivated
incapacitated
incarcerated
incarnated
incinerated
incorporated
incriminated
incubated
inculcated
inculpated
indicated
individuated
indoctrinated
indurated
inebriated
infatuated
infiltrated
inflated
infuriated
ingratiated
initiated
innervated
innovated
inoculated
inosculated
inseminated
insinuated
instigated
insulated
integrated

interdigitated
intermediated
interpolated
interrelated
interrogated
intimated
intimidated
intoxicated
inundated
invalidated
investigated
invigorated
iodinated
irradiated
irrigated
irritated
isolated
iterated
lacerated
lactated
laminated
lancinated
legated
legislated
levitated
liberated
ligated
liquidated
litigated
lobated
located
loculated
lubricated
lucubrated
luxated
luxuriated
macerated
machinated
maculated
mandated

manipulated
marinated
masticated
masturbated
mated
matriculated
maturated
mediated
medicated
meditated
meliorated
menstruated
mentholated
metricated
migrated
militated
misappropriated
miscalculated
misdated
mismated
misstated
mistranslated
mitigated
moderated
modulated
motivated
mutated
mutilated
myelinated
narrated
nauseated
navigated
necessitated
negated
negotiated
nitrated
nodulated
nominated
nonaffiliated
noncarbonated

nonsegregated
notated
novated
nucleated
numerated
obfuscated
objurgated
obligated
obliterated
obviated
officiated
operated
opinionated
orated
orchestrated
orientated
originated
oscillated
osculated
outdated
overcompensated
overdecorated
overeducated
overestimated
overinflated
overpopulated
overrated
overstated
overstimulated
ovulated
oxygenated
paginated
palliated
palpated
palpitated
participated
peculated
penetrated
pennated
perambulated

percolated
perforated
permeated
perpetrated
perpetuated
phonated
phosphated
pignorated
placated
plaited
plated
pollinated
pontificated
postdated
postulated
prated
precalculated
precipitated
predated
predesignated
predestinated
predicated
predominated
preestimated
prefabricated
premedicated
premeditated
preponderated
prevaricated
probated
procrastinated
procreated
prognosticated
proliferated
promulgated
pronated
propagated
propitiated
prorated
prostrated

pulsated
punctuated
pustulated
quadruplicated
radiated
rated
reactivated
rebated
recalculated
recapitulated
reciprocated
recirculated
reconciliated
recreated
recriminated
recuperated
redecorated
rededicated
redesignated
reduplicated
reeducated
reevaluated
reformulated
refrigerated
regenerated
regulated
regurgitated
rehabilitated
rehydrated
reincarnated
reinstated
reintegrated
reiterated
rejuvenated
related
relegated
relocated
remunerated
renegotiated
renominated

renovated	stated	unadulterated
repatriated	stimulated	unaffiliated
replicated	stipulated	unalleviated
repopulated	strangulated	unanimated
reprobated	striated	unaspirated
repudiated	subdelegated	uncalculated
resituated	subjugated	uncelebrated
resonated	sublimated	uncompensated
restated	subordinated	uncomplicated
resuscitated	substantiated	unconjugated
retaliated	suffocated	unconsecrated
reticulated	sulcated	unconsummated
revaluated	sulfated	uncrated
reverberated	sulphated	uncreated
rotated	sulphurated	uncultivated
ruminated	supinated	undated
rusticated	supplicated	undecorated
salivated	syncopated	underestimated
sanitated	syndicated	underrated
satiated	tabulated	understated
saturated	tailgated	undulated
scintillated	terminated	uneducated
sedated	titillated	unexcavated
segregated	titrated	unfederated
separated	tolerated	uninitiated
serrated	translated	unliberated
serrulated	transliterated	unlocated
sibilated	transmigrated	unmediated
simulated	transubstantiated	unmedicated
situated	triangulated	unmeditated
skated	trifurcated	unmitigated
slated	triplicated	unmotivated
somnambulated	truncated	unpopulated
sophisticated	turbinated	unrated
speculated	ulcerated	unregulated
spiculated	ululated	unrelated
spoliated	umbilicated	unsaturated
squamated	unabated	unsegregated
stagnated	unabbreviated	unseparated
stalemated	unaccentuated	unsophisticated

unstated
unstriated
unterminated
untranslated
unvaccinated
unventilated
updated
urinated
vacated
vaccinated
vacillated
vaginated
validated
valuated
variegated
vegetated
venerated
ventilated
vibrated
vindicated
violated
vitiated
waited
weighted
zonated

AT-ED
batted
chatted
combated
combatted
defatted
fatted
flatted
formatted
hatted
matted
patted
ratted
reformatted

scatted
slatted
spatted
tatted
unformatted
unplatted

AT-EN
batten
fatten
flatten
Latin
Manhattan
patten
Patton
platen
satin

Long A-TEST
greatest
latest
statist
straightest

Long AT-FUL
fateful
grateful
hateful
ungrateful

AT-HEAD
fathead
flathead

ATH-IK
empathic
homeopathic
naturopathic
osteopathic
photopathic

prognathic
psychopathic
telepathic

Long ATH-ING
bathing
lathing
scathing
sunbathing

ATH-LESS
bathless
pathless
wrathless

Long A-THOS
bathos
pathos

ATH-UR
blather
foregather
gather
lather
rather
slather

Long A-TEY
eighty
Haiti
imitatee
legatee
mandatee
matey
rete
weighty

AT-EY
batty
bratty

catty
chatty
Cincinnati
fatty
natty
patty
ratty

AT-IK
acrobatic
aerobatic
aristocratic
aromatic
asiatic
asthmatic
astigmatic
attic
autocratic
automatic
axiomatic
bacteriostatic
bureaucratic
charismatic
chromatic
cinematic
democratic
diagrammatic
diplomatic
dogmatic
dramatic
ecstatic
electrostatic
emblematic
emphatic
enigmatic
epigrammatic
erratic
fanatic
hanseatic
hematic

hemostatic
hepatic
hieratic
hippocratic
homeostatic
hydrostatic
idiocratic
idiomatic
idiosyncratic
judgmatic
kinematic
lymphatic
magmatic
mathematic
melodramatic
monochromatic
muriatic
nondiplomatic
nonidiomatic
numismatic
operatic
osmatic
overdramatic
overemphatic
panchromatic
pancreatic
phlegmatic
phosphatic
plasmatic
plutocratic
pneumatic
pragmatic
prismatic
problematic
protoplasmatic
psychosomatic
quadratic
rheostatic
rheumatic
sabbatic

schematic
schismatic
sciatic
semiautomatic
socratic
spasmatic
spermatic
static
stigmatic
symptomatic
systematic
technocratic
thematic
theocratic
thermostatic
traumatic
undemocratic
undiplomatic
undogmatic
unemphatic
unsystematic
vatic

AT-IKS
acrobatics
aerobatics
asthmatics
attics
automatics
cinematics
dramatics
electrostatics
fanatics
hydrostatics
kinematics
mathematics
melodramatics
numismatics
pneumatics
pragmatics

psychosomatics
quadratics
systematics

Long A-TIME
daytime
May-time
playtime

AT-IN
batten
fatten
flatten
Latin
Manhattan
Patten
Patton
platen
satin

Long AT-ING
abating
abbreviating
abdicating
abrogating
accumulating
actuating
adjudicating
administrating
adulterating
advocating
aerating
affiliating
agglutinating
aggravating
aggregating
agitating
alienating
alleviating
alliterating

allocating
alternating
amalgamating
ambulating
ameliorating
amputating
animating
annihilating
annotating
annunciating
antedating
anticipating
antiquating
appreciating
approbating
appropriating
approximating
arbitrating
arrogating
articulating
asphyxiating
aspirating
assassinating
assimilating
associating
attenuating
authenticating
automating
awaiting
backdating
baiting
bating
berating
bifurcating
calculating
calibrating
capacitating
capitulating
captivating
carbonating

carbureting
castigating
castrating
celebrating
checkmating
circulating
coagulating
cogitating
collaborating
collocating
commemorating
commiserating
communicating
compensating
complicating
concatenating
concentrating
conciliating
confederating
confiscating
conglomerating
congratulating
congregating
conjugating
consecrating
consolidating
constipating
consummating
contaminating
contemplating
contraindicating
cooperating
coordinating
copulating
correlating
corroborating
corrugating
crating
creating
cremating

criminating
culminating
cultivating
cumulating
dating
deactivating
debating
debilitating
decaffeinating
decapitating
decelerating
decimating
decontaminating
decorating
dedicating
defecating
defibrillating
deflagrating
deflating
defoliating
degenerating
dehydrating
delating
delegating
deliberating
delimitating
delineating
demarcating
demodulating
demonstrating
denigrating
denominating
depilating
depopulating
deprecating
depreciating
depredating
derating
deregulating
derogating

desecrating
desegregating
desiccating
designating
desolating
deteriorating
detonating
detoxicating
devaluating
devastating
deviating
dictating
differentiating
dilapidating
dilating
disaffiliating
discombobulating
discriminating
disintegrating
dislocating
disorientating
disseminating
dissimilating
dissipating
dissociating
domesticating
dominating
donating
duplicating
educating
ejaculating
elaborating
elating
electroplating
elevating
eliminating
elongating
elucidating
emaciating
emanating

emancipating
emasculating
emigrating
emulating
encapsulating
enervating
enumerating
enunciating
equating
equivocating
eradicating
eructating
escalating
estimating
evacuating
evaluating
evaporating
exacerbating
exaggerating
exasperating
excavating
excommunicating
excruciating
exculpating
execrating
exhilarating
exonerating
expatiating
expatriating
expectorating
expiating
explicating
expropriating
expurgating
extenuating
exterminating
extrapolating
extricating
fabricating
facilitating

fascinating
federating
felicitating
fibrillating
filtrating
fixating
flocculating
fluctuating
fluoridating
formulating
fornicating
freighting
frustrating
fumigating
geminating
generating
germinating
gestating
gesticulating
graduating
granulating
grating
gravitating
gyrating
habituating
hallucinating
halogenating
hating
herniating
hesitating
hibernating
humiliating
hydrating
hydrogenating
hyphenating
illuminating
illustrating
imbricating
imitating
immigrating

immolating
impersonating
implicating
imprecating
impregnating
inactivating
incapacitating
incarcerating
incarnating
incinerating
incorporating
incriminating
incubating
inculcating
inculpating
indicating
indiscriminating
individuating
indoctrinating
inebriating
infatuating
infiltrating
inflating
infuriating
ingratiating
initiating
innervating
innovating
inoculating
inosculating
inseminating
insinuating
instating
instigating
insulating
integrating
interdigitating
interpolating
interrelating
interrogating

intimating
intimidating
intoxicating
inundating
invalidating
investigating
invigorating
iodinating
irradiating
irrigating
irritating
isolating
iterating
lacerating
lactating
laminating
lancinating
legating
legislating
levitating
liberating
ligating
liquidating
litigating
locating
lubricating
lucubrating
luxating
luxuriating
macerating
machinating
maculating
mandating
manipulating
marinating
masticating
masturbating
mating
matriculating
maturating

mediating
medicating
meditating
meliorating
menstruating
metricating
migrating
militating
misappropriating
miscalculating
misdating
mismating
misstating
mistranslating
mitigating
moderating
modulating
motivating
mutating
mutilating
narrating
nauseating
navigating
necessitating
negating
negotiating
nitrating
nodulating
nominating
nondiscriminating
nonincriminating
nonirritating
nonparticipating
notating
novating
nucleating
numerating
obfuscating
objurgating
obligating

obliterating
obviating
officiating
operating
orating
orchestrating
orientating
originating
oscillating
osculating
overcompensating
overdecorating
overeducating
overestimating
overinflating
overpopulating
overrating
overstating
overstimulating
ovulating
oxygenating
paginating
palliating
palpating
palpitating
participating
peculating
penetrating
perambulating
percolating
perforating
permeating
perpetrating
perpetuating
phonating
phosphating
pignorating
placating
plaiting
plating

pollinating
pontificating
populating
postdating
postulating
precalculating
precipitating
predating
predestinating
predicating
predominating
preestimating
prefabricating
premedicating
premeditating
preponderating
prevaricating
probating
procrastinating
procreating
prognosticating
proliferating
promulgating
pronating
propagating
propitiating
prorating
prostrating
pulsating
punctuating
pustulating
quadruplicating
radiating
rating
reactivating
rebating
recalculating
recapitulating
reciprocating
recirculating

reconciliating
recreating
recriminating
recuperating
redecorating
rededicating
redesignating
reduplicating
reeducating
reevaluating
reformulating
refrigerating
regenerating
regulating
regurgitating
rehabilitating
rehydrating
reincarnating
reinstating
reintegrating
reiterating
rejuvenating
relating
relegating
relocating
remonstrating
remunerating
renegotiating
renominating
renovating
repatriating
replicating
repopulating
reprobating
repudiating
resituating
resonating
respirating
restating
resuscitating

retaliating
revaluating
reverberating
rotating
ruminating
rusticating
salivating
sanitating
satiating
saturating
scintillating
sedating
segregating
separating
sibilating
simulating
situating
skating
slating
somnambulating
speculating
spoliating
stagnating
stalemating
stating
stimulating
stipulating
strangulating
subdelegating
subjugating
sublimating
subordinating
substantiating
suffocating
sulfating
sulphating
sulphurating
supinating
supplicating
syncopating

syndicating
tabulating
tailgating
terminating
titillating
titrating
tolerating
translating
transliterating
transmigrating
transubstantiating
triangulating
trifurcating
triplicating
truncating
ulcerating
ululating
uncrating
underestimating
underrating
understating
undeviating
undulating
unhesitating
updating
urinating
vacating
vaccinating
vacillating
validating
valuating
variegating
vegetating
venerating
ventilating
vibrating
vindicating
violating
vitiating
vociferating

waiting

AT-ING
batting
catting
chatting
combating
combatting
defatting
fatting
flatting
formatting
matting
patting
platting
ratting
reformatting
scatting
slatting
spatting
tatting
wildcatting

AT-IS
apparatus
cirrostratus
gratis
lattice
status
stratus

Long A-TIV
connotative
dative
debilitative
denotative
devastative
disintegrative
educative
exaggerative

imitative
innovative
integrative
investigative
mitigative
mutative
native
nonnative
penetrative
significative
ulcerative

AT-EL
battle
brattle
cattle
chattel
embattle
prattle
rattle
seattle
striatal
tattle
tittle-tattle

Long AT-LESS
dateless
freightless
gateless
hateless
mateless
stateless
weightless

Long AT-LEY
greatly
inchoately
innately
insensately
irately

lately
oblately
ornately
philately
pinnately
plicately
sedately
stately
stellately
straightly
straitly

AT-LING
battling
fatling
flatling
prattling
tattling

AT-LUR
battler
prattler
rattler
tattler

Long AT-MENT
abatement
instatement
misstatement
overstatement
rebatement
reinstatement
restatement
statement
understatement

Long AT-NESS
greatness
innateness
insensateness

irateness
lateness
ornateness
plicateness
sedateness
straightness

AT-NESS
fatness
flatness
patness

Long AT-TO
nato
Plato
potato
tomato

AT-RIK
geriatric
iatric
Patrick

Long A-TRUN
matron
patron

AT-UM
atom
datum
erratum
stratum
substratum

Long A-TURE
denature
legislature
nature
nomenclature

Long A-TUR
abater
adjudicator
advocator
alligator
amputator
animater
animator
annotator
applicator
arbitrator
articulator
asphyxiator
aspirator
baiter
calculator
calibrater
calibrator
captivator
castigator
cater
celebrator
circulator
circumnavigator
collaborator
collator
commentator
communicator
compensator
complicator
confiscator
conjugator
consecrator
cooperator
corporator
corrugator
crater
creator
cremator
cultivator

dater
deactivator
debater
decapitator
decelerator
decontaminator
decorator
dedicator
deflator
defoliator
dehydrator
delegator
deliberator
demarcator
demonstrator
denigrator
denominator
depopulator
deprecator
depredator
desecrater
desecrator
desiccator
designator
detonator
detoxicator
devastator
dictator
dilapidator
dilator
discriminator
disintegrator
dissipater
dissipator
domesticator
dominator
donator
dumbwaiter
duplicator
educator

ejaculator
elaborator
elevator
eliminator
elucidator
emancipator
emasculator
emulator
enervator
enunciator
equator
equivocator
eradicator
escalator
estimator
evacuator
evaluator
evaporator
exaggerator
excavator
excommunicator
execrator
exonerator
expatiator
expectorator
expiator
explicator
expropriator
expurgator
exterminator
fabricator
felicitator
flagellator
formulator
fornicator
freighter
fumigator
gaiter
gator
generator

gladiator
graduator
granulator
grater
greater
gyrator
hater
headwaiter
hesitater
hesitator
hibernator
hydrator
illuminator
illustrator
imitator
impersonator
imprecator
inaugurator
incapacitator
incarcerator
incinerator
incorporator
incriminator
incubator
indemnificator
indicator
infiltrator
inflater
inflator
inhalator
initiator
innovator
inseminator
insinuator
inspirator
instigator
insulator
integrator
interpolator
interrogator

intimidator
invalidator
investigator
invigorator
irrigator
isolator
jurator
laminator
later
legislator
levator
liberator
liquidator
litigator
locator
lubricator
macerater
macerator
machinator
maitre
mandator
manipulator
masticator
masturbator
mater
medicator
migrator
mitigator
moderator
modulator
motivator
mutilator
narrater
narrator
navigator
negator
nominator
nullificator
numerator
obfuscator

obliterator
officiator
operator
orchestrator
originator
oscillator
oxygenator
participator
penetrator
perambulator
percolator
perforator
perpetrator
perpetuator
personator
pollinator
pontificator
postulator
prater
predicator
prestidigitator
prevaricator
procrastinator
procurator
prognosticator
pulsator
rater
rebater
refrigerator
regenerator
regulator
relater
relator
remonstrator
renovator
repudiator
resonator
revelator
reverberator
rotator

rusticator
satyr
separator
simulator
skater
spectator
speculator
stimulater
stimulator
stipulator
straighter
subjugator
substantiator
supinator
syndicator
tabulator
tater
terminator
testator
tidewaiter
tolerator
translator
transmigrator
triangulator
vaccinator
vacillator
valuator
ventilator
vibrator
vindicator
violator
vitiator
waiter

AT-UR
antimatter
batter
bespatter
chatter
clatter

fatter
flatter
formatter
hatter
latter
matter
patter
platter
ratter
scatter
shatter
smatter
spatter
splatter
tatter
wildcatter

AT-URN
pattern
Saturn
slattern

AT-US
apparatus
cirrostratus
gratis
lattice
status
stratus

Long AT-WAY
gateway
stateway
straightway

Long A-UR
allayer
assayer
ballplayer
betrayer

bilayer
bricklayer
cardplayer
conveyer
conveyor
crocheter
delayer
disobeyer
doomsayer
essayer
flayer
gainsayer
gayer
grayer
greyer
horseplayer
inveigher
layer
manslayer
mayor
minelayer
mislayer
obeyer
parlayer
payer
payor
player
portrayer
prayer
purveyor
ratepayer
sayer
slayer
soothsayer
sprayer
strayer
surveyor
taxpayer
underlayer
waylayer

weigher

AUN-CHEZ
haunches
launches
paunches
stanches

AUN-CHY
paunchy
raunchy

AUN-CHING
launching
stanching
staunching

AV-A
cassava
guava
java
kava
lava

AV-EL
gavel
gravel
ravel
travel
unravel

AV-ELD
gaveled
gavelled
graveled
raveled
ravelled
traveled
travelled
unraveled

unravelled
untraveled
untravelled

Long A-VEN
graven
haven
riboflavin
shaven
unshaven

Long A-VEY
gravy
jayvee
navy
wavy

AV-ID
avid
gravid

AV-IJ
lavage
ravage
savage
scavage

Long A-VING
behaving
braving
caving
craving
depraving
engraving
enslaving
laborsaving
lifesaving
misbehaving
paving
photoengraving

raving
reenslaving
repaving
saving
shaving
slaving
staving
timesaving
waiving
waving

AV-ING
calving
halving
having
salving

Long A-VIS
avis
Davis

AV-ISH
lavish
overlavish
ravish

Long AV-LEY
bravely
gravely

Long AV-MENT
depravement
enslavement
pavement

Long AV-NESS
braveness
concaveness
graveness

Long AV-UR
braver
craver
depraver
engraver
enslaver
lifesaver
misbehaver
paver
photoengraver
raver
saver
savour
shaver
slaver
waiver

AV-UR
cadaver
palaver
slaver

AV-URN
cavern
tavern

A-VYUR
behavior
misbehavior
savior
saviour
Xavier

A-YO
cacao
kayo
mayo
tko

AZ-A
Gaza
piazza
plaza

Long A-ZAL
appraisal
hazel
nasal
witch hazel

AZ-ARD
biohazard
haphazard
hazard
mazzard

AZ-EL
bedazzle
dazzle
frazzle
razzle-dazzle

Long A-ZEY
crazy
daisy
hazy
lazy
mazy
stir-crazy

Long A-ZEZ
amazes
appraises
blazes
braises
brazes
chaises
crazes
dazes

fazes
gazes
glazes
grazes
hazes
lazes
malaises
mazes
overglazes
overgrazes
overpraises
paraphrases
phases
phrases
polonaises
praises
raises
razes
reappraises
rephrases
stargazes
upraises

Long A-ZHUN
abrasion
dissuasion
equation
Eurasian
evasion
invasion
Malaysian
occasion
persuasion
pervasion
suasion

Long A-ZING
amazing

appraising
blazing
braising
brazing
crazing
dazing
fazing
fund-raising
gazing
glazing
grazing
hair-raising
hazing
hell-raising
house-raising
lazing
liaising
overgrazing
paraphrasing
phasing
phrasing
praising
raising
rasing
razing
rephrasing
stargazing
trailblazing
upraising

AZ-LING
dazzling
frazzling

AZ-MA
asthma
chiasma
miasma

phantasma
plasma

Long A-ZON
blazon
brazen
emblazon
raisin

AZ-UM
bioplasm
chasm
neoplasm
orgasm
phantasm
plasm
protoplasm
sarcasm
spasm

Long AZ-ER
appraiser
blazer
brazer
gazer
glazer
grazer
hair-raiser
hell-raiser
laser
paraphraser
phaser
praiser
raiser
razor
reappraiser
stargazer
trailblazer

Long E-A

absentia
acacia
academia
acrophobia
aerophobia
agromania
Albania
Alexandria
Algeria
algophilia
algophobia
alluvia
ambrosia
anaemia
anarithmia
anarthria
anemia
anglophilia
anglophobia
anorexia
aphasia
Appalachia
aquaria
Arabia
area
aria
Armenia
asphyxia
Assyria
Austria
azalea
Babylonia
bacchanalia
bacteria
bibliomania
bohemia
Bolivia
Brasilia
bronchia

brontophobia
Bulgaria
bulimia
cacodemonia
cafeteria
California
Cambodia
camellia
cancerphobia
cardia
cardiophobia
claustrophobia
cleptomania
cochlea
colloquia
Colombia
Columbia
compendia
cornea
cornucopia
crematoria
Crimea
criteria
cyclopedia
Czechoslovakia
diarrhea
diglossia
diphtheria
dyslexia
dyspepsia
dysphasia
echolalia
effluvia
egomania
emporia
encyclopedia
Estonia
Ethiopia
eupepsia
euphoria

fascia
forsythia
ganglia
Garcia
genitalia
giardia
Gloria
glossolalia
glycemia
gonorrhea
gonorrhoea
gymnasia
hemophilia
hemophobia
herbaria
hernia
honoraria
hydrophobia
hypochondria
hypoglycemia
hypothermia
hysteria
Iberia
idea
India
insignia
insomnia
intelligentsia
kinaesthesia
kinesthesia
kleptomania
kleptophobia
Korea
labia
Latakia
Latvia
leukemia
Liberia
Libya
Lithuania

lobelia	nymphomania	saturnalia
lymphorrhea	obeah	Scandinavia
macadamia	Olympia	schizophrenia
Macedonia	Ophelia	sepia
mafia	ophthalmia	septicaemia
malaria	orthodontia	septicemia
mammalia	pachydermia	Serbia
Manchuria	palladia	Siberia
mania	panacea	sinfonia
marginalia	panglossia	Sofia
Mauritania	paralalia	solaria
media	paralexia	somalia
melancholia	paramecia	spirea
melomania	paranomia	stadia
memorabilia	paraphasia	suburbia
memoria	paraphernalia	symposia
Mesopotamia	paraplegia	synesthesia
microbia	pedophilia	synovia
microphobia	Philadelphia	Syria
miliaria	phobia	Tanzania
millennia	phonophobia	theomania
minutia	photophobia	theophobia
miocardia	pizzeria	tibia
mitochondria	planetaria	tortilla
Mongolia	poinsettia	toxaemia
monomania	polyphagia	toxemia
moratoria	psalteria	trachea
multimedia	pseudoleukemia	trapezia
myalgia	pseudomania	triskaidekaphobia
myasthenia	pyromania	trivia
myocardia	raffia	trochlea
myopia	rauwolfia	utopia
Myotonia	regalia	uvea
mythomania	reptilia	via
narcomania	Rhodesia	Victoria
nausea	rickettsia	wisteria
necrophilia	rupiah	xenophobia
necrophobia	sabadilla	Yugoslavia
Nigeria	sanatoria	Zambia
nutria	Sardinia	zinnia

zoysia

Long E-AL
abacterial
accusatorial
actuarial
adverbial
aerial
alluvial
ambassadorial
ambrosial
arboreal
areal
armorial
arterial
asphyxial
axial
bacterial
baronial
bicentennial
biennial
binomial
biomaterial
boreal
bronchial
burial
cantorial
censorial
centennial
cereal
ceremonial
coaxial
collegial
colloquial
colonial
connubial
controversial
convivial
corneal
corporeal

cranial
custodial
dentilabial
diarrheal
dictatorial
diphtherial
editorial
effluvial
electorial
entrepreneurial
equatorial
esophageal
ethereal
extraterrestrial
Ezekiel
factorial
familial
finial
ganglial
genial
gonorrheal
gubernatorial
gustatorial
hernial
hierarchial
hymeneal
ideal
ileal
immaterial
immemorial
imperial
industrial
Israel
janitorial
jovial
labial
lacteal
laryngeal
lineal
luteal

magisterial
malarial
managerial
manorial
manubrial
marmoreal
marsupial
material
matrilineal
matrimonial
medial
memorial
menial
mercurial
microbial
millennial
ministerial
mitochondrial
monarchial
monasterial
monomial
myocardial
neocolonial
noncontroversial
nonindustrial
notarial
ordeal
oriel
oriole
osteal
pachydermial
pallial
parochial
participial
patrilineal
patrimonial
perennial
pharyngeal
pictorial
pineal

piscatorial
polynomial
predatorial
preindustrial
primordial
proctorial
professorial
proverbial
psalterial
purgatorial
quadrennial
quadricentennial
radial
real
remedial
sartorial
schlemiel
secretarial
sectorial
senatorial
sensorial
serial
sidereal
sponsorial
subcranial
suctorial
surreal
synovial
syzygial
terrestrial
territorial
testimonial
tibial
tracheal
transcutaneal
trapezial
tricentennial
triennial
trivial
tutorial

unfilial
unreal
uveal
uxorial
vectorial
venereal
venial
vestigial
vicarial

Long E-AN
accordion
Addisonian
Aegean
Aesopian
agrarian
Albanian
Alexandrian
Algerian
Algonquian
alien
Amazonian
Amerindian
amphibian
Andean
Anglian
antiquarian
Appalachian
Aquarian
Arabian
Arcadian
Argentinean
Aristotelian
Arizonian
Armenian
Arthurian
Aryan
Assyrian
Athenian
Augustinian

Australian
Austrian
authoritarian
avian
Babylonian
Bahamian
Baltimorean
barbarian
Bavarian
Bermudian
bohemian
Bolivian
Bostonian
Bulgarian
Burundian
caesarean
caesarian
Californian
Cambodian
Cambrian
Cameroonian
Canadian
Caribbean
Carolinian
Caspian
centenarian
centurion
cesarean
Chadian
champion
Chaucerian
Chilean
circadian
clarion
Colombian
Columbian
comedian
Corinthian
cornucopian
Crimean

criterion
custodian
Czechoslovakian
Darwinian
Delawarean
Devonian
Dionysian
Diphtherian
disciplinarian
draconian
Edwardian
egalitarian
epicurean
Episcopalian
equestrian
Estonian
Ethiopian
Euclidean
Euclidian
euphonium
European
Fabian
fallopian
Faustian
Freudian
Galilean
gallein
galleon
ganglion
grammarian
Gregorian
guardian
Guinean
halcyon
Hamiltonian
Herculean
historian
Hobbesian
humanitarian
Hungarian

hygeian
Iberian
Indian
isthmian
Jacksonian
Jacobean
Jeffersonian
Jordanian
Jungian
Kantian
Korean
lactovegetarian
Latvian
lesbian
Liberian
libertarian
librarian
Libyan
Lithuanian
lutein
Macedonian
Machiavellian
malarian
mammalian
Manchurian
Marxian
Mauritanian
Mediterranean
meridian
Mesopotamian
microbian
Mississippian
mitochondrion
monarchian
Mongolian
Napoleon
Neptunian
Newtonian
nickelodeon
Nigerian

nonsectarian
oblivion
obsidian
Oedipean
olein
Olympian
oratorian
Oregonian
Orwellian
ossein
ovarian
oxonian
Palestinian
Panamanian
paramedian
Parkinsonian
parliamentarian
Pavlovian
pedestrian
permian
Peruvian
Philadelphian
Pickwickian
plebeian
pogonion
Pomeranian
Precambrian
Presbyterian
procrustean
proletarian
promethean
protean
protein
Pygmalion
Pythagorean
quotidian
radian
reptilian
riparian
ruffian

Sadducean
Sagittarian
sanitarian
Sardinian
Scandinavian
scorpion
sectarian
seminarian
senatorian
Serbian
Shakespearean
Shakespearian
Shavian
Shoshonean
Siberian
silurian
simian
simoleon
Skinnerian
Slavonian
Smithsonian
Sophoclean
sparteine
stentorian
stygian
subclavian
subterranean
Swahilian
Swiftian
Syrian
Tanzanian
thespian
totalitarian
tragedian
Trinitarian
Ukrainian
Unitarian
utopian
vegetarian
veterinarian

Victorian
vulgarian
Wagnerian
Washingtonian
wolffian
wormian
Yugoslavian
zambian
zein
Zoroastrian
zunian

Long E-BA
ameba
amoeba
Sheba

Long E-BI
amoebae
CB
freebie
honeybee
KGB
PCB
Phoebe

EB-ING
ebbing
webbing

EB-LE
pebble
rebel
treble

Long E-BO
gazebo
placebo

Long E-BORD
freeboard
keyboard
seaboard

Long E-BORN
freeborn
reborn
seaborne

ECH-EY
sketchy
stretchy
tetchy

Long E-CHEZ
beaches
beeches
beseeches
bleaches
breaches
breeches
impeaches
leaches
leeches
outreaches
overreaches
peaches
preaches
reaches
screeches
speeches
teaches

Long E-CHI
beachy
litchi
peachy
preachy
reachy

screechy

Long E-CHING
beaching
beseeching
bleaching
breaching
I Ching
impeaching
leaching
leeching
outreaching
overreaching
preaching
reaching
schoolteaching
screeching
teaching

ECH-ING
etching
fetching
outstretching
retching
sketching
stretching

ECH-UP
catsup
ketchup

Long E-CHUR
beseecher
bleacher
feature
impeacher
leacher
overreacher
preacher
reacher

schoolteacher
screecher
teacher

ECH-UR
cowcatcher
dogcatcher
etcher
fetcher
fletcher
flycatcher
lecher
sketcher
stretcher

Long ED-BED
reed bed
seedbed
weed bed

ED-BEET
deadbeat

ED-BUG
bedbug
dead bug

Long E-DED
beaded
ceded
deeded
exceeded
heeded
impeded
impleaded
interceded
kneaded
needed
pleaded
proceeded

seceded
speeded
unconceded
unneeded
weeded

ED-ED
bareheaded
bedded
beheaded
bigheaded
bobsledded
breaded
bullheaded
clearheaded
coolheaded
dreaded
dunderheaded
embedded
empty-headed
featherbedded
hammerheaded
hardheaded
headed
hotheaded
imbedded
knuckleheaded
leaded
levelheaded
lightheaded
muddleheaded
pigheaded
pinheaded
shredded
threaded
towheaded
wedded
woodenheaded
wrongheaded

Long E-DEN
Eden
redone
Sweden

ED-EN
Armageddon
deaden
leaden
redden

Long ED-ENS
accedence
antecedence
credence
impedance
supersedence

Long ED-ENT
antecedent
credent
needn't
precedent

ED-EST
deadest
reddest

Long ED-FUL
heedful
needful
unheedful
unneedful

ED-HED
deadhead
redhead

ED-HEET
dead heat

red heat

Long ED-I
beady
greedy
needy
reedy
seedy
speedy
tweedy
weedy

ED-I
already
eddy
gingerbready
heady
ready
rough-and-ready
steady
teddy
thready
unready
unsteady

Long ED-IK
comedic
encyclopedic
Vedic

Long ED-IKT
edict
predict

Long ED-ING
acceding
beading
bleeding
breeding
conceding

crossbreeding
deeding
exceeding
feeding
heeding
impeding
impleading
inbreeding
interbreeding
interceding
kneading
leading
lipreading
misleading
misreading
needing
overfeeding
pleading
preceding
proceeding
proofreading
reading
receding
rereading
reseeding
seceding
seeding
speeding
stampeding
succeeding
superseding
underfeeding
unheeding
weeding

ED-ING
bedding
beheading
bloodshedding
bobsledding

breading
dreading
embedding
featherbedding
heading
imbedding
outspreading
overspreading
retreading
shedding
shredding
sledding
spearheading
spreading
steading
subheading
threading
treading
wedding
wide-spreading

ED-ISH
deadish
reddish

ED-IT
accredit
copy-edit
credit
discredit
edit
noncredit
reaccredit
reedit

Long EED-LE
beadle
needle
wheedle

ED-LE
bipedal
medal
meddle
pedal
peddle
quadrupedal
treadle

Long ED-LESS
creedless
heedless
needless
seedless
steedless
weedless

ED-LESS
bedless
breadless
headless

ED-LY
deadly
medley
redly

ED-LINE
breadline
deadline
headline
redline

Long ED-LING
needling
seedling
wheedling

ED-LING
meddling

peddling

ED-LITE
headlight
red light

ED-LOCK
deadlock
headlock
wedlock

Long ED-LUR
needler
wheedler

ED-LUR
meddler
peddlar
peddler

Long ED-O
credo
libido
Lido
speedo
Toledo
tuxedo

ED-REST
bed rest
headrest

Long ED-TIME
feed time
seed time
lead time

Long ED-UR
bleeder
breeder

cheerleader
copyreader
feeder
impeder
impleader
inbreeder
interceder
kneader
leader
lieder
misleader
needer
nonreader
pleader
proceeder
proofreader
reader
ringleader
seceder
seeder
speeder
stampeder
stockbreeder
superseder
weeder

ED-UR
bedder
bloodshedder
bobsledder
cheddar
deader
doubleheader
header
homesteader
mopeder
redder
shedder
shredder
sledder

spreader
threader
triple-header

Long E-EST
achiest
airiest
airworthiest
angriest
artiest
ashiest
atheist
baggiest
balkiest
balmiest
battiest
bawdiest
beadiest
beastliest
beefiest
bleariest
bloodiest
bloodthirstiest
bloomiest
blotchiest
blowiest
blowziest
blurriest
boggiest
boniest
bonniest
booziest
boskiest
bossiest
botchiest
bounciest
brainiest
brambliest
brassiest
brattiest

brawniest
breathiest
breeziest
briniest
bristliest
broodiest
broomiest
brothiest
bruskest
bubbliest
bulgiest
bulkiest
bumpiest
bunchiest
burliest
bushiest
busiest
cagiest
campiest
canniest
catchiest
cattiest
chalkiest
chanciest
chattiest
cheekiest
cheeriest
cheesiest
chewiest
chilliest
chintziest
choosiest
choppiest
chubbiest
chummiest
chunkiest
clammiest
classiest
cleanliest
clingiest

cliquiest
cloddiest
cloggiest
cloudiest
clumpiest
clumsiest
cockiest
comeliest
comfiest
copyist
corkiest
corniest
costliest
courtliest
coziest
crabbiest
crackliest
craftiest
craggiest
crankiest
crappiest
crawliest
craziest
creakiest
creamiest
creepiest
crinkliest
crispest
crispiest
croakiest
croupiest
crummiest
crunchiest
crustiest
cuddliest
curliest
curviest
cushiest
daffiest
daintiest

dandiest
deadliest
deist
dewiest
diciest
dingiest
dinkiest
dippiest
dirtiest
dizziest
dopiest
dottiest
doughiest
dowdiest
draftiest
draggiest
dreamiest
dreariest
dressiest
droopiest
drowsiest
duckiest
dumpiest
duskiest
dustiest
earliest
earthiest
earthliest
easiest
edgiest
eeriest
emptiest
enthusiast
fanciest
fattiest
faultiest
feistiest
filmiest
filthiest
finniest

fishiest
fizziest
flabbiest
flakiest
flashiest
fleeciest
fleshiest
fleshliest
flightiest
flimsiest
flintiest
floppiest
flossiest
fluffiest
flukiest
foamiest
foggiest
folksiest
foolhardiest
foxiest
freakiest
freest
friendliest
friskiest
frizziest
frostiest
frothiest
frowsiest
frowziest
fruitiest
frumpiest
fumiest
funkiest
funniest
furriest
fussiest
fustiest
fuzziest
gabbiest
gamiest

gassiest	gutsiest	kingliest
gaudiest	guttiest	kinkiest
gauziest	hairiest	knobbiest
gawkiest	hammiest	knottiest
germiest	handiest	kookiest
ghastliest	happiest	laciest
giddiest	hardiest	lakiest
gimpiest	hastiest	lankiest
glassiest	haughtiest	lardiest
gleamiest	haziest	laziest
gloomiest	headiest	leafiest
glossiest	healthiest	leakiest
gluiest	heartiest	leeriest
godliest	heaviest	leggiest
goodliest	heftiest	lengthiest
goofiest	hilliest	likeliest
gooiest	hoariest	limiest
goriest	hobbyist	lintiest
goutiest	hokiest	liveliest
grabbiest	holiest	loamiest
grainiest	homeliest	lobbyist
grassiest	homiest	loftiest
greasiest	horniest	logiest
greediest	horsiest	loneliest
grimiest	huffiest	looniest
gripiest	hungriest	lordliest
grippiest	huskiest	lousiest
grisliest	iciest	loveliest
grittiest	ickiest	lowliest
grizzliest	inkiest	luckiest
groggiest	itchiest	lumpiest
grooviest	jauntiest	lustiest
grouchiest	jazziest	mangiest
grubbiest	jerkiest	manliest
grumpiest	jolliest	marshiest
grungiest	jounciest	massiest
guiltiest	juiciest	mealiest
gummiest	jumpiest	measliest
gushiest	kickiest	meatiest
gustiest	kindliest	merriest

messiest	pearliest	readiest
mightiest	peatiest	reediest
milkiest	pebbliest	riskiest
mintiest	peppiest	ritziest
miriest	perkiest	rockiest
misoneist	peskiest	roomiest
mistiest	pettiest	rosiest
moldiest	phoniest	rowdiest
monotheist	pickiest	ruddiest
moodiest	piggiest	runniest
mopiest	pimpliest	runtiest
mossiest	pithiest	rustiest
mouldiest	pluckiest	ruttiest
mousiest	plumiest	saggiest
mouthiest	pointiest	saintliest
muckiest	pokiest	saltiest
muddiest	polytheist	sandiest
muggiest	porkiest	sappiest
murkiest	portliest	sassiest
mushiest	prettiest	sauciest
muskiest	prickliest	scabbiest
mustiest	prissiest	scaliest
nastiest	pudgiest	scantiest
nattiest	puffiest	scariest
naughtiest	pulpiest	schmaltziest
neediest	punchiest	scraggliest
nerviest	puniest	scrappiest
newsiest	pushiest	scratchiest
niftiest	pussiest	scrawniest
nippiest	quackiest	screechiest
noisiest	quakiest	screwiest
nosiest	queasiest	scrimpiest
nuttiest	quirkiest	scrubbiest
oiliest	raciest	scruffiest
ooziest	rainiest	scummiest
palmiest	randiest	scurviest
paltriest	rangiest	seamiest
pantheist	raspiest	seediest
pastiest	rattiest	seemliest
patchiest	raunchiest	sexiest

shabbiest	snazziest	stealthiest
shadiest	sneakiest	steamiest
shaggiest	sneeziest	steeliest
shakiest	snippiest	stickiest
shapeliest	snobbiest	stingiest
sheeniest	snoopiest	stinkiest
shiftiest	snootiest	stockiest
shiniest	snottiest	stodgiest
shoddiest	snowiest	stoniest
showiest	soapiest	stormiest
sickliest	soggiest	straggliest
sightliest	sootiest	streakiest
silkiest	soppiest	streamiest
silliest	sorriest	stretchiest
siltiest	soupiest	stringiest
sketchiest	speediest	stubbiest
skimpiest	spiciest	stuffiest
skinniest	spiffiest	stumpiest
slangiest	spikiest	sturdiest
slaphappiest	spindliest	sudsiest
sleaziest	spiniest	sulkiest
sleepiest	splashiest	sultriest
sleetiest	splotchiest	sunniest
slimiest	spongiest	surliest
slinkiest	spookiest	swampiest
slipperiest	sportiest	swankiest
sloppiest	spottiest	swarthiest
sloshiest	sprightliest	sweatiest
slouchiest	springiest	tackiest
sludgiest	spunkiest	talkiest
slushiest	squabbiest	tangiest
smeariest	squashiest	tardiest
smelliest	squattiest	tarriest
smoggiest	squeakiest	tastiest
smokiest	squirmiest	tawdriest
smudgiest	stagiest	tawniest
smuttiest	starchiest	teariest
snakiest	starriest	teeniest
snappiest	stateliest	testiest
snarliest	steadiest	tetchiest

theist
thirstiest
thorniest
threadiest
thriftiest
throatiest
tidiest
tiniest
tinniest
tipsiest
toothiest
touchiest
trashiest
trendiest
trickiest
trustiest
tubbiest
twangiest
tweediest
ugliest
unhealthiest
unruliest
wackiest
wariest
wartiest
washiest
wastiest
waviest
waxiest
weakliest
wealthiest
weariest
weediest
weeniest
weepiest
weightiest
wheeziest
whiniest
wiliest
windiest

winiest
wintriest
wiriest
wispiest
wittiest
wobbliest
woodiest
woodsiest
woolliest
wooziest
wordiest
worldliest
wormiest
worthiest
wriggliest
yeastiest
yummiest
zaniest
zestiest
zippiest

Long EF-DOM
chiefdom
fiefdom

Long EF-FY
beefy
leafy
reefy

Long EF-UR
briefer
reefer

EF-UR
deafer
heifer
zephyr

Long EG-ING
blitzkrieging
fatiguing
intriguing
leaguing
overfatiguing

EG-ING
begging
bootlegging
egging
legging
pegging
reneging
unpegging

Long E-GEL
eagle
illegal
legal
regal

EG-NANT
nonpregnant
pregnant
pseudopregnant
regnant

Long EG-RESS
egress
regress

Long EG-UR
eager
meager

EG-UR
beggar
bootlegger
reneger

E-ING

accompanying	filigreeing	pitying
agreeing	fleeing	prettying
anteing	flurrying	pureeing
atrophying	foreseeing	puttying
babying	freeing	quarrying
bandying	fricasseeing	querying
being	garnisheeing	rallying
bellying	glorying	readying
berrying	gussying	recopying
bloodying	harrying	reembodying
brandying	hurrying	refereeing
bullying	ill-being	remarrying
burying	intermarrying	remedying
busying	jellying	salarying
caddying	jeopardying	sallying
candying	jimmying	savvying
canopying	jockeying	scurrying
carrying	jollying	seeing
copying	journeying	sentrying
currying	keying	shimmying
curtseying	kneeing	shinnying
curtsying	levying	sightseeing
dairying	lobbying	skiing
dallying	marrying	steadying
decreeing	miscarrying	studying
dirtying	miscopying	stymieing
disagreeing	moneying	sullying
disembodying	monkeying	tallying
divvying	moseying	tarrying
dizzying	muddying	taxiing
eddying	mutinying	teeing
embodying	necropsying	tidying
emceeing	overseeing	toadying
emptying	parlaying	travestying
envying	parleying	treeing
fancying	parodying	trusteeing
farseeing	parrying	understudying
feeing	partying	unpitying
ferrying	photocopying	unseeing
	pillorying	unvarying

varying
volleying
waterskiing
wearying
well-being
whinnying
worrying

Long E-IST
achiest
airiest
airworthiest
angriest
artiest
ashiest
atheist
baggiest
balkiest
balmiest
battiest
bawdiest
beadiest
beastliest
beefiest
bleariest
bloodiest
bloodthirstiest
bloomiest
blotchiest
blowiest
blowziest
blurriest
boggiest
boniest
bonniest
booziest
boskiest
bossiest
botchiest
bounciest

brainiest
brambliest
brassiest
brattiest
brawniest
breathiest
breeziest
briniest
bristliest
broodiest
broomiest
brothiest
bruskest
bubbliest
bulgiest
bulkiest
bumpiest
bunchiest
burliest
bushiest
busiest
cagiest
campiest
canniest
catchiest
cattiest
chalkiest
chanciest
chattiest
cheekiest
cheeriest
cheesiest
chewiest
chilliest
chintziest
choosiest
choppiest
chubbiest
chummiest
chunkiest

clammiest
classiest
cleanliest
clingiest
cliquiest
cloddiest
cloggiest
cloudiest
clumpiest
clumsiest
cockiest
comeliest
comfiest
copyist
corkiest
corniest
costliest
courtliest
coziest
crabbiest
crackliest
craftiest
craggiest
crankiest
crappiest
crawliest
craziest
creakiest
creamiest
creepiest
crinkliest
crispest
crispiest
croakiest
croupiest
crummiest
crunchiest
crustiest
cuddliest
curliest

curviest	feistiest	fustiest
cushiest	filmiest	fuzziest
daffiest	filthiest	gabbiest
daintiest	finniest	gamiest
dandiest	fishiest	gassiest
deadliest	fizziest	gaudiest
deist	flabbiest	gauziest
dewiest	flakiest	gawkiest
diciest	flashiest	germiest
dingiest	fleeciest	ghastliest
dinkiest	fleshiest	giddiest
dippiest	fleshliest	gimpiest
dirtiest	flightiest	glassiest
dizziest	flimsiest	gleamiest
dopiest	flintiest	gloomiest
dottiest	floppiest	glossiest
doughiest	flossiest	gluiest
dowdiest	fluffiest	godliest
draftiest	flukiest	goodliest
draggiest	foamiest	goofiest
dreamiest	foggiest	gooiest
dreariest	folksiest	goriest
dressiest	foolhardiest	goutiest
droopiest	foxiest	grabbiest
drowsiest	freakiest	grainiest
duckiest	freest	grassiest
dumpiest	friendliest	greasiest
duskiest	friskiest	greediest
dustiest	frizziest	grimiest
earliest	frostiest	gripiest
earthiest	frothiest	grippiest
earthliest	frowsiest	grisliest
easiest	frowziest	grittiest
edgiest	fruitiest	grizzliest
eeriest	frumpiest	groggiest
emptiest	fumiest	grooviest
enthusiast	funkiest	grouchiest
fanciest	funniest	grubbiest
fattiest	furriest	grumpiest
faultiest	fussiest	grungiest

guiltiest
gummiest
gushiest
gustiest
gutsiest
guttiest
hairiest
hammiest
handiest
happiest
hardiest
hastiest
haughtiest
haziest
headiest
healthiest
heartiest
heaviest
heftiest
hilliest
hoariest
hobbyist
hokiest
holiest
homeliest
homiest
horniest
horsiest
huffiest
hungriest
huskiest
iciest
ickiest
inkiest
itchiest
jauntiest
jazziest
jerkiest
jolliest
jounciest

juiciest
jumpiest
kickiest
kindliest
kingliest
kinkiest
knobbiest
knottiest
kookiest
laciest
lakiest
lankiest
lardiest
laziest
leafiest
leakiest
leeriest
leggiest
lengthiest
likeliest
limiest
lintiest
liveliest
loamiest
lobbyist
loftiest
logiest
loneliest
looniest
lordliest
lousiest
loveliest
lowliest
luckiest
lumpiest
lustiest
mangiest
manliest
marshiest
massiest

mealiest
measliest
meatiest
merriest
messiest
mightiest
milkiest
mintiest
miriest
misoneist
mistiest
moldiest
monotheist
moodiest
mopiest
mossiest
mouldiest
mousiest
mouthiest
muckiest
muddiest
muggiest
murkiest
mushiest
muskiest
mustiest
nastiest
nattiest
naughtiest
neediest
nerviest
newsiest
niftiest
nippiest
noisiest
nosiest
nuttiest
oiliest
ooziest
palmiest

paltriest	rangiest	seamiest
pantheist	raspiest	seediest
pastiest	rattiest	seemliest
patchiest	raunchiest	sexiest
pearliest	readiest	shabbiest
peatiest	reediest	shadiest
pebbliest	riskiest	shaggiest
peppiest	ritziest	shakiest
perkiest	rockiest	shapeliest
peskiest	roomiest	sheeniest
pettiest	rosiest	shiftiest
phoniest	rowdiest	shiniest
pickiest	ruddiest	shoddiest
piggiest	runniest	showiest
pimpliest	runtiest	sickliest
pithiest	rustiest	sightliest
pluckiest	ruttiest	silkiest
plumiest	saggiest	silliest
pointiest	saintliest	siltiest
pokiest	saltiest	sketchiest
polytheist	sandiest	skimpiest
porkiest	sappiest	skinniest
portliest	sassiest	slangiest
prettiest	sauciest	slaphappiest
prickliest	scabbiest	sleaziest
prissiest	scaliest	sleepiest
pudgiest	scantiest	sleetiest
puffiest	scariest	slimiest
pulpiest	schmaltziest	slinkiest
punchiest	scraggliest	slipperiest
puniest	scrappiest	sloppiest
pushiest	scratchiest	sloshiest
pussiest	scrawniest	slouchiest
quackiest	screechiest	sludgiest
quakiest	screwiest	slushiest
queasiest	scrimpiest	smeariest
quirkiest	scrubbiest	smelliest
raciest	scruffiest	smoggiest
rainiest	scummiest	smokiest
randiest	scurviest	smudgiest

smuttiest	starchiest	teariest
snakiest	starriest	teeniest
snappiest	stateliest	testiest
snarliest	steadiest	tetchiest
snazziest	stealthiest	theist
sneakiest	steamiest	thirstiest
sneeziest	steeliest	thorniest
snippiest	stickiest	threadiest
snobbiest	stingiest	thriftiest
snoopiest	stinkiest	throatiest
snootiest	stockiest	tidiest
snottiest	stodgiest	tiniest
snowiest	stoniest	tinniest
soapiest	stormiest	tipsiest
soggiest	straggliest	toothiest
sootiest	streakiest	touchiest
soppiest	streamiest	trashiest
sorriest	stretchiest	trendiest
soupiest	stringiest	trickiest
speediest	stubbiest	trustiest
spiciest	stuffiest	tubbiest
spiffiest	stumpiest	twangiest
spikiest	sturdiest	tweediest
spindliest	sudsiest	ugliest
spiniest	sulkiest	unhealthiest
splashiest	sultriest	unruliest
splotchiest	sunniest	wackiest
spongiest	surliest	wariest
spookiest	swampiest	wartiest
sportiest	swankiest	washiest
spottiest	swarthiest	wastiest
sprightliest	sweatiest	waviest
springiest	tackiest	waxiest
spunkiest	talkiest	weakliest
squabbiest	tangiest	wealthiest
squashiest	tardiest	weariest
squattiest	tarriest	weediest
squeakiest	tastiest	weeniest
squirmiest	tawdriest	weepiest
stagiest	tawniest	weightiest

wheeziest
whiniest
wiliest
windiest
winiest
wintriest
wiriest
wispiest
wittiest
wobbliest
woodiest
woodsiest
woolliest
wooziest
wordiest
worldliest
wormiest
worthiest
wriggliest
yeastiest
yummiest
zaniest
zestiest
zippiest

Long E-ISM
abolitionism
absenteeism
absolutism
abstractionism
activism
agnosticism
alarmism
albinoism
alcoholism
altruism
amateurism
anabaptism
anabolism
anachronism

anarchism
aneurism
aneurysm
Anglicanism
Anglicism
animalism
antagonism
aphorism
archaism
asceticism
astigmatism
atheism
atomism
authoritarianism
autism
baptism
barbarianism
barbarism
behaviorism
betacism
biculturalism
biracialism
birchism
bisexualism
bolshevism
bossism
botulism
Brahmanism
Brahminism
briticism
Buddhism
bureaucratism
cabalism
Caesarism
Calvinism
cameralism
Canadianism
cannibalism
cannonism
capitalism

cartelism
Cartesianism
cataclysm
Catholicism
centralism
ceremonialism
chauvinism
chloralism
classicalism
classicism
collectivism
colloquialism
colonialism
commercialism
communalism
communism
conformism
Confucianism
congregationalism
conservationism
conservatism
constructionism
consumerism
conventionalism
cosmopolitanism
cretinism
criminalism
criticism
crowism
cubism
cultism
cynicism
czarism
Dadaism
dandyism
Darwinism
decentralism
defeatism
deism
Democratism

despotism
determinism
didacticism
dilettantism
dimorphism
dogmatism
druidism
dualism
dwarfism
dynamism
eclecticism
ecumenicalism
ecumenicism
ecumenism
egalitarianism
egocentrism
egoism
egotism
electromagnetism
elitism
emotionalism
empiricism
endomorphism
environmentalism
equestrianism
eroticism
erotism
escapism
eunuchism
euphemism
evangelicalism
evangelism
evolutionism
exhibitionism
existentialism
exorcism
exoticism
expansionism
expressionism
externalism

extremism
Fabianism
factionalism
fanaticism
fascism
fatalism
favoritism
federalism
feminism
fetichism
fetishism
feudalism
Fletcherism
formalism
fraternalism
Freudianism
fundamentalism
futurism
Gallicism
galvanism
gangsterism
gargoylism
geomagnetism
giantism
gigantism
globalism
Gothicism
Hasidism
heathenism
Hebraism
hedonism
heliotropism
Hellenism
heroinism
heroism
hierarchism
Hinduism
Hitlerism
Hobbism
holism

hooliganism
humanism
humanitarianism
hybridism
hypnotism
hypothyroidism
idealism
imperialism
impressionism
individualism
industrialism
infantilism
internationalism
invalidism
iotacism
isomorphism
jingoism
journalism
Judaism
Klanism
Labialism
Lamaism
landlordism
Leftism
legalism
Leninism
lesbianism
liberalism
libertarianism
literalism
lobbyism
localism
locoism
Lutheranism
lyricism
Machiavellianism
magnetism
malapropism
mannerism
Maoism

Martialism
Marxism
masochism
materialism
maternalism
mechanism
medievalism
melanism
Mendelism
mesmerism
metabolism
metamorphism
meteorism
Methodism
middlebrowism
militarism
misoneism
modernism
monarchism
Mongolianism
mongolism
monism
Monochromatism
monomorphism
monotheism
moralism
mormonism
mutism
mutualism
mysticism
narcism
narcissism
nationalism
nativism
naturalism
Naziism
necrophilism
negativism
neoclassicism
neologism

nepotism
neutralism
nicotinism
nihilism
nudism
obstructionism
occultism
officialism
onanism
opportunism
optimism
organism
pacifism
paganism
Paludism
panderism
pantheism
parallelism
paralogism
parochialism
pastoralism
paternalism
patriotism
pauperism
pedestrianism
perfectionism
pessimism
phobism
plagiarism
pluralism
pneumatism
polymorphism
polytheism
positivism
pragmatism
Presbyterianism
privatism
professionalism
protectionism
Protestantism

provincialism
pseudoclassicism
pugilism
purism
Puritanism
quackism
Quakerism
racialism
racism
radicalism
rationalism
realism
rebaptism
recidivism
relativism
republicanism
revisionism
rhotacism
robotism
romanticism
rotacism
rowdyism
ruralism
sadism
sapphism
satanism
saturnism
secularism
Semitism
separatism
sexism
Shintoism
Sikhism
skepticism
socialism
solecism
solipsism
somnambulism
sophism
specialism

spoonerism
Stalinism
Strychninism
surrealism
syllogism
symbolism
synchronism
synergism
Taoism
tarantism
teetotalism
terrorism
theism
tokenism
totalitarianism
tourism
traditionalism
traitorism
transcendentalism
transvestism
Trinitarianism
trophism
tropism
truism
ultraism
unionism
urbanism
utopianism
vagabondism
vandalism
veganism
vegetarianism
virilism
volcanism
voodooism
voyeurism
vulcanism
vulgarism
witticism
workaholism

Yankeeism
Zionism
Zoroastrianism

EJ-EZ
alleges
dredges
edges
featheredges
hedges
kedges
ledges
pledges
sedges
sledges
straightedges
swages
wedges

EJ-ING
dredging
edging
hedging
kedging
pledging
sledging
wedging

Long EJ-UN
collegian
legion
Norwegian
region
subregion

Long EK-A
ootheca
Costa Rica
eureka
paprika

Tanganyika
Topeka

EK-A
Mecca
Rebecca
Tribeca

Long EK-AL
fecal
treacle

Long EK-EN
archdeacon
beacon
Mohican
sleeken
weaken

Long EK-EST
bleakest
meekest
sleekest
weakest

Long EK-I
cheeky
freaky
leaky
reeky
screaky
sneaky
squeaky
streaky

Long EK-IDE
meek-eyed
weak-eyed

Long EK-ING
antiquing
bespeaking
creaking
freaking
leaking
nonspeaking
peaking
peeking
piquing
reeking
seeking
shrieking
sneaking
speaking
squeaking
streaking
tweaking
wreaking

EK-ING
bedecking
checking
decking
flecking
henpecking
necking
pecking
rechecking
rubbernecking
shipwrecking
specking
trekking
wrecking

Long E-KISH
freakish
weakish

EK-LE
freckle
Heckle
Jekyll
shekel
speckle

EK-LESS
checkless
feckless
necklace
reckless

Long EK-LI
antiquely
biweekly
bleakly
meekly
midweekly
obliquely
semiweekly
sleekly
treacly
triweekly
uniquely
weakly
weekly

EK-LI
freckly
nakedly
speckly

EK-LING
freckling
heckling
speckling

EK-MATE
checkmate

deck mate

Long EK-NESS
antiqueness
bleakness
chicness
meekness
obliqueness
sleekness
uniqueness
weakness

EK-NING
abandoning
apportioning
auctioning
auditioning
awakening
bargaining
battening
beckoning
betokening
blackening
blazoning
bludgeoning
brightening
broadening
burdening
burgeoning
captaining
captioning
casehardening
cautioning
chairmaning
chairmanning
championing
chastening
cheapening
chickening
christening

coarsening
commissioning
conditioning
cordoning
cottoning
counterconditioning
counteropening
crimsoning
cunning
curtaining
cushioning
dampening
darkening
deadening
deafening
deepening
determining
disburdening
disheartening
disillusioning
dunning
emblazoning
emboldening
enlightening
enlivening
envisioning
examining
fashioning
fastening
fattening
flattening
foretokening
freshening
frightening
functioning
gardening
garrisoning
gladdening
glistening
gunning

gunrunning
happening
hardening
harkening
harshening
hastening
hearkening
heartening
heightening
hoarsening
illumining
imagining
impassioning
imprisoning
jettisoning
ladening
leavening
lengthening
lessening
lightening
likening
listening
livening
loosening
maddening
malfunctioning
mentioning
moistening
motioning
occasioning
opening
orphaning
outbargaining
outgunning
outreasoning
outrunning
overburdening
pardoning
partitioning
pensioning

petitioning
pinioning
poisoning
portioning
positioning
preconditioning
predestining
predetermining
preexamining
proportioning
punning
questioning
quickening
rationing
rattening
ravening
reabandoning
reapportioning
reasoning
reawakening
rebuttoning
rechristening
reckoning
reconditioning
reddening
reenlightening
reexamining
refashioning
refastening
reopening
repositioning
requisitioning
rerunning
resharpening
ripening
rosining
roughening
ruining
rumrunning
running

saddening
sanctioning
seasoning
sectioning
sharpening
shortening
shunning
sickening
siphoning
slackening
smartening
softening
stationing
steepening
stiffening
straightening
straitening
strengthening
stunning
summoning
sunning
sweetening
syphoning
thickening
threatening
tightening
toughening
unburdening
unbuttoning
unfastening
unloosening
unquestioning
unreasoning
vacationing
visioning
wakening
wantoning
weakening
whitening
widening

worsening

EK-O
deco
echo
gecko
reecho
secco

Long EK-OK
peacock
poppycock
seacock

Long EK-ON
archdeacon
beacon
Mohican
sleeken
weaken

EK-ON
Aztecan
beckon
Meccan
reckon
Yucatecan

EK-OND
beckoned
fecund
microsecond
millisecond
nanosecond
picosecond
reckoned
second
unreckoned

Long EK-RAB
pea crab
seacrab
treecab

EK-SHUN
abjection
affection
bisection
circumspection
collection
complexion
confection
connection
convection
correction
defection
deflection
dejection
detection
direction
disaffection
disconnection
disinfection
dissection
ejection
election
erection
flection
flexion
genuflection
imperfection
indirection
infection
inflection
injection
inspection
insurrection
interconnection
interjection

intersection
introspection
midsection
misdirection
nondirection
objection
overcorrection
overprotection
perfection
predilection
preelection
projection
prosection
protection
recollection
redirection
reelection
reflection
reinspection
rejection
resection
resurrection
retroflection
retroflexion
retrospection
section
selection
subjection
subsection
transection
trisection
vivisection

EK-SING
annexing
flexing
hexing
indexing
perplexing
telexing

vexing

EK-STANT
extant
sextant

EK-STILE
sextile
textile

EK-SUS
nexus
plexus
sexes
solar plexus
Texas

EK-TANT
disinfectant
expectant
humectant
injectant
reflectant
suspectant

EK-TED
affected
bisected
collected
complected
connected
convected
corrected
defected
deflected
dejected
detected
directed
disaffected
disconnected

disinfected
dissected
effected
ejected
elected
erected
expected
genuflected
infected
inflected
injected
inspected
interconnected
interjected
intersected
misdirected
neglected
noninfected
noninflected
overprotected
perfected
preselected
projected
prospected
protected
recollected
reconnected
redirected
reelected
reflected
reinspected
rejected
respected
resurrected
selected
subjected
suspected
trisected
unaffected
unconnected

uncorrected
undetected
unexpected
uninflected
uninspected
unperfected
unprotected
unsuspected
vivisected

EKT-FUL
disrespectful
neglectful
respectful

EK-TIK
anorectic
apoplectic
dialectic
dyslectic
eclectic
hectic
pectic

EK-TING
affecting
bisecting
collecting
connecting
convecting
correcting
defecting
deflecting
detecting
directing
disaffecting
disconnecting
disinfecting
dissecting
effecting

effective
ejecting
electing
erecting
expecting
genuflecting
infecting
inflecting
injecting
inspecting
interjecting
intersecting
misdirecting
neglecting
objecting
overprotecting
perfecting
preselecting
projecting
prospecting
protecting
reconnecting
redirecting
reelecting
reflecting
reinspecting
rejecting
respecting
resurrecting
selecting
subjecting
suspecting
trisecting
unreflecting
unsuspecting
vivisecting

EK-TIVE
affective
collective

connective
convective
corrective
defective
deflective
detective
directive
effective
elective
ineffective
infective
introspective
invective
irrespective
nondirective
nonobjective
nonselective
objective
overprotective
perfective
perspective
prospective
protective
reflective
respective
retrospective
selective
subjective
unreflective

EK-TRUM
plectrum
spectrum

EK-TUR
affecter
bisector
collector
connecter
connector

corrector
defecter
defector
deflector
detector
director
dissector
effector
ejector
elector
erector
hectare
hector
infecter
infector
injector
inspector
interjector
nectar
neglecter
neglector
nonvector
objector
perfecter
projector
prosector
prospector
protector
rector
reflector
rejecter
rejector
respecter
sector
selector
specter
suspecter
vector
vivisector

Long EK-UR
beaker
bleaker
leaker
loudspeaker
meeker
reeker
seeker
sleeker
sneaker
speaker
streaker
weaker

EK-UR
checker
decker
double-decker
exchequer
pecker
rubbernecker
trekker
woodpecker
wrecker

Long EK-URZ
beakers
leakers
loudspeakers
reekers
seekers
sneakers
speakers
streakers

EK-URZ
checkers
rubberneckers
woodpeckers
wreckers

Long EK-WAL
equal
sequel
unequal

Long EK-WENSE
frequence
sequence

EL-A
a capella
bartonella
brucella
capella
cappella
cerebella
citronella
fellah
flagella
mozzarella
novella
panatella
patella
rubella
salmonella
sequela
umbrella

EL-ANT
appellant
propellant
repellent

EL-BA
Elba
Melba

EL-BOUND
hellbound
spellbound

EL-CHING
belching
squelching
welching

EL-CHUR
belcher
squelcher
welcher

Long EL-DED
fielded
outfielded
shielded
unshielded
wielded
yielded

Long EL-DING
fielding
outfielding
shielding
wielding
yielding

EL-DING
gelding
melding
welding

EL-DUR
elder
gelder
welder

EL-FIRE
hellfire
shellfire

Long E-LI
eely
freely
mealie
really
steely
swahili
wheelie

EL-I
belly
Delhi
deli
jelly
Kelly
potbelly
Shelley
shelly
smelly
underbelly
vermicelli

EL-IK
angelic
archangelic
evangelic
philatelic
psychedelic
relic

Long E-LINE
beeline
copyline
feline

Long E-LING
annealing
appealing
ceiling
concealing

dealing
double-dealing
feeling
freewheeling
healing
heeling
keeling
kneeling
misdealing
pealing
peeling
preconcealing
reeling
reheeling
repealing
resealing
revealing
sealing
self-revealing
self-sealing
snowmobiling
squealing
stealing
steeling
unappealing
unfeeling
unsealing
wheeling

EL-ING
compelling
dispelling
dwelling
excelling
expelling
felling
foretelling
fortunetelling
gelling
impelling

indwelling
jelling
knelling
misspelling
outselling
outspelling
outyelling
overselling
paralleling
parallelling
propelling
quelling
rebelling
repelling
reselling
retelling
selling
shelling
smelling
spelling
storytelling
swelling
telling
underselling
yelling

EL-ISH
embellish
hellish
overembellish
relish

EL-O
bedfellow
bellow
bordello
cello
fellow
jell-o
marshmallow

mellow
Othello
playfellow
schoolfellow
tangelo
yellow

EL-OT
appellate
helot
patellate
pellet
prelate
zealot

EL-PING
helping
whelping
yelping

Long EL-SKIN
eel-skin
real skin
sealskin

EL-TED
belted
melted
pelted
smelted
unmelted
welted

EL-THI
healthy
stealthy
unhealthy
wealthy

EL-TING
belting
melting
pelting
smelting
welting

EL-TUR
belter
melter
pelter
shelter
smelter
svelter
swelter
welter

EL-UM
antebellum
cerebellum
vellum

Long EL-UR
annealer
appealer
concealer
dealer
feeler
healer
heeler
keeler
peeler
reeler
repealer
revealer
sealer
snowmobiler
squealer
stealer
wheeler

EL-UR
best-seller
bookseller
cellar
cerebellar
compeller
dweller
expeller
flagellar
foreteller
fortuneteller
heller
impeller
interstellar
micellar
patellar
propeller
queller
rathskeller
repeller
saltcellar
seller
sheller
smeller
speller
stellar
storyteller
subcellar
teller
yeller

EL-US
jealous
overzealous
trellis
unzealous
zealous

EL-VING
delving

shelving

Long EM-A
eczema
edema
emphysema
lima
prima
schema

EM-A
dilemma
gemma

Long E-MAN
artilleryman
assemblyman
cavalryman
clergyman
committeeman
countryman
dairyman
demon
entryman
ferryman
freeman
hemin
infantryman
journeyman
juryman
laundryman
nurseryman
seaman
semen
tallyman
taximan
vestryman
zeeman

EM-BEL
assemble
disassemble
dissemble
preassemble
reassemble
resemble
semble
tremble

EM-BLI
assembly
disassembly
preassembly
reassembly
trembly

EM-BLING
assembling
disassembling
preassembling
reassembling
resembling
sembling
trembling

EM-BUR
December
dismember
ember
member
nonmember
November
remember
September
submember

Long EM-EST
extremest
supremest

Long EM-I
creamy
dreamy
gleamy
preemie
seamy
steamy
streamy

EM-IK
academic
biochemic
endemic
epidemic
nonacademic
pandemic
polemic
systemic
totemic
unacademic

Long EM-ING
beaming
beseeming
blaspheming
creaming
daydreaming
deeming
dreaming
esteeming
gleaming
reaming
redeeming
scheming
screaming
seaming
seeming
steaming
streaming
teaming

teeming

EM-ING
condemning
fleming
hemming
lemming
mayheming
mayhemming
precondemning
rehemming
stemming

EM-ISH
blemish
Flemish

Long EM-LESS
creamless
dreamless
seamless

Long EM-LI
extremely
seemly
supremely
unseemly

EM-O
demo
memo

EM-PLAR
exemplar
templar

EMP-SHUN
exemption
peremption
preemption

redemption

EMP-TED
attempted
exempted
preempted
reattempted
tempted
unattempted
untempted

EMP-TING
attempting
exempting
preempting
tempting
untempting

EMP-TIVE
preemptive
redemptive

Long EM-UR
blasphemer
creamer
daydreamer
dreamer
reamer
redeemer
schemer
screamer
teamer

Long EN-A
arena
Argentina
Athena
ballerina
concertina
czarina

farina
galena
hyena
kachina
marina
Messina
novena
patina
signorina
subpena
subpoena
Tina
tsarina

EN-A
antenna
Gehenna
henna
Ravenna
senna
sienna
Vienna

Long E-NAL
renal
subpoenal
venal

EN-AS
Dennis
menace
tennis
Venice

EN-CHING
benching
blenching
clenching
drenching
entrenching

quenching
retrenching
trenching
unclenching
wrenching

ENCH-MAN
Frenchman
henchman

EN-CHUR
adventure
backbencher
bencher
denture
indenture
misadventure
peradventure
trencher
venture

EN-DANS
ascendance
ascendence
attendance
condescendence
dependance
dependence
descendance
descendence
independence
independents
interdependence
resplendence
transcendence

EN-DANT
ascendant
ascendent
attendant

codefendant
defendant
dependant
dependent
descendant
descendent
independent
interdependent
overdependent
resplendent
superintendent
transcendent

EN-DED
amended
appended
apprehended
ascended
attended
befriended
blended
commended
comprehended
condescended
contended
defended
depended
descended
distended
emended
ended
expended
extended
fended
impended
intended
mended
misapprehended
offended
overextended

portended
pretended
reascended
recommended
rended
reprehended
splendid
subtended
superintended
suspended
tended
transcended
unamended
unattended
undefended
unended
unexpended
unextended
unintended
unmended
untended
upended
vended
wended

EN-DI
bendy
effendi
sendee
trendy
vendee

EN-DING
amending
appending
apprehending
ascending
attending
befriending
bending

blending
commending
comprehending
condescending
contending
defending
depending
descending
distending
emending
ending
expending
extending
fending
heartrending
impending
intending
lending
mending
misapprehending
misspending
offending
overextending
overspending
pending
portending
pretending
reascending
recommending
rending
reprehending
sending
spending
subtending
suspending
tending
transcending
unbending
unending
unpretending

upending
vending
wending

Long EN-DISH
fiendish

END-LESS
endless
friendless

END-MENT
amendment
befriendment
intendment

EN-DO
crescendo
diminuendo
innuendo

EN-DUM
addendum
agendum
referendum

EN-DUR
ascender
attender
bartender
bender
blender
contender
defender
engender
extender
fender
gender
goaltender
lender

mender
moneylender
offender
pretender
recommender
render
sender
slender
spender
splendor
surrender
suspender
tender
vender
vendor

EN-DUS
horrendous
stupendous
tremendous

EN-EL
antennal
fennel
kennel
lienal
phenyl

Long EN-ESS
cleanness
greenness
keenness
leanness
meanness
sereneness
uncleanness

Long E-NEST
cleanest
keenest

meanest

EN-ET
senate
tenet

ENG-THEN
lengthen
strengthen

Long EN-I
bikini
fettucine
genie
linguine
martini
meany
neoteny
Puccini
scaloppine
Sweeney
sweeny
tahini
teeny
teeny-weeny
weeny
wienie
zucchini

EN-I
antennae
any
benny
fourpenny
halfpenny
jenny
many
penney
penny
sixpenny

EN-IK
allergenic
antigenic
cacogenic
calisthenic
carcinogenic
eugenic
hallucinogenic
Hellenic
hygienic
mutagenic
nonallergenic
photogenic
saracenic
schizophrenic
telegenic
toxigenic
zoogenic

Long EN-ING
beaning
careening
cleaning
contravening
convening
damascening
demeaning
gleaning
guillotining
housecleaning
intervening
keening
leaning
machining
meaning
preening
quarantining
queening
reconvening
screening

silkscreening
supervening
unmeaning
weaning

EN-ISH
replenish
Rhenish
wennish

Long EN-LI
cleanly
greenly
keenly
leanly
meanly
obscenely
queenly
routinely
serenely

Long EN-O
amino
andantino
chino
Filipino
keno
maraschino
merino
palomino
Reno

EN-ON
pennon
tenon

EN-SEZ
condenses
consequences
defenses

dispenses
expenses
fences
incenses
offenses
pretenses
tenses

ENS-FORTH
henceforth
thenceforth

EN-SHAL
componential
confidential
consequential
credential
deferential
differential
essential
eventual
evidential
existential
experiential
exponential
inconsequential
inessential
inferential
influential
nonessential
nonresidential
pestilential
potential
preferential
presidential
providential
prudential
quintessential
referential
residential

reverential
sequential
subsequential
tangential
torrential
unessential

EN-SHUN
circumvention
contention
contravention
convention
detention
dissension
hypotension
inattention
indention
intention
intervention
invention
mention
nonintervention
prehension
pretension
pretention
prevention
prointervention
retention
roentgen
subvention
supervention
tension

EN-SHUND
aforementioned
intentioned
mentioned
unmentioned

EN-SHUS
contentious
licentious
noncontentious
overconscientious
pretentious
sententious
tendentious
unpretentious

EN-SIL
pencil
stencil
tensile
utensil

EN-SILD
penciled
pencilled
stenciled
stenciled

EN-SING
condensing
dispensing
fencing
incensing
recompensing
sensing
sequencing
tensing

EN-SIVE
apprehensive
coextensive
comprehensive
counteroffensive
defensive
expensive
extensive

hypertensive
hypotensive
inexpensive
inoffensive
intensive
offensive
overapprehensive
pensive
recompensive
reprehensive
suspensive
unoffensive

ENS-LESS
defenseless
fenceless
offenseless
senseless

ENS-NESS
denseness
intenseness
tenseness

EN-SUR
biosensor
censor
condenser
denser
dispenser
extensor
fencer
sensor
tensor

EN-TAL
accidental
bioenvironmental
coincidental
compartmental

complemental
consonantal
continental
dental
departmental
detrimental
developmental
documental
elemental
environmental
excremental
experimental
fragmental
fundamental
gentle
governmental
incidental
incremental
instrumental
interdental
judgmental
labiodental
labiomental
lentil
mental
monumental
nutrimental
occidental
oriental
ornamental
parental
placental
preplacental
regimental
rental
sacramental
segmental
sentimental
subcontinental
submental

supplemental
temperamental
transcontinental
ungentle
unsentimental

EN-TANS
repentance
sentence
unrepentance

EN-TED
accented
assented
augmented
cemented
circumvented
complemented
complimented
consented
contented
demented
dented
discontented
disoriented
dissented
documented
fermented
fomented
fragmented
implemented
indented
instrumented
invented
lamented
misrepresented
oriented
ornamented
presented
prevented

regimented
reinvented
relented
rented
reoriented
repented
represented
resented
scented
segmented
supplemented
tented
tormented
unaccented
undocumented
unfermented
unpigmented
unprecedented
unregimented
unrented
unscented
unsegmented
vented

ENT-FUL
eventful
resentful
uneventful
unresentful

EN-TI
aplenty
misrepresentee
plenty
representee
tnt
twenty

ENT-ING
accenting

assenting
augmenting
cementing
circumventing
complementing
complimenting
consenting
contenting
denting
disorienting
dissenting
documenting
experimenting
fermenting
fomenting
fragmenting
implementing
incrementing
indenting
instrumenting
inventing
lamenting
misrepresenting
nonconsenting
orienting
ornamenting
presenting
preventing
regimenting
reinventing
relenting
renting
reorienting
repenting
representing
resenting
scenting
segmenting
supplementing
tenting

tormenting
unconsenting
unrelenting
unrepenting
venting

EN-TIS
apprentice
momentous
portentous

EN-TIST
apprenticed
dentist

EN-TIVE
argumentive
attentive
circumventive
inattentive
incentive
inventive
overattentive
preventive
retentive
uninventive

ENT-LESS
incidentless
relentless
scentless

ENT-LI
aberrantly
abhorrently
absently
abundantly
acquiescently
adamantly
adherently

adjacently
adolescently
advertently
affluently
ambivalently
anciently
apparently
ardently
arrogantly
assonantly
attendantly
belligerently
beneficently
benevolently
blatantly
bluntly
brilliantly
buoyantly
clairvoyantly
clemently
cogently
coherently
competently
complacently
complaisantly
compliantly
concomitantly
concordantly
concurrently
confidently
congruently
consequently
consistently
constantly
constituently
contingently
conveniently
corpulently
counterinsurgently
currently

decadently
decently
defiantly
deficiently
delinquently
dependently
despondently
differently
diffidently
diligently
discordantly
discrepantly
disobediently
dissidently
dissonantly
distantly
divergently
dominantly
ebulliently
effervescently
efficiently
effulgently
elegantly
eloquently
eminently
equidistantly
equivalently
errantly
evanescently
evidently
excellently
exorbitantly
expectantly
expediently
exuberantly
exultantly
fervently
flagrantly
flamboyantly
flippantly

fluently
fragrantly
fraudulently
frequently
gallantly
grandiloquently
hesitantly
huntley
ignorantly
immanently
imminently
impatiently
impenitently
impermanently
impertinently
importantly
impotently
improvidently
imprudently
impudently
inadvertently
incandescently
incessantly
incoherently
incompetently
incongruently
inconsistently
incontinently
inconveniently
incumbently
indecently
independently
indifferently
indigently
indignantly
indolently
indulgently
inefficiently
inelegantly
ineloquently

infrequently
inherently
innocently
insignificantly
insistently
insolently
instantly
insufficiently
intelligently
intermittently
intransigently
irrelevantly
irreverently
jubilantly
lambently
latently
leniently
luxuriantly
magnificently
maleficently
malevolently
malfeasantly
malignantly
militantly
mordantly
munificently
negligently
nonviolently
obediently
obsolescently
omnipotently
omnisciently
opulently
overdiligently
overinsistently
patently
patiently
penitently
permanently
persistently

pertinently
petulantly
phosphorescently
piquantly
pleasantly
pliantly
poignantly
potently
predominantly
preeminently
pregnantly
preponderantly
presently
prevalently
proficiently
prominently
providently
prudently
pruriently
puissantly
pungently
purulently
quiescently
radiantly
recently
recreantly
recurrently
redolently
redundantly
refulgently
relevantly
reliantly
reluctantly
reminiscently
remittently
remonstrantly
repellently
repugnantly
resiliently
resistantly

resonantly
resplendently
reticently
reverently
saliently
sapiently
sentiently
sibilantly
significantly
silently
solvently
somnolently
stagnantly
stridently
stringently
subjacently
subsequently
subserviently
succulently
sufficiently
tolerantly
transcendently
transiently
translucently
transparently
trenchantly
triumphantly
truculently
turbulently
unpleasantly
urgently
vacantly
vagrantly
valiantly
vehemently
verdantly
vibrantly
vigilantly
violently
virulently

ENT-MENT
contentment
discontentment
resentment

EN-TO
divertimento
memento
pimento
portamento
pronunciamento
Sacramento

EN-TOR
centaur
mentor
stentor

EN-TRI
alimentary
complimentary
documentary
entry
gentry
reentry
rudimentary
sentry
subentry

EN-TUR
assentor
augmenter
centaur
center
complimenter
consenter
dissenter
documenter
enter
epicenter

experimenter
fomenter
hypocenter
implementer
implementor
indenter
indentor
inventer
inventor
lamenter
mentor
misrepresenter
presenter
reenter
renter
repenter
representor
segmenter
stentor
supplementer
tormenter
tormentor
venter

EN-TURE
adventure
backbencher
bencher
denture
indenture
misadventure
peradventure
trencher
venture

EN-TUS
apprentice
momentous
portentous

Long E-NUR
cleaner
gleaner
intervener
intervenor
keener
meaner
misdemeanor
wiener

Long E-NUS
achiness
airiness
airworthiness
almightiness
arbitrariness
artiness
ashiness
bagginess
balkiness
balminess
battiness
bawdiness
beastliness
beggarliness
blameworthiness
bloodiness
bloodthirstiness
blowiness
boniness
bonniness
bossiness
braininess
brattiness
brawniness
breeziness
brininess
brotherliness
bumpiness
burliness

busyness
cageyness
caginess
campiness
canniness
cattiness
chalkiness
chattiness
cheekiness
cheeriness
cheesiness
chilliness
choosiness
choppiness
chubbiness
chumminess
chunkiness
clamminess
cleanliness
cloudiness
clumsiness
cockiness
comeliness
contrariness
corniness
costliness
courtliness
cowardliness
coziness
crabbiness
craftiness
cragginess
crankiness
crappiness
craziness
creakiness
creaminess
creepiness
crinkliness
crispiness

croakiness
crotchetiness
crumbliness
curliness
cursoriness
curviness
cushiness
daffiness
daintiness
dastardliness
deadliness
derogatoriness
dewiness
dilatoriness
dinginess
dirtiness
disorderliness
dizziness
dopiness
dowdiness
draftiness
dreaminess
dreariness
dressiness
droopiness
drossiness
drowsiness
dumpiness
duskiness
dustiness
earliness
earthiness
earthliness
easiness
edginess
emptiness
fanciness
fatherliness
faultiness
featheriness

feistiness
fidgetiness
fieriness
filminess
filthiness
fishiness
flabbiness
flakiness
flashiness
fleeciness
fleshiness
flightiness
flimsiness
floppiness
floweriness
fluffiness
foaminess
fogginess
foolhardiness
foxiness
freeness
friendliness
frilliness
friskiness
frizziness
frostiness
frothiness
frowsiness
frowziness
fruitiness
funniness
furriness
fussiness
fustiness
fuzziness
gabbiness
gaminess
gassiness
gaudiness
gauziness

genus
ghastliness
ghostliness
giddiness
glassiness
gloominess
glossiness
godliness
goofiness
goriness
goutiness
graininess
greasiness
greediness
griminess
grittiness
grogginess
grouchiness
grubbiness
grumpiness
guiltiness
hairiness
handiness
happiness
hardiness
hastiness
haughtiness
haziness
headiness
healthiness
heartiness
heaviness
heftiness
hilliness
hoariness
holiness
homeliness
homeyness
housewifeliness
huffiness

huskiness
iciness
inkiness
intravenous
itchiness
jauntiness
jazziness
jerkiness
jolliness
juiciness
jumpiness
kindliness
kingliness
kinkiness
knobbiness
knottiness
kookiness
laciness
lankiness
laziness
leakiness
leatheriness
leeriness
lippiness
literariness
liveliness
loftiness
loginess
loneliness
looniness
lordliness
lousiness
loveliness
lowliness
luckiness
lumpiness
lustiness
maecenas
maidenliness
manginess

manliness
mannerliness
marshiness
massiness
matronliness
meatiness
mercenariness
merriness
messiness
mightiness
milkiness
miserliness
mistiness
moldiness
momentariness
moodiness
mossiness
motherliness
mousiness
muddiness
mugginess
murkiness
mushiness
muskiness
mussiness
mustiness
nastiness
nattiness
naughtiness
necessariness
neighborliness
nerviness
newsiness
niggardliness
noisiness
nosiness
noteworthiness
nuttiness
oiliness
ooziness

orderliness
ordinariness
orneriness
otherworldliness
overhastiness
paltriness
pastiness
patchiness
paunchiness
pearliness
penis
pepperiness
peppiness
perkiness
persnicketiness
peskiness
pettiness
phoniness
pitilessness
pluckiness
pokiness
portliness
praiseworthiness
predatoriness
prettiness
prickliness
priestliness
primariness
princeliness
prissiness
pudginess
puffiness
puniness
pushiness
queasiness
queenliness
quirkiness
raciness
raininess
ranginess

raunchiness
readiness
reediness
ricketiness
riskiness
ritziness
rockiness
roominess
rosiness
rowdiness
ruddiness
runtiness
rustiness
ruttiness
saintliness
saltiness
salutariness
sandiness
sappiness
sauciness
savoriness
scabbiness
scantiness
scariness
scholarliness
scrappiness
scratchiness
scrawniness
seaminess
seaworthiness
seediness
seemliness
sexiness
shabbiness
shadiness
shadowiness
shagginess
shakiness
shapeliness
shiftiness

shininess
shoddiness
showiness
sickliness
sightliness
silkiness
silliness
silveriness
sketchiness
skimpiness
skinniness
slanginess
sleaziness
sleepiness
slipperiness
slipshoddiness
sloppiness
slovenliness
slushiness
smelliness
smokiness
smuttiness
snappiness
sneakiness
snippiness
snootiness
soapiness
sogginess
solitariness
sorriness
speediness
spiciness
splashiness
spookiness
spottiness
sprightliness
springiness
spunkiness
starchiness
stateliness

steadiness
stealthiness
stickiness
stinginess
stockiness
stodginess
stoniness
storminess
streakiness
stringiness
stubbiness
stuffiness
sturdiness
subgenus
sugariness
sulkiness
sultriness
sunniness
surliness
swampiness
swarthiness
tackiness
tardiness
tarriness
tastiness
tawdriness
tawniness
temporariness
testiness
thirstiness
thriftiness
throatiness
tidiness
timeliness
tininess
tinniness
tipsiness
touchiness
transitoriness
trickiness

trustworthiness
tubbiness
ugliness
uncanniness
uncleanliness
uneasiness
unfriendliness
ungainliness
ungodliness
unhappiness
unhealthiness
unholiness
unlikeliness
unluckiness
unmanliness
unnecessariness
unreadiness
unruliness
unsavoriness
unseemliness
unsightliness
unsteadiness
untidiness
untimeliness
unwariness
unwieldiness
unworthiness
venous
venus
wackiness
wariness
washiness
waviness
wealthiness
weariness
weediness
weightiness
wheeziness
wiliness
windiness

wiriness
wittiness
wobbliness
womanliness
woodiness
woolliness
wooziness
wordiness
worldliness
worthiness
yeastiness
zaniness

EN-ZA
cadenza
credenza
influenza

EN-ZES
cadenzas
cleanses
credenzas
influenzas
lenses

E-O
adagio
arpeggio
audio
Boccaccio
Borneo
braggadocio
cameo
cheerio
curio
embryo
folio
impresario
mimeo
mustachio

nuncio
oleo
Ontario
oratorio
patio
Pinocchio
pistachio
polio
portfolio
presidio
punctilio
radio
ratio
Rio
rodeo
Romeo
scenario
Scorpio
solfeggio
stereo
studio
Tokyo
trio
video
vireo

E-ON
aeon
eon
freon
neon
nucleon
pantheon
peon
symbion

EP-ARD
leopard
peppered
shepherd

Long E-PEN
cheapen
deepen
steepen

Long E-PI
cheapy
creepy
sleepy
sweepy
tepee
weepy

EP-ID
intrepid
tepid

Long E-PIJ
seepage
sweepage

Long E-PING
beekeeping
beeping
bleeping
bookkeeping
cheeping
creeping
heaping
housekeeping
keeping
leaping
minesweeping
outleaping
oversleeping
peacekeeping
peeping
reaping
safekeeping
seakeeping

seeping
sleeping
steeping
sweeping
timekeeping
weeping

Long E-PL
kinspeople
people
steeple

Long E-PNESS
cheapness
deepness
steepness

EP-SHUN
conception
contraception
deception
exception
imperception
inception
interception
misconception
perception
preconception
preperception
reception

EP-TIK
analeptic
antiseptic
aseptic
dyspeptic
epileptic
eupeptic
narcoleptic
nympholeptic

peptic
proleptic
psycholeptic
septic
skeptic

Long E-PUR
barkeeper
beekeeper
beeper
bookkeeper
cheaper
cheeper
creeper
deeper
doorkeeper
gamekeeper
gatekeeper
goalkeeper
hotelkeeper
housekeeper
innkeeper
jailkeeper
keeper
leaper
minesweeper
peacekeeper
peeper
poundkeeper
reaper
scorekeeper
shipkeeper
shopkeeper
sleeper
steeper
stockkeeper
storekeeper
sweeper
timekeeper
weeper

zookeeper

EP-UR
hepper
leper
pepper
sidestepper
stepper

ER-AS
coheiress
derris
embarrass
eros
ferris
ferrous
heiress
millionaress
naris
nonferrous
Paris
polaris
sclerous
terrace

ER-BL
gerbil
gerbille
herbal
honorable

E-RENS
adherence
appearance
clearance
coherence
disappearance
incoherence
inherence
interference

perseverance
reappearance

E-RENT
adherent
coherent
incoherent

E-REST
clearest
dearest
nearest
queerest
severest
sincerest
theorist

E-RFUL
cheerful
fearful
sneerful
tearful
uncheerful

E-RI
ablutionary
abolitionary
actuary
adversary
aerie
airy
ancillary
antiquary
apiary
apothecary
arbitrary
aviary
axillary
barberry
bayberry

bearberry
beriberi
berry
bestiary
biliary
binary
blackberry
blueberry
boysenberry
bronchopulmonary
budgetary
bury
canary
Canterbury
capillary
cardiopulmonary
Carrie
carry
cautionary
cemetery
checkerberry
cherry
chokecherry
cloudberry
commissary
confectionery
consignatary
constabulary
contemporary
contrary
corollary
coronary
counterrevolutionary
cranberry
culinary
customary
dairy
deflationary
delusionary
depositary

devolutionary
dewberry
dictionary
dietary
dignitary
disciplinary
discretionary
diversionary
dromedary
dysentery
elderberry
elocutionary
emissary
evolutionary
expansionary
expeditionary
extraordinary
fairy
February
ferry
fragmentary
functionary
funerary
glairy
glary
gooseberry
hackberry
hairy
hereditary
honorary
huckleberry
imaginary
incendiary
inflationary
interdisciplinary
interlibrary
interplanetary
involuntary
itinerary
January

jerry
lamasery
lapidary
legendary
legionary
libationary
library
literary
loganberry
luminary
marry
maxillary
mercenary
merry
mesentery
miliary
military
millinery
miscarry
missionary
momentary
monastery
monetary
mortuary
mulberry
nary
necessary
nondisciplinary
nonmilitary
obituary
officiary
ordinary
ossuary
parry
pecuniary
pensionary
pituitary
planetary
prairie
precautionary

preliminary
primary
probationary
promilitary
pseudolegendary
pseudoliterary
pulmonary
quaternary
raspberry
reactionary
revisionary
revolutionary
rosemary
Salisbury
salivary
salutary
sanctuary
sanguinary
sanitary
scary
secondary
secretary
sedentary
seditionary
segmentary
seminary
sherry
signatary
solidary
solitary
stationary
stationery
statuary
strawberry
subsidiary
temporary
terry
tertiary
tributary
unitary

unmilitary
unnecessary
unwary
urinary
vary
very
veterinary
visionary
vocabulary
voluntary
voluptuary
vulnerary
wary
wherry

ER-ID
berried
buried
carried
ferried
married
miscarried
parried
serried
tarried
unburied
unmarried
unvaried
varied

E-RIJ
peerage
pierage
steerage

ER-IK
alphanumeric
barbaric
choleric
cleric

climacteric
copolymeric
derrick
dysenteric
Eric
esoteric
exoteric
generic
homeric
hysteric
icteric
isomeric
mesenteric
monomeric
numeric
tautomeric
trochanteric

ER-IKS
clerics
derricks
hysterics
numerics

E-RING
adhering
appearing
besmearing
bioengineering
blearing
careering
cashiering
cheering
clearing
cohering
commandeering
disappearing
domineering
electioneering
endearing

engineering
fearing
fleering
gearing
hearing
interfering
jeering
leering
mishearing
mountaineering
nearing
overhearing
peering
persevering
premiering
profiteering
queering
racketeering
reappearing
rearing
searing
shearing
sheepshearing
sheering
smearing
sneering
spearing
steering
tearing
unfearing

ER-IS
coheiress
derris
embarrass
eros
ferris
ferrous
heiress
millionaress

naris
nonferrous
Paris
polaris
sclerous
terrace

ER-ISH
bearish
bugbearish
cherish
garish
nightmarish
parish
perish
squarish

ER-IT
carat
carrot
demerit
disinherit
ferret
garret
inherit
merit
parrot

ER-IZ
actuaries
adversaries
aeries
ancillaries
antiquaries
apiaries
apothecaries
ares
aries
aviaries
axillaries

bayberries
bearberries
beneficiaries
berries
binaries
blackberries
blueberries
boysenberries
buries
canaries
capillaries
carries
cemeteries
checkerberries
cherries
commentaries
commissaries
consignataries
constabularies
contemporaries
contraries
coronaries
cranberries
dairies
depositaries
dewberries
dictionaries
dietaries
dignitaries
dromedaries
dysenteries
elderberries
emissaries
fairies
ferries
functionaries
gooseberries
huckleberries
incendiaries
itineraries

lapidaries
legionaries
libraries
loganberries
luminaries
marries
mercenaries
mesenteries
militaries
miscarries
missionaries
monasteries
mortuaries
mulberries
necessaries
obituaries
parries
prairies
preliminaries
primaries
raspberries
reactionaries
revolutionaries
sanctuaries
secondaries
secretaries
sherries
signataries
stationeries
statuaries
strawberries
subsidiaries
tarries
tributaries
varies
veterinaries
visionaries
vocabularies
wherries

E-RLESS
cheerless
earless
fearless
gearless
peerless
tearless

E-RLI
austerely
biyearly
cavalierly
clearly
dearly
insincerely
merely
nearly
queerly
severely
sheerly
sincerely
yearly

E-RNESS
austereness
cavalierness
clearness
dearness
nearness
queerness
severeness
sheerness

E-RO
antihero
hero
nero
zero

ER-OR
barer
bearer
carer
comparer
coswearer
crossbearer
cupbearer
darer
declarer
error
fairer
forbearer
pallbearer
preparer
rarer
repairer
seafarer
sharer
snarer
sparer
squarer
standard-bearer
starer
swearer
talebearer
terror
torchbearer
wayfarer
wearer

ER-UB
Arab
carob
cherub

E-RUR
adherer
clearer
dearer

hearer
interferer
mirror
nearer
queerer
rearer
severer
shearer
sheepshearer
sincerer
smearer
sneerer
spearer
steerer

E-RZMAN
frontiersman
privateersman
steersman

ES-CHUN
autosuggestion
congestion
question
suggestion

Long E-SEL
easel
measle
teasel
weasel

ES-ENS
acquiescence
adolescence
candescence
coalescence
convalescence
deflorescence
effervescence

efflorescence
essence
evanescence
florescence
fluorescence
incandescence
intumescence
iridescence
luminescence
obsolescence
opalescence
phosphorescence
pubescence
putrescence
quiescence
quintessence
recrudescence
rubescence
senescence
tumescence

Long E-SENT
decent
indecent
obeisant
recent

ES-SENT
acquiescent
adolescent
antidepressant
candescent
coalescent
convalescent
crescent
depressant
effervescent
efflorescent
evanescent
florescent

fluorescent
immunosuppressant
incandescent
incessant
intumescent
iridescent
lactescent
luminescent
obsolescent
phosphorescent
pubescent
putrescent
quiescent
recrudescent
rubescent
senescent
suppressant
tumescent
turgescent
viridescent

Long E-SEZ
altarpieces
caprices
ceases
centerpieces
chemises
creases
crosspieces
deceases
decreases
eyepieces
fieldpieces
greases
hairpieces
headpieces
increases
leases
mantelpieces
mantlepieces

masterpieces
mouthpieces
nieces
pieces
polices
releases
showpieces
sidepieces
subleases
surceases
timepieces

ES-FUL
distressful
stressful
successful
unsuccessful

ESH-ING
enmeshing
fleshing
freshing
intermeshing
meshing
refreshing
threshing

ESH-LI
fleshly
freshly

Long E-SHUN
accretion
completion
concretion
deletion
depletion
excretion
Grecian
magnesian

repletion
secretion
Tahitian
Venetian

ESH-UN
afterimpression
aggression
compression
confession
decompression
depression
digression
discretion
freshen
impression
indiscretion
ingression
nonaggression
oppression
possession
profession
progression
regression
repossession
retrogression
secession
self-possession
session
succession
suppression
transgression

ESH-UR
fresher
pressure
refresher
thresher

Long E-SHUS
capricious
facetious
specious

ES-I
addressee
assessee
dressy
Jesse
lessee
messy

Long E-SIDE
B-side
lee side
countryside
seaside

ES-IJ
message
presage

Long E-SING
ceasing
creasing
deceasing
decreasing
fleecing
greasing
increasing
leasing
piecing
policing
releasing
subleasing
unceasing

ES-SING
abscessing

accessing
acquiescing
addressing
assessing
blessing
caressing
coalescing
compressing
confessing
decompressing
depressing
digressing
distressing
dressing
effervescing
efflorescing
expressing
finessing
fluorescing
guessing
hairdressing
impressing
luminescing
messing
obsessing
oppressing
outguessing
overdressing
overimpressing
possessing
prepossessing
pressing
processing
professing
progressing
reassessing
recessing
recrudescing
redressing
regressing

repossessing
repressing
retrogressing
stressing
suppressing
transgressing
underdressing
undressing

Long E-SIS
anuresis
esthesis
exegesis
kinesis
kinesthesis
photokinesis
psychokinesis
rhesus
telekinesis
thesis

ES-IVE
aggressive
antidepressive
compressive
concessive
decompressive
depressive
digressive
excessive
expressive
impressive
inexpressive
ingressive
nonaggressive
obsessive
oppressive
overaggressive
possessive
progressive

regressive
repressive
retrogressive
successive
suppressive
transgressive
unexpressive
unimpressive
unpossessive

ESK-NESS
grotesqueness
picturesqueness

ES-L
nestle
pestle
sessile
trestle
vessel
wrestle

Long E-SLESS
ceaseless
creaseless
leaseless

ES-LING
nestling
wrestling

ES-LUR
nestler
wrestler

ES-MAN
chessman
pressman
yesman

ES-MENT
assessment
impressment
overassessment
reassessment

ES-TA
fiesta
podesta
siesta
Vesta

ES-TAL
festal
vestal

ES-TED
arrested
attested
breasted
congested
contested
crested
decongested
detested
digested
divested
infested
ingested
invested
jested
manifested
molested
nested
overinvested
predigested
pretested
protested
reinvested
requested

rested
retested
suggested
tested
unarrested
unattested
uncontested
undigested
uninvested
unmolested
unprotested
untested
vested
wrested

Long E-STI
beasty
yeasty

ES-TI
arrestee
chesty
contestee
teste
testee
testy
vestee
zesty

ES-TIK
anapestic
domestic
majestic

ES-TIN
clandestine
destine
intestine
predestine
progestin

Long E-STING
easting
feasting
yeasting

ES-TING
arresting
attesting
breasting
congesting
contesting
cresting
decongesting
detesting
digesting
divesting
infesting
ingesting
investing
jesting
manifesting
molesting
nesting
overinvesting
predigesting
pretesting
protesting
requesting
resting
retesting
suggesting
testing
unprotesting
vesting
wresting

ES-TIVE
congestive
decongestive
digestive

festive
indigestive
ingestive
postdigestive
restive
suggestive
unfestive

EST-LESS
crestless
guestless
jestless
questless
restless

Long E-STLI
beastly
priestly

ES-TO
manifesto
pesto
presto

Long E-STONE
cherrystone
freestone
holystone
keystone

ES-TRAL
ancestral
fenestral
kestrel
orchestral

Long E-STUR
Easter
feaster
northeaster

southeaster

ES-TUR
ancestor
arrester
arrestor
attester
attestor
detester
ester
Esther
fester
infester
investor
jester
Manchester
molester
nester
pester
polyester
protester
protestor
requester
requestor
rester
Rochester
semester
sequester
Silvester
southwester
Sylvester
tester
trimester
wester
wrester

EST-URD
festered
pestered
sequestered

westered

ES-TURE
gesture
vesture

ES-TUS
asbestos
asbestus

ES-UR
addresser
aggressor
antecessor
assessor
caresser
compressor
confessor
depressor
dresser
guesser
hairdresser
impresser
intercessor
lesser
microprocessor
obsessor
oppressor
possessor
predecessor
presser
processor
professor
redresser
regressor
repressor
stressor
successor
suppressor
transgressor

ET-A
Greta
operetta
poinsettia
vendetta

Long E-TED
bleated
cheated
competed
completed
conceited
defeated
deleted
depleted
entreated
feted
fleeted
greeted
heated
maltreated
meted
mistreated
overheated
pleated
preheated
receipted
reheated
repeated
retreated
seated
secreted
sleeted
treated
tweeted
uncompleted
undefeated
unheated
unseated
untreated

ET-ED
abetted
bayoneted
bayonetted
betted
coquetted
fetid
fretted
gazetted
indebted
jetted
netted
petted
pirouetted
regretted
silhouetted
stetted
sweated
vignetted
wetted
whetted

Long E-TEN
beaten
browbeaten
cretin
eaten
neaten
secretin
sweeten
unbeaten
uneaten
wheaten

Long E-TEST
completest
defeatist
fleetest
elitist
neatest

sweetest

ET-FUL
forgetful
fretful
regretful
threatful

Long E-THAL
bequethal
lethal

ETH-IL
Ethel
ethyl
methyl

Long E-THING
breathing
ensheathing
seething
sheathing
teething
wreathing

ETH-LESS
breathless
deathless

Long E-THUR
breather
either
neither

ETH-UR
altogether
bellwether
feather
heather
leather

nether
pinfeather
tether
together
weather
whether

Long E-TI
DDT
entreaty
gleety
meaty
rete
sleety
spermaceti
treaty

ET-I
betty
confetti
debtee
jetty
machete
petty
spaghetti
sweaty
yeti

ET-IK
aesthetic
alphabetic
anaesthetic
analgetic
anesthetic
antimagnetic
antithetic
anuretic
apathetic
apologetic
ascetic

athletic
biogenetic
cardiokinetic
cosmetic
cybernetic
diabetic
diarrhetic
dietetic
diuretic
eidetic
electromagnetic
empathetic
energetic
frenetic
gametic
genetic
geodetic
geomagnetic
gyromagnetic
hermetic
herpetic
homiletic
homogenetic
hyperkinetic
kinaesthetic
kinesthetic
kinetic
magnetic
monogenetic
nonathletic
nondiabetic
nonpoetic
ontogenetic
oogenetic
orthogenetic
parakinetic
parenthetic
paresthetic
pathetic
phonetic

photokinetic
photosynthetic
phrenetic
poetic
prediabetic
prophetic
prosthetic
psychogenetic
schizogenetic
sympathetic
synergetic
synesthetic
syngenetic
synthetic
theoretic
unaesthetic
unathletic
unesthetic

ET-IKS
apologetics
poetics

Long E-TING
beating
bleating
browbeating
cheating
competing
completing
defeating
deleting
depleting
eating
entreating
excreting
fleeting
greeting
heating
maltreating

meeting
mistreating
oilheating
overeating
overheating
pleating
preheating
receipting
reheating
repeating
retreating
seating
secreting
sheeting
sleeting
treating
tweeting
unseating

ET-ING
abetting
bayoneting
bayonetting
begetting
besetting
betting
bloodletting
coquetting
forgetting
fretting
gazetting
getting
insetting
jetting
letting
netting
offsetting
pacesetting
petting
pirouetting

presetting
regretting
resetting
setting
silhouetting
stetting
subletting
sweating
typesetting
upsetting
vignetting
wetting
whetting

ET-ISH
coquettish
fetich
fetish
sweetish

Long E-TL
Beatle
beetle
fetal
setal
spirochetal

ET-L
fettle
gunmetal
kettle
metal
mettle
nettle
nonmetal
petal
resettle
settle
teakettle
unsettle

Long E-TLI
completely
concretely
discreetly
discretely
effetely
fleetly
incompletely
indiscreetly
meetly
neatly
obsoletely
sweetly

ET-LING
nettling
resettling
settling
unsettling

ET-MENT
abetment
besetment
indebtness
revetment

Long E-TNESS
completeness
concreteness
discreetness
effeteness
fleetness
incompleteness
indiscreetness
neatness
repleteness
sweetness

Long E-TO
burrito

Hirohito
magneto
mosquito
neat-o
Quito
veto

ET-O
allegreto
amoretto
falsetto
ghetto
libretto
palmetto
stiletto
Tintoretto
zucchetto

ET-RIK
anthropometric
asymmetric
barometric
biotelemetric
calorimetric
cardiometric
diametric
ergometric
geometric
metric
millimetric
obstetric
parametric
phonometric
photometric
psychometric
stereometric

Long E-TUR
anteater
beater

beefeater
bleater
centimeter
cheater
decaliter
deciliter
defeater
dekaliter
eater
eggbeater
greeter
heater
hectoliter
hectometer
kiloliter
liter
litre
masseter
meter
milliliter
millimeter
neater
ohmmeter
overeater
Peter
receiptor
repeater
saltpeter
secretor
sweeter
teeter
treater
tweeter
worldbeater

ET-UR
begetter
better
bettor
bonesetter

codebtor
debtor
fetter
fretter
getter
letter
newsletter
pacesetter
petter
pinsetter
regretter
setter
sweater
tasksetter
typesetter
wetter
whetter

ET-WURK
fretwork
network

Long E-UR
achier
airier
airworthier
angrier
anterior
artier
ashier
balkier
ballcarrier
balmier
barrier
battier
bawdier
beadier
beastlier
beefier
binuclear

blearier
bloodier
bloodthirstier
bloomier
blotchier
blowier
blowzier
blurrier
boggier
bonier
bonnier
boozier
boskier
bossier
botchier
bouncier
brainier
bramblier
brassier
brattier
brawnier
breathier
breezier
brinier
bristlier
broodier
broomier
brothier
bubblier
bulgier
bulkier
bumpier
bunchier
burlier
bushier
busier
cagier
campier
cannier
carrier

catchier
cattier
chalkier
chancier
chattier
cheekier
cheerier
cheesier
chillier
chintzier
choosier
choppier
chubbier
chummier
chunkier
clammier
classier
cleanlier
cliquier
cloddier
cloggier
cloudier
clumpier
clumsier
cockier
collier
comelier
comfier
copier
corkier
cornier
costlier
courier
courtier
courtlier
cozier
crabbier
cracklier
craftier
craggier

crankier
crappier
crawlier
crazier
creakier
creamier
creepier
crinklier
crispier
croakier
croupier
crummier
crunchier
crustier
cuddlier
curlier
currier
curvier
cushier
daffier
daintier
dallier
dandier
deadlier
decreer
dewier
dicier
dingier
dinkier
dippier
dirtier
dizzier
dopier
dottier
doughier
dowdier
draftier
draggier
dreamier
drearier

dressier
droopier
drowsier
duckier
dumpier
duskier
dustier
earlier
earthier
earthlier
easier
edgier
eerier
embodier
emptier
envier
excelsior
exterior
fancier
fattier
faultier
feistier
filmier
filthier
finnier
fishier
fizzier
flabbier
flakier
flashier
fleecier
fleshier
fleshlier
flightier
flimsier
flintier
floppier
flossier
fluffier
flukier

foamier
foggier
folksier
foolhardier
foxier
freakier
freer
friendlier
friskier
frizzier
frostier
frothier
frowsier
frowzier
fruitier
frumpier
fumier
funkier
funnier
furrier
fussier
fustier
fuzzier
gabbier
gamier
gassier
gaudier
gauzier
gawkier
germier
ghastlier
giddier
gimpier
glassier
glazier
gleamier
gloomier
glossier
gluier
godlier

goodlier	heavier	leafier
goofier	heftier	leakier
gooier	hillier	leerier
gorier	hoarier	leggier
goutier	hokier	lengthier
grabbier	holier	levier
grainier	homelier	likelier
grassier	homier	limier
greasier	hornier	linear
greedier	horsier	lintier
grimier	huffier	livelier
gripier	hungrier	loamier
grippier	hurrier	lobbyer
grislier	huskier	loftier
grittier	icier	logier
grizzlier	ickier	lonelier
groggier	inferior	loonier
groovier	inkier	lordlier
grouchier	interior	lousier
grubbier	itchier	lovelier
grumpier	jauntier	lowlier
grungier	jazzier	luckier
guiltier	jerkier	lumpier
gummier	jollier	lustier
gushier	jouncier	mangier
gustier	journeyer	manlier
gutsier	juicier	marrier
guttier	jumpier	marshier
hairier	kickier	massier
hammier	kindlier	matrilinear
handier	kinglier	mealier
happier	kinkier	measlier
hardier	knobbier	meatier
harrier	knottier	merrier
hastier	kookier	messier
haughtier	lacier	meteor
hazier	lakier	mightier
headier	lankier	milkier
healthier	lardier	mintier
heartier	lazier	mirier

mistier
moldier
moodier
mopier
mossier
mouldier
mousier
mouthier
muckier
muddier
muggier
mulier
murkier
mushier
muskier
mustier
nastier
nattier
naughtier
needier
nervier
newsier
niftier
nippier
noisier
nosier
nuclear
nuttier
oilier
oozier
outlier
overseer
palmier
paltrier
pannier
paranuclear
parlayer
parleyer
pastier
patchier

patrilinear
pearlier
peatier
pebblier
peppier
perkier
peskier
pettier
phonier
photocopier
pickier
piggier
pimplier
pithier
pluckier
plumier
pointier
pokier
porkier
portlier
posterior
prettier
pricklier
prissier
pronuclear
pudgier
puffier
pulpier
punchier
punier
pushier
pussier
quackier
quakier
queasier
quirkier
racier
rainier
rallier
randier

rangier
rapier
raspier
rattier
raunchier
readier
reedier
riskier
ritzier
rockier
roomier
rosier
rowdier
ruddier
runnier
runtier
rustier
ruttier
saggier
saintlier
saltier
sandier
sappier
sassier
saucier
scabbier
scalier
scantier
scarier
schmaltzier
scragglier
scrappier
scratchier
scrawnier
screechier
screwier
scrimpier
scrubbier
scruffier
scummier

scurvier	smoggier	squattier
seamier	smokier	squeakier
seedier	smudgier	squirmier
seemlier	smuttier	stagier
sexier	snakier	starchier
shabbier	snakiest	starrier
shadier	snappier	statelier
shaggier	snarlier	steadier
shakier	snazzier	stealthier
shapelier	sneakier	steamier
sheenier	sneezier	steelier
shiftier	snippier	stickier
shinier	snobbier	stingier
shoddier	snoopier	stinkier
showier	snootier	stockier
sicklier	snottier	stodgier
sightlier	snowier	stonier
sightseer	soapier	stormier
silkier	soggier	stragglier
sillier	sootier	streakier
siltier	soppier	streamier
sketchier	sorrier	stretchier
skier	soupier	stringier
skimpier	speedier	stubbier
skinnier	spicier	studier
slangier	spiffier	stuffier
slaphappier	spikier	stumpier
sleazier	spindlier	sturdier
sleepier	spinier	sudsier
sleetier	splashier	sulkier
slimier	splotchier	sultrier
slinkier	spongier	sunnier
slipperier	spookier	superior
sloppier	sportier	surlier
sloshier	spottier	swampier
slouchier	sprightlier	swankier
sludgier	springier	swarthier
slushier	spunkier	sweatier
smearier	squabbier	tackier
smellier	squashier	talkier

tallier
tangier
tardier
tarrier
tastier
tawdrier
tawnier
tearier
teenier
terrier
testier
tetchier
thermonuclear
thirstier
thornier
threadier
thriftier
throatier
tidier
tinier
tinnier
tipsier
toothier
touchier
trashier
trendier
trickier
trochlear
trustier
tubbier
twangier
tweedier
uglier
ulterior
unhealthier
varier
vernier
volleyer
wackier
warier

warrior
wartier
washier
wastier
wavier
waxier
weaklier
wealthier
wearier
weedier
weenier
weepier
weightier
wheezier
whinier
wilier
windier
winier
wintrier
wirier
wispier
wittier
wobblier
woodier
woodsier
woollier
woozier
wordier
worldlier
wormier
worrier
worthier
wrigglier
xavier
yeastier
yummier
zanier
zestier
zippier

Long E-VA
diva
Geneva
Shiva
viva
yeshiva
yeshivah

Long E-VAL
evil
medieval
primeval
weevil

EV-EL
bedevil
bevel
bi-level
daredevil
devil
dishevel
level
revel
split-level

Long E-VEN
break-even
even
Genevan
Stephen
Steven
uneven

EV-EN
Devon
eleven
heaven
leaven
seven

EV-ENTH
eleventh
seventh

EV-I
bevy
Chevy
levee
levy
replevy

Long E-VIJ
cleavage
leavage

Long E-VIL
evil
medieval
primeval
weevil

Long E-VING
achieving
believing
bereaving
cleaving
conceiving
deceiving
disbelieving
grieving
hairweaving
heaving
interleaving
interweaving
leaving
misconceiving
overachieving
peeving
perceiving
preconceiving

receiving
reeving
relieving
reprieving
retrieving
thieving
unbelieving
underachieving
unperceiving
unweaving
weaving

EX-ING
annexing
flexing
hexing
indexing
perplexing
telexing
vexing

Long E-VISH
peevish
thievish

Long E-VMENT
achievement
bereavement

Long E-VUR
achiever
beaver
believer
cantilever
cleaver
conceiver
deceiver
disbeliever
griever
hairweaver

naiver
nonbeliever
overachiever
perceiver
receiver
reliever
repriever
retriever
transceiver
underachiever
weaver

EV-UR
cantilever
clever
dissever
endeavor
endeavour
ever
forever
however
howsoever
lever
never
sever
soever
whatever
whatsoever
whenever
whensoever
wheresoever
wherever
whichever
whichsoever
whoever
whomever
whomsoever
whosesoever
whosever
whosoever

Long E-WA
alleyway
anyway
entryway
freeway
leeway
milky-way
seaway
taxiway

Long E-ZAL
diesel
easel
measle
teasel
weasel

Long E-ZALZ
easels
measles
teasels
weasels

EZ-ANS
omnipresence
peasants
pheasants
presence

EZ-ANT
omnipresent
peasant
pheasant
pleasant
present
unpleasant

Long EZH-UR
leisure
seizure

E-ZHUR
countermeasure
displeasure
forepleasure
leisure
measure
pleasure
treasure

Long E-ZI
breezy
cheesy
easy
greasy
queasy
queazy
sleazy
uneasy

Long E-ZING
appeasing
breezing
displeasing
easing
freezing
greasing
nonfreezing
pleasing
seizing
sneezing
squeezing
stripteasing
subfreezing
teasing
tweezing
unfreezing
unpleasing
wheezing

Long E-ZMENT
appeasement
easement

Long E-ZON
preseason
reason
seisin
treason

Long E-ZUR
brainteaser
easer
freezer
geezer
greaser
misfeasor
pleaser
sneezer
squeezer
stripteaser
teaser
timepleaser
tweezer

I-A
ayah
Maya
messiah
Obadiah
papaya
pariah
rya
stria
via
Zachariah
Zechariah
Zephaniah

I-AD
diad
dyad
triad

I-AL
aisle
denial
dial
lisle
mistrial
phial
pial
predial
pretrial
retrial
sundial
trial
vial

I-AM
I am
iamb
Priam
Siam

Long I-ANS
alliance
appliance
bioscience
compliance
defiance
incompliance
misalliance
noncompliance
prescience
reliance
science

Long I-ANT
client
compliant
defiant
giant
incompliant
pliant
reliant
scient
supergiant
uncompliant

Long I-AS
bias
inebrious
pious
Pius
Zacharias

Long I-BING
ascribing
bribing
circumscribing
describing
gibing

imbibing
inscribing
jibing
oversubscribing
prescribing
proscribing
reinscribing
subscribing
superscribing
transcribing

IB-ING
ad-libbing
bibbing
cribbing
fibbing
jibbing
libbing
ribbing

IB-IT
exhibit
flibbertigibbet
gibbet
inhibit
prohibit

Long I-BL
bible
libel
tribal

IB-L
dibble
dribble
kibble
nibble
quibble
scribble
sibyl

Long IB-LD
dribbled
kibbled
nibbled
quibbled
ribald
scribbled

IB-LET
driblet
giblet

IB-LI
dribbly
glibly
quibbly
scribbly

IB-LING
dribbling
kibbling
nibbling
quibbling
scribbling
sibling

IB-LUR
dribbler
nibbler
quibbler
scribbler

Long I-BOL
eyeball
highball

IB-ON
gibbon
ribbon

Long I-BORN
highborn
skyborne

Long I-BROW
eyebrow
highbrow

Long I-BUR
briber
describer
giber
imbiber
inscriber
prescriber
subscriber
transcriber
Tiber

IB-UR
bibber
cribber
fibber
gibber
glibber
jibber
libber
ribber

ICH-EZ
bewitches
bitches
britches
ditches
enriches
flitches
glitches
hemistiches
hemstitches
hitches

itches
niches
ostriches
pitches
riches
sandwiches
snitches
stitches
switches
twitches
unhitches
witches

ICH-ING
backstitching
ditching
enriching
hemstitching
hitching
itching
pitching
snitching
stitching
switching
twitching
unhitching
witching

ICH-LESS
itchless
hitchless
stitchless
switchless

ICH-MENT
bewitchment
enrichment

ICH-UR
ditcher
enricher
hitcher
pitcher
richer
snitcher
stitcher
switcher
water-witcher

ID-ANS
forbiddance
riddance

Long I-DANS
abidance
guidance
misguidance
stridence

Long I-DED
abided
betided
chided
collided
confided
lopsided
misguided
presided
prided
resided
sided
subdivided
subsided
tided
undecided
undivided
unguided
unprovided

ID-ED
kidded
lidded
ridded

ID-EN
backslidden
bedridden
bidden
forbidden
hidden
joyridden
midden
outbidden
overbidden
overridden
ridden
stridden
unbidden
unforbidden

Long I-DENT
strident
trident

Long I-DI
tidy
untidy

ID-I
biddy
giddy
kiddy
middy
skiddy

ID-IK
bromidic
davidic
druidic

glyceridic
hasidic
iridic
meridic
nuclidic
pyramidic

Long I-DING
abiding
backsliding
betiding
chiding
coinciding
colliding
confiding
deciding
deriding
dividing
eliding
gliding
guiding
hiding
joyriding
misguiding
overriding
presiding
priding
providing
residing
riding
siding
sliding
striding
subdividing
tiding

ID-ING
bidding
forbidding
kidding

outbidding
overbidding
ridding
skidding
unforbidding

Long ID-INGZ
sidings
tidings

Long I-DL
bactericidal
bacteriocidal
bridal
bridle
feticidal
fratricidal
fungicidal
genocidal
germicidal
herbicidal
homicidal
idle
idyll
infanticidal
insecticidal
matricidal
pesticidal
sidle
spermicidal
sporicidal
suicidal
tidal
viricidal

ID-L
diddle
fiddle
griddle
middle

piddle
pyramidal
riddle
twiddle

Long ID-LING
bridling
idling
sideling
sidling

ID-NI
kidney
Sidney
Sydney

ID-O
kiddo
widow

Long I-DUR
abider
cider
eider
misguider
outrider
Schneider
slider
spider
subdivider

ID-UR
bidder
consider
forbidder
kidder
reconsider
ridder

Long I-ENS
alliance
appliance
bioscience
compliance
defiance
incompliance
misalliance
noncompliance
prescience
reliance
science

Long I-ET
diet
disquiet
quiet
riot
striate
unquiet

Long I-FEN
hyphen
siphon
siphon

IF-EN
griffin
griffon
stiffen

IF-I
iffy
jiffy
sniffy
spiffy

IF-IK
calcific
calorific

hieroglyphic
honorific
horrific
magnific
morbific
nonscientific
nonspecific
ossific
Pacific
prescientific
prolific
scientific
somnific
soporific
specific
sudorific
terrific
transpacific
unscientific
unspecific

IF-ING
miffing
riffing
sniffing
whiffing

Long I-FL
Eiffel
rifle
stifle
trifle

IF-L
piffle
riffle
sniffle
whiffle

Long I-FLESS
knifeless
lifeless
strifeless
wifeless

Long I-FLIKE
knifelike
lifelike
unlifelike

Long I-FLING
angling
annulling
appareling
apparelling
barreling
battling
bedazzling
bedraggling
befuddling
belittling
bespangling
beveling
bevelling
bicycling
bloodcurdling
bobbling
boggling
boodling
boondoggling
bottling
bridling
bugling
bumbling
bundling
bungling
burgling
caballing
cabling

cackling
canceling
cancelling
candling
capsuling
caroling
channeling
channelling
chiseling
chiselling
chortling
chucking
cobbling
coddling
commingling
counseling
counselling
cradling
cudgeling
cudgelling
culling
cycling
deviling
devilling
dialing
dialling
disemboweling
disembowelling
disheveling
dishevelling
doweling
driveling
drivelling
dueling
duelling
dulling
embezzling
empaneling
enabling
enameling

encapsuling
enfeebling
ennobling
entitling
equaling
equalling
fenagling
fiddling
finagling
fizzling
fondling
frazzling
freckling
frizzling
fuddling
fueling
fumbling
funneling
funnelling
gabbling
gambling
garbling
gargling
gaveling
gavelling
giggling
girdling
gobbling
goggling
grappling
graveling
groveling
grovelling
grumbling
gulling
gurgling
guzzling
hackling
haggling
handling

hassling
heckling
hobbling
hornswoggling
huddling
hulling
humbling
hurdling
hurtling
hustling
idling
impaneling
impanelling
imperiling
imperilling
initialing
initialling
jangling
jeweling
jiggling
jingling
jostling
juggling
jumbling
kibbling
labeling
labelling
ladling
leveling
levelling
libeling
libelling
lulling
manacling
marbling
marshaling
marshalling
martialing
martialling
marveling

marvelling
meddling
mingling
mishandling
mislabeling
mislabelling
modeling
modelling
mollycoddling
mottling
muddling
muffling
mulling
mumbling
muscling
muzzling
needling
nettling
nibbling
niggling
ogling
paddling
paneling
panelling
parceling
parcelling
pedaling
pedalling
penciling
pencilling
peopling
periling
pickling
piddling
piffling
pimpling
pinnacling
pommeling
pommelling
prattling

precanceling
puddling
pummeling
pummelling
puzzling
quadrupling
quarreling
quarrelling
quibbling
raffling
rambling
rattling
raveling
ravelling
recycling
redoubling
rekindling
relabeling
relabelling
remodeling
remodelling
rescheduling
resembling
resettling
reshuffling
reveling
revelling
riddling
riffling
rifling
rivaling
ruffling
rumbling
rumpling
rustling
sampling
scheduling
scrabbling
scrambling
scribbling

scuffling
sculling
scuttling
settling
shackling
shambling
shingling
shoveling
shovelling
shriveling
shrivelling
shuffling
shuttling
sideling
sidling
signaling
signalling
singling
sizzling
smuggling
sniffling
sniveling
snivelling
snorkeling
snuffling
snuggling
spangling
speckling
spiraling
spiralling
squabbling
squiggling
stabling
stapling
startling
stenciling
stencilling
stifling
stippling
stoppling

straddling
straggling
strangling
struggling
stumbling
subtitling
subtotaling
subtotalling
swaddling
swashbuckling
swindling
swiveling
swivelling
tabling
tackling
tasseling
tasselling
tattling
throttling
titling
toddling
toggling
toppling
totaling
totalling
toweling
trammeling
trammelling
trampling
traveling
travelling
trebling
trembling
trickling
trifling
tripling
troubling
trundling
tumbling
tunneling

tunnelling
tussling
twaddling
twiddling
unbuckling
uncoupling
unmuzzling
unraveling
unravelling
unscrambling
unsettling
unshackling
unsnarling
untangling
victualing
waddling
waffling
waggling
wailing
warbling
weaseling
whaling
wheedling
whiffling
whittling
wiggling
wobbling
wrangling
wrestling
wriggling
wrinkling
yodeling
yodelling
yowling

IF-LING
piffling
riffling
sniffling
whiffling

Long I-FLUR
stifler
trifler

IF-LUR
piffler
riffler
sniffler
whiffler

IF-TED
airlifted
downshifted
drifted
gifted
lifted
presifted
rifted
shifted
shoplifted
sifted
unsifted
uplifted
upshifted

IF-TI
drifty
fifty
nifty
shifty
spendthrifty
thrifty
unthrifty

IF-TING
airlifting
downshifting
drifting
lifting
presifting

rifting
shifting
shoplifting
sifting
uplifting
upshifting

IFT-LESS
shiftless
thriftless

IFT-UR
drifter
grifter
lifter
shifter
shoplifter
sifter
snifter
swifter
uplifter

Long I-FUR
cipher
decipher
encipher
fifer
knifer
lifer
rifer

IF-UR
differ
sniffer
stiffer

IG-FUT
bigfoot
pigfoot

IG-I
biggie
biggy
piggy
spriggy
twiggy

IG-ING
digging
jigging
reneging
rigging
swigging
wigging

IG-ISH
biggish
piggish
priggish
whiggish

IG-L
giggle
jiggle
niggle
squiggle
wiggle
wriggle

Long I-GLASS
eyeglass
spyglass

IG-LI
giggly
jiggly
prodigally
squiggly
wiggly
wriggly

Wrigley

IG-LING
angling
annulling
appareling
apparelling
barreling
battling
bedazzling
bedraggling
befuddling
belittling
bespangling
beveling
bevelling
bicycling
bloodcurdling
bobbling
boggling
boodling
boondoggling
bottling
bridling
bugling
bumbling
bundling
bungling
burgling
caballing
cabling
cackling
canceling
cancelling
candling
capsuling
caroling
channeling
channelling
chiseling

chiselling
chortling
chucking
cobbling
coddling
commingling
counseling
counselling
cradling
cudgeling
cudgelling
culling
cycling
deviling
devilling
dialing
dialling
disemboweling
disembowelling
disheveling
dishevelling
doweling
driveling
drivelling
dueling
duelling
dulling
embezzling
empaneling
enabling
enameling
encapsuling
enfeebling
ennobling
entitling
equaling
equalling
fenagling
fiddling
finagling

fizzling
fondling
frazzling
freckling
frizzling
fuddling
fueling
fumbling
funneling
funnelling
gabbling
gambling
garbling
gargling
gaveling
gavelling
giggling
girdling
gobbling
goggling
grappling
graveling
groveling
grovelling
grumbling
gulling
gurgling
guzzling
hackling
haggling
handling
hassling
heckling
hobbling
hornswoggling
huddling
hulling
humbling
hurdling
hurtling

hustling
idling
impaneling
impanelling
imperiling
imperilling
initialing
initialling
jangling
jeweling
jiggling
jingling
jostling
juggling
jumbling
kibbling
labeling
labelling
ladling
leveling
levelling
libeling
libelling
lulling
manacling
marbling
marshaling
marshalling
martialing
martialling
marveling
marvelling
meddling
mingling
mishandling
mislabeling
mislabelling
modeling
modelling
mollycoddling

mottling
muddling
muffling
mulling
mumbling
muscling
muzzling
needling
nettling
nibbling
niggling
ogling
paddling
paneling
panelling
parceling
parcelling
pedaling
pedalling
penciling
pencilling
peopling
periling
pickling
piddling
piffling
pimpling
pinnacling
pommeling
pommelling
prattling
precanceling
puddling
pummeling
pummelling
puzzling
quadrupling
quarreling
quarrelling
quibbling

raffling
rambling
rattling
raveling
ravelling
recycling
redoubling
rekindling
relabeling
relabelling
remodeling
remodelling
rescheduling
resembling
resettling
reshuffling
reveling
revelling
riddling
riffling
rifling
rivaling
ruffling
rumbling
rumpling
rustling
sampling
scheduling
scrabbling
scrambling
scribbling
scuffling
sculling
scuttling
settling
shackling
shambling
shingling
shoveling
shovelling

shriveling
shrivelling
shuffling
shuttling
sideling
sidling
signaling
signalling
singling
sizzling
smuggling
sniffling
sniveling
snivelling
snorkeling
snuffling
snuggling
spangling
speckling
spiraling
spiralling
squabbling
squiggling
stabling
stapling
startling
stenciling
stencilling
stifling
stippling
stoppling
straddling
straggling
strangling
struggling
stumbling
subtitling
subtotaling
subtotalling
swaddling

swashbuckling
swindling
swiveling
swivelling
tabling
tackling
tasseling
tasselling
tattling
throttling
titling
toddling
toggling
toppling
totaling
totalling
toweling
trammeling
trammelling
trampling
traveling
travelling
trebling
trembling
trickling
trifling
tripling
troubling
trundling
tumbling
tunneling
tunnelling
tussling
twaddling
twiddling
unbuckling
uncoupling
unmuzzling
unraveling
unravelling

unscrambling
unsettling
unshackling
unsnarling
untangling
victualing
waddling
waffling
waggling
wailing
warbling
weaseling
whaling
wheedling
whiffling
whittling
wiggling
wobbling
wrangling
wrestling
wriggling
wrinkling
yodeling
yodelling
yowling

IG-LUR
giggler
niggler
wiggler
wriggler

IG-MA
enigma
sigma
stigma

IG-MENT
figment
pigment

IG-MI
pygmy

IG-NANT
indignant
malignant
nonmalignant

IG-OR
bigger
chigger
digger
ditchdigger
jigger
outrigger
reneger
rigger
rigor
snigger
trigger
vigor
vigour

IG-OT
bigot
frigate
spigot

IG-UR
bigger
chigger
digger
ditchdigger
jigger
outrigger
reneger
rigger
rigor
snigger
trigger

vigor
vigour

Long I-ING
alibiing
allying
amplifying
applying
beautifying
belying
buying
calcifying
certifying
clarifying
classifying
codifying
complying
crucifying
crying
damnifying
dandifying
decalcifying
declassifying
decrying
defying
dehumidifying
deifying
denying
detoxifying
dignifying
disqualifying
dissatisfying
diversifying
drying
dyeing
dying
edifying
electrifying
emulsifying
espying

esterifying
exemplifying
eyeing
eying
falsifying
flying
fortifying
fructifying
frying
glorifying
gratifying
guying
hogtying
horrifying
humidifying
identifying
implying
indemnifying
intensifying
justifying
lignifying
liquefying
lying
magnifying
misapplying
misclassifying
modifying
mollifying
mortifying
multiplying
mummifying
mystifying
nitrifying
noncomplying
notifying
nullifying
occupying
ossifying
outlying
overbuying

overdiversifying
overflying
overlying
oversimplifying
oversupplying
pacifying
personifying
petrifying
plying
preoccupying
prettifying
prophesying
prying
purifying
putrefying
qualifying
quantifying
ramifying
rarefying
rarifying
ratifying
recertifying
reclassifying
rectifying
redrying
redyeing
refortifying
refrying
relying
remodifying
renotifying
reoccupying
replying
reunifying
reverifying
revivifying
sanctifying
saponifying
satisfying
shanghaiing

shying
sighing
signifying
simplifying
skying
solidifying
specifying
spying
stratifying
stultifying
stupefying
subclassifying
supplying
syllabifying
terrifying
testifying
tieing
torrifying
toxifying
trying
tying
typifying
underlying
undying
unedifying
ungratifying
unifying
untying
verifying
versifying
vilifying
vitrifying
vivifying
vying

IJ-ID
frigid
overrigid
rigid

IJ-ING
abridging
acknowledging
advantaging
averaging
bandaging
bridging
damaging
discouraging
disparaging
encouraging
envisaging
foraging
hemorrhaging
leveraging
managing
mismanaging
mortgaging
packaging
pillaging
portaging
prepackaging
privileging
ravaging
remortgaging
repackaging
ridging
rummaging
salvaging
scrimmaging
unacknowledging
voyaging

IJ-IT
digit
double-digit
fidget
midget
widget

IJ-ON
origin
pidgin
pigeon
religion
smidgen
smidgeon
smidgin
widgeon

IJ-US
irreligious
nonreligious
prestigious
prodigious
religious
sacrilegious

Long I-KA
balalaika
formica
mica
pica
plica
spica

IK-EN
awestricken
chicken
panic-stricken
poverty-stricken
publican
quicken
sicken
stricken
thicken

IK-ET
cricket
picket
spigot
thicket
ticket
wicket

I-KI
cliquey
dickey
doohickey
hickey
icky
kicky
Mickey
panicky
picky
quickie
sticky
tricky

Long I-KING
biking
disliking
hiking
hitchhiking
liking
overstriking
psyching
shunpiking
spiking
striking
Viking

IK-ING
bootlicking
brain-picking
bricking
clicking
cotton-picking
flicking
frolicking

handpicking
kicking
licking
mimicking
nicking
nitpicking
panicking
picking
picnicking
politicking
pricking
rollicking
siccing
sicking
slicking
sticking
ticking
trafficking
tricking
unpicking
unsticking

IK-LI
academically
acoustically
acrobatically
aerobically
aerodynamically
aeronautically
aesthetically
alcoholically
algebraically
allegorically
alphabetically
altruistically
anaerobically
analytically
anarchically
anatomically
anesthetically

angelically
antiheroically
antiseptically
antithetically
apathetically
aphoristically
apically
apologetically
apoplectically
archaeologically
archaically
aristocratically
arithmetically
aromatically
artistically
ascetically
aseptically
asthmatically
astronautically
astronomically
asymmetrically
athletically
atomically
authentically
autocratically
automatically
axiomatically
bacteriologically
ballistically
barbarically
barometrically
basically
bibliographically
biochemically
biologically
biotically
bombastically
bureaucratically
calorically
cannibalistically

capitalistically
catalytically
categorically
caustically
cephalically
characteristically
chauvinistically
choreographically
chronically
chronologically
cinematically
civically
classically
communistically
conically
cosmetically
cosmically
critically
cryptically
cryptographically
cybernetically
cylindrically
cytologically
democratically
demographically
despotically
diabolically
diagnostically
diagrammatically
diametrically
didactically
dietetically
diplomatically
diuretically
domestically
dramatically
drastically
dynamically
eccentrically
ecclesiastically

eclectically
economically
ecstatically
egoistically
egotistically
elastically
electrically
electrolytically
electromagnetically
electronically
elliptically
empathetically
emphatically
empirically
energetically
enigmatically
enthusiastically
entomologically
epidemically
epigrammatically
episodically
erotically
erratically
esoterically
ethnically
etiologically
euphemistically
euphorically
evangelically
evangelistically
exoterically
exotically
extrinsically
fanatically
fantastically
fatalistically
fluoroscopically
forensically
formalistically
frantically

frenetically
futuristically
galvanically
gametically
gastronomically
genealogically
generically
genetically
geocentrically
geographically
geologically
geometrically
gigantically
gothically
graphically
gymnastically
gyroscopically
harmonically
hebraically
hectically
hedonically
heliocentrically
heliotropically
heretically
hermeneutically
hermetically
heroically
heterotrophically
heuristically
hierarchically
hieratically
histologically
historically
holistically
holographically
humanistically
hydraulically
hygienically
hyperbolically
hypercritically

hypnotically
hypocritically
hypodermically
hypothetically
hypotonically
hysterically
idealistically
identically
ideologically
idiomatically
idiosyncratically
idiotically
illogically
inartistically
inimically
inorganically
intrinsically
ironically
isometrically
isotonically
isotopically
journalistically
judgmatically
juristically
kaleidoscopically
kinaesthetically
kinematically
lackadaisically
laconically
legalistically
lethargically
lexically
linguistically
lithographically
liturgically
logically
logistically
lunatically
lymphatically
lyrically

magically
magnetically
majestically
manically
masochistically
materialistically
mathematically
mechanically
mechanistically
medically
melancholically
melodically
melodramatically
meristically
metabolically
metallically
metallurgically
metaphorically
meteorically
methodically
metrically
misanthropically
mnemonically
monastically
monochromatically
monopolistically
monosyllabically
moralistically
moronically
morphemically
morphologically
musically
myopically
mystically
mythologically
narcissistically
narcotically
nationalistically
nautically
neoclassically

nepotistically
neurologically
neurotically
nihilistically
nomadically
nonethically
nonpolitically
nonsensically
nontechnically
numerically
ontogenetically
operatically
optically
optimistically
oratorically
organically
orthographically
orthopedically
osmotically
pacifically
panoramically
parenthetically
pathetically
pathologically
patriotically
patronymically
pedagogically
pedantically
pederastically
periodically
pessimistically
petrologically
phallically
pharmaceutically
pharmacologically
phenotypically
phlegmatically
phonemically
phonetically
phonically

phonographically
phonologically
photochemically
photoelectrically
photogenically
photographically
photolytically
photosynthetically
phototactically
physically
physiologically
platonically
pneumatically
poetically
polemically
polygraphically
polyphonically
pontifically
pornographically
practically
pragmatically
prehistorically
prickly
prolifically
prophetically
prophylactically
prosaically
prosthetically
psychedelically
psychiatrically
psychically
psychoanalytically
psychodynamically
psychologically
psychometrically
psychopathically
psychophysically
psychosomatically
psychotherapeutically
psychotically

publicly
puritanically
quickly
quixotically
rabbinically
radically
radiographically
rationalistically
realistically
rhetorically
rheumatically
rhythmically
ritualistically
romantically
rustically
sadistically
sarcastically
sardonically
satanically
satirically
scenically
schematically
schismatically
scholastically
scientifically
seismically
semantically
seraphically
sickly
simplistically
skeptically
slickly
sophomorically
spastically
specifically
spermatically
spherically
sporadically
statically
statistically

stenographically
stoically
strategically
strictly
stroboscopically
stylistically
subclinically
supersonically
surgically
surrealistically
syllogistically
symbiotically
symbolically
symmetrically
sympathetically
synaptically
synergically
synergistically
synthetically
systematically
systemically
tactically
technically
technologically
telegraphically
telepathically
telephonically
telescopically
terminologically
terrifically
theatrically
theistically
thematically
theocratically
theologically
theoretically
theosophically
therapeutically
thermostatically
thickly

tonically
topically
topographically
topologically
toxically
tragically
traumatically
tropically
typically
typographically
tyrannically
ultrasonically
undemocratically
unidiomatically
unpoetically
unrealistically
unromantically
unscientifically
unspecifically
unsympathetically
vertically
volcanically
whimsically
xenically
zoologically
zygotically
zymotically

IK-LING

bicycling
pickling
prickling
sickling
tickling
trickling

IK-LISH

pricklish
ticklish

IK-LUR
bicycler
prickler
stickler
strickler
tickler

IK-NESS
airsickness
carsickness
chaoticness
heartsickness
homesickness
lovesickness
prolificness
quickness
seasickness
sickness
slickness
strictness
thickness
trainsickness

IK-NING
abandoning
apportioning
auctioning
auditioning
awakening
bargaining
battening
beckoning
betokening
blackening
blazoning
bludgeoning
brightening
broadening
burdening
burgeoning

captaining
captioning
casehardening
cautioning
chairmaning
chairmanning
championing
chastening
cheapening
chickening
christening
coarsening
commissioning
conditioning
cordoning
cottoning
counterconditioning
counteropening
crimsoning
cunning
curtaining
cushioning
dampening
darkening
deadening
deafening
deepening
determining
disburdening
disheartening
disillusioning
dunning
emblazoning
emboldening
enlightening
enlivening
envisioning
examining
fashioning
fastening

fattening
flattening
foretokening
freshening
frightening
functioning
gardening
garrisoning
gladdening
glistening
gunning
gunrunning
happening
hardening
harkening
harshening
hastening
hearkening
heartening
heightening
hoarsening
illumining
imagining
impassioning
imprisoning
jettisoning
ladening
leavening
lengthening
lessening
lightening
likening
listening
livening
loosening
maddening
malfunctioning
mentioning
moistening
motioning

occasioning
opening
orphaning
outbargaining
outgunning
outreasoning
outrunning
overburdening
pardoning
partitioning
pensioning
petitioning
pinioning
poisoning
portioning
positioning
preconditioning
predestining
predetermining
preexamining
proportioning
punning
questioning
quickening
rationing
rattening
ravening
reabandoning
reapportioning
reasoning
reawakening
rebuttoning
rechristening
reckoning
reconditioning
reddening
reenlightening
reexamining
refashioning
refastening

reopening
repositioning
requisitioning
rerunning
resharpening
ripening
rosining
roughening
ruining
rumrunning
running
saddening
sanctioning
seasoning
sectioning
sharpening
shortening
shunning
sickening
siphoning
slackening
smartening
softening
stationing
steepening
stiffening
straightening
straitening
strengthening
stunning
summoning
sunning
sweetening
syphoning
thickening
threatening
tightening
toughening
unburdening
unbuttoning

unfastening
unloosening
unquestioning
unreasoning
vacationing
visioning
wakening
wantoning
weakening
whitening
widening
worsening

Long I-KON
icon
Nikon

IK-SEN
Nixon
vixen

IK-SHUN
addiction
affliction
benediction
constriction
contradiction
conviction
crucifixion
depiction
dereliction
diction
eviction
fiction
friction
infliction
interdiction
jurisdiction
malediction
nonfiction

prediction
reconviction
reliction
restriction
transfixion
valediction

IK-SI
Dixie
nixie
nixy
pixie
pixy
pyxie
tricksy

IK-SING
admixing
affixing
fixing
intermixing
matrixing
mixing
nixing
prefixing
premixing
sixing
suffixing
transfixing
unfixing

IKS-TURE
admixture
fixture
intermixture
mixture

IK-SUR
affixer
elixir

fixer
mixer

IK-TED
addicted
afflicted
conflicted
constricted
contradicted
convicted
depicted
evicted
inflicted
interdicted
nonrestricted
predicted
restricted
unconstricted
unpredicted
unrestricted

IK-TING
addicting
afflicting
conflicting
constricting
contradicting
convicting
depicting
evicting
inflicting
interdicting
nonaddicting
nonconflicting
predicting
restricting

IK-TIVE
addictive
adjective

afflictive
conflictive
constrictive
contradictive
fictive
inflictive
interdictive
jurisdictive
maledictive
nonaddictive
nonrestrictive
predictive
restrictive
unrestrictive
vindictive

IK-TUR
constrictor
depicter
evictor
inflicter
inflictor
interdictor
predictor
richter
stricter
victor

Long I-KUR
biker
hiker
hitchhiker
piker
shunpiker
striker

IK-UR
bicker
bootlicker
clicker

dicker
dropkicker
flicker
frolicker
goldbricker
kicker
licker
liquor
mimicker
nicker
nitpicker
picker
picnicker
pigsticker
placekicker
pricker
quicker
sicker
slicker
snicker
sticker
thicker
ticker
trafficker
tricker
vicar
wicker

IK-URZ
bickers
clickers
dickers
flickers
frolickers
goldbrickers
kickers
knickers
lickers
liquors
mimickers

nickers
nitpickers
pickers
picnickers
slickers
snickers
stickers
tickers
traffickers
trickers
vicars

IL-A
cedilla
chinchilla
flotilla
Godzilla
gorilla
guerilla
manila
manilla
maxilla
sabadilla
sarsaparilla
scilla
scintilla
spirilla
vanilla
villa

IL-AN
ampicillin
penicillin
vanillin
villain

Long I-LAND
highland
island

Long I-LDEST
mildest
wildest

IL-DING
bodybuilding
building
gilding
homebuilding
outbuilding
rebuilding
shipbuilding
unyielding

Long I-LDLI
mildly
wildly

Long I-LDLIKE
childlike
wildlike

Long I-LDNESS
mildness
wildness

Long I-LDUR
milder
wilder

IL-DUR
bewilder
bodybuilder
builder
gilder
guilder
shipbuilder

IL-EST
realest

shrillest
stillest

Long I-LET
autopilot
copilot
eyelet
islet
Pilate
pilot
stylet

IL-ET
billet
distillate
fillet
millet
skillet

Long I-LFUL
guileful
wileful

IL-FUL
skilful
skillful
unskillful
wilful
willful

Long I-LEE
drily
dryly
highly
shyly
slyly
spryly
strobili
wily
wryly

IL-I
billy
chili
chilly
dilly
filly
frilly
hillbilly
hilly
lily
piccalilli
shrilly
silly
stilly
willy-nilly

IL-IJ
millage
pillage
spillage
tillage
village

IL-IK
acrylic
cacodylic
cyrillic
dactylic
halophilic
idyllic
imbecilic
lipophilic
necrophilic
pedophilic
photophilic

Long I-LIN
byline
skyline

Long I-LING
beguiling
compiling
defiling
dialing
dialling
exiling
filing
hairstyling
misfiling
piling
profiling
reconciling
refiling
reviling
riling
smiling
stockpiling
styling
tiling
unpiling
unsmiling
whiling
wiling

IL-ING
billing
chilling
distilling
drilling
filling
fulfilling
grilling
instilling
killing
milling
overfilling
painkilling
prechilling
refilling

schilling
shilling
shrilling
spilling
stilling
swilling
thrilling
tilling
trilling
unwilling
winterkilling

Long I-LITE
highlight
skylight
twilight

IL-IZ
Achilles
Antilles
chilies
dillies
fillies
hillbillies
lilies
willies

IL-KI
milky
silky

IL-KING
bilking
milking

Long I-LLESS
guileless
smileless
styleless
wileless

Long I-LMENT
beguilement
defilement
reconcilement
revilement

IL-MENT
fulfillment
nonfulfillment
unfulfillment

IL-NESS
chillness
illness
shrillness
stillness

Long I-LO
high-low
silo

IL-O
armadillo
billow
cigarillo
kilo
pillow
willow

IL-TED
jilted
quilted
silted
stilted
tilted
wilted

IL-TI
guilty
silty

unguilty

IL-TING
jilting
quilting
silting
tilting
wilting

IL-TUR
filter
jilter
kilter
philter
philtre
quilter
refilter

I-LUM
asylum
phylum
subphylum
xylem

Long I-LUR
beguiler
defiler
filer
miler
reconciler
stockpiler
styler
tiler
viler

IL-UR
biller
caterpillar
chiller
distiller

driller
filler
fulfiller
griller
killer
miller
painkiller
pillar
rototiller
shriller
spiller
stiller
swiller
thriller
tiller

IL-YUN
billion
Brazilian
centillion
civilian
cotillion
million
multimillion
pavilion
pillion
postilion
quadrillion
quintillion
reptilian
sicilian
trillion
vaudevillian
vermilion
vermillion
zillion

IL-YUNT
brilliant
resilient

IL-YUNTH
billionth
millionth
quadrillionth
quintillionth
trillionth
zillionth

Long I-MAN
hymen
limen
pieman
Simon

Long I-MAT
acclimate
climate
primate

IM-BAL
cymbal
nimble
symbol
thimble
timbale
wimble

IM-BO
akimbo
bimbo
limbo

IM-BUR
limber
timber
timbre
unlimber

IM-EN
alderwomen

assemblywomen
batwomen
bondwomen
businesswomen
chairwomen
churchwomen
clanswomen
clergywomen
committeewomen
congresswomen
councilwomen
countrywomen
englishwomen
frenchwomen
gentlewomen
herdswomen
horsewomen
irishwomen
jurywomen
madwomen
mailwomen
markswomen
newswomen
noblewomen
oysterwomen
patrolwomen
persimmon
policewomen
spacewomen
spokeswomen
sportswomen
stateswomen
townswomen
tribeswomen
welshwomen
women
workingwomen
workwomen
yachtswomen

IM-EST
dimmest
grimaced
grimmest
pantomimist
primmest
slimmest
trimmest

Long I-MEY
grimy
limey
limy
rhymy
rimy
slimy
stymie

IM-I
gimme
Jimmy
shimmy

IM-IJ
afterimage
image
scrimmage
self-image

IM-IK
acronymic
bulimic
gimmick
homonymic
matronymic
mimic
pantomimic
patronymic

Long I-MING
chiming
climbing
miming
mistiming
pantomiming
priming
rhyming
timing

IM-ING
bedimming
brimming
outswimming
rimming
skimming
slimming
swimming
trimming

IM-IT
delimit
limit
prelimit

Long I-MLESS
chimelss
crimeless
grimeless
rhymeless
rimeless
slimeless
timeless

IM-LESS
brimless
limbless
rimless

Long I-MLI
sublimely
timely
untimely

IM-LI
dimly
grimly
primly
slimly
trimly

IM-NESS
dimness
grimness
primness
slimness
trimness

I-MON
hymen
limen
Simon

IM-PI
gimpy
limpy
scrimpy
skimpy
wimpy

IM-PING
crimping
limping
pimping
primping
scrimping
shrimping
skimping

IM-PL
dimple
oversimple
pimple
simple
wimple

IM-PLI
dimply
limply
pimply
simply

IM-PLING
dimpling
pimpling
wimpling

IM-PUR
crimper
limper
scrimper
shrimper
simper
skimper
whimper

Long IM-STUR
mimester
rhymester

Long I-MUR
chimer
climber
mimer
phototimer
primer
rhymer
timer

IM-UR
brimmer
dimmer
glimmer
grimmer
primer
primmer
shimmer
simmer
skimmer
slimmer
swimmer
trimmer

IM-ZI
flimsy
slimsy
whimsy

Long I-NA
angina
Carolina
China
Indochina
myna
pseudoangina
trichina
vagina

Long I-NAL
anginal
final
matutinal
quarterfinal
semifinal
supraspinal
vaginal

IN-CHING
cinching

clinching
flinching
inching
lynching
pinching
unflinching
winching

IN-CHUR
clincher
flincher
lyncher
pincher

Long I-NDED
absentminded
blinded
broad-minded
civic-minded
fair-minded
feebleminded
high-minded
masterminded
minded
narrow-minded
open-minded
reminded
simpleminded
social-minded
strong-minded
tender-minded
tough-minded
weak-minded
winded

IN-DED
absconded
broken-winded
long-winded
rescinded

winded

Long I-NDEST
blindest
kindest

IN-DI
Hindi
Lindy
windy

Long I-NDING
binding
blinding
bookbinding
faultfinding
finding
grinding
masterminding
minding
pathfinding
rebinding
reminding
rewinding
self-winding
spellbinding
unbinding
unwinding
winding

IN-DL
brindle
dwindle
enkindle
kindle
rekindle
spindle
swindle

Long I-NDLI
blindly
kindly
unkindly

IND-LING
dwindling
kindling
swindling

IND-LUR
dwindler
kindler
swindler

Long I-NDNESS
blindness
kindness
purblindness
unkindness

Long I-NDUR
binder
blinder
bookbinder
faultfinder
finder
grinder
highbinder
hinder
kinder
pathfinder
reminder
sidewinder
spellbinder
viewfinder

IN-DUR
cinder
flinder

hinder
Pindar
pinder
rescinder
tinder

Long I-NESS
Aquinas
dryness
highness
minus
shyness
sinus
slyness
spinous
spryness
trichinous
vinous
wryness

Long I-NEST
benignest
divinest
finest
malignest
supinest

IN-ET
linnet
minute
spinet

IN-FUL
sinful
unsinful

ING-GL
commingle
dingle
intermingle

jingle
mingle
shingle
single
surcingle
tingle

ING-GLI
jingly
shingly
singly
tingly

ING-GLING
commingling
intermingling
jingling
mingling
shingling
singling
tingling

ING-GLUR
intermingler
jingler
mingler
shingler
tingler

ING-GO
bingo
dingo
flamingo
gringo
jingo
lingo

ING-GUR
finger
forefinger

ladyfinger
linger
malinger

ING-I
clingy
dinghy
dingy
springy
stingy
stringy
swingy
zingy

ING-ING
bringing
clinging
flinging
gunslinging
hamstringing
mudslinging
pinging
ringing
singing
slinging
springing
stinging
stringing
swinging
upbringing
winging
wringing
zinging

ING-KI
blinky
dinghy
dinkey
dinky
Helsinki

inky
kinky
pinkie
pinky
slinky
stinky
winky

ING-KIDE
blink-eyed
pink-eyed

ING-KING
bethinking
blinking
chinking
clinking
countersinking
drinking
finking
freethinking
hoodwinking
inking
kinking
linking
nonthinking
overdrinking
pinking
prinking
rethinking
shrinking
sinking
slinking
stinking
syncing
thinking
unblinking
unthinking
winking
zincking

ING-KL
besprinkle
crinkle
sprinkle
tinkle
twinkle
unwrinkle
winkle
wrinkle

ING-KLI
crinkly
pinkly
tinkly
twinkly
wrinkly

ING-KLING
besprinkling
crinkling
inkling
sprinkling
tinkling
twinkling
wrinkling

ING-KLUR
sprinkler
tinkler
twinkler
wrinkler

ING-KSHUN
contradistinction
distinction
extinction
subdistinction

ING-KTIVE
contradistinctive

distinctive
instinctive

ING-KTNESS
distinctness
indistinctness
succinctness

ING-KUR
blinker
drinker
pinker
thinker

ING-LESS
kingless
meaningless
ringless
stringless
wingless

ING-LET
kinglet
ringlet
springlet
winglet

ING-LIKE
flinglike
kinglike
ringlike
springlike
stinglike
winglike

ING-TIME
ring time
springtime
swing time

ING-UR
bringer
clinger
flinger
gunslinger
humdinger
mudslinger
ringer
singer
stinger
stringer
swinger
winger
wringer

Long I-NI
assignee
briny
piney
shiny
signee
spiney
tiny
viney
whiney
winy

IN-I
finny
Guinea
ignominy
jinni
mini
Minnie
ninny
pickaninny
shinney
shinny
skinny
tinny

whinny

IN-IK
clinic
cynic
finnic
hologynic
misogynic
myelinic
nicotinic
olefinic
policlinic
polyclinic
rabbinic

Long I-NING
aligning
assigning
combining
confining
consigning
countersigning
declining
defining
designing
dining
divining
enshrining
entwining
fining
headlining
inclining
intertwining
lining
mainlining
maligning
mining
misdefining
moonshining
nonconfining

opining
outlining
outshining
pining
preassigning
predefining
realigning
reassigning
reclining
recombining
redefining
redesigning
redlining
refining
repining
resigning
shining
signing
streamlining
underlining
undermining
whining
wining

IN-ING
beginning
breadwinning
chagrining
chagrinning
chinning
dinning
disciplining
finning
ginning
grinning
pinning
prizewinning
shinning
sinning
skinning

spinning
thinning
tinning
twinning
underpinning
unpinning
winning

IN-ISH
bumpkinish
diminish
finish
Finnish
refinish

IN-JENT
astringent
constringent
contingent
stringent

IN-JEZ
binges
cringes
hinges
impinges
infringes
oranges
singes
syringes
tinges
twinges

IN-JI
cringy
dingy
stingy
twingy

IN-JING
cringing
fringing
hinging
impinging
infringing
scavenging
singeing
syringing
tingeing
twingeing
twinging
unhinging

INJ-MENT
impingement
infringement
unhingement

IN-JUR
cringer
fringer
ginger
infringer
injure

Long I-NKLAD
pine-clad
vine-clad

IN-LESS
chinless
kinless
sinless
skinless
windlass
winless

Long I-NLI
asininely

benignly
divinely
finely
supinely

Long I-NMENT
alignment
assignment
confinement
consignment
definement
designment
enshrinement
intertwinement
misalignment
nonalignment
overrefinement
realignment
reassignment
refinement

Long I-NO
albino
rhino
wino

IN-O
minnow
winnow

IN-SING
convincing
evincing
mincing
rinsing
unconvincing
wincing

INT-ED
blueprinted

glinted
hinted
imprinted
minted
misprinted
overprinted
printed
reprinted
splinted
sprinted
squinted
stinted
tinted
unstinted

IN-TI
flinty
linty
minty
squinty

INT-ING
blueprinting
fingerprinting
glinting
hinting
imprinting
minting
misprinting
overprinting
printing
reprinting
splinting
sprinting
squinting
stinting
tinting
unstinting

IN-TRI
splintrey
wintery
wintry

IN-TUR
hinter
imprinter
inter
midwinter
minter
printer
reinter
reprinter
splinter
sprinter
squinter
stinter
teleprinter
tinter
winter

IN-U
continue
discontinue
sinew

Long I-NUR
airliner
assigner
assignor
consignor
cosigner
decliner
definer
designer
diner
diviner
eyeliner
finer

forty-niner
headliner
incliner
jetliner
liner
mainliner
miner
moonshiner
one-liner
opiner
party-liner
recliner
refiner
repiner
resigner
shiner
shriner
sideliner
signer
streamliner
twiner
underminer

IN-UR
beginner
Berliner
breadwinner
dinner
discipliner
grinner
inner
pinner
prizewinner
sinner
skinner
spinner
thinner
winner

Long I-NUS
Aquinas
dryness
highness
minus
shyness
sinus
slyness
spinous
spryness
trichinous
vinous
wryness

IN-YUN
dominion
minion
opinion
pinion
pinon

Long I-ON
Brian
dandelion
Hawaiian
ion
lion
lyon
Mayan
Orion
scion
Zion

Long I-OR
acidifier
amplifier
applier
beautifier
briar
brier

buyer
certifier
clarifier
classifier
crier
dehumidifier
denier
detoxifier
drier
dryer
dyer
edifier
electrifier
emulsifier
eyer
falsifier
fire
flier
flyer
fortifier
friar
fryer
glorifier
higher
hire
humidifier
identifier
indemnifier
inquire
intensifier
justifier
liar
liquefier
magnifier
misapplier
modifier
mollifier
multiplier
mystifier
nigher

notifier
nullifier
occupier
pacifier
personifier
plier
preamplifier
prier
prior
prophesier
purifier
pyre
qualifier
ratifier
rectifier
replier
sanctifier
saponifier
satisfier
shier
shyer
sigher
signifier
simplifier
slier
slyer
sprier
spryer
supplier
sweetbrier
terrifier
testifier
trier
typifier
umpire
underlier
unifier
verifier
versifier
vilifier

vivifier

Long I-OT
diet
disquiet
quiet
riot
striate
unquiet

Long I-PEND
ripened
underripened
unripened

Long I-PEST
ripest
typist

IP-ET
snippet
tippet
whippet

IP-I
chippy
dippy
drippy
grippy
hippie
lippy
nippy
sippy
snippy
tippee
xanthippe
yippee
yippie
zippy

IP-IN
Nippon
pippin

Long I-PING
griping
hyping
mistyping
piping
retyping
sideswiping
sniping
stereotyping
striping
swiping
typing
wiping

IP-ING
blipping
chipping
clipping
dipping
dripping
equipping
flipping
gripping
gypping
horsewhipping
nipping
outstripping
quipping
ripping
shipping
sideslipping
sipping
skipping
slipping
snipping
stripping

tipping
tripping
unzipping
weatherstripping
whipping
yipping
zipping

IP-L
cripple
grippal
nipple
participle
ripple
stipple
tipple
triple

IP-LET
ripplet
triplet

IP-LI
fliply
ripply
triply

IP-LING
crippling
rippling
stippling
stripling
tippling
tripling

IP-LUR
crippler
tippler

IP-MENT
equipment
shipment

IP-SHUN
ascription
circumscription
conniption
conscription
description
egyptian
inscription
manuscription
oversubscription
prescription
proscription
subscription
superscription
transcription

IP-SI
dipsy
gipsy
gypsy
Poughkeepsie
tipsy

IP-TIK
apocalyptic
cryptic
ecliptic
elliptic
styptic
triptych

IP-TIVE
ascriptive
descriptive
nondescriptive
prescriptive

Long I-PUR
bagpiper
griper
hyper
riper
sideswiper
stereotyper
striper

IP-UR
chipper
clipper
dipper
double-dipper
dripper
flipper
gripper
hipper
kipper
nipper
ripper
shipper
sipper
skinny-dipper
skipper
slipper
snipper
stripper
tipper
tripper
whipper
zipper

IR-AH
hurrah
sirrah

I-RANT
arch-tyrant
aspirant

tyrant

Long I-RATE
circumgyrate
gyrate
irate
lyrate

IR-EL
conferral
deferral
demurral
doggerel
purl
referral
scurrile
sectoral
squirrel
transferal
transferal

Long I-REME
bireme
trireme

I-RI
accessory
adultery
advisory
alimentary
anniversary
antislavery
archery
armory
artery
artillery
augury
auxiliary
bakery
battery

beanery
beggary
benedictory
beneficiary
bewitchery
bicentenary
bindery
blistery
blubbery
blustery
boilary
bootery
boundary
bowery
brasserie
bravery
brewery
bribery
briery
buffoonery
buggery
burglary
buttery
cajolery
calgary
calorie
calory
calvary
camaraderie
camporee
cannery
cattery
celery
century
chancellery
chancellory
chandlery
cheatery
chicanery

cindery
clattery
complementary
complimentary
compulsory
comradery
conferee
connivery
contradictory
cookery
coppery
coterie
creamery
crockery
crookery
cursory
cutlery
daiquiri
deanery
debauchery
delivery
delusory
demagoguery
derisory
diary
directory
discovery
dispensary
dissatisfactory
distillery
documentary
doddery
doggery
drapery
drudgery
dungaree
eatery
electrosurgery
elementary
embracery

embroidery
emery
enquiry
equerry
every
exemplary
extrasensory
factory
fakery
feathery
fieri
fiery
finery
fishery
flattery
floury
flowery
fluttery
foolery
foppery
forgery
friary
frippery
gallery
gaucherie
gendarmerie
gimcrackery
gingery
glittery
glossary
granary
greenery
Gregory
grocery
gunnery
haberdashery
hatchery
heathery
hickory
Hillary

history
honoree
hosiery
housewifery
hungary
illusory
infirmary
injury
inquiry
intercessory
interdictory
interjectory
introductory
ivory
jamboree
japery
jittery
jobbery
judiciary
knavery
lampoonery
lathery
leathery
lechery
levorotary
littery
livery
lottery
luxury
machinery
maledictory
mammary
manufactory
martyry
mastery
memory
menagerie
mercury
microsurgery
midwifery

misery
mockery
Montgomery
multisensory
mummery
mystery
napery
notary
nunnery
nursery
offeree
olfactory
orangery
ornery
ovary
oystery
papery
parliamentary
peccary
penitentiary
penury
peppery
peremptory
perfumery
perfunctory
periphery
perjury
pessary
pettifoggery
phylactery
piggery
pillory
pinery
piscary
plastery
pledgery
plenary
possessory
pottery
powdery

precursory
preemptory
prehistory
priggery
prudery
psychoquackery
psychosurgery
quackery
quandary
quavery
quivery
recovery
rectory
redemptory
rediscovery
referee
refinery
refractory
rescissory
reverie
revery
robbery
rockery
roguery
rookery
rosary
rotary
rotisserie
rubbery
rudimentary
salary
salisbury
satisfactory
savory
savoury
scenery
sculduggery
scullduggery
scullery
scurry

secretory
sectary
sedimentary
self-flattery
sensory
shimmery
shivaree
shivery
showery
shrubbery
silvery
skulduggery
skullduggery
slavery
slippery
slithery
slobbery
smeltery
smothery
snobbery
soldiery
sorcery
spermary
spidery
spivery
spivvery
splintery
stannary
stitchery
strangury
sublunary
subtreasury
sugary
summary
summery
supervisory
supplementary
surgery
surrenderee
surrey

suspensory
tannery
ternary
thievery
thuggery
toggery
tomfoolery
tottery
towery
tracery
trajectory
treachery
treasury
trickery
trumpery
turbary
twittery
unsatisfactory
unsavory
upholstery
usury
vagary
valedictory
venery
victory
vinegary
votary
waggery
watery
whiggery
winery
wintery
wiry
witchery
zonary

IR-IK
atmospheric
blastospheric
chromospheric

empiric
exospheric
hemispheric
hydrospheric
ionospheric
lyric
photospheric
pyrrhic
satiric
stratospheric
xeric

Long I-RING
acquiring
admiring
aspiring
attiring
backfiring
bemiring
conspiring
desiring
enquiring
firing
hiring
inquiring
inspiring
miring
misfiring
overtiring
perspiring
reacquiring
refiring
rehiring
requiring
retiring
retrofiring
rewiring
siring
squiring
tiring

transpiring
umpiring
unaspiring
uninspiring
untiring
wiring

Long I-RNESS
direness
entireness

Long I-RO
autogiro
Cairo
gyro
tyro

Long I-RODE
byroad
highroad

Long I-RON
andiron
flatiron
gridiron
iron
radioiron
sadiron

IR-UP
chirrup
stirrup
syrup

Long I-RUR
desirer
direr
enquirer
hirer
inquirer

inspirer
wirer

Long I-RUS
Cyrus
desirous
iris
papyrus
poliovirus
poxvirus
virus

Long I-RWURKS
fireworks
wire works

Long IS-EST
concisest
nicest
precisesest

IS-EZ
abysses
benefices
dismisses
edifices
hisses
kisses
mantissas
misses
Mrs.
pisses
precipices
prejudices
reminisces
treatises

ISH-AL
artificial
beneficial

extrajudicial
initial
judicial
nonprejudicial
official
orificial
prejudicial
sacrificial
semiofficial
solstitial
superficial
unjudicial
unofficial

ISH-ENSE
omniscience
proficience

ISH-ENT
coefficient
deficient
efficient
inefficient
insufficient
omniscient
proficient
sufficient

ISH-FUL
dishful
wishful

ISH-I
fishy
garnishee
rubbishy
squishy
swishy
wishy

ISH-ING
abolishing
admonishing
anguishing
astonishing
banishing
blandishing
blemishing
brandishing
burnishing
cherishing
demolishing
diminishing
dishing
distinguishing
embellishing
establishing
extinguishing
famishing
finishing
fishing
flourishing
furbishing
furnishing
garnishing
impoverishing
languishing
lavishing
nourishing
overembellishing
overfurnishing
perishing
polishing
preestablishing
publishing
punishing
ravishing
reestablishing
refinishing
refurbishing

refurnishing
relinquishing
relishing
replenishing
republishing
revarnishing
skirmishing
swishing
tarnishing
vanishing
vanquishing
varnishing
wishing

ISH-UN
abolition
academician
admission
admonition
ambition
ammunition
attrition
audition
beautician
biometrician
bipartition
clinician
coalition
cognition
commission
competition
condition
contrition
cosmetician
cybernetician
decondition
definition
demolition
diagnostician
dietician

dietitian
edition
electrician
emission
erudition
exhibition
expedition
extradition
fission
geometrician
geriatrician
inhibition
intermission
intuition
malnutrition
mathematician
mission
monition
mortician
nonrecognition
nutrition
obstetrician
omission
optician
overnutrition
partition
pediatrician
perdition
permission
petition
phonetician
physician
politician
precognition
precondition
premonition
premunition
preposition
prohibition
readmission

recognition
recondition
redefinition
remission
rendition
repetition
requisition
resubmission
rhetorician
sedition
statistician
subcommission
subdefinition
submission
superstition
supposition
suspicion
tactician
technician
theoretician
tradition
transition
transmission
transposition
tuition
vendition
volition

ISH-UR
abolisher
accomplisher
admonisher
banisher
blandisher
brandisher
burnisher
cherisher
demolisher
embellisher
establisher

extinguisher
finisher
fisher
fissure
furnisher
impoverisher
kingfisher
languisher
lavisher
nourisher
polisher
publisher
ravisher
relinquisher
replenisher
republisher
skirmisher
vanisher
vanquisher
wisher

ISH-US
ambitious
auspicious
avaricious
delicious
expeditious
fictitious
inauspicious
injudicious
judicious
lubricous
malicious
meretricious
nutritious
officious
overambitious
oversuspicious
pernicious
propitious

repetitious
seditious
siliceous
silicious
superstitious
surreptitious
suspicious
unambitious
unauspicious
unjudicious
unofficious
unpropitious
unsuspicious
vicious

Long I-SI
dicey
icy
spicy

IS-I
hissy
missy
narcissi
prissy
sissy

IS-UL
bristle
dismissal
epistle
gristle
missal
missile
thistle
whistle

Long I-SING
deicing
dicing

enticing
icing
lysing
overpricing
pricing
sacrificing
slicing
spicing
splicing
sufficing

IS-ING
dismissing
hissing
kissing
missing
relinquishing
reminiscing

Long I-SIS
crises
crisis
Isis
lysis
nisus

IS-IT
elicit
explicit
implicit
licit
overexplicit
solicit
unexplicit

Long I-SIV
decisive
derisive
devisive
incisive

indecisive

IS-IVE
admissive
commissive
divisive
emissive
missive
permissive
submissive
transmissive
unpermissive
unsubmissive

ISK-ET
biscuit
brisket

IS-KI
frisky
risky
whiskey
whisky

IS-KING
frisking
risking
whisking

IS-KO
Cisco
disco
francisco
frisco

IS-KUR
bewhisker
brisker
frisker
risker

whisker

IS-KUS
discus
discuss
hibiscus
meniscus
viscous
viscus

IS-L
bristle
dismissal
epistle
gristle
missal
missel
missile
thistle
whistle

Long I-SLESS
diceless
iceless
priceless
spiceless
spliceless
viceless

Long I-SLI
concisely
imprecisely
nicely
precisely

IS-LI
bristly
gristly
thistly

IS-LING
brisling
bristling
whistling

IS-MUS
Christmas
isthmus

IS-N
christen
glisten
listen
rechristen

Long I-SNESS
conciseness
impreciseness
niceness
preciseness

IS-NING
abandoning
apportioning
auctioning
auditioning
awakening
bargaining
battening
beckoning
betokening
blackening
blazoning
bludgeoning
brightening
broadening
burdening
burgeoning
captaining
captioning

casehardening
cautioning
chairmaning
chairmanning
championing
chastening
cheapening
chickening
christening
coarsening
commissioning
conditioning
cordoning
cottoning
counterconditioning
counteropening
crimsoning
cunning
curtaining
cushioning
dampening
darkening
deadening
deafening
deepening
determining
disburdening
disheartening
disillusioning
dunning
emblazoning
emboldening
enlightening
enlivening
envisioning
examining
fashioning
fastening
fattening
flattening

foretokening
freshening
frightening
functioning
gardening
garrisoning
gladdening
glistening
gunning
gunrunning
happening
hardening
harkening
harshening
hastening
hearkening
heartening
heightening
hoarsening
illumining
imagining
impassioning
imprisoning
jettisoning
ladening
leavening
lengthening
lessening
lightening
likening
listening
livening
loosening
maddening
malfunctioning
mentioning
moistening
motioning
occasioning
opening

orphaning
outbargaining
outgunning
outreasoning
outrunning
overburdening
pardoning
partitioning
pensioning
petitioning
pinioning
poisoning
portioning
positioning
preconditioning
predestining
predetermining
preexamining
proportioning
punning
questioning
quickening
rationing
rattening
ravening
reabandoning
reapportioning
reasoning
reawakening
rebuttoning
rechristening
reckoning
reconditioning
reddening
reenlightening
reexamining
refashioning
refastening
reopening
repositioning

requisitioning
rerunning
resharpening
ripening
rosining
roughening
ruining
rumrunning
running
saddening
sanctioning
seasoning
sectioning
sharpening
shortening
shunning
sickening
siphoning
slackening
smartening
softening
stationing
steepening
stiffening
straightening
straitening
strengthening
stunning
summoning
sunning
sweetening
syphoning
thickening
threatening
tightening
toughening
unburdening
unbuttoning
unfastening
unloosening

unquestioning
unreasoning
vacationing
visioning
wakening
wantoning
weakening
whitening
widening
worsening

IS-PING
crisping
lisping

ISP-UR
crisper
lisper
whisper

IST-AL
Bristol
crystal
distal
pistil
pistol

IS-TANSE
assistance
coexistence
consistence
desistance
distance
equidistance
existence
inconsistence
insistence
nonexistence
outdistance
overinsistence

persistence
preexistence
resistance
subsistence

IS-TANT
assistant
coexistent
consistent
distant
equidistant
existent
inconsistent
insistent
nonexistent
overinsistent
persistent
preexistent
resistant
resistent
unresistant

IST-ED
assisted
blacklisted
closefisted
coexisted
consisted
desisted
enlisted
existed
hardfisted
insisted
ironfisted
listed
misted
persisted
preexisted
reenlisted
resisted

subsisted
tightfisted
twisted
unassisted
unlisted
untwisted
vistaed

IST-EM
ecosystem
filesystem
subsystem
system

IST-I
Christie
enlistee
misty
twisty

IS-TIK
absolutistic
activistic
altruistic
anachronistic
anarchistic
animalistic
animistic
anomalistic
antagonistic
aphoristic
archaistic
artistic
atheistic
atomistic
autistic
ballistic
behavioristic
belletristic

bigamistic
bolshevistic
cabalistic
calvinistic
cameralistic
cannibalistic
canonistic
capitalistic
characteristic
chauvinistic
communistic
contortionistic
criminalistic
cubistic
cystic
deistic
deterministic
dualistic
dynamistic
egoistic
egotistic
emotionalistic
eucharistic
eulogistic
euphemistic
evangelistic
expressionistic
fascistic
fatalistic
feministic
feudalistic
formalistic
functionalistic
futuristic
hedonistic
hellenistic
heuristic
holistic
humanistic
humoristic

idealistic
imperialistic
impressionistic
inartistic
individualistic
jingoistic
journalistic
juristic
legalistic
linguistic
logistic
masochistic
materialistic
mechanistic
melanistic
mentalistic
meristic
methodistic
militaristic
misogynistic
modernistic
monarchistic
monistic
monogamistic
monopolistic
monotheistic
moralistic
mystic
narcissistic
nationalistic
naturalistic
negativistic
nepotistic
neutralistic
nihilistic
nonrealistic
novelistic
onanistic
opportunistic
optimistic

overidealistic
overpessimistic
pacifistic
pantheistic
paternalistic
pessimistic
plagiaristic
pluralistic
polytheistic
pseudoartistic
pugilistic
puristic
racialistic
rationalistic
realistic
relativistic
revivalistic
ritualistic
romanistic
sadistic
scientistic
shintoistic
simplistic
socialistic
solipsistic
somnambulistic
sophistic
spiritualistic
statistic
stylistic
surrealistic
syllogistic
synergistic
terroristic
theistic
totalistic
totemistic
traditionalistic
unartistic
unionistic

unrealistic
vandalistic
voyeuristic
wholistic

IST-INE
Christine
cystine
pristine
Sistine

IST-ING
assisting
blacklisting
coexisting
consisting
desisting
enlisting
existing
insisting
listing
misting
nonexisting
persisting
preexisting
reenlisting
resisting
subsisting
twisting
unassisting
unresisting
untwisting

IST-UR
assister
assistor
blister
enlister
glister
insister

lister
mister
Mr.
persister
resister
resistor
sister
stepsister
transistor
twister

IS-U
issue
reissue
tissue

Long I-SUR
deicer
dicer
icer
nicer
sacrificer
slicer
splicer

Long I-TAL
entitle
mistitle
recital
requital
subtitle
title
vital

IT-AN
backbitten
bitten
Britain
Briton
frostbitten

ghostwritten
handwritten
kitten
mitten
overwritten
rewritten
smitten
typewritten
underwritten
unwritten
written

IT-ANSE
acquittance
admittance
intermittence
omittance
pittance
quittance
readmittance
remittance
submittance
transmittance

Long I-TED
alighted
benighted
blighted
cited
copyrighted
delighted
dynamited
excited
expedited
extradited
farsighted
floodlighted
foresighted
highlighted
ignited

incited
indicted
indited
invited
kited
knighted
lighted
longsighted
moonlighted
nearsighted
overexcited
plighted
proselyted
recited
reignited
requited
reunited
righted
sharpsighted
shortsighted
sighted
slighted
spited
unexcited
uninvited
united
unlighted
unrequited
unsighted
whited

IT-ED
acquitted
admitted
befitted
benefited
benefitted
committed
counterfeited
dimwitted

emitted
fitted
flitted
gritted
half-witted
intermitted
it'd
knitted
omitted
outfitted
outwitted
permitted
pitted
quick-witted
readmitted
recommitted
refitted
remitted
resubmitted
sharp-witted
slitted
slow-witted
spitted
submitted
thick-witted
transmitted
twitted
unaccredited
uncommitted
unfitted
unpermitted
unremitted
witted

Long I-TEN
brighten
enlighten
frighten
heighten
lighten

reenlighten
tighten
titan
whiten

IT-EN
backbitten
bitten
Britain
Briton
frostbitten
ghostwritten
handwritten
kitten
mitten
overwritten
rewritten
smitten
typewritten
underwritten
unwritten
written

Long I-TEST
brightest
lightest
politest
rightist
slightest
tightest
tritest
whitest

Long I-TFUL
delightful
despiteful
frightful
insightful
rightful
spiteful

Long I-THEST
blithest
lithest

ITH-I
pithy
prithee
smithy

Long I-THING
kithing
tithing
trithing
writhing

ITH-M
algorithm
biorhythm
logarithm
rhythm

Long I-THNESS
blitheness
litheness

Long I-THUR
blither
either
lither
neither
tither
writher

ITH-UR
come-hither
dither
hither
slither
whither
wither

zither

Long I-TI
almighty
Aphrodite
Blighty
flighty
mighty
nightie
nighty
whitey

IT-I
bitty
city
committee
ditty
gritty
intercity
intracity
itty-bitty
kitty
nitty
nitty-gritty
permittee
pity
pretty
remittee
self-pity
subcommittee
witty

IT-IDE
pitied
prettied
unpitied

IT-IK
analytic
anthracitic

arthritic
calcitic
catalytic
critic
dendritic
diacritic
dialytic
electrolytic
encephalitic
enclitic
epicritic
eremitic
graphitic
hermaphroditic
hypocritic
limonitic
lytic
mephitic
meteoritic
nephritic
paralytic
parasitic
pegmatitic
phagocytic
photolytic
psychoanalytic
semitic
sinitic
sodomitic
spondylitic
sulfitic
sybaritic
synclitic
syphilitic
ugaritic

Long I-TING
alighting
backbiting
biting

blighting
bullfighting
citing
cock-fighting
cockfighting
copyrighting
delighting
dynamiting
exciting
expediting
extraditing
fighting
floodlighting
frostbiting
ghostwriting
handwriting
highlighting
igniting
inciting
indicting
inditing
infighting
inviting
kiting
knighting
lighting
moonlighting
newswriting
outfighting
overexciting
overwriting
plighting
prizefighting
proselyting
reciting
reigniting
requiting
reuniting
rewriting
righting

sighting
skywriting
slighting
smiting
spiting
sportswriting
typewriting
underwriting
unexciting
uninviting
uniting
writing

IT-ING
acquitting
admitting
befitting
benefiting
benefitting
closefitting
committing
counterfeiting
earsplitting
emitting
fence-sitting
fitting
flitting
formfitting
gritting
hairsplitting
hard-hitting
hitting
housesitting
intermitting
knitting
omitting
outfitting
outhitting
outwitting
permitting

pitting
quitting
readmitting
recommitting
refitting
remitting
resubmitting
sidesplitting
sitting
slitting
spitting
splitting
submitting
transmitting
twitting
unbefitting
unfitting
unremitting
unwitting
witting

Long I-TIS
appendicitis
barotitis
bronchiolitis
bronchitis
bursitis
colitis
conjunctivitis
corditis
dermatitis
diverticulitis
encephalitis
enteritis
gastritis
gingivitis
hepatitis
laryngitis
mastitis
meningitis

myelitis
myocarditis
myositis
nephritis
osteitis
otitis
pancreatitis
peritonitis
phlebitis
pleuritis
sinusitis
situs
spondylitis
synovitis
tendinitis
tendonitis
tinnitus
tonsillitis
vaginitis

IT-ISH
British
skittish

IT-L
acquittal
belittle
brittle
committal
embrittle
hospital
it'll
kittle
lickspittle
little
noncommittal
recommittal
remittal
skittle
spital

spittle
submittal
tittle
transmittal
victual
whittle

Long I-TLESS
fightless
flightless
frightless
mightless
sightless
spiteless

Long I-TLI
brightly
contritely
eruditely
finitely
forthrightly
fortnightly
impolitely
knightly
lightly
nightly
politely
reconditely
rightly
sightly
slightly
sprightly
tightly
tritely
unsightly
uprightly

IT-LUR
brittler
belittler

Hitler
littler
whittler

IT-LZ
acquittals
belittles
committals
skittles
tittles
transmittals
victuals
whittles

Long I-TMENT
excitement
incitement
indictment

IT-MENT
acquitment
commitment
recommitment
remitment

Long I-TNESS
brightness
contriteness
finiteness
forthrightness
impoliteness
lightness
outrightness
politeness
reconditeness
rightness
slightness
tightness
triteness
uprightness

uptightness
whiteness

IT-NESS
counterfeitness
earwitness
eyewitness
fitness
unfitness
witness

IT-RIK
citric
vitric

Long I-TUR
backbiter
biter
blighter
braillewriter
brighter
bullfighter
copywriter
dynamiter
exciter
excitor
expediter
expeditor
fighter
first-nighter
fly-by-nighter
ghostwriter
gunfighter
inciter
indicter
indictor
infighter
inviter
kiter
lamplighter

lighter
miter
moonlighter
nighter
niter
nitre
one-nighter
politer
prizefighter
reciter
requiter
rewriter
righter
screenwriter
scriptwriter
skywriter
slighter
smiter
songwriter
sportswriter
tighter
triter
twinighter
typewriter
underwriter
whiter
writer

IT-UR
acquitter
admitter
aglitter
bitter
chitter
counterfeiter
critter
embitter
emitter
fitter
flitter

fritter
glitter
hairsplitter
hitter
jitter
knitter
litter
outfitter
pitter
quitter
quittor
remitter
sitter
skitter
spitter
submitter
switch-hitter
titter
transmitter
twitter

IT-URZ
admitters
bitters
counterfeiters
critters
embitters
emitters
fitters
flitters
fritters
glitters
hairsplitters
hitters
jitters
knitters
litters
outfitters
quitters
sitters

skitters
spitters
titters
transmitters
twitters

Long I-UR
acidifier
amplifier
applier
beautifier
briar
brier
buyer
certifier
clarifier
classifier
crier
dehumidifier
denier
detoxifier
drier
dryer
dyer
edifier
electrifier
emulsifier
eyer
falsifier
fire
flier
flyer
fortifier
friar
fryer
glorifier
higher
hire
humidifier
identifier

indemnifier
inquire
intensifier
ire
justifier
liar
liquefier
magnifier
misapplier
modifier
mollifier
multiplier
mystifier
nigher
notifier
nullifier
occupier
pacifier
personifier
plier
preamplifier
prier
prior
prophesier
purifier
pyre
qualifier
ratifier
rectifier
replier
sanctifier
saponifier
satisfier
shier
shyer
sigher
signifier
simplifier
slier
slyer

sprier
spryer
supplier
sweetbrier
terrifier
testifier
trier
typifier
umpire
underlier
unifier
verifier
versifier
vilifier
vivifier

Long I-URZ
amplifiers
appliers
beautifiers
briars
briers
buyers
certifiers
clarifiers
classifiers
criers
dehumidifiers
deniers
driers
dryers
dyers
edifiers
electrifiers
emulsifiers
eyers
falsifiers
fires
fliers
flyers

fortifiers
friars
fryers
glorifiers
hires
humidifiers
identifiers
intensifiers
liars
liquefiers
magnifiers
modifiers
mollifiers
multipliers
mystifiers
notifiers
nullifiers
occupiers
pacifiers
pliers
preamplifiers
priers
purifiers
pyres
qualifiers
ratifiers
rectifiers
repliers
shyers
sighers
simplifiers
suppliers
sweetbriers
terrifiers
testifiers
typifiers
umpires
unifiers
verifiers
versifiers

vivifiers

Long I-US
bias
inebrious
pious
Pius
Zacharias

Long I-VAL
adjectival
arrival
revival
rival
substantival
survival

Long I-VAT
private
semiprivate

IV-EN
driven
forgiven
given
riven
striven
thriven
unforgiven

IV-ET
divot
pivot
privet
rivet
trivet

IV-I
divvy
privy

skivvy

IV-ID
livid
vivid

IV-IL
civil
drivel
frivol
incivil
shrivel
snivel
swivel
uncivil

Long I-VING
arriving
conniving
contriving
depriving
deriving
diving
driving
gyving
hiving
jiving
midwiving
reviving
riving
skindiving
skydiving
striving
surviving
thriving
wiving

IV-LING
shriveling
sniveling

IV-OT
divot
pivot
privet
rivet
trivet

IV-RING
adventuring
altering
anchoring
angering
answering
armoring
badgering
bantering
barbering
bartering
battering
beggaring
belaboring
beleaguering
bespattering
bettering
bewildering
bickering
blistering
blubbering
blundering
blustering
bolstering
bordering
bothering
broidering
buffering
butchering
buttering
cambering
cankering
cantering

cantilevering
capering
capturing
catering
censoring
censuring
centering
chambering
chamfering
chartering
chattering
chauffeuring
checkering
ciphering
clamoring
clattering
clinkering
clobbering
cloistering
cloturing
clustering
cluttering
collaring
coloring
configuring
conjecturing
conjuring
conquering
considering
cornering
cosponsoring
countering
covering
cowering
culturing
cumbering
deciphering
delivering
denaturing
diapering

dickering
differing
discoloring
discovering
disencumbering
disfiguring
dishonoring
dismembering
disordering
dissevering
doctoring
doddering
embittering
embroidering
empowering
enamoring
enciphering
encountering
encumbering
endangering
endeavoring
engendering
enrapturing
entering
factoring
faltering
favoring
feathering
featuring
festering
fettering
figuring
filibustering
filtering
fingering
firing
fissuring
flattering
flavoring
flickering

floundering
flouring
flowering
flustering
fluttering
fostering
foundering
fracturing
frittering
garnering
gartering
gathering
gendering
gerrymandering
gesturing
gibbering
glimmering
glittering
glowering
haltering
hammering
hampering
hankering
harboring
hatemongering
hectoring
hindering
hollering
honoring
hovering
huckstering
humoring
hungering
hunkering
incumbering
indenturing
injuring
inquiring
jabbering
jittering

kippering
laboring
lacquering
laundering
lawyering
layering
lettering
levering
limbering
lingering
littering
loitering
lowering
lumbering
majoring
malingering
maneuvering
manoeuvering
manufacturing
martyring
massacring
mastering
mattering
maundering
meandering
measuring
metering
ministering
miring
mirroring
misnumbering
moldering
monitoring
mortaring
mothering
motoring
muggering
murdering
murmuring
mustering

muttering
neighboring
neutering
nickering
numbering
nurturing
offering
ordering
outmaneuvering
outnumbering
overpowering
oystering
palavering
paltering
pampering
pandering
papering
pasturing
pattering
peppering
perjuring
pestering
petering
philandering
picturing
pilfering
plastering
plundering
pondering
posturing
pottering
powdering
powering
prefiguring
preregistering
pressuring
proctoring
proffering
prospering
puckering

puncturing
puttering
quartering
quavering
quivering
recapturing
rechartering
recoloring
reconnoitering
reconquering
reconsidering
recovering
rediscovering
reentering
refiltering
registering
remaindering
remembering
rendering
renumbering
reordering
reupholstering
rumoring
rupturing
sandpapering
sauntering
savoring
scampering
scattering
scissoring
sculpturing
sectoring
sequestering
severing
shattering
shimmering
shivering
shouldering
showering
shuddering

shuttering
silvering
simmering
simpering
skewering
skittering
slandering
slathering
slaughtering
slavering
slithering
slivering
slobbering
smattering
smoldering
smothering
snickering
sniggering
sobering
soldering
soldiering
souring
spattering
splattering
splintering
spluttering
sponsoring
sputtering
squandering
staggering
stammering
steamrollering
structuring
stuttering
succoring
suffering
sugaring
sulfuring
sulphuring
summering

sundering
surrendering
suturing
swaggering
sweltering
tailoring
tampering
tapering
tattering
teetering
tempering
tendering
tethering
thundering
timbering
tincturing
tinkering
tiring
tittering
tottering
towering
transfiguring
treasuring
triggering
tutoring
twittering
ulcering
uncovering
unfaltering
unflattering
unwavering
upholstering
ushering
uttering
venturing
wagering
wallpapering
wandering
warmongering
watering

wavering
weathering
weltering
whimpering
whispering
wintering
wiring
withering
wondering
woolgathering
yammering

Long I-VUR

arriver
conniver
contriver
depriver
deriver
diver
driver
striver
thriver

IV-UR

almsgiver
deliver
downriver
flivver
forgiver
giver
lawgiver
liver
quiver
retriever
river
shiver
sliver
unbeliever
upriver

Long I-WAI

byway
flyway
highway
skyway
superhighway

IZ-ARD

blizzard
gizzard
lizard
scissored
vizard
wizard

IZ-EN

arisen
imprison
mizzen
prison
reimprison
risen
unprison

IZH-UN

circumcision
collision
concision
derision
division
elision
envision
fission
frisian
misprision
precision
provision
recision
rescission
revision

scission
subdivision
supervision
television
vision

IZ-I
busy
dizzy
fizzy
frizzy
tizzy

Long I-ZING
actualizing
advertising
advertizing
advising
aggrandizing
agonizing
alkalinizing
alkalizing
alphabetizing
amortising
amortizing
anaesthetizing
analyzing
anathematizing
anatomizing
anesthetizing
anglicizing
anodizing
antagonizing
anthologizing
apologizing
apostatizing
appetizing
apprising
apprizing
arborizing

arising
atomizing
authorizing
baptizing
barbarizing
bastardizing
bigamizing
brutalizing
burglarizing
cannibalizing
canonizing
capitalising
capitalizing
capsizing
caramelizing
carbonizing
categorizing
catheterizing
cauterizing
centralizing
channelizing
characterizing
chastising
christianizing
circumcising
civilizing
collectivizing
colonizing
commercializing
communalizing
comprising
compromising
computerizing
containerizing
conventionalizing
cretinizing
criticizing
crystallizing
customizing
decarbonizing

decentralizing
decriminalizing
defeminizing
dehumanizing
demagnetizing
demasculinizing
demilitarizing
demineralizing
demobilizing
democratizing
demonetizing
demoralizing
denationalizing
denaturalizing
deodorizing
deoxidizing
depersonalizing
deputizing
desensitizing
despising
devising
devitalizing
digitalizing
disguising
disorganizing
downsizing
dramatizing
economizing
editorializing
elasticizing
electrolyzing
elegizing
empathizing
emphasizing
energizing
enfranchising
enterprising
epitomizing
equalizing
eroticizing

eulogizing
evangelizing
excising
exercising
exorcising
factorizing
familiarizing
fanaticizing
fantasizing
federalizing
feminizing
fictionalizing
finalizing
fletcherizing
focalizing
formalizing
fossilizing
franchising
fraternizing
galvanizing
gelatinizing
generalizing
ghettoizing
glamorizing
globalizing
gormandizing
harmonizing
homogenizing
homologizing
hospitalizing
humanizing
hybridizing
hydrolyzing
hypersensitizing
hypnotising
hypnotizing
hypothesizing
hysterectomizing
idealizing
ideologizing

idolizing
immobilizing
immortalizing
immunizing
improvising
incising
individualizing
industrializing
intellectualizing
internalizing
iodizing
ionizing
italicizing
itemizing
jargonizing
jeopardizing
journalizing
keratinizing
legalizing
legitimatizing
legitimizing
liberalizing
libidinizing
lionizing
liquidizing
listerizing
lobotomizing
localizing
luteinizing
macadamizing
magnetizing
marbleizing
masculinizing
materializing
maximizing
mechanizing
melanizing
memorializing
memorizing
mercerizing

merchandising
merchandizing
mesmerizing
metabolizing
metastasizing
methodizing
metricizing
militarizing
mineralizing
miniaturizing
minimizing
misadvising
mobilizing
modernizing
moisturizing
monetizing
monopolizing
moralizing
motorizing
narcotizing
nasalizing
nationalizing
naturalizing
nebulizing
necrotizing
nesslerizing
neurologizing
neutralizing
nicotinizing
nitrogenizing
normalizing
notarizing
novelizing
organizing
ostracizing
overanalyzing
overcapitalizing
overdramatizing
overexercising
overgeneralizing

overindustrializing
overspecializing
oxidizing
ozonizing
paralysing
paralyzing
particularizing
pasteurizing
patronizing
pauperizing
pelletizing
penalizing
peptonizing
peritonizing
personalizing
philosophizing
phlebotomizing
photolyzing
photosynthesizing
plagiarizing
pluralizing
polarizing
politicizing
polymerizing
popularizing
pressurizing
privatizing
prizing
propagandizing
proselytizing
psychoanalyzing
psychologizing
publicizing
pulverizing
radicalizing
randomizing
rationalizing
realizing
rebaptizing
recognizing

reemphasizing
regularizing
remilitarizing
remising
remonetizing
reorganizing
reprising
reutilizing
revising
revitalizing
revolutionizing
rhapsodizing
rising
romanticizing
routinizing
rubberizing
sacrificing
sanitizing
satirizing
saucerizing
scandalizing
schismatizing
scrutinising
scrutinizing
sectionizing
secularizing
sensitizing
sentimentalizing
serializing
sermonizing
sexualizing
signalizing
simonizing
sizing
slenderizing
socializing
solarizing
solemnizing
soliloquizing
sovietizing

specializing
stabilizing
standardizing
sterilizing
stigmatizing
stylizing
subsidizing
sulfurizing
sulphurizing
summarizing
supervising
surmising
surprising
symbolizing
sympathizing
synchronizing
synthesizing
syphilizing
systematizing
systemizing
tantalizing
televising
temporizing
tenderizing
terrorizing
theorizing
totalizing
tracheotomizing
tranquilizing
tranquillizing
transistorizing
traumatizing
tyrannizing
unappetizing
uncompromising
unionizing
unsurprising
uprising
urbanizing
utilizing

valorizing
vandalizing
vaporizing
verbalizing
vernalizing
victimizing
virilizing
visualizing
vitalizing
vitaminizing
vocalizing
volatilizing
vulcanizing
vulgarizing
westernizing
winterizing
womanizing

IZ-ING
fizzing
frizzing
quizzing
whizzing

IZ-IT
exquisite
revisit
visit

IZ-L
chisel
drizzle
fizzle
frizzle
grizzle
sizzle

IZ-LI
drizzly
frizzly

grisly
grizzly

IZ-LING
chiseling
chiselling
drizzling
fizzling
frizzling
grizzling
quisling
sizzling

IZ-M
animism
ergotism
ism
ostracism
overoptimism
prism
rheumatism
schism
stigmatism
stoicism
tropism
vampirism

IZ-MAL
abysmal
aneurismal
baptismal
cataclysmal
catechismal
dismal
organismal

Long I-ZUR
advertiser
advertizer
adviser

aggrandizer
analyzer
apologizer
appetizer
assizer
atomizer
authorizer
baptizer
capitalizer
catalyzer
categorizer
centralizer
chastiser
circularizer
civilizer
colonizer
compromiser
criticizer
crystallizer
demoralizer
deodorizer
deoxidizer
desensitizer
deviser
devisor
disorganizer
divisor
economizer
editorializer
energizer
enterpriser
equalizer
eulogizer
exerciser
fertilizer
formalizer
franchiser
franchisor
fraternizer
galvanizer

generalizer
glamorizer
gormandizer
harmonizer
homogenizer
homologizer
humanizer
hybridizer
hypothesizer
idolizer
immobilizer
improviser
improvisor
ionizer
legitimizer
lionizer
localizer
magnetizer
maximizer
mechanizer
memorizer
mesmerizer
minimizer
mobilizer
modernizer

monopolizer
moralizer
nebulizer
neutralizer
normalizer
organizer
oxidizer
ozonizer
paralyzer
pasteurizer
patronizer
plagiarizer
polarizer
pressurizer
proselytizer
rationalizer
regularizer
reorganizer
reviser
revolutionizer
riser
sacrificer
sanitizer
satirizer
scandalizer

scrutinizer
secularizer
sermonizer
socializer
stabilizer
sterilizer
supervisor
surpriser
sympathizer
synchronizer
synthesizer
tenderizer
totalizer
tranquilizer
tranquillizer
tyrannizer
utilizer
vaporizer
victimizer
visualizer
vitalizer
vocalizer
vulcanizer
vulgarizer
wiser

O-A
balboa
boa
heliozoa
Iowa
Mesozoa
Noah
protozoa
Samoa
sporozoa

O-BALL
cobol
snowball

Long O-BI
adobe
Gobi
goby
Nairobi
Toby

OB-I
bobby
hobby
knobby
kohlrabi
lobby
Punjabi
Robby
snobby
squabby

OB-IN
bobbin
dobbin
robin
round-robin

Long O-BING
disrobing
probing
robing

OB-ING
bedaubing
blobbing
bobbing
daubing
fobbing
hobnobbing
jobbing
lobbing
mobbing
robbing
sobbing
stockjobbing
swabbing
throbbing

OB-L
bauble
bobble
cobble
gobble
hobble
squabble
wobble

OB-LING
cobbling
gobbling
hobbling
squabbling
wobbling

OB-LUR
cobbler
gobbler

hobbler
squabbler
wobbler

Long O-BOI
doughboy
lowboy

OB-STUR
lobster
mobster

Long O-BUR
disrober
October
prober
rober
sober

OB-UR
bobber
clobber
dauber
jobber
lobber
robber
sharejobber
slobber
sobber
stockjobber
swabber
throbber

Long O-CHEZ
approaches
broaches
brooches
coaches
cockroaches
encroaches

poaches
reproaches
roaches
stagecoaches

OCH-I
blotchy
botchy
debauchee
hibachi
mariachi
notchy
splotchy

Long O-CHING
approaching
broaching
coaching
encroaching
poaching
reproaching

OCH-ING
blotching
botching
debauching
notching
scotching
splotching
watching

OCH-MAN
Scotchman
watchman

Long O-CHUR
approacher
broacher
coacher
encroacher

poacher
reproacher

Long O-DA
coda
pagoda
Rhoda
soda

Long O-DAL
modal
nodal
yodel

OD-AL
caudle
dawdle
twaddle

Long O-DED
boded
coded
corroded
decoded
discommoded
eroded
exploded
foreboded
freeloaded
goaded
imploded
loaded
outmoded
overloaded

OD-ED
defrauded
nodded
plodded
prodded

sodded
wadded

OD-EN
broaden
downtrodden
sodden
trodden
untrodden

OD-ESS
bodice
goddess

OD-EST
broadest
immodest
modest
oddest
overmodest

OD-I
antibody
anybody
bawdy
body
busybody
cloddy
disembody
embody
everybody
gaudy
homebody
nobody
noddy
Peabody
reembody
shoddy
somebody
toddy

OD-IK
episodic
melodic
methodic
periodic
prosodic
rhapsodic
spasmodic
synodic

Long O-DING
boding
coding
corroding
decoding
discommoding
encoding
eroding
exploding
foreboding
freeloading
goading
imploding
loading
noncorroding
overloading
railroading
reloading
unloading

OD-ING
applauding
codding
defrauding
lauding
marauding
nodding
plodding
prodding
sodding

wadding

OD-IT
audit
plaudit

OD-L
caudal
caudle
coddle
dawdle
model
mollycoddle
noddle
remodel
swaddle
toddle
twaddle
waddle

OD-LI
broadly
godly
oddly
ungodly

OD-LING
coddling
codling
dawdling
mollycoddling
remodeling
swaddling
toddling
waddling

OD-LUR
coddler
dawdler
modeler

mollycoddler
toddler
twaddler
waddler

Long O-DOWN
hoedown
lowdown
showdown
slowdown

OD-ULE
module
nodule

Long O-DUR
encoder
odor
railroader
roader

OD-UR
applauder
broader
defrauder
dodder
fodder
lauder
marauder
nodder
odder
plodder
prodder
solder

Long O-EST
banjoist
egoist
frescoist
jingoist

judoist
lowest
maoist
mellowest
narrowest
oboist
shallowest
shintoist
slowest
soloist

Long O-ET
inchoate
poet

OF-ET
nonprofit
profit
prophet

OF-I
coffee
toffee

OF-IK
catastrophic
dystrophic
heterotrophic
philosophic
strophic
theosophic
trophic

OF-ING
coughing
doffing
quaffing
scoffing

OF-N
coffin
often
soften

OF-TI
lofty
softie
softy

OF-TUR
crofter
softer

OF-UL
awful
lawful
offal
unlawful

Long O-FUR
chauffeur
gofer
gopher
loafer
ophir

OF-UR
coffer
counteroffer
doffer
goffer
offer
proffer
quaffer
scoffer

Long O-GA
Saratoga
toga

yoga

Long O-GAN
blowgun
brogan
hogan
logan
shogun
slogan

OG-AN
noggin
toboggan

Long O-GI
bogey
bogy
dogie
fogy
hoagie
Hoagy
logy
stogie
yogi

OG-I
boggy
cloggy
demagogy
doggie
foggy
groggy
smoggy
soggy

OG-ING
backlogging
befogging
bogging
bulldogging

cataloging
cataloguing
clogging
defogging
dogging
flogging
fogging
hogging
jogging
leapfrogging
logging
pettifogging
slogging
togging
unclogging
waterlogging

Long O-GL
mogul
ogle

OG-L
boggle
boondoggle
goggle
hornswoggle
joggle
ogle
toggle

OG-LING
boggling
boondoggling
goggling
hornswoggling
joggling
ogling

O-GRESS
ogress

progress

OG-UR
cataloger
cataloguer
defogger
dogger
flogger
jogger
logger
pettifogger
slogger

Long O-I
billowy
blowy
bowie
Chloe
doughy
escrowee
furrowy
joey
meadowy
pillowy
shadowy
showy
snowy
tallowy
towhee
willowy

OI-AL
disloyal
Hoyle
loyal
royal
toil

OI-ANS
annoyance

clairvoyance
flamboyance
joyance

OI-ANT
buoyant
clairvoyant
flamboyant

OI-ING
alloying
annoying
buoying
convoying
decoying
deploying
destroying
employing
enjoying
octroying
overjoying
redeploying
reemploying
reenjoying
toying

OI-ISH
boyish
coyish

Long O-IJ
flowage
stowage
towage

Long O-IK
anechoic
antiheroic
azoic
echoic

Heliozoic
heroic
Mesozoic
Protozoic
stoic
unheroic
zoic

OI-LI
coyly
doily
oily
roily

OIL-ING
boiling
broiling
charbroiling
coiling
despoiling
embroiling
foiling
moiling
oiling
parboiling
preboiling
reboiling
recoiling
roiling
soiling
spoiling
toiling
uncoiling

OI-LUR
boiler
broiler
coiler
despoiler
oiler

potboiler
spoiler
toiler

OI-MENT
deployment
employment
enjoyment
reemployment
unemployment

Long O-ING
bellowing
bestowing
billowing
blowing
Boeing
borrowing
bowing
buffaloing
burrowing
churchgoing
crowing
easygoing
echoing
elbowing
embargoing
farrowing
flowing
following
foregoing
foreknowing
foreshadowing
forgoing
furloughing
furrowing
glassblowing
glowing
going
growing

hallowing
harrowing
hoeing
hollowing
imbargoing
ingrowing
kayoing
knowing
lassoing
lowing
mellowing
mimeoing
mind-blowing
moviegoing
mowing
narrowing
oceangoing
ongoing
outgoing
outgrowing
overflowing
overgrowing
overshadowing
overthrowing
owing
pillowing
radioing
reechoing
rowing
seagoing
sewing
shadowing
showing
slowing
snowing
soloing
sorrowing
sowing
stowing
stuccoing

swallowing
tangoing
thoroughgoing
throwing
tiptoeing
toeing
torpedoing
towing
undergoing
unknowing
vetoing
wallowing
whistle-blowing
windowing
winnowing
yellowing
zeroing

O-ING
awing
baaing
cawing
clawing
drawing
gnawing
guffawing
hawing
hurrahing
jawing
outlawing
overawing
overdrawing
pawing
sawing
seesawing
thawing
underdrawing
whipsawing
withdrawing
yawing

OI-NING
adjoining
coining
conjoining
disjoining
enjoining
joining
purloining
recoining
rejoining
subjoining

OIN-TED
anointed
appointed
counterpointed
disappointed
disjointed
double-jointed
jointed
lap-jointed
pinpointed
pointed
preappointed
unappointed
unjointed
unpointed

OIN-TING
anointing
appointing
checkpointing
counterpointing
disappointing
disjointing
jointing
pinpointing
pointing
preappointing

OINT-LESS
jointless
pointless

OINT-MENT
anointment
appointment
disappointment
ointment

OIN-TUR
anointer
appointer
disappointer
jointer
pointer

OI-NUR
coiner
joiner
purloiner

OI-SING
invoicing
rejoicing
unrejoicing
voicing

OIS-LESS
choiceless
voiceless

OI-STING
foisting
hoisting
joisting

OI-STUR
cloister
hoister

moister
oyster

OI-TRING
adventuring
altering
anchoring
angering
answering
armoring
badgering
bantering
barbering
bartering
battering
beggaring
belaboring
beleaguering
bespattering
bettering
bewildering
bickering
blistering
blubbering
blundering
blustering
bolstering
bordering
bothering
broidering
buffering
butchering
buttering
cambering
cankering
cantering
cantilevering
capering
capturing
catering

censoring
censuring
centering
chambering
chamfering
chartering
chattering
chauffeuring
checkering
ciphering
clamoring
clattering
clinkering
clobbering
cloistering
cloturing
clustering
cluttering
collaring
coloring
configuring
conjecturing
conjuring
conquering
considering
cornering
cosponsoring
countering
covering
cowering
culturing
cumbering
deciphering
delivering
denaturing
diapering
dickering
differing
discoloring
discovering

disencumbering
disfiguring
dishonoring
dismembering
disordering
dissevering
doctoring
doddering
embittering
embroidering
empowering
enamoring
enciphering
encountering
encumbering
endangering
endeavoring
engendering
enrapturing
entering
factoring
faltering
favoring
feathering
featuring
festering
fettering
figuring
filibustering
filtering
fingering
firing
fissuring
flattering
flavoring
flickering
floundering
flouring
flowering
flustering

fluttering
fostering
foundering
fracturing
frittering
garnering
gartering
gathering
gendering
gerrymandering
gesturing
gibbering
glimmering
glittering
glowering
haltering
hammering
hampering
hankering
harboring
hatemongering
hectoring
hindering
hollering
honoring
hovering
huckstering
humoring
hungering
hunkering
incumbering
indenturing
injuring
inquiring
jabbering
jittering
kippering
laboring
lacquering
laundering

lawyering
layering
lettering
levering
limbering
lingering
littering
loitering
lowering
lumbering
majoring
malingering
maneuvering
manoeuvering
manufacturing
martyring
massacring
mastering
mattering
maundering
meandering
measuring
metering
ministering
miring
mirroring
misnumbering
moldering
monitoring
mortaring
mothering
motoring
muggering
murdering
murmuring
mustering
muttering
neighboring
neutering
nickering

numbering
nurturing
offering
ordering
outmaneuvering
outnumbering
overpowering
oystering
palavering
paltering
pampering
pandering
papering
pasturing
pattering
peppering
perjuring
pestering
petering
philandering
picturing
pilfering
plastering
plundering
pondering
posturing
pottering
powdering
powering
prefiguring
preregistering
pressuring
proctoring
proffering
prospering
puckering
puncturing
puttering
quartering
quavering

quivering
recapturing
rechartering
recoloring
reconnoitering
reconquering
reconsidering
recovering
rediscovering
reentering
refiltering
registering
remaindering
remembering
rendering
renumbering
reordering
reupholstering
rumoring
rupturing
sandpapering
sauntering
savoring
scampering
scattering
scissoring
sculpturing
sectoring
sequestering
severing
shattering
shimmering
shivering
shouldering
showering
shuddering
shuttering
silvering
simmering
simpering

skewering
skittering
slandering
slathering
slaughtering
slavering
slithering
slivering
slobbering
smattering
smoldering
smothering
snickering
sniggering
sobering
soldering
soldiering
souring
spattering
splattering
splintering
spluttering
sponsoring
sputtering
squandering
staggering
stammering
steamrollering
structuring
stuttering
succoring
suffering
sugaring
sulfuring
sulphuring
summering
sundering
surrendering
suturing
swaggering

sweltering
tailoring
tampering
tapering
tattering
teetering
tempering
tendering
tethering
thundering
timbering
tincturing
tinkering
tiring
tittering
tottering
towering
transfiguring
treasuring
triggering
tutoring
twittering
ulcering
uncovering
unfaltering
unflattering
unwavering
upholstering
ushering
uttering
venturing
wagering
wallpapering
wandering
warmongering
watering
wavering
weathering
weltering
whimpering

whispering
wintering
wiring
withering
wondering
woolgathering
yammering

OI-TUR
exploiter
goiter
loiter
reconnoiter

OI-UR
annoyer
coyer
destroyer
employer
enjoyer
foyer
lawyer
voyeur

OJ-I
demagogy
dodgy
pedagogy
podgy
stodgy

OJ-IK
analogic
anthropologic
archaeologic
bacteriologic
biologic
cardiologic
chronologic
climatologic

cytologic
demagogic
dendrologic
ecologic
ethnologic
etiologic
geologic
histologic
horologic
hydrologic
ideologic
immunologic
logic
meteorologic
mineralogic
morphologic
mythologic
neurologic
pathologic
pedagogic
pedologic
petrologic
pharmacologic
phonologic
physiologic
proctologic
psychologic
radiologic
scatologic
serologic
sialagogic
sociologic
technologic
virologic
zoologic

OJ-ING
barraging
camouflaging
dislodging

dodging
garaging
lodging
massaging
outdodging
sabotaging

OJ-UR
codger
dodger
jolly-roger
lodger
massager
Roger

Long O-KAL
focal
subvocal
trifocal
univocal
vocal
yokel

Long O-KEN
bespoken
betoken
broken
foretoken
heartbroken
housebroken
oaken
outspoken
plainspoken
spoken
token
unbroken
unspoken

OK-ET
docket

locket
pickpocket
pocket
retrorocket
rocket
skyrocket
socket
sprocket

Long O-KI
choky
croaky
hokey
hokeypokey
hoky-poky
okey
okey-dokey
okeydokey
okie
pokey
poky
Skokie
smokey
smoky
soaky
troche
trochee
yolky

OK-I
chalky
gawky
talkie
talky
walkie
walkie-talkie

Long O-KING
backstroking
choking

cloaking
convoking
croaking
evoking
hoking
invoking
joking
pawnbroking
poking
presoaking
provoking
reinvoking
revoking
smoking
soaking
stockbroking
stoking
stroking
uncloaking
unyoking
yoking

OK-ING
balking
blocking
bluestocking
caulking
chalking
chocking
clocking
cocking
deadlocking
defrocking
docking
floccing
flocking
gawking
hawking
hocking
interlocking

jaywalking
knocking
locking
mocking
outwalking
overstocking
padlocking
rocking
shocking
sleepwalking
smocking
socking
spacewalking
squawking
stalking
stocking
streetwalking
talking
unblocking
unfrocking
unlocking
walking

OK-ISH
blockish
hawkish
mawkish

Long O-KLESS
cloakless
jokeless
smokeless
yokeless
yolkless

Long O-KO
coco
cocoa
loco
poco

rococo

OK-O
morocco
scirocco
shako
sirocco
socko
taco

OK-SHUN
auction
concoction
decoction

OK-SI
Biloxi
doxy
epoxy
foxy
heterodoxy
hydroxy
moxie
orthodoxy
proxy
unorthodoxy

Long O-KSING
coaxing
hoaxing

OK-SING
boxing
foxing
outboxing
outfoxing
shadowboxing
Xeroxing

Long O-KSUR
coaxer
hoaxer

OK-TUR
doctor
proctor

Long O-KUM
hokum
oakum

Long O-KUR
broker
choker
croaker
evoker
joker
nonsmoker
pawnbroker
provoker
revoker
smoker
soaker
stockbroker
stoker

OK-UR
balker
blocker
cakewalker
calker
caulker
clocker
cocker
deerstalker
docker
floorwalker
footlocker
hawker

jaywalker
knickerbocker
knocker
locker
mocker
rocker
shocker
sleepwalker
soccer
spacewalker
stalker
stocker
talker
walker

Long O-KUS
crocus
focus
hocus
hocus-pocus
locus
refocus

OK-US
caucus
glaucous
raucous

Long O-KUST
focused
focussed
locust
refocused
refocused

OK-WARD
awkward
dockward

Long O-LA
Angola
Coca-cola
cola
corolla
cupola
gladiola
gondola
granola
kola
Mazola
payola
Pepsi-cola
roseola
rubeola
viola

OL-AR
bawler
brawler
caller
collar
crawler
dollar
eurodollar
forestaller
hauler
holler
installer
mauler
scholar
scrawler
smaller
sprawler
squalor
taller
trawler

Long OL-ARD
bollard

collard
collared
hollered
Lollard

Long OL-DED
blindfolded
bolded
enfolded
folded
infolded
manifolded
molded
refolded
remolded
scolded
unfolded
unmolded

Long OL-DEN
beholden
embolden
golden
holden
olden
unbeholden

Long OL-DEST
boldest
coldest
oldest

Long OL-DING
beholding
blindfolding
enfolding
folding
holding
infolding
landholding

manifolding
molding
refolding
remolding
scolding
stockholding
unfolding
upholding
withholding

Long OLD-LI
boldly
coldly
manifoldly

Long OLD-NESS
boldness
coldness
manifoldness
oldness

Long OL-DUR
beholder
bolder
bondholder
boulder
cardholder
colder
copyholder
cupholder
enfolder
folder
freeholder
holder
householder
infolder
innholder
jobholder
landholder
leaseholder

lienholder
molder
officeholder
older
penholder
placeholder
pledgeholder
polder
policyholder
potholder
scolder
shareholder
shoulder
smolder
smoulder
stakeholder
stockholder
titleholder
toolholder
upholder
withholder

OL-DUR
alder
balder
Baldur

OL-EJ
acknowledge
college
foreknowledge
haulage
knowledge
precollege

Long O-LEN
Angolan
colon
semicolon
stolen

swollen

O-LEN
befallen
crestfallen
downfallen
fallen
Guatemalan
pollen

OL-ESS
aweless
braless
flawless
jawless
lawless

OL-EST
alcoholist
smallest
solaced
tallest

OL-FIN
dolphin

Long OL-FUL
bowlful
doleful
soulful

Long O-LI
gladioli
goalie
guacamole
holey
holy
lowly
mellowly
narrowly

ravioli
shoaly
slowly
solely
thoroughly
unholy
wholely
wholly

OL-I
Bali
brawly
collie
crawly
dolly
finale
folly
golly
holly
jolly
melancholy
molly
poly
Somali
squally
tamale
trolley
volley

OL-ID
solid
squalid
stolid

OL-IK
alcoholic
anabolic
apostolic
carbolic
colic

diabolic
diastolic
frolic
gallic
hydraulic
hyperbolic
melancholic
metabolic
mongolic
nonalcoholic
parabolic
rollick
symbolic
systolic
vitriolic
workaholic

Long O-LING
bankrolling
bowling
buttonholing
cajoling
condoling
consoling
controlling
decontrolling
enrolling
extolling
foaling
holing
logrolling
paroling
patrolling
pigeonholing
poling
polling
resoling
rolling
scrolling
soling

strolling
tolling
trolling
unrolling

OL-ING
appalling
balling
befalling
blackballing
brawling
caballing
calling
cannonballing
catcalling
crawling
dolling
drawling
enthralling
falling
forestalling
hauling
installing
lolling
mauling
overhauling
recalling
reinstalling
scrawling
snowballing
sprawling
squalling
stalling
stonewalling
trawling
walling

OL-ISH
abolish
demolish

dollish
polish
smallish
tallish

Long OL-MAN
coalman
dolman
dolmen
patrolman
tollman

Long OL-MENT
cajolement
condolement
enrollment

OL-MENT
enthrallment
forestallment
installment
reinstallment

OL-NESS
smallness
tallness

Long O-LO
bolo
nolo
polo
solo

OL-O
Apollo
follow
hollow
swallow
wallow

Long O-LON
Angolan
colon
semicolon
stolen

OL-OP
dollop
escallop
lollop
polyp
scallop
scollop
trollop
wallop

Long OL-STUR
bolster
holster
oldster
pollster
reupholster
upholster

Long OL-TED
bolted
jolted
molted
revolted
unbolted

OL-TED
assaulted
defaulted
desalted
exalted
faulted
halted
malted
oversalted

salted
somersaulted
stringhalted
unsalted
vaulted

OL-TI
faulty
malty
salty
vaulty

OL-TIK
asphaltic
Baltic
basaltic
peristaltic
systaltic

Long OL-TING
bolting
jolting
molting
revolting
unbolting

OL-TING
assaulting
defaulting
desalting
exalting
faulting
halting
oversalting
salting
somersaulting
vaulting

Long OL-TISH
coltish

doltish

OLT-LESS
faultless
maltless
saltless

OL-TUR
altar
alter
assaulter
defaulter
desalter
exalter
falter
Gibraltar
halter
palter
psalter
salter
vaulter

OL-UM
column
slalom
solemn
unsolemn

Long O-LUR
bowler
cajoler
circumpolar
holer
logroller
molar
multipolar
polar
poler
poller
premolar

roller
rubeolar
solar
steamroller
stroller
transpolar
troller
unipolar

OL-UR
bawler
brawler
caller
collar
crawler
dollar
eurodollar
forestaller
hauler
holler
installer
mauler
scholar
scrawler
smaller
sprawler
squalor
taller
trawler

OL-VING
absolving
devolving
dissolving
evolving
involving
redissolving
resolving
revolving
solving

OL-VUR
absolver
resolver
revolver
solver

OL-WAIZ
always
hallways

Long O-MA
aroma
carcinoma
chroma
coma
diploma
glaucoma
hematoma
lipoma
lymphoma
lymphosarcoma
melanoma
myoma
myosarcoma
noma
Oklahoma
sarcoma
Sonoma
stoma
stroma
syphiloma
Tacoma
xanthoma

OM-A
Brahma
comma
kama
llama
mama

squama
trauma
Yokohama

Long O-MAN
abdomen
bowman
foeman
gnomon
nomen
Oklahoman
omen
radioman
roman
showman
yeoman

OM-BAT
combat
noncombat
wombat

OM-BUR
omber
somber

Long O-MEN
abdomen
bowman
foeman
gnomon
nomen
Oklahoman
omen
radioman
roman
showman
yeoman

OM-ET
comet
grommet
vomit

Long O-MI
foamy
homey
loamy

OM-IK
anatomic
astronomic
atomic
carbamic
comic
economic
ergonomic
gastronomic
Islamic
metronomic
socioeconomic
taxonomic
tragicomic

Long O-MING
chroming
combing
currycombing
foaming
gloaming
homing
recombing
roaming
Wyoming

Long O-MUR
homer
misnomer
roamer

Long O-NA
Arizona
Barcelona
bona
corona
Cremona
Jonah
Mona
persona

ON-A
belladonna
donna
iguana
madonna
manana
prima donna
nirvana
piranha
zenana

Long O-NAL
atonal
hormonal
tonal
umbonal

ON-DA
anaconda
fonda
Honda
La Giaconda
Uganda

ON-DED
absconded
bonded
corresponded
desponded
responded

ON-DIJ
bondage
frondage
vagabondage

ON-DING
absconding
bonding
corresponding
responding

OND-NESS
blondness
fondness

ON-DUR
absconder
blonder
bonder
condor
fonder
launder
maunder
ponder
responder
squander
transponder
wander
yonder

Long O-NENT
component
deponement
exponent
opponent
proponent

ON-EST
dishonest
honest

wannest

ON-ET
bluebonnet
bonnet
sonnet
sultanate
sunbonnet
war-bonnet

ONG-ING
belonging
longing
prolonging
thronging
wronging

ONG-KUR
concur
conker
conquer
honker
reconquer

ONG-KURZ
bonkers
conquers
honkers
reconquers
Yonkers

ONG-GEST
longest
strongest

ONG-GUR
conger
fashionmonger
fishmonger
gossipmonger

hatemonger
ironmonger
longer
monger
newsmonger
rumormonger
scandalmonger
scaremonger
stronger
warmonger
whoremonger

Long O-NHED
bonehead
clonehead

Long O-NI
abalone
acrimony
alimony
baloney
bologna
bony
ceremony
coney
cony
crony
hegemony
macaroni
Marconi
matrimony
minestrone
palimony
pepperoni
phoney
phony
pony
sanctimony
Shoshone
Shoshoni

spumoni
stony
tony

ON-I
bonnie
bonny
brawny
Connie
Johnny
lawny
pawnee
scrawny
tawny

ON-IK
Aaronic
atonic
bionic
bubonic
Byronic
canonic
carbonic
catatonic
chronic
conic
demonic
diachronic
diatonic
dysphonic
electronic
harmonic
hedonic
hegemonic
histrionic
homophonic
hydroponic
hypersonic
hypotonic
infrasonic

ionic
ironic
isotonic
itaconic
ketonic
laconic
Masonic
mastodonic
mnemonic
monophonic
monotonic
moronic
Napoleonic
nucleonic
opsonic
philharmonic
phonic
planktonic
platonic
plutonic
pneumonic
polyphonic
pulmonic
quadraphonic
sardonic
Slavonic
sonic
stereophonic
subsonic
sulfonic
supersonic
symbionic
symphonic
syntonic
tectonic
telephonic
Teutonic
tonic
transonic
ultrasonic

zirconic

ON-IKS
bioelectronics
bionics
catatonics
cryonics
electronics
harmonics
histrionics
hydroponics
mnemonics
onyx
philharmonics
phonics
supersonics
tectonics
tonics
ultrasonics

Long O-NING
bemoaning
boning
chaperoning
cloning
condoning
dethroning
disowning
droning
enthroning
groaning
honing
intoning
jawboning
landowning
loaning
moaning
owning
phoning
postponing

reloaning
rezoning
stoning
telephoning
toning
upzoning
zoning

ON-ING
awning
conning
dawning
donning
fawning
pawning
spawning
yawning

ON-ISH
admonish
astonish
donnish
monish
premonish
wannish

Long O-NLESS
boneless
moanless
throneless
toneless
zoneless

Long O–NLI
lonely
only
pronely

Long O-NMENT
atonement

cantonment
dethronement
enthronement
postponement

ON-SOR
cosponsor
sponsor
tonsor

ON-TAL
fontal
horizontal

ON-TED
daunted
flaunted
haunted
jaunted
taunted
undaunted
unwanted
vaunted
wanted

ON-TING
daunting
flaunting
haunting
jaunting
taunting
vaunting
wanting

ON-TO
esperanto
portmanteau
pronto
Tonto
Toronto

ON-TUR
daunter
flaunter
gaunter
haunter
saunter
taunter

Long O-NUR
atoner
boner
condoner
deponer
dethroner
groaner
homeowner
honer
intoner
landowner
loaner
loner
telephoner

ON-UR
Afrikaner
dishonor
fawner
goner
honor
pawner
spawner
wanner
yawner

Long O-NUS
bonus
callowness
conus
hollowness
lowness

mellowness
narrowness
onus
sallowness
shallowness
slowness
thoroughness
tonus

OOD-ED
hooded
wooded

OOD-I
goodie
goody
goody-goody
woody

OOK-I
bookie
cookie
hookey
hooky
lookee
rookie

OOK-ING
booking
brooking
cooking
crooking
good-looking
hooking
looking
onlooking
overcooking
overlooking
precooking
recooking

rooking
undercooking
unhooking

OOK-UR
booker
cooker
good-looker
hooker
landlooker
looker
onlooker
snooker

OOL-EN
woolen
woollen

OOL-ET
bullet
pullet

OOL-I
bully
fully
pulley
woolly
wooly

OOL-ISH
bullish
coolish
foolish
fullish
ghoulish

OOL-UR
fuller
puller
wirepuller

OOT-ED
attributed
booted
commuted
computed
constituted
contributed
convoluted
deep-rooted
deputed
diluted
disputed
electrocuted
executed
fluted
fruited
hooted
imputed
instituted
involuted
looted
mooted
muted
parachuted
persecuted
polluted
prosecuted
prostituted
reconstituted
recruited
refuted
reputed
restituted
rooted
routed
saluted
scooted
substituted
suited
tooted

transmuted
undiluted
undisputed
unexecuted
unpolluted
unprosecuted
unrefuted
unsuited
uprooted

OOT-ING
footing
noncontributing
pussyfooting
putting

OP-ET
moppet
poppet

Long O-PI
dopey
hopi
mopey

OP-I
choppy
copy
floppy
jalopy
miscopy
photocopy
poppy
recopy
sloppy
soppy

OP-IK
bacteriotropic
chromoscopic

cytotropic
endoscopic
fluoroscopic
geotropic
gyroscopic
heliotropic
isotopic
isotropic
kaleidoscopic
macroscopic
microscopic
misanthropic
oscilloscopic
pantropic
philanthropic
phototropic
radioscopic
spectroscopic
stereoscopic
stethoscopic
stroboscopic
submicroscopic
subtopic
telescopic
thermotropic
topic
tropic

OP-IKS
subtopics
subtropics
topics
tropics

Long O-PING
coping
doping
eloping
groping
hoping

interloping
loping
moping
roping
scoping
sloping
soaping
telescoping
toping

OP-ING
airdropping
blacktopping
bopping
chopping
clodhopping
copping
cropping
dropping
eavesdropping
flopping
hedgehopping
hopping
joypopping
lopping
mopping
outcropping
overtopping
plopping
popping
propping
sharecropping
shopping
slopping
sopping
stopping
swapping
swopping
topping
unstopping

whopping
yawping

OP-L
hopple
popple
stopple
topple

Long O-PLESS
hopeless
ropeless
soapless

OP-SHUN
adoption
option
readoption

OP-SIS
synopsis
thanatopsis
coreopsis

OP-TED
adopted
coopted
opted
readopted

OP-TIK
bioptic
coptic
microptic
optic
preoptic
synoptic

Long O-PUR
doper

eloper
groper
hoper
interloper
moper
roper
soaper
soft-soaper
toper

OP-UR
bopper
chopper
clodhopper
copper
cropper
dropper
eavesdropper
eyedropper
eyepopper
flopper
grasshopper
hedgehopper
hopper
improper
job-hopper
joypopper
leafhopper
lopper
namedropper
popper
proper
sharecropper
shopper
showstopper
stopper
swapper
teenybopper
topper
wapper

whopper
window-shopper
woodchopper
yawper

Long O-PUS
Canopus
opus

OR-A
angora
aura
aurora
Devorah
fedora
flora
gomorrah
hora
Liorah
menorah
mora
pandora
senora
signora
Torah

OR-AKS
borax
storax
thorax

OR-AL
amoral
aural
auroral
chloral
choral
coral
floral
immoral

laurel
monaural
moral
oral
peroral
quarrel
sectoral
sorrel
subpectoral
unmoral
whorl

OR-BEL
corbel
doorbell

OR-BL
corbel
warble

OR-CHUR
scorcher
torcher

OR-CHURD
orchard
tortured

OR-DANT
accordant
concordant
discordant
mordant

OR-DED
accorded
afforded
awarded
boarded
corded

forded
outboarded
prerecorded
recorded
skateboarded
sordid
unrecorded
unrewarded
warded

OR-DING
according
affording
awarding
boarding
cording
fording
hoarding
hording
lording
outboarding
prerecording
recording
rewarding
skateboarding
unrewarding
warding

ORD-SHIP
boardship
lordship
wardship

OR-DUR
boarder
border
corder
disorder
order
recorder

reorder
skateboarder

OR-EL
amoral
aural
auroral
chloral
choral
coral
floral
immoral
laurel
monaural
moral
oral
peroral
quarrel
sectoral
sorrel
subpectoral
unmoral
whorl

OR-ENS
abhorrence
adulterants
antiperspirants
aspirants
belligerence
denaturants
deodorants
expectorants
Florence
ignorance
indifference
itinerants
Lawrence
operance
preponderance

protuberance
reference
refrigerants
reverence
severance
succorance
sufferance
tolerance
torrents
warrants

OR-ENT
abhorrent
torrent
warrant

OR-FIK
dimorphic
ectomorphic
endomorphic
heteromorphic
isomorphic
mesomorphic
metamorphic
monomorphic
morphic
orphic
pseudomorphic

OR-GAN
gorgon
organ
Morgan

OR-HED
forehead
sorehead
warhead

OR-HOUSE
poorhouse
storehouse
whorehouse

OR-I
accusatory
adjudicatory
advisatory
allegory
ambulatory
anticipatory
appreciatory
articulatory
auditory
aurae
cacciatore
capitulatory
castigatory
category
circulatory
compensatory
conciliatory
condemnatory
confirmatory
congratulatory
conservatory
consultatory
copulatory
corrie
corroboratory
cosignatory
crematory
criminatory
curie
dedicatory
defamatory
delegatory
denigratory
depository

derogatory
desiccatory
dictatory
dilatory
disclamatory
discriminatory
dory
dormitory
ejaculatory
eliminatory
excitatory
exclamatory
excretory
explanatory
exploratory
expository
glory
gory
gustatory
hallucinatory
hoary
hortatory
hunky-dory
incriminatory
inflammatory
initiatory
interrogatory
inventory
investigatory
judicatory
juratory
jury
laboratory
laudatory
lavatory
lorry
mandatory
manipulatory
migratory
minatory

mitigatory
modulatory
monsignori
montessori
morae
moratory
negotiatory
nondiscriminatory
nonpredatory
nugatory
obfuscatory
obligatory
observatory
offertory
oratory
oscillatory
participatory
perspiratory
Peter Lorre
predatory
predicatory
prefatory
preparatory
priori
prohibitory
promissory
promontory
propitiatory
pulsatory
punitory
purgatory
quarry
reformatory
regulatory
repertory
repository
respiratory
revelatory
salutatory
sanatory

signatory
sorry
statutory
stimulatory
stipulatory
story
subcategory
suppository
territory
Tori
tory
transitory
undulatory
vibratory
vindicatory

OR-ID
florid
forehead
horrid
torrid

OR-IJ
floorage
forage
moorage
porridge
storage

OR-IK
allegoric
boric
caloric
categoric
euphoric
Doric
folkloric
historic
metaphoric
meteoric

noncaloric
paregoric
phosphoric
prehistoric
pseudohistoric
sophomoric

OR-ING
abhorring
adoring
boring
contouring
coring
deploring
exploring
flooring
goring
ignoring
imploring
mooring
outpouring
outscoring
overinsuring
poring
pouring
prescoring
reassuring
restoring
rip-roaring
roaring
scoring
shoring
snoring
soaring
stevedoring
storing
touring
underscoring
unenduring
whoring

OR-JA
Borja
Georgia

OR-JI
Georgia Porgy
orgy

OR-JUN
Borgian
Georgian

OR-KING
corking
forking
torquing
uncorking

OR-LESS
coreless
doorless
oarless
oreless
scoreless
shoreless
warless

OR-LOK
forelock
oarlock
warlock

OR-MAL
abnormal
formal
informal
normal
semiformal
seminormal
subnormal

supernormal

OR-MAN
corpsman
doorman
floorman
foreman
longshoreman
longshoremen
Mormon
Norman

OR-MANT
conformant
dormant
informant

OR-MI
stormy
swarmy

OR-MING
barnstorming
brainstorming
chloroforming
conforming
deforming
forming
habit-forming
heartwarming
housewarming
informing
misinforming
nonconforming
outperforming
performing
preforming
prewarming
reforming
reinforming

storming
swarming
transforming
warming

ORM-LESS
formless
gormless
stormless

ORM-LI
lukewarmly
uniformly
warmly

OR-MUR
brainstormer
conformer
dormer
former
informer
performer
reformer
stormer
swarmer
transformer
warmer

OR-NET
cornet
hornet

ORN-FUL
mournful
scornful

OR-NI
corny
horny
thorny

OR-NING
borning
adorning
corning
dehorning
forewarning
horning
midmorning
morning
mourning
scorning
suborning
warning

ORN-LESS
hornless
scornless
thornless

OR-NUR
adorner
corner
horner
mourner
scorner
warner

OR-O
borrow
morrow
saguaro
sorrow
taro
tomorrow
toro

OR-OR
abhorrer
adorer
borer

coinsurer
corer
deplorer
explorer
floorer
furor
horror
ignorer
lurer
poorer
pourer
restorer
roarer
scorer
snorer
soarer
sorer
surer

OR-SAL
dorsal
morsel
subdorsal

OR-SEN
coarsen
hoarsen
whoreson

OR-SEST
coarsest
hoarsest

ORS-FUL
forceful
remorseful
resourceful
unremorseful

OR-SHUN
abortion
antiabortion
apportion
contortion
disproportion
distortion
extorsion
extortion
misproportion
portion
proportion
reapportion
retortion
torsion

OR-SING
coursing
deforcing
discoursing
divorcing
endorsing
enforcing
forcing
horsing
indorsing
reenforcing
reinforcing
unhorsing

OR-SLESS
forceless
horseless
remorseless
resourceless

OR-SMAN
horseman
Norseman

OR-SMENT
deforcement
divorcement
endorsement
enforcement
indorsement
reenforcement
reinforcement

OR-SNESS
coarseness
hoarseness

OR-SOME
boresome
dorsum
foursome

OR-SUR
coarser
courser
discourser
divorcer
endorser
enforcer
forcer
hoarser
indorser
reinforcer

OR-TAL
aortal
chortle
immortal
mortal
portal
postmortal
premortal
transportal

OR-TED
aborted
assorted
cavorted
consorted
contorted
courted
deported
distorted
escorted
exhorted
exported
extorted
imported
missorted
ported
purported
reported
resorted
shorted
snorted
sorted
sported
supported
thwarted
transported
unassorted
undistorted
unescorted
unreported
unsorted
unsupported

OR-TEKS
cortex
neocortex
subcortex
vortex

OR-TI
forty
shorty
snorty
sortie
sporty
warty

OR-TING
aborting
assorting
cavorting
consorting
courting
deporting
distorting
escorting
exhorting
exporting
extorting
importing
missorting
porting
purporting
reporting
resorting
retorting
self-supporting
shorting
snorting
sorting
sporting
supporting
thwarting
transporting
unsporting

OR-TIV
abortive
contortive

sportive
supportive

ORT-LI
courtly
portly
shortly

ORT-MENT
assortment
comportment
deportment

OR-TUNE
fortune
misfortune
importune

OR-TUR
distorter
exporter
extorter
forequarter
headquarter
hindquarter
importer
mortar
porter
quarter
reporter
ripsnorter
shorter
snorter
sorter
supporter
thwarter
transporter
woolsorter

OR-TURED
orchard
tortured

OR-UM
decorum
forum
indecorum
orem
quorum

OR-UR
abhorrer
adorer
borer
coinsurer
corer
deplorer
explorer
floorer
furor
horror
ignorer
lurer
poorer
pourer
restorer
roarer
scorer
snorer
soarer
sorer
surer

OR-US
boris
Brontosaurus
chorus
decorous
Dris

Horace
Ichtyosaurus
indecorous
loris
Morris
nonporous
Norris
oris
orris
phosphorous
porous
sonorous
stegosaurus
Taurus
thesaurus
torus
Tyrannosaurus

OR-WARD
foreword
forward
henceforward
shoreward
straightforward

Long O-SEST
closest
grossest

OS-ET
faucet

OSH-I
squashy
swashy
washy

OSH-ING
joshing
quashing

sloshing
squashing
swashing
washing

Long O-SHUR
gaucher
kosher

OSH-UR
brainwasher
dishwasher
josher
posher
swasher
washer
whitewasher

Long O-SHUN
commotion
demotion
devotion
emotion
goshen
laotian
locomotion
lotion
motion
notion
ocean
potion
promotion
scotian
slow-motion
transocean

Long O-SHUS
atrocious
ferocious
precocious

OS-I
bossy
drossy
flossy
glossy
mossy
posse

OS-IL
apostle
colossal
docile
fossil
glossal
jostle
wassail

OS-ING
bossing
crisscrossing
crossing
dossing
double-crossing
glossing
embossing
railway crossing
saucing
tossing

Long O-SIS
arteriosclerosis
autohypnosis
carcinosis
cirrhosis
diagnosis
halitosis
hypnosis
ichthyosis
ketosis
kyphosis
leucosis
leukosis
misdiagnosis
mitosis
mononucleosis
myosis
necrosis
nephrosis
neurosis
ornithosis
osmosis
perosis
pollinosis
polyhidrosis
prognosis
psychoneurosis
psychosis
ptosis
sclerosis
scoliosis
silicosis
stenosis
sycosis
symbiosis
thrombosis
trichinosis
tuberculosis
verminosis
virosis
zymosis

Long O-SIV
corrosive
erosive
explosive
implosive
nonexplosive

Long O-SNESS
bellicoseness
closeness
grandioseness
grossness
jocoseness
moroseness
verboseness

Long O-SO
amoroso
doloroso
mafioso
so-so
virtuoso

OS-OM
blossom
opossum
possum

Long O-STAL
coastal
postal

Long O-STED
boasted
coasted
ghosted
hosted
outboasted
overroasted
posted
roasted
toasted

OST-ED
accosted
defrosted
exhausted
frosted

OST-IK
acrostic
agnostic
caustic
diagnostic
gnostic
prediagnostic
prognostic

Long O-STING
boasting
coasting
ghosting
hosting
outboasting
overroasting
posting
roasting
toasting

OST-ING
accosting
costing
defrosting
exhausting
frosting

Long O-STLI
ghostly
mostly

OST-RUM
colostrum
nostrum
rostrum

Long O-STUR
boaster
coaster
ghoster

poster
roaster
roller-coaster
toaster
zoster

OST-UR
accoster
defroster
foster
Gloucester
imposter
impostor
paternoster
roster
zoster

Long O-SUR
closer
engrosser
grocer
grosser

OS-UR
Chaucer
crosser
double-crosser
embosser
saucer

Long O-TA
Dakota
iota
Kadota
Lakota
Minnesota
quota
Toyota

Long O-TAIT
notate
rotate

Long O-TAL
anecdotal
antidotal
motile
sclerotal
scrotal
subtotal
total

Long O-TED
bloated
boated
coated
connoted
demoted
denoted
devoted
doted
emoted
floated
footnoted
garroted
gloated
keynoted
misquoted
noted
outvoted
parotid
petticoated
promoted
quoted
sugarcoated
toted
undercoated
unnoted
voted

wainscoted

OT-ED
allotted
blotted
boycotted
clotted
counterplotted
dotted
garroted
jotted
knotted
parotid
plotted
potted
rotted
scotted
slotted
spotted
squatted
swatted
totted
trotted
unspotted
wainscoted
yachted

OT-EN
begotten
boughten
cotton
forgotten
gotten
gratin
guncotton
misbegotten
rotten
sauerbraten
tauten
unforgotten

Long O-THING
clothing
loathing
underclothing

Long OT-HOOK
boathook
coathook

OTH-UR
bother
forefather
godfather
grandfather
stepfather

Long O-TI
coyote
devotee
Don-Quixote
floaty
goatee
Quixote
throaty

OT-I
allottee
clotty
dotty
haughty
karate
knotty
lottie
naughty
potty
snotty
spotty
squatty
zloty

OT-IJ
cottage
frottage
plottage
pottage
wattage

OT-IK
aerobiotic
aeronautic
antibiotic
aquatic
arteriosclerotic
astronautic
biotic
chaotic
despotic
dichotic
erotic
escharotic
exotic
homozygotic
hypnotic
ichthyotic
idiotic
macrobiotic
melanotic
narcotic
neurotic
orthotic
patriotic
posthypnotic
prepsychotic
psychoneurotic
psychotic
quixotic
robotic
sclerotic
semiotic
subnarcotic

supraglottic
symbiotic
zygotic
zymotic

Long O-TING
bloating
boating
coating
connoting
demoting
denoting
devoting
doting
emoting
floating
footnoting
garroting
gloating
keynoting
misquoting
nonvoting
noting
outvoting
promoting
quoting
sailboating
speedboating
sugarcoating
toting
undercoating
voting
wainscoting

OT-ING
allotting
blotting
boycotting
clotting
counterplotting

dotting
garroting
globetrotting
jotting
knotting
plotting
potting
rotting
slotting
spotting
squatting
swatting
totting
trotting
wainscoting
yachting

OT-ISH
clottish
hottish
schottische
Scottish
sottish

Long O-TIST
anecdotist
noticed
protist
remotest

Long O-TIVE
automotive
electromotive
emotive
promotive
votive

OT-L
Aristotle
bluebottle

bottle
dottle
epiglottal
glottal
mottle
Nahuatl
supraglottal
throttle
tottle
twattle
wattle

OT-LESS
clotless
cotless
dotless
knotless
potless
rotless
spotless
thoughtless

OT-LI
hotly
motley
overwroughtly
squatly
tautly

Long O-TO
De-Soto
koto
Kyoto
photo
telephoto
toto
wirephoto

OT-O
blotto

grotto
legato
lotto
motto
mulatto
obbligato
pizzicato
sotto
staccato
vibrato

OTS-MAN
Scotsman
yachtsman

OT-UM
autumn
bottom

Long O-TUR
bloater
boater
doter
emoter
floater
garroter
gloater
keynoter
motor
neuromotor
oater
promoter
psychomotor
pulmotor
quoter
remoter
scapegoater
sensorimotor
servomotor
toter

voter

OT-UR
allotter
alma-mater
backwater
blackwater
blotter
boycotter
breakwater
cauter
clearwater
cotter
daughter
dishwater
dotter
firewater
floodwater
flyswatter
freshwater
garroter
globetrotter
goddaughter
granddaughter
headwater
heartwater
hotter
imprimatur
jerkwater
jotter
limewater
manslaughter
meltwater
otter
pinspotter
plotter
potter
rainwater
rosewater
rotter

saltwater
sandlotter
seawater
slaughter
spotter
squatter
stepdaughter
swatter
tatar
tauter
teeter-totter
tidewater
totter
trotter
underwater
water
yachter

OUCH-ING
avouching
couching
crouching
debouching
grouching
pouching
slouching
vouching

OUCH-UR
groucher
sloucher
voucher

OUD-ED
clouded
crowded
enshrouded
overcrowded
shrouded
uncrowded

OUD-EST
loudest
proudest

OUD-I
cloudy
cum laude
dowdy
howdy
pandowdy
rowdy

OUD-ING
beclouding
clouding
crowding
enshrouding
overclouding
overcrowding
shrouding

OUD-LI
loudly
proudly

OUD-NESS
loudness
proudness

OUD-UR
louder
powder
prouder

OU-EL
avowal
bowel
disavowal
disembowel
dowel

jowl
semivowel
towel
trowel
vowel
wildfowl
yowl

OU-ING
bellowing
bestowing
billowing
blowing
Boeing
borrowing
bowing
buffaloing
burrowing
churchgoing
crowing
easygoing
echoing
elbowing
embargoing
farrowing
flowing
following
foregoing
foreknowing
foreshadowing
forgoing
furloughing
furrowing
glassblowing
glowing
going
growing
hallowing
harrowing
hoeing

hollowing
imbargoing
ingrowing
kayoing
knowing
lassoing
lowing
mellowing
mimeoing
mind-blowing
moviegoing
mowing
narrowing
oceangoing
ongoing
outgoing
outgrowing
overflowing
overgrowing
overshadowing
overthrowing
owing
pillowing
radioing
reechoing
rowing
seagoing
sewing
shadowing
showing
slowing
snowing
soloing
sorrowing
sowing
stowing
stuccoing
swallowing
tangoing
thoroughgoing

throwing
tiptoeing
toeing
torpedoing
towing
undergoing
unknowing
vetoing
wallowing
whistle-blowing
windowing
winnowing
yellowing
zeroing

OUL-ING
befouling
cowling
disemboweling
disembowelling
doweling
fouling
fowling
growling
howling
prowling
scowling
yowling

OUL-UR
fouler
growler
howler
prowler
scowler
yowler

OUN-DED
abounded
astounded

bounded
compounded
confounded
dumbfounded
dumfounded
expounded
founded
grounded
hounded
impounded
mounded
overabounded
pounded
propounded
rebounded
resounded
rounded
sounded
surrounded
unbounded
unfounded
ungrounded

OUN-DEST
profoundest
roundest

OUN-DING
abounding
astounding
bounding
compounding
confounding
dumbfounding
dumfounding
expounding
founding
grounding
hounding
impounding

mounding
overabounding
pounding
propounding
rebounding
resounding
rounding
sounding
surrounding

OUND-LESS
boundless
groundless
soundless

OUND-LI
profoundly
roundly
soundly
unsoundly

OUND-LING
foundling
groundling

OUND-NESS
profoundness
roundness
soundness
unsoundness

OUN-DRI
boundary
foundry

OUN-DUR
bounder
confounder
expounder
flounder

founder
grounder
hounder
pounder
profounder
propounder
rounder
sounder

OUN-I
brownie
downy

OUN-ING
browning
clowning
crowning
downing
drowning
frowning
gowning

OUN-ISH
brownish
clownish

OUN-JING
lounging
scrounging

OUN-LESS
crownless
frownless
gownless

OUN-SEZ
announces
bounces
denounces
flounces

jounces
mispronounces
ounces
pounces
pronounces
renounces
trounces

OUN-SING
announcing
bouncing
denouncing
flouncing
jouncing
mispronouncing
pouncing
pronouncing
renouncing
trouncing

OUN-SUR
announcer
bouncer
denouncer
flouncer
renouncer

OUN-TED
accounted
amounted
counted
discounted
dismounted
miscounted
mounted
recounted
remounted
surmounted
unaccounted
uncounted

unmounted

OUN-TI
bounty
county
mountie
mounty

OUN-TIN
fountain
mountain

OUN-TING
accounting
amounting
counting
demounting
discounting
dismounting
miscounting
mounting
recounting
surmounting

OUN-WARD
downward
townward

Long O-UR
blower
boer
borrower
burrower
chipblower
churchgoer
echoer
filmgoer
flamethrower
follower
foregoer

foreshadower
frescoer
glassblower
grower
hallower
hoer
knower
lassoer
lower
mellower
mind-blower
mower
narrower
outgoer
overthrower
playgoer
rower
sewer
shadower
shallower
shower
slower
sower
swallower
thrower
tower
vetoer
widower
winegrower

O-UR
drawer
gnawer
rawer
sawer
withdrawer

OUR-I
avowry
bowery

cowrie
cowry
dowry
flowery
Maori

OUR-ING
adventuring
altering
anchoring
angering
answering
armoring
badgering
bantering
barbering
bartering
battering
beggaring
belaboring
beleaguering
bespattering
bettering
bewildering
bickering
blistering
blubbering
blundering
blustering
bolstering
bordering
bothering
broidering
buffering
butchering
buttering
cambering
cankering
cantering
cantilevering

capering
capturing
catering
censoring
censuring
centering
chambering
chamfering
chartering
chattering
chauffeuring
checkering
ciphering
clamoring
clattering
clinkering
clobbering
cloistering
cloturing
clustering
cluttering
collaring
coloring
configuring
conjecturing
conjuring
conquering
considering
cornering
cosponsoring
countering
covering
cowering
culturing
cumbering
deciphering
delivering
denaturing
diapering
dickering

differing
discoloring
discovering
disencumbering
disfiguring
dishonoring
dismembering
disordering
dissevering
doctoring
doddering
embittering
embroidering
empowering
enamoring
enciphering
encountering
encumbering
endangering
endeavoring
engendering
enrapturing
entering
factoring
faltering
favoring
feathering
featuring
festering
fettering
figuring
filibustering
filtering
fingering
firing
fissuring
flattering
flavoring
flickering
floundering

flouring
flowering
flustering
fluttering
fostering
foundering
fracturing
frittering
garnering
gartering
gathering
gendering
gerrymandering
gesturing
gibbering
glimmering
glittering
glowering
haltering
hammering
hampering
hankering
harboring
hatemongering
hectoring
hindering
hollering
honoring
hovering
huckstering
humoring
hungering
hunkering
incumbering
indenturing
injuring
inquiring
jabbering
jittering
kippering

laboring
lacquering
laundering
lawyering
layering
lettering
levering
limbering
lingering
littering
loitering
lowering
lumbering
majoring
malingering
maneuvering
manoeuvering
manufacturing
martyring
massacring
mastering
mattering
maundering
meandering
measuring
metering
ministering
miring
mirroring
misnumbering
moldering
monitoring
mortaring
mothering
motoring
muggering
murdering
murmuring
mustering
muttering

neighboring	puttering	silvering
neutering	quartering	simmering
nickering	quavering	simpering
numbering	quivering	skewering
nurturing	recapturing	skittering
offering	rechartering	slandering
ordering	recoloring	slathering
outmaneuvering	reconnoitering	slaughtering
outnumbering	reconquering	slavering
overpowering	reconsidering	slithering
oystering	recovering	slivering
palavering	rediscovering	slobbering
paltering	reentering	smattering
pampering	refiltering	smoldering
pandering	registering	smothering
papering	remaindering	snickering
pasturing	remembering	sniggering
pattering	rendering	sobering
peppering	renumbering	soldering
perjuring	reordering	soldiering
pestering	reupholstering	souring
petering	rumoring	spattering
philandering	rupturing	splattering
picturing	sandpapering	splintering
pilfering	sauntering	spluttering
plastering	savoring	sponsoring
plundering	scampering	sputtering
pondering	scattering	squandering
posturing	scissoring	staggering
pottering	sculpturing	stammering
powdering	sectoring	steamrollering
powering	sequestering	structuring
prefiguring	severing	stuttering
preregistering	shattering	succoring
pressuring	shimmering	suffering
proctoring	shivering	sugaring
proffering	shouldering	sulfuring
prospering	showering	sulphuring
puckering	shuddering	summering
puncturing	shuttering	sundering

surrendering
suturing
swaggering
sweltering
tailoring
tampering
tapering
tattering
teetering
tempering
tendering
tethering
thundering
timbering
tincturing
tinkering
tiring
tittering
tottering
towering
transfiguring
treasuring
triggering
tutoring
twittering
ulcering
uncovering
unfaltering
unflattering
unwavering
upholstering
ushering
uttering
venturing
wagering
wallpapering
wandering
warmongering
watering
wavering

weathering
weltering
whimpering
whispering
wintering
wiring
withering
wondering
woolgathering
yammering

OUR-UR
deflowerer
devourer
scourer
sourer

OUT-ED
clouted
doubted
flouted
outshouted
pouted
routed
scouted
shouted
spouted
sprouted
touted
undoubted

OUT-EST
devoutest
stoutest

OUT-I
doughty
gouty
grouty
pouty

OUT-ING
clouting
doubting
flouting
outing
outshouting
pouting
routing
scouting
shouting
spouting
sprouting
touting
undoubting

OUT-LI
devoutly
stoutly

OUT-NESS
devoutness
stoutness

OUT-UR
clouter
doubter
flouter
outer
pouter
router
scouter
shouter
stouter
touter

OU-UR
avower
bower
brainpower
candlepower

cauliflower
cornflower
cower
dayflower
deflower
dower
eisenhower
empower
endower
firepower
flour
flower
glower
horsepower
hour
hydropower
kowtower
manpower
mayflower
our
overpower
passionflower
plower
power
safflower
scour
shower
sour
sunflower
superpower
thundershower
tower
vower
wallflower
watchtower
waterpower
wildflower
willpower
windflower

OU-WOW
bow-wow
pow-wow

OU-ZAL
arousal
carousel
rearousal
spousal

OUZ-ZEZ
arouses
bathhouses
blouses
browses
carouses
chophouses
clearinghouses
clubhouses
courthouses
customhouses
douses
dowses
drowses
farmhouses
flophouses
henhouses
hothouses
houses
mouses
penthouses
rearouses
roughhouses
roundhouses
rouses
smokehouses
warehouses
workhouses

OU-ZI
blowsy
blowzy
drowsy
frowsy
frowzy
lousy
mousy

OUZ-ZING
arousing
blousing
browsing
carousing
dousing
dowsing
drowsing
espousing
housing
mousing
rearousing
roughhousing
rousing
warehousing

OUZ-UR
browser
carouser
dowser
mouser
rouser
towser
trouser
warehouser
wowser

OU-ZURZ
browsers
carousers
dowsers

mousers
rousers
trousers
trowsers
warehousers

OV-EL
grovel
hovel
novel
shovel

Long O-VEN
cloven
cordovan
rewoven
unwoven
woven

OV-EN
coven
oven
sloven

Long O-VINE
bovine
ovine

Long O-VUR
carryover
changeover
clover
dover
drover
flopover
hangover
holdover
layover
leftover
moreover

moveover
over
passover
popover
pullover
pushover
rollover
rover
slipover
stopover
strikeover
takeover
turnover
walkover

Long O-WAIR
hollowware
nowhere

O-YUR
lawyer
sawyer

Long O-ZEN
chosen
frozen
lederhosen
quickfrozen
refrozen
unchosen
unfrozen

Long O-ZEZ
exposes
Moses
roses

Long O-ZHUN
corrosion
erosion

explosion
implosion

Long O-ZI
cozy
dozy
nosey
nosy
posy
prosy
rosie
rosy

Long O-ZING
apposing
bulldozing
closing
composing
decomposing
deposing
disclosing
discomposing
disposing
dozing
enclosing
exposing
foreclosing
hosing
imposing
inclosing
juxtaposing
nosing
opposing
osmosing
overexposing
posing
predisposing
preexposing
presupposing
proposing

reimposing
reposing
sclerosing
superimposing
superposing
supposing
transposing
underexposing
unimposing

OZ-ING
causing
pausing

OZ-IT
closet
composite
deposit
posit
redeposit

OZ-L
causal
clausal
mazel
menopausal
nozzle
schnozzle
sozzle

Long O-ZUR
brownnoser
bulldozer
closer
composer
decomposer
deposer
discloser
disposer
dozer
exposer
imposer

opposer
poser
proposer
reposer

Long O-ZYUR
closure
composure
disclosure
enclosure
exclosure
exposure
foreclosure
inclosure
nondisclosure
osier
overexposure
preexposure
underexposure

U-AL

accrual
bejewel
crewel
cruel
dual
duel
eschewal
fuel
gruel
jewel
joule
lunule
mewl
newel
pilule
pursual
renewal
reviewal
schedule
vestibule
virgule

U-ANT

affluent
confluent
congruent
effluent
fluent
incongruent
obstruent
pursuant
suint
truant

U-BA

Cuba
scuba
tuba

U-BI

booby
ruby

UB-I

chubby
cubby
grubby
hubby
nubby
scrubby
shrubby
snubby
stubby
tubby

Long U-BIK

cherubic
cubic
pubic

Long U-BING

cubing
tubing

UB-ING

clubbing
dubbing
flubbing
grubbing
rubbing
scrubbing
snubbing
stubbing
subbing

UB-ISH

clubbish
rubbish

Long U-BIT

cubit
two-bit

UB-L

bubble
double
redouble
rubble
stubble
trouble

UB-LI

accountably
admirably
admissibly
adorably
advisably
affably
affirmably
agreeably
amenably
amiably
amicably
applicably
appreciably
apprehensibly
arguably
assumably
attainably
audibly
avoidably
bearably
believably
blamably
bubbly
capably
certifiably
charitably
colorably

comfortably
communicably
comparably
compatibly
conceivably
conformably
considerably
contemptibly
contestably
controllably
credibly
culpably
curably
damnably
debatably
defensibly
definably
delectably
demonstrably
dependably
deplorably
desirably
despicably
detachably
detectably
detestably
disagreeably
dishonorably
disputably
disreputably
distinguishably
doubly
durably
eligibly
enjoyably
enviably
equably
equitably
estimably
fallibly

fashionably
favorably
feasibly
flammably
flexibly
forcibly
formidably
gullibly
habitably
heritably
honorably
horribly
hospitably
identifiably
illegibly
imaginably
immeasurably
immovably
immutably
impalpably
impassibly
impeccably
impenetrably
imperceptibly
imperishably
impermeably
imperturbably
implacably
implausibly
imponderably
impossibly
impregnably
impressionably
improbably
inadmissibly
inadvisably
inalienably
inalterably
inapplicably
inaudibly

incalculably
incapably
incomparably
incompatibly
incomputably
inconceivably
inconsolably
incontestably
incontrovertibly
incorrigibly
incorruptibly
incredibly
incurably
indefatigably
indefensibly
indelibly
indescribably
indictably
indisputably
indistinguishably
indivisibly
indomitably
indubitably
ineffably
ineligibly
inequitably
inescapably
inestimably
inevitably
inexcusably
inexhaustibly
inexorably
inexplicably
inexpressibly
inextinguishably
inextricably
infallibly
inflexibly
inheritably
inhospitably

inimitably
insatiably
inscrutably
insensibly
inseparably
insolubly
insufferably
insurmountably
intangibly
intelligibly
interminably
intolerably
invaluably
invariably
invincibly
inviolably
invisibly
irreparably
irresistibly
irresponsibly
irretrievably
irreversibly
irrevocably
irritably
justifiably
knowledgeably
lamentably
laudably
laughably
legibly
lovably
loveably
malleably
manageably
measurably
memorably
miserably
movably
mutably
navigably

negligibly
noncontrollably
notably
noticeably
numerably
observably
operably
ostensibly
palatably
palpably
pardonably
passably
peaceably
penetrably
perceivably
perceptibly
perishably
permeably
permissibly
personably
persuadably
pitiably
plausibly
pleasurably
pliably
possibly
practicably
predictably
preferably
presentably
presumably
probably
profitably
proportionably
punishably
questionably
rateably
reasonably
recognizably
reconcilably

reducibly
refutably
regrettably
reliably
remarkably
reprehensibly
reputably
resistably
respectably
responsibly
rubbly
seasonably
sensibly
separably
serviceably
sizably
sociably
solubly
statutably
stubbly
suably
suitably
susceptibly
tangibly
tenably
terribly
thinkably
tolerably
traceably
tractably
treasonably
tunably
unacceptably
unaccountably
unalterably
unapproachably
unarguably
unassailably
unavoidably
unbearably

unbeatably
unbelievably
uncharitably
uncomfortably
unconquerably
unconscionably
uncontrollably
undeniably
understandably
undiscernibly
unendurably
unescapably
unexcusably
unexplainably
unfashionably
unfavorably
unflappably
unforgettably
unforgivably
unmistakably
unnoticeably
unpalatably
unperturbably
unpredictably
unprofitably
unquestionably
unreasonably
unreliably
unsatiably
unseasonably
unshakably
unsociably
unspeakably
unsuitably
unsurmountably
unsurpassably
unthinkably
untouchably
unworkably
variably

venerably
veritably
viably
violably
visibly
volubly
vulnerably

UB-LING
bubbling
doubling
redoubling
troubling

UB-LUR
bubbler
doubler
troubler

Long U-BRIK
lubric
rubric

Long U-BUR
goober
tuber

UB-UR
blubber
clubber
drubber
dubber
grubber
landlubber
lubber
money-grubber
rubber
scrubber
snubber
stubber

UCH-EZ
clutches
crutches
hutches
retouches
touches

UCH-I
archduchy
duchy
smutchy
touchy

UCH-ING
clutching
retouching
touching

Long U-DA
barracuda
Bermuda
Buddha

Long U-DED
brooded
concluded
deluded
denuded
duded
eluded
excluded
extruded
exuded
feuded
included
intruded
precluded
protruded

UD-ED
blooded
budded
cold-blooded
flooded
hot-blooded
pure-blooded
red-blooded
star-studded
thudded
warm-blooded

Long U-DENT
imprudent
jurisprudent
prudent
student

Long U-DEST
Buddhist
crudest
feudist
lewdest
nudest
nudist
rudest
shrewdest
Talmudist

Long U-DI
broody
Judy
moody

UD-I
bloody
buddy
cruddy
cuddy
duddie

duddy
fuddy
fuddy-duddy
hymnody
muddy
perfidy
ruddy
study
understudy

UD-ID
bloodied
muddied
unstudied

Long U-DING
alluding
brooding
concluding
deluding
denuding
eluding
excluding
extruding
exuding
feuding
including
intruding
obtruding
occluding
precluding
protruding
secluding
transuding

UD-ING
budding
flooding
scudding
studding

thudding

Long U-DL
boodle
caboodle
doodle
feudal
noodle
paludal
poodle
strudel
Yankee-Doodle

UD-L
befuddle
cuddle
fuddle
huddle
muddle
puddle
ruddle
synodal

Long U-DLI
crudely
lewdly
nudely
rudely
shrewdly

UD-LING
befuddling
cuddling
fuddling
huddling
muddling
puddling

UD-LUR
cuddler

fuddler
huddler
muddler
puddler

Long UD-NESS
crudeness
lewdness
nudeness
rudeness
shrewdness

Long U-DUR
brooder
concluder
cruder
deluder
eluder
excluder
intruder
lewder
nuder
ruder
shrewder

UD-UR
budder
rudder
shudder
solider
udder

Long U-E
bluey
bowie
buoy
chewy
chop-suey
dewy
flooey

gluey
gooey
hooey
interviewee
mildewy
phooey
screwy
sinewy
sloughy
suey
sui

Long U-EL
accrual
bejewel
crewel
cruel
dual
duel
eschewal
fuel
gruel
jewel
joule
lunule
mewl
newel
pilule
pursual
renewal
reviewal
schedule
vestibule
virgule

Long U-EST
altruist
bluest
canoeist
doest

fewest
newest
tattooist
truest
voodooist

Long U-ET
conduit
cruet
intuit
suet

UF-EN
muffin
puffin
ragamuffin
roughen
toughen

UF-EST
bluffest
gruffest
roughest
toughest

UF-I
buffy
chuffy
duffy
fluffy
huffy
puffy
scruffy
snuffy
stuffy
toughie

UF-IN
muffin
puffin

ragamuffin
roughen
toughen

Long U-FING
bulletproofing
goofing
proofing
roofing
soundproofing
spoofing
waterproofing
weatherproofing

UF-ING
bluffing
buffing
cuffing
fluffing
huffing
luffing
muffing
outbluffing
puffing
rebuffing
roughing
ruffing
scuffing
sloughing
snuffing
soughing
stuffing

UF-L
duffel
duffle
muffle
reshuffle
ruffle
scuffle

shuffle
snuffle
truffle
unmuffle

UF-LI
apocryphally
bluffly
gruffly
roughly
ruffly
snuffly
toughly

UF-LING
muffling
reshuffling
ruffling
scuffling
shuffling
snuffling
unmuffling

UF-LUR
muffler
ruffler
scuffler
shuffler

UF-NESS
bluffness
gruffness
roughness
toughness

Long U-FUR
goofer
hoofer
roofer
twofer

woofer

UF-UR
bluffer
buffer
duffer
gruffer
puffer
rougher
snuffer
stuffer
suffer
tougher

Long U-GAR
cougar
Lugar

UG-EST
druggist
smuggest
snuggest

UG-I
buggy
druggie
druggy
muggy
puggy
sluggy
thuggee

UG-ING
bugging
chugging
debugging
drugging
hugging
humbugging
jitterbugging

lugging
mugging
plugging
shrugging
slugging
tugging
unplugging

Long U-GL
bugle
frugal
fugal

UG-L
bugle
frugal
fugal

UG-LI
smugly
snugly
ugly

UG-LING
juggling
smuggling
snuggling
struggling

UG-LUR
juggler
smuggler
struggler

UG-NESS
smugness
snugness

UG-UR
bugger

hugger
huggermugger
humbugger
lugger
mugger
plugger
rugger
slugger
smugger
snugger
tugger

Long U-ID
Druid
fluid

Long U-IN
bruin
ruin
yuan

Long U-ING
accruing
arguing
ballyhooing
barbecuing
bedewing
bestrewing
blueing
bluing
booing
brewing
canoeing
clueing
cluing
construing
continuing
cooing
corkscrewing
cuing

curfewing
devaluing
discontinuing
doing
ensuing
eschewing
evildoing
ewing
gluing
hewing
imbuing
interviewing
issuing
mewing
mildewing
misconstruing
miscuing
misdoing
mooing
outdoing
overdoing
overvaluing
previewing
pursuing
queueing
queuing
redoing
reissuing
rendezvousing
renewing
rescuing
revaluing
reviewing
roughhewing
ruing
screwing
shampooing
shoeing
shooing
skewing

sloughing
sluing
snowshoeing
spewing
stewing
strewing
subduing
suing
tabooing
tattooing
trueing
truing
undervaluing
undoing
unscrewing
valuing
viewing
wooing
wrongdoing

UJ-EZ
begrudges
budges
drudges
fudges
grudges
judges
misjudges
nudges
prejudges
smudges
trudges

UJ-ING
adjudging
begrudging
budging
drudging
envisaging
fudging

grudging
imaging
judging
misjudging
nudging
prejudging
smudging
trudging
unbudging
ungrudging

UJ-ON
bludgeon
curmudgeon
dudgeon
gudgeon

UK-ET
bucket
ducat
Nantucket
Pawtucket

Long U-KI
fluky
kooky
pookie
pooky
spooky

UK-I
ducky
Kentucky
lucky
mucky
plucky
unlucky
yucky

UK-ING
bloodsucking
bucking
clucking
ducking
havocking
lucking
mucking
plucking
shucking
sucking
trucking
tucking
upchucking

UK-L
bare-knuckle
buccal
buckle
chuckle
honeysuckle
huckle
knuckle
pinochle
suckle
truckle
turnbuckle
unbuckle

UK-LD
buckled
chuckled
cuckold
knuckled
suckled
truckled
unbuckled

UK-LING
buckling

chucking
chuckling
duckling
knuckling
suckling
swashbuckling
truckling
unbuckling

UK-LUR
buckler
chronicler
chuckler
knuckler
swashbuckler
truckler

UK-SHUN
abduction
conduction
construction
deduction
destruction
induction
instruction
introduction
misinstruction
nonproduction
obstruction
preconstruction
preinduction
preinstruction
production
reconstruction
reduction
reproduction
seduction
subduction
suction
transduction

UK-TED
abducted
conducted
constructed
deducted
destructed
eructed
inducted
instructed
misinstructed
obstructed
preconstructed
preinstructed
reconstructed
unobstructed

UK-TING
abducting
conducting
constructing
deducting
destructing
ducting
eructing
inducting
instructing
misinstructing
obstructing
preconstructing
preinstructing
reconstructing

UK-TIVE
conductive
constructive
counterproductive
deductive
destructive
inductive
instructive

introductive
nonconstructive
nondestructive
nonproductive
obstructive
productive
reconstructive
reductive
reproductive
seductive
unproductive

UK-TRESS
conductress
instructress
seductress

UK-TUR
abductor
character
conductor
constructor
destructor
inductor
instructor
obstructer
obstructor
semiconductor
superconductor

Long U-KR
blucher
euchre
lucre
puker
rebuker

UK-UR
bloodsucker
bucker

chukker
mucker
plucker
pucker
sapsucker
seersucker
shucker
succor
sucker
trucker
tucker

Long U-LA
Ashtabula
Hula
hula-hula
moola
Missoula

Long U-LEP
julep
tulip

Long U-LESS
clueless
crewless
issueless
shoeless
valueless
viewless

UL-ET
gullet
mullet

UL-GAIT
promulgate
vulgate

Long UL-I
cooley
coolie
coulee
duly
newly
truly
unduly
unruly
untruly

Long U-LING
cooling
drooling
fooling
fueling
grueling
gruelling
mewling
misruling
overcooling
overruling
pooling
refueling
ridiculing
ruling
schooling
tooling

UL-ING
angling
annulling
appareling
apparelling
barreling
battling
bedazzling
bedraggling
befuddling
belittling

bespangling
beveling
bevelling
bicycling
bloodcurdling
bobbling
boggling
boodling
boondoggling
bottling
bridling
bugling
bumbling
bundling
bungling
burgling
caballing
cabling
cackling
canceling
cancelling
candling
capsuling
caroling
channeling
channelling
chiseling
chiselling
chortling
chucking
cobbling
coddling
commingling
counseling
counselling
cradling
cudgeling
cudgelling
culling
cycling

deviling
devilling
dialing
dialling
disemboweling
disembowelling
disheveling
dishevelling
doweling
driveling
drivelling
dueling
duelling
dulling
embezzling
empaneling
enabling
enameling
encapsuling
enfeebling
ennobling
entitling
equaling
equalling
fenagling
fiddling
finagling
fizzling
fondling
frazzling
freckling
frizzling
fuddling
fueling
fumbling
funneling
funnelling
gabbling
gambling
garbling

gargling
gaveling
gavelling
giggling
girdling
gobbling
goggling
grappling
graveling
groveling
grovelling
grumbling
gulling
gurgling
guzzling
hackling
haggling
handling
hassling
heckling
hobbling
hornswoggling
huddling
hulling
humbling
hurdling
hurtling
hustling
idling
impaneling
impanelling
imperiling
imperilling
initialing
initialling
jangling
jeweling
jiggling
jingling
jostling

juggling
jumbling
kibbling
labeling
labelling
ladling
leveling
levelling
libeling
libelling
lulling
manacling
marbling
marshaling
marshalling
martialing
martialling
marveling
marvelling
meddling
mingling
mishandling
mislabeling
mislabelling
modeling
modelling
mollycoddling
mottling
muddling
muffling
mulling
mumbling
muscling
muzzling
needling
nettling
nibbling
niggling
ogling
paddling

paneling
panelling
parceling
parcelling
pedaling
pedalling
penciling
pencilling
peopling
periling
pickling
piddling
piffling
pimpling
pinnacling
pommeling
pommelling
prattling
precanceling
puddling
pummeling
pummelling
puzzling
quadrupling
quarreling
quarrelling
quibbling
raffling
rambling
rattling
raveling
ravelling
recycling
redoubling
rekindling
relabeling
relabelling
remodeling
remodelling
rescheduling

resembling
resettling
reshuffling
reveling
revelling
riddling
riffling
rifling
rivaling
ruffling
rumbling
rumpling
rustling
sampling
scheduling
scrabbling
scrambling
scribbling
scuffling
sculling
scuttling
settling
shackling
shambling
shingling
shoveling
shovelling
shriveling
shrivelling
shuffling
shuttling
sideling
sidling
signaling
signalling
singling
sizzling
smuggling
sniffling
sniveling

snivelling
snorkeling
snuffling
snuggling
spangling
speckling
spiraling
spiralling
squabbling
squiggling
stabling
stapling
startling
stenciling
stencilling
stifling
stippling
stoppling
straddling
straggling
strangling
struggling
stumbling
subtitling
subtotaling
subtotalling
swaddling
swashbuckling
swindling
swiveling
swivelling
tabling
tackling
tasseling
tasselling
tattling
throttling
titling
toddling
toggling

toppling
totaling
totalling
toweling
trammeling
trammelling
trampling
traveling
travelling
trebling
trembling
trickling
trifling
tripling
troubling
trundling
tumbling
tunneling
tunnelling
tussling
twaddling
twiddling
unbuckling
uncoupling
unmuzzling
unraveling
unravelling
unscrambling
unsettling
unshackling
unsnarling
untangling
victualing
waddling
waffling
waggling
wailing
warbling
weaseling
whaling

wheedling
whiffling
whittling
wiggling
wobbling
wrangling
wrestling
wriggling
wrinkling
yodeling
yodelling
yowling

Long U-LIP
julep
tulip

Long U-LISH
coolish
foolish
ghoulish

UL-JENSE
indulgence
overindulgence

UL-JENT
effulgence
indulgence
overindulgence
refulgence

UL-JEZ
bulges
divulges
indulges
overindulges

ULK-I
bulky

hulky
sulky

ULK-ING
bulking
hulking
skulking
sulking

ULK-UR
sepulcher
sepulchre
skulker

UL-SHUN
avulsion
compulsion
convulsion
emulsion
evulsion
expulsion
impulsion
propulsion
repulsion
revulsion

UL-SING
avulsing
convulsing
pulsing
repulsing

UL-SIVE
compulsive
convulsive
emulsive
impulsive
propulsive
repulsive
revulsive

UL-TANT
consultant
exultant
resultant

UL-TED
consulted
exulted
insulted
resulted

UL-TING
consulting
exulting
insulting
resulting

UL-TURE
agriculture
anaculture
aquaculture
counterculture
culture
horticulture
multure
subculture
viticulture
vulture

Long U-LU
Honolulu
lulu
Zulu

Long U-LUR
cooler
crueler
crueller
preschooler

UL-UR
bottler
color
counsellor
counselor
crueler
crueller
discolor
dueler
duller
groveler
huller
jeweler
labeler
labeller
libeler
libeller
muller
puzzler
quarreler
quarreller
recolor
sculler
signaler
signaller
subtler
technicolor
traveler
tricolor
tunneler
tunneller
tutelar
twaddler
twiddler
versicolor
victualer
watercolor
yodeler

UL-URD
colored
discolored
dullard
multicolored
recolored
uncolored
varicolored
versicolored

UL-YUN
mullion
scullion

Long U-MA
duma
Montezuma
pneuma
puma
struma
Yuma

Long U-MAN
acumen
albumen
albumin
bitumen
crewman
human
inhuman
lumen
nonhuman
prehuman
subhuman
superhuman
Truman

UM-BA
rhumba
rumba

UM-BL
bumble
crumble
fumble
grumble
humble
jumble
mumble
rumble
stumble
tumble
umbel

UM-BLI
crumbly
grumbly
humbly
rumbly

UM-BLING
bumbling
crumbling
fumbling
grumbling
humbling
jumbling
mumbling
rumbling
stumbling
tumbling

UM-BLUR
fumbler
grumbler
humbler
mumbler
rumbler
stumbler
tumbler

UM-BO
gumbo
jumbo
mumbo
mumbo-jumbo
umbo

UM-BRUS
cumbrous
penumbrous
slumberous
slumbrous

UM-BUR
cucumber
cumber
disencumber
encumber
incumber
lumber
misnumber
number
outnumber
renumber
slumber
umber

Long U-MEN
acumen
albumen
albumin
bitumen
crewman
human
inhuman
lumen
nonhuman
prehuman
subhuman
superhuman

Truman

UM-EST
atomist
bummest
dumbest
glummest
handsomest
numbest

UM-ET
grummet
plummet
summit

Long UM-FUL
doomful
roomful

Long UM-I
fumy
gloomy
plumy
roomy
strumae

UM-I
blossomy
chummy
crumby
crummy
dummy
gummy
mummy
rummy
scummy
slummy
tummy
yummy

Long U-MID
humid
tumid

Long U-MING
assuming
blooming
booming
consuming
dooming
entombing
everblooming
exhuming
foredooming
fuming
grooming
looming
mushrooming
perfuming
pluming
presuming
resuming
rooming
subsuming
unassuming
vacuuming
zooming

UM-ING
becoming
benumbing
blossoming
bottoming
bumming
chumming
coming
crumbing
drumming
fathoming
forthcoming

gumming
homecoming
humming
incoming
numbing
oncoming
overcoming
plumbing
ransoming
shortcoming
slumming
strumming
succumbing
summing
thrumming
thumbing
unbecoming
upcoming
welcoming

UM-IT
grummet
plummet
summit

UM-LI
awesomely
comely
dumbly
fearsomely
gamesomely
gladsomely
glumly
gruesomely
handsomely
irksomely
lissomely
loathsomely
lonesomely
meddlesomely

noisomely
numbly
randomly
solemnly
tiresomely
troublesomely
unwholesomely
wearisomely
wholesomely
winsomely
worrisomely

UM-OK
hummock
stomach

UM-PASS
compass
encompass
gyrocompass
rumpus

UM-PET
crumpet
strumpet
trumpet

UM-PI
bumpy
clumpy
dumpy
frumpy
grumpy
jumpy
lumpy
stumpy

UMP-ING
bumping
clumping

dumping
humping
jumping
lumping
plumping
pumping
slumping
stumping
thumping
trumping

UM-PISH
dumpish
frumpish
grumpish
lumpish
plumpish

UMP-KIN
bumpkin
pumpkin

UM-PL
crumple
rumple

UM-PLING
crumpling
dumpling
rumpling

UMP-SHUN
assumption
consumption
gumption
presumption
resumption

UMP-SHUS
bumptious

scrumptious

UM-PUR
bumper
dumper
jumper
plumper
pumper
stumper
thumper

Long U-MUR
bloomer
boomer
consumer
costumer
groomer
perfumer

UM-UR
bummer
comer
drummer
dumber
glummer
handsomer
hummer
latecomer
midsummer
mummer
newcomer
number
plumber
plummer
rummer
scummer
slummer
strummer
succumber
summer

welcomer

Long U-MURD
humored
good-humored
ill-humored
rumored

Long U-MURS
bloomers
consumers
costumers
groomers
perfumers

UN-CHEZ
brunches
bunches
crunches
hunches
keypunches
lunches
punches
scrunches

UN-CHI
bunchy
crunchy
munchy
punchy

UN-CHING
bunching
crunching
hunching
keypunching
lunching
munching
punching
scrunching

UN-CHUN
luncheon
truncheon

UN-CHUR
buncher
cruncher
luncher
muncher
puncher

UN-DAI
Monday
sundae
Sunday

UN-DANS
abundance
overabundance
redundance

UN-DANT
abundant
overabundant
redundant

UN-DL
bundle
trundle

UN-DON
London
undone

UN-DUR
asunder
blunder
calendar
cylinder
Englander

hereunder
highlander
Hollander
husbander
Icelander
islander
lavender
lowlander
mainlander
plunder
refunder
sunder
thereunder
thunder
under
whereunder
wonder
woodlander
Zealander

UN-EL
funnel
gunnel
gunwale
hymenal
lienal
lumenal
promotional
propagational
proportional
propositional
runnel
transfusional
transportational
tunnel
turbinal
vicinal
virginal

Long U-NESS
blueness
fewness
newness
skewness
trueness

Long UN-FUL
spoonful
tablespoonful
teaspoonful
tuneful

UNG-GL
bungle
fungal
jungle

UNG-GUR
fashionmonger
fishmonger
hunger
monger
newsmonger
rumormonger
scandalmonger
scaremonger
warmonger
whoremonger
younger

UNG-KI
chunky
clunky
flunkey
flunky
funky
gunky
hunky
junkie

junky
monkey
spunky

UNG-KL
carbuncle
peduncle
truncal
uncle

UNG-KN
drunken
shrunken
sunken

UNG-KSHUN
adjunction
compunction
conjunction
disfunction
dysfunction
function
injunction
inunction
junction
malfunction
subfunction
subfunctions
unction

UNG-KSHUS
rambunctious
unctuous

UNG-KTUR
acupuncture
conjuncture
juncture
puncture

UNG-KUR
bunker
drunker
dunker
hunker

UNG-KURD
drunkard
hunkered

Long U-NI
loony
luny
moonie
moony
puisne
puny
spoony
zuni

UN-I
bargainee
barony
bunny
funny
gunny
honey
lineny
money
runny
scrutiny
sixpenny
sonny
sunny
tunney
tunny
unfunny

Long U-NIK
eunuch

Munich
Punic
runic
tunic

Long U-NING
attuning
ballooning
cartooning
communing
crooning
dragooning
festooning
harpooning
honeymooning
importuning
impugning
lampooning
marooning
mistuning
mooning
pruning
spooning
swooning
tuning

UN-ING
abandoning
apportioning
auctioning
auditioning
awakening
bargaining
battening
beckoning
betokening
blackening
blazoning
bludgeoning
brightening

broadening
burdening
burgeoning
captaining
captioning
casehardening
cautioning
chairmaning
chairmanning
championing
chastening
cheapening
chickening
christening
coarsening
commissioning
conditioning
cordoning
cottoning
counterconditioning
counteropening
crimsoning
cunning
curtaining
cushioning
dampening
darkening
deadening
deafening
deepening
determining
disburdening
disheartening
disillusioning
dunning
emblazoning
emboldening
enlightening
enlivening
envisioning

examining
fashioning
fastening
fattening
flattening
foretokening
freshening
frightening
functioning
gardening
garrisoning
gladdening
glistening
gunning
gunrunning
happening
hardening
harkening
harshening
hastening
hearkening
heartening
heightening
hoarsening
illumining
imagining
impassioning
imprisoning
jettisoning
ladening
leavening
lengthening
lessening
lightening
likening
listening
livening
loosening
maddening
malfunctioning

mentioning
moistening
motioning
occasioning
opening
orphaning
outbargaining
outgunning
outreasoning
outrunning
overburdening
pardoning
partitioning
pensioning
petitioning
pinioning
poisoning
portioning
positioning
preconditioning
predestining
predetermining
preexamining
proportioning
punning
questioning
quickening
rationing
rattening
ravening
reabandoning
reapportioning
reasoning
reawakening
rebuttoning
rechristening
reckoning
reconditioning
reddening
reenlightening

reexamining
refashioning
refastening
reopening
repositioning
requisitioning
rerunning
resharpening
ripening
rosining
roughening
ruining
rumrunning
running
saddening
sanctioning
seasoning
sectioning
sharpening
shortening
shunning
sickening
siphoning
slackening
smartening
softening
stationing
steepening
stiffening
straightening
straitening
strengthening
stunning
summoning
sunning
sweetening
syphoning
thickening
threatening
tightening

toughening
unburdening
unbuttoning
unfastening
unloosening
unquestioning
unreasoning
vacationing
visioning
wakening
wantoning
weakening
whitening
widening
worsening

Long U-NISH
baboonish
buffoonish
moonish
poltroonish

UN-ISH
hunnish
kittenish
paganish
punish

Long U-NIST
balloonist
bassoonist
cartoonist
immunist
lampoonist
opportunist
soonest

UN-JEZ
challenges
expunges

lozenges
lunges
plunges
sponges

UN-JING
challenging
expunging
lunging
plunging
scavenging
sponging
unchallenging

UN-JUN
dungeon
sponging

UN-JUR
lunger
plunger

Long U-NLESS
moonless
tuneless

Long U-NO
Juneau
Juno
numero uno
uno

UN-TAL
biparental
cliental
contrapuntal
disgruntle
frontal
infantile

UN-TED
absented
affronted
blunted
bunted
confronted
covenanted
frequented
grunted
hunted
patented
pigmented
punted
shunted
stunted
talented
unfrequented
unpatented
untalented
warranted

UN-TING
absenting
affronting
blunting
bunting
confronting
covenanting
frequenting
fronting
grunting
headhunting
hunting
patenting
punting
shunting
stunting
warranting

UN-TUR
blunter
carpenter
confronter
covenantor
frequenter
grunter
headhunter
hunter
patentor
punter
shunter
warranter

Long U-NUR
communer
crooner
honeymooner
impugner
kroner
kronor
lampooner
lunar
schooner
semilunar
sooner
spooner
sublunar
swooner
tuner

UN-UR
bargainer
beckoner
blackener
Dubliner
flattener
foreigner
forerunner
Gunnar

gunner
gunrunner
lightener
livener
Londoner
mentioner
pensioner
poisoner
questioner
reopener
roadrunner
rottener
rumrunner
runner
sanctioner
shunner
sickener
straightener
strengthener
sweetener
thickener
threatener
tightener

Long U-NYON
communion
prounion
reunion
union

UN-YON
bunion
Bunyan
grunion
onion
Paul-Bunyan
trunnion

Long U-PI
croupy

groupie
kewpie
loopy
rupee
snoopy
soupy
whoopee

UP-I
guppy
puppy
syrupy

Long U-PID
Cupid
stupid

Long U-PING
cooping
drooping
duping
grouping
looping
pooping
recouping
regrouping
scooping
snooping
souping
stooping
swooping
trooping
whooping

Long U-PL
duple
octuple
pupal
pupil
quintuple

sextuple

UP-L
couple
decouple
quintuple
septuple
supple
thermocouple
uncouple

UP-LET
couplet
octuplet
quintuplet
septuplet
sextuplet

UP-SHUN
corruption
disruption
eruption
incorruption
interruption
irruption

UPT-LI
abruptly
corruptly
incorruptly

UPT-NESS
abruptness
corruptness

Long U-PUR
blooper
cooper
grouper
hooper

looper
paratrooper
party-pooper
pooper
snooper
stupor
super
super-duper
swooper
trooper
whooper

UP-UR
crupper
developer
galloper
redeveloper
scalloper
scupper
supper
upper

UR-A
pleura
coloratura
bravura

U-RAL
caesural
extramural
intermural
intramural
jural
mural
neural
photomural
pleural
plural
puerile
rural

subneural
transmural
ural

UR-ANS
assurance
coinsurance
endurance
insurance
overinsurance
reassurance
securance

UR-BAN
bourbon
suburban
turban
turbine
urban

UR-BING
curbing
disturbing
perturbing

UR-BL
gerbil
gerbille
herbal
honorable

UR-CHEZ
besmirches
birches
lurches
perches
researches
searches
smirches

UR-CHUR
aperture
besmircher
bircher
nurture
overture
percher

UR-DED
forwarded
girded
hazarded
herded
placarded

UR-DI
bastardy
birdie
jeopardy
sturdy
wordy

UR-DING
forwarding
hazarding
herding
placarding
rewording
sheepherding
shepherding
undergirding
wording

UR-DL
curdle
girdle
hurdle

UR-DUR
forwarder

girder
herder
placarder
sheepherder

UR-ENS
concurrence
countertransference
deterrence
furtherance
inference
occurrence
recurrence
reoccurrence
transference

UR-ENT
concurrent
countercurrent
crosscurrent
currant
current
deterrent
occurrent
recurrent
undercurrent

U-REST
demurest
jurist
manicurist
maturest
miniaturist
obscurest
pedicurist
poorest
purest
purist
securest
surest

tourist

UR-GL
burgle
gurgle

U-RI
blurry
burry
buttery
curry
electrosurgery
feathery
floury
flurry
furriery
furry
fury
gingery
heathery
honoree
hurry
hurry-scurry
jugglery
jury
murderee
papery
scurry
slurry
surrey
transferee
vapory
watery
whirry
worry

U-RING
averring
bestirring
blurring

bolstering
burring
calendaring
calipering
concurring
conferring
deferring
deflowering
demurring
deterring
diapering
dismembering
disordering
dissevering
doddering
during
empowering
entering
erring
factoring
fathering
feathering
featuring
floundering
flouring
flowering
furring
furthering
gartering
gathering
glowering
hiring
huckstering
humoring
hungering
incurring
inferring
laboring
lacquering
lathering

laundering
lettering
littering
lowering
massacring
murmuring
occurring
preferring
purring
recurring
referring
reoccurring
sepulchering
sepulchring
sheltering
shirring
slumbering
slurring
souring
spurring
stirring
transferring
unerring
whirring

UR-ISH
amateurish
cleverish
feverish
flourish
nourish

UR-JENT
convergent
detergent
emergent
insurgent
resurgent
urgent

UR-JEZ
dirges
diverges
purges
reemerges
scourges
splurges
upsurges
urges

UR-JI
allergy
clergy
energy
lethargy
liturgy
metallurgy
synergy
zymurgy

UR-JIK
allergic
lysergic
metallurgic
synergic

UR-JING
converging
diverging
emerging
merging
purging
reemerging
scourging
splurging
submerging
surging
unmerging
urging
verging

UR-JUN
allergen
allergin
burgeon
microsurgeon
psychosurgeon
sturgeon
surgeon
virgin

UR-JUR
merger
perjure
verdure
verger

UR-KI
Albuquerque
jerky
murky
perky
quirky
turkey

UR-KIN
firkin
furkin
gherkin

UR-KING
clerking
hardworking
irking
jerking
lurking
metalworking
networking
outworking
overworking
perking

reworking
shirking
smirking
woodworking
working

UR-KUR
caseworker
dockerworker
glassworker
homeworker
houseworker
ironworker
jerker
metalworker
needleworker
outworker
pieceworker
shirker
smirker
steelworker
tearjerker
timeworker
woodworker
worker

UR-LI
demurely
early
immaturely
impurely
insecurely
maturely
obscurely
pearlie
poorly
prematurely
purely
purlie
securely

surely
unsurely

UR-LING
curling
fingerling
fosterling
furling
hireling
hirelings
hurling
impearling
purling
sterling
swirling
twirling
uncurling
underling
unfurling
whirling

UR-LISH
churlish
girlish
schoolgirlish

UR-LOIN
purloin
sirloin
tenderloin

UR-LU
curlew
purlieu

UR-LUR
curler
hurler
twirler
whirler

UR-MAL
isothermal
mesodermal
peridermal
photothermal
stenothermal
subdermal
thermal

UR-MAN
alderman
counterman
determine
doberman
ermine
fireman
fisherman
german
letterman
lumberman
merman
motorman
oysterman
predetermine
sermon
triggerman
vermin
wasserman

UR-MENT
accouterment
averment
betterment
bewilderment
conferment
deferment
determent
disfigurement
dismemberment
embitterment

empowerment
encipherment
endangerment
interment
measurement
peppermint
preferment
wonderment

UR-MI
germy
squirmy
taxidermy
wormy

UR-MIK
blastodermic
euthermic
mesodermic
peridermic
photothermic
thermic
tridermic
zoodermic

UR-MING
affirming
confirming
firming
reaffirming
squirming
terming
worming

UR-MIT
hermit
permit

UR-MITE
termite

thermite

UR-MUR
firmer
murmur
squirmer
termer

UR-NAL
diurnal
fraternal
hibernal
journal
maternal
paternal
sternal
vernal

UR-NESS
demureness
impureness
insecureness
matureness
prematureness
pureness
secureness
sureness
unsureness

UR-NI
attorney
ferny
gurney
journey
tourney

UR-NING
adjourning
burning
churning

concerning
discerning
earning
governing
interning
ironing
kerning
learning
misgoverning
overturning
patterning
readjourning
relearning
returning
sojourning
spurning
sunburning
turning
undiscerning
unlearning
upturning
yearning

UR-NISH
burnish
furnish
overfurnish

URN-MENT
adjournment
concernment
discernment
government
internment
misgovernment
progovernment
readjournment
secernent
sojournment

UR-NO
Inferno
Sterno

UR-NUR
afterburner
churner
earner
easterner
learner
southeasterner
southerner
southwesterner
stubborner
turner
westerner

UR-O
borough
burro
burrow
furrow
thorough

U-ROR
adjurer
adjuror
assurer
assuror
coinsurer
curer
demurer
fuhrer
furor
insurer
juror
lurer
maturer
obscurer
poorer

procurer
purer
reinsurer
securer
surer

UR-PING
burping
chirping
slurping
usurping

UR-SA
bursa
ursa
versa

UR-SAL
bursal
disbursal
dispersal
rehearsal
reversal
traversal
universal

UR-SEZ
asperses
coerces
converses
curses
disburses
disperses
hearses
immerses
intersperses
inverses
nurses
purses
rehearses

reimburses
reverses
submerses
transverses
traverses
universes
verses
versus

UR-SHAL
commercial
controversial

UR-SHUN
conversion
discursion
emersion
eversion
excursion
extraversion
extroversion
immersion
incursion
interspersion
introversion
inversion
persian
perversion
retroversion
reversion
submersion
subversion
version

UR-SI
controversy
mercy
oversee
undersea

UR-SING
aspersing
coercing
conversing
cursing
disbursing
dispersing
immersing
interspersing
nursing
pursing
rehearsing
reimbursing
submersing
traversing

UR-SIVE
cursive
extraversive
introversive
inversive
perversive
subversive

URS-NESS
adverseness
diverseness
perverseness
terseness

UR-STED
thirsted
worsted

UR-STING
bursting
thirsting
worsting

UR-SUR
bursar
coercer
curser
cursor
disburser
disperser
nurser
precursor
purser
rehearser
reverser
tercer
terser
traverser

UR-SUS
asperses
coerces
converses
curses
disburses
disperses
hearses
immerses
intersperses
inverses
nurses
purses
rehearses
reimburses
reverses
submerses
transverses
traverses
universes
verses
versus

UR-TAN
albertan
burton
certain
curtain
uncertain

UR-TED
adverted
alerted
asserted
averted
blurted
concerted
controverted
converted
deserted
discomforted
disconcerted
diverted
exerted
extraverted
extroverted
flirted
girted
inserted
introverted
inverted
miniskirted
overexerted
perverted
preinserted
reasserted
reconverted
reinserted
retroverted
skirted
spurted
squirted
subverted

uncomforted
unconverted

URTH-LESS
mirthless
worthless

UR-TI
dirty
flirty
thirty

UR-TING
adverting
alerting
asserting
averting
blurting
comforting
controverting
converting
deserting
discomforting
disconcerting
diverting
exerting
flirting
girting
hurting
inserting
inverting
overexerting
perverting
preinserting
reasserting
reconverting
reinserting
reverting
shirting
skirting

spurting
squirting
subverting
uncomforting

UR-TIVE
assertive
furtive

UR-TL
fertile
hurtle
infertile
kirtle
myrtle
turtle
unfertile

URT-LESS
shirtless
skirtless

URT-LI
alertly
covertly
curtly
expertly
inertly
inexpertly
malapertly
overtly
pertly
stalwartly

URT-NESS
alertness
covertness
curtness
expertness
inertness

malapertness
pertness

UR-TUR
alerter
assertor
converter
convertor
curter
deserter
diverter
frankfurter
inserter
invertor
perter
perverter
skirter
subverter

U-RUR
adjurer
adjuror
assurer
assuror
coinsurer
curer
demurer
fuhrer
furor
insurer
juror
lurer
maturer
obscurer
poorer
procurer
purer
reinsurer
securer
surer

UR-UR
alterer
answerer
armorer
barterer
bickerer
bitterer
blubberer
blunderer
blusterer
bolsterer
borderer
capturer
caterer
censurer
charterer
chatterer
clatterer
cleverer
coadventurer
conferrer
conjurer
conjuror
conqueror
coverer
deferrer
deliverer
demurrer
discoverer
disfigurer
dodderer
embroiderer
emperor
encounterer
enterer
favorer
filibusterer
flatterer
flutterer
fosterer

fritterer
gatherer
hammerer
hamperer
harborer
hinderer
hirer
honorer
hoverer
humorer
injurer
inquirer
jabberer
laborer
lacquerer
launderer
lecturer
letterer
lingerer
litterer
loiterer
malingerer
maneuverer
manufacturer
massacrer
maunderer
meanderer
measurer
multurer
murderer
murmurer
nurturer
offerer
offeror
orderer
pamperer
panderer
paperer
pasturer
patterer

perjurer
pesterer
philanderer
picturer
pilferer
plasterer
plunderer
ponderer
posturer
powderer
preferrer
profferer
putterer
quaverer
quiverer
referrer
registerer
rememberer
renderer
saunterer
scatterer
shelterer
shiverer
silverer
simperer
slanderer
slaughterer
slenderer
slumberer
soberer
solderer
sputterer
squanderer
staggerer
stammerer
stirrer
stutterer
sufferer
surrenderor
swaggerer

taborer
tamperer
temperer
tenderer
tinkerer
torturer
totterer
transferor
transferrer
treasurer
twitterer
upholsterer
utterer
venturer
wagerer
wanderer
waverer
wonderer
yammerer

UR-VENT

fervent
maidservant
manservant
observant
servant
unobservant

UR-VI

curvy
nervy
scurvy
turvy

UR-VING

conserving
curving
deserving
nerving
observing

preserving
reserving
serving
swerving
timeserving
undeserving
unnerving
unobserving
unswerving

UR-VUR
fervor
observer
server
timeserver

UR-ZHUN
conversion
discursion
emersion
eversion
excursion
extraversion
extroversion
immersion
incursion
interspersion
introversion
inversion
persian
perversion
retroversion
reversion
submersion
subversion
version

U-SEZ
adduces
cabooses

calabooses
conduces
deduces
deuces
duces
educes
gooses
induces
introduces
juices
looses
mongooses
mousses
nooses
outproduces
overproduces
papooses
produces
recluses
reduces
reinduces
reproduces
ruses
sluices
spruces
traduces
truces
unlooses
uses
vamooses

US-EZ
abacuses
anises
apprentices
archduchesses
artifices
asparaguses
baronesses
benefactresses

biases
blunderbusses
bodices
bonuses
burgesses
buses
businesses
busses
buttresses
calculuses
canvasses
captresses
choruses
christmases
chrysalises
citruses
cockatrices
congresses
cornices
crevices
crocuses
cusses
cutlasses
deaconesses
dentifrices
derrises
dinguses
discuses
discusses
duchesses
edifices
embarrasses
empresses
epiglottises
eucalyptuses
eyewitnesses
fetuses
focuses
focusses
fortresses

fracases
funguses
furnaces
fusses
geniuses
genuses
giantesses
gladioluses
glottises
goddesses
governesses
grimaces
gyrocompasses
harasses
harnesses
heiresses
hiatuses
hibiscuses
highnesses
hippopotamuses
hospices
hostesses
huntresses
iambuses
ibises
ictuses
ignoramuses
illnesses
impetuses
incubuses
injustices
irises
isthmuses
jaundices
judases
justices
kindnesses
lattices
laundresses
lettuces

likenesses
lionesses
lotuses
malefactresses
mantises
mattresses
mayoresses
menaces
meniscuses
minibuses
minuses
mistresses
mittimuses
mortises
murderesses
musses
narcissuses
necklaces
nexuses
nimbuses
nonpluses
notices
novices
octopuses
oedipuses
ogresses
omnibuses
orifices
orrises
palaces
pancreases
papyruses
patronesses
peeresses
penises
phalluses
pinnaces
plexuses
pluses
poetesses

porpoises
poultices
practices
precipices
prefaces
prejudices
premises
priestesses
protectresses
purchases
purposes
radiuses
rebuses
refocuses
resurfaces
rhinoceroses
roughnesses
ruckuses
rumpuses
sculptresses
seamstresses
seductresses
shepherdesses
sicknesses
sinuses
solstices
songstresses
sorceresses
statuses
stewardesses
styluses
subsurfaces
surfaces
surplices
surpluses
syllabuses
temptresses
terminuses
terraces
thesauruses

thicknesses
thymuses
tigresses
toastmistresses
tortoises
traitresses
treatises
trellises
trespasses
trusses
villainesses
viruses
waitresses
walruses
weaknesses
windlasses
witnesses

USH-EZ
blushes
brushes
bulrushes
crushes
flushes
gushes
hairbrushes
hushes
inrushes
lushes
mushes
paintbrushes
rushes
shushes
thrushes
toothbrushes

USH-I
gushy
mushy
plushy

rushy
slushy

USH-ING
airbrushing
blushing
brushing
crushing
flushing
gushing
hushing
inrushing
mushing
rushing
shushing
unblushing

Long U-SHUN
ablution
absolution
aleutian
attribution
circumlocution
confucian
constitution
contribution
convolution
counterrevolution
destitution
devolution
diminution
distribution
electrocution
elocution
evolution
execution
institution
interlocution
involution
irresolution

lilliputian
locution
persecution
pollution
prosecution
prostitution
reconstitution
redistribution
resolution
restitution
retribution
revolution
solution
substitution

USH-UN
byelorussian
concussion
discussion
percussion
prussian
repercussion
russian
succession

USH-UR
brusher
crusher
gusher
plusher
rusher
usher

Long U-SI
acey-deucey
goosey
goosy
lucy

US-I
fussy
gussie
gussy
hussy
jealousy
mussy
promise

Long U-SING
adducing
conducing
deducing
educing
goosing
inducing
introducing
juicing
loosing
outproducing
producing
reducing
reproducing
schussing
seducing
sluicing
sprucing
traducing
transducing
unloosing
vamoosing

US-ING
antibusing
apprenticing
biasing
biassing
busing
bussing
buttressing

callousing
callusing
canvasing
canvassing
caucusing
chorusing
compassing
cussing
discussing
embarrassing
encompassing
focusing
focussing
fussing
grimacing
harassing
harnessing
jaundicing
latticing
malpracticing
menacing
mussing
nonplusing
noticing
onrushing
poulticing
practicing
prefacing
prejudicing
premising
promising
purchasing
purposing
refocusing
refocussing
resurfacing
servicing
solacing
surfacing
terracing

trussing
unharnessing
unpromising
witnessing

Long U-SIV
abusive
allusive
conclusive
conducive
diffusive
effusive
elusive
exclusive
extrusive
illusive
inclusive
inconclusive
intrusive
nonexclusive
noninclusive
protrusive
reclusive
retrusive
seclusive
unobtrusive

US-IV
concussive
percussive
purposive
repercussive

US-KI
dusky
husky
musky

US-KING
busking

dusking
husking

US-KUR
brusker
husker
tusker

US-L
bustle
corpuscle
hustle
justle
muscle
mussel
rustle
tussle

US-LING
bustling
hustling
muscling
rustling
tussling

US-LUR
bustler
hustler
rustler

Long U-SNESS
diffuseness
looseness
obtuseness
profuseness

Long U-SOM
grewsome
gruesome
twosome

US-TED
adjusted
ballasted
breakfasted
busted
crusted
deforested
disgusted
disinterested
distrusted
dusted
encrusted
entrusted
forested
harvested
interested
intrusted
lusted
maladjusted
mistrusted
readjusted
reforested
rusted
trusted
unforested
unharvested

UST-FUL
distrustful
lustful
mistrustful
trustful
untrustful

US-TI
amnesty
busty
crusty
dishonesty
dusty

dynasty
fusty
gusty
honesty
immodesty
lusty
majesty
modesty
musty
rusty
trustee
trusty

US-TING
adjusting
ballasting
blockbusting
breakfasting
busting
crusting
deforesting
disgusting
distrusting
dusting
entrusting
harvesting
interesting
intrusting
lusting
mistrusting
readjusting
reforesting
rusting
thrusting
trustbusting
trusting

UST-LI
augustly
dishonestly

earnestly
embarrassedly
honestly
immodestly
justly
modestly
overmodestly
prejudicedly
robustly
unbiasedly
unjustly

UST-NESS
augustness
earnestness
honestness
justness
robustness
unjustness

US-TRUS
lustrous
robustness
sinistrous

Long U-STUR
booster
rooster

US-TUR
adjuster
adjustor
banister
blockbuster
bluster
broncobuster
buster
chorister
cluster
duster

filibuster
fluster
forester
harvester
lackluster
luster
lustre
muster
preregister
sinister
trustbuster
truster
trustor

US-TURD
blustered
clustered
custard
filibustered
flustered
mustard
mustered
preregistered

Long U-SUR
inducer
introducer
juicer
looser
producer
reducer
reproducer
seducer
sprucer
traducer
transducer

Long U-TAL
brutal
futile

isobutyl

Long U-TANT
disputant
mutant
pollutant

Long U-TED
attributed
booted
commuted
computed
constituted
contributed
convoluted
deep-rooted
deputed
diluted
disputed
electrocuted
executed
fluted
fruited
hooted
imputed
instituted
involuted
looted
mooted
muted
parachuted
persecuted
polluted
prosecuted
prostituted
reconstituted
recruited
refuted
reputed
restituted

rooted
routed
saluted
scooted
substituted
suited
tooted
transmuted
undiluted
undisputed
unexecuted
unpolluted
unprosecuted
unrefuted
unsuited
uprooted

Long U-TEST
acutest
cutest
flutist
lutist
minutest
parachutist
pharmaceutist
therapeutist

Long UTH-FUL
ruthful
toothful
truthful
untruthful
youthful

Long UTH-ING
smoothing
soothing

Long UTH-LESS
ruthless

toothless
truthless

Long UTH-UR
smoother
soother

UTH-UR
another
brother
godmother
grandmother
housemother
mother
other
smother
stepbrother
stepmother

Long U-TI
beauty
bootee
booty
cootie
cutie
duty
fluty
fruity
persecutee
rooty
snooty
tutti

UT-I
crotchety
gutty
maggoty
moribundity
nutty
puttee

putty
rutty
smutty
suety

Long U-TIK
hermeneutic
pharmaceutic
psychotherapeutic
scorbutic
therapeutic

Long U-TIL
brutal
futile
isobutyl
rutile
utile

Long U-TING
booting
commuting
computing
constituting
contributing
convoluting
disputing
distributing
electrocuting
executing
fluting
fruiting
hooting
imputing
instituting
looting
mooting
muting
overshooting
parachuting

persecuting
polluting
prosecuting
prostituting
reconstituting
recruiting
refuting
reputing
restituting
rooting
routing
scooting
sharpshooting
shooting
substituting
suiting
tooting
transmuting
trapshooting
troubleshooting
undershooting
uprooting

UT-ING
accrediting
attributing
auditing
balloting
banqueting
billeting
blanketing
bracketing
bucketing
budgeting
buffeting
butting
carpeting
circuiting
closeting
cohabiting

coveting
crediting
crosscutting
cutting
debiting
delimiting
depositing
dieting
discomfiting
discrediting
disquieting
docketing
editing
eliciting
exhibiting
exiting
faceting
fagoting
ferreting
fidgeting
forfeiting
gibbeting
glutting
gutting
haircutting
inhabiting
inheriting
inhibiting
interpreting
intuiting
junketing
jutting
legitimating
limiting
marketing
meriting
misinterpreting
orbiting
outpocketing
parroting

picketing
piloting
pirating
pivoting
plummeting
pocketing
positing
prelimiting
profiting
prohibiting
putting
quieting
rabbeting
rebutting
redistributing
reediting
revisiting
rioting
riveting
rivetting
rocketing
rutting
secreting
shutting
skyrocketing
soliciting
spiriting
stonecutting
strutting
surfeiting
surrebutting
targeting
ticketing
trumpeting
undercutting
visiting
vomiting
wainscoting
woodcutting

UT-ISH
ruttish
sluttish

Long U-TIST
acutest
cutest
flutist
lutist
minutest
parachutist
pharmaceutist
therapeutist

UT-L
cubital
rebuttal
sagittal
scuttle
shuttle
skeletal
subtle
surrebuttal
unsubtle

Long UT-LESS
bootless
fruitless
rootless

UT-LUR
butler
cutler
scuttler

Long UT-NESS
absoluteness
acuteness
astuteness
cuteness

destituteness
minuteness
muteness
mutinous
resoluteness

UT-ON
bellybutton
button
glutton
mutton
rebutton
unbutton

Long U-TUR
acuter
commuter
computer
crapshooter
cuter
disputer
executer
freebooter
hooter
instituter
looter
microcomputer
minicomputer
mooter
neuter
peashooter
persecutor
pewter
polluter
recruiter
refuter
rooter
router
saluter
scooter

sharpshooter
shooter
substituter
suitor
tooter
tributer
troubleshooter
tutor

UT-UR
aflutter
arbiter
banqueter
bucketer
budgeter
butter
circuiter
clutter
cutter
dieter
flutter
gutter
haircutter
heritor
junketer
limiter
marketer
mutter
orbiter
parroter
putter
quieter
rebutter
rioter
riveter
shutter
splutter
sputter
stonecutter
strutter

stutter
surrebutter
utter
visiter
visitor
woodcutter

Long U-TURE
future
moocher
suture

Long U-UR
bluer
brewer
chewer
construer
continuer
doer
eschewer
evildoer
ewer
fewer
hewer
horseshoer
interviewer
issuer
misdoer
newer
pursuer
renewer
rescuer
revenuer
reviewer
screwer
sewer
shampooer
shoer
skewer
snowshoer

spewer
suer
tattooer
televiewer
truer
valuer
viewer
wooer
wrongdoer

Long U-URD
skewered
steward

Long U-VAL
approval
disapproval
removal

UV-EN
oven
sloven

Long U-VI
groovy
movie

Long U-VING
approving
behooving
disapproving
disproving
earthmoving
grooving
improving
moving
proving
removing
reproving
unapproving

unmoving

UV-ING
loving
shoving
unloving

Long U-VUR
hoover
improver
louver
maneuver
manoeuver
mover
outmaneuver
prover

UV-UR
cover
discover
glover
hardcover
hover
lover
recover
rediscover
shover
slipcover
uncover
undercover

Long U-ZEZ
adduces
cabooses
calabooses
conduces
deduces
deuces
duces
educes

gooses
induces
introduces
juices
looses
mongooses
mousses
nooses
outproduces
overproduces
papooses
produces
recluses
reduces
reinduces
reproduces
ruses
sluices
spruces
traduces
truces
unlooses
uses
vamooses

Long UZ-EZ
accuses
bemuses
bruises
chooses
confuses
cruises
defuses
diffuses
disabuses
enthuses
excuses
fuses
fuzes
infuses

loses
masseuses
muses
oozes
overuses
peruses
reuses
ruses
suffuses
transfuses

UZ-EZ
buzzes
fuzzes

Long U-ZHUN
allusion
conclusion
confusion
contusion
diffusion
effusion
exclusion
extrusion
fusion
illusion
inclusion
infusion
intrusion
malthusian
obtrusion
perfusion
preclusion
profusion
protrusion
seclusion
suffusion
transfusion
venusian

Long U-ZI
boozy
floosie
floozie
floozy
fusee
jacuzzi
snoozy
woozy

UZ-IN
cousin
dozen

Long U-ZING
abusing
accusing
amusing
bemusing
boozing
bruising
choosing
confusing
cruising
defusing
defuzing
diffusing
disabusing
enthusing
excusing
fuzing
infusing
losing
misusing
musing
oozing
overusing
perfusing
perusing
refusing

reusing
snoozing
suffusing
transfusing
unamusing
using

Long U-ZL
accusal
bamboozle
perusal
refusal

UZ-L
guzzle
muzzle
nuzzle

puzzle
soremuzzle
unmuzzle

UZ-LING
guzzling
muzzling
nuzzling
puzzling
unmuzzling

UZ-LUR
guzzler
muzzler
nuzzler
puzzler

Long U-ZUR
abuser
accuser
amuser
bruiser
chooser
cruiser
infuser
loser
misuser
muser
nonuser
peruser
refuser
transfuser
user

Part Four:
Three-Syllable Rhymes

Long A-A-BL
conveyable
decayable
defrayable
displayable
obeyable
payable
playable
repayable
sayable
surveyable
unpayable
unplayable

Long A-BI-A
Arabia
labia

AB-I-EST
blabbiest
crabbiest
flabbiest
gabbiest
grabbiest
scabbiest
shabbiest

AB-I-LI
blabbily
crabbily
scabbily
shabbily

AB-I-NESS
blabbiness
crabbiness
flabbiness
gabbiness
scabbiness
shabbiness

AB-I-UR
blabbier
crabbier
flabbier
gabbier
grabbier
scabbier
shabbier

AB-U-LAIT
confabulate
tabulate

Long A-BUR-ING
laboring
neighboring

ACH-A-BLE
catchable
attachable
detachable
hatchable
matchable
nondetachable
patchable

Long A-DA-BL
aidable
biodegradable
braidable
degradable
dissuadable
fadable
invadable
persuadable
tradable
tradeable
unaidable
wadeable

Long A-DED-NESS
fadedness
degradedness
gradedness
jadedness
shadedness

Long A-DI-AN
arcadian
canadian
circadian

Long A-DI-ANT
Radiant

Long A-DI-UM
palladium
radium
stadium
vanadium

AF-I-KL
epigraphical
geographical
graphical
lexicographical
paleographical
pseudobiographical
topographical

AF-TI-NESS
craftiness
draftiness

AG-ED-LI
jaggedly
raggedly

AG-ED-NESS
jaggedness

raggedness

AG-I-NESS
bagginess
cragginess
shagginess

Long A-GRAN-SI
flagrancy
fragrancy
vagrancy

AG-UR-ING
staggering
swaggering

Long A-I-KL
algebraical
Hebraical

Long A-I-TI
gaity
laity

AJ-I-KL
magical
tragical

AJ-IL-NESS
agileness
fragileness

Long A-JUS-NESS
contagiousness
courageousness
outrageousness

Long A-KA-BL
breakable
mistakable

nonbreakable
shakable
shakeable
takable
takeable
unbreakable
unmistakable
unshakable

AK-A-BL
backable
crackable
smackable
trackable
uncrackable
untrackable

AK-ET-ED
bracketed
jacketed
packeted
racketed

AK-ET-ING
bracketing
jacketing
packeting
racketing

Long A-KI-NESS
achiness
flakiness
shakiness

AK-SA-BL
axable
relaxable
taxable
untaxable

AK-SHUN-L
factional
fractional

AK-SHUS-NESS
factiousness
fractiousness

AK-TA-BL
actable
attractable
compactible
contractible
extractable
infractible
intractable
retractable
tractable
untractable

AK-TI-KL
impractical
practical
syntactical
tactical

AK-TO-RI
dissatisfactory
factory
manufactory
olfactory
phylactery
refractory
satisfactory
unsatisfactory

AK-TU-AL
contractual
factual
tactual

AK-TUR-ING
fracturing
manufacturing

AK-U-LAIT
ejaculate
maculate

AK-U-LAR
macular
oracular
spectacular
unspectacular
vernacular

Long A-KUR-I
bakery
fakery

AK-UR-I
daiquiri
gimcrackery
psychoquackery
quackery

Long A-LA-BLE
assailable
available
bailable
mailable
resalable
sailable
unassailable
unavailable
unmailable
unsalable

Long A-LI-A
Australia
azalea

bacchanalia
echolalia
genitalia
glossolalia
paralalia
paraphernalia
regalia
saturnalia
Sedalia
Thalia

AL-I-ING
dallying
rallying
sallying
tallying

AL-IS-IS
analysis
dialysis
paralysis
pseudoparalysis
psychoanalysis

AL-I-TI
abnormality
actuality
amorality
animality
artificiality
asexuality
atonality
banality
bestiality
bilaterality
bipotentiality
bisexuality
brutality
carnality
causality

centrality
collegiality
commonality
commonalty
conditionality
confidentiality
congeniality
constitutionality
conventionality
conviviality
cordiality
criminality
criticality
dimensionality
duality
eventuality
fatality
finality
formality
frugality
generality
geniality
grammatically
heterosexuality
homosexuality
hospitality
hypersexuality
illegality
immorality
immortality
impartiality
impracticality
individuality
informality
instrumentality
irrationality
joviality
laterality
legality
lethality

liberality
locality
marginality
mentality
modality
morality
mortality
municipality
nasality
nationality
neutrality
normality
originality
partiality
personality
personalty
plurality
practicality
principality
provinciality
punctuality
rascality
rationality
reality
seasonality
sensuality
sentimentality
sexuality
spirituality
subnormality
technicality
temporality
tonality
topicality
totality
triviality
typicality
unmorality
unreality
venality

vitality
whimsicality

AL-I-UM
pallium
thallium
Valium

AL-JI-A
neuralgia
nostalgia

AL-O-EST
callowest
fallowest
hallowest
sallowest
shallowest

AL-O-GI
analogy
geneology

AL-O-GIST
anthologist
anthropologist
apologist
archaeologist
archeologist
audiologist
bacteriologist
biologist
cardiologist
chronologist
climatologist
cosmetologist
cosmologist
criminologist
cytologist
dermatologist

ecologist
embryologist
endocrinologist
entomologist
ethnologist
ethologist
etymologist
gemmologist
gemologist
genealogist
geologist
graphologist
gynecologist
hematologist
herpetologist
histologist
horologist
hydrologist
ichthyologist
ideologist
immunologist
kremlinologist
meteorologist
microbiologist
mineralogist
monologist
morphologist
mythologist
neurologist
numerologist
oceanologist
ophthalmologist
ornithologist
osteologist
paleontologist
pathologist
pedologist
penologist
petrologist
pharmacologist

philologist
phonologist
phrenologist
physiologist
planetologist
proctologist
protozoologist
psychologist
radiologist
seismologist
serologist
sexologist
sociologist
speleologist
syphilologist
technologist
toxicologist
urologist
virologist
zoologist

AL-O-NESS
callowness
fallowness
sallowness
shallowness

AL-O-UR
callower
hallower
sallower
shallower

AL-UR-I
calorie
calory
gallery
salary

Long A-MA-BL
blamable
blameable
claimable
nameable
reclaimable
tameable
unnameable

AM-A-TIV
amative
exclamative

AM-A-TIZE
dramatize
overdramatize

AM-BU-LAIT
ambulate
circumambulate
perambulate
somnambulate

AM-BU-LISM
ambulism
noctambulism
somnabulism

AM-BU-LIST
noctambulist
perambulist
somnambulist

AM-ET-UR
diameter
heptameter
hexameter
octameter
parameter
pentameter

tetrameter

AM-IN-NAIT
contaminate
decontaminate
laminate

AM-I-TI
amity
calamity

Long A-MLESS-NESS
aimlessness
blamelessness
shamelessness

AM-OR-ING
clamoring
hammering
stammering
yammering

AM-OR-UR
clamorer
hammerer
stammerer
yammerer

AM-OR-US
amorous
clamorous
glamorous
glamourous

AM-PUR-ING
hampering
pampering
scampering
tampering

AM-PUR-UR
hamperer
pamperer
tamperer

Long A-NA-BL
ascertainable
attainable
constrainable
containable
explainable
inexplainable
maintainable
obtainable
restrainable
retainable
retrainable
stainable
sustainable
trainable
unattainable
unexplainable
unobtainable
unsustainable

AN-DA-BL
expandable
mandible
understandable

AN-DI-NESS
handiness
sandiness

AN-DU-RING
meanderer
panderer
philanderer
slanderer

AN-DUR-UR
meanderer
panderer
philanderer
slanderer

AN-DUR-UR
launderer
maunderer
ponderer
squanderer
wanderer

Long A-NE-US
extemporaneous
extraneous
extraneus
instantaneous
miscellaneous
simultaneous
spontaneous
subcutaneous
subterraneous
transcutaneous

Long A-NFUL-I
disdainfully
gainfully
painfully

Long ANG-KUR-ING
anchoring
cankering
hankering

Long ANG-KUR-US
cankerous
cantankerous
rancorous

Long A-NI-A
agromania
Albania
bibliomania
cleptomania
egomania
kleptomania
lithuania
mania
mauritania
melomania
monomania
mythomania
narcomania
nymphomania
pseudomania
pyromania
theomania

Long A-NI-AK
egomaniac
kleptomaniac
maniac
monomaniac
mythomaniac
nymphomaniac
pyromaniac

Long A-NI-AN
Albanian
Iranian
Jordanian
Lithuanian
Mauritanian
Mediterranean
Pennsylvanian
Subterranean
Tasmanian
Transylvanian
Ukranian

AN-I-BL
cannibal
Hannibal
Plannable

AN-I-KL
mechanical
panicle
puritanical
sanicle
satanical
tyrannical

AN-I-MUS
animus
magnanimous
pusillanimous
unanimous

AN-ISH-ING
banishing
vanishing

AN-I-TI
Christianity
humanity
inanity
inhumanity
insanitary
insanity
profanity
sanity
urbanity
vanity

AN-JI-BL
frangible
intangible
tangible

AN-SHI-AIT
circumstantiate
substantiate
transubstantiate

AN-TUR-ING
bantering
cantering

AN-U-AL
annual
manual

AN-U-LAIT
annulate
granulate

AN-UR-I
cannery
granary
stannary
tannery

Long A-PA-BL
capable
drapable
drapeable
escapable
incapable
inescapable
shapable
shapeable
unescapable

AP-I-EST
chappiest
crappiest
flappiest
happiest
nappiest

rappiest
sappiest
scrappiest
slaphappiest
snappiest

AP-ID-LI
rapidly
vapidly

AP-I-LI
happily
scrappily
snappily
unhappily

AP-I-NESS
crappiness
happiness
sappiness
scrappiness
snappiness
unhappiness

AP-I-UR
crappier
flappier
happier
nappier
sappier
scrappier
slaphappier
snappier

Long A-PUR-I
drapery
japery
napery

Long A-PUR-ING
capering
tapering

AR-A-BL
arable
bearable
declarable
parable
repairable
sharable
shareable
spareable
tearable
terrible
unbearable
unwearable
wearable

AR-A-TIV
comparative
narrative
reparative

AR-BUR-ING
barbering
harboring

AR-DI-NESS
foolhardiness
hardiness
tardiness

AR-FUL-I
carefully
prayerfully

AR-I-A
aquaria

area
bulgaria
honoraria
hysteria
malaria
miliaria
planetaria
solaria

AR-I-AL
actuarial
aerial
areal
burial
malarial
ministerial
monasterial
notarial
secretarial
vicarial

AR-I-AN
agrarian
antiquarian
aquarian

ARYAN
authoritarian
barbarian
Bavarian
Bulgarian
caesarian
centenarian
Chaucerian
clarion
Delawarean
disciplinarian
egalitarian
grammarian
humanitarian

Hungarian
lactovegetarian
libertarian
librarian
malarian
nonsectarian
ovarian
parliamentarian
proletarian
riparian
Sagittarian
sanitarian
sectarian
seminarian
skinnerian
totalitarian
trinitarian
unitarian
vegetarian
veterinarian
vulgarian

AR-I-AT
chariot
commissariat
heriot
lariat
proletariat
secretariat

AR-I-FI
clarify
esterify
rarefy
rarify
reverify
scarify
terrify
verify

AR-I-ING
berrying
burying
carrying
dairying
ferrying
marrying
miscarrying
parrying
unvarying
varying

AR-I-NESS
airiness
arbitrariness
contrariness
hairiness
literariness
mercenariness
merriness
momentariness
necessariness
ordinariness
primariness
salutariness
scariness
solitariness
temporariness
unnecessariness
unwariness
wariness

AR-ING-LI
blaringly
caringly
daringly
despairingly
erringly
forbearingly
glaringly

overbearingly
sparingly
unerringly
unsparingly

AR-I-TI
angularity
austerity
barbarity
bipolarity
carroty
cellularity
charity
circularity
clarity
dexterity
disparity
dissimilarity
familiarity
granularity
hilarity
insularity
irregularity
jocularity
modularity
muscularity
overfamiliarity
parity
peculiarity
polarity
popularity
posterity
prosperity
rarity
regularity
similarity
sincerity
singularity
solidarity
temerity

unclarity
vascularity
verity
vulgarity

AR-I-UM
aquarium
barium
herbarium
honorarium
necessarium
planetarium
sanatarium
sanitarium
solarium
terrarium

AR-I-UR
airier
ballcarrier
barrier
carrier
hairier
merrier
scarier
tarrier
terrier
varier
warier

AR-I-US
Aquarius
barbarious
gregarious
hilarious
malarious
precarious
Sagittarius
vagarious
various

vicarious

AR-KI-KL
hierarchical
monarchical
oligarchical

AR-MING-LI
alarmingly
charmingly
disarmingly

AR-NISH-ING
garnishing
revarnishing
tarnishing
varnishing

AR-O-ING
harrowing
narrowing

AR-SHAL-IZM
anabolism
biracialism
cameralism
cannibalism
capitalism
centralism
ceremonialism
chloralism
classicalism
colonialism
congregationalism
conventionalism
decentralism
dualism
ecumenicalism
emotionalism
evangelicalism

evangelism
factionalism
fatalism
federalism
feudalism
fraternalism
fundamentalism
globalism
individualism
industrialism
infantilism
internationalism
journalism
labialism
legalism
liberalism
literalism
localism
martialism
materialism
maternalism
medievalism
mendelism
moralism
nationalism
naturalism
neutralism
officialism
parochialism
pastoralism
paternalism
pluralism
professionalism
radicalism
rationalism
specialism
traditionalism
transcendentalism
virilism

AR-TI-KL
article
particle

AR-TI-ZAN
artisan
bipartisan
bipartizan
nonpartisan
partisan

ART-LESS-LI
artlessly
heartlessly

AR-TUR-ING
bartering
gartering
martyring
rechartering

Long A-SHI-AIT
emaciate
expatiate
ingratiate
satiate

ASH-I-NESS
ashiness
flashiness
splashiness

Long A-SHUN-AL
aberrational
arbitrational
coeducational
computational
configurational
congregational
conjugational

conservational
conversational
declinational
dedicational
demonstrational
denominational
deputational
deviational
discriminational
durational
educational
emigrational
federational
fluctuational
foundational
generational
gradational
gravitational
hallucinational
ideational
imitational
improvisational
incubational
informational
inspirational
interpretational
invitational
lactational
lavational
maturational
mediational
migrational
motivational
multiplicational
mutational
navigational
nonvocational
notational
nutational
oblational

obligational
observational
occupational
operational
organizational
permutational
probational
recreational
reformational
relational
representational
respirational
revelational
rotational
salvational
sensational
situational
valuational
variational
vocational

ASH-UN-AL
binational
international
irrational
multinational
national
nonrational
rational
supranational

Long A-SHUN-LESS
congregationalist
conversationalist
emotionalist
functionalist
internationalist
professionalist
pronationalist
rationalist

traditionalist

Long A-SHUN-UR
probationer
stationer
vacationer

Long A-SHUS-NESS
audaciousness
curvaceousness
graciousness
inefficaciousness
loquaciousness
perspicaciousness
predaceousness
predaciousness
pugnaciousness
rapaciousness
salaciousness
spaciousness
ungraciousness
veraciousness
vexatiousness
vivaciousness
voraciousness

Long A-SI-BL
chaseable
braceable
effaceable
embraceable
erasable
irreplaceable
persuasible
placeable
replaceable
retraceable
traceable
untraceable

AS-I-BL
impassable
impassible
irascible
passable
passible
surpassable
unsurpassable

AS-I-NAIT
assassinate
deracinate
fascinate

Long A-SI-NESS
laciness
raciness
spaciness

AS-I-NESS
brassiness
classiness
gassiness
glassiness
grassiness
massiness
sassiness

AS-I-TEE
audacity
capacity
edacity
incapacity
loquacity
mendacity
opacity
overcapacity
perspicacity
pertinacity
predacity

pugnacity
rapacity
sagacity
tenacity
veracity
vivacity
voracity

AS-IV-LI
impassively
massively
passively

Long A-SIV-NESS
abrasiveness
assuasiveness
dissuasiveness
evasiveness
persuasiveness
pervasiveness
suasiveness

AS-IV-NESS
impassiveness
massiveness
passiveness

Long A-STFUL-I
distastefully
tastefully
untastefully
wastefully

AS-TI-KUL
ecclesiastical
fantastical
monastical

Long A-STIL-I
hastily

overhastily
tastily

AS-TI-SIZM
elasticism
fanaticism
fantasticism
monasticism
scholasticism

AS-TUR-ING
mastering
plastering

AS-UR-AIT
emacerate
lacerate
macerate

Long A-TA-BL
abatable
correlatable
cultivatable
datable
dateable
debatable
debateable
inflatable
manipulatable
ratable
rateable
relatable
rotatable
statable
stateable
translatable
undatable
unratable
untranslatable
updatable

vacatable

Long A-TFUL-I
fatefully
gratefully
hatefully
ungratefully

Long AT-FUL-NESS
fatefulness
gratefulness
hatefulness

ATH-UR-ING
gathering
lathering

ATH-UR-UR
blatherer
gatherer
latherer
slatherer

Long AT-I-BL
combatable
compatible
incompatible
uncombatable

AT-I-FI
beatify
gratify
ratify
stratify

AT-I-FIDE
gratified
ratified

AT-I-KA
Attica
hepatica
sciatica

AT-I-KUL
democratical
diagrammatical
emblematical
enigmatical
epigrammatical
fanatical
grammatical
hydrostatical
judgmatical
kinematical
mathematical
piratical
pragmatical
problematical
sabbatical
spasmatical
systematical

AT-I-NESS
battiness
brattiness
cattiness
chattiness
nattiness

AT-I-SIZM
agnosticism
anglicism
asceticism
betacism
catholicism
classicism
criticism
cynicism

ecumenicism
empiricism
eroticism
exoticism
fanaticism
iotacism
lyricism
mysticism
narcissism
rhotacism
romanticism
rotacism
skepticism
solecism
witticism

AT-I-TUDE
attitude
beatitude
gratitude
ingratitude
latitude
platitude

AT-OM-IST
anatomist
atomist

AT-RI-SIDE
fratricide
matricide
patricide

AT-UR-AIT
maturate
saturate
supersaturate
unsaturated

AT-URAL
bilateral
collateral
contralateral
equilateral
lateral
trilateral
unilateral

AT-UR-I
battery
cattery
clattery
flattery
self-flattery

AT-UR-ING
battering
bespattering
clattering
flattering
mattering
pattering
scattering
shattering
smattering
spattering
splattering
tattering
unflattering

AT-UR-UR
batterer
chatterer
clatterer
flatterer
patterer
scatterer
shatterer

spatterer
splatterer

AV-EL-ING
gavelling
graveling
raveling
ravelling
traveling
travelling
unraveling
unraveling

AV-EL-UR
caviler
raveler
traveler

Long A-VI-AN
avian
Scandinavian
Shavian
subclavian

AV-IJ-ING
ravaging
scavaging

AV-ISH-ING
lavishing
ravishing

AV-ISH-MENT
enravishment
lavishment
ravishment

Long A-VISH-NESS
knavishness

slavishness

AV-I-TI
antigravity
biconcavity
cavity
concavity
depravity
gravity

Long A-VUR-I
antislavery
bravery
knavery
savory
savoury
slavery

Long A-VUR-ING
favoring
flavoring
quavering
unwavering
wavering

A-VUR-US
cadaverous
flavorous
savorous

Long A-ZI-A
aphasia
athanasia
euthanasia
fantasia

Long A-ZI-NESS
craziness
laziness

Long E-A-BL
agreeable
amiable
appropriable
disagreeable
enviable
foreseeable
impermeable
inexpiable
invariable
leviable
malleable
permeable
pitiable
seeable
skiable
unenviable
unforeseeable
variable

Long E-AL-IST
aerialist
colonialist
editorialist
idealist
imperialist
industrialist
realist
surrealist

Long E-A-LIZE
editorialize
idealize
industrialize
materialize
memorialize
overindustrialize
realize

Long E-AL-IZM
animalism
biculturalism
bisexualism
botulism
cabalism
chloralism
colloquialism
commercialism
communalism
criminalism
environmentalism
existentialism
externalism
formalism
idealism
imperialism
metabolism
mongolism
mutualism
nihilism
provincialism
pugilism
racialism
realism
ruralism
socialism
somnambulism
surrealism
symbolism
teetotalism
vandalism

Long E-AL-TI
fealty
realty

Long E-AN-DUR
coriander
meander

oleander

Long E-CHA-BL
impeachable
reachable
teachable
unreachable
unteachable

ECH-I-NESS
catchiness
sketchiness
stretchiness

ECH-U-RI
lechery
treachery

ECH-U-RUS
lecherous
treacherous

Long E-DA-BL
feedable
pleadable
readable
unreadable

Long E-DFUL-NESS
heedfulness
needfulness

Long E-DI-AL
remedial

Long E-DI-AN
comedian
paramedian
tragedian

ED-I-BL
credible
edible
incredible
inedible
spreadable

Long E-DI-ENSE
disobedience
expedience
obedience

Long E-DI-ENT
disobedient
expedient
ingredient
obedient

Long E-DI-EST
beadiest
greediest
neediest
reediest
seediest
speediest
tweediest
weediest

ED-IEST
headiest
readiest
steadiest
threadiest

Long ED-I-KAIT
dedicate
medicate
predicate
premedicate
rededicate

Long E-DI-LI
greedily
needily
seedily
speedily
weedily

ED-I-LI
headily
medley
readily
steadily
unsteadily

ED-I-MENT
impediment
pediment
sediment

Long E-DI-NESS
greediness
reediness
seediness
speediness
weediness

ED-I-NESS
headiness
readiness
steadiness
unreadiness
unsteadiness

ED-I-TED
accredited
credited
discredited
edited
inedited
reedited

uncredited
unedited

ED-I-TING
accrediting
crediting
discrediting
editing
reediting

ED-I-TOR
creditor
editor
predator

Long E-DI-UM
medium
tedium

Long E-DI-UR
beadier
greedier
needier
reedier
seedier
speedier
tweedier
weedier

ED-I-UR
headier
readier
threadier

Long E-DLESS-LI
heedlessly
needlessly

Long E-DLESS-NESS
heedlessness

needlessness

ED-U-LUS
credulous
incredulous
sedulous

Long E-DUR-SHIP
leadership
readership

Long E-FI-NESS
beefiness
leafiness

EF-I-SENSE
beneficence
maleficence

EF-UR-ENSE
deference
preference
reference

Long E-GAL-IZM
anabolism
biracialism
cameralism
cannibalism
capitalism
centralism
ceremonialism
chloralism
classicalism
colonialism
congregationalism
conventionalism
decentralism
dualism
ecumenicalism

emotionalism
evangelicalism
evangelism
factionalism
fatalism
federalism
feudalism
fraternalism
fundamentalism
globalism
individualism
industrialism
infantilism
internationalism
journalism
labialism
legalism
liberalism
literalism
localism
martialism
materialism
maternalism
medievalism
mendelism
moralism
nationalism
naturalism
neutralism
officialism
parochialism
pastoralism
paternalism
pluralism
professionalism
radicalism
rationalism
specialism
traditionalism
transcendentalism

virilism

EG-NAN-SI
pregnancy
pseudopregnancy
regnancy

Long E-GUR-LI
eagerly
meagerly

Long E-GUR-NESS
eagerness
meagerness

Long E-I-TI
contemporaneity
deity
gaiety
homogeneity
simultaneity
spontaneity

Long E-JI-AN
collegian
Norwegian

EJ-I-BL
allegeable
illegible
legible

Long E-KI-LY
cheekily
creakily
sneakily
treacly

Long E-KI-NESS
cheekiness

creakiness
leakiness
sneakiness
streakiness

EK-ON-ING
beckoning
reckoning

EK-SHUN-AL
bisectional
complexional
convectional
correctional
cross-sectional
directional
inflectional
interjectional
multidirectional
nondirectional
noninflectional
objectional
protectional
sectional
selectional
subjectional
unidirectional

EK-SHUN-ISM
abolitionism
abstractionism
anachronism
antagonism
barbarianism
brahmanism
calvinism
cannonism
cartesianism
chauvinism
confucianism

constructionism
determinism
ecumenism
equestrianism
evolutionism
exhibitionism
expansionism
expressionism
feminism
galvanism
hellenism
humanism
humanitarianism
impressionism
mechanism
melanism
mormonism
obstructionism
onanism
perfectionism
revisionism
satanism
synchronism
totalitarianism
unionism
urbanism
veganism
volcanism
Zionism

EK-SHUN-IST
perfectionist
projectionist
protectionist
resurrectionist

EK-SI-TI
biconvexity
complexity
convexity

perplexity

EK-TED-NESS
affectedness
dejectedness
unaffectedness
unexpectedness

EK-TI-BL
collectable
collectible
correctable
deflectable
delectable
detectable
detectible
disrespectable
ejectable
erectable
expectable
injectable
perfectible
projectable
rejectable
resectable
respectable
suspectable
undetectable

EK-TI-FI
objectify
rectify

EK-TI-KAL
dialectical
spectacle

EK-TIV-LI
affectively
collectively

connectively
defectively
effectively
electively
ineffectively
introspectively
irrespectively
objectively
prospectively
protectively
reflectively
respectively
retrospectively
selectively
subjectively

EK-TIV-NESS
defectiveness
effectiveness
ineffectiveness
introspectiveness
objectiveness
protectiveness
selectiveness
subjectiveness

EK-TO-RAIT
directorate
electorate
protectorate

EK-TO-RAL
electoral
pectoral

EK-TO-RI
directory
interjectory
rectory
sectary

trajectory

EK-TU-AL
effectual
ineffectual
intellectual
pseudointellectual

EK-TUR-AL
architectural
conjectural

EK-U-LAIT
peculate
speculate

EK-U-LAR
bimolecular
molecular
monomolecular
multimolecular
nonsecular
secular
specular

EK-U-TIVE
consecutive
executive
inconsecutive
nonconsecutive

Long E-LA-BL
appealable
concealable
congealable
healable
repealable
revealable
sealable
stealable

EL-E-GAIT
delegate
relegate
subdelegate

EL-FISH-NESS
elfishness
selfishness
unselfishness

EL-I-BL
expellable
fellable
indelible
sellable
tellable

EL-ISH-ING
embellishing
overembellishing
relishing

EL-O-EST
mellowest
yellowest

EL-THI-EST
healthiest
stealthiest

EL-THI-LI
healthily
stealthily

EL-THI-UR
healthier
stealthier

EL-TUR-ING
sheltering

sweltering
weltering

EL-TUR-UR
shelterer
swelterer
welterer

EL-US-LI
jealously
unzealously
zealously

EM-BUR-ING
dismembering
remembering

Long E-MI-NESS
creaminess
dreaminess
seaminess
steaminess

Long E-MI-UR
dreamier
gleamier
seamier
steamier
streamier

EM-NI-TI
indemnitee
indemnity
solemnity

EM-UR-I
emery
memory

EN-A-TOR
primogenitor
progenitor
senator

END-A-BL
ascendable
comprehendible
dependable
descendible
emendable
expendable
extendable
extendible
recommendable
spendable
unamendable
vendable
vendible

ED-DEN-SI
indemnitee
indemnity
solemnity

END-LESS-LI
endlessly
friendlessly

END-LESS-NESS
endlessness
friendlessness

EN-DUR-EST
slenderest
tenderest

EN-DUR-ING
engendering
gendering

rendering
surrendering
tendering

EN-DUR-LI
slenderly
tenderly

EN-DUR-NESS
slenderness
tenderness

EN-DUR-UR
renderer
slenderer
surrenderor
tenderer

EN-DUS-LI
horrendously
stupendously
tremendously

Long E-NI-A
armenia
gardenia
myasthenia
Parthenia
schizophrenia
Xenia

Long E-NI-AL
genial
menial
venial

EN-I-AL
bicentennial
biennial
centennial

millennial
perennial
quadrennial
quadricentennial
tricentennial
triennial

Long E-NI-ENSE
convenience
inconvenience
lenience

Long E-NI-ENT
convenient
inconvenient

EN-I-SON
Tennyson
venison

EN-I-TI
amenity
lenity
obscenity
serenity

EN-I-TIVE
genitive
lenitive

EN-I-TUDE
lenitude
splenitude
serenitude

E-NI-UM
proscenium
selenium

Long E-NI-US
heterogeneous
homogeneous
genius
ingenious

EN-SA-TIV
compensative
hypersensitive
hyposensitive
insensitive
nonsensitive
oversensitive
photosensitive
sensitive
supersensitive
unsensitive

EN-SHI-AIT
licentiate
potentiate

EN-SHUN-AL
contentional
conventional
intentional
nonconventional
tensional
unconventional
unintentional

EN-SHUS-NESS
contentiousness
licentiousness
pretentiousness
sententiousness
tendentiousness
unpretentiousness

EN-SI-BL
compensable
condensable
undefensible

EN-SI-KL
forensical
nonsensical

EN-SI-TI
intensity
tensity

EN-SIV-NESS
apprehensiveness
comprehensiveness
defensiveness
extensiveness
inoffensiveness
intensiveness
offensiveness
overapprehensiveness
pensiveness

ENS-LESS-LI
defenselessly
senselessly

ENS-LESS-NESS
defenselessness
senselessness

EN-SU-RI
dispensary
extrasensory
multisensory
sensory
suspensory

EN-TA-BL
circumventable
dentable
documentable
fermentable
lamentable
presentable
preventable
preventible
rentable
representable
unpresentable
unpreventable

EN-TA-KL
pentacle
tentacle

EN-TA-LI
coincidentally
continentally
dentally
developmentally
elementally
environmentally
fragmentally
fundamentally
incidentally
instrumentally
mentally
monumentally
regimentally
supplementally
temperamentally

EN-TA-LIST
gentlest
instrumentalist
mentalist
sentimentalist

EN-TAL-IZM
elementalism
mentalism
Orientalism
sentimentalism
transcendalism

EN-TAL-NESS
gentleness
sentimentalness

EN-TA-RI
dysentery
fragmentary
involuntary
mesentery
momentary
sedentary
segmentary
voluntary

EN-TA-TIV
frequentative
preventative
representative
tentative

EN-TI-KL
denticle
identical
pentacle
tentacle

EN-TI-TI
entity
identity

EN-TIVE-NESS
attentiveness
inattentiveness

inventiveness
overattentiveness
preventiveness
retentiveness

EN-TU-AIT
accentuate
eventuate

EN-TUS-LI
momentously
portentously

EN-TUS-NESS
momentousness
portentousness

EN-UR-AIT
degenerate
generate
regenerate
venerate

Long E-NUR-I
beanery
greenery
machinery
scenery

EN-U-US
ingenuous
strenuous
tenuous

Long E-NYEN-SI
deviancy
expediency
incipiency
leniency
miscreancy

radiancy
saliency
subserviency
transiency

Long E-O-LA
gladiola
roseola
rubeola
viola

Long E-PI-LI
creepily
sleepily
weepily

Long E-PI-NESS
creepiness
sleepiness
weepiness

EP-TA-BL
acceptable
imperceptible
perceptible
susceptible
unacceptable

EP-TI-KL
dyspeptical
receptacle
skeptical

EP-UR-US
leperous
obstreperous

ER-FU-LI
cheerfully
fearfully

tearfully
uncheerfully

E-RFUL-NESS
cheerfulness
fearfulness

E-RI-AL
abacterial
arterial
bacterial
biomaterial
cereal
diphtherial
ethereal
immaterial
imperial
magisterial
managerial
material
monasterial
psalterial
serial
sidereal
venereal

E-RI-EST
bleariest
cheeriest
dreariest
eeriest
leeriest
smeariest
teariest
weariest

ER-I-ING
berrying
burying
carrying

dairying
ferrying
marrying
miscarrying
parrying
unvarying
varying

ER-I-KL
clerical
hysterical
numerical

E-RI-LI
cheerily
drearily
eerily
wearily

E-RI-NESS
cheeriness
dreariness
leeriness
weariness

ER-I-ON
Algerian
Assyrian
Caesarean
criterion
Diphtherian
Iberian
Liberian
Nigerian
Presbyterian
Shakespearean
Shakespearian
Siberian
Syrian
Wagnerian

E-RI-OR
anterior
blearier
cheerier
drearier
eerier
exterior
inferior
interior
leerier
posterior
smearier
superior
tearier
ulterior
wearier

ER-ISH-ING
cherishing
perishing

ER-I-TED
ferreted
inherited
merited
parroted
unmerited

ER-I-TI
angularity
austerity
barbarity
bipolarity
carroty
cellularity
charity
circularity
clarity
dexterity
disparity

dissimilarity
familiarity
granularity
hilarity
insularity
irregularity
jocularity
modularity
muscularity
overfamiliarity
parity
peculiarity
polarity
popularity
posterity
prosperity
rarity
regularity
similarity
sincerity
singularity
solidarity
temerity
unclarity
vascularity
verity
vulgarity

ER-I-TING
ferreting
inheriting
meriting
parroting

E-RI-UR
anterior
blearier
cheerier
drearier
eerier

exterior
inferior
interior
leerier
posterior
smearier
superior
tearier
ulterior
wearier

E-RI-US
deleterious
delirious
imperious
mysterious
serious

E-RLESS-NESS
cheerlessness
fearlessness

E-RYAL-IST
aerialist
colonialist
editorialist
idealist
imperialist
industrialist
realist
surrealist

E-RYAL-IZM
animalism
biculturalism
bisexualism
botulism
cabalism
chloralism
colloquialism

commercialism
communalism
criminalism
environmentalism
existentialism
externalism
formalism
idealism
imperialism
metabolism
mongolism
mutualism
nihilism
provincialism
pugilism
racialism
realism
ruralism
socialism
somnambulism
surrealism
symbolism
teetotalism
vandalism

ER-A-RI
accessory
intercessory
pessary
possessory

Long E-SENT-LI
decently
indecently
recently

ESH-UN-AL
compressional
confessional
congressional

depressional
discretional
nonprofessional
obsessional
processional
professional
progressional
pseudoprofessional
successional
unprofessional

ESH-UN-IST
expressionist
impressionist
neoimpressionist
postimpressionist
secessionist

Long E-SHUS-NESS
capriciousness
facetiousness
speciousness

ES-I-BL
accessible
assessable
compressible
confessable
depressible
expressible
impressible
inaccessible
inexpressible
irrepressible
possessable
possessible
repressible
suppressible
unaccessible
unsuppressible

ES-I-MAL
centesimal
decimal
infinitesimal

ES-IV-NESS
aggressiveness
excessiveness
expressiveness
impressiveness
inexpressiveness
obsessiveness
oppressiveness
possessiveness
progressiveness
regressiveness
repressiveness

ES-TI-BL
attestable
contestable
detestable
digestible
incontestable
indigestible
ingestible
investable
investible
manifestable
noncontestable
protestable
suggestible
testable
uncontestable

ES-TRI-AN
equestrian
pedestrian

ES-TUR-ING
festering
pestering
sequestering

ES-TU-US
incestuous
tempestuous

Long E-TA-BL
beatable
depletable
eatable
escheatable
heatable
reheatable
repeatable
treatable
unbeatable
uneatable
unrepeatable

ES-TRI-AN
equestrian
pedestrian

ES-TUR-ING
festering
pestering
sequestering

ES-TU-US
incestuous
tempestuous

Long E-TA-BL
beatable
depletable
eatable
escheatable

heatable
reheatable
repeatable
treatable
unbeatable
uneatable
unrepeatable

ET-A-BL
forgettable
getable
nettable
regrettable
unforgettable

ET-FU-LI
forgetfully
fretfully
regretfully

ET-FUL-NESS
forgetfulness
fretfulness
regretfulness

ETH-LESS-LI
breathlessly
deathlessly

ETH-LESS-NESS
breathlessness
deathlessness

ETH-U-RI
feathery
heathery

ETH-U-RING
feathering
tethering

weathering

EK-I-KL
aesthetical
alphabetical
antithetical
cybernetical
heretical
hermetical
hypothetical
parenthetical
poetical
prophetical
synthetical
theoretical

ET-I-NESS
pettiness
sweatiness

ET-ISH-LI
coquettishly
pettishly

ET-ISH-NESS
coquettishness
pettishness

ET-I-SIZM
agnosticism
anglicism
asceticism
betacism
catholicism
classicism
criticism
cynicism
ecumenicism
empiricism
eroticism

exoticism
fanaticism
iotacism
lyricism
mysticism
narcissism
rhotacism
romanticism
rotacism
skepticism
solecism
witticism

ET-RI-KL
asymmetrical
barometrical
calorimetrical
diametrical
geometrical
metrical
obstetrical

ET-UR-ING
bettering
fettering
lettering

Long E-VA-BL
achievable
believable
conceivable
deceivable
imperceivable
inconceivable
irretrievable
perceivable
receivable
retrievable
unbelievable

EV-EL-ING
beveling
bevelling
deviling
devilling
disheveling
dishevelling
leveling
levelling
reveling
reveling

EV-EL-UR
beveler
beveller
leveler
leveller
reveler
reveler

Long E-VI-AIT
abbreviate
alleviate
deviate

EV-I-LI
heavily
levelly
reveille

EV-IL-RI
devilry
revelry

Long E-VISH-LI
peevishly
thievishly

Long E-VISH-NESS
peevishness

thievishness

Long EV-I-TI
brevity
levity
longevity

Long E-VI-US
devious
previous

EV-O-LENSE
benevolence
malevolence
prevalence

EV-O-LENT
benevolent
malevolent
prevalent

EV-UR-MOR
evermore
nevermore

EV-UR-UR
cleverer
endeavorer
severer

Long E-ZA-BL
appeasable
defeasible
feasible
freezable
infeasible
unappeasable
unfeasible

EZ-AN-TRI
peasantry
pleasantry

Long E-ZI-A
amnesia
magnesia
Rhodesia

Long E-ZI-AN
Artesian
Austronesian
Cartesian
Polynesian

EZ-I-DENT
nonresident
president
resident

Long E-ZI-LI
breezily
easily
greasily
queasily
sleazily
uneasily

Long E-ZI-NESS
breeziness
cheesiness
easiness
greasiness
queasiness
sleaziness
uneasiness
wheeziness

Long E-ZING-LI
appeasingly
freezingly
pleasingly
teasingly
wheezingly

Long E-ZUN-ING
reasoning
unreasoning

EZ-YUR-ING
measuring
pleasuring
treasuring

EZ-YUR-UR
measurer
pleasurer
treasurer

Long I-A-BL
amplifiable
certifiable
clarifiable
classifiable
deniable
dryable
emulsifiable
falsifiable
flyable
friable
identifiable
inviable
justifiable
liable
liquefiable
modifiable
nonviable
notifiable
pacifiable
pliable
qualifiable
rectifiable
reliable
satisfiable
triable
unclassifiable
undeniable
unidentifiable
unreliable
unsatisfiable
verifiable
viable
vitrifiable

Long I-A-BLI
certifiably
identifiably
justifiably
pliably

reliably
undeniably
unreliably
viably

Long I-A-KL
demoniacal
maniacal
monomaniacal
paradisiacal
zodiacal

Long I-ANT-LI
compliantly
defiantly
pliantly
reliantly

Long I-BA-BL
ascribable
bribable
bribeable
describable
indescribable
prescribable
unbribable

IB-I-A
amphibia
fibia
Libya
tibia

ICH-I-NESS
bitchiness
itchiness
twitchiness
witchiness

ICH-U-RI
bewitchery
stitchery
witchery

ID-EN-NESS
forbiddenness
hiddenness

ID-I-AN
Gideon
Euclidean
Euclidian
Lydian
meridian
obsidian
quotidian

ID-I-FI
acidify
dehumidify
humidify
solidify

ID-I-KL
druidical
juridical
pyramidical
veridical

ID-I-TI
acidity
aridity
cupidity
fluidity
humidity
hyperacidity
hypoacidity
insipidity
invalidity

limpidity
liquidity
lucidity
morbidity
placidity
putridity
rabidity
rancidity
rapidity
rigidity
solidity
stolidity
stupidity
tepidity
timidity
torpidity
torridity
tumidity
turbidity
turgidity
validity
vapidity
viscidity

ID-I-UM
basidium
fastidium
idiom
presidium

ID-I-US
fastidious
hideous
insidious
invidious
overfastidious
perfidious

ID-U-AL
individual

residual

Long I-ET-AL
biparietal
parietal
societal
varietal

Long I-ET-ED
dieted
disquieted
quieted
rioted

Long I-E-TI
anxiety
impiety
impropriety
inebriety
insobriety
notoriety
piety
proprietary
propriety
satiety
sobriety
society
subvariety
variety

Long I-ET-ING
dieting
disquieting
quieting
rioting

Long I-ET-IST
pietist
quietist

Long I-ET-IZM
pietism
quietism

Long I-ET-UR
dieter
proprietor
quieter
rioter

IF-I-KAIT
pontificate
significate

IF-TI-LI
niftily
shiftily
thriftily

IF-TI-NESS
niftiness
shiftiness
thriftiness

IFT-LESS-NESS
shiftlessness

IF-UR-US
calciferous
coniferous
herbiferous
lactiferous
luminiferous
odoriferous
pestiferous
proliferous
sacchariferous
somniferous
soporiferous
sudoriferous

toxiferous
vociferous

IG-A-MI
bigamy
polygamy
trigamy

IG-AM-IST
bigamist
polygamist
trigamist

IG-A-MUS
bigamous
polygamous
trigamous

IG-MA-TIST
bigamist
polygamist
trigamist

IG-NI-FY
dignify
lignify
signify
stignify

IG-NI-TI
benignity
dignity
indignity
malignity

IG-NI-US
igneous
ligneous

IG-OR-US
rigorous
vigorous

IG-U-US
ambiguous
contiguous
exiguous
unambiguous

IJ-EN-US
caliginous
impetiginous
indigenous
polygynous
rubiginous
serpiginous
vertiginous

IJ-I-AN
Phrygian
Stygian

IJ-ID-LI
frigidly
rigidly

IJ-ID-NESS
frigidness
rigidness

IJ-UR-ENT
belligerent
refrigerant

IJ-US-NESS
prestigiousness
prodigiousness
religiousness
sacrilegiousness

IK-A-TIV
applicative
contraindicative
explicative
indicative
siccative
vindicative

IK-EN-ING
chickening
quickening
sickening
thickening

IK-E-TI
lickety
pernickety
persnickety
rickety
thickety

IK-E-TING
cricketing
picketing
ticketing

IK-E-TUR
cricketer
picketer

IK-I-LI
stickily
trickily

IK-I-NESS
pickiness
stickiness
trickiness

IK-LI-NESS
prickliness
sickliness

IK-SA-BLE
fixable
mixable

IK-SHUN-AL
dictional
fictional
frictional
jurisdictional
nonfictional

IK-SI-TI
fixity
prolixity

IK-TIV-LI
addictively
afflictively
contradictively
predictively
restrictively
vindictively

IK-TIV-NESS
addictiveness
predictiveness
restrictiveness
vindictiveness

IK-TO-RI
benedictory
contradictory
interdictory
maledictory
valedictory
victory

IK-U-LAIT
articulate
denticulate
folliculate
gesticulate
matriculate
reticulate
speculate

IK-U-LAR
articular
curricular
diverticular
extracurricular
extravehicular
follicular
lenticular
navicular
particular
pedicular
perpendicular
reticular
spicular
testicular
vehicular
ventricular

IK-WI-TI
antiquity
iniquity
ubiquity

IK-WI-TUS
iniquitous
ubiquitous

IL-A-BL
billable
decasyllable
distillable

fillable
monosyllable
polysyllable
spillable
syllable
tillable
unfulfillable
untillable
willable

IL-A-JUR
pillager
villager

Long I-LAN-DUR
highlander
islander

IL-ET-ED
billeted
filleted

IL-ET-ING
billeting
filleting

IL-FU-LI
skillfully
unskillfully
wilfully
willfully

IL-FUL-NESS
skillfulness
wilfulness
willfulness

IL-I-LAIT
affiliate
conciliate

disaffiliate
humiliate
reconciliate

IL-I-EST
chilliest
frilliest
hilliest
silliest

IL-I-NESS
chilliness
frilliness
hilliness
silliness

IL-ING-LI
chillingly
killingly
thrillingly
trillingly
willingly

IL-I-TAIT
debilitate
facilitate
militate
rehabilitate

IL-I-TI
ability
acceptability
accessibility
accountability
adaptability
adjustability
admissability
admissibility
adoptability
advisability

affability
agility
amicability
applicability
approachability
availability
believability
biodegradability
calculability
capability
civility
colorability
communicability
compatibility
compensability
comprehensibility
computability
conceivability
contractibility
controllability
corrodibility
corruptibility
corruptibly
countability
credibility
culpability
curability
debility
dependability
desirability
destructibility
disability
disputability
disreputability
docility
ductility
durability
edibility
educability
eligibility

extendibility
facility
fallibility
feasibility
fertility
flammability
flexibility
floatability
foreseeability
fragility
frangibility
futility
gentility
governability
gullibility
heritability
hostility
humility
identifiability
ignobility
imbecility
immobility
immutability
impalpability
impassability
impassibility
impeccability
imperceptibility
implacability
impossibility
impregnability
impressibility
improbability
inability
inaccessibility
incapability
incompatibility
incorruptibility
incredibility
inculpability

indivisibility
ineligibility
inevitability
infallibility
infertilely
infertility
inflexibility
infusibility
inhabitability
insensibility
instability
intelligibility
invariability
invisibility
irritability
juvenility
laudability
legibility
liability
likability
machinability
malleability
maneuverability
miscibility
mobility
motility
movability
moveability
mutability
navigability
negotiability
nobility
notability
operability
palatability
palpability
payability
perceptibility
perfectibility
perishability

permeability
permissibility
photostability
placability
plausibility
pliability
portability
possibility
potability
predictability
preferability
pregnability
probability
profitability
provability
puerility
punishability
rehabilitee
respectability
responsibility
salability
scurrility
sectility
senility
sensibility
separability
servility
sociability
solubility
stability
sterility
suggestibility
suitability
tactility
tangibility
teachability
testability
towability
traceability
tractability

tranquility
tranquillity
transportability
trustability
usability
utility
versatility
viability
virility
visibility
volatility
volubility
washability
workability

IL-KI-EST
milkiest
silkiest

IL-KI-UR
milkier
silkier

IL-O-I
billowy
pillowy
willowy

IL-O-ING
billowing
pillowing

IL-O-KWENSE
grandiloquence
magniloquence

IL-O-KWENT
grandiloquent
magniloquent

IL-O-KWI
soliloquy
somniloquy
ventriloquy

IL-U-RI
ancillary
artillery
capillary
distillery
Hillary
pillory

IL-YAN-SI
brilliancy
resiliency

IM-E-TUR
altimeter
dimeter
limiter
perimeter
scimitar
trimester

IM-IN-AIT
criminate
discriminate
eliminate
incriminate
recriminate

IM-I-NAL
criminal
liminal
subliminal
supraliminal

Long I-MI-NESS
griminess

sliminess

IM-I-TI
anonymity
equanimity
proximity
sublimity
unanimity

IM-PU-RING
simpering
whimpering

IM-PU-RUR
simperer
whimperer

IM-U-LAIT
overstimulate
simulate
stimulate

Long I-NA-BL
assignable
declinable
definable
finable
fineable
inclinable
indefinable
signable

IN-DI-KAIT
contraindicate
indicate
syndicate
vindicate

IN-E-AL
finial

lineal
matrilineal
patrilineal
pineal

ING-GU-RING
fingering
lingering
malingering

ING-GU-RUR
lingerer
malingerer

ING-I-NESS
dinginess
springiness
stinginess

ING-KA-BL
drinkable
nonsinkable
shrinkable
sinkable
thinkable
undrinkable
unshrinkable
unsinkable
unthinkable

ING-KI-NESS
inkiness
kinkiness

IN-I-A
Sardinia
Virginia
West Virginia
zinnia

Long I-NI-EST
briniest
liniest
shiniest
spiniest
tiniest
whiniest
winiest

IN-I-KL
binnacle
clinical
cynical
pinnacle
rabbinical

IN-ISH-ING
diminishing
finishing
refinishing

IN-IS-TUR
administer
minister
sinister

IN-I-TI
affinity
alkalinity
asininity
divinity
femininity
infinity
magnanimity
masculinity
saccharinity
salinity
trinity
vicinity
virginity

Long I-NI-UR
shinier
spinier
tinier
whinier
winier

IN-JEN-SI
astringency
contingency
stringency

IN-JIL-I
dingily
laryngeally
stingily

IN-JI-NESS
dinginess
stinginess

IN-TUR-I
splintery
wintery

Long I-NUR-I
binary
finery
pinery
refinery
winery

IN-U-US
continuous
discontinuous
sinuous

Long I-O-LET
inviolate
ultraviolet

violet

Long I-O-TUR
dieter
quieter
rioter

IP-TI-KL
apocalyptical
cryptical
eclyptical
elliptical

IP-U-LAIT
manipulate
stipulate

IP-U-LI
flippily
nippily
Tripoli
zippily

IP-U-RI
frippery
slippery

Long I-RA-BL
acquirable
desirable
desireable
expirable
fireable
tirable
untireable
wireable

IR-I-KL
empirical
hemispherical

lyrical
satirical
spherical

IS-EN-ING
christening
glistening
listening
rechristening

ISH-A-LI
artificially
beneficially
initially
judicially
officially
prejudicially
sacrificially
superficially
unjudicially
unofficially

ISH-EN-SI
deficiency
efficiency
inefficiency
insufficiency
proficiency
sufficiency

ISH-I-AIT
initiate
officiate
propitiate
vitiate

ISH-UN-AL
additional
attritional
coalitional

cognitional
conditional
nontraditional
nutritional
petitional
positional
prepositional
propositional
suppositional
traditional
transitional
unconditional
untraditional
volitional

ISH-UN-IST
abolitionist
coalitionist
exhibitionist
nutritionist
seditionist

ISH-UN-UR
commissioner
conditioner
exhibitioner
malpractitioner
parishioner
petitioner
practitioner
requisitioner

ISH-U-RI
beneficiary
fishery
judiciary

ISH-US-NESS
ambitiousness
auspiciousness

deliciousness
expeditiousness
inauspiciousness
injudiciousness
judiciousness
maliciousness
meretriciousness
nutritiousness
officiousness
perniciousness
repetitiousness
seditiousness
surreptitiousness
suspiciousness
viciousness

IS-I-BL
admissable
admissible
derisible
impermissible
inadmissable
inadmissible
kissable
miscible
omissible
permissible
rescissible
transmissible

Long I-SI-EST
diciest
iciest
spiciest

Long I-SI-KL
bicycle
icicle
tricycle

Long I-SIL-I
icily
spicily

IS-IM-O
bravissimo
fortissimo
generalissimo
pianissimo
prestissimo

Long I-SI-NESS
diciness
iciness
spiciness

IS-I-TI
authenticity
bioelectricity
canonicity
chronicity
complicity
concentricity
domesticity
duplicity
eccentricity
egocentricity
elasticity
electricity
ethnicity
felicity
heliocentricity
historicity
infelicity
lubricity
monochromaticity
multiplicity
plasticity
publicity
rusticity

seismicity
simplicity
specificity
tonicity
toxicity

IS-IT-NESS
explicitness
implicitness

IS-I-TUDE
solicitude
vicissitude

Long I-SIV-LI
decisively
incisively
indecisively

Long I-SIV-NESS
decisiveness
incisiveness
indecisiveness

ISK-I-EST
friskiest
riskiest

IS-TI-KL
egoistical
egotistical
eucharistical
linguistical
logistical
monistical
mystical
nepotistical
optimistical
pantheistical
sophistical

statistical
synergistical
theistical

IS-TO-RI
blistery
history
mystery
prehistory

Long I-TA-BL
copyrightable
excitable
hyperexcitable
ignitable
ignitible
indictable
unexcitable
writable

IT-A-BL
admittable
transmittable

Long I-TEN-ING
brightening
enlightening
frightening
heightening
lightening
reenlightening
tightening
whitening

Long I-TEN-UR
brightener
enlightener
whitener

Long I-TFUL-I
delightfully
despitefully
frightfully
rightfully
spitefully

IT-I-GAIT
litigate
mitigate

IT-I-KL
apolitical
critical
diacritical
geopolitical
hypocritical
levitical
mephitical
nonpolitical
parasitical
psychoanalytical
sociopolitical

Long I-TI-NESS
almightiness
flightiness
mightiness

Long I-TLI-NESS
sightliness
sprightliness
unsightliness

IT-L-NESS
brittleness
littleness

IT-U-AIT
habituate

resituate
situate

IT-U-AL
habitual
ritual
spiritual
unspiritual

IT-UR-AIT
alliterate
iterate
obliterate
reiterate
transliterate

IT-UR-ING
embittering
frittering
glittering
jittering
littering
skittering
tittering
twittering

Long I-UR-I
briery
diary
fiery
friary
inquiry
wiry

Long I-VA-BL
contrivable
deprivable
derivable
revivable

IV-A-BL
forgivable
giveable
livable
liveable
unforgivable
unlivable

IV-EL-UR
civiler
driveler
driveller
sniveler

IV-I-A
Bolivia
Livia
trivia

IV-I-AL
trivial
convivial

IV-ID-NESS
lividness
vividness

IV-I-TI
acclivity
activity
bioactivity
captivity
collectivity
conductivity
creativity
declivity
festivity
hyperactivity
hypersensitivity
hyposensitivity

impassivity
inactivity
insensitivity
nativity
objectivity
overactivity
passivity
perceptivity
privity
proclivity
procreativity
productivity
radioactivity
reactivity
receptivity
relativity
retroactivity
selectivity
sensitivity
subjectivity
transitivity

IV-I-US
lascivious
oblivious

IV-OR-US
carnivorous
granivorous
herbivorous
insectivorous
omnivorous

IV-UR-I
delivery
livery
quivery
shivaree
shivery
spivery

spivvery

IV-UR-ING
delivering
quivering
shivering
slivering

IV-UR-UR
deliverer
quiverer
shiverer

Long I-ZA-BL
advisable
analyzable
compromisable
criticizable
devisable
excisable
exercisable
hypnotizable
inadvisable
magnetizable
recognizable
sizable
sizeable
standardizable
surmisable
unadvisable
utilizable

IZ-A-BL
divisible
indivisible
invisible
nondivisible
nonvisible
subdivisible
visible

IZH-ON-AL
divisional
provisional
revisional
televisional
visional

IZ-I-EST
busiest
dizziest
fizziest
frizziest

IZ-I-KAL
metaphysical
paradisical
physical
psychophysical
quizzical

IZ-I-LI
busily
dizzily
frizzily

IZ-I-TOR
acquisitor
inquisitor
visiter
visitor

IZ-I-UR
busier
dizzier
fizzier
frizzier

Long I-ZOR-I
advisory
derisory

provisory
supervisory

Long O-BI-A
acrophobia
anglophobia
claustrophobia
hemophobia
hydrophobia
kleptophobia
obeah
phobia
photophobia
triskaidekaphobia
xenophobia

OB-UR-I
jobbery
robbery
slobbery
snobbery

OB-UR-ING
clobbering
slobbering

Long OD-I-FY
codify
modify

OD-I-KL
episodical
methodical
periodical
synodical
unmethodical

OD-I-NESS
bawdiness
gaudiness

OD-I-TI
commodity

oddity

Long O-DI-UM
monosodium
odium
podium

Long O-DI-US
commodious
incommodious
melodious
odious
unmelodious

OD-U-LAR
modular
nodular

OD-UR-ING
doddering
foddering

OF-A-GUS
esophagus
sarcophagus

OF-UL-I
awfully
lawfully
unlawfully

OF-UL-NESS
awfulness
lawfulness
unlawfulness

OF-UR-ING
offering
proffering

OG-A-MI
endogamy
exogamy
homogamy
misogamy
monogamy

OG-A-MIST
misogamist
monogamist

OG-AM-US
endogamous
exogamous
homogamous
monogamous

OG-A-TIVE
derogative
interrogative
prerogative

OG-RA-FI
autobiography
bibliography
biogeography
biography
cardiography
cartography
choreography
chronography
cinematography
cryptography
demography
geography
holography
kymography
lexicography
lithography
mammography

oceanography
orthography
paleography
photography
pneumography
pornography
radiography
reprography
seismography
skiagraphy
spectrography
stenography
tomography
topography
typography
xerography

OG-RA-FUR
bibliographer
biogeographer
biographer
cartographer
choreographer
cinematographer
cryptographer
demographer
geographer
lexicographer
lithographer
oceanographer
paleographer
photographer
pornographer
radiographer
skiagrapher
stenographer
topographer
typographer

OI-A-BL
destroyable
employable
enjoyable
unemployable
unenjoyable

OI-AL-IST
loyalist
royalist

OI-AL-IZM
loyalism
royalism

OI-AL-TI
disloyalty
loyalty
royalty
viceroyalty

Long O-I-KAL
heroical
stoical

OIN-TED-LI
disappointedly
disjointedly
pointedly

OIS-TUR-ING
cloistering
moistering
oystering
roistering

OJ-EN-I
cosmogony
hologyny
homogeny

misogyny
monogyny
ontogeny
orogeny
phylogeny
progeny

OJ-I-KAL
archaeological
bacteriological
biological
climatological
cytological
entomological
ethnological
ethological
etiological
etymological
genealogical
geological
graphological
histological
horological
hydrological
ideological
illogical
immunological
logical
meteorological
methodological
morphological
musicological
mythological
neurological
pedagogical
petrological
pharmacological
phonological
physiological
proctological

psychological
scatological
seismological
sociological
technological
terminological
topological
toxicological
typological
virological

Long O-KA-LIZ
focalize
localize
vocalize

Long O-KAL-IZM
anabolism
biracialism
cameralism
cannibalism
capitalism
centralism
ceremonialism
chloralism
classicalism
colonialism
congregationalism
conventionalism
decentralism
dualism
ecumenicalism
emotionalism
evangelicalism
evangelism
factionalism
fatalism
federalism
feudalism
fraternalism

fundamentalism
globalism
individualism
industrialism
infantilism
internationalism
journalism
labialism
legalism
liberalism
literalism
localism
martialism
materialism
maternalism
medievalism
mendelism
moralism
nationalism
naturalism
neutralism
officialism
parochialism
pastoralism
paternalism
pluralism
professionalism
radicalism
rationalism
specialism
traditionalism
transcendentalism
virilism

OK-A-TIVE
evocative
locative
provocative
talkative
vocative

Long O-KEN-LI
brokenly
outspokenly

OK-I-LI
broccoli
chalkily
cockily
gawkily
rockily
stockily

OK-I-NESS
balkiness
chalkiness
cockiness
rockiness
stockiness

OK-RA-SI
aristocracy
autocracy
bureaucracy
democracy
hypocrisy
idiocrasy
mobocracy
plutocracy
technocracy
theocracy

OK-U-LAR
binocular
floccular
jocular
monocular
monolocular
ocular
saccular
trilocular

OK-UR-I
crockery
mockery
rockery

Long O-LA-BL
consolable
controllable
inconsolable
noncontrollable
uncontrollable

Long O-LAR-IZE
polarize
solarize

Long O-LFUL-NESS
dolefulness
soulfulness

O-LI-A
magnolia
Mongolia

Long O-LI-AIT
defoliate
foliate
infoliate
spoliate

OL-ID-LI
solidly
squalidly
stolidly

OL-ID-NESS
solidness
stolidness
squalidness

OL-I-FI
disqualify
mollify
qualify

OL-I-FIDE
disqualified
mollified
overqualified
qualified
unmollified
unqualified

OL-I-KL
apostolical
diabolical
hyperbolical
follicle
metabolical
pollical
symbolical

OL-IK-SOM
frolicsome
rollicksome

Long O-LI-O
folio
oleo
polio

OL-ISH-ING
abolishing
demolishing
polishing

OL-I-TI
coequality
equality
frivolity

inequality
polity
quality

Long O-LI-UM
linoleum
petroleum

OL-O-ING
following
hollowing
swallowing
wallowing

OL-O-JI
anthology
anthropology
apology
archaeology
archeology
astrology
audiology
bacteriology
biology
biopsychology
biotechnology
cardiology
chronology
climatology
cosmetology
cosmology
criminology
cryptology
cytology
demonology
dendrology
deontology
dermatology
ecology
endocrinology

entomology
epistemology
ethnology
ethology
etiology
etymology
gemology
genealogy
geology
gerontology
graphology
gynecology
hematology
herpetology
histology
homology
horology
hydrology
hysterology
ichthyology
idealogy
ideology
immunology
kinesiology
kremlinology
lexicology
lithology
meteorology
methodology
microbiology
mineralogy
misology
morphology
musicology
mythology
necrology
neology
neurology
nosology
numerology

oceanology
oncology
ontology
ophthalmology
ornithology
osteology
paleontology
parapsychology
pathology
pedology
penology
pentalogy
petrology
pharmacology
philology
phonology
phraseology
phrenology
physiology
planetology
proctology
protozoology
psychology
radiology
reflexology
rheumatology
scatology
seismology
semiology
serology
sexology
sitology
sociology
speleology
syphilology
tautology
technology
teleology
terminology
tetralogy

theology
toxicology
urology
virology
xenobiology
zoology
zymology

OL-O-JIST
anthologist
anthropologist
apologist
archaeologist
archeologist
audiologist
bacteriologist
biologist
cardiologist
chronologist
climatologist
cosmetologist
cosmologist
criminologist
cytologist
dermatologist
ecologist
embryologist
endocrinologist
entomologist
ethnologist
ethologist
etymologist
gemmologist
gemologist
genealogist
geologist
graphologist
gynecologist
hematologist
herpetologist

histologist
horologist
hydrologist
ichthyologist
ideologist
immunologist
kremlinologist
meteorologist
microbiologist
mineralogist
monologist
morphologist
mythologist
neurologist
numerologist
oceanologist
ophthalmologist
ornithologist
osteologist
paleontologist
pathologist
pedologist
penologist
petrologist
pharmacologist
philologist
phonologist
phrenologist
physiologist
planetologist
proctologist
protozoologist
psychologist
radiologist
seismologist
serologist
sexologist
sociologist
speleologist
syphilologist

technologist
toxicologist
urologist
virologist
zoologist

OL-O-JIZE
anthologize
apologize
homologize
ideologize
neurologize
psychologize

OL-O-JUR
astrologer
philologer

OL-O-UR
follower
swallower

OL-TI-EST
faultiest
maltiest
saltiest

OL-TI-NESS
faultiness
saltiness

OL-TUR-ING
altering
faltering
haltering
paltering
unfaltering

OL-U-BL
insoluble

soluble
voluble

OL-VA-BL
insolvable
revolvable
solvable

OM-E-TRI
barometry
cardiometry
geometry
optometry
photometry
psychometry
seismometry
sociometry
stereometry
trigonometry

OM-E-TUR
barometer
biometer
chronometer
ergometer
hydrometer
inclinometer
kilometer
odometer
pedometer
picnometer
seismometer
speedometer
sphygmometer
tachometer
thermometer
vomiter

OM-I-KL
anatomical

astronomical
comical
economical
gastronomical
tragicomical

OM-I-NAIT
denominate
dominate
nominate
predominate
renominate

OM-IN-AL
abdominal
nominal
phenomenal
pronominal

OM-IN-ANS
dominance
predominance
prominence

OM-IN-ANT
dominant
predominant
prominent

OM-IN-I
dominie
hominy
ignominy
nominee
romany

ON-DUR-ING
laundering
maundering
pondering

squandering
wandering

ON-DUR-UR
launderer
maunderer
ponderer
squanderer
wanderer

Long O-NI-A
ammonia
aphonia
begonia
bronchopneumonia

IONIA
Patagonia
pneumonia

Long O-NI-AL
baronial
colonial
neocolonial
patrimonial
testimonial

Long O-NI-AN
Babylonian
Devonian
Draconian
Estonian
euphonium
Hamiltonian
Jacksonian
Macedonian
Oxonian
Pogonion
Shoshonean
Slavonian

ON-I-EST
bonniest
brawniest
scrawniest
tawniest

ON-IKA
Hanukkah
harmonica
Monica
Santa Monica
Veronica

ON-I-KAL
canonical
chronical
conical
demonical
ironical
mnemonical

ON-I-MUS
anonymous
antonymous
autonomous
homonomous
homonymous
synonymous

ON-ISH-ING
admonishing
astonishing

ON-ISH-MENT
admonishment
astonishment

Long O-NI-UM
euphonium
harmonium

pandemonium
plutonium
zirconium

Long O-NI-US
acrimonious
ceremonious
disharmonious
erroneous
euphonious
felonious
harmonious
inharmonious
parsimonious
polonius
sanctimonios
symphonious
unceremonious
unharmonious

ON-O-GRAF
chronograph
monograph

ON-O-MI
agronomy
astronomy
deuteronomy
economy
eponymy
gastronomy
homonymy
metonymy
synonymy
taxonomy
toponymy

ON-O-MIST
agronomist
autonomist

economist
ergonomist
gastronomist
taxonomist

ON-O-MIZE
astronomize
economize

OOK-UR-I
cookery
crookery
rookery

Long O-PI-A
cornucopia
Ethiopia
myopia
Utopia

Long O-PI-AN
Aesopian
cornucopian
Ethiopian
Fallopian

OP-I-KAL
anthropical
microscopical
misanthropical
nontropical
philanthropical
semitropical
subtropical
topical
tropical

Long O-PI-NESS
dopiness
soapiness

OP-I-NESS
choppiness
floppiness
sloppiness

OP-O-LIS
Acropolis
cosmopolis
megalopolis
metropolis
necropolis

OP-SI-KAL
dropsicle
mopsicle
popsicle

OP-U-LAIT
copulate
depopulate
overpopulate
populate
repopulate

OR-A-BL
adorable
deplorable
horrible
pourable
restorable
storable
unendurable

OR-A-LI
amorally
aurally
chorally
derogatorily
dilatorily
florally

gorily
immorally
mandatorily
monaurally
morally
orally
perorally
sorrily
transitorily

OR-DI-AL
cordial
flordial
primordial

OR-DI-NAIT
inordinate
insubordinate
ordinate
subordinate

OR-DUR-ING
bordering
disordering
ordering
reordering

O-RI-A
crematoria
emporia
euphoria
gloria
korea
memoria
moratoria
sanatoria
Victoria

O-RI-AL
accusatorial

ambassadorial
arboreal
armorial
boreal
cantorial
censorial
corporeal
dictatorial
editorial
electorial
equatorial
factorial
gubernatorial
gustatorial
immemorial
janitorial
manorial
marmoreal
memorial
oriel
oriole
pictorial
piscatorial
predatorial
proctorial
professorial
purgatorial
sartorial
sectorial
senatorial
sensorial
sponsorial
suctorial
territorial
tutorial
uxorial
vectorial

O-RI-AN
Baltimorean

Gregorian
historian
Korean
oratorian
senatorian
stentorian
Victorian

OR-ID-LI
floridly
horridly
torridly

OR-I-FI
glorify
horrify
torrify

OR-I-KAL
allegorical
categorical
coracle
historical
metaphorical
oracle
oratorical
rhetorical

OR-I-NESS
derogatoriness
dilatoriness
goriness
hoariness
predatoriness
sorriness
transitoriness

OR-I-TI
authority
exteriority

inferiority
interiority
majority
minority
posteriority
priority
seniority
sonority
sorority
superiority
surety

OR-I-UM
auditorium
crematorium
emporium
moratorium
sanatorium
sanitorium

OR-I-US
glorious
inglorious
laborious
meritorious
notorious
uncurious
uproarious
uxorious
victorious

ORM-A-TIVE
formative
informative
reformative

ORM-I-TI
deformity
enormity
nonconformity

uniformity

OR-O-ING
borrowing
sorrowing

OR-O-UR
borrower
sorrower

OR-SA-BL
endorsable
enforceable
forcible
unenforceable

OR-TI-FI
fortify
mortify
refortify

ORT-LI-NESS
courtliness
portliness

OR-TU-NATE
fortunate
unfortunate

OR-US-LI
adulterously
adventurously
barbarously
boisterously
cadaverously
cancerously
cantankerously
carnivorously
clamorously
dangerously

decorously
generously
glamorously
herbivorously
humorously
indecorously
languorously
lecherously
malodorously
murderously
numerously
obstreperously
odoriferously
odorously
omnivorously
pestiferously
ponderously
preposterously
proliferously
prosperously
rancorously
rapturously
rigorously
slanderously
somniferously
sonorously
thunderously
timorously
torturously
traitorously
treacherously
valorously
vaporously
venturously
vigorously
viviparously
vociferously

OR-YUS-LI
beauteously

bounteously
ceremoniously
commodiously
contemporaneously
copiously
courteously
curiously
cutaneously
deleteriously
deliriously
deviously
discourteously
dubiously
duteously
enviously
erroneously
extemporaneously
extraneously
fastidiously
feloniously
furiously
gaseously
gloriously
gregariously
harmoniously
hideously
hilariously
ignominiously
illustriously
impecuniously
imperiously
imperviously
impiously
industriously
ingeniously
ingloriously
injuriously
insidiously
instantaneously
invidiously

laboriously
lasciviously
lugubriously
luxuriously
melodiously
meritoriously
miscellaneously
multifariously
mysteriously
nauseously
nefariously
notoriously
obliviously
obsequiously
obviously
odiously
osseously
parsimoniously
penuriously
percutaneously
perfidiously
piteously
precariously
prestigiously
previously
punctiliously
salubriously
seriously
spontaneously
spuriously
studiously
subcutaneously
tediously
unenviously
uproariously
uxoriously
variously
vicariously
victoriously

Long O-SHUN-AL
devotional
emotional
notional
unemotional

Long O-SHUS-NESS
atrociousness
ferociousness
precociousness

OS-I-NESS
bossiness
drossiness
glossiness
mossiness
sauciness

OS-I-TI
animosity
atrocity
bellicosity
curiosity
ferocity
generosity
gibbosity
grandiosity
jocosity
luminosity
monstrosity
nervosity
onerosity
pomposity
porosity
precocity
reciprocity
serosity
speciosity
varicosity
velocity

verbosity
virtuosity
viscosity
zygosity

Long O-SIV-NESS
corrosiveness
erosiveness
explosiveness

Long O-TA-BL
boatable
floatable
notable
potable
promotable
quotable
unquotable

OT-AN-I
botany
cottony
monotony

Long O-TA-RI
coterie
levorotary
notary
rotary
votary

Long O-TED-LI
bloatedly
devotedly
notedly
rotedly

OT-I-EST
dottiest
haughtiest

knottiest
naughtiest
snottiest
spottiest
squattiest

OT-I-LI
haughtily
naughtily

OT-I-NESS
haughtiness
knottiness
naughtiness
spottiness

OT-I-UR
dottier
haughtier
knottier
naughtier
snottier
spottier
squattier

OT-OM-I
arteriotomy
dichotomy
lithotomy
lobotomy
phlebotomy
tracheotomy

OT-UR-I
lottery
pottery
tottery
watery

OT-UR-ING
pottering
slaughtering
tottering
watering

OUD-I-NESS
cloudiness
dowdiness
rowdiness

OUND-LESS-LI
boundlessly
groundlessly
soundlessly

OUND-LESS-NESS
boundlessness
groundlessness
soundlessness

OUNT-A-BL
countable
discountable
mountable
surmountable
unaccountable
uncountable
unsurmountable

OUT-I-NESS
doughtiness
goutiness

OU-UR-I
bowery
floury
flowery
showery
towery

OU-UR-ING
cowering
empowering
flouring
flowering
glowering
overpowering
powering
showering
souring
towering

OU-ZI-NESS
drowsiness
lousiness

Long O-ZI-EST
coziest
nosiest
rosiest

Long O-ZI-LI
cozily
nosily
rosily

Long O-ZI-NESS
coziness
doziness
nosiness
prosiness
rosiness

Long O-ZI-UR
cozier
nosier
rosier

Long U-A-BL
accruable
chewable
construable
doable
issuable
pursuable
renewable
reviewable
suable
unarguable
viewable

UB-I-NESS
chubbiness
grubbiness
stubbiness

Long U-BRI-US
insalubrious
lugubrious
salubrious

Long U-BUR-US
protuberous
tuberous

Long UD-I-LI
bloodily
cuddly
puddly
ruddily

Long U-DI-NAL
attitudinal
longitudinal

UD-I-NESS
bloodiness
muddiness

ruddiness

Long U-DI-NUS
fortitudinous
multitudinous
platitudinous
vicissitudinous

Long U-DI-TI
crudity
nudity
seminudity

Long U-EL-UR
crueler
crueller
dueler
jeweler

UF-I-NESS
fluffiness
huffiness
puffiness
stuffiness

UG-UR-I
buggery
sculduggery
scullduggery
skulduggery
skullduggery
thuggery

Long U-I-TI
acuity
ambiguity
annuity
congruity
contiguity
continuity

discontinuity
exiguity
fortuity
gratuity
incongruity
ingenuity
perpetuities
perpetuity
perspicuity
promiscuity
superfluity
vacuity
viduity

Long U-I-TUS
circuitous
fatuitous
fortuitous
gratuitous

UK-I-LI
epochally
luckily
pluckily
unluckily

UK-SHUN-AL
constructional
inductional
instructional

UK-TI-BL
conductible
deductible
destructible
indestructible
nondeductible
reconstructible

UK-TIV-LI
constructively
counterproductively
deductively
destructively
inductively
nonconstructively
nondestructively
obstructively
productively
reproductively
seductively
unproductively

UK-TIV-NESS
constructiveness
counterproductivene
destructiveness
inductiveness
nondestructiveness
obstructiveness
productiveness
reproductiveness
seductiveness
unproductiveness

UK-TOR-I
introductory
reproductory

UK-UR-ING
puckering
succoring

Long U-LISH-NESS
bullishness
foolishness
ghoulishness
mulishness

Long U-LI-TI
credulity
garrulity
incredulity

UL-MI-NAIT
culminate
fulminate

UL-SIV-LI
compulsively
convulsively
impulsively
repulsively

UL-SIV-NESS
compulsiveness
impulsiveness
repulsiveness

UM-BUR-ING
cumbering
disencumbering
encumbering
incumbering
lumbering
misnumbering
numbering
outnumbering
renumbering

Long U-MI-NAIT
illuminate
luminate
ruminate

Long U-MI-NANT
luminant
illuminant
ruminant

Long UM-I-NESS
gloominess
roominess

UM-ING-LI
becomingly
numbingly
unbecomingly

Long U-MI-NUS
leguminous
luminous
voluminous

UMP-SHUS-LI
bumptiously
scrumptiously

Long U-MUR-AL
humoral
numeral
tumoral

UM-UR-I
montgomery
mummery
summary
summery

Long U-MUR-US
humerus
humorous
numerous
tumorous

UN-DI-TI
fecundity
jocundity
orotundity
profundity

rubicundity

UN-DUR-ING
blundering
plundering
sundering
thundering
wondering

UN-DUR-UR
blunderer
plunderer
wonderer

UN-DUR-US
blunderous
thunderous
wonderous

UNGK-U-LAR
avuncular
carbuncular

Long U-NI-FORM
uniform
cuneiform
luniform

UN-I-LI
constitutionally
funnily
marginally
notionally
personally
proportionally
sunnily

Long U-NI-TI
community
immunity

importunity
impunity
opportunity
unity

Long UN-UR-I
buffoonery
lampoonery
sublunary

Long U-PUR-AIT
recuperate
vituperate

U-RA-BL
curable
demurrable
endurable
incurable
insurable
securable
unendurable
uninsurable

UR-A-BL
deferable
deferrable
enterable
factorable
filterable
honorable
inferable
nontransferable
pleasurable
referable
transferable
transferrable
untransferable

U-RAL-IST
muralist
pluralist
ruralist

UR-BAL-IST
cruciverbalist
herbalist
verbalist

UR-BAL-IZM
cruciverbalism
herbalism
verbalism

UR-DI-LI
sturdily
wordily

U-RI-AIT
infuriate
luxuriate
muriate

U-RI-AL
entrepreneurial
mercurial
seigneurial

UR-I-ING
currying
flurrying
hurrying
scurrying
worrying

UR-ISH-ING
flourishing
nourishing

U-RI-TI
immaturity
impurity
insecurity
maturity
obscurity
prematurity
purity
security
surety

UR-I-UR
blurrier
courier
currier
furrier
hurrier
worrier

U-RI-US
curious
furious
incurious
injurious
luxurious
overcurious
penurious
spurious
uncurious
uninjurious

UR-JEN-SI
convergency
emergency
insurgency
urgency

UR-JI-KAL
liturgical
metallurgical

surgical
synergical

UR-JUR-I
perjury
surgery

UR-KU-LAR
circular
semicircular
tubercular

UR-LI-EST
burliest
curliest
earliest
pearliest
surliest

UR-LI-NESS
beggarliness
brotherliness
burliness
curliness
disorderliness
earliness
fatherliness
mannerliness
miserliness
motherliness
neighborliness
orderliness
pearliness
scholarliness
surliness

UR-LISH-LI
churlishly
girlishly

UR-LISH-NESS
churlishness
girlishness

UR-MI-NAIT
exterminate
germinate
terminate

UR-MI-NAL
germinal
subterminal
terminal

UR-MI-NUS
conterminous
terminus
verminous

UR-NA-BL
burnable
discernable
discernible
earnable
governable
indiscernible
learnable
nonreturnable
returnable
undiscernible
unreturnable

UR-NAL-IZM
anabolism
biracialism
cameralism
cannibalism
capitalism
centralism
ceremonialism

chloralism
classicalism
colonialism
congregationalism
conventionalism
decentralism
dualism
ecumenicalism
emotionalism
evangelicalism
evangelism
factionalism
fatalism
federalism
feudalism
fraternalism
fundamentalism
globalism
individualism
industrialism
infantilism
internationalism
journalism
labialism
legalism
liberalism
literalism
localism
martialism
materialism
maternalism
medievalism
mendelism
moralism
nationalism
naturalism
neutralism
officialism
parochialism
pastoralism

paternalism
pluralism
professionalism
radicalism
rationalism
specialism
traditionalism
transcendentalism
virilism

UR-NISH-ING
burnishing
overfurnishing

UR-NISH-UR
burnisher
furnisher

UR-NI-TI
confraternity
eternity
fraternity
modernity
paternity
taciturnity

UR-PEN-TINE
serpentine
turpentine

UR-SA-RI
anniversary
bursary
cursory
nursery
precursory

UR-SI-BL
coercible
irreversible

nonreimbursable
reimbursable
reversible
submersible
traversable

UR-SIV-NESS
coerciveness
discursiveness

URTH-LESS-NESS
mirthlessness
worthlessness

UR-VA-TIVE
conservative
overconservative
preservative

UR-ZHUN-IST
excursionist
reversionist

Long U-SHUN-AL
constitutional
executional
institutional

Long U-SHUN-UR
evolutioner
executioner
revolutioner

Long U-SI-BL
adduceable
adducible
crucible
deducible
educible
inducible

introducible
irreducible
producible
reducible
reproducible
seduceable
seducible

Long U-SID-LI
deucedly
lucidly
pellucidly

Long U-SIV-NESS
abusiveness
allusiveness
conclusiveness
effusiveness
elusiveness
exclusiveness
illusiveness
inclusiveness
inconclusiveness
intrusiveness
unobtrusiveness

US-KI-LI
duskily
huskily
muskily

US-KU-LAR
corpuscular
crepuscular
muscular
neuromuscular

Long U-SO-RI
conclusory
delusory

elusory
illusory

UST-FUL-I
distrustfully
lustfully
mistrustfully
trustfully

UST-I-BL
adjustable
combustible
harvestable
readjustable

US-TI-EST
crustiest
dustiest
fustiest
gustiest
lustiest
mustiest
rustiest

US-TI-NESS
bustiness
crustiness
dustiness
fustiness
lustiness
mustiness
rustiness

US-TRI-US
illustrious
industrious

US-TUR-ING
blustering
filibustering

flustering
mustering
preregistering

Long U-TA-BL
commutable
computable
confutable
disputable
executable
immutable
imputable
incomputable
indisputable
inscrutable
mutable
prosecutable
refutable
scrutable
substitutable
suitable
transmutable
unrefutable
unsuitable

Long UTH-FUL-LI
truthfully
untruthfully
youthfully

Long UTH-FUL-NESS
truthfulness
youthfulness

Long UTH-LESS-LI
ruthlessly
truthlessly

UTH-UR-HOOD
brotherhood

motherhood

UTH-UR-ING
brothering
mothering
smothering

UTH-UR-LI
brotherly
motherly
southerly

Long U-TU-FUL
beautiful
dutiful
undutiful

Long U-TI-KL
cuticle
hermeneutical
pharmaceutical
therapeutical

Long U-TI-NEER
mutineer
scrutineer

Long U-TI-NUS
glutinous
mutinous

Long U-TI-US
beauteous
duteous
gluteus

UT-UR-ING
buttering
cluttering
fluttering

muttering
puttering
shuttering
spluttering
sputtering
stuttering
uttering

UT-UR-UR
flutterer
mutterer
putterer
sputterer
splutterer
stutterer
utterer

Long UV-A-BL
approvable

disprovable
immovable
immoveable
improvable
movable
moveable
provable
removable
unmovable
unprovable
unremovable

Long U-VI-AL
alluvial
antediluvial
effluvial
fluvial
pluvial

Long U-VI-AN
antedeluvian
Peruvian

Long U-ZA-BL
abusable
accusable
diffusible
excusable
inexcusable
infusible
reusable
transfusable
transfusible
unaccusable
unexcusable
unusable
usable
useable

ACKNOWLEDGMENTS

This book is dedicated to the two loves of my life, my son — Joshua Zollo, who makes rhyming and living fun, and my wife, Leslie Diller Zollo, who helps me get through every day.

My sincere gratitude is extended here to many people, but must begin with Andrea Rotondo, my editor and friend at Omnibus Books; it's Andrea's vision, patience, and encouragement that led me to take on this project, and to complete it. Thanks to my other friends and supporters at Omnibus, especially Alison Wofford, a publicist who has the rare combination of warmth and efficiency, and Sara Resnick. Also many heartfelt thanks: to Mr. Mark Salerno, a great poet and an even greater friend, who knows more about rhymes and poetry than I do, and who kindly contributed his acumen to this volume, to all the following Zollos, for your love and enduring support: my parents Burt and Lois, Peter and Debbie, Benjamin, Sarah and Jimmy, and to the Millers: Peggy and David, Jason and Katy, Liza and Robbie, and to the many friends who made the long bricklaying epoch of creating this book a much happier one: Scott Docherty, Howard Diller, Jean Stawarz, Jeff and Holly Gold, Andy and Anne Kurtzman, Barbara Nassman, Tomas Ulrich, Geoffrey Owens, Henry Diltz, Scott Eyerly, Sean Heaney, Janet Heaney, Amy O'Neill, Marketa Janska, Veronique Chevalier, Ben Schafer at Da Capo, Michael Dorr, Billy Salisbury, Craig Eastman, Kirke Jan, Bobby Malone, Sandy Ross, Lee Hirsch, Rob Pongi, Paul Kulak, Franne Golde, Nurit Wilde, Judy Close, Mo Golden & Henry Crinkle, Jack Frost, Robert Milkwood Thomas, Doug Waterman, Wade Smith, Mary Klauzer, Jay Silverman, Steve Schalchlin, Darryl Purpose, Rik Lawrence, Lucy Hagan, James Hurley, Smokey Miles, Eddie Simon, Danny Shorago, Jill Freeman, Debbie Kruger, Noah Stone, Paul Kulak, Severin Browne, Allan Harris, James Coberly Smith, Bruce Lewitt, Dr. Nareshkumar Arulampalam, Adam Block, Purlie Olloz, and my friends at the Aspen Writer's Foundation—Lisa Consiglio, Daniel Shaw and Meredith Carroll.

To the many authors of fine rhyming dictionaries, especially Gene Lees and Sammy Cahn, and to the many songwriters and poets whose wisdom and whose achievement in the art and craft of rhyming fed me and provided me with good examples of great rhymes, especially Bob Dylan, Paul Simon, Stephen Sondheim, Van Dyke Parks, Randy Newman, Leonard Cohen, Tom Petty, Bruce Springsteen, John Lennon, Paul McCartney, Aimee Mann, Yoko Ono, Sammy Cahn, Cole Porter, Yip Harburg, Ira and George Gershwin, Peter Case, Irving Gordon, Lorenz Hart, W.H. Auden, Ogden Nash, Tom Lehrer, Laura Nyro, Busta Rhymes, Ralph Waldo Emerson, John Keats, Lord Byron, Willie "The Shake" Shakespeare, Steve Goodman, Michael Smith, Jacques Levy, Rickie Lee Jones, and Harry Nilsson.